Lecture Notes in Computer Science   10885

Commenced Publication in 1973
Founding and Former Series Editors:
Gerhard Goos, Juris Hartmanis, and Jan van Leeuwen

More information about this series at http://www.springer.com/series/7410

Cristiano Giuffrida · Sébastien Bardin
Gregory Blanc (Eds.)

Detection of Intrusions and Malware, and Vulnerability Assessment

15th International Conference, DIMVA 2018
Saclay, France, June 28–29, 2018
Proceedings

 Springer

Editors
Cristiano Giuffrida
Vrije Universiteit Amsterdam
Amsterdam
The Netherlands

Gregory Blanc
Université Paris-Saclay
Evry
France

Sébastien Bardin
CEA
Palaiseau
France

ISSN 0302-9743   ISSN 1611-3349   (electronic)
Lecture Notes in Computer Science
ISBN 978-3-319-93410-5   ISBN 978-3-319-93411-2   (eBook)
https://doi.org/10.1007/978-3-319-93411-2

Library of Congress Control Number: 2018946629

LNCS Sublibrary: SL4 – Security and Cryptology

Preface

On behalf of the Program Committee, it is our pleasure to present the proceedings of the 15th International Conference on Detection of Intrusions and Malware and Vulnerability Assessment (DIMVA), which took place on Campus Paris-Saclay, France, during June 28–29, 2018. Since 2004, DIMVA has been bringing together leading researchers and practitioners from academia, industry, and government to present and discuss novel security research in the broader areas of intrusion detection, malware analysis, and vulnerability assessment. DIMVA is organized by the Special Interest Group – Security, Intrusion Detection, and Response (SIDAR) of the German Informatics Society (GI).

This year, DIMVA received 59 valid submissions from academic and industrial organizations from 25 different countries. Each submission was carefully reviewed by at least three Program Committee members or external experts. The submissions were evaluated on the basis of scientific novelty, importance to the field, and technical quality. The final selection of papers was decided during a day-long Program Committee meeting that took place at Vrije Universiteit Amsterdam, The Netherlands, on April 9, 2018. In all, 17 full papers and one extended abstract were selected for presentation at the conference and publication in the proceedings, resulting in an acceptance rate of 30.5%. The accepted papers present novel ideas, techniques, and applications in important areas of computer security, including malware analysis, mobile and embedded security, attacks, detection and containment, Web and browser security, and reverse engineering. The conference program also included two insightful keynote talks by Manuel Costa (Microsoft Research Cambridge) and Alex Halderman (University of Michigan).

A successful conference is the result of the joint effort of many people. We would like to express our appreciation to the Program Committee members and external reviewers for the time spent reviewing papers, participating in the online discussion, attending the Program Committee meeting in Amsterdam, and shepherding some of the papers to ensure the highest quality possible. We also deeply thank the members of the Organizing Committee for their hard work in making DIMVA 2018 such a successful event. We are wholeheartedly thankful to our sponsors EDF, Thales, Trail of Bits, ERNW, CNRS, and the CyberCNI chair for generously supporting DIMVA 2018. We also thank Springer for publishing these proceedings as part of their LNCS series and the DIMVA Steering Committee for their continuous support and assistance.

Finally, DIMVA 2018 would not have been possible without the authors who submitted their work and presented their contributions, as well as the attendees who came to the conference. We would like to thank them all, and we look forward to their future contributions to DIMVA.

June 2018

Cristiano Giuffrida
Sébastien Bardin
Gregory Blanc

Organization

DIMVA was organized by the special interest group Security – Intrusion Detection and Response (SIDAR) of the German Informatics Society (GI).

Organizing Committee

General Chairs

Sébastien Bardin   CEA, France
Gregory Blanc   Télécom SudParis, France

Program Chair

Cristiano Giuffrida   Vrije Universiteit Amsterdam, The Netherlands

Publicity Chair

Manolis Stamatogiannakis   Vrije Universiteit Amsterdam, The Netherlands

Sponsor Chair

Hervé Debar   Télécom SudParis, France

Steering Committee (Chairs)

Ulrich Flegel   Infineon Technologies, Germany
Michael Meier   University of Bonn and Fraunhofer FKIE, Germany

Steering Committee

Magnus Almgren   Chalmers University of Technology, Sweden
Herbert Bos   Vrije Universiteit Amsterdam, The Netherlands
Danilo M. Bruschi   Università degli Studi di Milano, Italy
Roland Bueschkes   RWE AG, Germany
Juan Caballero   IMDEA Software Institute, Spain
Lorenzo Cavallaro   Royal Holloway, University of London, UK
Hervé Debar   Télécom SudParis, France
Sven Dietrich   City University of New York, USA
Bernhard Haemmerli   Acris GmbH and HSLU Lucerne, Switzerland
Thorsten Holz   Ruhr-Universität Bochum, Germany
Marko Jahnke   CSIRT, German Federal Authority, Germany
Klaus Julisch   Deloitte, Switzerland
Christian Kreibich   ICSI, USA
Christopher Kruegel   UC Santa Barbara, USA

Pavel Laskov	Huawei European Research Center, Germany
Federico Maggi	Trend Micro, Italy
Konrad Rieck	TU Braunschweig, Germany
Robin Sommer	ICSI/LBNL, USA
Urko Zurutuza	Mondragon University, Spain

Program Committee

Magnus Almgren	Chalmers University of Technology, Sweden
Elias Athanasopoulos	University of Cyprus, Cyprus
Leyla Bilge	Symantec Research Labs, France
Lorenzo Cavallaro	Royal Holloway, University of London, UK
Lucas Davi	University of Duisburg-Essen, Germany
Hervé Debar	Télécom SudParis, France
Sven Dietrich	City University of New York, USA
Brendan Dolan-Gavitt	NYU, USA
Adam Doupé	Arizona State University, USA
Manuel Egele	Boston University, USA
Ulrich Flegel	Infineon Technologies AG, Germany
Aurélien Francillon	Eurecom, France
Yanick Fratantonio	Eurecom, France
Flavio Garcia	University of Birmingham, UK
Thorsten Holz	Ruhr-Universität Bochum, Germany
Alexandros Kapravelos	North Carolina State University, USA
Vasileios Kemerlis	Brown University, USA
Erik van der Kouwe	LIACS, The Netherlands
Anil Kurmus	IBM Research, Switzerland
Pavel Laskov	Huawei European Research Center, Germany
Corrado Leita	Lastline, UK
Zhiqiang Lin	University of Texas at Dallas, USA
Martina Lindorfer	University of California, Santa Barbara, USA
Federico Maggi	Trend Micro, Italy
Clémentine Maurice	IRISA, France
Michael Meier	University of Bonn and Fraunhofer FKIE, Germany
Matthias Neugschwandtner	IBM Research, Switzerland
Nick Nikiforakis	Stony Brook University, USA
Roberto Perdisci	University of Georgia and Georgia Tech, USA
Jason Polakis	University of Illinois at Chicago, USA
Georgios Portokalidis	Stevens Institute of Technology, USA
Sanjay Rawat	Vrije Universiteit Amsterdam, The Netherlands
Konrad Rieck	University of Göttingen, Germany
Christian Rossow	Saarland University, Germany
Yan Shoshitaishvili	Arizona State University, USA
Asia Slowinska	IBM, The Netherlands
Gianluca Stringhini	University College London, UK

Additional Reviewers

Ioannis Agadakos
Wissam Aoudi
William Blair
Kevin Borgolte
Andrea Continella

Seulbae Kim
Pierre Laperdrix
Enrico Mariconti
Jeremy Seideman
Guillermo Suarez-Tangil

Contents

Detection and Containment

Web and Browser Security

Reverse Engineering

Malware Analysis

MALREC: Compact Full-Trace Malware Recording for Retrospective Deep Analysis

Giorgio Severi[1]($\boxtimes$), Tim Leek[2], and Brendan Dolan-Gavitt[3]

[1] Sapienza University of Rome, Rome, Italy
severi.1462794@studenti.uniroma1.it
[2] MIT Lincoln Laboratory, Lexington, USA
tleek@ll.mit.edu
[3] New York University, New York, USA
brendandg@nyu.edu

Abstract. Malware sandbox systems have become a critical part of the Internet's defensive infrastructure. These systems allow malware researchers to quickly understand a sample's behavior and effect on a system. However, current systems face two limitations: first, for performance reasons, the amount of data they can collect is limited (typically to system call traces and memory snapshots). Second, they lack the ability to perform *retrospective analysis*—that is, to later extract features of the malware's execution that were not considered relevant when the sample was originally executed. In this paper, we introduce a new malware sandbox system, MALREC, which uses whole-system deterministic record and replay to capture high-fidelity, whole-system traces of malware executions with low time and space overheads. We demonstrate the usefulness of this system by presenting a new dataset of 66,301 malware recordings collected over a two-year period, along with two preliminary analyses that would not be possible without full traces: an analysis of kernel mode malware and exploits, and a fine-grained malware family classification based on textual memory access contents. The MALREC system and dataset can help provide a standardized benchmark for evaluating the performance of future dynamic analyses.

Keywords: Malware analysis · Record and replay
Malware classification

1 Introduction

As the number of malware samples seen each day continues to grow, automated analyses have become a critical part of the defenders' toolbox. Typically,

Tim Leek's work is sponsored by the Assistant Secretary of Defense for Research and Engineering under Air Force Contract #FA8721-05-C-0002 and/or #FA8702-15-D-0001. Opinions, interpretations, conclusions and recommendations are those of the author and are not necessarily endorsed by the United States Government.

© Springer International Publishing AG, part of Springer Nature 2018
C. Giuffrida et al. (Eds.): DIMVA 2018, LNCS 10885, pp. 3–23, 2018.
https://doi.org/10.1007/978-3-319-93411-2_1

these analyses can be broadly divided into static and dynamic analyses. Static analyses, which do not need to actually execute a sample, have the benefit of being often highly scalable, but are easily foiled by obfuscation and packing techniques. On the other hand, dynamic malware analysis systems can quickly extract behavioral features of malware by running them inside an instrumented virtual machine or full-system emulator, but are less scalable since each sample must run for a certain amount of real (wall-clock) time.

However, current sandbox systems suffer from several limitations. First, they must choose between deep analysis (in the form of heavyweight monitoring) and transparency. The sandbox may take a very light hand and only observe what malware does at a gross level, such as files read or written, configuration changes, network activity, etc. Or the sandbox may attempt to gather very detailed information about behavior, such as the sequence of function calls and their arguments. However, the instrumentation we may wish to perform while the malware is running might be invasive and slow down the sandbox to much slower than real time performance, which may mean the malware will behave differently than it would when not under instrumentation (for example by causing network connections to time out). This means that expensive analyses such as dynamic taint analysis [25] are out of reach for malware sandbox systems.

Second, the effective "shelf life" of malware samples is limited under dynamic analysis. Modern malware is typically orchestrated via communication with remote command-and-control servers. When these servers go down (e.g., because they are taken down due to anti-malware efforts), the malware is less likely to work correctly and will display a stunted range of behaviors. Hence, dynamic analyses of malware must be done while the malware is new. This means that new analyses and features can only be employed on new samples; *retrospective* analysis is not possible, since older samples will not exhibit their original behavior when re-run. We believe this problem to be particularly relevant in the context of forensic analysis and when new, previously unknown, samples are encountered.

This latter problem also leads to a severe shortage of standard datasets for dynamic malware analysis. Such datasets cannot consist merely of the malware binaries, since these will go stale. Summaries of observed behavior, such as those provided by online services like Malwr[1], necessarily capture only a subset of the malware's activity in the sandbox. And while detailed logs, such as full instruction and memory traces, may provide sufficient fidelity to perform retrospective analyses, their cost is prohibitive, requiring many gigabytes of storage per trace and imposing a large overhead on the sandbox's runtime performance. Dynamic analysis datasets are therefore limited to the features their creators thought to include and cannot be extended, which limits their utility for future research.

A solution to this problem is dynamic analysis under deterministic replay [16, 35]. If we run a malware sample while collecting enough information to permit us to replay the whole system execution with perfect fidelity, then we are free to use expensive dynamic analysis after the fact. We can even iterate, performing

---

[1] https://malwr.com/.

one cheap dynamic analysis to determine if another, more expensive one is likely to be worthwhile and feeding intelligence gleaned from shallower analysis to deeper ones. There is no worry about slowing down the sandbox overly since we perform all analyses under replay. And since no code is introduced into the guest to instrument or interpose to collect dynamic features, the malware is more likely to behave normally. If the recording, which consists of an initial snapshot plus the log of nondeterministic inputs to the system, can be made small enough, we can not just collect but also store these recordings in order to apply new analyses dreamt up at later dates, as well as retrospective analyses in general. We can share the whole-system malware recordings with other researchers and, if we also provide code to collect and analyze dynamic features, enable them to reproduce our results perfectly.

In this paper, we present MALREC, a system that captures dynamic, whole-system behavior of malware. Although none of its technical features (whole system emulation, virtual machine introspection, and deterministic record and replay) are wholly novel, their combination permits deeper analyses than are currently possible. We demonstrate this by presenting a dataset of 66,301 full-system malware traces that capture all aspects of dynamic execution. Each trace is compact—the entire dataset can be represented in just 1.3 TB. We also describe three novel analyses of this dataset: an analysis of how many unique blocks of code are seen in our dataset over time, a comprehensive accounting of kernel malware and how each sample achieved kernel privileges, and a novel technique for malware classification and information retrieval based on the textual content (i.e., English words) read from and written to memory as each sample executes. Each of these analyses is currently too heavyweight to be run on a traditional malware sandbox, but we show that they can be performed at a reasonable price and a relatively short amount of time by taking advantage of the embarrassingly parallel nature of the computations.

By providing full-trace recordings, we hope to enable new research in dynamic analysis by making it easier for researchers to obtain and analyze dynamic execution traces of malware. Moreover, we believe that the dataset we provide can serve as a standard benchmark for evaluating the performance of new algorithms. And although ground truth is always elusive in malware analysis, a fixed dataset that captures all dynamic features of interest allows us to steadily improve our understanding of the dataset over time.

2   Design

2.1   Background: Record and Replay

The MALREC sandbox is built on top of PANDA [11], a whole-system dynamic analysis platform. The key feature of PANDA for our purposes is *deterministic record and replay*. Record and replay, as implemented in PANDA, captures compact, whole-system execution traces by saving a snapshot of the system state at the beginning of the recording and then recording all sources of *non-determinism*: interrupts, input from peripherals, etc. At replay time, the snapshot is loaded and the system is run with all peripherals disabled; the stored non-deterministic events are replayed from the log file at the appropriate times. This ensures that as long as we have accounted for all sources of non-determinism, the replayed execution will follow the exact path as the original execution.

The 66,301 traces in our dataset can be compactly represented in just 1.3 TB, but are sufficient to capture every aspect of the 1.4 quadrillion instructions executed. This allows us to decouple our analyses from the execution of each sample, an idea first proposed by Chow et al. [9]. In Sects. 4 and 5 discuss the results of several analyses that would be too heavyweight to run on a live execution but are practical to run on a replay.

Although the record/replay system in PANDA is relatively robust, there are still some sources of non-determinism which are not captured (i.e., bugs in our record/replay system). As a result, some recordings cannot be correctly replayed. In our dataset, 2,329 out of 68,630 (3.4%) of our recordings cannot be replayed and hence are omitted from the analyses presented in this paper. With additional engineering it should be possible to fix these bugs and guarantee deterministic replay for all samples.

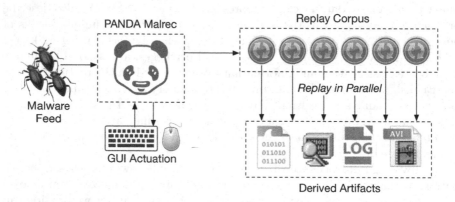

Fig. 1. The MALREC recording system. Malware samples are ingested and recorded; our actuation attempts to stimulate behavior by clicking on GUI elements. The resulting recordings can then be replayed to produce may different kinds of derived artifacts: network logs, screenshots, memory dumps, etc.

2.2   Recording Setup

Unlike many sandboxes, MALREC is *agentless*: no special software is installed inside the guest virtual machine. Instead, behavioral reports are generated later by PANDA plugins that run on the replayed execution. This increases the transparency of the emulated environment, though it is still vulnerable to sandbox evasion techniques that target the underlying emulator (QEMU). In Sect. 3.2 we provide upper and lower bounds on the number of evasive samples in our dataset.

Malware samples are loaded into MALREC via a virtual CD-ROM and then copied into the guest filesystem. Next, time synchronization is performed; this is needed both to improve transparency and because many protocols (e.g., HTTPS) depend on the client's clock being set correctly. Finally, the sample is executed with Administrator privileges. All commands are entered by simulating key-presses into the virtual machine. The recording setup is depicted in Fig. 1.

Once the malware has been started, we allow it to run for ten minutes (real time). During this time period, we periodically use virtual machine introspection (specifically, a module based on Volatility's Windows GUI support [1]) to look for buttons on screen that we should click on. This is accomplished by parsing the Windows kernel's GUI-related data structures and looking for elements that contain text such as "OK", "I agree", "Yes", "Go", etc. The goal is to get higher coverage for samples that require some user interaction.

Each PANDA replay consists of an initial VM snapshot and a log of non-deterministic events. After the recording has ended, we compress the log of nondeterministic events using xz. For the initial snapshot, we observe that each recording starts off with a nearly identical initial system snapshot. Thus, rather than trying to compress and store the snapshot for each recording, we instead store the differing bytes from a set of reference images. In a test on a subset of our data (24,000 recordings), we found that this provides savings of around 84% (i.e., a 6x reduction) in the storage required. This gives us an effective storage rate of around 1048 instructions per byte.

2.3 Offline Analyses

Once we have our recordings of malware, we can perform decoupled, offline analyses to extract features of interest. Because our recordings are made with the PANDA dynamic analysis system, our analyses take the form of PANDA plug-ins, but we anticipate that analyses from other QEMU-based dynamic analysis platforms (e.g., DECAF) should be relatively straightforward to port. An analysis plugin can extract any feature that would have been available at the time of the original recording; hence, the features available from a replay are a *superset* of those collected by traditional sandboxes—from the replay, we can re-derive network traffic logs, videos of what was on screen during the recording, system call traces, etc.

Although some of our analyses can be relatively expensive, an additional benefit of a replay-based system is that a corpus of recordings acquired over a long period can be replayed in a much shorter time by simply running each replay in parallel. There is also a practical benefit of replay here: whereas most cloud providers and HPC clusters are unwilling to run live malware samples, *replayed* malware executions cannot interact with the outside world and are hence safe to run anywhere.

For the case studies presented in this paper, we used New York University's "Prince" HPC cluster; processing the full corpus of 66,301 samples took between two days (for a bare replay with no analysis plugins) and eight days (for the unique basic block and malwords analyses). A rough calculation suggests that at the time of this writing, Amazon EC2 `m4.large` spot instances could be used instead at a cost of around $200 (USD); this seems easily within reach of most research groups.[2]

A final benefit of offline analysis via replay is that *multi-pass* analyses can be created. In cases where some analysis is too expensive to be run on every sample, we can often find some more lightweight analysis that selects a subset of samples where the heavier analysis is likely to bear fruit. For example, in our kernel malware case study (Sect. 4) we initially build a coverage bitmap that tracks what kernel code is executed in each replay. This analysis is cheap but allows us to quickly identify any replays that executed code outside of a kernel module that was present before we executed the malware. Once we have identified this (much smaller) subset, we can then apply more sophisticated and expensive analyses, such as capturing full-system memory dumps and analyzing them with Volatility.

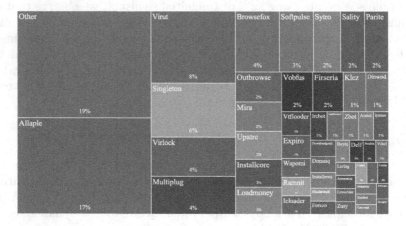

Fig. 2. The distribution of malicious samples.

3   Dataset

Our dataset consists of 66,301 full-system PANDA recordings captured at between December 7, 2014 and December 3, 2016. The samples are provided in a daily feed by the Georgia Tech Information Security Center (GTISC) and come from ISPs and antivirus vendors; from this feed we randomly select 100 executables per day.

The total number of instructions executed across the entire corpus is 1.4 quadrillion. Each recording contains, on average, 21 billion instructions, but there is significant variance among the samples: the standard deviation is 18

---

[2] Note that this calculation does not include the cost of storing the recordings on some EC2-accessible storage medium such as Elastic Block Store.

billion instructions, with a min of 4 billion instructions and a max of more than 330 billion instructions. The vast majority (all but 261 recordings) are of 32-bit samples. This makes sense, since on Windows, 32-bit samples can run on a 64-bit system but not vice versa.

Considering only the portions of each trace where the malware or some derived process was executing, each sample executes an average of 7 billion instructions with a standard deviation of 16 billion. Among these, 3,474 (5.2%) execute no instructions in the malware itself, indicating that they crashed on startup or were missing some necessary components.

In the remainder of this section we describe notable features of the dataset: the amount unique code, the prevalence of evasive malware, and the number and distribution of families (as determined by antivirus labels).

3.1 Unique Code Executed

PANDA replays of malware allow us to accurately measure exactly how much new code each malware sample actually represents. By this we mean the actual code that executes, system-wide, dynamically, when the malware sample is activated. We can use PANDA recordings to perform a detailed analysis of this aspect of the MALREC corpus.

Each recording was replayed under PANDA with the ubb plugin enabled, which performs an accounting of the code actually executed, at the basic block level. The plugin considers each basic block of code immediately before it is to be executed by the emulator. If the block has not been seen before in this replay, then we add it to a set, Ubb_i, the unique basic blocks for malware sample i. For every novel block encountered, we attempt to *normalize* it to undo relocations applied by the linker or loader. We use Capstone [27] to disassemble each basic block of code, considering each instruction in sequence, and then zero out any literals. This should permit comparison both within and between replays for different malware samples that are really running the same code.

In addition to the set of unique basic blocks in a replay (and thus associated with a malware sample), we also maintain the set of unique, normalized basic blocks. At the end of each replay, the set of normalized basic blocks, Nbb_i, for malware i, is marshaled. After collecting Nbb_i for each malware sample, the results were merged, in time order, to observe how much new code is added to a running total by each sample.

The number of unique (not normalized) basic blocks identified in a recording, $|Ubb_i|$, is plotted as a function of time in Fig. 3a. The average number of unique blocks in a sample is around 553,203 and it seems fairly stable across all 66,031 samples. This is a lot of code per sample, and it is in stark contrast to the number of new blocks of normalized code we see for each additional sample, as depicted in Fig. 3b. The average, here, is 3,031 new blocks per sample. In addition, we seem to see two similar regimes, the first from 0 to 150 days, and the other from 150 to 320 days. These two start with higher average per-sample contribution, perhaps close to 10000 blocks, and gradually relax to a lower value. The final average (at the far right of the plot) seems to be around 2000 blocks of new (normalized) code per additional sample.

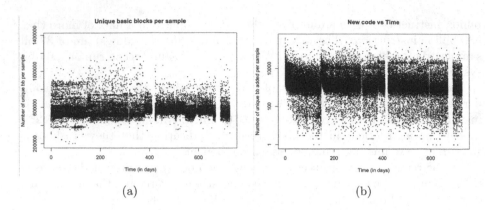

Fig. 3. A plot of the number of unique basic blocks of code per sample recording, Ubb_i, as a function of time, both before (a) and after (b) normalization.

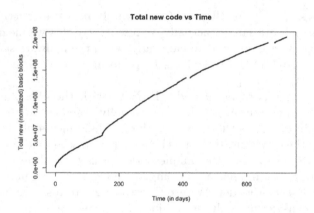

Fig. 4. A plot of the new code contribution for each malware sample, considered in time order. New code is the number of not seen before basic blocks, after normalizing to remove the effect of code relocation

The total amount of novel code seen so far in the MALREC corpus is plotted in Fig. 4. Time, in days, is on the horizontal axis, and on the vertical is the total accumulated number of unique, normalized basic blocks. Thus, e.g., after 200 days, we have about 75 million unique, normalized basic blocks of code; after 400 days we have about 130 million basic blocks, and at the end of the MALREC corpus, at about 727 days, we have collected over 200 million unique normalized blocks of code. We can see here the same effect observed in Fig. 3b: there appear to be two distinct regions, one from 0 to 150 days, and another beginning at 150 days. Both regions have similar shape, with the slope at the beginning higher than later in the region. Over time, both appear to seek a linear (but not horizontal) asymptote.

We investigated the cause of the jump at the 150 day mark, and found that this corresponded to the date we made a configuration change to the VM image and took a new snapshot (specifically, we made a configuration change to disable mouse pointer acceleration so that our GUI actuation could accurately target on-screen elements). The jump in new code, then, is likely not related to any feature of the incoming malware samples but rather an artifact of the recording environment.

3.2 Evasiveness

A concern with dynamic malware analysis is that samples may detect that they are being analyzed and refuse to show their true behavior. With MALREC, this may happen only during the recording phase, since the behavior during replay is deterministically equal to the one previously registered, regardless of the analysis plugins employed during replay. Although some previous work [4] has attempted to uncover evasive behavior in malware by running it in both a sandbox and on a reference (non-emulated) system and comparing the resulting traces, here we attempt a more difficult task: measuring the prevalence of evasive malware from a single trace of each sample. In this initial work, we do not completely succeed in characterizing all evasive behavior, but we are able to provide an estimate for the lower and upper bounds on the number of evasive samples by checking for known evasion techniques and clear signs of malicious behavior, respectively.

We first checked the execution traces of our samples against a few well-known, recognizable indicators of emulation awareness. In particular, we looked for Windows Registry accesses to keys related to the configuration of virtual machines:

```
HARDWARE\\ACPI\\DSDT\\VBOX__
HARDWARE\\ACPI\\FADT\\VBOX__
HARDWARE\\ACPI\\RSDT\\VBOX__
iSOFTWARE\\Oracle\\VirtualBox Guest Additions
```

We also kept track of registry queries containing key values like VMWARE and VBOX. Finally, we checked whether the malware ever executed the icebp instruction. This is an undocumented instruction, originally intended for hardware debugging, which is known to be handled incorrectly by QEMU and is therefore almost exclusively used as a "red pill" to detect emulation. Using these criteria, we identified 1,370 samples (approximately 2% of our dataset) which showed strong signs of sandbox awareness.

To obtain the upper bound, we compared the reports obtained from Virus-Total[3] behavior API with the analysis logs extracted from our dynamic analysis environment. We focused on keeping track of the actions on the file-system (written files) and the processes created by each sample. We also filtered out those samples which we could not clearly identify as malicious and assign a malware family label to (Sect. 3.3). Comparing those data sources we were able to identify 7,172 samples (10.81% of the dataset) showing the exact same written files and created processes both in the VirusTotal sandbox and in our platform. This

---

[3] https://www.virustotal.com.

allows us to conclude that those samples are unlikely to be evasive. This kind of approach, it must be noted, does not provide information regarding those samples which are able to evade VirusTotal, and may or may not evade MALREC.

We conclude that evasive malware makes up between 2% and 87.2% of our dataset. We acknowledge that these are not particularly tight bounds, but they can be improved over time with help from the research community to approach a full, ground-truth accounting of evasive malware and its sandbox avoidance techniques.

3.3 Malware Labeling

The labeling of malicious software samples is a long-standing problem in malware categorization tasks. Since our dataset is too large to be manually analyzed, we rely on labels provided by antivirus (AV) scanners from VirusTotal Using AVs labels as a reference classification, poses some well known challenges. Different AV vendors use different naming schemes with proprietary label formats, multiple aliases for the same software classes, generic names (e.g., "Downloader"), and often conflicting identification results. The ubiquity of this problem has encouraged an abundance of research efforts [15,19,22,28]. For the analyses in this paper we employed the AVClass tool [28] to perform malware family name de-aliasing, normalization, and plurality voting amongst the retrieved labels. AVClass assigns a unique label to 58,187 samples belonging to 1,270 distinct families in our dataset. Figure 2 shows the distribution of samples over malicious families.

4 Case Study: Kernel Malware and Privilege Escalation

Kernel mode malware is a powerful threat to the security of end users' systems. Because it runs at the same privilege level as the operating system, it can bypass any OS access control mechanisms and monitoring. Existing malware sandbox systems are not well-suited to analyzing malware with kernel mode components because their instrumentation focuses on system calls or higher-level user mode APIs. By contrast, the recordings in our data set capture the whole-system execution, and so we can perform analyses on any kernel-mode code. In addition, because of the lack of instruction-level granularity, current sandboxes cannot analyze privilege escalation exploits that may allow malware to load its kernel mode components in the first place.

We performed an analysis aimed at detecting any kernel mode malware in the MALREC dataset. We created an analysis plugin, kcov, which used a bitmap to shadow each byte of kernel memory and track whether it was ever executed. This allows the kernel code coverage of all replays that start from the same snapshot to be compared; furthermore, we can use introspection (e.g., Volatility [33]) to map the list of loaded kernel modules on the uninfected image and check whether any code outside a known module was executed. Any code executed outside of these kernel modules must therefore be a results of the malware's activity (though, as we will see, it does *not* necessarily mean that those modules are malicious).

Comparing kernel code executed to the list of modules loaded before the malware infection yielded 574 recordings that might contain kernel malware. We then systematically examined the replays to determine whether the kernel code was malicious and how it achieved kernel-mode execution.

Of our 574 candidates, 71 did not contain malicious kernel code. The unknown kernel code could be attributed, in these cases, to side effects of normal operation, such as starting a legitimate user-land service with a kernel-mode component, loading a signed driver, installing a new font, etc. In some cases it is possible that a benign driver is being loaded for malicious purposes. For example, one sample installed the tap0901.sys tap driver bundled with OpenVPN; while this is not malicious by itself, some older versions contain security vulnerabilities that could then be used to load further unsigned code into the kernel.

Malicious kernel code is loaded in a variety of different ways. Because our replays allow us to reproduce instruction-level behavior, we can potentially identify new techniques used by kernel malware. The load mechanisms we found are listed in Table 1. The most common technique by far is to simply call NtLoadDriver; because our samples are run with administrator privilege and the 32-bit version of Windows 7 does not enforce driver code signing, this is a straightforward and successful way to load a kernel module. More exotic techniques were also used, however: four samples modified the Windows Registry keys that determine the driver used for the built-in high definition audio codec, causing the rootkit to be loaded.

Table 1. Load techniques of kernel-mode malware

Technique	Count
NtLoadDriver	497
Replace legitimate driver	4
Kernel exploit	2

The final and most interesting technique for loading malicious code was to exploit a vulnerability in the Windows kernel. We found just two samples in our dataset that used this technique; both exploited MS15-061, a vulnerability in win32k.sys, which implements the kernel portion of the Windows GUI subsystem. It is surprising that this technique is used at all: all samples are executed with administrator privileges, so there is no reason for malware to attempt kernel exploits. This indicates that the malware samples in question simply do not bother checking for more straightforward means of achieving kernel code execution before launching an exploit.

Overall, we find that rootkits are very uncommon in our dataset, and most achieve kernel privileges using standard APIs. We note, however, that these analyses would be difficult to perform with traditional sandbox systems, which typically monitor at the system call boundary and may miss kernel code. In particular, we know of no existing sandbox analysis that can capture kernel mode exploits, but our system can as a byproduct of reproducing full system executions. In the future, we hope to run more samples *without* Administrator privileges and then apply analyses such as checking for violations of system-wide Control Flow Integrity [3,26] to detect exploits automatically.

5 Case Study: Classification with Natural Language Features

In this section, we introduce a novel approach to the task of malware behavioral modeling for the identification of similar samples. Our guiding intuition is to model malware behaviors as textual documents by isolating textual features (natural language words) from the byte content of memory accessed during the sample execution. Our goal is to effectively transform the problem of classifying malware samples into a task which could be tackled with techniques derived from the well studied domains of text mining and document classification. The overwhelmingly high percentage of code reuse in malicious software discovered in the wild [30,31,36] will lead to a high occurrence of the same words in malware samples belonging to the same families.

5.1 Acquiring the Features

We first identified the subsets of each whole-system trace where the malware was actually executing. To do so, we monitored system calls and tracked:

- the original malware process;
- any process directly created by a tracked process;
- any process whose memory was written by another tracked process (in order to catch instances of code injection attacks).

For each of these processes, we record the portion of the replay (indexed by instruction count) where the process was running.

Next, we replayed our corpus with a plugin that monitored memory reads and writes and checked for byte sequences that matched an entry in our wordlist. We initially used the technique reported in [12] but found that it was unable to scale to large wordlists. Instead, we built an optimized string search plugin that first creates an index of valid four-byte prefixes from the wordlist and stores them in a hash set; because the vast majority of memory writes will not match one of our prefixes, this allows us to quickly ignore memory writes that cannot possibly match. If the prefix does match, then we proceed to look up the string in a crit-bit tree (a variant of a Patricia Tree) and update a count for any matching word. We also perform normalization by converting each character to its uppercase equivalent, ignoring punctuation characters, and skipping NULL bytes (this last normalization step allows us to recognize the ASCII subset of UTF-16 encoded strings, which are common on Windows). The optimized version of our plugin imposes a relatively small (40%) overhead on the replay and easily handles wordlists with millions of entries.

Our wordlist consists of words between 4 and 20 characters long appearing in the English version of Wikipedia, a total of 4.4 million terms. Wikipedia was chosen because it encompasses both generic English words and proper nouns such as names of companies, software, etc.

5.2   Preprocessing

The *bag-of-words* representation, thus obtained, uses a vectors of dimension $N_{w,d}$ for each sample. Across the whole dataset, the total number of unique words is around 1.4 million. These high-dimensional feature vectors are computationally expensive to manage and often provide a noisy representation of the data. We therefore performed several preprocessing steps to reduce the dimensionality of our data. We first removed all words seen in a baseline recording of a clean, operating system only, run of the analysis platform, which allowed us to avoid words not correlated with the actual malicious behaviors. Next, we eliminated words found in more than 50% or less than 0.1% of the corpus (D). In the former case, a word that is present in a huge number of samples cannot be characteristic of a single family (or of a small group of families) and hence does not provide any valuable information. At the same time, very rare words, found only in a insignificant fraction of samples, would not provide a clear indication of affinity with a specific class. Finally, we removed strings which were purely numerical or contained non-ASCII characters, since these features are less likely to be interpretable. This procedure lowered the dimensionality of our feature vectors to ≈460,000.

Rather than dealing with raw word counts, information retrieval typically assigns each word a Term Frequency Inverse Document Frequency (TF-IDF) score, which evaluates the importance of a word in relation to a document collection. Essentially, a higher score implies that the word appears many times in a small fraction of documents, thus conveying a high discriminative power. Conversely, a low score indicates that the word appears either in very few or very many documents. TF-IDF is computed for each word w and document d as:

$$tf(w,d) = a + (1 - a)\frac{freq(w,d)}{max_{w\prime \in d}(freq(w\prime, d))}, \ a = 0.4 \tag{1}$$

$$idf(w,D) = \log \frac{|D|}{|d \in D : w \in d|} \tag{2}$$

$$tfidf(w,d) = tf(w,d) \cdot idf(w,D) \tag{3}$$

Because the vast majority of memory accesses consist of non-textual data, some shorter words will match by coincidence. To adjust for these "random" matches, we measured the frequency of each 3-byte sequence in the memory accesses in our corpus. We then compute a likelihood score for each word w as the sum of the logarithms of the frequencies of each 3-gram g composing the word:

$$randlike(w) = \sum_{g \in w} \log(freq(g)) \tag{4}$$

And finally combine the two scores to obtain a single word score:

$$wordscore(w, d) = tfidf(w, d) \cdot (-1) \cdot randlike(w) \tag{5}$$

5.3 Classification Model

Before attempting any classification task, the dataset was divided into 3 subsets: a training set, a test set, and a validation set (which was held out and not used during training), by randomly sampling 70%, 15%, 15% of the elements, respectively. Because machine learning algorithms deal poorly with class imbalance (which is present in our dataset, as seen in Sect. 3), we rebalanced it by undersampling the over-represented classes to a maximum of 1000 samples per class and imposing a hard lower threshold on under-represented families, considering only those categories represented by at least 100 samples. The balanced dataset consists of 28,582 malware samples belonging to 65 families.

Despite the preprocessing described previously, the feature vectors still posed a serious problem due to their high dimensionality. We additionally used Incremental Principal Component Analysis (PCA) to further reduce dimensionality while preserving the greatest amount of variance in the new dataset. Based on empirical experiments on a small subset of the dataset, we chose to reduce each vector to 2048 components for classification.

Our classification model is based loosely on the Deep Averaging Network used by Iyyer et al. [14] for sentiment analysis. The model is a 5-layer feed-forward artificial neural network, with 2048, 1024, 512, 256, and 65 nodes in each layer. A final *Softmax* layer was used for multi-class classification. We implemented the network in Tensorflow [2] and trained it on our dataset. Given the different shape of our input vectors from the ones used in the sentiment analysis context, we performed a classical feature scaling normalization instead of vector averaging. In addition to the regular application of dropout to the hidden layers, in our model the dropout is applied also to the input layer, by randomly setting to zero some of the features, similar the technique suggested by Iyyer et al. [14].

5.4 Results

The Deep Network classifier achieves an overall F1 score of 94.26% on the validation set, and its median F1 score is 97.2%. Figure 5 shows the confusion matrix for the classifier. This is a remarkably positive result considering that malware family classification was performed on such a high number of different classes (65). The average F-Score is lowered by a few isolated families: only 6 are below 0.75 and just 2 below 0.5. The reported results seem to confirm the ability of the model to exploit the peculiarities of the dataset, obtaining a good predictive capacity.

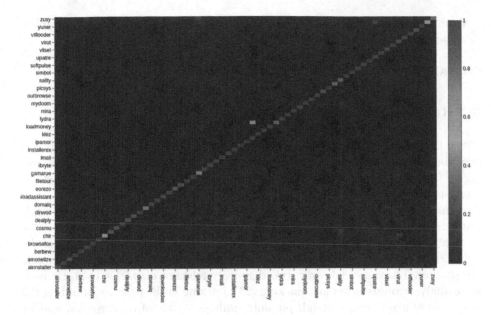

Fig. 5. Confusion matrix for deep network classification of the validation set.

5.5 Textual Search in Malware Samples

In order to further show the usefulness of this approach to the characterization of malicious software behavior, we experimented with employing a full-text search engine to explore the natural language feature data. Using Elasticsearch,[4] we indexed the words recovered during execution. This enabled us to efficiently retrieve the details of malicious programs by specifying particular strings.

We performed two kind of queries. First, we looked for relevant strings regarding the 20 most represented malware families, found in reports and white-papers by antivirus vendors. The ransomware Virlock is clearly identifiable by the strings included in the reports, with the word "bitcoin" appearing in 1,420 samples, of which 74% are Virlock. Other classes like Virut, Sality and Upatre showed words which appeared in samples of those families around 15% of the times. On the other hand, some words which were found in a large number of samples of different families were also found inside almost all the samples of a specific family. For instance, the word "mira", found in 24,000 samples, appeared also in each of the 1,109 samples of the class Mira.

We also searched for a list of 10 well-known antivirus vendors and U.S. bank names. In this case we noted that the Virut[5] family showed a very high propensity to contain names of AV products. Words like "McAfee", "Sophos", "Norton", and "Symantec" were found in multiple samples belonging to that family (from 15% to 37% of the retrieved samples). Bank names, instead, were often found in

---

[4] https://www.elastic.co/products/elasticsearch.
[5] Virut is a malware botnet that spreads through html and executable files infection.

different families, with "Wells Fargo" appearing prevalently in Firseria samples, "Paribas" in Lydra, and "Barclays" in Lamer.

We plan to make this search engine available as a public interface to our dataset in order to help researchers quickly locate samples of interest.

6   Related Work

Given the relevance of the threat posed today by malicious software distributed over the Internet, a wide number of different attempts have been made at studying it. Two main approaches exists for the analysis of software samples: static analysis, where the binary file is thoroughly inspected but not executed, and dynamic analysis where the unknown program is run in an instrumented environment in order to acquire information regarding its behavior.

Static analysis, in theory, allows a thorough, and complete, exploration of the behavior of the analyzed sample, and is often more cost-efficient than dynamic approaches. There are, however, two definitely relevant obstacles to static malware analysis: obfuscation and packing [23]. Packing is the practice of hiding the real code of a program through possibly multiple levels of compression and/or encryption. Obfuscation is the process of taking an arbitrary program and converting it to a new program, with the exact same functionality, that is unintelligible, by some definition of that characteristic [5]. Due to the still unsolved nature of those issues, in this work we focused our attention on dynamic analysis platforms.

6.1   Dynamic Analysis Platforms

Over the years a noticeable wealth of research work has been produced in the field of dynamic malware analysis systems. Instrumentation of user level programs at runtime was firstly conceived as a technique for profiling, performance evaluation and debugging. It has been deeply studied with systems like Pin [20], Valgrind [24] and DynamoRIO [7]. Those systems, while achieving good performance and enabling heavyweight analyses, were limited to single user level processes. Successively, in the late 2000s, dynamic analysis platforms aimed at the identification of malicious software started to become common.

A remarkable example of one of such platforms, which allowed the collection of whole system execution trace, was Anubis [21]. Anubis was based on the QEMU emulator and is now discontinued. The platform was employed in [6] which represented a milestone in research regarding automated malware analysis. The proposed approach abstracted system calls traces with the definition of a set of operating systems objects, useful to avoid the high variability of traces describing similar behaviors, and performed the clustering operation using Locality Sensitive Hashing, which allowed the system to scale easily with large datasets.

A different technique was proposed with Ether [10], which leveraged hardware virtualization extensions to eliminate in-guest software components, in order to appear as transparent as possible to the analyzed malware sample. This approach was specifically targeted at thwarting sandbox evasion attempts from virtualization-aware malicious programs. Another, distinct, method is the one found in BitBlaze [29], by Song et al. which fuses together elements of static and dynamic analysis. The structure of this complex system was composed by three main elements: Vine, a static analysis tool providing an intermediate language for assembly; TEMU, built on the QEMU whole system emulator, which provided the dynamic analysis capabilities; Rudder for on-line dynamic symbolic execution. The maintenance of all these platforms seems to have ceased.

Other relevant dynamic analysis systems are still currently actively used in academia and industry contexts. CWSandbox [34] was developed in 2007 to track malicious software behavior through API hooking. Contrary to Anubis, CWSandbox was designed to use virtualization, instead of CPU emulation. Cuckoo Sandbox[6] is another widely used automated malware analysis environment, which powers the on-line analysis service Malwr.[7] Similar to its predecessors, Cuckoo produces comprehensive reports containing information regarding: system call traces, network and file-system activity, screenshots, and memory dumps.

All the platforms mentioned above, however, lack the flexibility provided by the incremental and retrospective analysis capabilities of MALREC. These advanced functionalities are granted by the use of PANDA [11] (Platform for Architecture-Neutral Dynamic Analysis) which implements the concept of deterministic replay to allow the recording, compressed storage, and unmodified replay of full-system execution traces. In the next subsection we will look with particular attention at those sandbox systems which allow the recording and instrumented replay of execution traces.

6.2   Deterministic Replay Systems

Usage of the record and replay methodology was firstly introduced for debugging purposes by LeBlanc and Mellor-Crummey [18] to tackle non-determinism in execution flows. Different solutions to the problem of providing deterministic executions of computer programs in presence of nondeterministic factors were developed over time. A comprehensive overview of those methodologies is provided by [8]. A particularly interesting examples of these techniques, is the use of time-traveling virtual machines (TTVM) for operating systems debugging [17], which allowed whole system recording. VMWare also used to support the Record and Replay feature in its Workstation products [32]. This capability, however, was removed in the Workstation 8 release.

Pioneering work in the field of recording and replaying whole system traces for intrusion detection was provided by ReVirt [13] by Dunlap et al. The Aftersight project [9], in 2008, was the first to apply the approach of decoupling heavyweight trace analyses from the actual sand-boxed execution. The architecture if this

---

[6] https://cuckoosandbox.org/.
[7] https://malwr.com/.

system was based on two main components: a recording step executed inside a VMWare virtualized environment, and a replay phase on a system emulated through QEMU to enable deep instrumentation.

The concept of decoupled dynamic analysis was further expanded in V2E [35] by Yan et al. V2E exploits hardware virtualization to achieve good recording performance and software emulation to support heavily instrumented analyses. The presented implementation, which conceptually resembles that of Aftersight, is based on the use of Linux KVM (Kernel Virtual Machines) during the recording phase and the TEMU emulator to enable heavyweight analyses during replay.

7 Conclusion

Automated malware analysis systems have become increasingly crucial in dealing with the triage of computer attacks. In this paper we introduced a novel sandbox platform, MALREC that overcomes several shortcomings of traditional malware analysis systems by leveraging high-fidelity, whole-system record and replay. MALREC enables the development of complex, iterative analyses that would be infeasible in standard dynamic analysis platforms. We also introduced a new dataset of 66,301 full-system recordings of malicious software. This dataset, along with accompanying documentation, can be found at:

http://giantpanda.gtisc.gatech.edu/malrec/dataset

We presented two case studies based on this dataset which highlight the usefulness of whole-system record and replay in malware analysis. In the first, we comprehensively catalog the kernel-mode malware present in our dataset. We discovered 503 samples which loaded malicious kernel modules using 3 different techniques, including exploiting a vulnerability in the Windows kernel for privilege escalation. The second analysis takes advantage of the ability to monitor every memory access without disrupting the execution of the malware by extracting fine-grained features based on the natural language words read from or written to memory during execution. We then showed that we could employ those features to train a Deep Neural Network classifier that achieved a global F1-Score of 94.2%.

It is our hope that this system and dataset will enable future research in dynamic malware analysis by providing a standard benchmark and a large supply of test data. This will allow researchers to directly compare the results of competing dynamic analyses, reproduce each others' work, and develop deep, retrospective analyses of malware.

Acknowledgments. We would like to thank our anonymous reviewers for their helpful feedback, as well as Paul Royal and the Georgia Tech Institute for Information Security and Privacy for their help in obtaining malware samples for MALREC. Funding for this research was provided under NSF Award #1657199.

References

1. Volatility command reference - GUI. https://github.com/volatilityfoundation/volatility/wiki/Command-Reference-Gui
2. Abadi, M.N., Agarwal, A., Barham, P., Brevdo, E., Chen, Z., Citro, C., Corrado, G.S., Davis, A., Dean, J., Devin, M., Ghemawat, S., Goodfellow, I., Harp, A., Irving, G., Isard, M., Jia, Y., Jozefowicz, R., Kaiser, L., Kudlur, M., Levenberg, J., Mane, D., Monga, R., Moore, S., Murray, D., Olah, C., Schuster, M., Shlens, J., Steiner, B., Sutskever, I., Talwar, K., Tucker, P., Vanhoucke, V., Vasudevan, V., Viegas, F., Vinyals, O., Warden, P., Wattenberg, M., Wicke, M., Yu, Y., Zheng, X.: TensorFlow: Large-Scale Machine Learning on Heterogeneous Distributed Systems. arXiv: 1603.04467 [cs], March 2016
3. Abadi, M., Budiu, M., Erlingsson, U., Ligatti, J.: Control-flow integrity. In: ACM Conference on Computer and Communications Security (2005)
4. Balzarotti, D., Cova, M., Karlberger, C., Kirda, E., Kruegel, C., Vigna, G.: Efficient detection of split personalities in malware. In: NDSS (2010)
5. Barak, B., Goldreich, O., Impagliazzo, R., Rudich, S., Sahai, A., Vadhan, S., Yang, K.: On the (im)possibility of obfuscating programs. In: Kilian, J. (ed.) CRYPTO 2001. LNCS, vol. 2139, pp. 1–18. Springer, Heidelberg (2001). https://doi.org/10.1007/3-540-44647-8_1
6. Bayer, U., Comparetti, P.M., Hlauschek, C., Kruegel, C., Kirda, E.: Scalable, behavior-based malware clustering. In: NDSS, vol. 9, pp. 8–11. Citeseer (2009)
7. Bruening, D., Garnett, T., Amarasinghe, S.: An infrastructure for adaptive dynamic optimization. In: International Symposium on Code Generation and Optimization, CGO 2003, pp. 265–275. IEEE (2003)
8. Chen, Y., Zhang, S., Guo, Q., Li, L., Wu, R., Chen, T.: Deterministic replay: a survey. ACM Comput. Surv. 48(2), 1–47 (2015)
9. Chow, J., Garfinkel, T., Chen, P.M.: Decoupling dynamic program analysis from execution in virtual environments. In: USENIX 2008 Annual Technical Conference on Annual Technical Conference, pp. 1–14 (2008)
10. Dinaburg, A., Royal, P., Sharif, M., Lee, W.: Ether: malware analysis via hardware virtualization extensions. In: Proceedings of the 15th ACM Conference on Computer and Communications Security, pp. 51–62. ACM (2008)
11. Dolan-Gavitt, B., Hodosh, J., Hulin, P., Leek, T., Whelan, R.: Repeatable reverse engineering with PANDA. In: Program Protection and Reverse Engineering Workshop (PPREW), pp. 1–11. ACM Press (2015)
12. Dolan-Gavitt, B., Leek, T., Hodosh, J., Lee, W.: Tappan zee (north) bridge: mining memory accesses for introspection. In: ACM Conference on Computer and Communications Security (CCS), pp. 839–850. ACM Press (2013)
13. Dunlap, G.W., King, S.T., Cinar, S., Basrai, M.A., Chen, P.M.: ReVirt: enabling intrusion analysis through virtual-machine logging and replay. SIGOPS Oper. Syst. Rev. 36(SI), 211–224 (2002)
14. Iyyer, M., Manjunatha, V., Boyd-Graber, J., Daumé III, H.: Deep unordered composition rivals syntactic methods for text classification. In: Proceedings of the 53rd Annual Meeting of the Association for Computational Linguistics and the 7th International Joint Conference on Natural Language Processing (vol. 1: Long Papers), pp. 1681–1691 (2015)
15. Kantchelian, A., Tschantz, M.C., Afroz, S., Miller, B., Shankar, V., Bachwani, R., Joseph, A.D., Tygar, J.D.: Better malware ground truth: techniques for weighting anti-virus vendor labels. In: ACM Workshop on Artificial Intelligence and Security (AISEC), pp. 45–56. ACM Press (2015)

16. King, S.T., Chen, P.M.: Backtracking intrusions. ACM Trans. Comput. Syst. (TOCS) **23**(1), 51–76 (2005)
17. King, S.T., Dunlap, G.W., Chen, P.M.: Debugging operating systems with time-traveling virtual machines. In: Proceedings of the Annual Conference on USENIX Annual Technical Conference, p. 1 (2005)
18. LeBlanc, T.J., Mellor-Crummey, J.M.: Debugging parallel programs with instant replay. IEEE Trans. Comput. **36**(4), 471–482 (1987)
19. Li, P., Liu, L., Gao, D., Reiter, M.K.: On challenges in evaluating malware clustering. In: Jha, S., Sommer, R., Kreibich, C. (eds.) RAID 2010. LNCS, vol. 6307, pp. 238–255. Springer, Heidelberg (2010). https://doi.org/10.1007/978-3-642-15512-3_13
20. Luk, C.K., Cohn, R., Muth, R., Patil, H., Klauser, A., Lowney, G., Wallace, S., Reddi, V.J., Hazelwood, K.: Pin: building customized program analysis tools with dynamic instrumentation. In: ACM SIGPLAN Notices, vol. 40, pp. 190–200. ACM (2005)
21. Mandl, T., Bayer, U., Nentwich, F.: ANUBIS ANalyzing unknown BInarieS the automatic way. In: Virus Bulletin Conference, vol. 1, p. 2 (2009)
22. Mohaisen, A., Alrawi, O.: AV-meter: an evaluation of antivirus scans and labels. In: Dietrich, S. (ed.) DIMVA 2014. LNCS, vol. 8550, pp. 112–131. Springer, Cham (2014). https://doi.org/10.1007/978-3-319-08509-8_7
23. Moser, A., Kruegel, C., Kirda, E.: Limits of static analysis for malware detection. In: Twenty-Third Annual Computer Security Applications Conference, ACSAC 2007, pp. 421–430. IEEE (2007)
24. Nethercote, N., Seward, J.: Valgrind: a framework for heavyweight dynamic binary instrumentation. In: ACM SIGPLAN Notices, vol. 42, pp. 89–100. ACM (2007)
25. Newsome, J.: Dynamic taint analysis for automatic detection, analysis, and signature generation of exploits on commodity software. In: Network and Distributed System Security Symposium (NDSS) (2005)
26. Prakash, A., Yin, H., Liang, Z.: Enforcing system-wide control flow integrity for exploit detection and diagnosis. In: ACM SIGSAC Symposium on Information, Computer and Communications Security (2013)
27. Quynh, N.A.: Capstone: Next-Gen Disassembly Framework. Black Hat USA (2014)
28. Sebastián, M., Rivera, R., Kotzias, P., Caballero, J.: AVCLASS: a tool for massive malware labeling. In: Monrose, F., Dacier, M., Blanc, G., Garcia-Alfaro, J. (eds.) RAID 2016. LNCS, vol. 9854, pp. 230–253. Springer, Cham (2016). https://doi.org/10.1007/978-3-319-45719-2_11
29. Song, D., et al.: BitBlaze: a new approach to computer security via binary analysis. In: Sekar, R., Pujari, A.K. (eds.) ICISS 2008. LNCS, vol. 5352, pp. 1–25. Springer, Heidelberg (2008). https://doi.org/10.1007/978-3-540-89862-7_1
30. Tian, K., Yao, D., Ryder, B.G., Tan, G.: Analysis of code heterogeneity for high-precision classification of repackaged malware. In: 2016 IEEE Security and Privacy Workshops (SPW), pp. 262–271, May 2016
31. Upchurch, J., Zhou, X.: Malware provenance: code reuse detection in malicious software at scale. In: 2016 11th International Conference on Malicious and Unwanted Software (MALWARE), pp. 1–9, October 2016
32. VMWare: Enhanced Execution Record/Replay in Workstation 6.5, April 2008
33. Walters, A.: The Volatility framework: Volatile memory artifact extraction utility framework. https://www.volatilesystems.com/default/volatility

34. Willems, C., Holz, T., Freiling, F.: Toward automated dynamic malware analysis using CWSandbox. IEEE Secur. Priv. **5**(2), 32–39 (2007)
35. Yan, L.K., Jayachandra, M., Zhang, M., Yin, H.: V2E: combining hardware virtualization and software emulation for transparent and extensible malware analysis. ACM SIGPLAN Not. **47**(7), 227–238 (2012)
36. Zhou, Y., Jiang, X.: Dissecting android malware: characterization and evolution. In: 2012 IEEE Symposium on Security and Privacy, pp. 95–109, May 2012

MEMSCRIMPER: Time- and Space-Efficient Storage of Malware Sandbox Memory Dumps

Michael Brengel$^{(\boxtimes)}$ and Christian Rossow

CISPA, Saarland University, Saarbrücken, Germany
{michael.brengel,rossow}@cispa.saarland

Abstract. We present MEMSCRIMPER, a novel methodology to compress memory dumps of malware sandboxes. MEMSCRIMPER is built on the observation that sandboxes always start at the same system state (i.e., a sandbox snapshot) to analyze malware. Therefore, memory dumps taken after malware execution inside the same sandbox are substantially similar to each other, which we can use to only store the differences introduced by the malware itself. Technically, we compare the pages of those memory dumps against the pages of a reference memory dump taken from the same sandbox and then deduplicate identical or similar pages accordingly. MEMSCRIMPER increases data compression ratios by up to 3894.74% compared to standard compression utilities such as 7zip, and reduces compression and decompression times by up to 72.48% and 41.44%, respectively. Furthermore, MEMSCRIMPER's internal storage allows to perform analyses (e.g., signature matching) on compressed memory dumps more efficient than on uncompressed dumps. MEMSCRIMPER thus significantly increases the retention time of memory dumps and makes longitudinal analysis more viable, while also improving efficiency.

1 Introduction

As of 2018, the number of new and potentially malicious files has risen to over 250,000 per day [2]. Naturally, defenders strive to analyze as many of these files as possible. Malware sandboxes play a key role in this process and represent *the* prevalent mechanism to study the behavior of unknown programs. To cope with the daily flood of unknown files, malware sandboxes can utilize hardware virtualization (e.g., Intel VT) to speed up parallel processing. While significant progress has been made in scaling malware analysis [5,6,9,13,14], mechanisms how to efficiently store the results of malware analysis has received little attention so far. Obviously, without detailed planning and well-tuned mechanisms, long-term storage of analysis results hardly scales. This is particularly challenging for unstructured and space-consuming outputs such as memory snapshots ("images" or "dumps") taken during or after malware analysis. Although storing memory images seems unfeasible at first, a persistent storage is appealing. First,

C. Giuffrida et al. (Eds.): DIMVA 2018, LNCS 10885, pp. 24–45, 2018.
https://doi.org/10.1007/978-3-319-93411-2_2

a long-term storage of memory dumps enables for a large variety of promising forensic analyses, such as on the evolution of malware over time (e.g., lineage), extracting malware configuration files (e.g., to see targets of banking trojans), or group similar malware files by clustering them on unpacked malware code [10]. Second, a long-term storage of memory artifacts aids to grasp the concept drift in malware, e.g., to reevaluate the accuracy of code signatures (e.g., YARA) over a long-term data set. Yet, as compelling as it sounds, naïvely storing memory dumps for each malware analysis run does not scale. Given that the storage footprint of regular memory dumps equals to the virtual memory given to a sandbox, merely analyzing 10,000 malware samples requires already about 5 TiB of disk space (assuming 512 MiB per dump) to persistently store malware dumps.

To tackle this problem, we propose time- and space-efficient storage methodologies for dumps stemming from malware sandboxes. We first study the straw man solution to the problem and assess how regular file compression algorithms perform. While existing compression utilities reduce storage demands by an order of magnitude, they (i) have a relatively poor computation performance, and (ii) do not achieve compression ratios that would allow for persistent data storage. We thus propose novel methodologies that (i) better utilize the structure of memory dumps (i.e., memory pages), and (ii) leverage the fact that we are actually only interested in *changes* caused by the malware under analysis.

Our main idea is borrowed from genome data processing in biology, which faces similar scaling problems for persistently storing genomes. While a human's genome consists of about 3 *billion* pairs, only very few (around 0.1%) of these pairs are actually different per human. Thus, by just storing these *mutations*, one can significantly reduce the space footprint of a genome. Transposing this idea to malware, we observed that malware changes the memory only slightly compared to a system *before* infection. Our general idea is thus to store only these differences compared to a base snapshot that is taken before analyzing a particular file. That is, given that sandboxes usually use snapshots to restore to a clean state after analyzing a file [22], we first save a so called reference memory dump from this state. This reference dump is identical for all files analyzed with a given sandbox and thus needs to be persisted only once. Then, after having analyzed a malware in the sandbox, we compare the memory dump of the malware-infected system with the reference dump and only store the differences between the two. Furthermore, we can leverage page-wise memory deduplication, as deployed in operating systems or incremental checkpoints of hypervisors [16, 17,20], to reduce the dump size. As a final optimization, we search for pages that have only slightly been altered compared to the reference dump, and if so, we store only the changes instead of the entire page.

We implement MEMSCRIMPER, a prototype for this methodology. Our results show that MEMSCRIMPER outperforms standard compression utilities such as 7zip in our sandbox context. MEMSCRIMPER improves the data compression ratio by up to 3894.74%, while reducing compression and decompression times by up to 72.48% and 41.44%, respectively. Storing a 2 GiB memory dump with MEMSCRIMPER requires roughly 5 MiB (<0.3%) on average. Finally, we measure

if forensic analysis can be carried out on such compressed dumps by matching
YARA [1] rules on them. This demonstrates how we can speed up the forensic
analysis with our methodology due to the smaller file size of the compressed
memory dumps.

2   Methodology

We first motivate our idea and give technical preliminaries which are required
to grasp the concepts of our approach. We then describe the two main compression ideas, namely *intra-deduplication* and *inter-deduplication*, which are implemented by MEMSCRIMPER (Sect. 3) and which will be evaluated in Sect. 4.

2.1   Motivation and High-Level Idea

Our proposed methodology is designed to be used in large-scale malware analysis
systems. In such a setting, the following high-level workflow is usually deployed:

1. **Set up an analysis environment.** This involves installing an operating system and configuring it to run the malware. The latter includes disabling security mechanisms such as firewalls or built-in anti-virus solutions to increase
   the likelihood that the malware will expose its malicious behavior.
2. **Create a snapshot.** To ensure that malware exposes its malicious behavior
   and to ease the analysis, the malware should be executed in an untampered
   environment. This allows to eliminate side effects where one malware might
   hinder another malware from executing and also reduces noise in the behavioral data. To guarantee such a clean state, snapshots can revert the state of
   the system to the one immediately after the setup process (step 1). Snapshots
   are common in both virtualization-based and bare-metal sandboxes [12].
3. **Analyze the malware.** The first two steps will be executed once per analysis
   machine. After that, the malware is executed for a predefined amount of time
   after which the analysis data (including the memory dump) is collected, and
   finally, the system is restored to its original snapshot state. This procedure is
   repeated for every malware sample that will be executed.

The core design principle of MEMSCRIMPER is based on two intuitive assumptions. First, the snapshot guarantees that the memory will be bit-by-bit identical
every time the execution of a malware sample starts. Second, it is unlikely that a
malware will modify huge parts of the memory of the analysis machine. This follows the intuition that malware usually has a small memory footprint to operate
stealthily and to ensure that it runs on a variety of systems including systems
where memory is scarce. These two observations imply that the memory dumps
resulting from executions of different malware samples on the same analysis
environment will share a significant amount of their memory contents. By simply storing memory dumps in plain, the space is not efficiently used, as the same
memory content is stored over and over again. This is also true if the memory
dump is deflated with standard compression utilities such as `gzip` or `7zip`, since
the same memory content is redundantly compressed. With MEMSCRIMPER we
fill this gap.

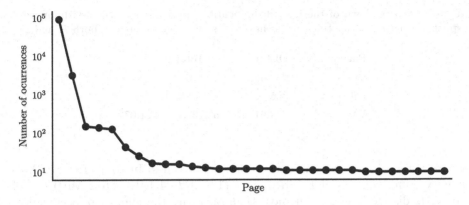

Fig. 1. The number of occurrences of the 30 most common pages of a 512 MiB memory dump taken from a Windows XP analysis machine.

2.2   Terminology

The central objects that MEMSCRIMPER works on are *memory dumps*. A memory dump is a bit-by-bit copy of the *physical memory* of a system taken at some point in time. Modern operating systems and hardware use the concept of *virtual memory*, which gives each running process the impression of having a large contiguous space of memory. This virtual memory space is then mapped to the physical memory space, which does not have to be contiguous. The granularity of this mapping is determined by the *page size*. The page size is an important piece of structural information that dictates the way we process memory dumps. We will focus on the x86 platform, which has a page size of 4,096 bytes. Formally, we consider a memory dump $\mathcal{D}$ as an ordered sequence of pages, i.e., $\mathcal{D} = [P_1, \ldots, P_n]$ where $P_i \in \mathcal{D}$ is the ith page of $\mathcal{D}$—we will also call i a *page number*. A page is an ordered sequence of bytes, i.e. $P_i = [b_{i,1}, \ldots, b_{i,ps}]$ where $b_{i,j} \in [0, 255]$ and ps is the page size.

2.3   Intradeduplication

As a first mean of compressing a memory dump, we leverage two observations. First, sandboxes usually have a small memory footprint, since they do not have a lot of software executing on them. Hence, the majority of the physical memory is unused, which usually means that the vast majority of the pages contain only 0-bytes. Second, some of the pages inside the memory dump besides the 0-byte pages are likely to appear multiple times. This is because of technical issues like the usage of different library versions or memory-mapped files.

To illustrate this, Fig. 1 shows the number of occurrences of the 30 most-common pages of a 512 MiB memory dump of a Windows XP analysis system we created. The most common page is the page which contains only 0-bytes and occurs 91,698 times. While this is expected, also other, non-zero pages occur several times. For example, the second most common page also contains mostly

Table 1. A breakdown of the inter-deduplicatable pages of a Carbanak dump with respect to whether or not those pages have the same page number in both $\mathcal{R}$ and $\mathcal{D}$.

Page number	Distinct	Total
Same	23,695	118,685
Different	365	8,500
$\sum$	23,991/27,776	127,185/131,072

0-bytes with a few exceptions and occurs 3,173 times. In total, the 512 MiB memory dump consists of 131,072 pages ($131,072 \cdot 4$ KiB $= 512$ MiB) out of which 942 distinct pages occur more than once and the number of occurrences sum up to 97,663. This means that 97,663 out of 131,072 pages (74.51%) can be represented by storing only 942 (0.72%) pages plus some metadata overhead.

We call this way of compressing a memory dump *intra-deduplication*, as it deduplicates pages *within* a given memory dump. While intra-deduplication seems promising, we will see that this compression idea is inferior to the one we will describe next—given that common compression methods work similarly. However, it is very efficient and gives a basic understanding of the modus operandi of MemScrimper. In particular, it shows how we can leverage the structure of memory dumps, i.e., the concept of pages, to achieve a compression with simple means. We just need to read the memory dump page-wise, keep track of pages that occur more than once, and finally, write a data structure which leverages this deduplication idea (cf. Sect. 3.2 for more details).

2.4   Interdeduplication

We now describe *inter-deduplication*, which is a second, more evolved compression method implemented in MemScrimper. The idea of inter-deduplication is to compare a memory dump $\mathcal{D}$ that we want to compress with the help of a reference dump $\mathcal{R}$ of the analysis machine. That is, we parse the sequence of pages $[P_1, \ldots, P_n]$ of $\mathcal{D}$ and check for each P_i if it is present in the reference dump $\mathcal{R}$, i.e., we check if $P_i \in \mathcal{R}$ is true. If this is the case, it means that we do not have to store P_i. Instead, we only need to store referential information that links the deduplicated page from $\mathcal{D}$ to the correct page number of $\mathcal{R}$.

To illustrate the effectiveness of this idea, Table 1 shows how many pages of a memory dump resulting from an execution of a Carbanak APT malware can be deduplicated when compared against the reference dump. In total, 23,991 distinct pages occur more than once and the number of occurrences sum up to 127,185. This means that 127,185 out of 131,072 pages (97.03%) can be represented by storing only referential information. In fact, as we will see later in the implementation details in Sect. 3.3, we only need to store referential information if the deduplicated page has a different page number in $\mathcal{D}$ than it has in $\mathcal{R}$. The vast majority of deduplicatable pages ($118,685/127,185 \approx 93.32\%$) share the page number between $\mathcal{R}$ and $\mathcal{D}$, which means that we do not need to store a single byte to represent those pages. We will only need to store referential information for the 8,500/127,185 (6.68%) pages which have a different page number in $\mathcal{R}$ than they do have in $\mathcal{D}$.

Combining Interdeduplication with Intradeduplication: In our example, inter-deduplication leaves 3,887 (2.97%) that cannot be deduplicated as they do not appear in $\mathcal{R}$. To further reduce the amount of information required to represent those pages one could apply the intra-deduplication technique between those 3,887 pages. In this example, 101 (2.60%) of the distinct pages occur more than once and the number of total occurrences sums up to 202. This means that intra-deduplication might only add a slight improvement, and as we will show in Sect. 4, might even reduce the compression ratio if we add standard compression utilities on top.

Differential Interdeduplication: So far we have deduplicated *identical* pages. We now search for *similar* pages, and if possible, only store differential information to a similar page. Such a differential view is particularly helpful if pages are only slightly modified when the malware executed. While a strict page comparison would interpret such slight changes as failure to deduplicate, a differential deduplication likely requires less space than saving the entire updated page. Thus, for each page P_i, we check if we can find a similar page $P'_j \in R$ and only store the diff $\delta(P_i, P'_j) = [b'_{j,k} \mid 1 \le k \le ps, P_i \ni b_{i,k} \ne b'_{j,k} \in P'_j]$, i.e., the byte-wise difference of both pages. The diff function δ captures the type of modifications we expect, i.e., patches which just replace a few bytes as opposed to more complex modifications which completely move data inside a page. Additionally, we expect the closest candidate to reside at the same page number in the reference dump. Hence, we let $j = i$, which also makes the candidate selection less costly. Since we need some metadata for storing a diff, i.e., the offsets of the bytes which will need to be patched, we only store a diff if the number of bytes plus the metadata overhead is smaller than the page size.

In our running Cabernak example, 3,811 out of 3,887 pages (98.04%) yield a diff (including overhead) which is smaller than the page size. On average, the size of the diff without overhead, i.e. $|\delta(P_i, P'_i)|$, is 891.39 bytes (median 317, std 1,099.4). The sum of all $\delta(P_i, P'_i)$ is 3,397,094 bytes, which is $3,811 \cdot 4,096 - 3,397,094 = 12,212,762 \approx 11.65$ MiB less than what would be needed to store those pages without our diffing idea (ignoring metadata overhead). To foreshadow a bit, however, the overhead of storing diffs is not negligible and would account for 527.21 KiB in this example.

After performing all of these steps, only a negligible fraction of pages, i.e., 76/131,072 (0.06%), need to be stored without any of the previous optimizations being applied to them. The remaining 130,996/131,072 pages (99.94%) could either be deduplicated page-wise, or a similar page was found in $\mathcal{R}$ such that storing the diff is less costly than storing the entire new page.

3 Implementation

We will now describe the implementation details of MEMSCRIMPER. We implemented a reference prototype in Python, which includes the design of a file format for memory dumps compressed with MEMSCRIMPER.

3.1 File Format Overview

The compressed memory dump files of MEMSCRIMPER consist of two components, the *header* and the *body*. The header contains metadata which is shared among the different compression methods, while the body contains method-specific metadata as well as the actual compressed memory dump. We first define the header, which contains the following information:

Magic Number. A zero-terminated string (*str*) (currently "MBCR"), which aids file identification.

Method. The name of the method (*str*) that the memory dump has been compressed with (e.g., "intradedup" for intra-deduplication).

Major Version Number. A two-byte integer describing the version of MEMSCRIMPER, which can, e.g., be used to track changes to the header format.

Minor Version Number. A two-byte integer version number that can be used to track changes to the compression method implementation.

Page Size. The page size (in bytes, usually 4096) that has been assumed for the compression represented with a four-byte integer (4B).

Uncompressed Size. The size of the uncompressed dump in bytes represented with an eight-byte integer (8B).

3.2 Intradeduplication

Intra-deduplication finds pages which are shared *within* the same memory dump. Technically, we read the memory dump page-wise and keep track of duplicate appearances. To reduce the memory footprint of pages that already appeared previously in the memory dump, we can store hashes instead of the entire page contents. The file format that we use for intra-deduplication memory dumps is depicted in Fig. 2. The integer n stores the number of distinct pages used as reference during deduplication and corresponds to the number of page contents that appear in more than one page in the given dump. For each such page, we can deduplicate all other identical pages. After the number n, we write all these n reference pages next to each other in the file (*ps* is the page size in bytes).

Once we have stored all reference pages, we now also have to encode how these pages were referred to in the original memory dump. That is, we need to denote at which offset(s) each reference page was stored such that we can (during decompression) reconstruct the original file. A naïve solution would be storing a list of original page numbers for each reference page. Yet such lists waste space if we face large contiguous ranges where the same page occurs repeatedly, as for example in the case of 0-pages. To account for this, for each reference

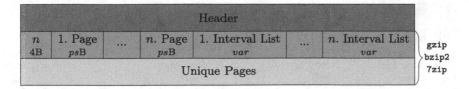

Fig. 2. File format of a memory dump, which was compressed with intra-deduplication.

t	d	l	r − l
1b	2b	29b	{0,1,2,4}B

Fig. 3. Encoding of an interval $[l, r]$.

page, we store a list of page number intervals. A list of page number intervals is an ordered sequence of intervals $I = [l, r]$, in which each interval represents the page numbers at which a deduplication page occurs. Figure 3 depicts how we encode an interval. First, we store the termination bit t, which indicates whether this interval is the last item of the contiguous interval list. This enables the decompressor to detect the end of an interval list without the need to store the length of the interval. After that we store a two bit number d, which describes the number of bytes that is required to store the size of the interval (the four possible states are mapped to an interval length size of 0, 1, 2 or 4 bytes). To encode the actual interval, we store the left side of the interval l, i.e., the page number at which the interval starts. Finally, we encode the size of the interval in number of pages (minus 1), i.e., $r - l$. We omit the size encoding if the interval is just one page (determined by d), such that we can store single-page intervals in just four bytes.

To parse an interval list, the decompressor would proceed as follows: First, t, d and l are read. Then, the size of the interval can be deduced depending on the value of d. If $d = 0$, the interval is $[l, l]$ and the $r - l$ field is omitted. For $d = 1$, the $r - l$ field is a single byte long and can indicate a page range of maximum 256 pages. For the maximum $d = 3$, the $r - l$ field is four bytes long and can indicate a size of up to 2^{32} pages. With this information, the decompressor can reconstruct the interval $[l, r]$. If $t = 0$, this process is repeated until the final entry that has $t = 1$ and thus terminates the list of page intervals.

The notion of intervals serves as a zero-overhead alternative to plainly storing page numbers. If a deduplicated page occurs only twice at non-consecutive page numbers, for example, we would represent this with two interval lists which would be 4-bytes each, which is the same number of bytes that we would require if we simply stored the page numbers directly. Since we use 29 bits to denote the left side of the interval l, the maximum number of pages that MEMSCRIMPER can handle with this method is $2^{29} - 1$, which roughly corresponds to 2 TiB memory dumps if we consider a page size of 4 KiB. Any changes to size constraints made in the file format can be reflected by the minor version field of the header.

Header						
Reference	n	PageNr List	1. Interval List	...	n. Interval List	gzip
str	4B	var	var		var	bzip2
Interval List		1. New Page	...	l. New Page		7zip
var		psB		psB		

Fig. 4. File format of memory dump, which was compressed with inter-deduplication.

After the interval lists, the unique pages, i.e., the pages which cannot be deduplicated, are written next to each other in the same order as they appear in the memory dump. We do not need to store any referential information for those pages. To reconstruct the memory dump, the decompressor would first parse all the pages and intervals. The page numbers which are not contained in those intervals are then chronologically mapped to those unique pages.

Finally, to further compress the inter-deduplicated memory dump, we can optionally add standard compression utilities like gzip, bzip2 or 7zip on top of this method. This is achieved by simply compressing the body of the file with those utilities, while the header is left untouched to give the decompressor the necessary metadata for reconstructing the memory dump.

3.3 Interdeduplication

To compress a memory dump $\mathcal{D}$ with inter-deduplication, we need to compare the pages of $\mathcal{D}$ against the pages of a reference memory dump $\mathcal{R}$. To achieve this, we first parse the pages of $\mathcal{R}$ and then iterate over all pages in $\mathcal{D}$ and check if a page occurs in $\mathcal{R}$. If so, we can inter-deduplicate this page. If the page number of such a page is identical in $\mathcal{R}$ and $\mathcal{D}$, we do not need to store any information about the page. Only if the page numbers differ, we need to store the respective page number in the compressed memory dump.

The file format of the inter-deduplication method is depicted in Fig. 4. We first store the path of $\mathcal{R}$ so that the decompressor knows against which memory dump the compressed memory dump was compared. Similar to the intra-deduplication implementation, we again store the number of distinct reference pages n that are used as basis for (inter-)deduplication. Again, similarly, we store n page number interval lists which denote for each of the n reference pages where it occurs in $\mathcal{D}$. The missing bit of information, i.e., where the deduplication page occurs in $\mathcal{R}$ (its page number), is stored in a *page number list* that maps the n interval lists to n offsets in $\mathcal{R}$.

For space-efficiency reasons, the page number list is a sequence of n variable-sized integers. The first page number is absolute and all subsequent page numbers are relative to the page number given by the previous entry. If such a relative page number (or the first absolute page number) fits into 7 bits, the page number is encoded as a single-byte integer and the most significant bit is set to 1. This gives the decompressor the information that the page number can be recovered by only reading a single byte. Otherwise, the most significant bit is 0 and the page number is encoded with 4 bytes.

Finally, we need to store the new pages, i.e., pages which are not covered by inter-deduplication. We thus store a page number interval list that encodes the page numbers of all new pages, followed by the sequence of new pages. The number of page numbers encoded by the interval list is the same as the number of new pages, i.e., l in Fig. 4, which tells the decompressor where to put each new page. If a page number is not covered by this interval list or the page number list of the deduplicated pages, then this page is identical to the page in $\mathcal{R}$ at the same page number. This is also why we need to store referential information for the new pages, which we did not need to do for intra-deduplication.

Combined Inter- and Intradeduplication: The new pages in the basic inter-deduplication format are not deduplicated within themselves. That is, if a new page occurs multiple times, we still store that page redundantly multiple times. This can be fixed by applying intra-deduplication to those pages, similar as described before by storing an interval list for each of the l new pages. This idea is depicted in Fig. 5, where we also need to store the integer l to tell the decompressor how many new pages exist, which was previously given implicitly by the single interval list for the new pages. However, we noticed in our experiments that intra-deduplication applied to the new pages adds little to no benefit, since the new pages usually do not occur multiple times. In fact, if we use standard utilities to compress the body, this combined inter- and intra-deduplication might result in worse compression ratios due to locality issues.

Header						
Reference	n	PageNr List	1. Interval List	...	n. Interval List	
str	4B	var	var		var	gzip
l	1. Interval List	...	l. Interval List	1. New Page	...	bzip2
4B	var		var	psB		7zip
l. New Page						
psB						

Fig. 5. File format of a memory dump, which was compressed with inter-deduplication and intra-deduplication applied to the new pages.

Differential Interdeduplication: A more effective optimization is to look for *similar* pages in $\mathcal{R}$ and $\mathcal{D}$ and store only their differences. To do this, we compare each page P_i of $\mathcal{D}$ with the corresponding page P_i' of $\mathcal{R}$, which resides at the same page number i. We then compare each byte $b_{i,j} \in P_i$ with the corresponding byte $b_{i,j}' \in P_i'$ at the same offset and remember the byte if it is different. This yields the difference $\delta(P_i, P_i') = [b_{i,k} \mid 1 \leq k \leq ps, P_i \ni b_{i,k} \neq b_{i,k}' \in P_i']$.

To encode the difference such that we can use it later to restore the actual page P_i, we also need to store the offsets of the patched bytes. A simple solution for this problem would be to store pairs of offsets and bytes. While this

Header						
Reference str	n 4B	PageNr List var	1. Interval List var	...	n. Interval List var	
d 4B	1. Diff var	...	d. Diff var	PageNr List var	Interval List var	1. New Page psB
...		l. New Page psB				

gzip bzip2 7zip

Fig. 6. File format of a compressed memory dump with inter-deduplication and diffing.

n 2B	$l_1 - 1$	o_1 2B or 3B	p_1 l_1B	...	$l_n - 1$	o_n 2B or 3B	p_n l_nB

Fig. 7. Encoding of a diff $d = [(o_1, l_1, p_1), \ldots, (o_n, l_n, p_n)]$

would work, it would incur a significant overhead, as we would have overhead for each byte. Instead, we reshape the difference of a page to look as follows: $D = [(o_1, l_1, p_1), \ldots, (o_n, l_n, p_n)]$, i.e., a a sequence of triples (o, l, p) that each represents a patch. A patch is a sequence of bytes p of length l which needs to be applied at offset o to restore the original page content at a particular offset in the page. It is straight forward to compute D from δ by simply looking for long streaks, i.e., bytes $b_{i,k}$, which appear consecutively. Additionally, the offsets o_i are relative to the offset given by the previous entry plus the length of the previous entry, i.e., $o_{i-1} + l_{i-1}$, with the exception of o_1, which is absolute.

Figure 7 shows the diff encoding. An integer n stores the number of patches of the diff. This is followed by n patches, i.e., (o, l, p) triples. The offset o and the length l are packed into a single two-byte integer if they both fit into 7 bits each, otherwise they are packed into a 3-byte integer and the most significant bit of this integer is set to 1. To ensure that the length and the offset always fit in 3 bytes, we guarantee that no streak is longer than 2048 bytes and partition longer streaks. Since we store $l - 1$, as shown in Fig. 7, we ensure that the decompressor can recover the correct value of l since $l - 1$ fits in 11 bits and therefore the most significant bit of the three-byte integer does not overlap.

Figure 6 shows how this diffing idea is incorporated into the file format. The file format is similar to the previous one with the only addition being that the interval list of deduplicated page numbers is followed by a list of d diffs. Again, we add a page number list to encode the position of the d pages that can be recovered by applying those diffs. The page number list and the diffs are ordered so that the nth diff corresponds to the nth page number of the page number list. To recover the original pages, the decompressor reads the page numbers from the page number list, read the corresponding pages from the reference dump and apply the corresponding diffs. Similar to before, intra-deduplication can optionally be applied to the new pages, which is depicted in Fig. 8.

Header						
Reference *str*	*n* 4B	PageNr List *var*	1. Interval List *var*	...	*n*. Interval List *var*	gzip
d 4B	1. Diff *var*	... *d*. Diff *var*	PageNr List *var*	*l* 4B	1. Interval List *var* ...	bzip2
l. Interval List *var*	1. New Page *psB*	...	*l*. New Page *psB*			7zip

Fig. 8. File format of a compressed memory dump with inter-deduplication, diffing and intra-deduplication applied to the new pages.

4 Evaluation

In the following, we will now evaluate MEMSCRIMPER with respect to several aspects. First, we will evaluate the *data compression ratio*, i.e., the ratio between compressed size and uncompressed size of a memory dump and we will compare this ratio against the ratios of the standard compression utilities gzip, bzip2 and 7zip. For each of these utilities, we add a compression method to MEMSCRIMPER where the body contains the memory dump after compressing it with the respective utility. For each utility we used the strongest compression flags, e.g., mx=9 for 7zip or -9 for gzip. Second, we will evaluate the compression time, i.e., how long it takes to compress and decompress a memory dump with MEMSCRIMPER.

As discussed in Sect. 3, there are several different methods that we will need to compare. First, there are the three standard compression methods gzip, bzip2 and 7zip. Then, we have the intra-deduplication method, for which we have an additional method if we add the above mentioned standard compression utilities, which gives us 4 additional methods. We will refer to this method and its variations with Intra^x where $x \in \{\text{gz}, \text{bz}, \text{7z}, -\}$, to denote the compression method that was used on top[1]. In the case of the inter-deduplication method, we have 4 different variations. The one which applies no intra-deduplication on the new pages, the one which does and for both of them an additional variation which applies diffing. On each of those four variations, we can again apply the above standard compression utilities as before, which results in 16 additional methods. We will refer to this method and its variations with Inter^x_y where $x \in \{\text{gz}, \text{bz}, \text{7z}, -\}$ and $y \subseteq \{\circlearrowleft, \delta\}$, i.e., $\circlearrowleft$ denotes intra-deduplication applied to the new pages and δ indicates that diffing was used[2]. In total, this gives us 23 methods, which we will need to consider.

---

[1] For the sake of brevity, we denote the absence of an additional compression layer with Intra instead of Intra^-.

[2] For the sake of brevity, we write Inter^x instead of $\text{Inter}^x_\varnothing$.

Table 2. The average data compression ratio of the different methods (larger is better, best ratio is highlighted) grouped by the analysis machine the memory dump was taken from (Windows XP and Windows 7).

Windows XP (512 MiB)				Windows 7 (2 GiB)			
Method	gzip	bzip2	7zip	Method	gzip	bzip2	7zip
–	9.54	10.71	16.15	–	9.34	9.51	14.54
Intra	10.20	11.15	16.55	Intra	9.73	9.74	15.27
Inter	121.72	134.37	206.18	Inter	140.08	147.93	232.61
Inter$_\circlearrowleft$	117.41	121.04	195.12	Inter$_\circlearrowleft$	132.15	128.19	216.55
Inter$_\delta$	427.53	459.90	645.15	Inter$_\delta$	351.73	361.11	505.82
Inter$_{\circlearrowleft,\delta}$	446.60	469.65	644.75	Inter$_{\circlearrowleft,\delta}$	358.91	363.49	503.14

4.1   Experimental Setup

For evaluation we collected a data set of 236 labelled samples from 20 malware families in total (Foreign, Tedroo, Fareit, Ghost, Kelihos, Kuluoz, Nitol, NJRat, Nymaim, Virut, ZeusP2P, Kronos, Pushdo, Carbanak, LuminosityLink, SpyEye, Dridex, ISRStealer, Palevo, Tinba). We executed each sample for 2 min in a virtual machine (VM) starting from a snapshot using the VirtualBox hypervisor. Additionally, we ran an idle execution on the VM for 2 min as well to collect the reference dump $\mathcal{R}$. Using manual forensic analysis, we carefully verified that each sample became active and that it indeed belongs to the labelled family. By doing so, we ensure that MEMSCRIMPER will operate on actually infected memory dumps. If malware for example shows evasive behavior and will not start on the virtual machine, MEMSCRIMPER would operate on a memory dump where the malware has left little to no memory footprint, which would in turn skew our results as the resulting memory dump would be more similar to the reference memory dump $\mathcal{R}$. By verifying the family and the activity of the sample, we therefore simulate a worst case behavior where MEMSCRIMPER operates on memory dumps with a real malware footprint.

We performed this whole process for a Windows XP and a Window 7 VM where 512 MiB of memory was assigned to the former and 2 GiB of memory was assigned to the latter. We did so as we want to evaluate how MEMSCRIMPER scales for larger memory dumps.

4.2   Data Compression Ratio

The data compression ratio is defined as $\frac{u}{c}$ where u is the size of the uncompressed memory dump in bytes and c is the size of the compressed memory dump in bytes. To compute the compression ratio, we ran all methods of MEM-SCRIMPER on all collected memory dumps and compared the sizes. The average compression ratio of each method is depicted in Table 2. A first (rather unsurprising) observation is that 7z is superior to both gz and bz2, which is also why

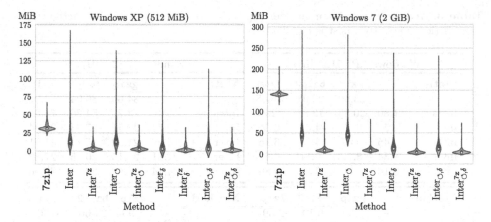

Fig. 9. A violin plot depicting the distribution of the actual file sizes of memory dumps compressed with MEMSCRIMPER (lower is better).

we will only consider 7z for the remaining data compression ratio evaluation. Another observation is that while Intra^x yields a better compression ratio than the individual compression methods alone, the improvement is not significant. The standalone 7z method yields a compression ratio of 16.15 on the Windows XP memory dumps and 14.54 on the Windows 7 memory dumps, while Intra^{7z} achieves a ratio of 16.55 (2.42% improvement) and 15.27 (5.02% improvement) respectively. The Inter$_\delta$ method on the other hand yields compression ratios as high as 645.15 (212.91% improvement) in the case of Windows XP and 505.82 (117.45% improvement) if we use 7z as the inner compression. Another observation is the fact that the usage of diffing (δ) greatly improves the compression ratio. In the case of Inter^{7z} and Inter$_\delta^{7z}$, it increases the compression ratio from 206.18 to 645.15 (212.91% improvement) in the Windows XP case and from 232.61 to 505.82 (117.45% improvement) in the Windows 7 case. The usage of intra-deduplication within the new pages ($\circlearrowleft$) adds little to no improvement and even more interesting, it might also decrease the compression ratio, which we can see if we compare Inter$_\delta^{7z}$ against Inter$_{\circlearrowleft,\delta}^{7z}$ for example or Inter^{7z} against Inter$_\circlearrowleft^{7z}$. We suspect that the reason for this is that by intra-deduplicating the new pages, we remove locality information, which can be used by the 7z utility to achieve a better compression.

The violin plot in Fig. 9 depicts the distribution of the file sizes of the compressed memory dumps. We focus here only on 7z and the relevant inter-deduplication variations as the previous discussion has shown that these are the most relevant candidates. The plot also contains the file sizes for the Inter$_x$ variations, i.e., without any inner compression applied – something we have omitted in Table 2. An interesting observation here is that these variants are already better than 7z alone on average. For example, in the Windows 7 case, 7z yields an average size of 141.12 MiB (median 139.72, std 6.65) whereas the Inter$_{\circlearrowleft,\delta}$ method yields an average size of 21.26 MiB (median 12.58, std 24.10). However, as shown

Table 3. Average compression and decompression times of the different methods in seconds (lower is better, best is highlighted).

	Windows XP (512 MiB)				Windows 7 (2 GiB)			
Compression	**Method**	–	gzip	bzip2	7zip	**Method**	–	gzip	bzip2	7zip
	–	–	23.99	22.08	35.68	–	–	84.66	86.04	53.02
	Intra	1.80	20.43	13.82	32.37	Intra	7.40	73.21	54.26	75.63
	Inter	2.54	6.87	4.67	6.06	Inter	10.73	22.51	17.73	20.94
	$Inter_\circlearrowleft$	2.45	6.57	4.03	6.16	$Inter_\circlearrowleft$	10.97	21.92	15.71	21.91
	$Inter_\delta$	8.34	8.78	9.11	9.82	$Inter_\delta$	24.11	27.15	26.15	27.82
	$Inter_{\circlearrowleft,\delta}$	8.16	8.66	9.15	9.86	$Inter_{\circlearrowleft,\delta}$	24.14	26.98	26.38	27.90
Decompression	**Method**	–	gzip	bzip2	7zip	**Method**	–	gzip	bzip2	7zip
	–	–	2.35	6.19	2.69	–	–	8.99	24.66	10.86
	Intra	0.52	1.41	4.90	2.60	Intra	1.63	5.23	19.87	10.41
	Inter	1.12	1.27	1.82	1.46	Inter	4.74	5.18	6.68	5.07
	$Inter_\circlearrowleft$	1.04	1.18	1.71	1.44	$Inter_\circlearrowleft$	4.36	4.86	6.28	5.14
	$Inter_\delta$	1.90	2.94	4.22	2.19	$Inter_\delta$	5.94	8.03	10.71	6.36
	$Inter_{\circlearrowleft,\delta}$	1.90	2.87	4.16	2.17	$Inter_{\circlearrowleft,\delta}$	5.92	8.00	10.63	6.37

in the violin plot, the methods without any inner compression applied to them suffer from outliers, which results in a high standard deviation. This standard deviation can be greatly reduced by applying 7z as the inner compression, which takes care of compressable data that we missed with our methodology. To put this into perspective consider the $Inter_\delta$ method, which has a standard deviation of 25.34 which can be reduced to 6.27 by applying 7z as the inner compression, which gives the $Inter_\delta^{7z}$ method. The best performing method in both cases, i.e. $Inter_\delta^{7z}$, yields an average size of 2.81 MiB (median 0.94, std 4.26) in the case of Windows XP and an average size of 5.57 MiB (median 3.63, std 6.27) in the case of Windows 7, which is a large improvement over 7z alone (WinXP: 32.21 avg, 30.49 med, 4.61 std, Win7: 141.12 avg, 139.72 med, 6.66 std).

4.3   Compression and Decompression Time

To further assess the performance of MEMSCRIMPER, we measured how long it takes to compress and to decompress a memory dump. To this end, Table 3 depicts the average compression and decompression time of the different methods in seconds. To collect this data, we randomly sampled 4 memory dumps per family (i.e., a pair of a Windows XP and a Windows 7 memory dump for 2 samples per family), and ran all methods on the resulting memory dumps. We had to sample, as a precise compression and decompression time analysis required us to run the methods sequentially. Parallel processing would introduce variance of our results due to concurrent disk reads/writes, caching issues and scheduling and load problems. Since running all methods on all memory dumps sequentially would take too long, we decided to follow this sampling approach, which still gives us a reasonable number of $20 \cdot 4 = 80$ memory dumps per method.

Table 3 shows that the fastest compression method by far is Intra with average compression times of 1.8 s for Windows XP and 7.4 s for Windows 7. This is followed by Inter with compression times of 2.54 s for Windows XP and 10.73 s for Windows 7. Although Intra and Inter are conceptually quite similar in that they only look for deduplicatable pages, Inter is slightly slower, since it has to process two memory dumps, i.e., the one we want to compress $\mathcal{D}$ and the reference memory dump $\mathcal{R}$. In a real world deployment of MemScrimper one could pre-process the reference memory dump $\mathcal{R}$ once and put the result (i.e., a hashmap of the pages) in memory to eliminate overhead. Due to the bad data compression ratio, Intra also gets significantly slower as soon as we add inner compression to the method, which becomes evident if we compare Intra with Intra^{7z} where we observe a slowdown of 922.03% in the Windows 7 case—the costly inner compression has to work on large data, which is inevitably slow. Conversely, if we consider Inter_δ, i.e., the method with the best data compression ratio, we can see that the overhead of adding inner compression is less significant with the largest being the difference to Inter_δ^{7z} with 3.71 s (15.39%) in the case of Windows 7. Another observation is that intra-deduplicating the new pages adds little to no overhead, since the difference between Inter and $\text{Inter}_\circlearrowleft$ and between Inter_δ $\text{Inter}_{\circlearrowleft,\delta}$ can be considered negligible. The usage of diffing on the other hand incurs a significant overhead of up to 124.70% if we compare Inter against Inter_δ in the case of Windows 7. This can be explained by the fact that diffing adds more complexity to the compression, as it has to compare each page that cannot be directly deduplicated with the corresponding page in the reference memory dump $\mathcal{R}$. As we have seen in the compression ratio analysis, this turns out to be very effective, which means that many diffs have to be created and serialized – all of which contributes to additional complexity.

If we compare the numbers of Windows XP to the numbers of Windows 7, we can see that the methods scale linearly with the size of the memory dump, which confirms our expectations given the way we have implemented those methods (cf. Sect. 3). All of the Inter_y^x methods perform better than any of the standalone compression methods in both compression and decompression. In particular, Inter_δ^{7z}, i.e., the method with the best data compression ratio, has an average compression and decompression time of 9.82/2.19 s (Windows XP) and 27.82/6.36 s (Windows 7) as opposed to 7zip alone, which yields average compression and decompression times of 35.68/2.69 s (Windows XP, 72.48%/18.59% improvement) and 53.02/10.86 (Windows 7, 47.53%/41.44% improvement). This also shows that decompression is much faster than compression, which also stems from the fact that we have written the decompressed memory dumps to memory in our decompression runs as opposed to writing them to disk. We did so, because we envision a workflow where a memory dump is compressed once for storage and then decompressed multiple times over time for historical analysis, e.g., consider a case where a sandbox operator retrieves new signatures and wants to apply them on archived memory dumps. In our evaluation, the Inter_y^x methods also benefited from the fact that we put the reference memory dump $\mathcal{R}$ for both Windows XP and Windows 7 in memory rather than on disk, which we believe is a realistic option for sandbox vendors (cf. Sect. 5.1 for a detailed discussion on this matter).

Finally, note that while the standalone compression tools gzip, bzip2 and 7zip are all written in C or C++ and are heavily optimized, our prototype of MEMSCRIMPER is written in Python and can therefore not achieve the same level of optimization. It is therefore likely that an optimized implementation in a non-interpreted language would further amplify the performance benefit.

4.4 Soundness and Efficiency of Analyses on Compressed Dumps

In the previous evaluation step, we have measured how long it takes to decompress an entire memory dump. In fact, however, for several analyses such as signature matching it is not actually required to work on the entire dump, but just on the memory parts that were changed by the malware. To demonstrate this, we collected a total of 17 YARA [1] signatures for 17 out of 20 malware families of our data set using Malpedia [18] and various other online resources. We then matched all those YARA signatures against the previously sampled 80 memory dumps and verified that 24/80 memory dumps matched the correct signature for the given family. Since our methodology only stores memory pages in plain if they cannot be deduplicated or stored differentially, it is reasonable to assume that only these pages contain the relevant memory footprint of the given malware. To verify this, we matched all the YARA signatures against the memory dumps of the Intra and Inter$_x$ methods without inner compression. We discovered that the compressed memory dumps matched all YARA rules perfectly, i.e., the matching yielded the same results as the completely uncompressed ones.

Performance-wise, the matching was also faster than on uncompressed memory dumps. While the uncompressed ones took 6.6 s on average to match all signatures, Intra yielded an average matching time of 1.57 s, Inter took 0.14 s followed by Inter$_{\circlearrowright}$ (0.14 s). The best results were yielded by the Inter$_\delta$ method with 0.064 s and the Inter$_{\delta,\circlearrowright}$ method with 0.067 s on average. These results nicely reflect the data compression ratio, i.e., the better the compression, the smaller the file size, the faster the matching. Even if we consider the overhead of removing the inner compression, the matching is still faster than on raw uncompressed memory dumps. Consider, for example, the Inter$_\delta^{7z}$ method in the Windows 7 case (i.e., the worst case) where 7zip adds compression time overhead of $27.82 - 24.11 = 3.71$ s (cf. Table 3) in which case the matching is still $6.6 - (0.064 + 3.71) = 2.826$ s (43.36%) faster.

5 Discussion

In this secion we briefly discuss some aspects of MEMSCRIMPER regarding its limitations, use cases, deployment and future work.

5.1   Use Case and Limitations

MEMSCRIMPER is not a general purpose compression tool and is primarily meant to compress memory dumps of snapshot-based sandboxes. The underlying assumption of the inter-deduplication methods is that dumps share a common "predecessor" which contains a substantial amount of similar data, i.e., the reference memory dump $\mathcal{R}$. In other settings, intra-deduplication is still applicable, which does however not yield the same compression ratio as inter-deduplication.

Furthermore, we assume that the malware execution starts from a well-defined snapshot. This snapshot was taken with great care to ensure that the system was in a stable idling state to limit the forensic noise that subsequent malware executions would create. This means that we verified no background process was executing and disabled services that had a large memory or performance footprint, as this would hinder differential analysis and would ultimately increase the size of the resulting memory dumps. We did not evaluate how MEMSCRIMPER would perform in a setting where the snapshot was not taken at such a stable point, e.g., when the snapshot would be created during the boot process.

One could question whether it is practical that MEMSCRIMPER keeps the reference dump in memory to speed up inter-deduplication. If the number of analysis environment and their memory footprint grows, sandbox operators might not have sufficient memory to store all dumps. However, note that (i) the number of environments and their assigned memory is usually small, (ii) intra-deduplication of the reference dump can be applied, and (iii) hashing the pages (except for diffing methods) significantly reduces the footprint. Therefore, maintaining reference dumps on the heap should always be feasible. Even if not, disk caches could partially mitigate this problem and maintain the substantial performance improvement compared to standard compression utilities.

5.2   Deployment

Adding MEMSCRIMPER to existing infrastructures should not pose a major challenge. At its core, MEMSCRIMPER can be considered a black box which receives a memory dump as input and yields a compressed memory dump as output, which can easily be integrated into an existing pipeline. The only manual effort which needs to be done is to take a reference memory dump per analysis machine and per snapshot and optionally putting this reference memory dump in memory to speed up the inter-deduplication process. Additionally, fine-tuning the snapshot as described above to ensure an optimal data compression ratio might be required. However, this is a one-time effort per analysis machine and per snapshot, after which MEMSCRIMPER operates completely automatic. To foster a wide-spread deployment of MEMSCRIMPER in sandbox environments, we publish the source code of our reference implementation[3].

---

[3] Available at https://github.com/mbrengel/memscrimper.

5.3   Future Work

We have left open a few extensions open for future work. First, in our current inter-deduplication implementation, we compare against a single reference dump. However, it might be beneficial to also compare against other memory dumps in general, as similar malware instances will likely create similar (or identical) memory changes. Adding this to MEMSCRIMPER is simple and promising to gain more space, yet it might incur a performance penalty.

Second, the presented methodology is *lossless* and does not discard any information from memory dumps. Depending on the actual use case, such as signature matching, it might be sensible to disregard small changes to memory pages (e.g., changes of pointers or small data items) in a lossy compression method. Lossy compression has the potential to even further reduce memory footprint, would however not allow the analyst to entirely restore the original memory dump.

6   Related Work

To the best of our knowledge, we are the first to leverage the similarity of malware sandbox memory dumps for compression. While the concept of data deduplication is well-known and extensively studied [3,8,11,21], we do not know of any prior work which applied similar methodologies in the context of sandbox malware analysis. The closest work we found in this area is given by Park et al. [15], who discuss fast and space-efficient virtual machine checkpointing. The authors propose a deduplication mechanism for shared pages between the memory of a virtual machine and its page cache on disk, which is different from our approach and also not as effective.

We have introduced several new deduplication aspects, including (i) a file format for compressed memory dumps, (ii) the possibility to compare memory dumps against reference snapshots, and (iii) differential deduplication. In the malware context, the closest works to ours study the differential behavior (e.g., system activity) of malware on multiple sandboxes to discover evasive malware [4,12]. While the objective of these works is not to compress data, and both do not consider memory dumps, they also extract an essential footprint of the malware by considering the differences in behavioral profiles—similar to how we only store the differences introduced by the malware in the forensic sense.

Despite the lack of otherwise related work in this area, we argue that our results are highly relevant. Apart from the primary use case of our work—saving memory dumps time- and space-efficiently—it also allows for other interesting insights. By only storing the forensic differences introduced by a malware, we enable a more targeted and more efficient analysis, which can only focus on those differences. Forensic analysis techniques such as digital forensic text string searching as proposed by Beebe and Clark [7], or data structure content reverse engineering such as proposed by Saltaformaggio et al. [19], can significantly benefit from our approach. For example, after inter-deduplication, these techniques only have to consider the new pages, i.e., the ones which could not be (differentially) deduplicated—similar to how we matched YARA signatures more efficiently.

7 Conclusion

MEMSCRIMPER is a novel methodology for compressing malware sandbox memory dumps by exploiting their snapshot mechanism and the resulting similarity of the memory dumps. MEMSCRIMPER achieves data compression ratios which are one order of magnitude better than the ones yielded by standalone compression utilities such as 7zip, while at the same time significantly improving their performance. We believe that MEMSCRIMPER is a promising addition to existing malware sandbox analysis infrastructures as it is easy to deploy and enables a longer storage time and a more viable longitudinal analysis of memory dumps.

Acknowledgements. This work was supported by the European Union's Horizon 2020 research and innovation programme, RAMSES, under grant agreement No. 700326 and by the European Union's Horizon 2020 research and innovation programme, SISSDEN, under grant agreement No. 700176.

References

1. YARA - The pattern matching swiss knife for malware researchers. https://virustotal.github.io/yara/. Accessed 27 Feb 2018
2. Malware Statistics & Trends Report — AV-TEST (2018). https://www.av-test.org/en/statistics/malware/. Accessed 27 Feb 2018
3. Aronovich, L., Asher, R., Bachmat, E., Bitner, H., Hirsch, M., Klein, S.T.: The design of a similarity based deduplication system. In: Proceedings of the Israeli Experimental Systems Conference (SYSTOR) (2009)
4. Balzarotti, D., Cova, M., Karlberger, C., Christopher, K., Kirda, E., Vigna, G.: Efficient detection of split personalities in malware. In: Proceedings of the Annual Network and Distributed System Security Symposium (NDSS) (2010)
5. Bayer, U., Comparetti, P.M., Hlauschek, C., Kruegel, C., Kirda, E.: Scalable, behavior-based malware clustering. In: Proceedings of the Annual Network and Distributed System Security Symposium (NDSS) (2009)
6. Bayer, U., Kirda, E., Kruegel, C.: Improving the efficiency of dynamic malware analysis. In: Proceedings of the ACM Symposium on Applied Computing (SAC) (2010)
7. Beebe, N.L., Clark, J.G.: Digital forensic text string searching: improving information retrieval effectiveness by thematically clustering search results. In: Proceedings of the Digital Forensic Research Conference (DFRWS) (2007)
8. Bhagwat, D., Eshghi, K., Long, D., Lillibridge, M.: Extreme binning: scalable, parallel deduplication for chunk-based file backup. In: Proceedings of the International Symposium on Modeling, Analysis and Simulation of Computer and Telecommunication Systems (MASCOTS) (2009)

9. Jacob, G., Comparetti, P.M., Neugschwandtner, M., Kruegel, C., Vigna, G.: A static, packer-agnostic filter to detect similar malware samples. In: Flegel, U., Markatos, E., Robertson, W. (eds.) DIMVA 2012. LNCS, vol. 7591, pp. 102–122. Springer, Heidelberg (2013). https://doi.org/10.1007/978-3-642-37300-8_6

10. Jang, J., Brumley, D., Venkataraman, S.: BitShred: feature hashing malware for scalable triage and semantic analysis. In: Proceedings of the Conference on Computer and Communications Security (CCS) (2011)

11. Jayaram, K.R., Peng, C., Zhang, Z., Kim, M., Chen, H., Lei, H.: An empirical analysis of similarity in virtual machine images. In: Proceedings of the International Middleware Conference (MIDDLEWARE) (2011)

12. Kirat, D., Vigna, G., Kruegel, C.: BareCloud: bare-metal analysis-based evasive malware detection. In: Proceedings of the USENIX Security Symposium (2014)

13. Kolbitsch, C., Comparetti, P.M., Kruegel, C., Kirda, E., Zhou, X., Wang, X.: Effective and efficient malware detection at the end host. In: Proceedings of the USENIX Security Symposium (2009)

14. Neugschwandtner, M., Comparetti, P.M., Jacob, G., Kruegel, C.: ForeCast - skimming off the malware cream. In: Proceedings of the Annual Computer Security Applications Conference (ACSAC) (2011)

15. Park, E., Egger, B., Lee, J.: Fast and space-efficient virtual machine checkpointing. In: Proceedings of the International Conference on Virtual Execution Environments (VEE) (2011)

16. Plank, J.S., Beck, M., Kingsley, G., Li, K.: Libckpt: transparent checkpointing under unix. In: Proceedings of the USENIX Technical Conference (TCON) (1995)

17. Plank, J.S., Chen, Y., Li, K., Beck, M., Kingsley, G.: Memory exclusion: optimizing the performance of checkpointing systems. Softw.: Pract. Exp. **29**(2), 125–142 (1999)

18. Plohmann, D., Clauß, M., Enders, S., Padilla, E.: Malpedia: a collaborative effort to inventorize the malware landscape. In: Proceedings of the Botconf (2017)

19. Saltaformaggio, B., Gu, Z., Zhang, X., Xu, D.: DSCRETE: automatic rendering of forensic information from memory images via application logic reuse. In: Proceedings of the USENIX Security Symposium (2017)

20. Meyer, D.T., Aggarwal, G., Cully, B., Lefebvre, G., Feeley, M.J., Hutchinson, N.C., Warfield, A.: Parallax: virtual disks for virtual machines. In: Proceedings of the European Conference on Computer Systems (EuroSys). Association for Computing Machinery (ACM) (2008)

21. Xia, W., Jiang, H., Feng, D., Hua, Y.: SiLo: a similarity-locality based near-exact deduplication scheme with low RAM overhead and high throughput. In: Proceedings of the USENIX Annual Technical Conference (USENIX ATC) (2011)

22. Yokoyama, A., Ishii, K., Tanabe, R., Papa, Y., Yoshioka, K., Matsumoto, T., Kasama, T., Inoue, D., Brengel, M., Backes, M., Rossow, C.: SandPrint: fingerprinting malware sandboxes to provide intelligence for sandbox evasion. In: Monrose, F., Dacier, M., Blanc, G., Garcia-Alfaro, J. (eds.) RAID 2016. LNCS, vol. 9854, pp. 165–187. Springer, Cham (2016). https://doi.org/10.1007/978-3-319-45719-2_8

Spearphishing Malware: Do We Really Know the Unknown?

Yanko Baychev[1]($\boxtimes$) and Leyla Bilge[2]

[1] Airbus CyberSecurity, Taufkirchen, Germany
yanko.baychev@airbus.com
[2] Symantec Research Labs, Sophia Antipolis, France
leyla_bilge@symantec.com

Abstract. Targeted attacks pose a great threat to governments and commercial entities. Every year, an increasing number of targeted attacks are being discovered and exposed by various cyber security organizations. The key characteristics of these attacks are that they are conducted by well-funded and skilled actors who persistently target specific entities employing sophisticated tools and tactics to obtain a long-time presence in the breached environments. Malware plays a crucial role in a targeted attack for various tasks. Because of its stealthy nature, malware used in targeted attacks is expected to act differently compared to the traditional malware. However, to our knowledge, there is no previous study that performed an empirical validation to this assumption.

In this paper, we perform a study to understand whether malware used in targeted attacks is any different than traditional malware. To this end, we dynamically analysed a set of targeted and traditional malware to extract more than 700 features to be able to measure their discriminative power. These features are calculated from the network, host and memory behavior of malware. The rigorous experimentation we performed with several machine learning algorithms suggest that targeted malware indeed behaves differently and even with raw features extracted from the dynamic analysis reports, fairly good classification accuracy could be achieved to distinguish them from traditional malware.

Keywords: Targeted attacks · Malware · Dynamic analysis

1 Introduction

Since 2010, we witnessed a dramatic change in the cyber threat landscape. Before that, the main motivation of cyber attacks was financial gain and therefore, the goal was to infect as many computers as possible. While this kind of attacks still exist and constitute the majority of the cyber attacks seen in the wild [25], a new class of attacks has emerged and became the top priority risk for both governmental and commercial organizations: targeted attacks. In targeted attacks,

© Springer International Publishing AG, part of Springer Nature 2018
C. Giuffrida et al. (Eds.): DIMVA 2018, LNCS 10885, pp. 46–66, 2018.
https://doi.org/10.1007/978-3-319-93411-2_3

well-organized operators target specific entities persistently with high motivation, evade security defenses in place, employ advanced tools and tactics, maintain long-time presence in target environment and operate slow and stealthy to avoid detection [26].

Malware plays a vital role in the success of a targeted attack and is employed almost in every phase of the attack lifecycle until the operator's goal is achieved. It is used to perform a wide range of tasks including compromising systems, escalating privileges, maintaining presence, exfiltrating data, communicating with the operators over command and control servers, carrying out commands, etc. Even though these tasks are not peculiar to targeted malware per se, targeted malware is expected to act differently compared to traditional malware and in this paper, we seek to understand whether this common belief is aligned with the reality or not.

As the sophistication level of targeted attacks rises gradually in time, increasing number of targeted attacks are being discovered using malware with advanced stealth techniques or even non-persistent malware that only resides in memory [27]. Recently cyber security professionals came up with a new term for targeted attacks employing non-persistent in-memory malware and named them as Advanced Volatile Threats [36], because there is no easy way to detect them other than analyzing the volatile memory. In order to detect fileless malware and also malware that hides its presence on the system by using advanced malware stealth techniques such as hooking, injection, hollowing, etc., memory analysis is a must and needed to be conducted along with dynamic analysis. In this paper, we used popular open-source memory forensics tool called The Volatility Framework [34], which can be integrated with the Cuckoo Sandbox [11] and offers wide range of plugins for various memory related analysis tasks to be able to detect fileless malware that remains solely in memory. Cuckoo Sandbox was configured to dump full memory of the guest analysis machine just before the execution finishes and run Volatility with selected plugins on the memory dump. We additionally utilized YARA tool [32] to supplement behavioral characterization of malware and included YARA rules that match certain behavioral patterns during the execution.

Past evidence suggests that targeted attacks are significantly more impactful compared to traditional malware attacks for the victims [33]. Therefore, they deserve more attention and there is an immediate need for methodologies that can distinguish them from traditional malware. However, before that we need to first find out whether they are different at all such that depending on the result more effort could be put to devise new detection methodologies. In this paper, we aim at identifying the differences between targeted and traditional malware. Unfortunately, obtaining a large-scale dataset that is representative for the real targeted malware that is used in advanced persistent threats is difficult. One one hand such attacks are more rare to see compared to the volume of other cyber attacks. One the other hand, as this kind of attacks might include actions done by a more skilled attacker manually, it might be even hard to identify them. For this reason, in this paper, we employ a set of malware that is used in spearphishing attacks. We believe that the general spearphishng malware will share some behavioral similarities to more advanced targeted malware as they are both carefully choosing their victims and also some of the advanced persistent threats use spearphishing as means of the infection vector. Therefore, it is possible that in our data we actually include some examples for more sophisticated targeted malware. Our assumption here is that by analysing this dataset, it is possible to achieve an approximation to how general targeted attacks behave differently than the traditional malware.

We investigate the behavioral differences between targeted and traditional malware by running them in a controlled environment. During the analysis period, we extract a wide range of features from both the dynamic analysis and memory analysis traces. Afterwards, we experiment with a number of machine learning algorithms to find the most discriminative features and test the feasibility of distinguishing targeted malware. The result of the extensive evaluation made on spearphishingmalware used in the wild indicates that targeted malware behaves differently and can be distinguished from the traditional malware. Note that our goal with this paper is not to propose a detection method for targeted malware but to obtain insights about their differences. However, the classification accuracy achieved using the raw features extracted from the dynamic analysis reports is good enough for many real-world threat intelligence applications. For example, the methodology explained in this paper could be used as a filtering step during targeted attack detection that involves in more sophisticated analysis.

In summary, this paper makes the following contributions:

- We present the first study on understanding the differences of targeted malware from traditional malware.
- We extract an extensive list of dynamic analysis features from a broad perspective including behavioral patterns when fed to a machine learning classifier are capable of distinguishing targeted malware.
- We present a novel set of memory features extracted from memory analysis that could be incorporated to targeted malware detection systems.
- We provide a comprehensive evaluation of the features using different machine learning algorithms and provide a detailed discussion about the most discriminative features and their reasoning behind them.

2   Analyzing the Malware

Figure 1 illustrates the architecture of the system we devised to obtain insights about malware that is used in spearphishing attacks. Before digging into the details about which features we focus on and why, we will briefly summarize each step in the process of analyzing the malware samples. These malware samples were provided to us by Symantec and each of them were categorized by human analysts whose main goal is to mine large amounts of e-mail data to identify spearphishing attacks. This process does not only consist of data mining but also reverse-engineering the binary that is attached to the mail. While we do not know the details about the methodology adopted to identify the samples provided to us, we are confident that the false positives in the data is fairly low as each of them were carefully analyzed by these human analysts. The traditional malware data, on the other hand, was build by randomly choosing malware that is observed by Symantec during the targeted malware collection period. Unfortunately, we could not acquire the binaries for these samples and therefore, we needed to search for them ourselves.

To obtain the binaries of the malware samples, we download them from Virus Total [31] and store them in our malware repository. Easy but also very efficient way to reveal malware's behavior once it infects a system is to run it in a controlled environment and capture all the changes on the host and the network during the analysis process [10]. Despite its obvious limitations, dynamic analysis of malware in a sandbox environment is extensively used in malware analysis field due to its convenience on analyzing malware in fast and automated manner. For our work, we utilize a modified version of Cuckoo Sandbox [24]. Cuckoo Sandbox is a very powerful and highly customizable open-source dynamic analysis sandbox backed by a large community of researchers and developers. It leverages memory analysis framework for conducting memory analysis. Each malware is analyzed in the cuckoo sandbox and their analysis reports that contain both information about their dynamic analysis behavior and the memory analysis are stored in our database. Then, the reports are processed to extract a large number of features that can capture the behavioral characteristics of malware. Finally, as a last step, we employ a number of machine learning classifiers to test whether targeted malware could be distinguished using the features we will explain in the following section.

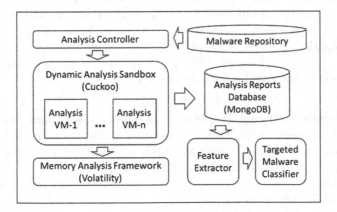

Fig. 1. System architecture.

2.1 Features

A wide range of system-level artifacts are captured during the whole analysis process of each malware sample. We examined the analysis reports in detail to identify useful features for our purpose. Instead of utilizing high granularity

Table 1. Network features.

#	Feature name
1	Number of UDP connections
2	Number of distinct IP addresses
3	Number of distinct UDP destination ports
4	Number of IRC connections
5	Number of HTTP connections
6	Number of SMTP connections
7	Number of TCP connections
8	Number of ICMP connections
9	Number of hosts
10	Number of hosts with reverse DNS
11	Number of DNS requests
12–17	DNS request type frequency
18	Number of domains
19–22	Domain level frequency
23–27	Domain name length frequency
28	Is top websites visited

features that represent low level atomic operations [5,22], we decided to utilize low granularity and mostly quantitative features that could represent malware behavior from a wider aspect [18]. We identified a total of 754 features either by defining new dynamic and memory features or adopting the existing ones from state-of-the-art in malware classification [2,13,18,29]. These features are divided into six categories: network features (28), file system features (174), registry features (4), system call features (289), memory features (71) and miscellaneous features (208). At total we have extracted 754 features.

Network Features. During the execution of malware, we captured all incoming and outgoing network traffic. From the network traffic we extracted a total of 28 network features such as number of DNS requests, TCP/IRC/SMPT/HTTP connections, IPs contacted, etc. Most of these features are single features and represent counts, therefore the name of each feature in Table 1 provides sufficient information about the feature itself.

In the course of the analysis, we encountered only the following DNS requests types; A, AAAA, MX, SRV, TXT, PTR. For each of these DNS record types, we counted the number of DNS requests and kept them as features. For each second, third, forth level domain name and the fully qualified domain names we observed in the network, we counted number of queries as well. Finally, we extracted some features to express the length of the domain names used by malware. We calculated the number of domain names whose lengths fall into the following ranges: 0–10, 11–16, 17–20, 20–32 and 32–∞.

File System Features. Cuckoo Sandbox employs several injection and hooking techniques while executing the malware in order to detect and capture the file system operations including, access, read, create, modify and delete operations. From these file system artifacts we extracted a total of 174 file system features (see Table 2). We came across a wide range of file extensions of the created, modified or deleted files throughout the analysis process. In order to characterize this behavior, we defined a feature vector, which we call the top extension frequency, composed of top 34 extensions varying from "dll", "exe", "jpg" to "tmp", "txt" each corresponding to a specific extension and representing its count. During the analysis of malware, it creates files under specific paths in the file systems and typically these are good features to identify malware. These paths are usually associated with environment variables and named as common folder or known folder in Windows operating system [16]. We counted number of times file operations were done on specific file paths and used them as features in our analysis. For example, the following paths are some of the well-known paths where malware often copies itself;

- C:\Windows\System32\
- C:\DOCUME~1\<user name>\LOCALS~1\Temp\
- C:\Documents and Settings\All Users\

Another observation we had during the analysis phase is that files are created in varying sizes from bytes to megabytes. After examining the file sizes in detail, we decided not to utilize the size as a whole but in ranges and we picked the following four size ranges in bytes; 0–64, 65–4096, 4097–262144 and 262144–∞. We have also identified five types of files that malware often interacts with. These file types are the files, the directories, the drivers, the pipes and the alternate stream types. For each of these file types, we counted number of reads, accesses and modify operations.

Malware samples in general read and access an extensive number of files which are mostly duplicates or a noise because of the nested path traversal. To obtain the unique list of such operations, we pre-processed and filtered out these duplicates from the data. While five types of file artifacts are captured during the analysis, in terms of access, read, modify, create and delete operations, we did not build the frequency vectors for all of the file operations, but only for the ones that are more characterizing for malware. For instance, the known path frequency vector is constructed only for the file create, modify or delete operations but not for the read or access operations.

Registry Features. We extracted 4 features from the registry operations conducted by malware. Similar to the file operations, malware samples read and access an extensive number of registry keys. After we pre-processed them to exclude the duplicates and noise, we counted the number of registry keys deleted, modified, read and accessed.

System Call Features. We have also included some features that we extracted from the system call traces malware produces during its execution. To decrease

Table 2. File system features.

#	Feature name
1	Number of files deleted
2	Number of files modified
3	Number of files deleted in distinct paths
4	Number of files deleted with distinct extensions
5–38	Top extension frequency of deleted files
39–52	Known path frequency of deleted files
53	Number of files modified in distinct paths
54	Number of files modified with distinct extensions
55–88	Top extension frequency of modified files
89–102	Known path frequency of modified files
103–107	File type frequency of modified files
108	Number of files created
109	Number of files created with distinct extension
110	Number of files created in distinct path
111–114	File size frequency
115–148	Top extension frequency of created files
149–162	Known path frequency of created files
163	Number of files read
164–168	File type frequency of read files
169	Number of files accessed
170–174	File type frequency of accessed files

the number of features, we performed an aggregation over the system call types (network, threading, hooking etc.) and counted number of system calls that fall into one of the 16 categories we have identified.

Although tracking counts of system calls in individual categories can provide good insights about the malware, some categories have disproportionally high counts of system calls. To capture this behavior at a higher level, we calculated proportion of number of system calls in each of the 16 categories over the total number of system calls as well.

As system calls are generally not directly accessed by programs but via APIs, we have also extracted the API calls made by the binaries. In our data, we have observed 256 different API functions called by malware samples and for each of these API calls we included a feature which represents the number of times the particular API call was made by malware.

Miscellaneous Features. In addition to the features explained above, Cuckoo sandbox generates analysis reports enriched with several other malware related static or dynamic artifacts including API functions resolved, mutexes created, services started, commands executed, etc. In order to incorporate these rich artifacts into our analysis, we extracted a total of 208 miscellaneous features that include the total number of resolved API functions and API files, the number of times each of these API functions are resolved, the total number of commands executed, number of services/mutexes created and started, number of YARA signatures matched and for each signature how many times the matches were identified. Although majority of the features in this category are based on the dynamic analysis reports, we were also able to include few simple static analysis features such as resolved API files and functions, strings included in the binaries.

We also leveraged the YARA tool [32] that comes with the Cuckoo Sandbox. YARA is capable of identifying particular malicious behavior or generic techniques adopted by malware. These signatures can provide valuable insights into malware behavior when utilized as a feature. Note that we only include the yara signatures that are related to behavioral characteristics. The malware specific yara signatures are excluded from our analysis so that they are not used by the classifier to distinguish the malware family from the targeted malware rather than the general traditional malware. For the sake of brevity, we do not list the whole list of YARA signatures that are matched, however, in the evaluation section we demonstrate the ones that are the most useful during the classification process.

Memory Features. We leveraged the infamous Volatility Framework [34] to extract a large number of features from the memory introspection we performed during our analysis. The targeted attacks typically perform obfuscation on the malware they use and for that reason, without memory analysis it would be very hard to fully observe the malicious behavior. Getting motivated from this insight, we investigated memory indicators that could identify a malicious activity and selected 13 Volatility plugins. The reason for this is that some plugins can take very long time to complete and are not feasible to perform on thousands of samples. From outputs of these plugins, we identified and extracted a total of 51 features. In Table 3, all extracted memory features are listed along with the name of the Volatility plugin used for the feature. These features are a novel set of features that have not been used in any other works before to our knowledge.

3   Experiments and Results

3.1   Experimental Setup

Dynamic analysis of the malware samples and experiments were performed on a server with two quad-core Intel Xeon E5440 2.83 GHz processors, 16 GB DDR2 RAM, three 146 GB 10,000 RPM SAS hard drives and two Gigabit network adapters. The server was running Ubuntu 12.04 LTS as host operating system along with headless-mode VirtualBox (version 4.2.22) as the hypervisor.

We utilized a heavily modified and improved [20] version of Cuckoo Sandbox (Cuckoo 1.3-dev by Brad Spengler) for dynamically analyzing the malware

Table 3. Memory features.

#	Feature name	Vol. Plugin
1	Number of mutexes	Mutantscan
2–5	Mutex length frequency	Mutantscan
6	Number of processes exited	Pslist
7	Number of processes running	Psxview
8–14	Process list frequency	Psxview
15–21	Module in common Windows process freq	Dlllist
22–28	Avg. mod. in common Windows proc. freq	Dlllist
29–31	Injection VAD tag frequency	Malfind
32	Number of injections	Malfind
33	Average number of injections per process	Malfind
34	Number of processes with privileges	Privs
35	Number of proc. with Administrator SID	Getsids
36–38	Hidden DLL type frequency	Ldrmodules
39	Number of services	Svcscan
40	Number of driver names	Devicetree
41	Found duplicate driver name (0 or 1)	Devicetree
42	Number of device offsets	Devicetree
43	Number of device names	Devicetree
44	Number of kernel drivers	Modscan
45	Number of timers	Timers
46	Number of distinct timer periods	Timers
47	Number of distinct timer modules	Timers
48	Number of callbacks	Callbacks
49	Number of distinct callback types	Callbacks
50	Number of distinct callback modules	Callbacks
51	Number of distinct callback details	Callbacks

samples and Volatility Framework (version 2.4) for analyzing the memory dumps acquired at the end of execution. Malware was allowed to access the Internet during the analysis. Note that we did not allow the malware to do large scale attacks such as denial of service attacks. With the help of Pafish tool [21], we assessed the analysis environment against several anti-vm and anti-sandbox techniques and hardened the environment to avoid detection by fixing the identified issues. After the Cuckoo Sandbox was configured properly, all malware samples were executed in parallel, each for a period of five minutes, on two virtual analysis machines.

3.2   Data Set

Obtaining malware samples that are attached to targeted attacks is a challenging task. While there are several malware repositories such as VirusShare [30] that share a big volume of malware samples, information regarding their category is not provided for most cases. Some cyber security firms dealing with targeted attacks publish reports on attack campaigns and disclose hashes of files involved. Although this is useful, the number of malware hashes in those reports is too small for generalization.

To increase our knowledge about malware samples that are used in targeted attacks, we obtained a list of manually chosen malware that are used in sophisticated spearphishing attacks. As we mentioned before, by analyzing these spearphising malware we hope to achieve an approximation to how targeted attacks behave as a spearphishing attack is a form of targeted attack itself. The analyst in Symantec also provided an additional list of traditional malware samples for comparison. It is important to note that all of the targeted malware samples were vetted and labeled manually by an analyst, not by an automated process. We obtained 2032 targeted and 10 K traditional malware hashes. Afterwards, we searched Virustotal [31] for hashes and managed to find 709 targeted malware samples in Virustotal. We believe not finding the majority of the targeted samples but the traditional samples in Virustotal is a good indicator for the targetedness property of these malware samples.

After submitting them to our deployed Cuckoo Sandbox for analysis, only 471 were executed properly on our guest virtual machines by producing reports containing system-wide artifacts. Dynamic analysis of the other 238 samples were failed because either the analysis task was terminated shortly after the start or no single process was created throughout the analysis period. It is possible that these malware samples employ techniques for detecting the sandbox environment or require newer operating system to execute. In order to have balanced sets of targeted and traditional malware samples, we searched for only randomly picked small fraction of the traditional malware hashes and downloaded 618 malware samples from Virustotal. 550 out of 618 traditional malware samples were executed in the sandbox without any problems. Compared to the scale of malware seen in the wild this is definitely a very small number, however, unfortunately the number of spearphishing malware we were able to obtain was very small and that was the reason for limiting ourselves to these numbers.

To be sure that our traditional malware set is not composed of a big cluster of samples from the same category, therefore, we are not distinguishing the behavior of a particular malware family from the targeted malware, we investigated the AV labels of those 550 malware samples. From the selected top keywords from all traditional malware samples, we constructed a global list of keywords and number of their occurrences. Our traditional malware set includes a balanced distribution over various malware types including some downloaders, backdoors, zeus, password-stealers, autorun, autoit, etc. We also investigated keywords of targeted malware samples to make sure that our targeted malware set is not comprised of malware mostly with same type or functionality, e.g. "dropper", "downloader", etc. The top 20 keywords we identified have at least 10 and average of 40 matches each.

3.3   Leveraging Machine Learning

To evaluate the proposed method and the discriminative power of the features extracted in terms of targeted malware classification, we conducted experiments using the following supervised learning algorithms: Support Vector Machine (SVM), Logistic Regression, k-Nearest-Neighbor (kNN), Decision Tree and Random Forest. In all of our experiments, we used 5-fold cross validation where the dataset is divided into five equally sized partitions with four partitions used to train the classifier and the remaining partition used for validation. This process was repeated five times and resulting scores were averaged. Because we have extracted a wide-variety of features each lying in differing ranges of value, we employed standard feature scaling and centered the feature values around 0 with zero mean and unit variance to avoid biasing toward any feature resulting misclassification.

Table 4. Targeted malware classification results.

Algorithm	Accuracy	Precision	Recall	F1	False-Pos.	AUC
SVM RBF	89.27%	93.51%	80.90%	86.75%	4.31%	92.50%
SVM Linear	89.27%	91.36%	83.15%	87.06%	6.03%	94.20%
K-NN	88.29%	84.95%	88.76%	86.81%	12.07%	88.35%
Log. Regression	88.78%	90.24%	83.15%	86.55%	6.90%	91.85%
Decision Tree	87.80%	84.78%	87.64%	86.18%	9.73%	87.41%
Random Forest	89.17%	91.33%	82.92%	86.92%	6.03%	93.88%

The obtained experiment results in Table 4 show that supervised learning algorithms exhibited similar performance on accuracy measure and they all achieved above 87% accuracy rate. There is also not a single algorithm that outperformed others in most of the measures. Performance not being dependent on a single algorithm suggests that the identified set of features are comprehensive enough to characterize malware from different aspects and therefore ensure high level of accuracy independent of the algorithm used for classification.

While both SVM algorithms achieved best result on accuracy with 89.27%, SVM RBF yielded highest precision and lowest false-positive rate with 93.51% and 4.31%, respectively. SVM Linear yielded best f-1 measure with 87.06% and k-Nearest Neighbor algorithm yielded best recall rate. As a measure representing overall performance, computed AUC for SVM Linear algorithm was the highest followed by Random Forest algorithm with a small margin.

3.4   Why Is Spearphishing Malware Different?

The results of the machine learning experiments suggest that the targeted malware can be distinguished from the traditional malware using the set of features utilized in this study. In the following section, we will look into the list of most discriminative features to understand why targeted malware is different than the traditional malware and how this difference is captured by these top features.

Table 5. Top 20 features.

Ind.	Cat.	Description
672	Misc	Matched signature frequency: infostealer_mail
553	Misc	Resolved top API function frequency: oleaut32.dll
680	Misc	Matched signature frequency: injection_runpe
666	Misc	Matched signature frequency: antidbg_windows
421	Call	API function frequency: SHGetFolderPathW
395	Call	API function frequency: FindWindowW
547	Misc	Resolved top API function frequency: urlmon.dll
267	Call	API function frequency: NtSetContextThread
468	Call	API function frequency: InternetConnectW
459	Call	API function frequency: HttpSendRequestW
411	Call	API function frequency: RtlDecompressBuffer
360	Call	API function frequency: HttpOpenRequestW
80	File	Number of files modified in distinct paths
52	File	Top extension frequency of deleted files: tmp
434	Call	API function frequency: CryptCreateHash
237	Call	System call category percentage frequency: com
586	Misc	Resolved top API function frequency: sxs.dll
723	Mem	Module in common Win. proc. freq: winlogon.exe
749	Mem	Number of distinct timer modules
668	Misc	Matched signature frequency: disables_uac

In order to determine contribution of each feature to the prediction of targeted malware, we performed feature selection using the Recursive Feature Elimination (RFE) technique [1] which is commonly used for problems with small sample size and high dimensionality along with Support Vector Machines [8]. As its name suggests, RFE recursively eliminates features with smaller weights and constructs the model repeatedly to compute the model accuracy. We employed RFE with SVM Linear classifier which yielded best result in terms of area under ROC curve and identified most discriminative 20 features in classifying targeted malware. Top 20 features are presented in Table 5 in descending order starting with the most discriminative feature.

Most of the identified top features in Table 5 align well with the behavioural characteristics of modern malware [4]. In this section, we will provide a discussion about the most interesting discriminative features going over the plots of the empirical cumulative distribution functions (ECDF) for both targeted and traditional malware (in ascending order according to index of feature in feature vector).

Top Extension Frequency of Deleted Files - Tmp: This feature corresponds to the number of files deleted during the malware execution with extension "tmp". It is known that malware can download or drop temporary files which can be used as additional payload or configuration files. Because of this known characteristic, antivirus software can flag files having extension "tmp" as suspicious or malicious. Therefore, it is expected for a targeted malware to delete temporary files after they are consumed to avoid getting the attention of the antivirus software or the security analyst. This behavioral pattern is captured with this feature and it is revealed in Fig. 2 that targeted malware tends to delete at least one temporary file almost twice as many times as the traditional malware. Because while only 20% of the traditional malware samples deleted at least one file with extension "tmp", it is 38% for the targeted malware samples.

System Call Category Percentage Frequency - Com: This feature corresponds to the proportion of number of system calls in communication category to the total number of system calls triggered by the malware. Difference between the targeted and traditional malware's empirical cumulative distribution functions suggests that percentage of system calls initiated by traditional malware related to the communication is almost 8 times more than the targeted malware. It can be deduced from this behavior that targeted malware avoids initiating too many communication attempts to avoid triggering any alarms which aligns well with its stealthy nature.

API Function Frequency - NtSetContextThread: This feature corresponds to the number of times NtSetContextThread function is called by the malware. As the "Nt" prefix implies, NtSetContextThread is an Windows Native API system call that is used for modifying an existing thread's context, e.g. CPU registers. Malware utilizes this function for performing various advanced actions including evading Microsoft's EMET to execute shellcode, injecting code into processes or anti-debugging. It is important to note that this particular function is also used in process hollowing technique [17] for changing a thread's EIP and EAX registers which is widely employed by the sophisticated and targeted malware, i.e. Duqu. Difference in the traditional and targeted malware behavior with regards to this feature is very clear in Fig. 2 showing that while only 8% of the traditional malware samples called NtSetContextThread API function, 59% of the targeted malware samples called it at least once which reveals the sophisticated and state-of-the art nature of targeted malware.

API Function Frequency - HttpOpenRequestW: This feature corresponds to the number of times HttpOpenRequestW function called by the malware. HttpOpenRequestW is an Windows Internet (WinInet) API function that is used for creating an HTTP request. It is called by malware while accessing a web resource or downloading a file. It is also known that malware hooks this function to perform a wide variety of information theft attacks. Because WinInet is a higher level API and also used by browsers, it allows malware to hide itself in the regular network traffic.

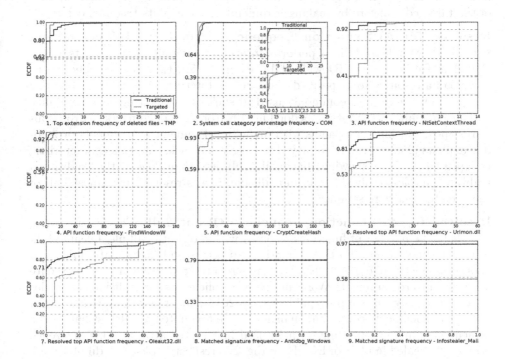

Fig. 2. ECDF of top features for targeted and traditional samples.

API Function Frequency - FindWindowW: This feature corresponds to the number of times FindWindowW function is called by the malware. Find-WindowW is an Windows API function that is used to get a handle to the window with the given name or class. It is usually called by malware to search for a window that belongs to a specific security tool used in malware analysis, mostly a debugger as an anti-debugging trick. It is also utilized in code injection in a very stealthy manner. Only 8% of the traditional malware samples called FindWindowW API function. On the other hand, almost half of the targeted malware samples called it at least once, mostly more than once. This difference in plots of ECDFs in Fig. 2 indicates that targeted malware takes additional measures to avoid being detected and analyzed which matches well with the previously discussed characteristic of the targeted malware.

API Function Frequency - CryptCreateHash: CryptCreateHash is an Windows API function that is used to initiate hashing of a stream of data.

It is called by malware to perform cryptographic hashing functions to generate encryption keys or obfuscating key internal data. In a report published about evasive malware [9], obfuscating internal data is found among the four most common evasive behaviours. Figure 2 shows that whereas only around 7% of the traditional malware samples called CryptCreateHash function, it was called by more than 40% of the targeted malware samples confirming the evasive nature of the targeted malware by making it difficult to identify its true behaviour.

Resolved Top API Function Frequency - Urlmon.dll: URLmon.dll provides URL Monikers API to perform Internet communications and its URL-DownloadToFile (or URLDownloadToCacheFile) function is very effective to download a resource to a specified filename via Internet Explorer with just one call [15]. Therefore, it is commonly used in shellcode exploiting a vulnerability and also in malicious scripts embedded in Office or PDF documents to drop malware. Spear phishing campaigns with malicious document attachments or zero-day exploits [25] are widely employed in targeted attacks and this characteristic is captured in Fig. 2 showing that while only less than 20% of the traditional malware samples resolved the urlmon.dll file, it was resolved by almost half of the targeted malware samples.

Resolved Top API Function Frequency - Oleaut32.dll: This feature corresponds to the number of functions resolved within oleaut32.dll file. Oleaut32.dll provides a mechanism, OLE Automation, to access and manipulate objects in another application, e.g. ActiveX, Word macro, etc. It allows malware to execute VBScript macros in remote Word and Excel applications for malicious activities in a hidden way. In a report published in 2016 [25], it was found that Word and Excel documents containing malicious code accounted for almost half of the attachments in spear-phishing attacks used in targeted attacks. This difference is clearly revealed in plots of ECDFs in Fig. 2 in respect to oleaut32.dll file where 70% of the targeted malware samples resolved this API file, while only less than 30% of the traditional malware samples used it. When this and the previous features are both taken into account, it gives a clear picture of the attackers techniques to target individuals or organisations via spear-phishing attacks.

Matched Signature Frequency - Antidbg_Windows: This feature corresponds to the occurrence of a match of antidbg_windows YARA signature. Antidbg_windows signature checks if the malware contains strings of windows names of popular debuggers and forensic tools which are indication of malware employing anti-debugging tricks. Figure 2 shows that whereas only around 20% of the traditional malware samples were discovered having anti-debugging tricks, almost 70% of the targeted malware samples contained strings that are used to determine the presence of debuggers or other security tools in the execution environment. This difference in plots of ECDFs, similar to FindWindowW feature, aligns well with the targeted malware characteristics of making it hard for the analysts or automated systems to detect and analyze it.

Matched Signature Frequency - Infostealer_Mail: This feature corresponds to the occurrence of a match of infostealer_mail YARA signature. Infostealer_mail signature checks if the malware attempts to collect credentials from various local email client programs. Whereas only 3% of the traditional malware samples were stealing information regarding the email, more than 40% of the targeted malware samples as shown in Fig. 2 were found harvesting email credentials and addresses possibly to be used in spearphishing campaigns which are widely conducted in targeted attacks such as APTs. It was found out in a report published in 2016 that while the number of spearphishing campaings were increased by 55% in year 2015, they became more stealthier and number of recipients as well as the average duration of the campaigns fell by 39% and 33%, respectively [25].

Matched Signature Frequency - Injection_Runpe: This feature corresponds to the occurrence of a match of injection_runpe YARA signature. Injection_runpe signature checks if the malware launches a new process and injects code into it which can also include unpacking of code. The API functions filtered in this signature including NtUnmapViewOfSection, NtSetContextThread, NtResumeThread, etc. [12] are commonly used in process hollowing technique which allows stealthy code execution within another process' address space and is frequently used in targeted attacks. Only around 7% of the traditional malware samples were matched. On the other hand, more than 40% of the targeted malware samples were identified as employing such sophisticated injection techniques.

4   Related Work

Finding a suitable way to represent binary files lies at the heart of every method or system presented so far to detect or classify malware via machine learning. In this section a literature background about malware classification is provided with a focus on the use of static and dynamic features in malware classification.

4.1   Static Feature Extraction

Static analysis is the process of examining a binary file without actually executing it in order to determine if it is malicious or not. Extracting static features from a binary file to perform malware classification is carried out by static analysis tools or techniques.

[23] were among the first who introduced static features for malware detection by employing several different classifiers. They conducted experiments based on three different types of static features including Portable Executable (PE), strings and byte sequence n-grams. From PE header of a binary, they extracted dynamic link library (DLL) information and constructed three different feature vectors representing if a DLL was used, if a specific function inside a DLL was called and count of unique function calls inside each DLL. Encoded strings inside a binary was extracted and used as a feature. They also converted binary files into hexadecimal codes and used byte sequences of codes as n-gram features. Based on these three features, different classifiers are employed to classify new

binaries as malicious or clean. While string features yielded the highest accuracy, the best detection rate was achieved by using byte sequence n-grams.

Their work inspired and encouraged others to try similar approaches for malware classification. [14] adopted and enhanced the byte sequence n-grams technique. They achieved better results in detecting malicious binaries via classifiers including Support Vector Machine, Decision Tree and boosted versions of them. [37] extracted API calls from PE header of a binary file similar to what [23] did in their work and used them as features for classifying a binary as malicious or not.

[28] disassembled the binary and then extracted the length and frequency of function names. Based on the function name length features, they perform malware classification between different malware families and their results suggested that function name length is significant as a feature in distinguishing malware families.

While static features have been widely used to detect or classify malware via machine learning, there exists some limitations. Authors assume that the malware is unpacked or not encrypted and static features can be extracted right away from the binary. However, it is very common for a malware to be packed or encrypted and in some cases it is not possible to fully unpack or decrypt malware. There also exists a wide variety of obfuscation techniques that can thwart the whole process [19].

4.2   Dynamic Feature Extraction

Dynamic analysis is the process of examining a binary file by executing it in a controlled environment and capturing its behavior in order to determine if it is malicious or not. Controlled environment where the analysis is conducted could be a specially designed sandbox [6,11,35] offering virtual, emulated or even bare-metal environment, but also a single computer equipped with dynamic analysis tools.

[3] constructed a high level behavior profile consisting of system change counts for process, file, registry and network categories for each binary sample after running it in a virtual environment and collecting system events. Using the behavioral profiles representing malware behavior as features and Normalized Compression Distance (NCD) as distance metric, they conducted hierarchical clustering on malware samples to cluster them into families. [5] extended the previous work [3] by constructing a low level behavior profile using a generalized form of system resources and system calls after running the sample in a dynamic analysis sandbox [6]. They achieved high run-time performance by performing hierarchical clustering using Locality Sensitive Hashing (LSH) and Jaccard index as distance metric. While both of the previous works used an unsupervised algorithm for the malware classification, [22] performed malware classification using Support Vector Machines (SVM) by extracting features from analysis report generated after running a malware sample in a dynamic analysis system [35].

Feature vectors in the works [5, 22] were representing malware behavior using a generalized form of the system calls and their parameters captured during the analysis.

[29] executed binaries in a virtual environment and captured system calls and their parameters with the help of an automated tool. A global list with strings representing captured system calls and parameters is compiled. Feature vector for each binary was constructed using this list and consisted of boolean values for each string in the global list specifying whether it was encountered during the analysis of the sample or not. They used supervised learning classifiers both for classifying a binary as malicious or not and for classifying malware into malware families. [13] extended the previous work by incorporating static features including printable strings and function length frequency into the dynamic system call features. Function length frequency feature vector consists of counts of functions for fixed length ranges. They conducted experiments for each feature separately and also for the integrated features using different supervised learning classifiers. All experimented classifiers achieved best results using the integrated features. [2] presented a method for combining features from six different sources including three static sources, two dynamic sources and one source containing statistics about the other sources. They achieved high accuracy classifying binaries as malicious or not using SVM classifier.

[18] proposed a system consisting of two components, one for analyzing binaries dynamically and one for classification and clustering. 65 features in three categories including file, registry and network were extracted from the artifacts captured during the dynamic analysis. Extracted features were in low granularity, mostly counts, e.g. number of files created, unique number of extensions of the created files, file size, etc. Memory artifacts were also collected during the analysis phase but used only for signature matching to enhanced labeling, but not included in the feature vector. Experiments conducted using wide range of supervised learning classifiers in order to classify binaries as malicious or not and achieved high accuracy. They also performed clustering using several different distance metrics and parameters and presented results in terms of accuracy and performance.

There is also considerable amount of work that utilizes DNS features for classification. [7] identified malicious domains by monitoring the DNS traffic passively, extracted 15 features from the monitored traffic and achieved high detection rate. Types of features defined in terms of granularity are similar to the features presented in this paper.

5   Conclusion

Targeted attacks constitute one of the greatest risks for many organizations. As they are typically carefully prepared and designed particularly for the victims, they are harder to detect both during the infection and the further phases of the attacks. In this paper, we put an effort in understanding whether the malware that is used in targeted attacks could be distinguished from traditional malware. In big organizations, the security products in place produce many malware detection alerts. Unfortunately, the number of alerts in general is too high and therefore too overwhelming for the security analysts who are responsible for prioritizing the most risky attacks. Hence, a methodology to identify correctly targeted attacks from the haystack of attacks organizations everyday face with would be very beneficial for the organizations.

In this paper, we first aimed at understanding whether malware that is used in targeted attacks is different from traditional malware. To achieve this, we dynamically analyzed a substantial amount of targeted and traditional malware and compared their behavior. We profiled the behavior of malware and their execution characteristics by extracting over 700 features that could represent the network, host and memory behavior of the malware analyzed. We then, experimented with a number of machine learning algorithms and found out that while not perfectly, targeted malware could be distinguished from traditional malware. Furthermore, we have shown that using raw simplistic features that could be easily calculated from the dynamic analysis traces of executables, it is possible to achieve good classification accuracies. This is a very important finding as it opens the door for future works that could focus on improving the methodology we proposed in this paper.

References

1. Ambroise, C., McLachlan, G.J.: Selection bias in gene extraction on the basis of microarray gene-expression data. Proc. Natl. Acad. Sci. **99**(10), 6562–6566 (2002)
2. Anderson, B., Storlie, C., Lane, T.: Improving malware classification: bridging the static/dynamic gap. In: Proceedings of the 5th ACM Workshop on Security and Artificial Intelligence, pp. 3–14. ACM (2012)
3. Bailey, M., Oberheide, J., Andersen, J., Mao, Z.M., Jahanian, F., Nazario, J.: Automated classification and analysis of internet malware. In: Kruegel, C., Lippmann, R., Clark, A. (eds.) RAID 2007. LNCS, vol. 4637, pp. 178–197. Springer, Heidelberg (2007). https://doi.org/10.1007/978-3-540-74320-0_10
4. Barbosa, G.N., Branco, R.R.: Prevalent characteristics in modern malware. Black Hat USA (2014)
5. Bayer, U., Comparetti, P.M., Hlauschek, C., Kruegel, C., Kirda, E.: Scalable, behavior-based malware clustering. In: NDSS, vol. 9, pp. 8–11 (2009)
6. Bayer, U., Kruegel, C., Kirda, E.: TTAnalyze: a tool for analyzing malware. na (2006)
7. Bilge, L., Kirda, E., Kruegel, C., Balduzzi, M.: Exposure: finding malicious domains using passive DNS analysis. In: Ndss (2011)
8. Chen, X.W., Jeong, J.C.: Enhanced recursive feature elimination. In: Sixth International Conference on Machine Learning and Applications, ICMLA 2007, pp. 429–435. IEEE (2007)
9. Christopher, K.: Evasive malware exposed and deconstructed. In: RSA Conference (2015)
10. Egele, M., Scholte, T., Kirda, E., Kruegel, C.: A survey on automated dynamic malware-analysis techniques and tools. ACM Comput. Surv. (CSUR) **44**(2), 6 (2012)

11. Guarnieri, C., Tanasi, A., Bremer, J., Schloesser, M.: The cuckoo sandbox (2012)
12. Harrell, C.: Prefetch file meet process hollowing (2014). https://journeyintoir. blogspot.be/2014/12/prefetch-file-meet-process-hollowing_17.html
13. Islam, R., Tian, R., Batten, L.M., Versteeg, S.: Classification of malware based on integrated static and dynamic features. J. Netw. Comput. Appl. **36**(2), 646–656 (2013)
14. Kolter, J.Z., Maloof, M.A.: Learning to detect malicious executables in the wild. In: Proceedings of the Tenth ACM SIGKDD International Conference on Knowledge Discovery and Data Mining, pp. 470–478. ACM (2004)
15. M-Labs: Reversing malware command and control: From sockets to com. Fire-Eye (2010). https://www.fireeye.com/blog/threat-research/2010/08/reversing-malware-command-control-sockets.html
16. Microsoft: Common folder variables (2015). https://www.microsoft.com/security/ portal/mmpc/shared/variables.aspx
17. MITRE: Process hollowing (2016). https://attack.mitre.org/wiki/Technique/ T1093
18. Mohaisen, A., Alrawi, O., Mohaisen, M.: Amal: high-fidelity, behavior-based automated malware analysis and classification. Comput. Secur. **52**, 251–266 (2015)
19. Moser, A., Kruegel, C., Kirda, E.: Limits of static analysis for malware detection. In: Twenty-Third Annual Computer Security Applications Conference, ACSAC 2007, pp. 421–430. IEEE (2007)
20. Optiv: Improving reliability of sandbox results (2014). https://www.optiv.com/ blog/improving-reliability-of-sandbox-results
21. Ortega, A.: Pafish (paranoid fish) (2012). https://github.com/a0rtega/pafish/
22. Rieck, K., Holz, T., Willems, C., Düssel, P., Laskov, P.: Learning and classification of malware behavior. In: Zamboni, D. (ed.) DIMVA 2008. LNCS, vol. 5137, pp. 108–125. Springer, Heidelberg (2008). https://doi.org/10.1007/978-3-540-70542-0_6
23. Schultz, M.G., Eskin, E., Zadok, F., Stolfo, S.J.: Data mining methods for detection of new malicious executables. In: Proceedings of 2001 IEEE Symposium on Security and Privacy, S&P 2001, pp. 38–49. IEEE (2001)
24. Spengler, B.: Modified edition of cuckoo. Github (2013). https://github.com/brad-accuvant/cuckoo-modified
25. Symantec: Internet Security Threat Report, vol. 21, April 2016. https://www. symantec.com/security-center/threat-report
26. Tankard, C.: Advanced persistent threats and how to monitor and deter them. Netw. Secur. **2011**(8), 16–19 (2011)
27. Teller, T., Hayon, A.: Enhancing Automated Malware Analysis Machines with Memory Analysis. Black Hat, USA (2014)
28. Tian, R., Batten, L.M., Versteeg, S.: Function length as a tool for malware classification. In: 3rd International Conference on Malicious and Unwanted Software, MALWARE 2008, pp. 69–76. IEEE (2008)
29. Tian, R., Islam, R., Batten, L., Versteeg, S.: Differentiating malware from clean-ware using behavioural analysis. In: 2010 5th International Conference on Malicious and Unwanted Software (MALWARE), pp. 23–30. IEEE (2010)
30. VirusShare: Virusshare.com - because sharing is caring (2017). https://virusshare. com/
31. Virustotal: Virustotal - free online virus, malware and URL scanner (2012). https://www.virustotal.com/
32. Virustotal: YARA - the pattern matching swiss knife for malware researchers (2014). https://virustotal.github.io/yara/

33. Virvilis, N., Gritzalis, D., Apostolopoulos, T.: Trusted computing vs. advanced persistent threats: can a defender win this game? In: 2013 IEEE 10th International Conference on Ubiquitous Intelligence and Computing and 10th International Conference on Autonomic and Trusted Computing (UIC/ATC), pp. 396–403. IEEE (2013)
34. Walters, A.: The volatility framework: volatile memory artifact extraction utility framework (2007)
35. Willems, C., Holz, T., Freiling, F.: CWSandbox: towards automated dynamic binary analysis. IEEE Secur. Privacy **5**(2), 32–39 (2007)
36. Wilson, T.: Move over, apts - the ram-based advanced volatile threat is spinning up fast. DarkReading (2013). www.darkreading.com/vulnerabilities--threats/move-over-apts--the-ram-based-advanced-volatile-threat-is-spinning-up-fast/d/d-id/1139211
37. Ye, Y., Wang, D., Li, T., Ye, D., Jiang, Q.: An intelligent pe-malware detection system based on association mining. J. Comput. Virol. **4**(4), 323–334 (2008)

Mobile and Embedded Security

Honey, I Shrunk Your App Security: The State of Android App Hardening

Vincent Haupert[1(✉)], Dominik Maier[2], Nicolas Schneider[1], Julian Kirsch[3], and Tilo Müller[1]

[1] Friedrich-Alexander University Erlangen-Nürnberg (FAU), Erlangen, Germany
vincent.haupert@cs.fau.de
[2] TU Berlin, Berlin, Germany
dmaier@sect.tu-berlin.de
[3] TU Munich, Munich, Germany
kirschju@sec.in.tum.de

Abstract. The continued popularity of smartphones has led companies from all business sectors to use them for security-sensitive tasks like two-factor authentication. Android, however, suffers from a fragmented landscape of devices and versions, which leaves many devices unpatched by their manufacturers. This security gap has created a vital market of commercial solutions for *Runtime Application Self-Protection* (RASP) to harden apps and ensure their integrity even on compromised devices. In this paper, we assess the RASP market for Android by providing an overview of the available products and their features. Furthermore, we describe an in-depth case study for a leading RASP product—namely *Promon Shield*—which is being used by approximately 100 companies to protect over 100 million end users worldwide. We demonstrate two attacks against Promon Shield: The first removes the entire protection scheme statically from an app, while the second disables all security measures dynamically at runtime.

1 Introduction

Mobile platforms based on the Google Android and Apple iOS operating systems (OSs) have matured in recent years. They are now omnipresent and form a part of our daily lives. In contrast to desktop platforms, however, some vendors still consider their mobile devices as embedded platforms without rolling security updates. Particularly on Android, device owners may face a problem when the manufacturer leaves a device unpatched, or at least vulnerable, for a long time [17,29,33]. Even in the case where an OS is fully updated, recent history has taught us that new attack vectors can still be uncovered: Rowhammer [14,27] and Spectre [15] are prominent examples of this. Vulnerable end-user devices lead to a challenging situation for companies that promote security apps—such as two-factor authentication apps—which rely on the integrity of the underlying OS. Instead of changing the business logic, for example, by shipping secure hardware tokens or leveraging a phone's *trusted execution environment* (TEE), we noticed

© Springer International Publishing AG, part of Springer Nature 2018
C. Giuffrida et al. (Eds.): DIMVA 2018, LNCS 10885, pp. 69–91, 2018.
https://doi.org/10.1007/978-3-319-93411-2_4

a trend toward applying app-hardening solutions that are purely software-based. These solutions are frequently referred to as *Runtime Application Self-Protection* (RASP), and they have already given rise to a vital market.

To the best of our knowledge, our work is the first to challenge the claims of the RASP market by assessing the features commonly offered by RASP products. Furthermore, we provide a detailed security analysis of an internationally leading product called *Promon SHIELD*, which is currently used in more than 30 apps worldwide. In general, we find that RASP solutions cannot protect against their own threat model. In particular, we developed a tool called NOMORP, which is able to automatically disable all security measures employed by Promon Shield.

2   App Hardening

In this section, we discuss the features commonly offered by app-hardening solutions. App hardening, and RASP in general, aim to ensure the security of an app even on a hostile or breached OS. Even though most products are available for Android and iOS, we focus on Android in this work, as many implementations are highly specific to the OS and the ecosystem. We chose Android because of its larger market share and the significant fragmentation of Android versions, both of which lead to a greater demand for app hardening.

App-hardening products are typically provided as *software development kits* (SDKs) with binary libraries, or sometimes as build environment patches that offer the automated integration of security features into an app without the assistance of developers. A central part of an app-hardening solution is obfuscation as it stalls reversing and cracking for a certain period. This is adequate in the gaming industry, for example. In the case of security apps like two-factor authentication apps and financial apps, however, merely increasing the period of protection is not enough. So, app-hardening solutions enrich obfuscation with a variety of defenses against dynamic analysis and best practices.

2.1   The RASP Market

In the course of this research, we analyzed the feature set of 10 commercial app-hardening solutions [9]. The initial goal—to give definite answers about the strength of the provided features—was quickly dismissed, for app-hardening solutions differ vastly per license and app. Some apps protected by the same RASP solution have features enabled that others do not have. Similarly, we noticed apps bearing hardening features in addition to the RASP provider. For all these reasons, the following overview builds on available marketing documents of the RASP products rather than manual analyses of their features.

Table 1 lists market-leading hardening solutions and compares their official feature sets. Additionally, Promon Shield was taken as a case study for in-depth manual reverse engineering, as discussed in later sections. While investigating Promon Shield, we noticed features that were not mentioned in the official documentation. In other words, a feature not being listed in Table table:securityspssolutions does not necessarily imply that a feature is not present.

Table 1. Overview of RASP products and their advertised features.

Product	Anti-Tampering	Anti-Hooking	Anti-Debugging	Anti-Emulator	Code Obfuscation	White-Box Cryptography	Device Binding	Root Detection	Anti-Keylogger	Anti-Screen Reader	Data Encryption	Secure Communication
Arxan for Android	✓	✓	✓	.	✓	✓	.	✓	.	.	✓	.
DNP HyperTech CrackProof	✓	.	✓	✓	.	.	.	✓	.	.	.	.
Entersekt Transakt	✓	.	.	.	.	.	✓	✓	✓	.	.	✓
Gemalto Mobile Protector	.	✓	✓	.	✓	.	✓	✓	✓	.	✓	✓
GuardSquare DexGuard	✓	✓	✓	✓	✓	✓	.	✓	.	.	.	✓
Inside Secure Core for Android	✓	.	✓	.	✓	✓	.	✓	.	.	.	.
Intertrust WhiteCryption	✓	.	✓	.	✓	✓	✓	✓	.	.	.	.
PreEmptive DashO	✓	.	✓	✓	✓	.	✓	✓	.	.	.	.
Promon SHIELD	✓	✓	✓	✓	✓	✓	✓	✓	✓	✓	✓	✓
SecNeo AppShield	✓	.	✓	.	✓	.	.	.	.	.	✓	.

Anti-tampering. If attackers manage to alter the code at runtime, they acquire the same privileges as the underlying app. They can then manipulate data that gets exchanged in the backend, or disable license and security checks. Anti-tampering solutions use a variety of methods to ensure that a third party did not alter an app's code. If tampering the code is possible, other dynamic defenses can be patched out. Therefore, anti-tampering technology is the cornerstone of current app security solutions, and every library in the set offers it.

An obvious anti-tampering approach is to check the signature of the *Android application package* (APK) at startup. If the signature does not match the expected developer certificate, then a third party likely altered the app. More sophisticated measures scatter signature checks throughout the app or use watermarks, thus making the check itself harder to strip [22].

Promon Shield assesses the integrity of the installed `base.apk` by loading the developer's certificate from an encrypted entry in a configuration file at startup. In addition to verifying the APK, it checks the hash sums of certain Android-specific files—such as `AndroidManifest.xml` and `classes.dex`—and its own native library, `libshield.so`.

Anti-hooking Even if the code inside the app has not been altered, an attacker can still run code within the app by hooking certain calls and inserting functionality at runtime. The hooking of functions, *Application programming interfaces* (APIs), or system calls allows attackers to modify many elements. For example, they can alter the method parameters and the return values of calls or completely swap out methods. On Android, a variety of open source hooking frameworks exists. Since hooks are usually inserted from the outside, potentially at a higher privilege level, detection is not easy. Anti-hooking solutions for Android typically attempt to find traces of well-known hooking frameworks in the file system or memory. Promon Shield, for example, checks for artifacts of *Xposed* and *Cydia Substrate* but does not scan the app's memory. Therefore, our analysis based on *Frida* remained undetected.

Anti-debugging. Like in hooking, debuggers can alter the control flow and change the return values of functions that have not been tampered with otherwise. Furthermore, debugging gives attackers insights into the operation of the hardening framework and app. For this very reason, app-hardening solutions try to detect the presence of a debugger and abort the execution if needed. Android has two worlds where a debugger can attach: the native code debugger based on `ptrace` for C and C++, and the Java debugger based on the JDWP protocol.

For the Java part, a trivial implementation merely checks if the `isDebuggerConnected` API returns `true`; if it does not, then the execution is aborted. Promon Shield modifies native code data structures to prevent JDWP debugging. In the `JdwpState` struct, it replaces the function pointers that are responsible for handling debugger packets with a pointer to a function that always returns the value `false`, leading to the immediate termination of unaltered debugger sessions. To hinder the debugging of native code, libraries usually trace their own code path using `ptrace`. The `ptrace` API allows only a single debugger at a given time. Therefore, if the hardening library already debugs the binary, no other debugger can attach to it. In Promon, the main Promon Shield process SHIELD−1 forks a child process SHIELD−2, which then attaches to all threads of its parent via `ptrace`.

Anti-emulator. Running an app inside an emulator, a virtual machine, or sandbox allows an attacker to hook or trace program execution. For apps running inside an Android emulator, it is easy to inspect the state of the system, reset it to a saved image, or monitor how the app operates. Several mechanisms for detecting sandboxes are known to be used by malware [18,19,28], and RASP solutions usually implement a subset of the same mechanisms. Promon Shield, for example, immediately crashes the app if it runs inside an Android emulator.

Code Obfuscation. The Android toolchain comes with *ProGuard*, an obfuscation tool that renames all class and method names at compile time. As renaming is a well-known obfuscation method, the techniques used to deobfuscate it have been well researched [3]. Obfuscation, in general, tries to obscure code as much as possible, as do app-hardening solutions. Besides renaming, some other obfuscation methods are, for example, control-flow flattening, opaque and random predicates, and function merging and splitting [5].

While perfectly obfuscating code running on the same machine as the attacker is impossible according to Barak et al. [1], it can notably increase the effort an attacker has to invest. Krügel et al. state that "[o]bfuscation and de-obfuscation is an arms race [...] usually in favor of the de-obfuscator" [16]. This statement still holds true, as Schrittwieser et al. discussed fairly recently [24].

Another category of obfuscation is DEX packing that aims at mitigating static and dynamic analysis and is particularly popular among malware authors to hide their malicious code from both automatic and manual analysis, e.g., an automated sandbox or a reverse engineer, respectively. The popularity of Android packers is unbroken; hence, research has proposed various approaches for automatic unpacking [6, 30–32].

The native part of Promon Shield is encrypted and the unpacked code is obfuscated further. The Java part of the `no.promon.shield` package is slightly obfuscated, depending on the target app. If it is, then all packages, classes, methods, and fields are renamed to random eight-character strings. However, Promon Shield does not obfuscate the customer's app using any of the obfuscation techniques mentioned above; at most, *ProGuard* is used independently.

White-Box Cryptography. Like code obfuscation, white-box cryptography aims to obscure secrets [23]. It does not obfuscate the business logic, but tries to prevent cryptographic secrets from leaking [4]. Implementations try to provide a one-way function, making it easy to apply cryptographic operations but hard to reverse the input keys. Like in the case of code obfuscation, attackers can reverse most implementations [10]. While white-box cryptography makes reverse engineering of the key significantly harder, an attacker can still copy the whole implementation blob and apply the cryptographic operations without having to learn the keys used.

Device Binding. Device binding does not prevent copying but stops execution on other devices. For apps like banking, it is desired that they work only on a device that is explicitly paired with the account. So, to comply with the demand of physical second factors, app-hardening solutions try to achieve device binding. They usually fingerprint the device and then store unique identifiers at the first start of the app. If any identifier does not match on app start, the app refuses to run. A common approach is to use the `ANDROID_ID` and `IMEI` as they are unique and very robust [11]. The disadvantage of device fingerprinting compared to approaches that leverage, for example, the hardware-backed key store, is that they rely on information that is accessible to any application running on the same device [2]. In Promon Shield, device binding is rudimentary. It only consists of the `Build.SERIAL` of the device and, if permissions allow it, the IMEI.

Root Detection. On Android, every app runs in its own user context as part of the sandboxing concept. Users who still want to alter certain aspects of their OS often have to *root* their phone, creating a user with elevated privileges. Since rooting breaks the sandboxing concept and allows the user to alter arbitrary app data, hardening solutions often try to prevent the app from running on rooted phones. Mostly, artifacts of root management applications are checked (e.g., `SuperSU.apk`), or binaries only present on rooted phones (e.g., `/system/bin/su`).

Promon Shield additionally iterates all processes using the `proc` file system and checks for processes like `daemonsu`, belonging to *SuperSU*, a root management app. It also scans `/proc/self/exe`, which resolves to the `app_loader` binary, and scans for *SuperSU* and *Magisk Manager* artifacts. Not only are these checks easy to bypass by renaming the files but they also prevent the execution of protected apps on phones deliberately rooted by their users; however, they cannot prevent privilege escalation exploits on non-rooted phones [7,26].

Anti-keylogger. The possibility to install third-party keyboard apps on Android opens the system up to malicious keyboards that grab sensitive information entered in the apps. To counteract this, RASP solutions often ship their own keyboards that apps can use in a more trusted fashion. In Promon Shield, if an app uses the provided `SecureEditText` and `SecureKeyboard` classes, Promons built-in keyboard shows up. As a different line of defense, Promon Shield offers to check the installed keyboard apps against a whitelist. If one of the installed keyboards is not whitelisted in the configuration, the app quits.

Anti-screen Reader. Malware can use accessibility services, as demonstrated by *Cloak and Dagger* [8], to read the contents on a screen. Anti-screen reader methods try to mitigate these attacks. Promon Shield, for example, iterates through all installed apps that provide accessibility services and checks them against a whitelist provided by the configuration, including their name and signature. Another way to prevent screen content grabbing is by disabling screenshots. When this feature is enabled, Promon Shield sets the `FLAG_SECURE` property on the application's window object at runtime, instructing Android to disallow screenshots and to show a black rectangle in place of media created through the recording API instead of the actual window content.

Data Encryption. App-hardening products sell the idea that data stored encrypted within the app is more secure than data that is encrypted by the system. The idea is to try to prevent attackers with higher privileges from reading stored data. For example, attackers might do this to gain knowledge about possibly sensitive data like transaction histories or encryption keys. The main problem is where the key should be stored so as to remain inaccessible to an attacker. Hence, if not derived at runtime from a user-provided secret, data encryption uses a sort of obfuscation to hide the keys and inner workings as a best-effort solution. Promon Shield provides its customer with the `SecureStorage` class that allows data encryption that also leverages Promon's white-box cryptography. We provide more details on its implementation in Sect. 3.5.

Secure Communication. Secured communication lowers the possibility of man-in-the-middle attacks not only on the network but also against attackers on the phone. Promon Shield has two distinct features for this. First, it offers its own HTTPS networking API for Java. If the app developers switch from using `HttpURLConnection` to `PromonHttpUrlConnection`, all requests get automatically routed through the native lib where certificate pinning is enforced. The native library only connects to servers for which certificates are present in the encrypted configuration file. Additionally, the app developers can choose to add a client certificate to the configuration file in such a way that the server knows whether it is communicating with a genuine app or a third-party client. Second, Promon Shield offers its own protocol based on the `DeviceManagement` class that relies on native methods into `libshield.so`. This Java class allows APIs to register an app at the server and performs signed transactions afterward.

2.2   Threat Model

Based on the diverse mitigations that different hardening solutions claim, we try to synthesize their threat model in this chapter. Hence, we infer our threat model from the one commonly employed by RASP products.

Attacks Against Intellectual Property. The first adversary aims at the intellectual property or other secrets, such as the hardcoded credentials, of an app. She has privileged access to her own device and tries to gather insights into the app by means of reverse engineering, including static and dynamic analysis. Her goals are, for example, circumventing licensing checks to pirate an app, cloning the integral functionality of the business logic, or publishing information like hardcoded API keys. She may even be able to offer third-party apps that are fully compatible with the original app by analyzing API calls, leading to potential monetary gain and critical insights into a company's infrastructure.

Attacks Against the User Account. The second adversary is a remote attacker who tries to gather user information or execute transactions in the name of the legitimate user. Such attackers usually apply social engineering, drive-by downloads, app piggybacking or any other method to achieve code execution on the victim's device. This attacker is omnipotent as she has access to privilege escalation exploits and can take complete control of the operating system the app is running on. She may trie to run code in the context of the app, communicate to the backend server with the user's credentials, or clone the complete state of the app to her own device for further analysis and use. Additionally, she might use man-in-the-middle attacks to gather sensitive information.

3   Unpacking Promon Shield with Nomorp

Large international finance and public law institutions place their trust in Promon Shield. To demonstrate how this popular RASP product can be thwarted, we propose NOMORP, a tool that automatically disables all protection features from a hardened app. To that end, we developed a static and a dynamic attack to address both threats described in Sect. 2.2. The static version aims at attacking intellectual property, while the dynamic version is after the user's data.

3.1   Promon Shield

Promon, a company from Norway specializing in the security of mobile and desktop applications, is a global player in the RASP market with approximately 100 individual business customers protecting the apps of around 100 million end users [25]. The large number of users, as well as the companys focus on the critical banking sector, makes their product a perfect fit for our in-depth case study analysis. Since Promon does not disclose the names of its customers, we crawled the official Google Play Store for apps using Promon Shield. These are identifiable simply by the inclusion of Promon's characteristic native library, `libshield.so`. After downloading over 150,000 free apps from all Play Store categories, we found 31 apps that include Promon Shield at the time of writing.

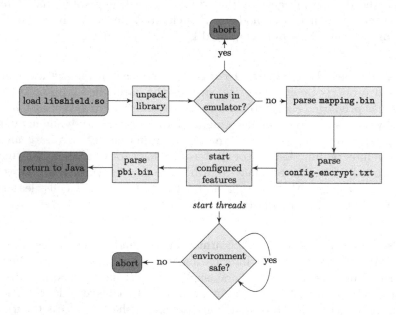

Fig. 1. Life cycle of Promon Shield's native library.

Interestingly, even though Promon advertises its solution to other fields—for example, to car manufacturers—all 31 apps in the Google Play Store belong to the finance category. Twenty apps are from Germany, two apps from Norway and Finland, and one app each is from the Netherlands, Sweden, Great Britain, United States, Mexico, Brazil, and Hong Kong. The app s high popularity in Germany is striking; Promon Shield protects most of the banking apps on the German market. As of April 23, 2018, four out of the top ten financial apps in Germany make use of Promon's solution.

The integration process is claimed to be very easy for app developers [20]. After a customer has received Promon's integration tool, developers simply have to specify a configuration file to enable or disable security features. Later, the Promon integration tool takes the app's APK and the configuration file and outputs a hardened APK with the specified protection mechanisms applied. The customer can now publish the resulting APK to the Google Play Store, and no further steps are needed.

The life cycle of an app protected by Promon Shield is illustrated in Fig. 1. The app first loads the native library `libshield.so`. For this, the integration tool adds initializing Java code to the `onCreate` method of the main activity, as specified in `AndroidManifest.xml`. The native library relies on three files which are a product of the integration tool and are added encrypted to the assets of the APK: `mapping.bin`, `config-encrypt.txt`, and `pbi.bin`. After the initialization routine has decrypted and parsed the configuration file, Promon Shield starts a series of threads that realize the enabled features—for example, the anti-debugging or root detection. The configuration defines how Promon Shield should treat anomalies, by allowing the execution of callbacks or directly crashing the app with the possibility to open a web browser with a given URL.

3.2   Static Nomorp

In this section, we propose the use of NOMORP, a fully automated tool intended to strip Promon Shield's app hardening from all apps. We had access to neither the Promon Shield integration tool nor any insider information or internal source code. An adversary could leverage the same tooling and knowledge which makes the tool and analysis particularly relevant. To create NOMORP, we analyzed multiple apps that were hardened by Promon Shield. We combined static reverse engineering with dynamic analysis based on a custom Android runtime (ART) and the *Frida* dynamic instrumentation tool. Our analysis quickly revealed that Promon Shield adds a native library to the app that gets loaded first. As stated, this library is easily detected, for the naming of the file always follows the pattern `libshield_{ID}.so`. We leveraged this knowledge to detect additional apps in the Google Play Store that use Promon Shield. As described in Sect. 3.5, we used this library and all calls from Java to it as a starting point in the analysis. After discovering that Promon left the Java part largely untouched, we focussed on either removing `libshield.so` statically or disabling it dynamically at runtime. We ended up implementing both methods in NOMORP. This section presents sNOMORP, a tool that is capable of producing a version that is easier to analyze. In Sect. 3.3, we describe dNOMORP, a tool to disable Promon Shield at runtime.

The native library `libshield.so` implements most app-hardening features internally. Stripping it automatically disables almost all security measures.

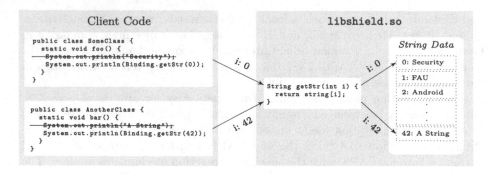

Fig. 2. Visualization of Promon Shield's string externalization.

Promon is aware of the attack scenario and seeks to prevent it by introducing a binding between the customer's Java code and their own native code implemented in `libshield.so`. This mainly consists of two mechanisms: externalization of strings, and externalization of constants. Hereinafter, we explain how Promon Shield implements each feature and how we circumvented them.

String Externalization. Promon Shield's string externalization is visualized in Fig. 2 and works as follows: When the integration tool applies Promon Shield's protection, it looks for strings inside the client's Java code. For each string, it creates an entry in an index-string dictionary with a linear increasing index. This also applies to strings of the same value. The string declaration is then removed from the byte code and replaced by a method invocation that points to `libshield.so`. This method takes an integer as an argument and returns the corresponding string value whenever it gets called with a key of the previously created index-string dictionary. Due to its semantics, we dubbed this function `getStr`. For example, a previous declaration of the Java string ``Hello World'' gets replaced by a call to `getStr(123)`, which returns ``Hello World'' as a result.

Constant Externalization. Apart from the substitution of strings with method calls to Promon's `getStr` method, it also externalizes Java constants in a clever way. This works as follows and the process is further illustrated in Fig. 3: (1) The Promon integration tool replaces any class member field declared as `static` and `final` with a random value of the correct type. Similar to the string externalization, the replaced values of a class are stored in a nested dictionary: While the first level takes the fully qualified class name as a key, its value is a dictionary that maps the constant names of the class to their original value, including the type. To restore these values prior to the first use of the class, Promon Shield adds a call with the `Class` object as an argument to its Java glue code in the static constructor of the class. The ART executes the static constructor as soon as the class gets loaded, enabling execution of the code even before a static field is accessed. (2) The Java wrapper code of

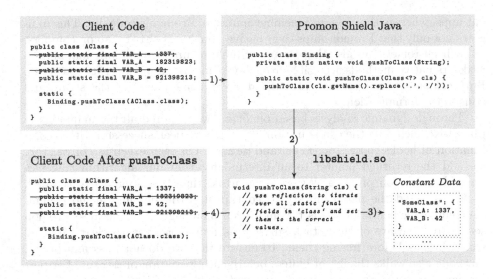

Fig. 3. Visualization of Promon Shield's constant externalization.

Promon Shield replaces the dots in the fully qualified class name as returned by `Class.getName()` with slashes and invokes the corresponding native method. The string alternation likely remains compatible with the previously created dictionary. (3) Inside `libshield.so`, the method looks up the class name and reads out all the key-value pairs for this class. (4) In the last step, the native code replaces the random constant value with the original values by means of reflection. Given the way the method works, it is dubbed `pushToClass`. Notably, it is not possible to dynamically alter the value of fields declared as `final` using Java. The Java Native Interface (JNI), however, does not have this restriction.

Rewriting the App. To rewrite the app using *dexlib2*, we have to apply the mappings of the Promon integration tool in reverse. The trivial and straightforward method for string externalization is to statically determine the highest index N for the argument of the `getStr` method. Next, we use *Frida* to dynamically invoke `getStr` with each value in the range $[0; N]$, thus creating an index-string mapping. The required mapping for the constant obfuscation can be created similarly: After determining all the classes with a static constructor that calls `pushToClass`, we dynamically access these classes. Alternatively, we could just iterate all the classes. The resultant mapping is sufficient to assign the original values to the constants.

A subtle detail that hindered the straightforward usage of *dexlib2* to rewrite the DEX bytecode of the app was the renaming obfuscation of Promon Shield's own Java code. As the renaming always differed between apps and even between versions, we would have needed heuristics to identify the class and method names we wished to rewrite. In the course of our analysis, however, we realized that the hash sum of the bundled `libshield.so` did not always differ between two different apps, whereas the class and member names of Promon's code did. This indicates not only that Promon ships their native library `libshield.so` precompiled to their customers but also that Promon Shield requires a renaming mapping to make its native methods accessible from Java code by calling `RegisterNatives`. Furthermore, it implies that `libshield.so` has mappings for the string and constant externalization.

Through dynamic analysis based on *Frida*, we acquired all the mappings in plain text, including the configuration file. We have been successful with a combination of hooks to `malloc`, `free`, and `memset`. On each execution of `malloc`, we add the returned pointer to an internal list that our algorithm traverses on each execution of `free`. We were surprised that this approach succeeded, as we expected the native library to contain its own dynamic memory management implementation. This becomes even more significant because Promon seems to be aware of the attack surface, as it uses `memset` to clear (at least some) buffers before freeing them. To ensure that we do not miss any buffer, our code also walks the list of buffers before each execution of `memset`. For performance reasons, we implemented our *Frida* hooks in C instead of JavaScript. This happens through our own native library `libnomorp.so`, which gets loaded first and particularly before `libshield.so`. With this approach, we were able to quickly retrieve the plain text configuration file and the two mappings. The file `config-encrypt.txt` contains the customer-defined configuration file in the CSV format, while `mapping.bin` and `pbi.bin` are both JSON dictionaries: The first stores information about the client code's string and constant obfuscation, as explained earlier, and the second contains a renaming mapping of Promon Shield's Java code obfuscation—for example, its original class and method names.

Evaluation. Using sNomorp, an adversary can produce an app version that is easier to analyze statically. The entire process is fully automated and takes no longer than five minutes from the start of the download of the APK until the output of the rewritten app. Apart from that—even though not a declared goal of the applied threat model—the majority of apps processed using sNomorp is even fully runnable after our tool stripped Promon Shield from the app.

During the large scale analysis, however, 9 Apps used a different version of Promon Shield that registers the device at the backend from inside the library. Stripping the library completely breaks the HTTP communication channel. This means that sNomorp is less useful in this case, because the HTTP requests are performed from within `libshield.so`. Dynamic analysis of the communication is, however, possible using dNomorp that we present in Sect. 3.3.

3.3 Dynamic Nomorp

While the previous approach, sNomorp, explained how to remove Promon Shield from an app, this section is dedicated to a dynamic procedure; hence, we call it dNomorp. In contrast to sNomorp, we keep using `libshield.so` but disable all its features at runtime.

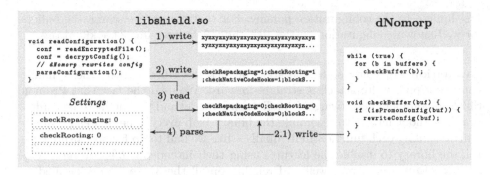

Fig. 4. Visualization of rewriting Promon Shield's configuration at runtime.

To alter the execution dynamically, we still need to insert our custom native library in order to hook functionality. Similar to SNOMORP, this library extracts the configuration file and the mapping. Instead of dumping them for further analysis, however, DNOMORP then rewrites the configuration file on the fly as soon as it gets decrypted. This clear text configuration file consists of key-value pairs separated by a semicolon.

In the configuration of Promon Shield, most security features have three entries: a binary value indicating if the features are enabled, another binary value indicating if the app should crash, and a third value that may contain a percent-encoded URL that would be opened if the app crashes. For app repackaging, these entries may look like `checkRepackaging=1`, `exitOnRepackaging=0`, and `exitOnRepackagingURL=https%3A%2F%2Ffau.de`.

The objective of our attack is to disable all features of Promon Shield by replacing values of 1 with 0 at loading time using a hook that rewrites the plain text configuration file after decryption but before evaluation. The parsing of the configuration file consists of four steps, which are shown in Fig. 4:

(1) Read the encrypted content of the file `config-encrypt.txt` from the APK and write it to a `malloc`-allocated buffer.
(2) Decrypt the configuration file using Promon Shield's white-box cryptography. The result is once again written to a dynamically allocated buffer at the heap.
(3) The native library reads the cleartext configuration file.
(4) The data gets parsed into the library's internal data structures.

Right after the configuration file has been decrypted in (2), it is copied to another buffer using `memcpy` before `libshield.so` starts to read the decrypted content in (3). To that end, we installed a hook to `memcpy` just before the content of the old buffer gets copied into the new one. By modifying the source buffer in our `memcpy` hook before delegating to the real `memcpy` function, we can effectively modify the content of the target buffer and, therefore, the configuration file (Step 2.1) in Fig. 4. Obviously, `memcpy` is a frequently used function, and its use is not just limited to the configuration parsing. For that reason, we search the buffers for well-known configuration entries like `checkDebugger` and `checkRooting`.

Evaluation. In contrast to the static attack described earlier, the dynamic configuration rewrite attack is straight-forward. We used the fact that Promon Shield is commercial software with a licensing model and the intent to be configurable without having to recompile the binary blob every time. Instead of manually disabling each function individually—like we had to do for sNOMORP—we ask the library to disable the features using their intended configuration.

DNOMORP works very well and reliably on all the 31 apps we identified to use Promon Shield. In contrast to the static approach, DNOMORP does not help static analysis, for it does not internalize the constants and strings as they are defined in `pbi.bin`. In return, however, the dynamic approach produces an APK that is fully compatible with the original version where Promon Shield is still part of the app, including all of its own functionality. Values secured by the white-box cryptography inside `libshield.so`, for example, can still be used. An attacker can now modify the app at will (e.g., add malicious code) or dynamically analyze it (e.g., run a man-in-the-middle attack against the network communication).

3.4 Coordinated Disclosure

We informed Promon about our results in close cooperation with Hakan Tanriverdi, a journalist at *Süddeutsche Zeitung* who frequently writes articles in the area of information security. He first made contact with Promon and later asked the affected German financial institutions for their opinion on the case. Finally, Mr. Tanriverdi published an article [25] about our findings in the business section of Süddeutsche Zeitung on November 24, 2017, describing our attack in an abstract way without disclosing technical details. We decided to not disclose any of our source codes to third parties, in order to avoid supporting cybercriminals.

When we let Promon know that our proposal to present the attacks at the *34th Chaos Communication Congress (34c3)* had been accepted, we agreed to not disclose any further information before the 34c3 talk. Additionally, we provided Promon with a detailed description of the weaknesses of their RASP product. On December 27, 2017, we presented our attack to the audience at 34c3.

3.5 Inside Past and Present Libshield.so

This section is dedicated to the internals of `libshield.so`, the core part of Promon's hardening solution. In reaction to our findings, Promon introduced some modifications to its native library and we describe these changes at the end of this section. At the time of writing, however, large parts of our past analysis still apply to recent versions of Promon Shield.

During normal mode of operation, Promon Shield uses a variety of cryptographic primitives to secure the contents of `libshield.so`: several files in the

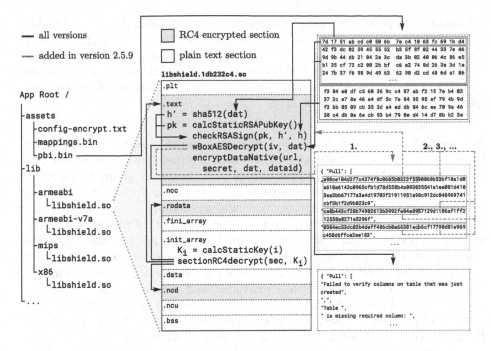

Fig. 5. Cryptographic functions protecting `libshield.so` and selected assets.

`assets` directory, and the contents of the secure storage feature Promon offers. Figure 5 shows an overview of `libshield.so` and depicts the decryption of the mapping file `pbi.bin`. Promon, however, processes the other files similarly.

Executable. Encryption protects various sections of the shared library `libshield.so`. After loading the image into memory and resolving all its dependencies, the dynamic loader dispatches the constructors specified in `.init_array`. One constructor invokes an obfuscated version of the RC4 cipher to decrypt the `.rodata`, `.text`, and `.ncd` sections of the binary employing three distinct keys that are specific to the version of Promon Shield used.

Assets. As part of the integration process of Promon Shield into the target app, Promon creates three files and stores them encrypted in the `assets` folder of the app: `config-encrypt.txt`, `mappings.bin`, and `pbi.bin`. Section 3.2 explains the purpose of each file. The initialization procedure of `libshield.so` applies the following steps to these files to decrypt them: First, a SHA512 hash h' over all but the last 64 bytes is calculated. Second, a fixed DER-encoded public RSA key pk is generated using the same combination of arithmetic operations and loops that conceal all other constant strings needed. This public RSA key is used afterwards to decrypt the last 64 bytes h of the file, to allow the comparison of the result and h'. This third step effectively constitutes a signature validation, and is only decrypted using a white-box implementation of AES128 if h and $RSA_D(h', pk)$ match the contents. The white-box relies on OpenSSL and a custom implementation of the block cipher that uses the secret symmetric key in an expanded version only. AES128 is applied in CBC mode with the first 16 bytes of the data serving as initialization vector (IV). The result is expanded using the `inflate` algorithm of `zlib`.

Secure Storage. Applications can request Promon Shield to encrypt data through the Java class `SecureStorage` which internally uses `libshield.so`'s native function `encryptDataNative`. Apart from the data requested for encryption (`dat`), the function requires a URL parameter of a Promon Shield server endpoint (`url`), and two byte strings: one chosen randomly at runtime (`secret`), and another one to identify the data to store (`dataid`). Promon Shield first applies an HMAC to `dataid` using `secret` as the HMAC key and stores the result in `dataid`. This step is repeated 4096 times in total before calculating a 16 byte hard-coded device identifier (again using the obfuscation technique described earlier). Together with a `protocol` and a `msg` variable, as well as the version of Promon Shield, the device and data id serve as HTTP form data (`application/x-www-form-urlencoded`) that `libshield.so` submits via HTTPS (with an optional TLS client certificate). After successfully transferring this information to the server specified by the `url` parameter, the backend responds with a key specific for the combination of all parameters used in the corresponding request. This key is then used for AES256 in CBC mode to encrypt the data specified by `dat`.

Changes Introduced in Later Versions of Promon Shield. In response to our attacks, Promon introduced a few countermeasures. To the best of our knowledge, the changes were introduced in version 2.5.9 and all apply to Promon Shield's handling of the encrypted configuration `config-encrypt.txt` and the push and pull bindings contained in `pbi.bin`. Promon's renaming mapping for its Java obfuscation, `mapping.bin`, remains untouched.

First, Promon Shield now uses two layers of its AES white-box for both files to prevent revealing the configuration's location via easy to recognize strings in memory. For this purpose, all configuration keys have additionally been replaced by a combination of 16 + 4 byte identifiers. Second, the configuration parameters indicating whether Promon Shield should perform certain runtime checks—for example `checkRooting`—were removed and are now directly compiled into the code of `libshield.so`.

Altogether, these modifications to Promon Shield aim at making NOMORP stop working. Even though neither sNOMORP nor dNOMORP function for recent versions of Promon Shield, we are confident that the required adjustments are minor. To substantially increase the effort an adversary has to take, Promon should implement further improvements as suggested in the following section.

4   Discussion and Improvements

In this section, we discuss the findings and show what RASP providers can do to improve their offerings. Attackers will always have an advantage over the defending RASP solution as they only need to find single failures and can look at the implementation statically. App developers therefore should consider two-factor authentication and server-based solutions where possible.

In the following, we use the term *RASP provider* for developers of RASP solutions, *customer* for app developers using RASP to secure their apps and *end user* for the user of an app developed by customers. Our treat model outlined in Sect. 2.2 implies the following goals for a RASP provider: First, make analysis harder and more expensive so that an adversary cannot easily steal the customer's nor the RASP provider's intellectual property (IP). Second, mitigate automated large scale attacks against the customers' products.

With increased value of the protected contents, the motivation to break the protection increases; hence, defense mechanisms which are sufficient for one app might not be enough for another. The possibility to steal money, for example, increases the literal payout of successful attacks. The more valuable a successful attack is, the stronger RASP protection needs to be.

Of course, with more customers using a certain RASP implementation in their apps, the value of a generalized attack against a RASP solution increases. This does not only demand that RASP providers continuously improve their libraries, but also calls for diversification of their product on a per customer per app basis. On top, randomness should be introduced in the build steps to make sure all updates of an app look different. Another main way to hinder automated unpacking is to interweave the code of the RASP provider and the customer tightly. Both measures, individualization and interweaving the RASP providers and the customer's code, would frustrate reverse engineering and mitigate automatic attacks. In the following, we give more detailed suggestions on how to strengthen the security of RASP solutions.

Avoid Easy to Track Resource Files. The NOMORP unpacker was very effective once we found out at which point the configuration was processed. At that point, our tool could disable features by simply altering the configuration. RASP solutions should never offer options to deactivate features at runtime as an attacker can always leverage them for their benefit. Instead of loading a configuration as asset that can be traced, RASP providers should not include features in the binary that the customer disabled. On the other hand, activated features should not have single points where an adversary can disable them.

In addition to the configuration file, we could recover the mappings of obfuscated strings and constants by tracing accesses to the asset files. Compiling the mappings into the main binary blob at random positions would already have increased the attack complexity.

Since an attacker can still iterate over all elements and recreate the mappings dynamically, a RASP solution could call the next JNI functions directly instead of returning the value [21]. For this purpose, a function for each constant could be created in native code, taking additional parameters forwarded to the next function call and then filling in the needed parameter with the constant value.

Anti-tampering. Measures to assert the integrity of the customer and RASP code are already widely applied. A good defense checks the integrity of certain code blocks often and in different ways to make it harder to disable or alter it.

Anti-hooking and Anti-debugging. Anti-debugging and anti-hooking are close relatives. An attacker can replace debugging tasks like reading from memory using hooks. Likewise, if an app allows debugging, adding hooks is trivial. As for anti-hooking, RASPs already implement detections for hooks through LD_PRELOAD, *Xposed* or *Cydia Substrate* and *Frida*, however are not yet resilient against simple changes in those frameworks. Generally speaking, RASP providers should employ more general detection mechanisms. Adding more runtime integrity checks, raising alarms from obfuscated code, checking they have actually fired after the anticipated time and more can add enough complexity to make hooking and debugging a burden. Code obfuscation can help obscuring the location of anti-hooking and anti-debugging checks. Most importantly, the RASP provider should interweave their code and the included checks with the client's code so that no obvious interfaces are exposed that an adversary can disable, e.g., on startup. Similarly, once the integrity is breached, the app should fail fast. Since callbacks could be hooked to keep the app running, crashing the app without an explicit exit call or any status report is the safest option.

Anti-emulator. If the app runs inside an emulator, debugging and hooking remains trivial. A perfect emulator can hardly exist, so emulator fingerprinting can add manual work to the analysis. For this, many environment checks can be added at random positions in the code [18]. Research in automatic unpacking of malware samples based on whole-system emulation suggests that anti-emulation techniques are effective [6].

Device Binding. To mitigate running a cloned app on a different device that was used for registration, an app can make use of device binding. For this, aggressive fingerprinting can be employed, aggregating multiple environment values. On modern hardware apps should create asymmetric keys in the trusted environment, if available. From there, keys can hardly be extracted. Adding a signature to the network configuration using this key lets the server know it is still talking to the same device.

Code Obfuscation. RASP should not only obfuscate and strip its own but also the customer's code. The larger and more interwoven the obfuscated code is, the harder it is to reverse. This means that the integration tool of the RASP provider should even include third party libraries to create one entangled unit where possible. Interweaving can be done within native libraries, DEX bytecode and between the native library and Java using JNI. Modern Android specific obfuscation methods like DEX packing and VM-based obfuscation should be considered [31,32]. Another aspect is the randomization of compilation passes. If every version of an app looks different, it will be hard to automate unpackers and to adapt to the latest changes of apps. Some of the steps discussed may require RASP providers to ship source code or intermediate language together with a toolchain to their customers. In turn, it requires that RASP providers value the IP of the customer higher than their own.

Root Detection. Root detection can help to slow down reverse engineering. Many analysis frameworks require root. It does, however, not defend the user against attacks that use privilege escalation exploits. App developers have to decide if they really need to block rooted users or if it is enough to warn the user of possible consequences. As for root detection, relying on the presence of certain files, like su, is too easy to circumvent. Instead, two alternatives appear useful:

(1) Google SafetyNet is an API that allows apps to check the integrity of the device they are running on. To prevent an attacker from hooking the decision, the implementation must check the attestation result on the server rather than on the client side. This means RASP Providers and app manufacturers need to support this in their backend.
(2) Privilege escalation exploits cannot be prevented or detected. The only way to reduce the likelihood is to require a sound minimum version of Android and its security patch level. Instead of comparing a string, the app should rely on a new API to talk to its backend. That way, the app crashes if its communication does not employ the new API.

Anti-keylogger and Anti-screen Reader. An internal keyboard or keyboard whitelists are reasonable. An attacker, however, may still overlay it with their own app [8].

Secure Communication. RASP solutions can automatically upgrade TLS communications with certificate pinning. If client and server certificate are obfuscated and hidden at random positions, the effort the attacker needs to invest to build a man-in-the-middle server for analysis and therefore reversing the API is increased. Requiring newer client certificates on the server side often additionally increases the complexity.

Encryption. Storing data encrypted makes it considerably harder for attackers. Newer phones can create and store encryption material securely inside the hardware-backed key store. If attackers is on the system before keys are created, however, they can hook the API calls for key creation and provide their own. A RASP may, for this reason or to support older hardware, choose to employ white-box cryptography. White-box cryptography obfuscates a static key making it more difficult to recover it. An attacker, however, may use the whole crypto mechanism as a black box and decrypt secrets with it. The white-box code should therefore be tightly interwoven with the rest of the code and entry points to the crypto functionality as well as their use should not be obvious. Just like for constants, the RASP solution can call Java functions directly using JNI instead of returning the decrypted secrets from a function. The white-box and the mechanisms to harden it should be changed often and a previous version should only be accepted by the server for a limited period of time.

5   Conclusion

Taking into account the threat model from Sect. 2, we showed, based on a case study of Promon Shield, that RASP solutions do not uphold their security promises. Relying on obfuscation and other software-based hardening techniques cannot replace established security practices like two-factor authentication if the stakes are high, e.g., in financial apps.

During our evaluation, we systematically broke all security guarantees of our case study. Our tool NOMORP is capable of dynamically disabling all security measures of Promon Shield by altering protected apps at runtime. Other frameworks discussed in Sect. 2 were not vetted as thoroughly. While they might make use of stronger obfuscation and hardening we still believe their defenses can be broken one way or another. Similar, fully automated tools can therefore be built for all app-hardening solutions. Application layer security mechanisms will always lose against elaborated attackers [12], since they operate at the same privilege level as the attackers or at an even lower one. Worse, research has shown that RASP providers perform can even introduce severe security vulnerabilities [13].

As a short-term line of defense, RASP providers can use stronger obfuscation, improve their detection measures for hooking, debugging and rooting and add additional hardening steps to the client app as we discussed in Sect. 4. These measures make attacks harder but RASP solutions should still not claim security-sensitive apps can be used on compromised devices under all circumstances. Instead, they need to communicate to their clients clearly that they will only raise the bar for attackers for a certain time. Of course, this can be a valid defense, according to the companies thread model. RASP providers need to develop methods that are less scalable through automated attacks by providing individualized solutions for their customers.

For the future of two-factor authentication, the only way forward is to shift the security vectors toward secure tokens in hardware, like TEEs, as well as backend-based fraud detection, instead of relying on solutions that appear good enough but are conceptually flawed.

For the time being, users should make sure to run the latest updates and security patches and to upgrade their mobile devices if they are no longer patched.

RASP providers need to develop methods that are less scalable through automated attacks by providing individualized solutions for their customers. While we showed all RASP systems can theoretically be broken, in practice not all is lost: RASP providers will have reached their goals to secure the mobile app market once adversaries do not consider reversing hardened apps worth it as it is simply too complex with very little gain.

Acknowledgments. We wish to thank our shepherd Yanick Fratantonio and the anonymous reviewers for their helpful comments. Furthermore, we appreciate Felix Freiling's support during the disclosure process.

The work presented in this paper was conducted within the research project "Software-based Hardening for Mobile Applications" and was partially funded by the German Federal Ministry of Education and Research (BMBF).

References

1. Barak, B., Goldreich, O., Impagliazzo, R., Rudich, S., Sahai, A., Vadhan, S., Yang, K.: On the (im)possibility of obfuscating programs. In: Kilian, J. (ed.) CRYPTO 2001. LNCS, vol. 2139, pp. 1–18. Springer, Heidelberg (2001). https://doi.org/10.1007/3-540-44647-8_1
2. Bianchi, A., Gustafson, E., Fratantonio, Y., Kruegel, C., Vigna, G.: Exploitation and mitigation of authentication schemes based on device-public information. In: Proceedings of the 33rd Annual Computer Security Applications Conference, ACSAC 2017, pp. 16–27. ACM, New York (2017)
3. Bichsel, B., Raychev, V., Tsankov, P., Vechev, M.T.: Statistical deobfuscation of android applications. In: Proceedings of the 2016 ACM SIGSAC Conference on Computer and Communications Security, Vienna, Austria, 24–28 October 2016, pp. 343–355 (2016)
4. Chow, S., Eisen, P., Johnson, H., Van Oorschot, P.C.: White-box cryptography and an AES implementation. In: Nyberg, K., Heys, H. (eds.) SAC 2002. LNCS, vol. 2595, pp. 250–270. Springer, Heidelberg (2003). https://doi.org/10.1007/3-540-36492-7_17
5. Collberg, C., Nagra, J.: Surreptitious Software: Obfuscation, Watermarking, and Tamperproofing for Software Protection, 1st edn. Addison-Wesley Professional, Boston (2009)
6. Duan, Y., Zhang, M., Bhaskar, A.V., Yin, H., Pan, X., Li, T., Wang, X., Wang, X.: Things you may not know about android (un)packers: a systematic study based on whole-system emulation. In: 25th Annual Network and Distributed System Security Symposium, NDSS 2018, 18–21 February 2018, San Diego, California, USA (2018)
7. Felt, A.P., Finifter, M., Chin, E., Hanna, S., Wagner, D.A.: A survey of mobile malware in the wild. In: Jiang, X., Bhattacharya, A., Dasgupta, P., Enck, W. (eds.) Proceedings of the 1st ACM Workshop Security and Privacy in Smartphones and Mobile Devices, Co-located with CCS 2011, SPSM 2011, 17 October 2011, Chicago, IL, USA, pp. 3–14. ACM (2011)
8. Fratantonio, Y., Qian, C., Chung, S.P., Lee, W.: Cloak and dagger: from two permissions to complete control of the UI feedback loop. In: 2017 IEEE Symposium on Security and Privacy, SP 2017, 22–26 May 2017, San Jose, CA, USA, pp. 1041–1057 (2017)

9. Gartner Inc.: Market guide for application shielding, June 2017. https://www.gartner.com/doc/3747622/market-guide-application-shielding

10. Goubin, L., Masereel, J.-M., Quisquater, M.: Cryptanalysis of white box DES implementations. In: Adams, C., Miri, A., Wiener, M. (eds.) SAC 2007. LNCS, vol. 4876, pp. 278–295. Springer, Heidelberg (2007). https://doi.org/10.1007/978-3-540-77360-3_18

11. Haupert, V., Müller, T.: On app-based matrix code authentication in online banking. In: Furnell, S., Mori, P., Camp, O. (eds.) Proceedings of the 4th International Conference on Information Systems Security and Privacy, ICISSP 2018, 22–24 February 2018, Funchal, Madeira, Portugal, pp. 149–160 (2018)

12. Jung, J., Kim, J.Y., Lee, H., Yi, J.H.: Repackaging attack on android banking applications and its countermeasures. Wireless Pers. Commun. **73**(4), 1421–1437 (2013)

13. Kim, T., Ha, H., Choi, S., Jung, J., Chun, B.: Breaking ad-hoc runtime integrity protection mechanisms in android financial apps. In: Proceedings of the 2017 ACM on Asia Conference on Computer and Communications Security, AsiaCCS 2017, 2–6 April 2017, Abu Dhabi, United Arab Emirates, pp. 179–192 (2017)

14. Kim, Y., Daly, R., Kim, J., Fallin, C., Lee, J., Lee, D., Wilkerson, C., Lai, K., Mutlu, O.: Flipping bits in memory without accessing them: an experimental study of DRAM disturbance errors. In: ACM/IEEE 41st International Symposium on Computer Architecture, ISCA 2014, 14–18 June 2014, Minneapolis, MN, USA, pp. 361–372 (2014)

15. Kocher, P., Genkin, D., Gruss, D., Haas, W., Hamburg, M., Lipp, M., Mangard, S., Prescher, T., Schwarz, M., Yarom, Y.: Spectre attacks: exploiting speculative execution. CoRR abs/1801.01203 (2018). http://arxiv.org/abs/1801.01203

16. Krügel, C., Robertson, W.K., Valeur, F., Vigna, G.: Static disassembly of obfuscated binaries. In: Proceedings of the 13th USENIX Security Symposium, 9–13 August 2004, San Diego, CA, USA, pp. 255–270 (2004)

17. Luu, D.: How out of date are android devices? (2017). https://danluu.com/android-updates

18. Maier, D., Müller, T., Protsenko, M.: Divide-and-conquer: why android malware cannot be stopped. In: Ninth International Conference on Availability, Reliability and Security, ARES 2014, 8–12 September 2014, Fribourg, Switzerland, pp. 30–39. IEEE Computer Society (2014)

19. Petsas, T., Voyatzis, G., Athanasopoulos, E., Polychronakis, M., Ioannidis, S.: Rage against the virtual machine: hindering dynamic analysis of android malware. In: Balzarotti, D., Caballero, J. (eds.) Proceedings of the Seventh European Workshop on System Security, EuroSec 2014, 13 April 2014, Amsterdam, The Netherlands, pp. 5:1–5:6. ACM (2014)

20. Promon AS: Shield: application protection and security for mobile apps. https://promon.co/products/mobile-app-security

21. Protsenko, M., Kreuter, S., Müller, T.: Dynamic self-protection and tamperproofing for android apps using native code. In: 10th International Conference on Availability, Reliability and Security, ARES 2015, 24–27 August 2015, Toulouse, France, pp. 129–138 (2015)

22. Ren, C., Chen, K., Liu, P.: Droidmarking: resilient software watermarking for impeding android application repackaging. In: Crnkovic, I., Chechik, M., Grünbacher, P. (eds.) ACM/IEEE International Conference on Automated Software Engineering, ASE 2014, 15–19 September 2014, Vasteras, Sweden, pp. 635–646. ACM (2014)

23. Saxena, A., Wyseur, B.: On white-box cryptography and obfuscation. CoRR abs/0805.4648 (2008). http://arxiv.org/abs/0805.4648
24. Schrittwieser, S., Katzenbeisser, S., Kinder, J., Merzdovnik, G., Weippl, E.R.: Protecting software through obfuscation: can it keep pace with progress in code analysis? ACM Comput. Surv. **49**(1), 4:1–4:37 (2016)
25. Tanriverdi, H.: Überweisung vom Hacker. Süddeutsche Zeitung **73**(270), (2017)
26. Thomas, D.R., Beresford, A.R., Rice, A.C.: Security metrics for the android ecosystem. In: Lie, D., Wurster, G. (eds.) Proceedings of the 5th Annual ACM CCS Workshop on Security and Privacy in Smartphones and Mobile Devices, SPSM 2015, 12 October 2015, Denver, Colorado, USA, pp. 87–98. ACM (2015)
27. van der Veen, V., Fratantonio, Y., Lindorfer, M., Gruss, D., Maurice, C., Vigna, G., Bos, H., Razavi, K., Giuffrida, C.: Drammer: deterministic rowhammer attacks on mobile platforms. In: Proceedings of the 2016 ACM SIGSAC Conference on Computer and Communications Security, 24–28 October 2016, Vienna, Austria, pp. 1675–1689 (2016)
28. Vidas, T., Christin, N.: Evading android runtime analysis via sandbox detection. In: Moriai, S., Jaeger, T., Sakurai, K. (eds.) 9th ACM Symposium on Information, Computer and Communications Security, ASIA CCS 2014, 03–06 June 2014, Kyoto, Japan, pp. 447–458. ACM (2014)
29. Wu, L., Grace, M.C., Zhou, Y., Wu, C., Jiang, X.: The impact of vendor customizations on android security. In: 2013 ACM SIGSAC Conference on Computer and Communications Security, CCS 2013, 4–8 November 2013, Berlin, Germany, pp. 623–634 (2013)
30. Xue, L., Luo, X., Yu, L., Wang, S., Wu, D.: Adaptive unpacking of android apps. In: 2017 IEEE/ACM 39th International Conference on Software Engineering (ICSE), pp. 358–369 (2017)
31. Yang, W., Zhang, Y., Li, J., Shu, J., Li, B., Hu, W., Gu, D.: AppSpear: bytecode decrypting and DEX reassembling for packed android malware. In: Bos, H., Monrose, F., Blanc, G. (eds.) RAID 2015. LNCS, vol. 9404, pp. 359–381. Springer, Cham (2015). https://doi.org/10.1007/978-3-319-26362-5_17
32. Zhang, Y., Luo, X., Yin, H.: DexHunter: toward extracting hidden code from packed android applications. In: Pernul, G., Ryan, P.Y.A., Weippl, E. (eds.) ESORICS 2015. LNCS, vol. 9327, pp. 293–311. Springer, Cham (2015). https://doi.org/10.1007/978-3-319-24177-7_15
33. Zhou, X., Lee, Y., Zhang, N., Naveed, M., Wang, X.: The peril of fragmentation: security hazards in android device driver customizations. In: 2014 IEEE Symposium on Security and Privacy, SP 2014, 18–21 May 2014, Berkeley, CA, USA, pp. 409–423 (2014)

GuardION: Practical Mitigation of DMA-Based Rowhammer Attacks on ARM

Victor van der Veen[1(✉)], Martina Lindorfer[3], Yanick Fratantonio[4],
Harikrishnan Padmanabha Pillai[2], Giovanni Vigna[3], Christopher Kruegel[3],
Herbert Bos[1], and Kaveh Razavi[1]

[1] Vrije Universiteit, Amsterdam, The Netherlands
{vvdveen,herbertb,kaveh}@cs.vu.nl
[2] Amrita University, Coimbatore, India
hpadmanabhapillai@gmail.com
[3] University of California, Santa Barbara, USA
martina@iseclab.org, {vigna,chris}@cs.ucsb.edu
[4] EURECOM, Biot, France
yanick.fratantonio@eurecom.fr

Abstract. Over the last two years, the Rowhammer bug transformed
from a hard-to-exploit DRAM disturbance error into a fully weaponized
attack vector. Researchers demonstrated exploits not only against desktop computers, but also used single bit flips to compromise the cloud
and mobile devices, all without relying on any software vulnerability.

Since hardware-level mitigations cannot be backported, a search for
software defenses is pressing. Proposals made by both academia and
industry, however, are either impractical to deploy, or insufficient in stopping all attacks: we present RAMPAGE, a set of DMA-based Rowhammer
attacks against the latest Android OS, consisting of (1) a root exploit,
and (2) a series of app-to-app exploit scenarios that bypass all defenses.

To mitigate Rowhammer exploitation on ARM, we propose GUARDION,
a lightweight defense that prevents DMA-based attacks—the main attack
vector on mobile devices—by isolating DMA buffers with guard rows. We
evaluate GUARDION on 22 benchmark apps and show that it has a negligible memory overhead (2.2 MB on average). We further show that we can
improve system performance by re-enabling higher order allocations after
Google disabled these as a reaction to previous attacks.

1 Introduction

For decades, defensive research on memory corruption could brush aside the
threat of exploitation via hardware bugs as "outside the threat model," if not
science fiction entirely. The frightening list of devastating Rowhammer attacks,
however, published at one security venue after another [5,12,16,24,28,30], suggests that we are in urgent need of practical defenses. Anything new? In this
paper, we propose a practical, isolation-based protection that stops DMA-based
Rowhammer attacks by carefully surrounding DMA buffers with DRAM-level

© Springer International Publishing AG, part of Springer Nature 2018
C. Giuffrida et al. (Eds.): DIMVA 2018, LNCS 10885, pp. 92–113, 2018.
https://doi.org/10.1007/978-3-319-93411-2_5

guard rows. We focus our work on mobile devices as here, the problem is even more worrisome: unlike desktop and server machines, it is impossible to perform hardware upgrades.

Rowhammer on Mobile Devices. The Rowhammer hardware bug at its core consists of the leakage of charge between adjacent memory cells on a densely packed DRAM chip [19]. Thus, whenever the CPU reads or writes one row of bits in the DRAM module, the neighboring rows are ever so slightly affected. Normally, this does not create problems as DRAM periodically refreshes the charge in its cells, well in time to preserve data integrity. However, an attacker who deliberately hits the same rows many times within a refresh interval may cause the charge leakage to accumulate to the point that a bit flips in an adjacent row and modify memory that she does not own. Initially considered a curiosity of relatively minor importance, researchers have shown that attackers can harness Rowhammer to completely subvert a system's security [5,8,16,24,26,28,30].

Clearly, the threat of Rowhammer attacks for smartphones and tablets is particularly serious, as replacing the memory chips of such devices is not an option. In addition, power consumption is a prime concern in the mobile world, and many of the hardware-level solutions (such as ECC memory or higher DRAM refresh rates) consume more power. Furthermore, even though newer standards such as LPDDR4 [18] discuss the adoption of Rowhammer mitigations, i.e., Target Row Refresh (TRR), they do so only as an *optional* protection mechanism, thus making LPDDR4 chips vulnerable as well [20,28].

Existing Software Defenses are Not Effective. Given the challenges of deploying hardware solutions, the development of effective software-based defenses is particularly important to protect mobile users against Rowhammer attacks. In our analysis, we systematically explore existing proposals, which fall into two categories: techniques that attempt to prevent attackers from triggering bit flips, and those that focus on making it impossible for a bit flip to bring physical memory into an exploitable state (Sect. 4). We argue that both directions have limitations, either in terms of practicality (for instance because they require specific hardware features), or worse, in terms of effectiveness (as they still allow for Rowhammer exploitation). We demonstrate this ineffectiveness by presenting novel attacks that circumvent all existing proposed and implemented defense techniques (Sect. 5).

The Need for *Practical* Solutions. Security solutions need to strike a balance between security and practicality—a defense against Rowhammer attacks should not incur unacceptable performance overhead, nor should it severely reduce the amount of available memory. Conversely, it should be effective and hard to bypass. In this work, we propose GUARDION, which effectively and efficiently blocks all known DMA-based Rowhammer attacks against mobile devices (Sect. 6).

GUARDION builds on the observation that triggering bit flips on ARM-based mobile platforms is facilitated by using uncached memory, accessible through DMA allocations [28]. Albeit other techniques exist, most are either impractical or easily addressable on ARM. For example, the `cacheflush()` system call that is exposed to userland by the Android kernel, only flushes up to the Level 2 cache, and thus fails to force repetitive DRAM accesses for a single address. Additionally, ARMv8's unprivileged cache flush instruction can easily be disabled by the kernel and thus do not pose a security risk.

We thus explicitly limit our defense to the more generic class of DMA-based Rowhammer attacks that rely on uncached memory. Doing so has an important implication for our design: instead of attempting to isolate all sensitive information, which is impractical, we can instead isolate only DMA allocations. As we will show, DMA allocations constitute only a very small fraction of all allocations in the system, and we can hence afford to apply expensive fine-grained isolation for *each* DMA allocation using guard rows. In our design, we isolate DMA allocations from the rest of the system by using two guard rows, one at the top and another at the bottom. With this scheme, an attacker can no longer use DMA allocations to trigger bit flips in any memory page in the system except in the guard rows. In effect, this design defends against Rowhammer by eradicating the ability to inject bit flips in sensitive data.

Can GuardION Defend Against Any Rowhammer Exploit? No. GUARDION only enforces that DMA-based Rowhammer attacks can no longer flip bits in another process or kernel memory. Attacks that induce bit flips by means of cache eviction sets—another popular Rowhammer technique on x86—are still possible. The (1) lento, and (2) idiosyncratic nature of these attacks, however, make them harder to launch in practice. First, increased access times will result in less flipped bits at a slower rate. Second, a substantial amount of reverse engineering is required for such attacks, and this work must be repeated for each target architecture [12,28]. Thus, although not stopping all possible attacks, GUARDION reduces the attack surface significantly.

Contributions. In summary, we make the following contributions:

- We systematically explore the design of software defenses, and show that existing proposals are either not practical or not effective.
- To back our claims, we present RAMPAGE, a set of DMA-based Rowhammer attack variants on ARM. RAMPAGE consists of (1) a root exploit, and (2) a series of app-to-app attacks.
- We introduce GUARDION, a software-based defense that prevents DMA-based Rowhammer attacks. GUARDION is simple, efficient, and has low memory overhead.

In the spirit of open science, we provide our modifications to the Android source code for implementing GUARDION at https://github.com/vusec/guardion.

2   Threat Model

We consider an attacker with full control over a zero-permissions holding, unprivileged Android app that is running on the victim's device. She seeks to mount a DMA-based Rowhammer attack, similar to recent work [28], to either (1) escalate her privileges to root, or (2) compromise other apps present on the device. The victim device is hardened against other classes of Rowhammer attacks (e.g., GLitch [12]) and has the latest Android security updates installed.

3   Background

This section describes the relevant background information about the Rowhammer vulnerability and its exploitation. This is meant to provide only a brief introduction, for a more in-depth discussion, we point the interested reader to papers exclusively focusing on this topic [19,22,30].

3.1   The Rowhammer Vulnerability

Rowhammer is a hardware fault in dynamic random-access memory (DRAM) chips. DRAM chips work by storing charges in an array of *cells*. The charge state of a given cell encodes a binary value, a memory bit. Cells are organized in *rows*, which, at the hardware level, is the smallest unit for a memory access. When a memory row is accessed, the content of its cells is copied to a so-called *row buffer*. During this copy operation, the row's cells are discharged, and they are then recharged with their initial values.

Independently from the row access process, memory cells tend to leak their charged state (due to their nature), and their content thus needs to be refreshed regularly. Kim et al. [19] observed that the increasing density of memory chips makes them prone to disturbance errors due to charge leaking into adjacent cells on every memory access. In particular, they show that, by repeatedly accessing, i.e., "hammering," the same memory row (the aggressor row), an attacker can cause enough of a disturbance in a neighboring row (the victim row) to cause bits to flip. The Rowhammer vulnerability is thus a race against the DRAM memory refresh: if an attacker can cause sufficient disturbance, the refresh process may not be fast enough to recharge the cells with their initial values. Kim et al. show that it is possible to flip bits in memory by solely performing software-induced memory read operations, bypassing common memory isolation mechanisms.

3.2   Rowhammer Exploitation

Triggering the Rowhammer bug is different than exploiting it. Most bits in memory are irrelevant for an attacker, as flipping them would often just trigger a memory corruption, without obtaining any concrete security advantage. For successful exploitation, the attacker must first land a security-sensitive memory page (e.g., a page owned by the operating system or by another privileged process) into a vulnerable physical memory page. In the general case, software exploitation of this kind is challenging, and, as outlined by van der Veen et al. [28], requires the implementation of the following primitives:

Fast Uncached Memory Access. The attacker must access the DRAM chip "fast enough." One of the biggest challenges here is bypassing CPU caches, which, if not handled properly, would "block" any read attempt. The attacker thus needs to either flush them (to make sure that the next memory read access propagates to DRAM), or use uncached DMA memory to bypass CPU caches altogether.

Physical Memory Massaging. For successful exploitation, the attacker must land a security-sensitive page into a physical memory location that is vulnerable to Rowhammer. This entails that the attacker somehow massages the physical memory so that she can probabilistically [26] or deterministically [24] determine where security-sensitive memory pages would land in physical memory.

Physical Memory Addressing. To make Rowhammer exploitation more practical, the attacker can mount a so-called double-sided Rowhammer attack in which the victim row gets hammered by not one, but both adjacent rows. While this increases the chances of triggering bit flips, it is more challenging: the attacker must either be able to allocate physically contiguous memory, or determine how virtual addresses of an unprivileged process are mapped to physical addresses. In other words, the attacker must determine which virtual addresses map to the two physical rows adjacent to the victim row. We note that, while this primitive is not strictly necessary to implement Rowhammer attacks, its implementation is often required to make these attacks practical.

Security researchers demonstrated that a variety of different system environments are vulnerable to Rowhammer exploitation. Seaborn and Dullien [26] were the first to demonstrate two practical attacks: one to gain local privilege escalation, and another to escape native client sandboxes. Other researchers then used Rowhammer to bypass in-browser JavaScript sandboxes [5,16], and even to perform cross-VM attacks [24,30]. While most work focuses on the x86 platform, Van der Veen et al. show that also ARM-based mobile devices are vulnerable to the Rowhammer bug [28]. This last attack, Drammer, is the most problematic as it does not rely on any special hardware or software features. It shows that it is possible to mount a deterministic privilege escalation technique by relying only on basic memory management functions available in typical modern operating systems that cannot easily be turned off.

3.3   Android Memory Management

Android, as any other Linux platform, manages physical memory via the buddy allocator, whose goal is to minimize memory fragmentation [15]. In addition, starting from Android 4.0, Google introduced ION [31], a high-level interface that aims at replacing and unifying the several memory management interfaces exposed by each hardware manufacturer. One of the main features implemented by ION is a number of DMA Buffer Management APIs, which allows userland apps to obtain uncached memory. ION organizes its memory pools in several in-kernel heaps, such as the *kmalloc heap* (SYSTEM_CONTIG) and the *system heap* (SYSTEM). These heaps allocate memory at different memory locations and, in general, behave differently. For example, van der Veen et al. [28] observed how an app can use the *kmalloc heap* to obtain physically contiguous memory (now disabled by Google [14]), while this is not possible when using the *system heap*.

4   Overview of Software-Based Rowhammer Defenses

Proposed software-level Rowhammer mitigations try to (1) prevent Rowhammer from triggering bit flips, or (2) prevent massaging of physical memory into an exploitable state (i.e., bit flips in security-sensitive data structures). We now discuss these defenses in more detail and expose their limitations in terms of practicality—*What are the limitations for deploying this technique in practice?*—and security—*Does this technique stop all attacks?* Table 1 summarizes our discussion and shows that no previous solution is both practical *and* secure.

Table 1. Summary of existing defenses and their limitations when deployed to prevent DMA-based Rowhammer attacks on ARM

Class	Defense	Practical	Secure
¬flips	ANVIL [4]	✗	✓[a]
	B-CATT [6]	✗	✗
	Disabling the contiguous heap [14]	✓	✗
	Pool size reduction [14]	✓	✗
¬massage	CATT [7]	✗	✗
	Separation of lowmem/highmem [14]	✓	✗
	Our approach (GUARDION)	✓	✓

[a] Assuming a modified implementation that monitors DRAM accesses instead of cache misses.

4.1   Preventing Bit Flips (¬flips)

ANVIL [4] is a two-step mitigation technique that relies on the processor's performance monitoring unit (PMU) to (1) monitor last-level cache misses (LLC misses). If the number of LLC misses per time period exceeds a predefined value, it marks the offending load/store instructions as a potential Rowhammer attack. It then (2) instructs the PMU to also record virtual addresses accessed, and data sources used by those instructions. ANVIL analyzes the results of the latter, and, if it concludes that a Rowhammer attack is ongoing, it accesses neighboring rows to force an early refresh, effectively preventing any bit from flipping.

ANVIL could prevent DMA-based Rowhammer attacks by monitoring DRAM accesses instead of LLC misses. Such a defense would be secure, as it would successfully prevent bits from flipping. We were unsuccessful, however, in our search for PMU features on ARM that allow an efficient implementation of ANVIL's second stage: we were unable to locate any feature that allows us to keep track of which virtual or physical addresses are read from or written to. As such, we conclude that ANVIL is impractical as a mitigation against DMA-based Rowhammer attacks.

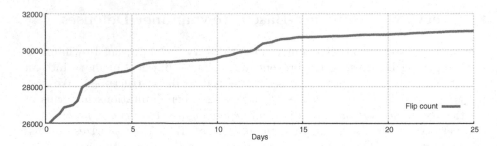

Fig. 1. Number of unique bit flips found while repeatedly hammering the same 4 MB chunk using double-sided Rowhammer on a Nexus 5 over a time-period of 25 days. Results were obtained by using Drammer's source code [3].

B-CATT [6] instructs the bootloader to run a Rowhammer test over the entire physical memory to identify memory pages with vulnerable cells. It then instructs the operating system to mark these pages as unavailable, forcing the system to never use them. This effectively removes the ability of an attacker to induce bit flips.

To evaluate B-CATT's security guarantees, we ran an experiment in which we search for bit flips on a Nexus 5 device by repeatedly performing double-sided Rowhammer on the same 4 MB chunk of contiguous memory. We ran our test for little less than a month while keeping track of each bit flip. Figure 1 shows our results: it depicts the number of unique bit flips over time, where a bit flip is unique if the physical address at which it was reported has not been flipped during an earlier round. Our results show that unique flips indeed do increase over time, and proves that mitigations based on blacklisting vulnerable memory, such as B-CATT, do not scale and are inherently insecure. Furthermore, it shows that any technique that relies on observations and thresholds derived during a testing period, can be subverted as the attacker can trigger different bit flips during runtime. This is on par with related work that discusses the importance of different bit patterns unique to every device when hammering [20,25]), which makes generic hammering techniques not always effective in finding all vulnerable memory regions.

In parallel, there are many issues that make B-CATT impractical. First, since devices may average close to one bit flip per page [28,30], B-CATT would have to disable *all* of physical memory for those. Second, blacklisted pages contribute to physical memory fragmentation, making it harder—or impossible—for apps that require physically contiguous memory to run properly. Third, doing a single sweep of a devices's physical memory may take over a day to complete—as we experienced when scanning the entire 4 GB of LPDDR4 memory of a Google Pixel, which is in line with observations of related work [30].

Disabling the Contiguous Heap was Google's first reaction to Drammer [28] and is a third defense that tries to prevent the attacker from flipping bits. In the November 2016 security update for Android, Google disabled the *kmalloc heap*, removing an attacker's primitive to allocate contiguous memory [14]. Without access to the `pagemap` interface—a special file in `procfs` for retrieving physical addresses—this update effectively disables an attacker's ability of performing double-sided Rowhammer, greatly reducing the number of bits she can flip [5].

As this was Google's first attempt at mitigating Drammer, disabling the contiguous heap is proven to work in practice on a variety of devices. We will show in Sect. 5, however, that it is not secure: it possible to implement primitives for obtaining contiguous memory allocations even when using the regular *system heap* (which does not guarantee the allocation of contiguous memory). In concurrent work, Frigo et al. [12] present another side channel for detecting contiguous memory.

Pool Size Reduction was part of a second round of Drammer mitigations by Google which reduced the number of internal *system heap* pools to two. Before, ION could allocate and pool memory using many different pool sizes (4 KB, 8 KB, 16 KB, ..., 4 MB). If one requested a large chunk of memory, say 4 MB, from an empty pool, ION would request these large chunks from the underlying allocator directly, increasing the likelihood for an attacker to obtain physically contiguous memory. By reducing the maximum pool size to 64 KB, the attacker is more likely to obtain fragmented memory pieces that are not physically contiguous.

Although this is a proven practical solution, it does not eradicate the problem at its root. We show in Sect. 5 how a determined attacker can still force the system to allocate contiguous memory to launch double-sided Rowhammer. Moreover, we show how limiting system allocations to low orders (up to 64 KB) is not effective when memory is not heavily fragmented. In fact, a request for 200 MB would get split up in many 64 KB allocations, some of which will very likely be allocated right next to each other in physical memory.

4.2 Preventing Physical Memory Massaging (¬massage)

CATT proposes a static partitioning of physical memory between different security domains [6]. In principle, its design allows for an arbitrary *finite* number of security domains. However, only a prototype for the special case of two security domains was implemented and evaluated: *lowmem* (kernel memory) and *highmem* (user memory). By design, this system guarantees that, under any circumstance, the kernel never touches userland memory, and vice versa.

Modern operating system kernels are designed to make all possible resources available to an app or to the kernel itself. For example, in Linux, the memory management code moves physical memory between zones (e.g., highmem and lowmem) to alleviate memory pressure in them, as a function of the current workload. Due to its *static* partition, CATT severely limits this capability, making it unlikely to be used in practice. Moreover, as acknowledged by the authors, the generalization of CATT to more than two security domains presents a number of significant practicality and complexity challenges. For example, to prevent app-to-app attacks that we will discuss in Sect. 5, CATT must enable as many domains as there are apps installed. To support this, the prototype must be able to pass additional arguments to the kernel's memory allocator to specify the security domain of the process requesting the allocation. This would result in memory fragmentation, which would in turn lead, among other problems, to performance issues: the memory allocator must scan the memory to find a "suitable" memory region for each memory allocation.

Not only is CATT impractical, recent work also demonstrates that so-called *double-ownership* kernel buffers (e.g., video buffers that are shared between user and kernel) allow an attacker to bypass CATT's security guarantees [9].

Separation of Highmem/Lowmem was part of Google's mitigations against Drammer. Android now enforces that the *system heap*—which is exposed to userland apps—only returns memory pages from highmem, separating attacker-controlled memory for critical data structures in lowmem.

The highmem/lowmem separation suffers from the same issues as described before. Additionally, we show in the next section that an attacker can allocate many ION chunks to deplete the highmem pool and force the kernel to serve new requests from lowmem. Thus, despite Android's latest security updates, an unprivileged app can still force the system to allocate userland pages in lowmem.

5   RAMpage: Breaking the State-of-the-Art

This section elaborates on the security limitations of existing defenses as discussed in the previous section. We document new attack strategies, showing that the defense mechanisms that appear to be practical are not effective for preventing Rowhammer attacks. We first show how it is possible to mount Rowhammer-based attacks even when ION memory allocations are not contiguous and served from highmem. Next, we discuss several app-to-app attack scenarios that show kernel-owned data is not the only target memory to protect.

5.1   Exploiting Non-contiguous Memory

Before Drammer, the ION subsystem allowed userland apps to allocate a large number of contiguous chunks. As described previously, to mitigate Drammer, Google disabled the ION *kmalloc heap*. The ION *system heap*, however, is still available. This heap has two features that make the Drammer attack more challenging: (1) ION allocations from this heap are no longer guaranteed to be physically contiguous, preventing attackers from performing double-sided Rowhammer; (2) the system heap allocates memory from a different zone (highmem, as opposed to lowmem for the kmalloc heap).

We now detail our first RAMPAGE variant, R0: a reliable Drammer implementation that shows how disabling contiguous memory allocations does not prevent Rowhammer-based privilege escalation attacks.

Exhausting the System Heap. We observe that once ION's internal pools are drained, subsequent allocations are handled directly by the buddy allocator. In this state, we rely on the predictable behavior of the buddy allocator to get contiguous pages [28]. With access to contiguous chunks of memory, we then perform double-sided Rowhammer to find exploitable bit flips. However, as mentioned, the system heap initially allocates memory from highmem while the interesting data structures reside in the lowmem zone. To force lowmem allocations, we simply continue allocating memory until no highmem is left (which we detect by monitoring `procfs`). Once this is the case, the kernel serves subsequent requests from lowmem, allowing us to find bit flips in physical memory that may later hold a page table.

Shrinking the Cache Pool. Armed with an exploitable bit flip in lowmem, we perform *Phys Feng Shui* to trick the kernel in storing a page table in the vulnerable page. For this, we need to free the vulnerable row so that the buddy allocator may use it as a page table later. Simply releasing the chunk, however, is not sufficient: after freeing, it ends up in the ION memory pool. We thus require a primitive to shrink system heap pools.

On Android, the low-memory killer (LMK) [29] handles low-memory conditions that arise in the system before the more severe Linux Out-of-Memory (OOM) killer is triggered. The LMK works similarly to the OOM killer, but keeps track of additional information, such as various shrinkers that are available. Shrinkers are registered by memory subsystems or drivers that reserve an amount of memory from the system RAM [1]. When the system is close to running out of memory, the LMK calls the registered shrinkers to release and regain cached memory.

We now construct a primitive to release physical memory of the system heap pools back to the kernel: (1) we read from `/proc/meminfo` to learn how much free memory is available and use this to (2) trigger a `mmap` allocation from userland which is large enough to trigger the LMK. This indirectly forces the ION subsystem to release its preallocated cached memory, including the row with the vulnerable page.

Rooting a Google Pixel. By combining our primitives with the *Phys Feng Shui* methodology of Drammer [28], we implement the remaining steps of the attack (i.e., finding exploitable chunks and landing page tables in vulnerable locations) and develop a root exploit. We were successful in mounting our proof of concept against a Google Pixel running the latest version of Android (7.1.1. at the time of our experiments).

The implementation of these steps involves solving a number of engineering challenges that, from a conceptual point of view, are similar to what was presented in Drammer. We report the details of our attack in Appendix A.

5.2 Exploiting System-Wide Isolation

In this section, we detail how defense solutions that only protect specific parts of system memory (e.g., the CATT prototype) do not provide a comprehensive protection mechanism. We present three more RAMPAGE variants that illustrate how one can bypass these defenses.

ION-to-ION (R1). In this scenario, we use ION allocations to corrupt ION buffers that belong to another app or process. We start with allocating ION memory to search for exploitable bit flips. Next, we release the vulnerable page to which this bit belongs so that our victim may reuse it. Depending on our victim process, we must then either wait for it to allocate ION memory, or we can trigger allocations by sending an app-specific *intent*.

To investigate the feasibility of this attack, we developed a proof-of-concept in which we trigger bit flips in ION memory that is in use by a victim process. During a real attack, an attacker will likely target a privileged app, such as the media server, in which case she must investigate what bits are sensitive to flip. We acknowledge that it may not be trivial to perform such an attack, and we believe this to be an interesting direction for future research. However, we argue that this scenario and our proof of concept provide a concrete example showing how current defense mechanisms are not comprehensive enough.

CMA-to-CMA Attack (R2). The Contiguous Memory Allocator (CMA) is another kernel mechanism to implement DMA-like primitives [10,11,21] and thus provides another venue for attackers. Mounting CMA attacks is technically more challenging since it uses a bit map for deciding allocations: depending on the internal state of the bit map, the victim may not get the same chunk of memory that the attacker releases after the templating, i.e., the probing for vulnerable memory locations. However, the attacker can exhaust the CMA bit map before releasing the vulnerable range to make sure that the victim will reuse the attacker's vulnerable target chunk.

CMA-to-System Attack (R3). Although challenging, it is also possible to corrupt system memory from CMA-allocated memory, leading to our last RAMPAGE variant. In fact, the buddy allocator is designed to migrate pages from the CMA heap when the system is close to out-of-memory situations. These pages can be claimed back at any time by the CMA heap (in other words, they are moveable). We note that this attack cannot directly target page tables (because they are unmovable); however, the attacker might be able to target other sensitive system-owned data structures (e.g., `struct cred`).

6 GuardION: Fine-Grained Memory Isolation

As discussed, the main reason for which defenses fail in practice is because they aim to protect *all* sensitive information by making sure that they are not affected by Rowhammer bit flips. Hence, they are either impractical or they miss

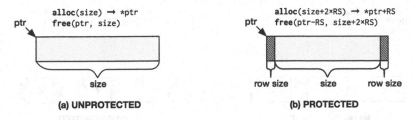

Fig. 2. Allocations on ION's contiguous heap (a) without and (b) with GUARDION (RS = row size).

cases (e.g., variants R1–R3). As RAMPAGE shows, ARM devices are still widely exposed, and providing an adequate software protection is particularly pressing.

We propose GUARDION, a mitigation against DMA-based Rowhammer exploits on mobile devices. Instead of trying to protect all physical memory, we focus on limiting the capabilities of an attacker's uncached allocations. As we will show in Sect. 7, these only constitute a small fraction of all allocations in the system. We can hence afford to apply expensive fine-grained isolation for *each* DMA allocation. GUARDION isolates such buffers with two *guard rows*, one at the 'top' (the first n bytes before an allocation), and another at the 'bottom' (n additional bytes starting at the last address of the allocation). This enforces a strict containment policy in which bit flips that are triggered by reading from uncached memory cannot occur outside the boundaries of that DMA buffer. In effect, this design defends against Rowhammer by eradicating the ability of the attacker to inject bit flips in sensitive data.

Note that GUARDION works under the assumption that bit flips never occur in memory pages that are physically more than one row 'away' from the aggressor rows. This is in the same spirit as other defenses and we believe a sane assumption: such flips have never been reported before, and the electrical properties of Rowhammer make this unlikely to ever occur. Additionally, our current prototype assumes that physical addresses are linearly mapped to DRAM addresses. While this is true for most ARM-based chipsets [22,28], a next version of GUARDION should use a kernel allocator that is aware of DRAM geometry.

We now describe our implementation of this fine-grained isolation for the Android kernel. Specifically, we modify three allocators that potentially hand contiguous uncached memory to userland apps: the ION contiguous heap, the ION system heap, and the contiguous memory allocation heap (i.e., the CMA heap). In all cases, we need modifications in the allocation and deallocation routines, which we now discuss in more detail.

6.1 Isolating ION's Contiguous Heap

Google disabled ION's contiguous heap, the *kmalloc heap* (SYSTEM_CONTIG), as part of their efforts to thwart the Drammer attack. This was possible since most devices do not require physically contiguous memory allocations to be available for regular userland apps. Device configurations that do require this, however,

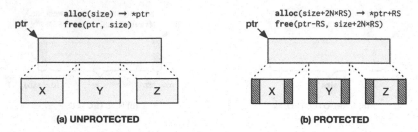

Fig. 3. Allocations on ION's system heap (a) without and (b) with GUARDION (N = number of pool members, size = X + Y + Z, RS = row size).

remain exposed. Since isolating these allocations is simple, we explore them first before describing our more elaborate efforts for isolating ION's system and CMA heaps.

For each request, the contiguous heap allocator takes the requested size and computes the smallest buddy order that satisfies this. The allocator then requests the required number of pages from that buddy order. To free a previously allocated buffer, the allocator simply returns the pages back to the buddy allocator. To isolate bit flips in these buffers, we allocate two guard rows that sandwich the allocation as shown in Fig. 2. At allocation time for a given size s, we request two extra rows, i.e., $s + 2 \times RS$ (RS being the row size), and return the buffer starting after the guard row to the user. Note that the user process will not have access to these guard rows, as they are never mapped to virtual memory.

For this to work, we need to round up the allocation size to at least the row size. Hence, to protect a 4 KB buffer, we need to allocate 3×64 KB (assuming a row size of 64 KB). Fortunately, at runtime, many requested buffers have a larger size, amortizing the overhead of guard rows. Further, given that DMA buffers constitute a small fraction of an entire app's memory, this overhead becomes negligible as we will show in Sect. 7.

6.2 Isolating ION's System Heap

There are two main limitations with ION's contiguous heap: (1) it is not possible to satisfy requests if physically contiguous memory is not available due to fragmentation, and (2) the interaction with the buddy allocator is expensive. To address these limitations, the *system heap* (SYSTEM) provides its users with virtually contiguous memory backed by memory pools of various sizes.

Figure 3(a) shows how the system heap satisfies an allocation of a given size by stitching multiple smaller physically contiguous allocations together. These smaller allocations are satisfied from pools with pre-defined sizes. The system heap makes an attempt to use pools of the largest suitable size before resorting to pools with smaller sizes to reduce management overhead for each allocation. These pools act as a cache of the buddy allocator in order to improve the allocation performance. Whenever the system is under memory pressure, free memory from these pools is reclaimed and given back to the buddy allocator.

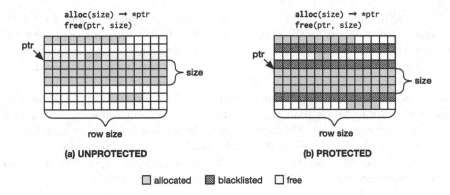

Fig. 4. Allocations on ION's CMA heap (a) without and (b) with GUARDION.

Currently, in order to thwart Drammer, Android only enables pools of size 4 KB and 64 KB, instead of previously-supported larger sizes. Since the size of a memory row is usually 64 KB on ARM, it was expected that attackers cannot allocate large-enough physically contiguous buffers to perform the templating step reliably. We showed that this is not the case in Sect. 4 and we now discuss how we can protect the system heap with GUARDION.

We extend our design for the contiguous heap to protect each physically contiguous allocation from each pool, as depicted in Fig. 3(b). We extended the pool allocation and deallocation routines to isolate every pool member, similar to how we isolated each allocation from the contiguous heap. Our modifications are mostly straightforward, given that we do not introduce an additional state in the pool allocator. During `free` operations, we return the extra guard rows back to the system.

The overhead of isolating uncached allocations in the system heap depends on the number of allocations from the pools for each request. Given that we are isolating each sub-allocation, we now safely re-enable pools with larger sizes. On top of reducing per-allocation management overhead in the system heap, enabling larger pools reduces the overhead of GUARDION given that it reduces the number of sub-allocations for each request.

6.3 Isolating ION's CMA Heap

While it was possible to disable ION's contiguous heap for newer mobile devices, there are still drivers that may require physically contiguous memory allocations. These allocations, however, mostly happen in the kernel and are handled by the *CMA heap* (`CMA`). The CMA heap has a statically-defined size which is reserved in physical memory at boot time. These pages may be used by other users when necessary but can always be claimed back by the kernel. While the CMA heap is currently only used by the kernel, we found that recent Android versions still expose it to unprivileged apps. Although we did not find any userland app on a Google Pixel that requires it, we still implement isolation for this heap to provide complete protection.

Figure 4(a) shows how the CMA allocator handles requests using a bit map that tracks free memory in the CMA region. The CMA allocator scans this bit map to find the first fit for a requested allocation size. This means that over time, this bit map gets fragmented. To provide isolation in this heap, we follow the following strategy: we blacklist all odd rows in the bit map during initialization. This provides isolation for all allocations that are smaller than the size of the row. To support allocations larger than the row size, we scan the bit map to find a first fit assuming we can allocate blacklisted rows. We use a secondary bit map for the rows to keep track of odd rows that are allocated as part of a large allocation and maintain it during free operations of these large allocations. Figure 4(b) shows an isolated allocation from the CMA heap with GUARDION in place.

7   Evaluation

We now evaluate GUARDION under several aspects: security, performance, and ease of adoption.

7.1   Security Evaluation

GUARDION provides an isolation primitive that makes it impossible for attackers to use uncached DMA allocations to flip bits in memory that is in use by the kernel or any userland app. Within our threat model, where attacks are only possible by attacking uncached memory, GUARDION protects all known Rowhammer attack vectors, and, to the best of our knowledge, no existing technique can bypass it. We verify this by mounting the exploits detailed in Sect. 5 which all failed: we were unable to flip bits in the memory of another process.

7.2   Performance and Memory Footprint

We now evaluate the overhead of GUARDION, focusing on both performance and memory overhead.

Dataset. To evaluate GUARDION, we execute 22 Android benchmark apps that we selected as follows: (1) we built a dataset of 135 benchmark apps, obtained by searching for the *benchmark* keyword on Google Play; (2) by profiling the ION subsystem, we found that only 28 of them use uncached DMA memory; (3) we discarded two of them as they perform the same tests, one because it does not produce a score, and three because they do not produce reproducible numbers for our baseline.

We run each benchmark app thrice on a Google Pixel running Android 7.1.1 without GUARDION (baseline) and reboot the device after each execution. We then enable GUARDION and repeat this experiment. We compute the median over the three runs and use this as the benchmark score. Since some benchmarks report higher scores for better performance, while for others a lower score indicates better performance, we normalize the scores across benchmarks. Finally, we calculate the geometric mean (geomean) over all benchmark results.

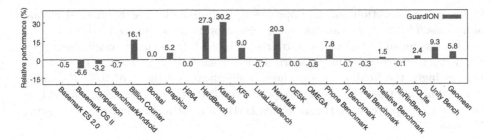

Fig. 5. Performance results of applying GUARDION. The numbers show the relative improvement (positive number) or degradation (negative number) of the performance according to each benchmark app. The last column reports the geometric mean of these results (5.8%), which shows that the performance generally increases.

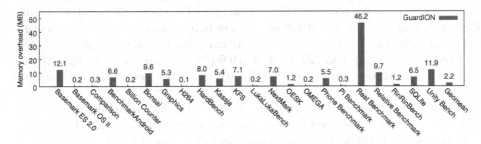

Fig. 6. Memory overhead of DMA isolation with GUARDION. The numbers show the overhead in MB. The last column reports the geometric mean of these results (2.2 MB), which indicates that the memory overhead is, in the general case, negligible.

Performance Overhead. Figure 5 shows the overall performance impact of GUARDION. In particular, the figure shows the relative performance compared to the baseline, where a positive value indicates an improvement, while a negative value indicates a performance degradation.

In the worst case, GUARDION results in a performance degradation of 6.6%, which we believe is still acceptable. The geomean, however, indicates a performance improvement of 5.8%, likely caused by the fact that GUARDION allows us to revert Google's second series of patches, which reduced pool size as outlined in Sect. 4. This allows the ION subsystem to use higher order allocations again in case a process files a request for DMA memory larger than 64 KB: for example, the Kassja benchmark triggers many 2 MB uncached allocations. With large order allocations enabled, each such request triggers the ION subsystem to call the underlying page allocator only once, at most (if the request cannot be processed by the pool). Without GUARDION, however, the request would get split up in $\frac{2\,MB}{64\,KB} = 32$ allocations, each one introducing additional overhead.

Memory Overhead. Figure 6 shows the memory overhead of GUARDION. We determine the memory footprint of an app by modifying the ION subsystem to log every allocation and free operation, including the kernel affected virtual addresses. This way, we can map each allocation to its associated free operation.

The geomean of the memory overhead is 2.2 MB, which is negligible, especially when considering that modern devices usually have at least 2 GB of RAM. Interestingly, the RealBench app shows a significant overhead of 46.2 MB, which is much higher than the average. Upon investigation, we determine that this is because the app pressures the uncached DMA, allocating about 190.2 MB during the test.

Impact on UI Performance and Everyday Usage. Google measures UI performance of apps mainly in terms of frames per second (fps) and number of "janky," i.e., delayed or dropped, frames [13]. A consistent rate of 60 fps is considered ideal for smooth UI animations. Android provides measurements of these values for a specific app through `adb shell dumpsys gfxinfo <packagename>`. We evaluate the performance of web browsing with Google Chrome on the Google Pixel with and without GUARDION and aggregated the results [2]. Averaged over five runs each, we did not notice any significant differences in UI performance: 22.4 out of 266.8 (8.4%) and 22.0 out of 279.0 (7.9%) frames were janky without and with GUARDION, respectively, with the frame rate remaining constant at 60 fps.

Finally, we evaluated the impact of GUARDION on day-to-day device use. For this test, we performed several "everyday" operations on a Google Pixel with and without GUARDION. These operations include taking a photo, shooting and watching a video, watching a video through the YouTube app, making a phone call, making a video call through the Skype app, and browsing the web with Chrome. In all scenarios, we did not notice any difference. Moreover, we did not notice any sign of slowdown or instability.

7.3 Patch Complexity and Adoption

We believe that it is easy to integrate GUARDION with the current Android code base. In particular, our prototype implementation for Android 7.1.1 consists of only 844 lines of code. The patch is mostly contained in the ION subsystem, and adds functionality to the bit map data structure of the kernel. Touching only 9 files in the Android source code, it is thus well contained. We also note that a significant part of our patch (422 lines, 5 files) relates to augmenting the bit map data structure to protect the CMA heap, which we believe should not be exposed to userland apps in the first place (thus possibly reducing the size of our patch even more).

We are currently in the process of submitting our patch to Google, and we hope that Google adopts our proposal either as a security patch for existing versions or in newer versions of Android.

8 Related Work

This section provides an overview of related work in the field of Rowhammer exploitation and prevention that were not yet discussed in Sects. 3.2 and 4.

8.1 Rowhammer Attacks

After Kim et al. [19] performed the first systematic study on the Rowhammer hardware fault, and Seaborn and Dullien [26] demonstrated the first practical attacks, Qiao and Seaborn [23] showed how to use non-temporal access instructions such as `movnti`, to bypass the cache (instead of relying on `clflush`, which was disabled in the Google Native Client browser sandbox following the first Rowhammer attacks). Aweke et al. [4] showed that it is possible to trigger bit flips without using special instructions: they show how an attacker can force the cache to invalidate its content by accessing memory addresses belonging to the same cache eviction set. Another recent technique abuses Intel's Cache Allocation Technology (CAT) to reduce the number of active ways in the last-level cache, which in turn significantly decreases the number of memory accesses required to trigger a bit flip [27]. As discussed in Sect. 3.2, related work has also shown how the Rowhammer vulnerability can be exploited in a number of different scenarios [5,16,24,28,30].

8.2 Rowhammer Defenses

The aforementioned attacks have demonstrated the severity of the Rowhammer vulnerability and prompted the research community to propose a number of defense mechanisms, both in hardware and in software.

Hardware-Level Defenses. One of the most obvious defense mechanism is the production of memory chips that do not suffer from the Rowhammer vulnerability. Kim et al. [19] discuss the various aspects that could be improved: for example, one could increase the row refresh rate. The DDR3 standard [17] specifies that rows should be refreshed at least every 64 ms, while Kim et al. suggest to refresh the rows at least every 32 ms. Other proposals are Error-Correcting Code (ECC) memory and Target Row Refresh (TRR). One last protection mechanism is PARA [19], which probabilistically activates rows adjacent to a potential victim row.

Unfortunately, all these techniques have significant limitations. First, many of these techniques rely on hardware modifications: ECC and TRR require the production of new memory chips, while PARA requires a change in the memory controller. This makes their deployment less practical, mainly because these chips would be more expensive, would require new development and production pipelines, and they cannot be easily adopted by existing systems, especially mobile devices. Moreover, newer standards such as LPDDR4 [18] already discuss the adoption of TRR, but only as an *optional* protection mechanism, thus leaving LPDDR4 chips still vulnerable to Rowhammer. Protecting mobile devices through hardware protection mechanisms is even more challenging due to the energy consuming nature of these mechanisms and the importance minimizing the device's battery consumption.

Second, these mechanisms are not always effective, even when deployed. For example, Aweke et al. [4] show that they could perform Rowhammer exploitation under 32 ms, making the faster refresh rate ineffective. Instead, mechanisms like ECC memory have the limitations of protecting only from one-bit memory corruption, which is not enough since Kim et al. could induce multiple bit flips. These limitations provided strong incentives to develop software-level defenses.

Software-Level Defenses. The research community has started to propose software-based solutions only recently. The first concrete solution is ANVIL [4], which we discussed in Sect. 4. Unfortunately, ANVIL is not applicable to mobile devices. Furthermore, we discussed B-CATT and CATT [6, 7], as well as Google's patches in reaction to Drammer, in Sect. 4, and demonstrated why they are not effective in Sect. 5.

9   Conclusion

In recent years, the Rowhammer vulnerability gathered a lot of attention from both the academic and industrial community. While researchers have demonstrated exploits for a range of devices in a variety of settings [5,16,19,24,26,28, 30], the Drammer attack on mobile devices [28] is particularly worrying, since it allows for a deterministic attack on very popular systems, by just relying on basic memory management features. Given that it is impossible to perform hardware upgrades on these devices, there is a clear need for effective and efficient software-based defenses.

In this paper, we showed that existing software mitigations do not solve the problem: they are either impractical to deploy, or do not provide adequate protection. To back our claims, we presented RAMPAGE, a set of DMA-based Rowhammer attacks against the latest Android OS. As a mitigation, we proposed GUARDION, a lightweight, software-only defense to prevent Rowhammer exploitation on mobile devices. Our evaluation shows that GUARDION introduces negligible memory overhead, improves performance compared to Google's mitigation in reaction to previous attacks, and prevents all known DMA-based Rowhammer attacks, even when considering app-to-app attacks. We release our modifications as open source, and are in the process of sharing our patches with Google, hoping they will adopt our proposal in newer versions of Android.

Acknowledgments. We thank the anonymous reviewers for their valuable comments and input to improve the paper, as well as Pietro Frigo for his help on understanding GLitch.

This work was supported by the Netherlands Organisation for Scientific Research through grants NWO CSI-DHS 628.001.021, by the European Commission through project H2020 ICT-32-2014 "SHARCS" under Grant Agreement No. 644571, the NSF under Award No. CNS-1408632, the ONR under Award No. N00014-17-1-2897, DARPA under agreement number FA8750-15-2-0084, and a Security, Privacy and Anti-Abuse award from Google. The U.S. Government is authorized to reproduce and distribute reprints for Governmental purposes notwithstanding any copyright notation thereon. Any opinions, findings, and conclusions or recommendations expressed in this publication are those of the authors and do not necessarily reflect the views, position, official policies, or endorsements, either expressed or implied, of the U.S. Government, DARPA, ONR, NSF, or Google.

A   RAMpage Attack Details

This section provides additional details on RAMPAGE variant R0, our end-to-end exploit that bypasses Google's deployed defenses against Drammer. We rely on primitives and steps discussed in Sect. 5: how to exhaust the *system heap*, how to shrink the cache pool, and how to trigger the Low Memory Killer (LMK). We now discuss the remaining steps: how to find exploitable chunks, how to land a page table in the vulnerable page, and how to obtain root access.

With the help of the primitives defined in Sect. 5, we can allocate memory chunks directly from the buddy allocator. We exploit the deterministic behavior of buddy to obtain large contiguous chunks of memory that we then template for exploitable bit flips. Typically, Android ARMv8 devices are configured to use 3 levels of translation tables with 4 KB pages, resulting in 39 bits that are available for virtual addressing. Page table entries are 64 bits wide, but since most devices are shipped with only 4 GB of RAM or less, half of those bits are never used. We thus ignore those during the templating phase.

The exploitation steps for RAMPAGE R0 now involve the following sequence:

1. Exhaust ION memory page pools.
2. Monitor /proc/pagetypeinfo and allocate chunks using ION's SYSTEM heap with large orders that span at least 3 or more physical rows, e.g., chunks of at least 256 KB if the row size is 64 KB. As soon as ION's internal pools are drained, we will see each of these large order allocations immediately affecting pagetypeinfo. From this point, each subsequent request for (large) ION chunks is likely to be contiguous as they are being served by buddy directly.
3. Optionally, to confirm that allocated chunks are contiguous, we could either (1) perform double-sided Rowhammer to check if there are any flips, or (2) use the bank-conflict side-channel [12].
4. Template the memory using double-sided Rowhammer to find an exploitable page.
5. Perform *Phys Feng Shui* so that the large chunk that contains the vulnerable page is split in multiple smaller chunks (of the row size) that we can release individually [28].
6. Confirm that the aggressor rows are still accessible by performing a second templating round.
7. Release the vulnerable row. This will give it back to the ION cache.
8. Perform a *cache pool shrink* operation. This will release memory from all registered shrinkers—including the ION cache—back to buddy.
9. Perform page table spraying while monitoring /proc/pagetypeinfo until the first chunk of the row size is touched.
10. Allocate page tables until all chunks of the row size are used.

Once page tables using row size chunks are allocated, we could set those page tables with values that point it back to itself when hammered. Once we are able to get access to the page table, we scan the kernel memory for struct cred bytes and overwrite the UID's to that of root.

References

1. Low-Memory Shrinker API, October 2013. http://www.phonesdevelopers.info/1815288. Accessed 5 May 2017
2. cookie-butter: Python Script for Making Graphics Performance Charts for an Android App (2016). https://github.com/Turnsole/cookie-butter
3. Drammer: Native Binary for Testing Android Phones for the Rowhammer Bug (2016). https://github.com/vusec/drammer
4. Aweke, Z.B., Yitbarek, S.F., Qiao, R., Das, R., Hicks, M., Oren, Y., Austin, T.: ANVIL: software-based protection against next-generation Rowhammer attacks. In: Proceedings of ACM International Conference on Architectural Support for Programming Languages and Operating Systems (ASPLOS) (2016)
5. Bosman, E., Razavi, K., Bos, H., Giuffrida, C.: Dedup Est Machina: memory deduplication as an advanced exploitation vector. In: Proceedings of IEEE Symposium on Security and Privacy (S&P) (2016)
6. Brasser, F., Davi, L., Gens, D., Liebchen, C., Sadeghi, A.R.: CAn't touch this: practical and generic software-only defenses against Rowhammer attacks, November 2016. arXiv:1611.08396 [cs.CR]
7. Brasser, F., Davi, L., Gens, D., Liebchen, C., Sadeghi, A.R.: Can't touch this: practical and generic software-only defenses against Rowhammer attacks. In: Proceedings of USENIX Security Symposium (2017)
8. Cai, Y., Ghose, S., Luo, Y., Mai, K., Mutlu, O., Haratsch, E.F.: Vulnerabilities in MLC NAND flash memory programming: experimental analysis, exploits, and mitigation techniques. In: Proceedings of International Symposium on High-Performance Computer Architecture (HPCA) (2017)
9. Cheng, Y., Zhang, Z., Nepal, S.: Still hammerable and exploitable: on the effectiveness of software-only physical kernel isolation, February 2018. arXiv:1802.07060 [cs.CR]
10. Corbet, J.: Contiguous Memory Allocation for Drivers, July 2010. https://lwn.net/Articles/396702/
11. Corbet, J.: A Reworked Contiguous Memory Allocator, June 2011. https://lwn.net/Articles/447405/
12. Frigo, P., Giuffrida, C., Bos, H., Razavi, K.: Grand Pwning unit: accelerating microarchitectural attacks with the GPU. In: Proceedings of IEEE Symposium on Security and Privacy (S&P) (2018)
13. Google: Testing UI Performance. https://developer.android.com/training/testing/performance.html
14. Google: ion: Disable ION_HEAP_TYPE_SYSTEM_CONTIG, November 2016. https://android.googlesource.com/device/google/marlin-kernel/
15. Gorman, M.: Understanding the Linux Virtual Memory Manager. Prentice Hall PTR, Upper Saddle River (2007)
16. Gruss, D., Maurice, C., Mangard, S.: Rowhammer.js: a remote software-induced fault attack in JavaScript. In: Proceedings of Conference on Detection of Intrusions and Malware & Vulnerability Assessment (DIMVA) (2016)
17. JEDEC Solid State Technology Association: DDR3 SDRAM Specification. JESD79-3F (2012)
18. JEDEC Solid State Technology Association: Low Power Double Data 4 (LPDDR4). JESD209-4A (2015)

19. Kim, Y., Daly, R., Kim, J., Fallin, C., Lee, J.H., Lee, D., Wilkerson, C., Lai, K., Mutlu, O.: Flipping bits in memory without accessing them: an experimental study of DRAM disturbance errors. In: Proceedings of International Symposium on Computer Architecture (ISCA) (2014)
20. Lanteigne, M.: How Rowhammer Could Be Used to Exploit Weaknesses in Computer Hardware, March 2016. http://www.thirdio.com/rowhammer.pdf
21. Nazarewicz, M.: A Deep Dive into CMA, March 2012. https://lwn.net/Articles/486301/
22. Pessl, P., Gruss, D., Maurice, C., Schwarz, M., Mangard, S.: DRAMA: exploiting DRAM addressing for cross-CPU attacks. In: Proceedings of USENIX Security Symposium (2016)
23. Qiao, R., Seaborn, M.: A new approach for Rowhammer attacks. In: Proceedings of IEEE International Symposium on Hardware Oriented Security and Trust (HOST) (2016)
24. Razavi, K., Gras, B., Bosman, E., Preneel, B., Giuffrida, C., Bos, H.: Flip Feng Shui: hammering a needle in the software stack. In: Proceedings of USENIX Security Symposium (2016)
25. Schaller, A., Xiong, W., Salee, M.U., Anagnostopoulos, N.A., Katzenbeisser, S., Szefer, J.: Intrinsic rowhammer PUFs: leveraging the Rowhammer effect for improved security. In: Proceedings of IEEE International Symposium on Hardware Oriented Security and Trust (HOST) (2017)
26. Seaborn, M., Dullien, T.: Exploiting the DRAM Rowhammer bug to gain kernel privileges. In: Black Hat USA (BH-US) (2015)
27. Aga, M.T., Aweke, Z.B., Austin, T.: When good protections go bad: exploiting anti-DoS measures to accelerate Rowhammer attacks. In: Proceedings of IEEE International Symposium on Hardware Oriented Security and Trust (HOST) (2017)
28. van der Veen, V., Fratantonio, Y., Lindorfer, M., Gruss, D., Maurice, C., Vigna, G., Bos, H., Razavi, K., Giuffrida, C.: Drammer: deterministic Rowhammer attacks on mobile platforms. In: Proceedings of ACM Conference on Computer and Communications Security (CCS) (2016)
29. Vorontsov, A.: Android Low Memory Killer vs. Memory Pressure Notifications, December 2011. https://lkml.org/lkml/2011/12/18/173
30. Xiao, Y., Zhang, X., Zhang, Y., Teodorescu, M.R.: One bit flips, one cloud flops: cross-VM Rowhammer attacks and privilege escalation. In: Proceedings of USENIX Security Symposium (2016)
31. Zeng, T.M.: The Android ION Memory Allocator, February 2012. https://lwn.net/Articles/480055

BinArm: Scalable and Efficient Detection of Vulnerabilities in Firmware Images of Intelligent Electronic Devices

Paria Shirani[1]([✉]), Leo Collard[1], Basile L. Agba[2], Bernard Lebel[3],
Mourad Debbabi[1], Lingyu Wang[1], and Aiman Hanna[1]

[1] Security Research Centre, Concordia University, Montreal, Canada
p_shira@encs.concordia.ca
[2] Institut de recherche d'Hydro-Québec, Montreal, Canada
[3] Thales Canada Inc., Montreal, Canada

Abstract. There is a widespread adoption of intelligent electronic devices (IEDs) in modern-day smart grid deployments. Consequently, any vulnerabilities in IED firmware might greatly affect the security and functionality of the smart grid. Although general-purpose techniques exist for vulnerability detection in firmware, they usually cannot meet the specific needs, e.g., they lack the domain knowledge specific to IED vulnerabilities, and they are often not efficient enough for handling larger firmware of IEDs. In this paper, we present BinArm, a scalable approach to detecting vulnerable functions in smart grid IED firmware mainly based on the ARM architecture. To this end, we build comprehensive databases of vulnerabilities and firmware that are both specific to smart grid IEDs. Then, we propose a multi-stage detection engine to minimize the computational cost of function matching and to address the scalability issue in handling large IED firmware. Specifically, the proposed engine takes a coarse-to-fine grained multi-stage function matching approach by (i) first filtering out dissimilar functions based on a group of heterogeneous features; (ii) further filtering out dissimilar functions based on their execution paths; and (iii) finally identifying candidate functions based on fuzzy graph matching. Our experiments show that BinArm accurately identifies vulnerable functions with an average accuracy of 0.92. The experimental results also show that our detection engine can speed up the existing fuzzy matching approach by three orders of magnitude. Finally, as a practical framework, BinArm successfully detects 93 real-world CVE vulnerability entries, the majority of which have been confirmed, and the detection takes as little as 0.09 s per function on average.

1 Introduction

Intelligent electronic devices (IEDs) play an important role in typical smart grids by supporting SCADA communications, condition-based monitoring, and polling for event-specific data in the substations. The firmware (software) running on

© Springer International Publishing AG, part of Springer Nature 2018
C. Giuffrida et al. (Eds.): DIMVA 2018, LNCS 10885, pp. 114–138, 2018.
https://doi.org/10.1007/978-3-319-93411-2_6

IEDs is subject to a wide range of software vulnerabilities, and consequently security attacks exploiting such vulnerabilities may have debilitating repercussions on national economic security and national safety [6]. In fact, a startling increase in the number of attacks against industrial control systems (ICS) equipment has been observed (e.g., a 110% increase when comparing 2016 to 2015 [10]). A prime example of such an attack is *Industroyer* [2] targeting Ukraine's power grid, which is capable of directly controlling substation switches and circuit breakers. As other examples, the *Black Energy* [40] APT took control of operators' control stations, and utilized them to cause a blackout; and *Stuxnet* [24,36] targeted Siemens ICS equipment in order to infiltrate Iranian nuclear facilities. In addition to those real-world attacks, industrial analysis demonstrates similar threats in other countries, e.g., with 50 power generators taken over by attackers, as many as 93 million US residents may be left without power [47]. These real-world attacks or hypothetical scenarios indicate a clear potential and serious consequences for future attacks against critical infrastructures including smart grids.

Identifying security-critical vulnerabilities in firmware images running on IEDs is essential to assess the security of a smart grid. However, this task is especially challenging since the source code of firmware is usually not available. In the literature, general-purpose techniques have been developed to automatically identify vulnerabilities in embedded firmware based on dynamic analysis (e.g., [14,19,49,55]) or static analysis (e.g., [17,23,25,44,54]). To the best of our knowledge, none of the existing approaches focuses on the smart grid context. Although such general purpose techniques are also applicable to the firmware of smart grid IEDs, they share some common limitations as follows. (i) *Applicability:* They lack sufficient domain knowledge specific to smart grids and IEDs, such as a database of known vulnerabilities in such devices and that of the IED firmware. Therefore (a) no prior knowledge about the scope is required; (b) no additional effort to gather and analyse the relevant IED firmware images is needed. They can easily crawl and download any firmware from the wild; and (c) no study on the used libraries in the IED firmware images is performed; it is highly likely that most relevant libraries are not included in their vulnerability dataset, which might result in higher false negative rates. (ii) *Scalability:* Those approaches typically rely on expensive operations, such as semantic hashing [44], and they typically lack effective filtering steps to speed up the function matching. Consequently, those techniques are usually not efficient enough to handle the much larger sizes of IED firmware (e.g., compared to that of network routers) and not scalable enough for a large scale application to real-world smart grids. (iii) *Adaptability:* Handling the presence of a new CVE and efficiently indexing it poses another challenge to some existing works (e.g., [54]).

In this paper, we present BINARM, a scalable approach to detecting vulnerable functions in smart grid IED firmware based on the ARM architecture. To this end, we first build a large-scale vulnerability database consisting of common vulnerabilities in IED firmware images. The design of our vulnerability database is highly influenced and guided by the prominent libraries used in the

IED firmware images. To identify these IEDs and obtaining the corresponding firmware images significant efforts is required to: (i) identify relevant manufacturers; (ii) collect and analyze the corresponding IED firmware images; (iii) identify the used libraries in these images; and (iv) compile the list of CVE vulnerabilities.

Second, to ensure BINARM is efficient and scalable enough to handle IED firmware images, we design a detection engine that employs three increasingly complex stages in order to speed up the process by filtering out mismatched candidates as early as possible. Third, BINARM does not only provide a similarity score as prior efforts, such as [23,54], but also presents in-depth (at instruction, basic block and function levels) details to justify the results of the matching and to assist reverse engineers for further investigation. We conduct extensive experiments with a large number of real-world smart grid IED firmware from various vendors in order to evaluate the effectiveness and performance of BINARM.

Contributions. Our main contributions are as follows:

- To the best of our knowledge, we develop the first large-scale vulnerability database specifically for IEDs firmware covering most of the major vendors. In addition, we build the first IED firmware database, which gives an overview of the state of the industry. Such effort can be leveraged for future research on smart grid IEDs, and can be beneficial to IED vendors as well as utilities to assess the security of elaborated and deployed IED firmware.
- We propose a multi-stage detection engine to efficiently identify vulnerable functions in IED firmware, while maintaining the accuracy. The experiments demonstrate this engine is three orders of magnitude faster than the existing fuzzy matching approach [31].
- Our experimental results ascertain the accuracy of the proposed system, with an average total accuracy of 0.92. In addition, the real-world applicability of BINARM is confirmed in our study, which successfully detects 93 potential CVEs among real-world IED firmware within 0.09 s per function on average, the majority of which have been confirmed by our manual analysis.

2   Approach Overview

An overview of our approach is depicted in Fig. 1, which consists of two major phases: *offline preparation* and *online search*. The *offline preparation* phase consists in the creation of two comprehensive databases; one containing a set of IED firmware and the other known vulnerabilities specific to IEDs. To this end, we:

Fig. 1. BINARM overview

- Identify a set of manufacturers that provides equipment for smart grids.
- Collect relevant IED firmware produced by the identified manufacturers, and store the images in the *Firmware Database*.

Such information further provides insight about which libraries might be utilized by each manufacturer in their released firmware, which enables us to build our vulnerability database. For this purpose, we:

- Determine reused libraries in the IED firmware from manufacturers' websites or available documentations.
- Collect the identified open-source and vulnerable libraries, and cross-compile them for the ARM processor in order to build the *Vulnerability Database*.

We demonstrate how the aforementioned process works by applying it to the following motivating example. Suppose a fictitious utility company would like to deploy several phasor measurement units (PMUs) and is concerned about potential vulnerabilities inside those units. Following our methodology depicted in Fig. 1, we would first identify the manufacturer, e.g., given by the utility as National Instruments (NI) in this particular example. Second, we would collect the IED firmware, which is given by the utility as NI PMU1_0_11 firmware image [8]. Third, we would identify the reused libraries in this firmware, e.g., the `libcurl` v7.50.2 library. Fourth,

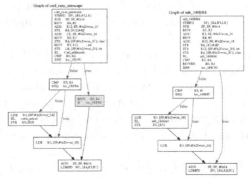

we would identify vulnerable functions inside each library, e.g., a vulnerable function inside the `libcurl` v7.50.2 library as depicted in Fig. 2a. Finally, we employ our detection engine to find matching functions in the provided firmware image, e.g., a matched function shown in Fig. 2b. As shown, the two functions have a high degree of similarity; indeed, the only difference is the presence of an additional basic block consisting of two instructions (highlighted in Fig. 2a) in the `curl_easy_unescape` function. This similarity implies that the

(a) `curl_easy_unescape` CFG in `libcurl` v7.50.2 with CVE-2016-7167

(b) `sub_149BB4` CFG in NI PMU1_0_11.`libws_repl`

Fig. 2. An example of function reuse in IED firmware (Color figure online)

function in Fig. 2b may also have the CVE-2016-7167 vulnerability, which provides useful information for the utility to take corresponding actions.

We note that, although this particular example may make it seem relatively straightforward to detect vulnerable functions in a firmware, this is usually not the case in practice due to two main challenges. First, the needed information about manufacturer, libraries, and vulnerabilities may not be readily available from the utility company as in this example. For this reason, we will build our vulnerability and firmware databases in Sect. 3. Second, the function matching process may be too expensive for utility companies, since they may be dealing with the constant deployment or upgrade of thousands of IEDs from different manufacturers. Cross checking such a large number of firmware images[1] with an even larger number of library functions (e.g., 5,103 vulnerable functions) can take significant effort. To address this challenge, we will propose our efficient multi-stage detection engine in Sect. 4.

3   Building IED Firmware and Vulnerability Databases

Identifying the IEDs and obtaining their corresponding firmware can help vendors and utilities in assessing the security of elaborated or deployed IEDs firmware. However, this process requires significantly more effort than simply acquiring firmware from any consumer devices by crawling and downloading from the wild. In this section, we provide the background of smart grid IEDs, and then elaborate on the creation and content of our firmware and vulnerability databases.

3.1   Intelligent Electronic Devices in the Smart Grid

A power grid is a complex and critical system to provide generated power to a diverse set of end users. It is composed of three main sectors: generation, transmission and distribution. The role of a distribution substation is to transform received high voltage electricity to a lower more suitable voltage for distribution to customers. With the introduction of IEC 61850 [1] standard technologies such as Ethernet, high speed wide area networks (WANs), and powerful but cheap computers are leverage in order to define a modern architecture for communication within a substation [39]. Consequently, a vast set of devices labelled as intelligent electronic devices (IEDs) are emerged, which are coupled with traditional ICS and power equipment which enables their integration into the network.

There exists three non-exclusive categories of IEDs: (i) *Control:* send and receive commands to control the system behaviour remotely, such as load-shedding, circuit breaker, and switch; (ii) *Monitoring and relay:* convert received analog input (e.g., currents, voltages, power values) from primary equipment into a digital format that can be used throughout the network, such as phasor measurement units (PMUs), and phasor data concentrators (PDCs); and (iii) *Protection:* detect faults that need to be isolated from the network in a specific and timely manner, such as busbar, generator, line distance and breaker.

---

[1] *Linksys WRT32X* with 39 kb size contains 47,025 functions, whereas *NI PMU1_0_11* firmware comprises 226,496 functions and is 256 kb large.

3.2   Manufacturer Identification

In order to identify a set of relevant manufacturers and market dynamics, we study the categorization of smart grid vendor ecosystem by using different sources, such as *GTM Research* [28] and *Cleantech Group* [41] reports. This information provides the necessary insights in order to identify top smart grid manufacturers, as listed in Table 1. Such knowledge becomes the foundation to further determine relevant libraries, vulnerabilities and IED firmware images.

Table 1. Identified major smart grid manufacturers and their supported components

Relevant component	Manufacturer													
	ABB	Aclara	Cisco	EI	Elster	GE	Honeywell	Itron	L + G	NI	SE	SEL	Sensus	Siemens
Automation hardware	•									•	•	•		•
Smart meters	•		•	•	•			•	•			•		
Automation software			•		•				•					
Communication			•		•			•	•			•		
Demand response						•								

(ABB): ABB Schweiz AG. (EI): Electro Industries. (GE): General Electric. (L+G): Landis+Gear. (NI): National Instruments. (SE): Schneider Electric. (SEL): Schweitzer Engineering Laboratories.

Heterogeneous hardware architectures are used in firmware images, however, many ICSs are based on the ARM architecture [13,35,58]. Additionally, as reported in Fig. 3, most of our collected IED firmware images are identified as targeting the ARM architecture (82%), followed by PowerPC (9%). On the other hand, Linux is the most encountered operating system in our firmware dataset, with 90% of frequency amongst others, such as Windows. Therefore, this work mainly focuses on the ARM-based and Linux-based firmware images.

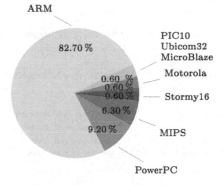

Fig. 3. Distribution of hardware architectures among collected IED firmware

3.3   Vulnerability Database

Our study shows that many of the listed manufacturers reuse existing open-source software in their product implementations. This generally entails the legal obligation of publishing documents containing the licenses of all utilized open-source software. By investigating several sources of information pertaining to these manufacturers, such as corporate websites, product documentations, and FTP search tools, we extract large amounts of open-source usage declarations that are related to the current smart grid scope, such as simple network management protocol (SNMP), and network time protocol (NTP).

The top 25 relevant, vulnerable, and popular open-source libraries are illustrated in Table 2, which are ordered by their relative significance considering which ones are more frequently used in the recognized manufacturers. We download the source code of reused libraries with different versions, and cross-compile them for the ARM architecture using GCC compiler with four optimization flags ($O0 - O3$). We utilize the CVE database to identify the number of known CVEs for each of these libraries. It is worth mentioning that all the functions of each library are stored in our *Vulnerability Database*, and the vulnerable functions are labelled by their corresponding identified CVEs. Our *Vulnerability Database* consists of 3,270,165 functions, 5,103 of which are marked as vulnerable. This results in a total of 235 unique vulnerabilities after discarding the duplicates that are created due to the use of different compilers and optimization flags.

Table 2. Vulnerable open-source libraries in identified manufacturers

Library	#CVEs	Manufacturers	Library	#CVEs	Manufacturers
php	601	Cisco, Honeywell, Siemens	qemu	225	Cisco
imagemagick	402	Cisco, GE, Honeywell	libxml2	44	ABB, Cisco, GE, Honeywell, Siemens
openssl	189	ABB, Cisco, GE, Honeywell, SE, Siemens	bind	102	Cisco, Siemens
mysql	564	Cisco	binutils	97	Cisco, Siemens
tcpdump	162	Cisco, GE, Siemens	libcurl	34	ABB, Cisco, Honeywell, SE, Siemens
openssh	87	ABB, Cisco, GE, Honeywell, Siemens	freetype	83	Cisco, Siemens
ntp	79	Cisco, GE, Honeywell, SE, Siemens	libpng	47	Cisco, Honeywell, Siemens
libtiff	149	Cisco, GE	samba	124	Honeywell
postgresql	98	Cisco, Honeywell, Siemens	utillinux	15	ABB, Cisco, GE, Honeywell, SE, Siemens
ffmpeg	274	Siemens	cups	88	Cisco
pcre	49	ABB, Cisco, GE, Honeywell, Siemens	lighttpd	28	ABB, Cisco, Honeywell
python	81	Cisco, Honeywell, Siemens	netsnmp	21	Cisco, GE, SE, Siemens
glibc	81	Cisco, Honeywell, Siemens			

Note: (GE): General Electric. (SE): Schneider Electric.

It has not escaped our notice that the acquired firmware images contain various kinds of binaries, such as kernel, application-level, open-source as well as proprietary libraries. Consequently, based on the CVE database [5], we have identified 4,344 CVE vulnerabilities in kernel-level, 5,581 CVEs in application-level, and CVEs 2,336 in open-source libraries amongst the identified manufacturers, considering the fact that some of the open-source libraries are reused in applications. Additionally, we have prepared an initial list of IED-specific proprietary libraries (e.g., NI). However, our list of such proprietary libraries is not yet comprehensive. Further effort would also be required in order to verify identified vulnerabilities, since the source code of such proprietary libraries is not publicly available. This task remains the subject of our future work.

3.4 Firmware Database

The proposed methodology is not necessarily specific to smart grid IEDs and therefore could be applied to any ARM-based firmware, such as IoT devices, routers, and IEDs. However, since the goal of this work is to assess the security of IEDs in the smart grid, we shift the focus to IED-specific firmware. We first utilize popular FTP search engines to leverage publicly accessible corporate FTP servers. We then create a simple website scraper and apply it to specific parts of each manufacturers' website. Finally, we perform a manual inspection for dynamically generated websites, which mostly applies to each manufacturers' download centre. All retrieved images are filtered based on the relevance to the smart grid context, and 2,628 firmware packages are extracted.

Firmware Analysis Challenges. Performing firmware analysis with the objective of complete disassembly is a challenging task [17]. This is partially due to a large requirement of time, domain specific knowledge and research [34]. Furthermore, binaries are often stored in proprietary formats, obfuscated or encrypted for protection. These processes effectively make it extremely difficult (e.g. obfuscation [34]), or even impossible (e.g. uncrackable encryption [51], indecipherable formats [37]) to directly access the contents of a given blob. Encrypted binaries can sometimes be identified by their use of specific headers. For instance, a file encrypted with `openssl` starts with the first 8-byte signature of ``Salted__''. In order to process all acquired firmware, we follow well-known procedures such as the ones presented in [51,56]. This process has several main steps: (i) unpacking and extraction, which consists of removing all files from another compressed file; (ii) firmware identification, that can be located amongst or within the extracted files; (iii) hardware architecture identification and scanning for op-code signatures to be identified as ARM; (iv) image base identification in order to know where the binary should be loaded; and (v) disassembling using IDA PRO [7], where using the properly identified architecture and entry point is required. A given binary blob can contain several entry points [49], and it may not be possible for tools such as IDA PRO to automatically identify them. In these cases entry point discovery should be performed [34,49], which is one of the most challenging parts of this entire procedure and required leveraging various techniques (e.g., [58]).

4 Multi-stage Detection Engine

We propose an efficient multi-stage detection engine to identify vulnerable functions in firmware images, which conducts from a coarse to granular detection stages. To this end, our key idea is to start with light-weight feature extraction and function matching operations, and to perform the most expensive operations in the end for selected candidates. More specifically, (i) function shape-based detector extracts the simplest and more distinguishable features that quickly eliminates dissimilar candidates with less computational overhead. (ii) branch-based detector performs more expensive matching operations, however, still not as expensive as graph matching. It specifically extracts execution paths, including the instruction-set and turns them into hash values, and simply employs a binary search. (iii) fuzzy matching-based detector performs the most expensive operations, which mainly include careful examination of basic blocks, their neighbours, and graph matching for a selected and relatively smaller number of candidates.

The details of each stage are explained in the following.

4.1   Function Shape-Based Detection

The function shape-based detection is performed based on a collection of heterogeneous features extracted at different levels of a function, namely, function *shape* [48], as explained in the following.

Table 3. An excerpt of function shape features

Feature category	Examples
Instruction-level	#instructions, #arguments, #strings, #mnemonics, #callees, #constants
Structural	#nodes, #edges, cyclomatic complexity, average_path_length, graph_energy, link_density
Statistical	skewness, kurtosis, Z-score, standard deviation, mean, variance

Feature Extraction. To capture the topology of a function and to extract the *structural* features, we employ a set of graph metrics [27]. However, some functions might have the same structural shape, while being semantically different. As a result, we consider additional features in order to also include semantic information. The *instruction-level* features carry the syntax and semantic information of a function [11]. For instance, the strings frequencies have been used to classify malware based on their behaviour [46]. Finally, *statistical features* are used in order to capture the semantics of a function [45], such as skewness and kurtosis [3], which are extracted as $S_k = (\frac{\sqrt{N(N-1)}}{N-1})(\frac{\sum_{i=1}^{N}(Y_i-\overline{Y})^3/N}{s^3})$, and $K_z = \frac{\sum_{i=1}^{N}(Y_i-\overline{Y})^4/N}{s^4} - 3$ respectively, where N is the number of data points, Y_i is the frequency of each instruction, $\overline{Y}$ represents the *mean*, and s is *standard deviation*. An excerpt of the extracted features is listed in Table 3. For the sake of space, the details of other features are omitted and can be found in [48].

Normalization. In the ARM instruction set, each assembly instruction consists of a mnemonic and a sequence of up to five operands. Two fragments of code might be identical both structurally and syntactically, but differ in terms of memory references or registers. Hence, it is essential to normalize the instruction sets prior to comparison. For this purpose, we normalize the operands according to the mapping sets provided by IDA PRO. We further categorize the 'general' registers based on their types.

Feature Selection. In order to identify the most differentiable features, mutual information (MI) [43] is leveraged to measure the dependency degree between the aforementioned features and the functions in *Vulnerability Database*. Based on the results, we choose three top-ranked features, graph_energy, skewness (sk), and kurtosis (kz), as a 3-tuple feature for each function. It is worth mentioning that there is a dependency between the next two top-ranked features (e.g., rich_club_metric and link_density) and graph_energy. Additionally, since our goal is to perform coarse detection at this stage, and extracting more features would affect the time complexity, we choose the first three top-ranked features. Our experiments confirm the effectiveness of three chosen features (Sect. 5.6).

Function Matching. All functions that surpass a predetermined threshold distance, λ, from a given target function are deemed dissimilar in shape-based detection stage. Euclidean distance of $d(p,q) = \sqrt{\sum_{i=1}^{n}(q_i - p_i)^2}$ is used to calculate the similarity between two functions, where $p = (p_1, p_2, p_3)$ and $q = (q_1, q_2, q_3)$ are 3-tuple associated with each function consisting of graph_energy, sk, and kz features. In order to calculate the threshold distance, we employ K-Means clustering on the extracted features and, based on the distance between the clusters, the final threshold value of $\lambda = 26.45$ is obtained as the following.

Threshold Selection. We acquire the threshold value by leveraging K-Means clustering. K-Means clustering algorithm partitions n observations into k clusters, $C_1, \ldots, C_k$, such that the total within-cluster sum of square $WSS = \sum_{i=1}^{k} \sum_{p \in C_i} dist(p, c_i)^2$ [29] is minimized, where p represents a given observation; c_i is the centroid of cluster C_i, and $dist$ is the Euclidean distance. To identify the optimal number of clusters, we employ the elbow method [20], where the goal is to get a small WSS while minimizing k. The K-means clustering is applied to our data points for each value of k starting from one to 100, and the WSS is calculated. The optimal value for k is at the location of the knee which is equal to 11. To achieve the threshold value of λ, first we calculate the average Euclidean distances of all 3-tuple points in each cluster separately to measure the distances between similar functions. Then, according to *Vulnerability Database*, the average of eleven obtained distances is considered as threshold value of $\lambda = 26.45$.

4.2 Branch-Based Detection

In the next stage, BinArm incorporates a branch-based detection to reduce the graph comparison effort during the final detection stage. The idea behind branch-based detector is that similar functions have similar execution paths. In addition, analyzing the execution paths has been used to identify function vulnerabilities as well as stealthy program attacks [50,53].

Weighted Normalized Tree Distance (WNTD). The normalized tree distance (NTD) [57] is proposed for comparing phylogenetic trees with

124   P. Shirani et al.

the same topology and same set of N taxonomic groups, as depicted in
Fig. 4. Consider two trees A and B with the same topology and same
set of taxa denoted by $A = \{a_1, a_2, \ldots, a_N\}$ and $B = \{b_1, b_2, \ldots, b_N\}$,
where N is equal to path lengths. In order to compare trees A and
B, the distance is measured as $NTD = \frac{1}{2}(\sum_{i=1}^{N}|\frac{a_i}{\sum_{j=1}^{N} a_j} - \frac{b_i}{\sum_{j=1}^{N} b_j}|)$ [57],
where a_i and b_i are the lengths of path i from trees A and B,
respectively. Such a dissimilarity metric
scales from 0 (identical trees) to 1 (distinct trees). However, NTD is originally
designed for two trees with the same
topology (the same number of paths).
Additionally, NTD does not consider the
contents of nodes.

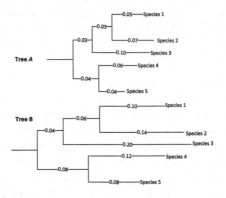

Therefore, we propose a weighted normalized tree distance (WNTD) metric to
measure dissimilarity between two functions W and V. First, we represent the
CFGs as a directed acyclic graph, and
then all possible paths are extracted from
the two CFGs using breadth first search.

Fig. 4. An example of two trees with
the same topology

Based on the contents of basic blocks
along the path and their neighbours, a
weight is calculated (will be discussed later) and assigned to each path. The
dissimilarity between $W = \{w_1, w_2, \ldots, w_N\}$ and $V = \{v_1, v_2, \ldots, v_M\}$ functions, containing N and M ($N \leq M$) number of weights representative of each
path (which is called "weighted paths"), is measured as the following:

$$WNTD = \frac{1}{2}(\sum_{i=1}^{N}|\frac{w_i}{\sum_{j=1}^{N}(w_j)} - \frac{v_{BM}}{\sum_{j=1}^{M}(v_j)}|)$$

where w_i and v_i are the weighted paths in functions W and V, respectively; and
v_{BM} is the best match for weighted path w_i amongst the other weighted paths
in function V as the following:

$$v_{BM} = \begin{cases} excatMatch(w_i, \boldsymbol{V}) & \text{, if there is any exact match} \\ inexactMatch(w_i, \boldsymbol{V}, \delta) & \text{, if there is any inexact match} \leqslant \delta \\ 0 & \text{, else} \end{cases} \quad (1)$$

WNTD considers a weight for each node (basic block) and finally a single
weight for each path of a function. Moreover, even if the two CFGs do not have
the same number of paths, it can still find a match for that path as either the
best match or zero. Once the WNTD comparison is performed, the functions
with a distance less than γ are preserved for the final detection step. Performed
experiments (Sect. 5.7) suggest 50% cut off is the best.

Mnemonic Instructions Grouping. Instruction mnemonics carry information about the semantics of a function, for instance, cryptographic functions perform more logical and mathematical operations compared to a function which opens a file. However, due to different factors, such as compiler effects, various mnemonics might be used interchangeably. Therefore, we identify the list of ARM instruction sets [4], and group them based on their functionality, e.g., arithmetic instructions. As a result, we obtain seventeen groups of mnemonics and then the mutual information (MI) is leveraged to measure the dependency degree between mnemonic group frequencies and functions in our *Vulnerability dataset*. Accordingly, we choose the 7-top-ranked mnemonic groups as the final features to be extracted from each basic block in a path.

Algorithm 1. Weight Assignment	**Algorithm 2.** WNTD
Input: $Path_a$: A path extracted from the CFG. **Output**: w : Branch weight. **Initialization** 1 $f[] \leftarrow 0; nn$ PDF of top-ranked instruction groups; 2 $weights[] \leftarrow 0; nn$ Feature vector of the weights; 3 $w \leftarrow 0; nn$ Initialize the path weight to zero; **begin** 4 　**foreach** $node[i] \in Path_a$ **do** 5 　　$f \leftarrow node[i].getPDF(); U[] \leftarrow 0;$ 　　$J[] \leftarrow f;$ 6 　　**while** *(node[i].hasParents())* **do** 7 　　　$J \leftarrow$ 　　　$J \cap node[i][].getParent().getPDF();$ 8 　　**end** 9 　　**while** *(node[i].hasChildren())* **do** 10 　　　$U \leftarrow$ 　　　$U \cup node[i][].getChild().getPDF();$ 11 　　**end** 12 　　$f \leftarrow J + U; weights[i] \leftarrow TLSH(f);$ 13 　**end** 14 　**foreach** $wt[i] \in weights$ **do** 15 　　$w \leftarrow w + wt[i];$ 16 　**end** 17 　**return** w; 18 **end**	**Input**: $W[]$: Branch weights of function W 　　stored in a linked list. **Input**: $BTree_V$: Branch weights of function 　　V stored in a B$^+$tree. **Output**: $WNTD$: Dissimilary score between 　　functions W and V. 1 **Function** WNTD(W,$BTree_V$) 2 　$sum \leftarrow 0 ; sum_W \leftarrow \sum_{j=1}^{N}(w[j]);$ 3 　$sum_V \leftarrow \sum_{j=1}^{M}(v[j]);$ 4 　**foreach** $w[i] \in W$ **do** 5 　　$v_{BM} = $ exactMatch($BTree_V$, w_i) ; 6 　　**if** v_{BM} != -1 **then** 7 　　　$sum+ = \mid \frac{w[i]}{sum_W} - \frac{v_{BM}}{sum_V} \mid$; ; 　　　$W.remove(w[i]);$ 8 　　**end** 10 　**end** 11 　$v_{BM} \leftarrow 0 ;$ 12 　**foreach** $w[i] \in W$ **do** 13 　　$v_{BM} = $ inexactMatch($BTree_V$, w_i, δ); 14 　　$sum+ = \mid \frac{w[i]}{sum_W} - \frac{v_{BM}}{sum_V} \mid$ 15 　**end** 16 　**return** $WNTD = sum/2$; 17 **end**

Weight Assignments. To condense all the information of a node and its neighbours into a single hash value, a graph kernel with linear time complexity is proposed in [26,30]. Inspired by this approach, we calculate the accumulated weights of each node along the path and assign a single hash value to each path. The weight assigned to each node is calculated based on the top-ranked instruction groups of the node itself and its neighbours (parents and children) that could be out of the current path. For this purpose, we first extract the top-ranked instruction groups and create a feature vector of their probability density function (PDF) for each node and its neighbours. We further distinguish between the in-degrees (parents) and out-degrees (children) by calculating the joint and the union of the PDFs, respectively. Finally, TLSH [42] is applied on the obtained feature vector and a weight is assigned to each node. This process is performed on all the nodes in a given path, and the final weighted path is obtained by the summation of all hash values along the path. The details are presented in Algorithm 1.

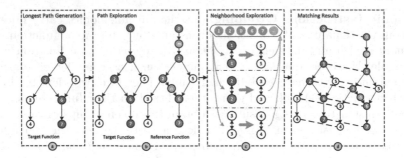

Fig. 5. Fuzzy matching

Finding the Best Match. In order to find the best match for each path, we pre-calculate all the weights of all paths for both reference and target functions foremost, and then store the obtained weighted paths of the larger function V in a B$^+$tree. Afterwards, we perform exact and inexact matching to acquire the best match for weighted paths. First, we search in the B$^+$tree to find the exact match for each weight in function W, and then remove it from the B$^+$tree. Second, we perform inexact matching by considering *backward* and *forward* sibling pointers to each leaf node, which points to the previous and next leaf nodes, respectively. The number of neighbours is obtained by a user-defined distance δ (Eq. 1). If there is not any match for a given path, the best match would be zero. The details of calculating the WNTD is presented in Algorithm 2. The time complexity to find the best match is $O(n \log m)$.

4.3 Fuzzy Matching-Based Detection

The results of the branch-based detection stage, which are a relatively small set of candidate functions, are passed to the final detection stage. In order to compare a given target function with the reference functions in the candidate set, inspired by [31], we perform fuzzy matching on each pair of functions and obtain the similarity score. Functions with the highest similarity scores are returned as the final matching pairs. The details are described in the following.

Path and Neighbourhood Exploration. The fuzzy matching approach is composed of three main phases: (i) longest path extraction; (ii) path exploration; and (iii) neighbourhood exploration, which is illustrated with an example in Fig. 5. First, we unroll all the loops and employ depth first search on the CFG of target function to extract the longest path (as depicted in Fig. 5 part a). A path represents one complete particular execution, where its functionality is the result of executing all its basic blocks. Therefore, retrieving two equivalent paths is an initiation to further match their nodes. The longer the path is, the more matching pairs would be acquired.

Second, the reference function is explored to find the best match for the longest path in the target function. Inspired by [31,38], a breadth-first search combined with longest common subsequence (LCS) method of dynamic programming [16] is executed. In order to satisfy the requirements of the LCS algorithm, since any path is a sequence of basic blocks, each basic block is treated as a letter. Two basic blocks are compared based on their instructions, and a similarity score (which will be discussed later) is returned. Therefore, all the possible paths in the reference function are explored and the one with the highest similarity score is returned as the best matched path (including basic blocks pairs) [31]. Additionally, we put all the obtained matching basic blocks pairs in a priority queue. As an example, the best match for the given longest path with a reference function is highlighted in Fig. 5 part b.

Finally, we further perform neighbourhood exploration and leverage Hungarian algorithm in both the target and reference functions to improve and extend the mapping. Since all the mapping basic block pairs are obtained as the result of path exploration, we explore the neighbours of the most similar basic block pairs (priority queue shown in Fig. 5 part c) to initiate the search and find more matched pairs for their successors and predecessors by considering the in-degrees and out-degrees and leveraging Hungarian algorithm. If there is a new match, we put the paired match in the priority queue to explore their neighbours later on. We continue the same algorithm for the rest of nodes until the priority queue is empty. The outcome of neighbourhood exploration is the basic block matching pairs in the control flow graph (Fig. 5 part d) and the corresponding similarity scores. To obtain the final similarity score between the f_T and f_r functions with n_T and n_r number of basic blocks, respectively, we apply the following formula:

$$similarity\ (f_T, f_r) = \frac{2 \times \sum_{i=1}^{k} WJ(S,T)}{n_T + n_r} \tag{2}$$

where k is the number of matched basic blocks between functions f_T and f_r, and $WJ(S,T)$ returns the similarity score between the matching basic block pairs. Moreover, BinArm provides all the differences between two functions at instruction level, basic blocks level and function level.

Basic Block Matching. For basic block matching, we could adopt the LCS method of dynamic programming on the instructions of two basic blocks as in [31]. However, the accuracy of this approach might be affected by *instruction reordering* and *instruction substitutions* [31]. Moreover, the time complexity of the LCS algorithm is $O(mn)$, where m and n represent the number of instructions in the two basic blocks. Consequently, to accurately and efficiently perform basic block matching, we use the weighted Jaccard similarity [32] between the two basic blocks. Let two sets of S and T contain the mnemonic frequencies of the two basic blocks, with n and m number of elements in each blocks. The weighted Jaccard similarity (WJ) between the two vectors is calculated as follows:

$$WJ(S,T) = \frac{\sum_{k=1}^{N} \min(S_k \cap T_k)}{\sum_{k=1}^{N} \max(S_k \cup T_k)}, \ N = \max\{m,n\}$$

The usage of WJ similarity together with instruction grouping could over-come *instruction reordering* and some *instruction substitutions*. Moreover, the time complexity of the WJ similarity is of order $O(N)$.

5   Evaluation

This section details our experiments and analysis.

5.1   Experimental Setup

All of our experiments are conducted on machines running Windows 7 and Ubuntu 15.04 with Intel Xenon $E5$ 2.4 GHz CPU and 16 GB RAM. BINARM is written in C++ and utilizes a *Cassandra* database to store all the functions along with their features. *Vagrant* is used to create a specialized environment used for firmware reverse engineering as well as library cross compilation for the *ARM* architecture. The utilized cross compiler is *gcc-arm-linux-gnueabi* version 4.7.3 using the debug flag, the static flag , and all compatible optimization flags (*O0-O3*). The symbol names are preserved during the compilation process for metric validation. A custom python script is used in tandem with IDA PRO to extract function CFGs in the desired JSON format. *Docker* is used to create a containerized version of the CVE database and its associated search tools.

Dataset. The experiments are performed on different datasets, which are explic-itly indicated in each section. In order to evaluate the scalability of BINARM, a large quantity of IED and non-IED firmware images are collected from the wild, 5, 756 of which were successfully disassembled to construct our *General Dataset*.

Evaluation Metrics. To evaluate the accuracy of BINARM, we use the total accuracy $TA = \frac{TP+TN}{TP+TN+FP+FN}$ measure, where TP is the number of relevant functions retrieved correctly; FP represents the number of irrelevant functions that are incorrectly detected; and FN indicates the number of relevant functions that are not detected, and TN is the number of not-detected irrelevant functions.

Time Measurement. The execution time for function indexing is measured by adding the time required for each step, including feature extraction and func-tion indexing. The search time includes time required for feature extraction and function discovery. The time taken to disassemble the binaries using IDA PRO is excluded, where it takes on the order of seconds on average to disassemble a binary file and can be distributed over all functions in a binary file.

5.2   Function Identification Accuracy

We evaluate the accuracy of BINARM by examining a randomly selected set of binaries from our *Vulnerability Database*, where the source code and the symbol names are provided in order to validate the results. We randomly select 10% of libraries from *Vulnerability Database* as targets, and match them against the remaining 90% of libraries in our repository. We repeat this process various times. The average accuracy results are summarized in Table 4. As can be seen, the average of total accuracy is 0.92. According to our experiments, the results are affected due to different versions and the degree of changes in the new versions. Since the libraries are randomly selected, in some cases the differences between versions are relatively high that cause a drop in the accuracy.

Table 4. Average accuracy results

Project	glibc	libcurl	libxml2	lighttpd	ntp	openssh	openssl	postgresql	zlib	Average
Total accuracy	0.96	0.93	0.89	0.92	0.87	0.89	0.93	0.98	0.89	0.92

5.3   Efficiency

In this section, we conduct experiments to measure the efficiency of BINARM for function matching. To this end, we test the 5, 103 vulnerable functions against all functions in our *Vulnerability Database* and Netgear ReadyNAS v6.1.6 firmware separately, and measure the search time for each function.

Table 5. Baseline comparison on indexing time of `ReadyNAS v6.1.6`

	MULTI-MH [44]	GENIUS [25]	BINARM	DISCOVRE [23]
Time (minutes)	5,475	89.7	78.65	54.1
Hardware specification	Intel Core $i7 - 2640M$ at 2.8 GHz 8 GB DDR3-RAM	24 Cores at 2.8 GHz 65 GB RAM	Intel Xenon $E5 - 2630v3$ at 2.4 GHz 16 GB RAM	Intel Core $i7 - 2720QM$ at 2.20 GHz 8 GB DDR3 RAM

The obtained results are reported in Fig. 6, where the x-axis represents the percentage of number of functions, and the y-axis shows the cumulative distribution function (CDFs) of search time. The average searching time per function for each scenario are 0.01 s and 0.008 s, respectively. Note that the search time of BINARM is firmly related to the CFG complexity of target function. If the target function has a large value of

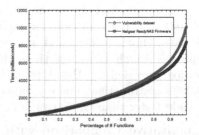

Fig. 6. CDF of vulnerable function search time

`graph_energy`, the search time would be higher. However, search time of a small function against a very complex CFG would not be costly, since the complex functions are deemed dissimilar in the shape-based detection stage and filtered out, and no heavy graph matching would be performed.

5.4 Comparison

Indexing Time Comparison. In order to compare the indexing time of BIN-ARM with the state-of-the-art DISCOVRE [23], GENIUS [25], and MULTI-MH [44] approaches, we choose the Netgear ReadyNAS v6.1.6 [9] firmware image. The reasons of this choice are threefold: (i) the firmware is publicly available and is based on the ARM architecture; (ii) all the aforesaid works have measured the indexing time of Netgear ReadyNAS based on their techniques; and (iii) the hardware specifications of the machines of conducted experiments are provided. Altogether these facilitate comparison. We index ReadyNAS in our database and record the indexing time. Table 5 illustrates the preparation time along with the hardware specifications that are reported by the aforementioned approaches, as well as those of BINARM. As taking machines computational capacity into account, BINARM is more efficient with respect to indexing time when compared to aforesaid approaches with the exception of DISCOVRE. The reason is that DIS-COVRE only considers CFG extraction time, while BINARM extracts additional features, such as the weighted paths. Nevertheless, the evaluation performed by [25] demonstrate DISCOVRE's inaccuracy in large scale setup.

Search Time Comparison. We further compare the search time of our prototype system with that of BINSEQUENCE [31]. The reason for this comparison is to verify the efficiency of the first two stages of detection prior to the third stage of fuzzy matching, as BINSEQUENCE employs fuzzy matching approach after a pre-filtering process. In this experiment, we compare three different versions of `zlib` library (v1.2.5, v1.2.6, v1.2.7) with their next version using BINARM with the same setup performed in BINSEQUENCE. For instance, we test `zlib` v1.2.5 against its successive version `zlib` v1.2.6 together with two million noise functions in the database. We collect the search time for each scenario, and obtain the average time of 0.0002 s per function as reported in Table 6. On the other hand, the average of optimal search times for these three scenarios provided by BINSEQUENCE [31] is

Table 6. Baseline comparison on search time (seconds) per function

zlib Version	BINARM	BINSEQUENCE [31]
1.2.5	0.00057	0.897
1.2.6	0.00016	0.913
1.2.7	0.00009	0.918
Average	0.00027	0.909

0.909 s per function. These results confirm that BINARM is three orders of magnitude faster than BINSEQUENCE.

Qualitative Comparison with GEMINI. GEMINI [54] is one of the latest iterations in code similarity detection in binaries, which extracts attributed control flow graphs and feeds them into a siamese neural network. Since the tool is not publicly available in order to perform a direct comparison, a qualitative comparison is performed as follows. (i) The required training time of Gemini, which is performed on a powerful server with two CPUs and one GPU card, is significant compared to BinArm. (ii) The time required to constantly retrain the neural network and re-generate the embeddings is a major disadvantage in a real-world scenario. As such, BinArm greatly outperforms Gemini with respect to the indexing of new vulnerable functions. (iii) Gemini has a total of 154 vulnerable functions and presents a use case that employs two of them. In contrast, BinArm's *Vulnerability Database* contains 235 vulnerable functions, all of which are used for vulnerability identification. (iv) Gemini solely relies on a few basic features and the use of a siamese neural network to perform the comparison. Such feature choices are reflected through the reported vulnerability identification accuracy of about 82% [54], whereas BinArm's much richer collection of features and the rigorous feature selection process help to obtain a 92% accuracy. This is partially due to the fact that BinArm takes into account a much broader scope of information relative to a given function.

5.5   Detecting Vulnerabilities in Real Firmware

In this section, we demonstrate BinArm's capability to facilitate the vulnerability identification process in real-world IED firmware. We randomly select five firmware images from our *Firmware Database* and compare them to all vulnerable functions in our *Vulnerability Database*. Each resulting function pair is ranked by similarity score. We consider a candidate as a potential match, if the matching score is higher than 80%. We successfully identify 93 potential CVEs, the majority of which are confirmed by our manual analysis.

Table 7. Identifying CVEs in real-world firmware images

Firmware	CVE	Score	Firmware	CVE	Score
NI PMU1_0_11	CVE-2016-6303	1.00	Schneider Link150	CVE-2015-0208	0.68
	CVE-2014-8176	1.00	Schneider M251	CVE-2014-2669	0.65
	CVE-2014-6040	0.92	ReadyNAS v6.1.6	CVE-2015-7497	0.98
	CVE-2016-7167	0.91		CVE-2014-2669	0.97
	CVE-2015-0288	0.91		CVE-2015-7941	0.95
Honeywell.RTUR150	CVE-2016-0701	1.00		CVE-2014-6040	0.93
	CVE-2016-2105	0.99		CVE-2010-1633	0.93
	CVE-2010-1633	0.94		CVE-2014-0160	0.92
	CVE-2016-6303	0.94		CVE-2015-0288	0.91
	CVE-2015-0287	0.92		CVE-2014-3566	0.76

Due to lack of space, a subset of obtained results are presented in Table 7. As shown, BinArm is able to successfully identify different vulnerabilities in the NI PMU1_0_11, Honeywell.RTUR150, and Ready-NAS v6.1.6 firmware images. For instance, a critical heap-based buffer overflow vulnerability (CVE-2016-7167) with 0.91 similarity score is identified in NI PMU1_0_11 firmware. The obtained matching results

of vulnerable function X509_to_
X509_REQ (CVE-2015-0288) in
NI PMU1_0_11 firmware are
depicted in Fig. 7, which illustrates BINARM's capability
for providing in-depth mapping
results for the verification purposes. Additionally, our experiments demonstrate that BIN-
ARM can identify CVE-2014-
0160 (Heartbleed vulnerability) and CVE-2014-3566 (POO-
DLE vulnerability) in Ready-
NAS firmware (as also demonstrated by the state-of-the-art

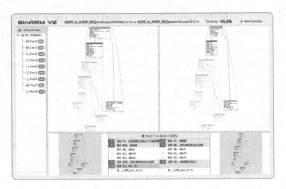

Fig. 7. A snapshot of BINARM's in-depth results
for bug search in NI PMU1_0_11 firmware

approaches [23, 25]) in less than 0.5 ms. The results confirm the capability of
BINARM to be applied in real-world scenarios in order to perform vulnerability
analysis on the IED firmware embedded in the smart grid.

5.6   Impact of Multiple Detection Stages

In order to study the impact of proposed multi-stage detection engine,
we employ four experiments by
enabling and disabling shape-based
and branch-based detectors (we
always keep the fuzzy matching-
based detector enabled), and mea-

Table 8. Impact of detection stages

Shape-based	Branch-based	Accuracy	Time (s)
True	True	0.929	626.72
True	False	0.928	3649.80
False	True	0.925	44823.34
False	False	0.924	50671.66

Note: The Fuzzy-based detector is always enabled.

sure both the accuracy and efficiency of BINARM on *Vulnerability Database*. To
this end, we perform the tests on randomly selected projects with different versions and optimization settings. As shown in Table 8, the total accuracy remains
the same as it is not affected by any of the prior detection stages. On the other
hand, the proposed multi-stage detection improves the efficiency of BINARM.

5.7   Impact of Parameters

In this subsection, we further study the impact of λ and γ parameters on BIN-
ARM accuracy. We perform experiments by (i) disabling the branch-based detector, and incrementing the value of λ by 5 starting from 5; (ii) disabling the
shape-based detector and incrementing the value of γ by 5 each time, starting
from 25%. We randomly select 10% of libraries from our *Vulnerability Database*
as the test set, and perform the matching against remaining libraries in our
dataset. We repeat this process multiple times and record the accuracy. The
experimental results illustrated in Figs. 8 and 9 demonstrate that the values of
$\lambda = 26.45$ and $\gamma = 50\%$ return the highest accuracy among other values.

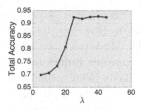

Fig. 8. Impact of λ

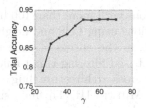

Fig. 9. Impact of γ

5.8 Scalability Study

We further investigate the time required for both indexing and retrieving matched functions to demonstrate BINARM capability to handle firmware analysis at a large scale. To this end, we randomly index one million functions from *General Dataset*, and collect the indexing time per function. Figure 10 depicts the CDF of the preparation time for the randomly selected functions, and most of the functions are indexed in less than 0.1 s, where the median indexing time is 0.008 s, and it takes 0.02 s on average to index a function.

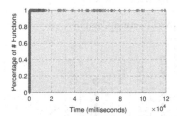

Fig. 10. CDF of indexing time

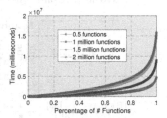

Fig. 11. CDF of search time

Moreover, we perform several scalability benchmarks, each utilizes a randomly selected set of 10,000 target functions. For each evaluation, we employ a randomly selected set of reference functions, where its size increases in increments of 0.5 up to 2 million, as plotted in Fig. 11.

6 Related Work

We briefly describe most recent existing works to identify known vulnerable functions in program binaries. BINDIFF [21] performs graph isomorphism on function pairs of two binaries in the cross architecture setting. However, it is not designed to be applied on large scale datasets. RENDEZVOUS [33] performs function matching based on different features. Nevertheless, it is sensitive to structural changes and instruction reordering. TRACY [18] employs LCS algorithm to align two tracelets obtained from decomposed CFGs. However, this approach is suitable for functions with more than 100 basic blocks [18]. BINSEQUENCE [31] compares two functions using LCS and neighbourhood exploration. However, its accuracy drops due to the effects of code transformation [31]. Moreover, the proposed MinHash-based filtering is not efficient for large and complex functions.

Some cross-architecture bug search approaches have been proposed. For instance, MULTI-MH [44] finds similar code by capturing the input and output variables at basic block level. However, finding semantic similarities is performed by MinHash, which is slow to be applicable to large code base. DISCOVRE [23] applies maximum common subgraph isomorphism for function matching, whereas the utilized pre-filtering to speed up the subgraph isomorphism causes significant reduction in accuracy [25]. GENIUS [25] generates attributed control flow graphs, where each basic block is labelled with statistical and structural features, and then converts them into embeddings using LSH. However, graph embedding and distance matrix is expensive [54], and changes in the CFG structure affect its accuracy [25]. Most recently, a neural network-based approach called GEMINI [54] computes numeric vectors based on the CFGs and addresses the efficiency issue of GENIUS. We compare BINARM with the aforementioned proposals in Table 9.

Table 9. Comparing existing solutions with BINARM

PROPOSALS	Feature				Feature Level			Architecture			Compiler			
	Syntactic	Semantic	Structural	Statistical	Instruction	Basic Block	Function	x86-64	ARM	MIPS	VS	GCC	ICC	Clang
BINDIFF [21]		•	•			•	•	•			•	•		
RENDEZVOUS [33]	•	•	•		•		•	•				•		
TRACY [18]		•	•			•	•	•				•		
BINSEQUENCE [31]	•	•	•		•	•	•	•				•		
MULTI-MH [44]		•				•		•	•	•		•		•
DISCOVRE [23]			•	•	•	•		•	•	•	•	•		
GENIUS [25]			•	•	•	•		•	•	•		•		•
BINSHAPE [48]	•	•	•	•			•	•			•	•		
GEMINI [54]			•	•	•	•		•	•	•		•		•
BinArm	•	•	•	•	•	•	•		•			•		

Note: Symbol (•) indicates that system supports the corresponding feature, otherwise it is empty.

All of the aforesaid approaches employ static analysis, while some dynamic analysis techniques have been proposed. For instance, BLEX [22] executes functions for several calling contexts and deems functions with the same side effects as similar. However, dynamic analysis approaches are often computationally expensive, and are difficult for firmware images [23].

7   Conclusion

In this paper, we presented BINARM, a scalable and efficient vulnerability detection technique for smart grid IED firmware. We proposed two substantial databases of smart grid firmware and relevant vulnerabilities. We then introduced a multi-stage detection engine that leveraged this data and identified vulnerable functions in IED firmware accurately and efficiently. This was further ramified by its evaluation on real-world IED firmware images which resulted in the identification of 93 potentially vulnerable functions. However, BinArm has the following limitations: (i) We do not currently support function inlining. However, this problem can be circumvented by leveraging data flow analysis. (ii) Our system deals only with the ARM architecture, since most of IEDs firmware leverage these processors. An intermediate representation could be utilized to support multiple architectures. (iii) We do not consider type inference in our features, which is important to mitigate some types of vulnerabilities [12,52]. (iv) The proposed detection approach fails to detect runtime data-oriented exploits, due to the lack of runtime execution semantics checking [15]. Proposing a hybrid approach including dynamic analysis could overcomes this limitation.

Acknowledgement. We would like to thank our shepherd, Dr. Yan Shoshitaishvili, and the anonymous reviewers for the invaluable comments. This research is the result of a fruitful collaboration between members of the Security Research Centre (SRC) of Concordia University, Hydro-Québec, and Thales Canada under the *NSERC/Hydro-Québec/Thales Senior Industrial Research Chair in Smart Grid Security: Detection, Prevention, Mitigation and Recovery from Cyber-Physical Attacks.*

References

1. IEC 61850 - Communication Networks and Systems for Power Utility Automation. https://webstore.iec.ch/publication/6028. Accessed 2018
2. WIN32/INDUSTROYER: A New Threat for Industrial Control Systems. https://www.welivesecurity.com/wp-content/uploads/2017/06/Win32_Industroyer.pdf
3. NIST/SEMATECH e-Handbook of Statistical Methods (2015). http://www.itl.nist.gov/div898/handbook/
4. ARM Instruction Reference (2017). http://infocenter.arm.com/help/index.jsp?topic=/com.arm.doc.dui0068b/CIHEDHIF.html
5. Common Vulnerabilities and Exposures (2017). https://nvd.nist.gov/
6. ICS-CERT: Critical Infrastructure Sectors (2017). https://www.dhs.gov/critical-infrastructure-sectors
7. IDA Pro (2017). https://www.hex-rays.com/products/ida/
8. NI   PMU1_0_11.lvappimg   (2017).   http://digital.ni.com/public.nsf/allkb/5391E8424944D0BC86257E45000B025C
9. ReadyNAS Firmware Image v6.1.6 (2017). http://www.downloads.netgear.com/files/GDC/READYNAS-100/ReadyNASOS-6.1.6-arm.zip
10. Security Intelligence (2017). https://securityintelligence.com/attacks-targeting-industrial-control-systems-ics-up-110-percent/
11. Alrabaee, S., Shirani, P., Wang, L., Debbabi, M.: FOSSIL: a resilient and efficient system for identifying FOSS functions in malware binaries. ACM Trans. Priv. Secur. (TOPS) **21**(2), 8 (2018)
12. Caballero, J., Lin, Z.: Type inference on executables. ACM Comput. Surv. (CSUR) **48**(4), 65 (2016)

13. Chen, B., Dong, X., Bai, G., Jauhar, S., Cheng, Y.: Secure and efficient software-based attestation for industrial control devices with arm processors. In: ACSAC (2017)
14. Chen, D.D., Egele, M., Woo, M., Brumley, D.: Towards automated dynamic analysis for Linux-based embedded firmware. In: NDSS (2016)
15. Cheng, L., Tian, K., Yao, D.D.: Orpheus: enforcing cyber-physical execution semantics to defend against data-oriented attacks (2017)
16. Cormen, T.H.: Introduction to Algorithms. MIT Press, Cambridge (2009)
17. Costin, A., Zaddach, J., Francillon, A., Balzarotti, D., Antipolis, S.: A large-scale analysis of the security of embedded firmwares. In: USENIX Security (2014)
18. David, Y., Yahav, E.: Tracelet-based code search in executables. In: ACM SIGPLAN Notices, vol. 49, pp. 349–360. ACM (2014)
19. Davidson, D., Moench, B., Ristenpart, T., Jha, S.: FIE on firmware: finding vulnerabilities in embedded systems using symbolic execution. In: USENIX, Security, pp. 463–478 (2013)
20. Dimitriadou, E., Dolničar, S., Weingessel, A.: An examination of indexes for determining the number of clusters in binary data sets. Psychometrika **67**(1), 137–159 (2002)
21. Dullien, T., Rolles, R.: Graph-based comparison of executable objects (English version). SSTIC **5**, 1–3 (2005)
22. Egele, M., Woo, M., Chapman, P., Brumley, D.: Blanket execution: dynamic similarity testing for program binaries and components. In: Usenix, Security, pp. 303–317 (2014)
23. Eschweiler, S., Yakdan, K., Gerhards-Padilla, E.: discovRe: Efficient cross-architecture identification of bugs in binary code. In: NDSS (2016)
24. Falliere, N., Murchu, L.O., Chien, E.: W32. stuxnet dossier. White paper, vol. 5, p. 6. Symantec Corp., Security Response (2011)
25. Feng, Q., Zhou, R., Xu, C., Cheng, Y., Testa, B., Yin, H.: Scalable graph-based bug search for firmware images. In: CCS. ACM (2016)
26. Gascon, H., Yamaguchi, F., Arp, D., Rieck, K.: Structural detection of android malware using embedded call graphs. In: AISEC. ACM (2013)
27. Griffin, C.: Graph theory: Penn state math 485 lecture notes (2011–2012). http://www.personal.psu.edu/cxg286/Math485.pdf
28. Groarke, D.G.R.: The Networked Grid 150: The End-to-end Smart Grid Vendor Ecosystem Report and Rankings (2013). https://www.greentechmedia.com/research/report/the-networked-grid-150-report-and-rankings-2013
29. Han, J., Pei, J., Kamber, M.: Data Mining: Concepts and Techniques. Elsevier, New York (2011)
30. Hido, S., Kashima, H.: A linear-time graph kernel. In: ICDM (2009)
31. Huang, H., Youssef, A.M., Debbabi, M.: BinSequence: fast, accurate and scalable binary code reuse detection. In: ASIACCS. ACM (2017)
32. Ioffe, S.: Improved consistent sampling, weighted minhash and l1 sketching. In: ICDM (2010)
33. Khoo, W.M., Mycroft, A., Anderson, R.: Rendezvous: a search engine for binary code. In: MSR (2013)
34. Kruegel, C., Robertson, W., Valeur, F., Vigna, G.: Static disassembly of obfuscated binaries. In: USENIX Security (2004)
35. Kwon, Y., Kim, H.K., Koumadi, K.M., Lim, Y.H., Lim, J.I.: Automated vulnerability analysis technique for smart grid infrastructure. In: ISGT 2017 (2017)
36. Langner, R.: Stuxnet: dissecting a cyberwarfare weapon. In: IEEE SP (2011)

37. Liu, M., Zhang, Y., Li, J., Shu, J., Gu, D.: Security analysis of vendor customized code in firmware of embedded device. In: SecureComm (2016)
38. Luo, L., Ming, J., Wu, D., Liu, P., Zhu, S.: Semantics-based obfuscation-resilient binary code similarity comparison with applications to software plagiarism detection. In: ACM SIGSOFT (2014)
39. Mackiewicz, R.: Overview of IEC 61850 and benefits. In: PSCE (2006)
40. Nazario, J.: Blackenergy DDOS bot analysis. Arbor Networks (2007)
41. Neichin, G., Cheng, D., Haji, S., Gould, J., Mukerji, D., Hague, D.: 2010 US Smart Grid Vendor Ecosystem (2010)
42. Oliver, J., Cheng, C., Chen, Y.: TLSH-a locality sensitive hash. In: CTC (2013)
43. Peng, H., Long, F., Ding, C.: Feature selection based on mutual information criteria of max-dependency, max-relevance, and min-redundancy. IEEE TPAMI **27**, 1226–1238 (2005)
44. Pewny, J., Garmany, B., Gawlik, R., Rossow, C., Holz, T.: Cross-architecture bug search in binary executables. In: IEEE SP (2015)
45. Rad, B.B., Masrom, M., Ibrahim, S.: Opcodes histogram for classifying metamorphic portable executables malware. In: ICEEE (2012)
46. Rieck, K., Holz, T., Willems, C., Düssel, P., Laskov, P.: Learning and classification of malware behavior. In: DIMVA (2008)
47. Series, I.: Business blackout. https://www.lloyds.com/~/media/files/news-and-insight/risk-insight/2015/business-blackout/business-blackout20150708.pdf
48. Shirani, P., Wang, L., Debbabi, M.: BinShape: scalable and robust binary library function identification using function shape. In: DIMVA (2017)
49. Shoshitaishvili, Y., Wang, R., Hauser, C., Kruegel, C., Vigna, G.: Firmalice-automatic detection of authentication bypass vulnerabilities in binary firmware. In: NDSS (2015)
50. Shu, X., Yao, D., Ramakrishnan, N.: Unearthing stealthy program attacks buried in extremely long execution paths. In: CCS. ACM (2015)
51. Shwartz, O., Mathov, Y., Bohadana, M., Elovici, Y., Oren, Y.: Opening Pandora's box: effective techniques for reverse engineering IoT devices. In: Eisenbarth, T., Teglia, Y. (eds.) CARDIS 2017. LNCS, vol. 10728, pp. 1–21. Springer, Cham (2018). https://doi.org/10.1007/978-3-319-75208-2_1
52. Slowinska, A., Stancescu, T., Bos, H.: Body armor for binaries: preventing buffer overflows without recompilation. In: USENIX Annual Technical Conference, pp. 125–137 (2012)
53. Wang, T., Wei, T., Lin, Z., Zou, W.: Intscope: automatically detecting integer overflow vulnerability in x86 binary using symbolic execution. In: NDSS (2009)
54. Xu, X., Liu, C., Feng, Q., Yin, H., Song, L., Song, D.: Neural network-based graph embedding for cross-platform binary code similarity detection. In: Proceedings of the 2017 ACM SIGSAC Conference on Computer and Communications Security, pp. 363–376. ACM (2017)
55. Zaddach, J., Bruno, L., Francillon, A., Balzarotti, D.: AVATAR: a framework to support dynamic security analysis of embedded systems' firmwares. In: NDSS (2014)
56. Zaddach, J., Costin, A.: Embedded devices security and firmware reverse engineering. Black-Hat USA (2013)

57. Zheng, Y., Ott, W., Gupta, C., Graur, D.: A scale-free method for testing the proportionality of branch lengths between two phylogenetic trees. arXiv preprint arXiv:1503.04120 (2015)
58. Zhu, R., Zhang, B., Mao, J., Zhang, Q., Tan, Y.-A.: A methodology for determining the image base of arm-based industrial control system firmware. Int. J. Crit. Infrastruct. Prot. **16**, 26–35 (2017)

Attacks

Update State Tampering: A Novel Adversary Post-compromise Technique on Cyber Threats

Sung-Jin Kim[1]([✉]), Byung-Joon Kim[1], Hyoung-Chun Kim[1],
and Dong Hoon Lee[2]

[1] National Security Research Institute of South Korea,
P.O.Box 1, Yuseong, Daejeon, Republic of Korea
{ksj1230, bjkim, khche}@nsr.re.kr
[2] Graduate School of Information Security, Korea University,
Seoul, Republic of Korea
donghlee@korea.ac.kr

Abstract. With modern cyber threats, attackers should gain persistency in target systems to achieve attack objectives. Once an attacker's zero-day vulnerabilities on target systems are patched, the attacker may lose control over the system. However, systems remain vulnerable when an attacker manipulates the component resources on a Windows system. We found methods to generate invisible vulnerabilities on a victim's system. Our findings are as follows: first, we found ways to replace a component to an old vulnerable version while maintaining the current update records; second, we found that the Windows system does not recognize the replaced components. We define the first issue as a package-component mismatch and the second issue as a blind spot issue on the Windows update management. They have been identified on all version of Vista and later, including desktop platforms and server platforms. Based on our findings, we reveal an Update State Tampering technique that can generate invisible security holes on target systems. We also offer corresponding countermeasures to detect and correct package-component mismatches. In this paper, we introduce the problems with the current Windows update management mechanism, the Update State Tampering technique from the attacker's point of view, and an Update State Check scheme that detects and recovers the package-component mismatches. We stress that our proposed Update State Check scheme should be deployed immediately in order to mitigate large-scale exploitation of the proposed technique.

Keywords: Post-compromise · Windows update · Cyber threat

1 Introduction

In modern cyber threats [3–5], the post-compromise phase [1, 2, 6] comes after the exploitation of a victim's system. During this phase, an attacker should gain persistency on target systems while maintaining stealth. The ATT&CK matrix [7] provided by MITRE introduces 38 persistence techniques and 40 defense evasion techniques that were used in various APT attack campaigns during the post-compromise phase. As a persistence tactic, an attacker can use the "Accessibility Features" technique [8] to

© Springer International Publishing AG, part of Springer Nature 2018
C. Giuffrida et al. (Eds.): DIMVA 2018, LNCS 10885, pp. 141–161, 2018.
https://doi.org/10.1007/978-3-319-93411-2_7

launch a malicious program before a user logs in. For example, by modifying a specific registry key, an attacker can allow a debugger program to be executed with SYSTEM privileges at the login screen [9]. As a defense evasion tactic, APT attack campaigns can use the "Modify Registry" technique [10] to hide information within registry keys or to neutralize the UAC. For example, Regin [11] hides malware payloads in the registry. CHOPSTICK [12], used by APT28, stores the configuration block in the registry with RC4 encryption. And Shamoon [13] changes a specific registry value to disable remote restrictions on target systems. These persistence techniques reveal to attackers that can be used against targets even after system updates and reboots. Except for some rootkit attacks, such as hooking or bootkit, these techniques fall into the categories of misconfiguration or abuse.

We present a novel post-compromise technique that exploits the structural problems of the Windows update management mechanism that are not yet known. We modify registry values related to component resources and the pending.xml file to replace target components with old vulnerable versions. Consequently, the known vulnerabilities of those components can be revived. Moreover, the target system's defense mechanisms cannot detect the revived vulnerabilities. Ultimately, our technique allows an attacker to exploit hidden vulnerabilities, even when the target system is fully patched and the attacker's initial vulnerability is removed.

Package-Component Mismatch. In Microsoft Windows, a component is the smallest unit of a software module. When security vulnerabilities are reported, Microsoft deploys update packages that include some higher version components. When users install the update, the Windows Installer saves the new versions of the component in the component store and projects them to the appropriate locations. On the surface, the process appears simple; however, behind the scenes are complicated registry settings that are not well known. We focus on the fact that the Windows update mechanism relies on specific registry settings to determine the current configuration of system components. If an attacker intentionally alters the version names of target components in the registry during the system update, either the target components will be rolled back to the old vulnerable versions, or the system will not update the target components. At this time, the installation history of the update packages remains unchanged. We define this problem as a package-component mismatch. In this paper, we expose three update state tampering methods that cause the package-component mismatches. The identified methods are affected by component dependency issues. We address the issues in Sect. 8.

Blind Spot Issue. To make matters worse, Windows does not provide a means to detect and recover from package-component mismatches. Because the replaced components are normal Windows binaries, they are loaded without any alert to the system. Built-in tools such as the system file checker (SFC) [14] and Windows Update Check [15] cannot verify the package-component mismatches. Further, security compliance tools, such as the Microsoft baseline security analyzer (MBSA) [16], do not check the consistency between update packages and components installed in the system. We call these issue blind spots of the Windows update management mechanism. In this paper, we describe the impact of blind spots on both server platforms and desktop platforms.

Assumptions and Attack Scenario. The proposed technique requires administrator privileges to modify specific component resources. Therefore, an attacker must first exploit a known vulnerability or a zero-day on the target system with local privilege escalation, before using the proposed technique. We also present an attack scenario that re-infects the target system after the attacker's initial exploit has been removed. In our scenario, we assume that only the attacker's initial exploit and its payloads are removed when the target system is restored. This scenario does not include the case where all system components are re-installed in the recovery phase. Moreover, the attacker must be in a position to gain access to vulnerable service ports on the target system for re-infections.

Contributions. The following contributions are made in this paper:

- *Problems in Windows update management*
  To the best of our knowledge, the package-component mismatch and the blind spot issue are the first structural problems with the Windows update management mechanism that have not been reported. We outline the concept of a package-component mismatch and two types of blind spots with Windows update management and reveal the potential threats associated with them. The blind spot issue occurs because Windows neglects consistency between update packages and components installed on the system. These issues affect all server and desktop platforms.
- *Update State Tampering technique*
  We outline three update state tampering methods and a toy example. The toy example describes how an attacker can generate a package-component mismatch on a target system. Finally, we show that the vulnerability lifecycle on a local system can be extended by exploiting the blind spot issue.
- *Countermeasures to eliminate the blind spots*
  The blind spot issue can be resolved by mutually verifying the package information and component information. We could extract package-component mapping information from the registry settings scattered inside a local system. We also propose an Update State Check scheme, which detects and corrects package-component mismatches by using this package-component mapping information.

Outline. The remainder of this paper is structured as follows: In Sect. 2, we introduce background on the Windows update management mechanism. In Sect. 3, we describe the fundamental problems pertaining to the current Windows update management mechanism. In Sect. 4, we reveal an Update State Tampering technique and an attack scenario. In Sect. 5, we measure the impact of the Update State Tampering technique on several different versions of Windows. In Sect. 6, we revisit previous studies to determine whether they can detect tampered components. In Sect. 7, we propose an Update State Check scheme as a countermeasure. Section 8 summarizes features of the Update State Tampering technique and its countermeasures, and Sect. 9 presents our conclusions.

2   Background

In this section, we provide the background on Component-Based Servicing (CBS) [17, 18] and pending file rename operations [19] that govern Windows Update. We then introduce fundamental problems with the current Windows update management mechanism. Details are provided based on Windows 7, 64-bit versions.

Component-Based Servicing. Upon installing an update package, TrustedInstaller. exe, the CBS agent, runs the component copy and registry settings. CBS controls the entire installation and deletion of Windows components. Within a local system, component resources managed by CBS span a vast area. Within this area, we focus on specific component resources to explain the blind spot issue. Each resource notation is as shown in Table 1.

All component files in a local system are hard-linked from the component store (*CS*) to the destination path. For example, the "ntoskrnl.exe" file for the component named "amd64_microsoft-windows-os-kernel_31bf3856ad364e35_6.1.601.17514_no ne_ca56670fcac29ca9" is hard-linked under the system32 folder. Here, P_n contains the installed package names. Each sub-key of P_n designates a package name. For example, the sub key "Package_109_for_KB4012215 ~ 31bf3856ad364e35 ~ amd64 ~ ~ 6. 1.1.2" represents the 109th package included in the rollup security update KB4012215. Likewise, C_n provides the component names that make up the system. For example, the sub key "amd64_microsoft-windows-os-kernel_31bf3856ad364e35_none_2003 e93c9e12938" represents the component name that contains the "ntoskrnl.exe" file. The current component version can be found on the registry value in C_v.

Table 1. Component resources

Resource	Path	Notation
Component store (files)	\Windows\WinSxS\[*Component Name*]\[*File name*]	*CS*
Registry key for package name	HKLM\SOFTWARE\Microsoft\Windows\CurrentVersion \Component based servicing\Packages\[*Package Name*]	P_n
Registry key for component name	HKLM\SOFTWARE\Microsoft\Windows\CurrentVersion \SideBySide\Winners\[*Component Name*]	C_n
Registry value for component version	HKLM\SOFTWARE\Microsoft\Windows\CurrentVersion \SideBySide\Winners\[*Component Name*]\[*Windows Version*]\(default)	C_v

Pending File Rename Operations. After a system shutdown or reboot, the poqexec. exe process performs the component resource replacement. The pending file rename operations place the replacement of the current memory-mapped file to the point after the reboot event. The TrustedInstaller.exe process generates a pending.xml file when installing an update package. The pending.xml file contains essential information for component resource replacement. The tag name refers to the native API, and the ensuing key-value pairs indicate the arguments referenced by the corresponding API. In Table 2, the tag name "HardlinkFile" refers to the NtSetInformationFile function with the FileLinkInformation argument, and the tag name "SetKeyValue" refers to NtSet-ValueKey function. The tags T_f and T_v are performed by the poqexec.exe process. The Windows system considers these sets of operations a transaction. When the execution of the transaction is completed, the installation status of the package is changed from "pending" to "installed".

Table 2. Tags listed in the pending.xml file when replacing a component

Action	Format	Notation
Replace component file	<HardlinkFile source="\SystemRoot\WinSxS\[*Component Name*]\[*File Name*]" destination="\??\C:\[*Destination Pa-th*]\[*File Name*]">	T_f
Replace component version name	<SetKeyValue path="\Registry\Machine\Software \Micro-soft\Windows\Current Version\SideBySide\Winners \[*Component Name*]\[*Windows Version*]" name="" type = "0x00000001" encoding="base64" value="[*base64 encoded Version Name*]">	T_v

3   Windows Update Management Problems

In this section, we present the concept of a package-component mismatch. We also present the blind spot issue whereby the system's defense mechanisms cannot detect a package-component mismatch.

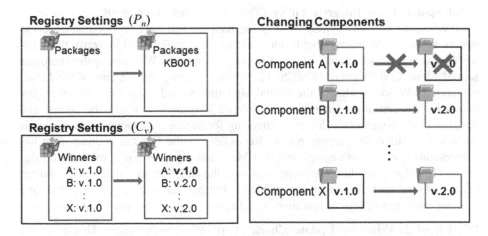

Fig. 1. Simplified illustration of a package-component mismatch

3.1   Package-Component Mismatch

A package-component mismatch refers to a state in which a part of the component is different from the system that is usually updated. The concept of a simple package-component mismatch is illustrated in Fig. 1. It shows the registry and component changes that occur when installing the update KB001, which includes components A through X. When installing KB001, the system adds package information about KB001 to P_n, and the value of C_v is updated from v.1.0 to v.2.0. Ultimately, the poqexec.exe process projects the newer versions from the CS to the destination paths with hardlinks. However, during the update procedure of KB001, if an attacker modifies the pending.xml file to set the destination file name to "A_1.0" in T_f and the component version name to "1.0" in T_v, the poqexec.exe process leaves component A unchanged. The system works fine despite the package-component mismatch. Indeed, package-component mismatches rarely occur in normal update procedures. However, by obtaining access rights to the component resources, an attacker can manipulate package-component information. If the replaced component is an older version of the component that contains a known vulnerability, the problem becomes more severe.

3.2   Blind Spots on Windows Update Management

Can the package-component mismatch be detected or corrected? As we have seen, the logic to diagnose the package-component mismatch does not exist inside Windows. In this paper, we identify this as a blind spot of the Windows update management mechanism. We have discovered two types of blind spots.

- *(Type I)* The system loads the components that do not match the current update state.
- *(Type II)* The system does not provide a means for detecting the package-component mismatch.

Blind Spot 1. Code Integrity Policy (Type I). Kernel components must be trustworthy because they can bypass security mechanisms and have unrestricted access to system resources. Windows applies the code integrity policy [20] to verify the trustworthiness of drivers and applications. For example, a 64-bit Windows system enforces Kernel Mode Code Signing (KMCS) [21] policy. During the loading of the kernel component, Windows checks the digital signature signed with the encryption key issued by the certificate authority. This allows Windows to verify the source and integrity of the component. However, checking for package-component consistency is not a role of the code integrity policy. Regardless of the fact that a component has vulnerabilities, every core component that Microsoft provides has a valid digital signature. Therefore, the old components will pass the code integrity mechanism and get loaded into the system without any problems. Further, the system will not leave any warning messages or logs at that time. We diagnose this as the first blind spot.

Blind Spot 2. Windows Update Check (Type II). The Windows Update Agent checks the status of the update packages installed on the system, sends them to the update server, and receives the update packages. The Windows update check performs the following operations:

1. *Collect package information*
   The Windows update check refers to the registry path P_n to determine the packages installed on the system and the installation status.
2. *Download and install packages*

Based on the information gathered, it identifies the missing updates and downloads the update packages.

From the above operations, the Windows Update Check only references the package information; it does not check the component information. Therefore, even if an attacker changes components and component registry settings, the Windows Update Check cannot detect the package-component mismatch. We diagnose this as the second blind spot.

Blind Spot 3. System file checker (Type II). Windows system administrators can use the "SFC/SCANNOW" command to check for, and repair damaged components. SFC performs the following operations.

1. *Check component information*
   The SFC refers to the registry path C_n and C_v to check a component name and its version name installed on the system.
2. *Verify component damage*
   After confirming the component information, the SFC ensures that the component information obtained from the registry settings matches the component that is hard-linked to the destination path from the CS.
3. *Repairs corrupted components*
   If the SFC detects any corruption, it finds the correct version of the component in the component store, then hard-links and reboots.

From the above operations, the SFC only detects and repairs damage to components; it does not take the installed package history into account. Thus, the SFC cannot play any role in detecting the package-component mismatch. We diagnose this as the third blind spot.

4 Update State Tampering Technique

In this section, we introduce a toy example and three update state tampering methods. In each method, we specify the component resources that an attacker can manipulate to cause a package-component mismatch. The goal of the attack is as follows.

- *Replace current components with previous versions that have vulnerabilities while maintaining the record of updates*

When this goal is achieved, the system is affected by all the vulnerabilities that the replaced component has. Further, the blind spots make it impossible for the system to detect this as an update status abnormality.

4.1 Toy Example of Update State Tampering

We start with a toy example to expose an invisible SMB vulnerability in Windows 10, 64-bit versions. The replaced target components are the srv.sys file and the srv2.sys file with an SMB vulnerability known as Eternal Blue [22]. The proposed example assumes that an attacker has gained Administrator privileges.

Identify the Target Component. Before tampering with the update state, the attacker should ensure that the system has a vulnerable version of the target component. The Windows system leaves the previous version of the component in the *CS* for recovery, rather than removing it. If the target system has not performed a *CS* cleanup, the vulnerable component will be present inside the *CS*. Figure 2 shows the target srv.sys file with the SMB vulnerability under the *CS*. The version name of the vulnerable sys. srv file is "10.0.0.14393.0". Next, we check the value of C_v. Figure 3 shows the current version name of the srv.sys file. To downgrade the current srv.sys file, the attacker replaces the value "10.0.0.14393.953" with "10.0.0.14393.0", and then uses additional methods.

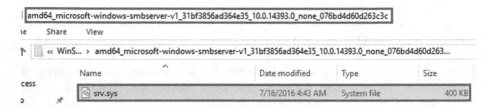

Fig. 2. srv.sys file with Eternal Blue vulnerability

Fig. 3. Current version name of the srv.sys file

Use SFC Tool. The System File Checker (SFC) tool detects and recovers component damage based on the version name recorded in C_v. After replacing the value of C_v, the attacker can execute the "SFC/SCANNOW" command with Administrator privileges. The SFC then creates the pending.xml file that downgrades the version of the srv.sys file according to the value of C_v.

```
zgZhMLLXGwjbVcAd27AAmSH" flags="0x00000080"/>
        <HardlinkFile source="\SystemRoot\WinSxS\amd64
_microsoft-windows-smbserver-v1_31bf3856ad364e35_10.0.14393.0
_none_076bd4d60d263c3c\srv.sys" destination="\??\C:\Windows
\System32\drivers\srv.sys"/>
        <HardlinkFile source="\SystemRoot\WinSxS\amd64
_microsoft-windows-smbserver-v2_31bf3856ad364e35_10.0.14393.0
_none_076bd4d60d263c3c\srv2.sys" destination="\??\C:\Windows
\System32\drivers\srv2.sys"/>
        <SetKeyValue path="\Registry\Machines\Software\Microsoft
\Windows\Current Version\SideBySide\Winners\amd64_microsoft-
windows-smbserver-v2_31bf3856ad364e35_none_9d3efb7f0929174a
```

Fig. 4. Inserted component rollback tasks in the pending.xml file

Tamper at a Single Point. After the pending.xml file is generated, the attacker can register additional component rollback operations in the pending.xml file. Only TrustedInstaller, which is one of the NT service accounts can modify the pending.xml file. Therefore, an attacker who gains Administrator privileges must change file ownership, add file modification rights, and make modifications to the pending.xml file. In this example, we assume that the attacker also downgrades the srv2.sys file. Figure 4 shows an example of additionally registered component rollback tasks in the pending.xml file. In Fig. 4, the attacker adds the tag T_f with the vulnerable component name "amd64 _microsoft-windows-smbserver-v2_31bf3856ad364e35_10.0.14393.0_none_076104e a0d2e582d", and adds the tag T_r with the vulnerable component version "10.0.0.14393.0". Manipulating pending.xml has several advantages for attackers. It eliminates the need to access and change the scattered component resources individually. Instead, the pending.xml file can be manipulated to let the poqexec.exe process execute arbitrary pending jobs. This means that the tampering point can be minimized to a single file.

Reboot System. After the system reboot replaces the components, srv.sys and srv2.sys are properly loaded into the system due to the Blind Spot 1. Because of Blind Spot 2, the Windows update check reports the same result as the update status before the system was compromised. The hidden Eternal Blue vulnerability is now generated. Even if the attacker's initial exploit is removed, the attacker can exploit the remote execution vulnerability in the SMB components to re-compromise the system. In this example, we assume that the target system's SMB service is enabled and that the attacker is in a location accessible to the SMB service port of the target system.

4.2   Update State Tampering Methods

We organized the techniques used in the above toy example by three update state tampering methods.

Method 1. Using SFC to Tamper with the Update State. The SFC detects and recovers corrupted components. However, an attacker can abuse it to tamper with the update state. As stated in Sect. 3.2, the SFC restores components based on the version information listed in the registry value C_v. The procedure of method 1 is as follows.

1. *Change component version information*
   Access registry path C_v, and then change the target version of a component you wish to replace.
2. *Run the "SFC/SCANNOW" command*
   After the command runs, the system will request a reboot to replace the component. At this point, the pending.xml file will contain a tag T_v with the same component version name in C_v.
3. *Reboot the system*
   The pending jobs are executed to replace the component. The Update Check determines that the package installation is complete. SFC determines that there is no damage to the components. By running the SFC command, attackers can tamper with an update state.

Method 2. Leave Components Unchanged. As stated in Sect. 4.1, an attacker who gains administrator privileges can arbitrarily add or remove pending jobs in pending. xml. Assume that the attacker removes certain component replacement jobs from pending.xml during package installation. When this occurs, the component will remain unchanged. The procedure of method 2 is as follows.

1. *Delete the target component replacement tag*
   Delete the target component replacement tag listed in the pending.xml file just before rebooting after installing the package. The tag T_f should be deleted to omit the replacement of system files.
2. *Delete the target registry setting tag*
   Delete the target component replacement tag listed in the pending.xml file just before rebooting after installing the package. The tag T_v of a target component should be deleted to omit the operation of target registry settings.
3. *Reboot the system*
   After the system reboot, target components are not replaced, but package information is normally updated. The Update Check determines that the package installation is complete, and the SFC determines that there is no damage to the components.

   Method 2 is only applicable if the update creates a pending job for component replacement. The pending job is generated only when there are some changes in kernel components.

Method 3. Revert Components to the Past. During the update package installation, additional tags can be inserted into the pending.xml file to replace components. The procedure of method 3 is as follows.

1. *Insert the target component replacement tag*
   Insert the target component replacement tag listed in the pending.xml file just before rebooting. The tag T_f with a target version name should be added to revert a target component to an old vulnerable version.
2. *Insert the target registry setting tag*
   Insert the target component replacement tag listed in the pending.xml file just before rebooting after installing the package. The tag T_v of a target component should be added to revert the target components to the old vulnerable versions.
3. *Reboot the system*
   After the system reboot, the target components are replaced, and the Update Check determines that the package installation is complete. The SFC determines that there is no damage to the components.

   Method 3 is similar to method 2 described above but differs in that it can add component replacement work without limits. When using the methods 2 and 3, the T_f tag that modifies the component file should always be listed together with the T_v tag which changes the version of the associated component.

4.3   Attack Scenario

Based on these update state tampering methods, we introduce an attack scenario.

- Step 1. The attacker uses a zero-day exploit and his malware to launch the first attack on the target system.
- Step 2. One of the update state tampering methods is performed along with the execution of the malware. The replacement target is a previous version of the component that has a remote code execution vulnerability.
- Step 3. The system is patched and the attacker's initial exploit is deleted.
- Step 4. The attacker exploits the hidden remote code execution vulnerability to continue malicious activities.

The attacker compromises the target system once with the zero-day exploit (Step 1). In Step 2, the attacker replaces target components with old vulnerable versions. Unlike with Method 1, which simply runs the SFC after manipulated component resource C_v, Methods 2 and 3 need to wait for the moment the target system is updated. In Step 3, based on the periodic update policy of the target organization, the target system performs an update, and the attacker's initial exploit is removed. In Step 4, the attacker must be in a position to access the vulnerable service port of the target.

4.4   Extending the Life Cycle of a Vulnerability

We here describe the best time to use the Update State Tampering technique in the life cycle of vulnerabilities [23, 24]. Suppose an attacker discovered a new vulnerability, A, created an exploit and malware, and infected the target system for information-stealing purposes. After a certain amount of time, the software vendors distribute patches. The user tries to recover the infected system by removing the malware and updating vulnerable system components. At this point, the system is no longer affected by the attacker's exploit. This procedure is a typical case of following the vulnerability lifecycle.

What if an attacker tampers with the update status before the target system is recovered? After the recovery procedure, the vulnerability and malware will be removed from the system. However, vulnerable components replaced by the identified methods remain intact. The target system is now subject to known vulnerabilities in those components. If the exposed vulnerabilities contain the remote code execution, the attacker can easily re-compromise the target system. Figure 5 shows the life cycle of vulnerabilities extended by the Update State Tampering technique. Typically, the life of Vulnerability A (a 0-day) ends at the patch phase after the discovery-disclosure-exploit phases. However, if an attacker tampers with the update status between the exploit and the patch phases, existing Vulnerabilities B and C can be resurrected, and the target system cannot detect the revived vulnerabilities due to the blind spot issue.

In Fig. 5, Vulnerabilities B and C are resurrected by the Update State Tampering technique and maintained until at least one of following obtains.

1. The next cumulative update replaces the tampered components
2. The operating system of a target host is re-installed
3. The user detects and recovers the tampered components by himself/herself.

If even one of the above conditions is met, Vulnerabilities B and C are removed. Otherwise, they will remain in the system permanently.

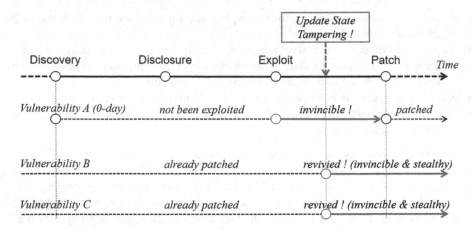

Fig. 5. Illustration of the process of extending a vulnerability life cycle

5   Evaluation

In this section, we evaluate the impact of the identified problems and Update State Tampering methods on different Windows platforms. We applied the latest version of the update to all test platforms in October 2017.

5.1   Impact of the Blind Spots on the Windows Platforms

Since Vista, Windows systems have managed updates based on the CBS. Thus, the presence of blind spots may affect all versions of Windows. Tables 3 and 4 show the Windows versions that are affected by the outlined blind spots.

Table 3. Impact of blind spots on desktop platforms.

Version	Blind spot 1	Blind spot 2	Blind spot 3
Windows 7	O	O	O
Windows 8	O	O	O
Windows 8.1	O	O	O
Windows 10	O	O	O

Table 4. Impact of blind spots on server platforms.

Version	Blind spot 1	Blind spot 2	Blind spot 3
Windows Server 2008	O	O	O
Windows Server 2012	O	O	O
Windows Server 2012 R2	O	O	O
Windows Server 2016	O	O	O

We have confirmed that the blind spots exist not only on desktop platforms but also on server platforms. Therefore, this issue affects enterprise environments as well as desktop users.

5.2   Impact of the Identified Methods on Windows Platforms

Tables 5 and 6 show the Windows versions that are affected by the identified methods. Windows 8.1 and later do not create a pending.xml file when installing an update; therefore, methods 2 and 3 cannot be applied. This is the same in Windows Server 2012 R2 and later versions. However, method 1 is still valid for all versions of Windows.

All the update state tampering methods described above require the administrative privileges. Therefore, it is recommended to use the proposed methods together with known exploits or 0-days. 0-day attacks are one shot only. Once patched, holes are closed. However, the proposed methods can widen the attack choices. Because of the blind spots, the tampered update state cannot be detected or fixed. The exposed vulnerabilities will persist until the next update to the replaced components.

Table 5. Impact of the identified methods on desktop platforms.

Version	Method 1	Method 2	Method 3
Windows 7	O	O	O
Windows 8	O	O	O
Windows 8.1	O	X	X
Windows 10	O	X	X

Table 6. Impact of the identified methods on server platforms.

Version	Method 1	Method 2	Method 3
Windows Server 2008	O	O	O
Windows Server 2012	O	O	O
Windows Server 2012 R2	O	X	X
Windows Server 2016	O	X	X

6   Previous Work

Before introducing measures to solve the blind spot issue, we checked whether previous studies have proposed solutions to this issue.

Microsoft Baseline Security Analyzer (MBSA). MBSA is a free security compliance tool that detects insecure configurations and missing security updates in the system. This tool provides a report of security vulnerabilities and solutions that exist in the system. However, we investigated whether MBSA checks the update state. We used Process Monitor [25] to monitor the behavior of MBSA v.2.3 in Windows 7, 64-bit versions and checked the results. When MBSA begins a scan, it calls the TrustedInstaller.exe process to test the update status and check the package installation status. The registry paths referenced are shown in Table 7. They are the same registry paths that Windows Update Check verifies. Similarly, MBSA does not play any role in detecting package-component mismatches. We tampered with the components according to the toy example in a test VM and then executed MBSA on the system. As a result, the tool does not detect any update status abnormalities.

Table 7. Registry paths frequently referenced by MBSA and MyPCInspector

HKLM\SOFTWARE\Microsoft\Windows\CurrentVersion\Component Based Servicing \Packages\[*Package Name*]
HKLM\SOFTWARE\Microsoft\Windows\CurrentVersion\Component Based Servicing \PackagesPending\[*Package Name*]
HKLM\SOFTWARE\Microsoft\Windows\CurrentVersion\Component Based Servicing \PackageDetect\[*Package Name*]
HKLM\SOFTWARE\Microsoft\Windows\CurrentVersion\Component Based Servicing \ApplicabilityEvaluationCache\[*Package Name*]

MyPCInspector. MyPCInspector [26] is a third-party security compliance tool used by Korean government offices to check the security status of Windows-based PCs. It provides functionality similar to MBSA and examines the security settings and security update status of Windows, as well as the security settings of commonly used third-party applications.

We used the process monitor tool to observe the behavior of MyPCInspector v.3.0 Windows 7, 64-bit versions and checked the results. MyPCInspector calls the TrustedInstaller.exe process to check the update status. The registry paths it references when checking the update status are the same as those in Table 7. Thus, MyPCInspector does not perform any extra work to detect package-component mismatches. We tampered with the components according to the toy example in a test VM and then executed MyPCInspector on the system. As a result, the tool does not detect any update status abnormalities.

Penetration Testing. Unlike the above tools, Metasploit [27] is a type of penetration testing tool. There are also remote vulnerability scanners such as OpenVAS [28], Greenbone [29], Nessus [30], and Nexpose [31]. Performing penetration tests is the most obvious way to verify vulnerabilities in target systems. The scanning result will not be able to determine, whether there is a package-component mismatch. Nevertheless, if, after a scan, the administrator must remove the vulnerability and updates the system, and if the vulnerability still exists, then there will be a more in-depth investigation. Therefore, penetration testing cannot immediately detect package-component mismatches but provides an opportunity to solve the problem.

7 Countermeasures

In this section, we propose the schemes that detect and fix the blind spot issue. The proposed schemes can deal with the blind spot type II.

7.1   Package-Component Mappings

To ensure package-component consistency, knowledge of which component configuration is appropriate for the current update state is crucial. Figure 6 shows the registry paths for package-component mappings, where it can be determined which version of a particular component belongs to which update package. The subkeys of "ComponentDetect" represent component names. The red box to the right lists the version of the component installed by the particular package. For example, the name of the package that installed version 6.1.7200.21980 of the amd64_microsoft-windows-os-kernel is KB3046480.

We can refer to the file information for updates provided by Microsoft. Since October 2016, Windows supports the cumulative update method [32]. Microsoft began to provide file information with the monthly cumulative update. The file information for a cumulative update is in CSV format. It contains the information about files to be updated, versions, and release dates. By collecting that information, we can extract the package-component mapping list.

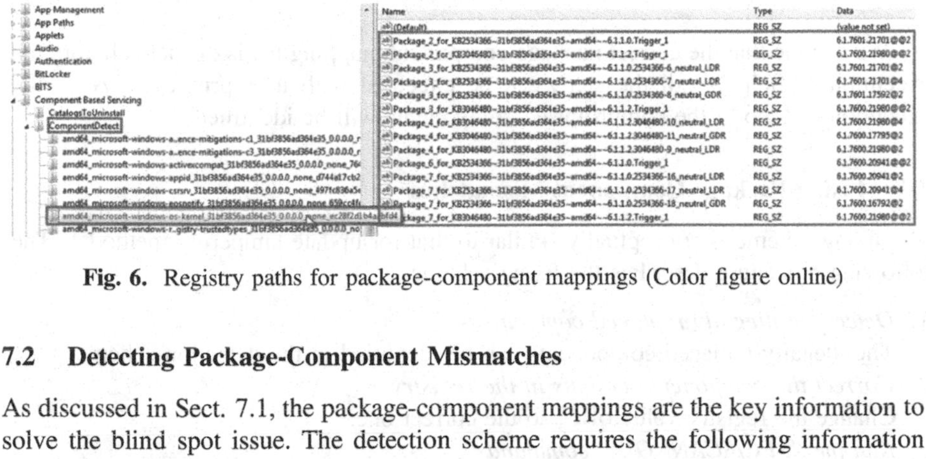

Fig. 6. Registry paths for package-component mappings (Color figure online)

7.2   Detecting Package-Component Mismatches

As discussed in Sect. 7.1, the package-component mappings are the key information to solve the blind spot issue. The detection scheme requires the following information described in Table 8. The following procedure describes the detection scheme.

1. *List the installed packages on the system*
   The package installation information can be found in the registry path P_n. Alternatively, if you run the command "dism/online/get-packages", the servicing agent queries the registry keys and values under the path P_n.
2. *Check the package-component mappings*
   It must be ensured that your system has component configurations that match the installed package. The mapping list introduced in Table 8. provides the answer. If all component configurations match the package-component mapping list, the update status is normal; unmatched items should be considered to have a package-component mismatch.
3. *Verify the hardlink information of components*

Finally, the hardlink information for each component needs to be verified. The "fsutil hardlink list [component file path]" command tells us the hardlink information. If the hardlink sources in the component store have the correct versions of the target components, the update status is normal. Otherwise, the update status has been compromised.

Table 8. Preparations for a detection scheme.

Item	Description
List of package-component mapping	• Information about which package contain which components • A record in the list comprises a package name, a component name, and a component version name. (For example, {KB001, Component_A, 1.0})
Package information	• Information of the components that make up the system (including component names and component versions)
Component information	• Information about all update packages installed on the system (including package names)

We assume that the correct package-component mapping list is extracted before the execution of Step 2. All the steps can be executed with user privileges. After the execution of Step 3, the compromised components will be identified.

7.3 Fixing Package-Component Mismatches

The fixing scheme is conceptually similar to that for update tampering method 1. The following procedure describes the fixing scheme.

1. *Detect the illegally replaced components*
   The illegally replaced components can be identified in the detection scheme.
2. *Correct the component versions in the registry*
   Change the registry value of C_v to the correct one.
3. *Run the "SFC/SCANNOW" command*
   Let SFC replace the component files with the correct ones. After the execution of SFC, the system will require a reboot. Through the pending file rename operations after the reboot event, the mismatched components will be restored.

   Because TrustedInstaller permissions are required to modify the component version names, Step 2 and 3 should be executed with Administrator privileges.

8   Discussion

In this section, we summarize features of Update State Tampering technique, matters that defenders should consider, and limitations of this work.

Attack Feature. The characteristics of the Update State Tampering technique are shown in Table 9. Adversaries can tamper with the Windows registry and the pending.xml file to generate known but invisible vulnerabilities on a victim's system, or as part of other techniques to aid in persistence and execution. The technique we describe affects all versions of Vista and later version of Windows. An adversary must already be a privileged user (i.e., Administrator). The result of the technique bypasses the code integrity policy, SFC, Windows Update Check, and security compliance tools. An adversary can use this technique to revive a remote code execution vulnerability as described in Sect. 4.

Table 9. Characteristics of the update state tampering technique.

Update state tampering technique	
Tactic	Persistence, defense evasion
Platform	Windows
Permissions required	Administrator, TrustedInstaller
Data sources	Windows registry (C_v), pending.xml file (T_f, T_v)
Defense bypassed	Code integrity policy, SFC, windows update check, security compliance tools

Defender Considerations. Systems that have package-component mismatches are at heightened risk because of invisible security holes. A user can self-check file versions of components, looking for major vulnerabilities such as Eternal Blue [33]. Moreover, users can utilize the Update State Check scheme described in Sect. 7 to verify the batch of component versions. The scheme can be created easily in the form of a Powershell script. We recommend that users periodically check the consistency between update packages and components installed in the system.

Limitations. Section 3 identifies issues that are not security vulnerabilities, but rather structural problems with the current Windows update management mechanism. Therefore, we recommend using the identified methods together with known exploits or zero-day attacks. Zero-day attacks are one shot only. Once patched, holes are closed. However, our technique allows attackers more time and a variety of choices. Because of blind spots, a tampered update state cannot be detected or fixed. Exposed vulnerabilities will persist until the next update to the replaced components.

As discussed in Sect. 4, it is most advantageous for an attacker to replace a component with an older version that has a remote code execution vulnerability. However, there are a few cases where the Update State Tampering technique will not apply. If only individual components are replaced, the system will not work properly, owing to inconsistencies with other components patched together. Therefore, an attacker must ensure that a system is running reliably after generating a package-component mismatch. We address this issue in the next subsection. Moreover, the Update State Tampering technique assumes that there is a vulnerable version of the component inside the component store. This technique cannot be applied if the user has recently cleaned up the *CS* or if the operating system installed on the system is the latest version and does not require additional update installations. We address this issue in detail below.

The Update State Check scheme proposed in Sect. 7 collects the component resource information and identifies differences with the correct configuration values. Our scheme does not consider rootkit attacks. For example, if an attacker installs a malicious filter driver on a target system that already has control, the attacker could manipulate the target such that it always returns the correct value when checking the component resource information. In this case, the Update State Check scheme will be disabled.

Furthermore, the proposed scheme deals exclusively with type II blind spots. However, it does not handle type I blind spots. To remove type 1 blind spots, a filtering module in the form of a kernel driver should be deployed. However, filtering loaded components is a sensitive issue. Careless design can cause a new security module to be bypassed or system performance to degrade. Eliminating type I blind spots will be pursued in future work.

Component Dependency Problem. In this study, we have not yet found an explicit method or theoretical model to identify component dependency problems. Security patches for components are implementation dependent. For example, in a security update, with code that has weaknesses that correspond to CWE-120 [34], a developer will only need to add logic to check the length of the input values without adding or removing any features. In this case, you can expect the system to function normally even if the attacker replaces the component with a previous version of the component. However, not all updates will be the same as in this example, and it cannot be guaranteed that the system will work. Moreover, Microsoft does not officially provide information regarding the identification of component dependencies. Therefore, attackers will need to perform tests in the same environment as the target system before performing the attack. For testing purposes, the attacker should collect the base version name of OS, the list of installed packages, and the presence of previous version components on the target system. In our future work, we will cover a VM-based automated testing system that can identify component dependencies.

Applicability of the Attack Scenario. In SP 800-61 [35], NIST introduces several example actions in the recovery phase of the incident response. Table 10 shows the applicability of the proposed attack scenario when each action in the recovery phase is taken. We assume the case of ④ in the attack scenario. The attack scenario is not affected by the actions of ⑤ and ⑥. The actions of ① and ② involve re-imaging the machine. In such cases, the proposed scenario is of no use. Further, the attack scenario considers the actions of ③ but assumes that tampered components are left undetected due to the blind spots.

Table 10. Applicability of the proposed attack scenario due to actions at a recovery phase

Action		Applicability	Action		Applicability
①	Restoring system from clean backups	X	④	Installing patches	O
②	Rebuilding systems from scratches	X	⑤	Changing passwords	O
③	Replacing compromised files with clean versions	Δ	⑥	Tightening network perimeter security	O

Real World Survey. To the best of our knowledge, the Windows update management problems identified in this paper have not yet been reported. Indeed, there is the possibility that this issue has already been exploited without being disclosed. We have not determined whether the proposed techniques have being utilized in the real world. In future research, we plan to deploy a detection script for the proposed technique, collect data from actual cases, and then evaluate the effectiveness and practical impact of the proposed technique and the attack scenario. The Powershell script for detections has been publicly uploaded to GitHub.[1]

9 Conclusion

In this paper, we presented Update State Tampering, a novel post-compromise technique that exploits package-component mismatches and blind spots. Were an attacker to implement the Update State Tampering technique, the target system would load the older versions of components that contain vulnerabilities. Further, Update Check, System File Check, and security compliance tools will not detect any abnormalities. These issues affect all versions of Vista and later versions of Windows. To rectify these problems, we proposed an Update State Check scheme, that detects and corrects package-component mismatches.

Acknowledgement. We would like to thank our shepherd Adam Doupe and our anonymous reviewers for their valuable comments and suggestions. We would also like to thank Sungryoul Lee, Seunghun Han, Junghwan Kang, Hyunyi Yi and Wook Shin for their feedback and advice.

References

1. Strom, B.E., Battaglia, J.A., Kemmerer, M.S., Kupersanin, W., Miller, D.P., Wampler, C., Whitley, S.M., Wolf, R.D.: Finding Cyber Threats with ATT&CKTM-Based Analytics, MITRE Technical report (2017)
2. The MITRE Corporation. Presentation: Detecting the Adversary Post-Compromise with Threat Models and Behavioral Analytic. https://www.mitre.org/publications/technical-papers/presentation-detecting-the-adversary-post-compromise-with-threat. Accessed 27 Feb 2018
3. Yadav, S., Mallari, D.: Technical aspects of cyber kill chain. Commun. Comput. Inf. Sci. **536**, 438–452 (2016)
4. Chen, P., Desmet, L., Huygens, C.: A study on advanced persistent threats. In: De Decker, B., Zúquete, A. (eds.) CMS 2014. LNCS, vol. 8735, pp. 63–72. Springer, Heidelberg (2014). https://doi.org/10.1007/978-3-662-44885-4_5
5. Malone, S.: Using an Expanded Cyber Kill Chain Model to Increase Attack Resiliency. Black Hat US (2016)
6. Smith, V., Ames, C.: Meta-Post Exploitation, Black Hat US (2008)
7. The MITRE Corporation. ATT&CK Matrix. https://attack.mitre.org/wiki/ATT&CK_Matrix. Accessed 27 Feb 2018

[1] Update State Checker Project GitHub: https://github.com/ksj1230/Update-State-Checker.

8. Speulstra, P.: Accessibility Features. https://attack.mitre.org/wiki/Technique/T1015. Accessed 27 Feb 2018
9. Tilbury, C.: Registry Analysis with CrowdResponse. https://www.crowdstrike.com/blog/registry-analysis-with-crowdresponse/. Accessed 27 Feb 2018
10. Jerzman, B., Smit, T.: Modify Registry. https://attack.mitre.org/wiki/Technique/T1112. Accessed 27 Feb 2018
11. Kaspersky Lab. The Regin Platform Nation-State Ownage of GSM Networks. https://securelist.com/files/2014/11/Kaspersky_Lab_whitepaper_Regin_platform_eng.pdf. Accessed 27 Feb 2018
12. FireEye Threat Intelligence. APT28: A Window Into Russia's Cyber Espionage Operations? https://www.fireeye.com/content/dam/fireeye-www/global/en/current-threats/pdfs/rpt-apt28.pdf. Accessed 27 Feb 2018
13. Falcone, R.: Shamoon 2: Return of the Disttrack Wiper. https://researchcenter.paloaltonetworks.com/2016/11/unit42-shamoon-2-return-disttrack-wiper. Accessed 27 Feb 2018
14. Microsoft. Use the System File Checker tool to repair missing or corrupted system files. https://support.microsoft.com/eu-es/help/929833/use-the-system-file-checker-tool-to-repair-missing-or-corrupted-system-files. Accessed 27 Feb 2018
15. Microsoft. How to get an update through Windows Update. https://support.microsoft.com/en-us/help/3067639/how-to-get-an-update-through-windows-update. Accessed 27 Feb 2018
16. Microsoft. Microsoft Baseline Security Analyzer. https://technet.microsoft.com/en-us/security/cc184924.aspx. Accessed 27 Feb 2018
17. Microsoft. Understanding Component-Based Servicing. https://blogs.technet.microsoft.com/askperf/2008/04/23/understanding-component-based-servicing/. Accessed 27 Feb 2018
18. Microsoft. Manage the Component Store. https://technet.microsoft.com/en-us/library/dn251569.aspx. Accessed 27 Feb 2018
19. Russinovich, M.E., Solomon, D.A., Ionescu, A.: Windows Internals, Part 2, 6th edn, p. 525 (2012)
20. Microsoft. Code Integrity. https://technet.microsoft.com/en-us/library/dd348642(v=ws.10).aspx. Accessed 27 Feb 2018
21. Microsoft. Kernel-Mode Code Signing Walkthrough. https://msdn.microsoft.com/en-us/library/windows/hardware/dn653569(v=vs.85).aspx. Accessed 27 Feb 2018
22. The MITRE Corporation. CVE-2017-0114. https://www.cve.mitre.org/cgi-bin/cvename.cgi?name=CVE-2017-0144. Accessed 27 Feb 2018
23. Frei, S., May, M., Fiedler, U., Plattner, B.: Large-scale vulnerability analysis. In: SIGCOMM Workshop on LSAD (2006)
24. Joh, H., Malaiya, Y.K.: Defining and assessing quantitative security risk measures using vulnerability lifecycle and CVSS metrics. In: International Conference on Security and Management (SAM) (2011)
25. Microsoft. Process Monitor v3.50. https://docs.microsoft.com/en-us/sysinternals/downloads/procmon. Accessed 27 Feb 2018
26. AhnLab. MyPCInspector. http://www.ahnlab.com/kr/site/product/productView.do?prodSeq=86. Accessed 27 Feb 2018
27. Rapid7. Metasploit. https://www.metasploit.com/. Accessed 27 Feb 2018
28. OpenVAS. OpenVAS. http://www.openvas.org/. Accessed 20 Apr 2018
29. Greenbone Networks. Greenbone. https://www.greenbone.net/en/. Accessed 20 Apr 2018
30. Tenable. Nessus Home. https://www.tenable.com/products/nessus/nessus-professional. Accessed 20 Apr 2018
31. Rapid7. Nexpose. https://www.rapid7.com/products/nexpose/. Accessed 20 Apr 2018

32. Microsoft. Further simplifying servicing models for Windows 7 and Windows 8.1. https://blogs.technet.microsoft.com/windowsitpro/2016/08/15/further-simplifying-servicing-model-for-windows-7-and-windows-8-1/. Accessed 20 Apr 2018
33. Microsoft. How to verify that MS17-010 is installed. https://support.microsoft.com/en-us/help/4023262/how-to-verify-that-ms17-010-is-installed. Accessed 27 Feb 2018
34. The MITRE Corporation. CWE-120. https://cwe.mitre.org/data/definitions/120.html. Accessed 20 Apr 2018
35. Cichonski, P., Millar, T., Grance, T., Scarfone, K.: Computer security incident handling guide. NIST Special Publication, 800-61 (2012)

Evasive Malware via Identifier Implanting

Rui Tanabe[1]([✉]), Wataru Ueno[1], Kou Ishii[1], Katsunari Yoshioka[1],
Tsutomu Matsumoto[1], Takahiro Kasama[2], Daisuke Inoue[2],
and Christian Rossow[3]

[1] Yokohama National University, YNU, Yokohama, Japan
`{tanabe-rui-nv,ueno-wataru-tn,ishii-kou-yf}@ynu.jp,`
`{yoshioka,tsutomu}@ynu.ac.jp`
[2] National Institute of Information and Communications Technology,
NICT, Koganei, Japan
`{kasama,dai}@nict.go.jp`
[3] Center for IT-Security, Privacy, and Accountability, CISPA, Saarland University,
Saarbrücken, Germany
`rossow@cispa.saarland`

Abstract. To cope with the increasing number of malware attacks that organizations face, anti-malware appliances and sandboxes have become an integral security defense. In particular, appliances have become the *de facto* standard in the fight against targeted attacks. Yet recent incidents have demonstrated that malware can effectively detect and thus evade sandboxes, resulting in an ongoing arms race between sandbox developers and malware authors.

We show how attackers can escape this arms race with what we call *customized malware*, i.e., malware that only exposes its malicious behavior on a targeted system. We present a web-based reconnaissance strategy, where an actor leaves marks on the target system such that the customized malware can recognize this particular system in a later stage, and only then exposes its malicious behavior. We propose to *implant* identifiers into the target system, such as unique entries in the browser history, cache, cookies, or the DNS stub resolver cache. We then prototype a customized malware that searches for these implants on the executing environment and denies execution if implants do not exist as expected. This way, sandboxes can be evaded without the need to detect artifacts that witness the existence of sandboxes or a real system environment. Our results show that this prototype remains undetected on commercial malware security appliances, while only exposing its real behavior on the targeted system. To defend against this novel attack, we discuss countermeasures and a responsible disclosure process to allow appliances vendors to prepare for such attacks.

1 Introduction

Malware, in its various forms, is equally a threat to consumers (e.g., banking trojans, ransomware), businesses (e.g., targeted attacks, denial-of-service bots),

C. Giuffrida et al. (Eds.): DIMVA 2018, LNCS 10885, pp. 162–184, 2018.
https://doi.org/10.1007/978-3-319-93411-2_8

and society (e.g., spambots). As a response, malware sandboxes have been widely deployed as a vital component in the fight against malware. Sandboxes help to obtain threat information, such as previously unseen malware, inputs for supervised detection mechanisms, malware C&C servers, targets of banking trojans, intelligence on spreading campaigns, or simply to assist in the manual processes of reverse engineering. In addition, organizations face so many security incidents that vendors use sandboxes as an integral part of malware security appliances. As a consequence, the anti-virus industry and security companies heavily rely on sandboxes to detect the maliciousness of an unknown program under analysis.

Seeing sandboxes' utility to defenders, malware authors naturally have been trying to evade sandbox analyses to fly under the radar. There are various types of sandbox implementations, most prominently sandboxes that use virtual machine technologies or CPU emulators. Whereas, malware may include indicators to detect a sandbox, e.g., using artifacts that show the presence of virtualization solutions. Consequently, sandbox designers have tried to design stealthier sandboxes, such as those hiding virtualization artifacts [21,24] or using bare-metal systems for malware analysis [33,34,54]. However, recent research demonstrates that characteristics other than virtualization hint at sandboxes. For example, Yokoyama et al. show that snapshotting features can reveal a sandbox [60], while Najmeh et al. search for wear-and-tear artifacts of user systems [42]. This demonstrates an ongoing arms race between sandbox maintainers and attackers.

We show that this cat-and-mouse game can be won by attackers once and for all if they implement malware that is tailored to a specific target system. Instead of malware that distinguishes between sandboxes and actual user systems, we envision *customized malware* that is carefully crafted such that it only reveals its malicious behavior on a specific target system. In fact, malware campaigns that follow a similar idea have already been observed [29]. For example, the Gauss malware computed MD5 hashes over directories, assuming a certain identifier only present on the target system, and using this information to unpack/decrypt itself [6]. The difference between these approaches and ours is that we do not use machine-specific keys that are difficult to exfiltrate before infection. Instead, we aim to *implant* marks in the target system. We propose an automated web-based reconnaissance phase, in which an actor uniquely marks a target system so that it can be reidentified later. After doing so, the customized malware is created such that it hides the malicious payload until it can verify that the previously placed characteristics match with the execution environment. This way, not only sandboxes, but any type of non-targeted systems are subject to evasion, without the need to enter the battle of sandbox detection. Such an attack might become especially attractive for targeted attacks, where attackers aim to compromise single individuals in sophisticated attacks.

We instantiate a reconnaissance strategy tailored towards both heterogeneous and homogeneous environments, i.e., a methodology that even works when most systems in the target environment (including the appliances' sandboxes) share the same configuration. Especially homogeneous environments are a highly-controlled setting that are common in large organizations that aim to reduce maintenance costs. This way, traditional evasion attacks that aim to detect artifacts of sandboxes are ineffective in such a setting, as the users and the sandbox are cloned from each other. However, with our proposal to implant an identifier into the target system, we show that adversaries can even evade analysis in such homogeneous settings. We show that attackers can place unique and characteristic marks in the browser's history, cache, or cookies, or place delicate traces in the DNS stub resolver cache. Implants are, for example, triggered via email, where a target user is tricked into clicking on an attacker-controlled URL that performs a reconnaissance phase and places an implant.

To prototype the attack, we create customized malware that checks the execution environment and search for certain marks/traces. We experimentally show that this malware becomes active on a previously-explored target system, but remains silent and does not raise security warnings on any malware security appliance. Our results demonstrate that implants escape the battle of sandbox detection and remain fully undetected on modern anti-malware appliances. This provides a new angle to the ongoing arms race and calls for completely novel anti-evasion strategies. We discuss several such defenses, ranging from enhancing the sandbox with alerts upon detection of a reconnaissance phase, to how implants can be reliably destroyed. To allow appliance vendors to prepare for such attacks, we discuss a responsible disclosure process to notify affected vendors.

Summarizing, the contributions of this paper are as follows:

- We propose a stealth reconnaissance strategy that places unique *implants* in the target system. This methodology allows attackers to create target-specific malware for both heterogeneous and homogeneous environments.
- We envision the general concept of *customized malware* that presents a completely new angle in the context of malware sandbox evasion. We instantiate the concept with a web-based reconnaissance strategy and demonstrate perfect evasion of three popular commercial malware security appliances.
- We discuss several defenses and a responsible disclosure process. We inform appliances vendors about this new threat to collaborate on countermeasures.

2   Background

We first describe the terminology that we use throughout the paper. We use the term *sandbox* to refer to a dynamic analysis environment that executes unknown programs to observe their behavior. Sandboxes are extensively leveraged to obtain threat information, such as current campaigns [19], recent C&C servers and traffic patterns [43,49,51], or attack targets [26]. Similarly, sandboxes can be used to group behavior into malware families [16,50], or to identify suspicious behavioral patterns [36].

Sandbox Analysis: To cope with the daily feed of hundreds of thousands of previously-unseen malware samples, sandboxes are highly automated. To scale the analysis, most sandboxes rely on some form of virtualization. To this end, sandboxes rely on various virtualization techniques such as VMWare [10] and VirtualBox [8] or CPU emulators [3,17]. Cuckoo Sandbox [5] is a popular open-source sandbox. However, many security organizations operate other sandboxes, either choosing from commercial sandboxes or designing their own solution. Virtualization offers the benefit that many virtual machines (VMs) can run in parallel on a single system, each analyzing one piece of malware. Egele *et al.* give a comprehensive overview of known sandboxes [25].

Malware Security Appliances: By now, sandbox analysis is widely used in academia, the anti-virus industry, and finally, also by commercial malware security appliances (henceforth simply "appliances"). Such appliances protect endpoints by analyzing unknown files and inspecting their behavior for suspicious actions. They are frequently deployed at the network layer and are used orthogonally as anti-virus scanners, e.g., to protect endpoints from opening malicious email attachments and malicious file downloads from the Internet. Internally, appliances also use a sandbox to analyze the malware behavior, such as its system interactions or network communication.

Given the importance of preventing malware intrusions, these appliances play an ever-increasing role as security defenses. This motivates malware authors to find ways to detect and evade sandboxes. Typically, malware detects sandboxes by checking the execution environment. For example, Barbosa *et al.* reported that about 80% of evasive malware detects VM environments [13]. By now, many appliances have resilience to such simple sandbox evasion techniques. Still, as we will show, it is fundamentally difficult to prevent targeted attacks that can gather information about the target system prior to compromising the target.

Targeted Attack: Adversaries with an outstanding interest to infiltrate a target will continuously and persistently attack the target using various types of malware in several attack phases. Security vendors have defined this type of attack as Advanced Persistent Threat (APT) [1,2]. The purpose of a targeted attack varies per attack campaign, such as leaking information related to financial and intellectual property, destroying a target's core system, or altering data saved in the target system. Although attacks are complex and can be divided into several phases, it is common that attackers gather pieces of information related to the target user(s) and their setup. This makes it possible to plan an attack scenario in which the targeted malware bypasses existing security measures. New vulnerabilities (zero-day attacks) and human weaknesses (social engineering) are then abused to infect a victim. Once the malware has infected a target system, backdoors or C&C channels are created. Further attacks may abuse this stepping stone to propagate to and monitor other target systems.

3 Sandbox Evasion via Implants

We use this section to explain the general concept of *customized malware* that presents a completely new angle in the battle of sandbox evasion. In our context, customized malware can identify a target-specific system in both heterogeneous and homogeneous environments. We will first explain the attack scenario that follows two phases, starting with a phase to place identifiers into the target system and then using them in the next phase. We then describe how to leave unique and characteristic features in the target system. To prototype the attack, we implement customized malware that checks the execution and search for certain marks/traces. Finally, we test these samples against commercial appliances and see if stealth evasion is possible in practice (Fig. 1).

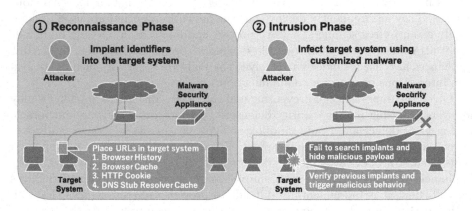

Fig. 1. Overview of our attack scenario. Adversaries first implant identifiers into the target system using an out-of-band channel. We propose to place URLs in the browser history, cache, cookie, and DNS stub resolver cache(①). Attackers then send customized malware that search for the previously placed characteristics, and trigger its malicious behavior only if the features match. This way, not only malware security appliances, but any type of not-targeted systems are evaded(②).

3.1 Attack Scenario

We first explain the threat model that we follow in our work and the assumptions that we make about the capabilities of sandboxes. We start with an overview of how sandboxes are used in practice, and then detail the setting of our new concept of customized malware.

To defend against the ever-increasing number of malware attacks, malware security appliances have become an integral part of many organizations' security strategies. Seeing their prevalence, malware authors put significant effort into detecting (and evading) such sandboxes. For example, malware can deploy detection routines for VM-based or emulation-based sandboxes and change its behavior if a sandbox environment is found. Similarly, malware that evades sandbox analysis based on the lack of user interaction has been seen. In addition, recent academic works propose further more systematic sandbox detection strategies [42,60]. To cope with the problem, stealthier or even bare-metal sandboxes [7,34] have arisen, and security vendors have entered an ongoing arms race to become resilient against sandbox evasion techniques.

Whereas it seems that this evasion arms race will continue for a while, in this paper, we call attention to the next-stage problem of target-specific malware. That is, we envision *customized malware* that is tailored towards infecting one particular system. To this end, we assume that the customized malware first places an implant into the target system using an out-of-band channel (e.g., triggered via email). Later on, when executed, the customized malware first gathers information on the executed environment, matches these features against the previous implants of the target system, and triggers its malicious activities only if the features match. Regardless of the efforts put into hiding the presence of a sandbox, as long as the sandbox is not an exact copy of the target system, the customized malware will not reveal its normal behavior. That is, our work is fundamentally different from previous approaches in that our key idea is to identify the target system instead of separating sandboxes from normal systems.

Individual malware campaigns have already been observed to follow a similar idea, e.g., by computing MD5 hashes over directories, assuming a certain SID (a unique per-system identifier in Windows), and by comparing specific and current paths to decrypt themselves [6,29]. Chengyu *et al.* show some system unique properties that can be used to obfuscate malware samples [23]. However, these features are difficult to exfiltrate remotely (before infection) and thus pose costs for the attacker or even render such evasions infeasible. We hence revisit this attack pattern and augment it with new techniques. Most importantly, we propose to place unique marks on the target system prior to infection instead of merely using existing ones.

The novel concept of customized malware follows a two-phase approach, starting with the *reconnaissance phase* and then using its results in the *intrusion phase*. This attack scenario is common for targeted attacks such as Advanced Persistent Threats (APTs), in which the attackers aim to infiltrate specific systems after spying on their victims first. In our context, we require that the reconnaissance target and the attack target are the same (specific user). As we will show, this assumption can be easily satisfied, e.g., when both reconnaissance phase and infection phase share the same communication channel (e.g., email or HTTP). We will describe the two phases in the following:

Reconnaissance Phase: In this phase, adversaries first *implant* certain marks on the target system. The Internet has become a necessary technology for daily business, including email communication and web browsing. In fact, obtaining the email address of an attack target is already a vital step for targeted attacks. To perform the reconnaissance, we assume that a targeted email successfully tricks a user into clicking the URL of an attacker-controller reconnaissance web site. This web site will then use a web-based reconnaissance procedure that implants features to the host, e.g., via email or via web sites. That is, if target users click on an attacker-provided URL in an email, an unique identifier is implanted on the target system. Such an implant can be stealthy, e.g., by leaving certain marks/traces in the browser or system. Later on, customized malware can recognize the target-specific system based on these implants.

During the reconnaissance phase, we assume that sandboxes either do not click on URLs provided in emails (e.g., as this would otherwise cause bad side effects, such as automated unsubscriptions from mailing lists, etc.). Or, if sandboxes indeed follow links provided in emails, we assume that the intrusion and reconnaissance phase would *not* be run within the same execution unit of the sandbox. This follows the reasoning that sandboxes have to differentiate the behavior of different inputs (emails, malware files, etc.) and restore their snapshot after analyzing a particular input. In fact, this relaxation allows us to place implants without even requiring the user to click on URLs. We observed that it is possible to carefully craft emails that automatically load external content from attacker-controlled URLs (e.g., loading embedded external images, as enabled by default in Apple Mail), which then can be used to place implants. In an attempt to collect implants, sandboxes could also automatically open emails and access the URLs, but again, if this happens on a freshly-restored snapshot, both phases would still not be linked. We will motivate this further in Sect. 4.

Intrusion Phase: After the reconnaissance phase, adversaries have sufficient characteristic information to reidentify a specific target. The purpose of the intrusion phase is thus to create stealth customized malware that only executes on the target system, while not triggering suspicious activity on other systems and thereby also evading anti-malware appliances. As we will show, we can even hide the actual malicious payload by encrypting/decrypting it with the characteristic information. That is, also a manual analyst lacking the true characteristics of the actual target system could not reverse engineer the malicious payload.

To assess how stealthy the customized malware is, we assume that the crafted customized malware is tested by any (combination of) appliance(s) and sandbox(es). We further assume that adversaries have no insights on which (if any) sandboxes are deployed, which also makes it difficult to implant features. Although some expert knowledge might be helpful to guess which activity in the intrusion phase might raise an alert in the sandbox, an attacker might use blackbox tests to identify viable strategies that survive sandbox checks.

Hetegerogeneous vs. Homogeneous Target Environments: Targeted attacks are usually easier to perform in heterogeneous environments compared to homogeneous environments, as systems in the heterogeneous setting can be easily distinguished from each other. Yet we propose a methodology for customized malware that also performs well if the target system has identically-configured clones. For example, organizations that deploy preconfigured configurations to their end users to minimize maintenance and license costs and to ease security management create such a *homogeneous environment*. High-end security appliances adapt to such settings in that their sandbox operates on exact copies of the actual production systems of the organization they aim to protect. In such a setting, traditional fingerprinting methods may fail to distinguish target systems from any other system of the organization—including the sandbox.

3.2   Feature Implantation

We will now describe and evaluate our implant-based methodology to develop customized malware that implicitly evades sandboxes. The key idea of the proposed *implants* is to add unique and characteristic marks into the target system, such that the customized malware can recognize them during the infection stage. An important detail is that the implants should look benign to the target system (and to the sandbox when looking them up), while the customized malware has to be able to query implants. We now consider four non-invasive methods to realize such implants.

Browser History: Web browsers typically record histories of web accesses to ease lookups of visited sites in the future. By sending a unique (not necessarily attacker-controlled) URL to the target and leading him to access it, the URL will be recorded in the log of the target system. Since adversaries only need to implant the URL in the access history, the web site does not have to be malicious, so that no network appliances will be able to detect such implants. As the implant just has to be unique, it could even be a legitimate web site with a unique identifier added within the URL (e.g., `google.com/12345`). Another way to abuse browser history is to use the access date as an implant, if browsers record the last access date per URL.

Browser Cache: Most web browsers cache web content to speed up subsequent visits. By luring the target system into clicking a unique URL, one can place identifiers that are stored in the cache of the target system. The implant could be benign but unique URLs or resources (images, CSS files, etc.). As caches might be refreshed or deleted after a certain time and may thus not last long, attackers would likely aim to shorten the time between the reconnaissance phase and the intrusion phase.

HTTP Cookie: Cookies are a well-known technique for tracking browsers. They are stored on the user's computer as a file and store stateful information that is specific to the pair of a client and a specific web site. Cookies are usually saved when a new web site is loaded and can be queried by the web server or accessed by the client computer. By now, most legitimate web sites use cookies, so their usage is not suspicious. Although they can be destroyed when the current web browser is closed, the lifetime of cookies is configurable (unless overridden by manual browser configurations). Attackers can also use cookies to implant an identifier in a stealth manner using attacker-controlled web sites. This way, malware authors could search for an implant in cookie databases of browsers.

Supercookies (Evercookies) are similar to cookies in that they are stored on the user's computer. They are usually harder to delete from the device, as they are realized using multiple storage mechanisms [31]. For example, a supercookie can implant a user-specific identifier using a Flash Local Shared Object. Alternatively, web servers can abuse a security improvement function like HSTS or HPKP for supercookies [9]. The data size can be larger than normal cookies, showing that supercookies are suited to track devices and place implants.

DNS Stub Resolver Cache: The Domain Name System (DNS) is widely used to resolve domains to IP addresses, e.g., when accessing web sites. On Windows, by default the Windows DNS stub resolver is used to query domains and cache results according to their lifetime, as specified in the Time-to-Live (TTL) value in DNS responses. Thus by sending a specific URL to the target and leading him to access it, the domain will be cached by the DNS stub resolver. In fact, the domain does not have to lead to a malicious web site, just feature a sufficiently long cache duration (i.e., TTL) to bridge the time between reconnaissance and infection. Malware authors could then check if the resolver cached a particular domain, e.g., using common DNS cache snooping techniques.

Beside implanting features, when it becomes important for malware authors to learn if the target has accessed a specific web site, the situation is trickier. The obvious solution is using an attacker-controlled URL. Alternatively, one could use unique benign web sites that state the date of the most recent visit, deploy a publicly-visible visitor counter, or even abuse a timing-based side channel to infer whether a certain page has been visited. By preparing an attacker-controlled URL, malware authors can also find out which web browser the target is using and make it easier to search for such implants. Therefore, malware authors may carefully send an attacker-controlled URL and effectively implant identifiers into the target system.

3.3   Customized Malware

We envision that customized malware first gathers information of the executed environment and then matches these features against the implants placed previously during the intrusion phase. Most basic, malware authors could simply check if the implant exists, and if so, follow a binary decision to either unpack the malicious payload or not. However, a manual analyst could then still reverse engineer the customized malware, reverse the decision to not unpack, and then obtain the malicious payload. In fact, malware sandboxes and appliances already have similar functionalities to scan malware binaries for malicious payloads, or to execute several branches (multi-path execution [41]).

To strengthen this naïve approach, malware authors can not only check for the existence of an implant. In fact, they can retrieve a value from the implant, which can then be used as decryption key for malicious payloads. This way, it would be impossible to decrypt the malicious payload even for a human analyst or multi-path execution. Embedding such implant values is trivial for cookies, caches and browser history, where adversaries just need to configure the implant URLs in the reconnaissance phase accordingly. For DNS caches, storing implant values is bit more evolved, but also possible. For example, the value of a cached `AAAA` record (which stores an IPv6 address) could be used as a 128-bit AES key.

3.4 Malware Security Appliance Evasion

Seeing that one can implant identifiers through web-based techniques and implement customized malware, we now test if such implants can be used to evade commercial appliances.

Implementation: We first prepared a legitimate web site, which prototypes an attacker-controlled URL and gives an attacker the highest flexibility. We accessed our web site from a user machine that is used on a daily basis at a real organization (henceforth simply "target"). To compare the results, we accessed the web site from three different web browsers (Chrome, Firefox, and IE) and implanted a URL in the target system's browser history, cache, cookie, and DNS stub resolver cache. We then implemented Windows 32-bit PE programs written in C/C# that use the Windows API, commands, and custom functions to search for URLs that perfectly match our web site. We implemented samples that open the browser history by searching for `preferences` for Chrome, `sessionstore.js` for Firefox, and `%HISTORY%` for IE. Our web site has an image file embedded in the top page, and therefore the samples search for such cached items in `entries` for Firefox and `%TEMPORARY INTERNET FILES%` for IE. We furthermore implemented samples that read a cookie from `Cookies` for Chrome and `cookies.sqlite` for Firefox. To inspect the stub resolver's DNS cache, our prototype uses the Windows `ipconfig` utility and the undocumented Windows API `DnsGetCacheDataTable`.

Evaluation Setup: We first executed the samples on the target host and verified that all implants could be found. We then submitted the samples to three popular appliances from well-known vendors[1] (henceforth simply appliance A, B, and C). We gained access to various sandbox configurations (Windows 10, Windows 7, Windows XP, 32/64 bit, different service packs, etc.) of the appliances, totaling nine distinct sandboxes. Since the appliances did not allow for network communication (which supports our threat model that even collecting implants might be impractical for most sandboxes), we investigated the analysis report which was produced by the appliance after execution. Although the appliances were *not* cloned from actual user machines, this methodology would similarly work in a fully-homogeneous environment.

---

[1] We omit the vendor names not to pinpoint to weaknesses of individual appliances.

Table 1. Security alerts reported from the three appliances including nine sandboxes (Windows 10, Windows 7, and Windows XP) which executed samples that searched for implants of browser history, cache, cookie, and DNS cache.

Feature		Appliance A	Appliance B	Appliance C
History	Chrome	*Hardware Access*	no alert	no alert
	Firefox	*Hardware Access*	no alert	no alert
	IE	*Hardware Access*	no alert	no alert
Cache	Firefox	*Hardware Access*	no alert	no alert
	IE	*Hardware Access*	no alert	no alert
Cookie	Chrome	*Hardware Access* *Browser Access*	no alert	no alert
	Firefox	*Hardware Access* *Browser Access*	no alert	no alert
DNS		*Hardware Access*	*Directory Access*	no alert

Table 2. Security alerts reported from the three appliances including five sandboxes (Windows 10 and Windows 7) which executed samples that searched for implants of browser history, cache, and DNS cache and decrypts malicious payload when previous implants are found.

Feature		Appliance A	Appliance B	Appliance C
History	Chrome	no alert	no alert	no alert
	Firefox	no alert	no alert	no alert
	IE	no alert	no alert	no alert
Cache	Firefox	no alert	no alert	no alert
	IE	no alert	no alert	no alert
DNS		no alert	no alert	no alert

Evaluation Results: When manually inspecting the analysis reports, not surprisingly, the implants were not found in any of the sandboxes. After verifying the evasion capabilities, we then checked if our implant checks triggered any security alerts from the appliances. We summarize the results in Table 1. The first column contains the implant technique, and the last three columns show the result per vendor. We first implemented test samples that are executable on systems that are backwards-compatible to earlier Windows versions, down to Windows XP. We had a look at the reports produced by the appliances and found that a security alert about *Hardware access* was reported for every single sample. The alert was reported from Windows XP, by one of the nine sandboxes which belonged to appliance A. For samples that check HTTP cookies, we obtained another alert about *Browser access* from three sandboxes, which belonged to appliance A. The sample that checks the DNS stub resolver cache raised an alert about *Hardware access* from two sandboxes (including Windows

XP) which belonged to appliance A, and an alert about a Windows command (`ipconfig`) from three sandboxes which belonged to appliance B.

For further analysis, we implemented test samples that not only searched for implants, but also encapsulated an encrypted version of a malicious payload that all sandboxes would detect if it was not hidden. That is, we chose to use malware that was seen in a real attack campaign targeting organizations in Japan and Taiwan [4]. We submitted the malware sample to the appliances and verified that it indeed was detected as such by all sandboxes. We then wrapped the malware in the customized malware, protected by a decryption that would only trigger if implants were found. Technically, the sample searches for the implant, and when the URL is found, decrypts and executes the actual malware. In fact, adversaries could include the decryption key in implants, such that even multi-path execution or manual analysts would fail to obtain the malicious packed payload. In our evaluation, the implants are the same as for the previous experiment and searched for in the browser history (for Chrome, Firefox, and IE), browser cache (for Firefox and IE), and DNS stub resolver cache. Seeing that one of the three appliances reported alerts when accessing cookies, we excluded the HTTP cookie from further analysis. Assuming that the target host operates Windows 7 or newer, we implemented these samples using libraries that do not work on earlier Windows versions, leaving us to five sandboxes of three appliances in our test setting. Using this new API, only a single sandbox raised an alert when our sample tried to inspect the DNS stub resolver using `ipconfig`. To counter this alert, we used `DnsGetCacheDataTable`, which did not raise any alert. In summary, as Table 2 shows, our updated implant search did not trigger any alerts. We manually inspected the analysis reports of all sandboxes and verified that none of the sandboxes decrypted the malware sample, meaning that our implant checking mechanism worked as expected.

Evaluation Summary: To summarize, an attacker can *implant* several identifiers into the target-specific system using web-based techniques. The implanted features can be used to implement *customized malware* that can stealthily evade malware security appliances. Adversaries with insider knowledge on anti-malware appliances, or having an oracle that tells whether their customized malware is detected as such, can tweak their implant mechanism such that the evasion is stealthy and remains undetected.

4   Discussion and Limitations

4.1   Defenses Against the Attack

As we have shown, attackers could reliably distinguish between a target-specific system from others based on *implanted* identifiers. As an option to solve these problems, we consider three solutions. First, we envision raising the bar for creating implants. Second, sandboxes and appliances can be tuned against such attacks. Third, appliance could be included in the reconnaissance phase to learn implants. We will discuss those ideas and their limitations in the following.

Destroying Implants: Adversaries can implant features into the target system using web-based techniques. An important detail is that the implant looks benign to the target system and sandboxes when looking them up. Therefore, detecting the implant itself require additional care and cannot be easily thwarted. Potential targets could aim to destroy implants by periodically deleting the cookies and browser history, or disabling caching to destroy cache-based implants. However, especially disabling browser and DNS caches would likely degrade user experience due to increased communication latencies, showing a fine line between utility and security. It is possible to change where to store browser cache and make malware authors difficult to find. In our experiment, we found that Chrome stores browser cache randomly. Although, we note that an attacker could combine multiple implants, and if a single implant survives, any attempts to hide other implants would be rendered ineffective. Alternatively, one could use a proxy service to make the tracking difficult. This technique would even destroy most of the proposed implant strategies. Still, proxy services leaves records into the target system. An attacker can search for this identifier instead of tracing implants.

Reconnaissance Detection in Sandboxes: An orthogonal solution to destroy implants would be for sandboxes to become aware of the reconnaissance phases. Such detection would allow the sandbox to identify suspicious behavior in the customized malware, regardless of whether it unpacks the malicious payload. At the risk of raising false alerts, sandboxes could aim to identify the various strategies that customized malware has to use in order to find an implant. Our work can help sandbox developers to become aware of implant strategies and assist them in raising alerts when seeing such behavior. By now, appliances detect sandbox evasion techniques by monitoring access to credential files and the registry. We show that the monitoring search space needs to be significantly extended, including browser-related files (cookies, cache, history) and Windows internals such as the DNS stub resolver's cache.

An obvious challenge is to keep up with all potential implant techniques that attackers could use. Our list of possible implants is by no means complete. For example, during experiments, we also inspected the Windows system log that includes various system events. We found that one can create log entries by trying to resolve a domain for which the authoritative name server times out. This would be another excellent way to place an attacker-controllable implant in a system, and demonstrate how creative attackers might become when choosing implant techniques. By adapting to these techniques, sandbox operators can aim to *detect* potential customized malware samples. Unfortunately, this does *not* help in unpacking encrypted payloads that depend on the value of certain implants that are missing in the sandbox or are unknown to the manual analyst.

Including Sandboxes in the Reconnaissance Phase: At the core of our threat model, we assume that the target system undergoes the reconnaissance, whereas the appliance does not. Although the appliances did not allow for network communication, we did not observe any actions that tries accessing to our web site, while the target host was protected by the appliances. This could be changed if appliances are included in the typical reconnaissance steps, e.g., when they automatically follow URLs listed in emails sent to targets. The dangers of such automated URL visits make them impractical, though, as they will cause undesired side effects such as unsubscribing from mailing lists, or mistakenly confirming email-based authentication requests. Other drawbacks, such as attackers being able to learn which email address is protected by an appliance, and requiring the appliance to have Internet access (which none in our testbed had), give us the impression that this idea is only a last resort.

Suppose that despite these drawbacks a sandbox would indeed visit the URLs, and by doing so, collect implants. Even then, one complication is that sandboxes typically use snapshots to clean the system after each analysis to properly differentiate and to avoid side-effects between two malicious inputs, respectively. As a sandbox cannot correlate reconnaissance and intrusion phases, both phases would be executed separately in a clean system snapshot. Therefore, the intrusion phase would not see implants placed in the reconnaissance phase.

4.2 Ethical Considerations

Our research may seem offensive in the sense that we reveal a methodology that adversaries can use for targeted attacks. However, with our insights, sandbox operators will have a heads-up to implement stealthier analysis systems. While it will always be possible to find artifacts that can identify an individual sandbox or user machines, it is significantly harder to distinguish the target-specific system, especially if vendors synchronize the characteristics of the sandbox with user systems. However, attackers may not need profiles of the target, but could *implant* an identifier. Therefore, it is important to be more sensitive to programs that conduct sensitive data acquisitions that is used to discover implants. A responsible disclosure process (see next subsection) informed vendors of the appliances to prepare for attacks described in this paper. We gave suggestions on which activities to monitor for detecting programs that conduct implant acquisitions to appliances vendors prior to the conference. Finally, We anonymize the appliance vendors to avoid exposing weaknesses of specific vendors or products.

4.3 Responsible Disclosure

Appliance vendors are immediately affected by our research results and we thus considered them as the target of our responsible disclosure process. We chose to disclose our result to the three appliance vendors from our experiments, and to additional eleven popular appliance vendors. To notify these organizations, we contacted them 120 days prior to the publishing date of this paper, detailing the proposed attack and including hints on how to protect against potential adversaries in the future. We used direct contacts whenever possible and available. Alternatively, we resorted to contact details stated on the organization's web sites, notably including Web-based contact forms. If we did not hear back after four weeks, we retried to contact the organizations, if possible using alternative communication channels (e.g., using generic email addresses like info@organization.com or email addresses found in the WHOIS database for the organization's web site domain) and received a feedback. If we did not hear back after eight weeks from the first process, we contacted the national CERT(s) that are in the same country as the affected organization in order to notify the party via the CERT as a trusted intermediary.

We provided each organization an executive summary of our research results as well as a full description of our research methodology (i.e., a copy of this paper in the pre-print version). We made sure to highlight the implications of our work with respect to future operations of the appliance. We also specified our contact details for both research institutions, including physical address, phone number, and the email address of a representative for the research activities. We allowed organizations to download the latest version of the test samples and their source code. Such auxiliary data helps to build protection mechanisms against customized malware. We removed all organization and product names as well as precise messages (security alerts) that were reported by the appliances. To this end, we received feedbacks from most of the organizations and provided test samples and their source code.

4.4   Limitations of the Attack

Enforcement of Reconnaissance Phase: Our attack makes use of emails that contain a URL in order to create an implant. We assume that the targeted mail attracts the user, such that the target host will access the URL and complete the reconnaissance phase. We consider the way the attacker tricks the user into clicking the URL a separate research topic that is out of the scope of this work. In practice, however, sophisticated attacks involving social engineering would succeed with this task. Even if a user does *not* click, adversaries can make the target host automatically access the URL. For HTML mail, most email clients support techniques to prefetch web access or download images from the Internet. For example, Apple Mail has prefetching of external email content enabled by default. Attackers can easily create emails that use these techniques to complete the reconnaissance as soon as the user opens the email. On occasions where the email is opened through web browsers, the accessed URL or image is saved in caches. Even for some mailers, the accessed URL is saved in a temporary file, so the attacker can implant a specific URL. However, for services that use proxy servers for access (e.g., Gmail), serving implants is difficult. Similarly, the functionality of external email content prefetching is not always (and should not be) allowed, again requiring an active click on a URL as fallback. We leave the problem of luring a user into clicking such an implant URL as future work.

Stability of Implants: After the malware author has accomplished the reconnaissance phase, the intrusion phase is started. If the phases are far apart from each other, certain implants may get lost. However, we argue that the typical gap between reconnaissance and intrusion is in the range of several days, which is a short enough period for implants to remain stable. Most of the implants do not decay over time, unless action is taken by the user or they are blocked from the beginning. For example, the browser history and cache file may not record access histories, which prevents implants from being created. Cookies could be configured to be deleted periodically, which disturbs the implants being recorded. The DNS stub resolver cache may be cleaned, which implicitly destroys implants. We argue that a combination of *multiple* implants would survive most of these individual deletions and decays. Note that this does not sacrifice accuracy, as any individual implant out of a set of multiple unique implants is still unique. That is, the customized malware could search for multiple implants and trigger its malicious behavior when *any* implant was found.

False Positives: It is not in question that implants can be made unique with an attacker-controlled (high) entropy. We thus consider that the possibility of a non-targeted host to be falsely recognized as the targeted host is low. Even if such a coincidental match happens, assuming that the malware spreads to hundreds of other systems (including sandboxes), it is still unlikely that the coincidentally matching system will ever get in contact with the customized malware.

5   Related Work

5.1   Sandbox Evasion Techniques

Seeing the wide use of sandboxes, malware authors have been trying to evade sandbox analyses. There are various types of sandbox implementations, and Egele *et al.* give a comprehensive overview [25]. Most sandboxes use virtual machine (VM) technology [8,10,14] or CPU emulators [3,17]. Techniques to check for artifacts that indicate the presence of virtualization solutions are seen in modern malware [13,15,18,20,35,53,55,56]. Accordingly, there have been a number of studies about how to distinguish between a real machine and a virtual environment. RedPill [52] is one of the most well-known methods, and determines whether it is executed on VMware using the `sidt` instruction. Many other detection methods have also been developed not only for VMware [32,48], but also for famous system emulators such as QEMU [11,28,32,40,45,48], and BOCHS [28,40,45]. There are also some detection methods for emulation-based Android sandboxes [30,47,59]. Garfinkel *et al.* [27] surveyed the wide range of dissimilarities between real and virtualized platforms, and Chen *et al.* [22] developed a taxonomy of anti-virtualization and anti-debugging techniques that are used by modern malware. Although these techniques work against classical sandboxes, malware security appliances are designed to protect endpoints from recent threats and may not be as susceptible.

On the other hand, evading sandboxes does not necessarily require searching for virtualization or emulation artifacts. Malware has already started to evade sandboxes based on the lack of user interaction, such as checking for mouse events [53,55,56] or waiting for a user to close a dialog box [20,56]. Recent research identifies features that are common on user systems [44]. These types of evasions are based on seeing that the system is used by a real user, and thus may seem similar to our approach. The fundamental difference is that we do not try to identify if malware executes on just *any* (non-)sandbox system. Instead, we show that attackers can tailor their malware to specific target systems.

In addition to identifying sandboxes, fingerprinting has also become popular. Maier *et al.* [39] gathered several features of Android sandboxes and showed that Android malware can bypass the existing sandboxes by using the fingerprints. Regarding sandboxes for Windows malware, Yoshioka *et al.* [61] clustered and detected sandboxes by their external IP addresses. Yokoyama *et al.* clustered sandbox fingerprints and created a classifier that can distinguish user machines from sandboxes [60]. They gathered fingerprints from sandboxes to user machines and proposed sandbox-inherent features so that even appliances placed in real networks can be classified as sandboxes. Najmeh *et al.* collected user and sandbox fingerprints to assess the degree of system use and age [42]. They developed statistical models that capture how realistic the system's past use looks to aid sandbox operators in creating system images that exhibit a realistic wear-and-tear state. We were inspired by these works and swifted the problem to homogeneous target environments. To this end, we aim to use implant-based techniques to identify the *target* systems, instead of any sandboxes or any benign systems. Our work extends existing ideas in that we show how an attacker might escape the typical arms race of identifying sandboxes using customized malware.

5.2   Transparent/Bare-Metal Sandboxes

Seeing the threat of VM evasion, researchers started to explore transparent sandboxes that are stealthy against detection. Vasudevan and Yerraballi proposed Cobra [58], which is a first dynamic analysis system focused on countering anti-analysis techniques. Dinaburg *et al.* proposed Ether [24], a transparent sandbox using hardware virtualization extensions such as Intel VT. Those systems focus on how to conceal the existence of analysis mechanisms from malware. Pek *et al.* introduced a timing-based detection mechanism to detect Ether [46]. Orthogonal to stealth VM-based sandboxes, Kirat *et al.* proposed to use actual hardware to analyze malware [7,34]. The proposed system, called BareBox, is based on a fast and rebootless system restore technique. Since the system executes malware on real hardware, it is not vulnerable to any type of VM/emulation-based detection attacks. In the context of Android sandboxes, Bordoni *et al.* proposed Mirage [38], an architecture that aims to arm an Android analysis system to tackle evasion by reproducing characteristics of real devices as much as possible into the Android emulator. These sandboxes increase evasion resilience in the classical setting, but would be evaded by customized malware.

5.3   Evasive Malware Detection

Separately from our work, researchers have identified the threat of evasive malware and studied its evasion attempts. As evasive malware became more popular, the demand for distinguishing whether malware has evasive functionality increased. Many of the evasive malware detection methods are based on comparison of behaviors between analysis and non-analysis environments. Balzarotti *et al.* proposed a method to detect malware that behaves differently in an analysis environment vs. a bare-metal reference host [12]. They first execute a malware sample on a reference host and compare its system call behavior with the execution in a virtual environment, revealing split behaviors in malware. Sun *et al.* proposed the behavior distance algorithm [57], which is based on generic string matching, for calculating the difference between two environments for the same malware. DISARM [37] compares behaviors in four emulation-based analysis systems and detects those differences. Barecloud [33] is a similar method to DISARM, but uses four fundamentally different analysis platforms, including bare-metal sandboxes. All these studies support the conclusion that malware already deploys evasion attempts. As we have shown, it will be difficult to detect customized malware. In fact, even advanced techniques such as multi-path execution [41] do not help in our threat model, as attackers can derive (strong) keys from implants to decrypt the piggybacked malicious payload.

6   Conclusion

The novel concept of *customized malware* might gain attention from malware authors in the future, as it solves many of their daily problems of evading increasingly stealthy and professional sandboxes. A fundamental challenge of malware authors remains evading anti-malware solutions that are based on sandboxes. Whereas our focus was email as infection vector, the problem scope goes beyond this. In fact, similar concepts could be integrated (much more easily, and fully automatically) into other popular ways of infections such as browser exploit kits. We thus think it is important to shed light on this potential new area which might add another burden to malware sandbox engineers, and to aid sandbox operators with ideas for protecting against such attacks. This is not only relevant for targeted attacks; also consumer malware could facility similar ideas by slightly sacrificing the implant accuracy to broader the set of accepted systems.

Implant techniques that we presented have been fairly successful in evading even the most modern malware security appliances. In settings like small agile organizations (startups, academia, etc.), where employees bring and configure their own devices: heterogeneous environment, an attacker can distinguish target system from others. Furthermore, it helps to infiltrate all kinds of environments, even those that require strict homogeneity. Regardless of the precise customization strategy being used, it is the simplicity of the proposed attack concept and its ease of automation that make it appealing for attackers. To give sandbox operators a timely heads-up before publishing our work, we have planned a rigorous responsible disclosure process.

Acknowledgements. We would like to thank the anonymous reviewers for their constructive feedback. This work was supported by the European Union's Horizon 2020 research and innovation program, project SISSDEN, under grant agreement No. 700176. A part of this work was funded by the WarpDrive: Web-based Attack Response with Practical and Deployable Research Initiative project, supported by the National Institute of Information and Communications Technology (NICT).

References

1. Advanced persistent threats: how they work. https://www.symantec.com/theme.jsp?themeid=apt-infographic-1
2. APT [Advanced Persistent Threat]. http://www.trendmicro.com/vinfo/us/security/definition/advanced-persistent-threat
3. bochs: The open source IA-32 emulation project. http://bochs.sourceforge.net
4. Darwins favorite APT group. https://www.fireeye.com/blog/threat-research/2014/09/darwins-favorite-apt-group-2.html
5. Malwr - malware analysis by cuckoo sandbox. https://malwr.com/
6. The mystery of the encrypted gauss payload. https://securelist.com/the-mystery-of-the-encrypted-gauss-payload-5/33561/
7. NVMTrace: Proof-of-concept automated baremetal malware analysis framework. https://code.google.com/p/nvmtrace/
8. Oracle VM VirtualBox. https://www.virtualbox.org
9. Public key pinning extension for http. https://tools.ietf.org/html/rfc7469
10. VMware. http://www.vmware.com/
11. Detecting android sandboxes (2012). http://www.dexlabs.org/blog/btdetect
12. Balzarotti, D., Cova, M., Karlberger, C., Kruegel, C., Engin, K., Vigna, G.: Efficient detection of split personalities in malware. In: Proceedings of the Symposium on Network and Distributed System Security, ser. NDSS 2010 (2010)
13. Barbosa, G.N., Branco, R.R.: Prevalent characteristics in modern malware (2014). https://www.blackhat.com/docs/us-14/materials/us-14-Branco-Prevalent-Characteristics-In-Modern-Malware.pdf
14. Barham, P., Dragovic, B., Fraser, K., Hand, S., Harris, T., Ho, A., Neugebauer, R., Pratt, I., Warfield, A.: Xen and the art of virtualization. SIGOPS Oper. Syst. Rev. **37**(5), 164–177 (2003)
15. Bayer, U., Habibi, I., Balzarotti, D., Kirda, E., Kruegel, C.: A view on current malware behaviors. In: Proceedings of the 2nd USENIX Conference on Large-Scale Exploits and Emergent Threats: Botnets, Spyware, Worms, and More, ser. LEET 2009, p. 8 (2009)
16. Bayer, U., Comparetti, P.M., Hlauschek, C., Kruegel, C., Kirda, E.: Scalable, behavior-based malware clustering. In: Proceedings of the Symposium on Network and Distributed System Security, ser. NDSS 2009 (2009)
17. Bellard, F.: QEMU, a fast and portable dynamic translator. In: Proceedings of the Annual Conference on USENIX Annual Technical Conference, ser. ATEC 2005, p. 41 (2005)
18. Branco, R.R., Barbosa, G.N., Neto, P.D.: Scientific but academical overview of malware anti-debugging, anti-disassembly and anti-vm technologies (2012). http://research.dissect.pe/docs/blackhat2012-paper.pdf
19. Caballero, J., Grier, C., Kreibich, C., Paxson, V.: Measuring pay-per-install: the commoditization of malware distribution. In: Proceedings of the 20th USENIX Security Symposium (2011)

20. Candid, W.: Does malware still detect virtual machines? (2014). https://www.symantec.com/connect/blogs/does-malware-still-detect-virtual-machines
21. Carsten, W., Ralf, H., Thorsten, H.: CXPInspector: Hypervisor-Based, Hardware-Assisted System Monitoring (2012)
22. Chen, X., Andersen, J., Mao, Z., Bailey, M., Nazario, J.: Towards an understanding of anti-virtualization and anti-debugging behavior in modern malware. In: Proceedings of the 38th Annual IEEE International Conference on Dependable Systems and Networks, ser. DSN 2008, pp. 177–186 (2008)
23. Chengyu, S., Paul, R., Wenke, L.: Impeding automated malware analysis with environment-sensitive malware. In: Proceedings of the 7th USENIX Conference on Hot Topics in Security, ser. HotSec 2012 (2012)
24. Dinaburg, A., Royal, P., Sharif, M., Lee, W.: Ether: malware analysis via hardware virtualization extensions. In: Proceedings of the 15th ACM Conference on Computer and Communications Security, ser. CCS 2008, pp. 51–62 (2008)
25. Egele, M., Scholte, T., Kirda, E., Kruegel, C.: A survey on automated dynamic malware-analysis techniques and tools. ACM Comput. Surv. $44(2)$, 6:1–6:42 (2008)
26. Freiling, F.C., Holz, T., Wicherski, G.: Botnet tracking: exploring a root-cause methodology to prevent distributed denial-of-service attacks. In: di Vimercati, S.C., Syverson, P., Gollmann, D. (eds.) ESORICS 2005. LNCS, vol. 3679, pp. 319–335. Springer, Heidelberg (2005). https://doi.org/10.1007/11555827_19
27. Garfinkel, T., Adams, K., Warfield, A., Franklin, J.: Compatibility is not transparency: VMM detection myths and realities. In: Proceedings of the 11th USENIX Workshop on Hot Topics in Operating Systems, ser. HOTOS 2007, pp. 6:1–6:6 (2007)
28. Hao, S., Abdulla, A., Jelena, M.: Cardinal pill testing of system virtual machines. In: Proceedings of the 23rd USENIX Security Symposium (2014)
29. Ishimaru, S.: Why corrupted (?) samples in recent APT? case of Japan and Taiwan. https://hitcon.org/2016/pacific/0composition/pdf/1201/1201%20R1%201500%20why%20corrupted%20samples%20in%20recent%20apt.pdf
30. Jing, Y., Zhao, Z., Ahn, G.-J., Hu, H.: Morpheus: automatically generating heuristics to detect android emulators. In: Proceedings of the 30th Annual Computer Security Applications Conference, ser. ACSAC 2014 (2014)
31. Mayer, J.R., Mitchell, J.C.: Third-party web tracking: policy and technology. In: Proceedings of the 33rd IEEE Symposium on Security and Privacy, ser. S&P 2012, pp. 413–427 (2012)
32. Jung, P.: Bypassing sandboxes for fun. https://www.botconf.eu/wp-content/uploads/2014/12/2014-2.7-Bypassing-Sandboxes-for-Fun.pdf
33. Kirat, D., Vigna, G., Kruegel, C.: BareCloud: bare-metal analysis-based evasive malware detection. In: Proceedings of the 23rd USENIX Security Symposium (2014)
34. Kirati, D., Vigna, G., Kruegel, C.: Barebox: efficient malware analysis on bare-metal. In: Proceedings of the 27th Annual Computer Security Applications Conference, ser. ACSAC 2011, pp. 403–412 (2011)
35. Kruegel, C.: Evasive malware exposed and deconstructed (2015). https://www.rsaconference.com/writable/presentations/file_upload/crwd-t08-evasive-malware-exposed-and-deconstructed.pdf
36. Lanzi, A., Balzarotti, D., Kruegel, C., Christodorescu, M., Kirda, E.: Access-Miner: using system-centric models for malware protection. In: Proceedings of the 17th ACM Conference on Computer and Communications Security, ser. CCS 2010 (2010)

37. Lindorfer, M., Kolbitsch, C., Milani Comparetti, P.: Detecting environment-sensitive malware. In: Sommer, R., Balzarotti, D., Maier, G. (eds.) RAID 2011. LNCS, vol. 6961, pp. 338–357. Springer, Heidelberg (2011). https://doi.org/10.1007/978-3-642-23644-0_18

38. Bordoni, L., Conti, M., Spolaor, R.: Mirage: toward a stealthier and modular malware analysis sandbox for android. In: Foley, S.N., Gollmann, D., Snekkenes, E. (eds.) ESORICS 2017. LNCS, vol. 10492, pp. 278–296. Springer, Cham (2017). https://doi.org/10.1007/978-3-319-66402-6_17

39. Maier, D., Müller, T., Protsenko, M.: Divide-and-conquer: why android malware cannot be stopped. In: Proceedings of the 9th International Conference on Availability, Reliability and Security, ser. ARES 2014 (2014)

40. Martignoni, L., Paleari, R., Roglia, G.F., Bruschi, D.: Testing CPU emulators. In: Proceedings of the Eighteenth International Symposium on Software Testing and Analysis, ser. ISSTA 2009, pp. 261–272 (2009)

41. Moser, A., Kruegel, C., Kirda, E.: Exploring multiple execution paths for malware analysis. In: Proceedings of the 28th IEEE Symposium on Security and Privacy, ser. S&P 2007 (2007)

42. Najmeh, M., Mahathi, P.A., Nick, N., Michalis, P.: Spotless sandboxes: evading malware analysis systems using wear-and-tear artifacts. In: Proceedings of the 38th IEEE Symposium on Security and Privacy, ser. S&P 2017 (2017)

43. Neugschwandtner, M., Comparetti, P.M., Platzer, C.: Detecting malware's failover C&C strategies with squeeze. In: Proceedings of the 27th Annual Computer Security Applications Conference, ser. ACSAC 2011 (2011)

44. Nikiforakis, N., Joosen, W., Livshits, B.: Privaricator: deceiving fingerprinters with little white lies. In: Proceedings of the 24th International Conference on World Wide Web, ser. WWW 2015, pp. 820–830 (2015)

45. Paleari, R., Martignoni, L., Roglia, G.F., Bruschi, D.: A fistful of red-pills: how to automatically generate procedures to detect CPU emulators. In: Proceedings of the 3rd USENIX Conference on Offensive Technologies, ser. WOOT 2009 (2009)

46. Pék, G., Bencsáth, B., Buttyán, L.: nEther: in-guest detection of out-of-the-guest malware analyzers. In: Proceedings of the 4th European Workshop on System Security, ser. EUROSEC 2011, pp. 3:1–3:6 (2011)

47. Petsas, T., Voyatzis, G., Athanasopoulos, E., Polychronakis, M., Ioannidis, S.: Rage against the virtual machine: hindering dynamic analysis of android malware. In: Proceedings of the 7th European Workshop on System Security, ser. EUROSEC 2014 (2014)

48. Raffetseder, T., Kruegel, C., Kirda, E.: Detecting system emulators. In: Garay, J.A., Lenstra, A.K., Mambo, M., Peralta, R. (eds.) ISC 2007. LNCS, vol. 4779, pp. 1–18. Springer, Heidelberg (2007). https://doi.org/10.1007/978-3-540-75496-1_1

49. Rieck, K., Schwenk, G., Limmer, T., Holz, T., Laskov, P.: Botzilla: detecting the phoning home of malicious software. In: Proceedings of the 2010 ACM Symposium on Applied Computing, ser. SAC 2010, pp. 1978–1984 (2010)

50. Rieck, K., Trinius, P., Willems, C., Holz, T.: Automatic analysis of malware behavior using machine learning. J. Comput. Sec. 19(4), 639–668 (2011)

51. Rossow, C., Dietrich, C.J., Bos, H.: Large-scale analysis of malware downloaders. In: Proceedings of the 9th Conference on Detection of Intrusions and Malware & Vulnerability Assessment, ser. DIMVA 2012 (2012)

52. Rutkowska, J.: Red pill... or how to detect VMM using (almost) one CPU instruction (2004). http://www.securiteam.com/securityreviews/6Z00H20BQS.html

53. Shinotsuka, H.: Malware authors using new techniques to evade auto-mated threat analysis systems (2012). http://www.symantec.com/connect/blogs/malware-authors-using-new-techniques-evade-automated-threat-analysis-systems
54. Simone, M., Yanick, F., Antonio, B., Luca, I., Jacopo, C., Dhilung, K., Christopher, K., Giovanni, V.: Baredroid: large-scale analysis of android apps on real devices. In: Proceedings of the 31st Annual Computer Security Applications Conference, ser. ACSAC 2015 (2015)
55. Singh A., Khalid, Y.: Don't click the left mouse button: introducing trojan upclicker (2012). https://www.fireeye.com/blog/threat-research/2012/12/dont-click-the-left-mouse-button-trojan-upclicker.html
56. Singh, A., Bu, Z.: Hot knives through butter: evading file-based sandboxes (2013). https://media.blackhat.com/us-13/US-13-Singh-Hot-Knives-Through-Butter-Evading-File-based-Sandboxes-WP.pdf
57. Sun, M.K., Lin, M.J., Chang, M., Laih, C.S., Lin, H.T.: Malware virtualization-resistant behavior detection. In: Proceedings of the 17th IEEE International Conference on Parallel and Distributed Systems, ser. ICPADS 2011, pp. 912–917 (2011)
58. Vasudevan, A., Yerraballi, R.: Cobra: fine-grained malware analysis using stealth localized-executions. In: Proceedings of the 27th IEEE Symposium on Security and Privacy, ser. S&P'06, pp. 264–279 (2006)
59. Vidas, T., Christin, N.: Evading android runtime analysis via sandbox detection. In: Proceedings of the 9th ACM Symposium on Information, Computer and Communications Security, ser. ASIA CCS 2014 (2014)
60. Yokoyama, A., et al.: SandPrint: fingerprinting malware sandboxes to provide intelligence for sandbox evasion. In: Monrose, F., Dacier, M., Blanc, G., Garcia-Alfaro, J. (eds.) RAID 2016. LNCS, vol. 9854, pp. 165–187. Springer, Cham (2016). https://doi.org/10.1007/978-3-319-45719-2_8
61. Yoshioka, K., Hosobuchi, Y., Orii, T., Matsumoto, T.: Your sandbox is blinded : Impact of decoy injection to public malware analysis systems. J. Inf. Process. 52(3), 1144–1159 (2011)

On the Weaknesses of Function Table Randomization

Moritz Contag$^{(\boxtimes)}$, Robert Gawlik, Andre Pawlowski, and Thorsten Holz

Horst Görtz Institute (HGI), Ruhr-Universität Bochum, Bochum, Germany
moritz.contag@rub.de

Abstract. Latest defenses against code-reuse attacks focus on information hiding and randomization as important building blocks. The main idea is that an attacker is not able to find the position of the code she wants to reuse, hence thwarting successful attacks. Current state-of-the-art defenses achieve this by employing concepts such as execute-only memory combined with booby traps.

In this paper, we show that an attacker is able to abuse symbol metadata to gain valuable information about the address space. In particular, an attacker can mimic dynamic loading and manually resolve symbol addresses. We show that this is a powerful attack vector inherent to many applications using symbol resolving at runtime, an ubiquitous concept in today's systems. More importantly, we utilize this approach to resolve and reuse functions otherwise unavailable to an attacker due to *function table randomization*. To confirm the practical impact of this attack vector, we demonstrate how dynamic loading can be exploited to bypass Readactor++, the state-of-the-art defense against code-reuse attacks, despite its use of booby traps and virtual function table (*vtable*) randomization. Furthermore, we present a novel approach to protect symbol metadata to defend against such attacks. Our defense, called Symtegrity, is able to safeguard symbols from an attacker, whilst preserving functionality provided by the loader. It is both orthogonal to existing defenses and applicable to arbitrary binary executables. Empirical evaluation results show that our approach has an overhead of roughly 8% during application startup. At runtime, however, no noticeable performance impact is measured, as evident from both browser and SPEC benchmarks.

1 Introduction

The continuous arms race between more sophisticated attacks and subsequent defense mechanisms has led to several new primitives both sides can make use of. More fine-grained ASLR [16] has been tackled by just-in-time ROP (JIT-ROP), which discloses memory pages at runtime and builds a ROP sequence on the fly [32]. In turn, several exploit mitigation systems have attempted to prevent such disclosure using *information hiding*. Most notably, *XnR* [3] and *HideM* [15] provide *execute-only* memory to mitigate *direct* code disclosure. *Heisenbyte* [33] also distinguishes memory access patterns, but implements *destructive code reads*

© Springer International Publishing AG, part of Springer Nature 2018
C. Giuffrida et al. (Eds.): DIMVA 2018, LNCS 10885, pp. 185–207, 2018.
https://doi.org/10.1007/978-3-319-93411-2_9

instead of restricting access per se. Thus, it ensures that information read by an adversary cannot be directly used in her exploit. *TASR* [4], on the other hand, is a randomization-based approach, which indirectly prevents an attacker from using the information she obtained before re-randomization. Finally, the *Readactor* system employs multiple techniques (namely, *execute-only* memory and trampolines) in order to overcome both *direct* and *indirect* memory disclosure attacks [10].

Nonetheless, any form of fine-grained randomization or diversification is inherently limited when aiming to prevent attacks based on *function reuse*. While an attacker will be limited in finding gadgets ending on a return, which reside at any offset within a function, she can resort to building an exploit chain only consisting of gadgets starting at a function beginning. The underlying idea is that it is still possible to build a payload this way and, what is more, that there are more sources leaking function addresses. Known function-reuse attacks [25,30] may obtain function addresses from functions imported from shared objects or virtual function tables as used in C++ binaries, respectively. This has led to the development of the state-of-the-art defense Readactor++ [11], which introduces booby traps [9] and function table randomization on top of Readactor in order to counter advanced function-reuse attacks. In particular, it prevents an attacker from re-using functions at virtual function callsites in case of an information leak. We consider Readactor++ to be the most complete mitigation to date.

On a more general note, any code-reuse attack requires an attacker to harvest pointers to code sequences of her interest in order to perform the desired computation. However, depending on the application layout as well as defenses present, not all interesting code sequences may be accessible via a pointer exposed by the application itself. Hence, an attacker might be able to obtain the required information by traversing the data structures present in the program's address space to obtain further pointers. Especially, the *symbol table* in Linux and the *export table* in Windows applications provide valuable information for an attacker. The symbols contained in this structure may refer to both functions and data, whereas arguably, the former is of higher interest for an attacker. As the loader parses the symbol table to serve symbol requests at runtime, it is naturally mapped into the application's address space. In Linux, symbol requests may be dispatched due to the first attempt to execute a lazily-bound function imported from another module (*dynamic linking*) or even explicitly upon a programmer's request (*dynamic loading*). Microsoft Windows uses a similar concept.

In this paper, we demonstrate that dynamic loading represents an attack surface not considered before in detail. If an attacker is equipped with capabilities to read from the symbol table, she is able to mimic the loader's symbol-resolving facilities and obtain function pointers of her choice exported by the module in question. Consequently, dynamic loading can be considered an Achilles' heel inherent to most applications: while strictly required in many practical scenarios, we show that it represents a powerful attack vector against many defenses. More specifically, we discuss the attack vector induced by dynamic loading in general, along with the required background. To demonstrate the practical impact, we show how the attack vector can be used to successfully exploit web browsers protected by the state-of-the-art exploit-mitigation system Readactor++. Along the way, we also demonstrate how booby traps inserted into the vtables are ineffective against *vtable crafting* (i.e., the usage of fake vtables) attacks on Linux. To ascertain feasibility on Windows the attack has also been implemented against Internet Explorer successfully, but had to be omitted due to space limitations.

To counter this type of attack, we discuss potential defenses and propose Symtegrity. In contrast, our defense leverages execute-only memory for hiding information about symbols: we replace readable symbol metadata with references to so-called *oracles* that return the symbol address when executed. The oracles are protected via execute-only memory and booby traps, thus an attacker is not able to disclose them (even in the presence of an arbitrary read/write primitive). To demonstrate the practical feasibility of the approach, we implemented a prototype of this defense for binary executables in a tool called Symtegrity. While our defense induces a start-up overhead of around 8% for the Chromium browser, the overhead during runtime is negligible in several browser benchmarks and SPEC. To foster research on this topic, we make our implementation freely available at https://github.com/RUB-SysSec/symtegrity.

In summary, we make the following contributions in this paper:

- **Dynamic Loading as an Attack Vector.** We show that dynamic loading is a potential attack vector inherent to many applications and has to be considered in the design of modern defenses.
- **Overcoming function table randomization and boopy traps.** We demonstrate a novel attack against the Readactor++ system. Our generic bypass is based on information used to implement dynamic loading and circumvents protective mechanisms present in Readactor++, such as booby traps and function table randomization.
- **Legacy-compatible, light-weight defense.** We propose a robust defense mechanism to mitigate the attack vector. It induces low overhead and can be added to arbitrary binary executables. Additionally, it is orthogonal to most proposed defenses.

2   Technical Background

2.1   Dynamic Loading

The linking process at build time, as well as the loading process at run time, both allow for a variety of different approaches. In the following, we provide an overview of both aspects and discuss why dynamic linking using lazy binding and dynamic loading are the preferred approaches in practice.

Static linking describes the process of resolving symbols imported by a binary object at compile time. The code or data belonging to the declared symbol is copied verbatim into the object that uses the symbol. In contrast, *dynamic linking* defers this process to runtime. Instead of copying the corresponding data into the object that *uses* the symbol, the data lies in the object *declaring* it, commonly called *shared object* or *shared library*. If a symbol is used for the first time (e.g., by calling an exported function), its address is resolved and cached for further use (called *lazy binding*). Although it is possible to resolve the addresses of all symbols during load time (so-called *eager binding*), it is not used per default because it significantly slows down the loading process.

Dynamic linking using lazy binding is in practice the de-facto standard for multiple reasons. For one, startup speed increases considerably, as symbols are merely loaded on demand, and only necessary shared libraries are loaded to improve responsiveness. Furthermore, when the same shared libraries are used by multiple processes, they are only copied once into physical memory and shared by these processes. In addition, dynamic linking has security implications: Delaying symbol resolution to run time—as opposed to compile time—results in more modular applications. Hence, if one component of an application is affected by a security-critical vulnerability, this component can easily be updated without having to recompile and redistribute the whole application. *Dynamic loading* provides the programmer with capabilities comparable to those used by the dynamic linker. Namely, he can load or unload shared objects into process memory and resolve symbols at runtime. This approach is mostly taken if, due to program logic, the choice of shared object is dependent on runtime state and cannot be made at link-time. For example, an optional feature in a shared object may only be loaded if said object file actually exists on disk. If the object is missing, the feature it provides is not available, but the application as a whole remains usable. To implement dynamic loading, the *glibc* standard library exposes, amongst others, the APIs `dlopen` and `dlclose` for loading and unloading objects, respectively. Furthermore, *glibc* provides APIs such as `dlsym` for resolving the address of a symbol within an object. Every object that exposes symbols contains a *symbol table* describing metadata associated with a symbol. `dlsym` parses said table upon looking up a symbol, which is why the information has to be loaded into (readable) memory.

2.2 Execute-Only Memory and Booby Traps

Execute-only memory is a technique that allows the operating system to protect memory pages such that they are neither readable nor writable, but still executable. This enables a plethora of use cases. Most notably, this concept goes well with schemes relying on *information hiding* (e.g., of *safe regions* [19]). Discovery of a hidden page does not immediately lead to disclosure of the page's content to the attacker. Consequently, execute-only memory protects against *direct* memory disclosure as used in the just-in-time ROP (JIT-ROP) attack [32].

Booby traps, a concept proposed by Crane et al. [9], are a mechanism to actively detect and respond to attacks against a given application. The main idea of booby traps is as follows: in a diversified application, code sequences—the actual booby traps—are added that trigger an active response, such as terminating the program or generating an alert. In a regular program run, these code snippets lie dormant and do not interfere with the normal program execution. However, if an attacker blindly executes a memory location, such as an entry in a randomized vtable, chances are high that she will hit a booby trap early on. This can be the case, for example, if the memory layout differs from what the attacker expects due to diversification.

2.3   Readactor++ Overview

Readactor [10] and its follow-up, Readactor++ [11], are state-of-the-art exploit mitigation systems. Due to space reasons, we can only briefly present the underlying approach, for a more detailed overview we refer to the corresponding papers and our technical report [8]. Readactor is a source-based solution and consists of several components. Its compiler applies fine-grained code diversification such that an attacker cannot make assumptions about the application's memory layout. Further, code and data are separated. This enables execute-only memory, which is implemented using extended page tables (EPT). Consequently, *direct* memory disclosure (as used in, e.g., JIT-ROP) is mitigated. Further, code pointers are hidden by replacing direct code references with *trampolines* lying in execute-only memory. This mitigates *indirect* memory disclosure, which leaks code layout via code pointers stored on the stack or heap (e.g., return addresses). The attacker can now merely leak the addresses of the trampolines. Readactor++ improves the system in order to mitigate function reuse attacks such as RILC [25] and COOP [30]. The core insight is that knowing the layout of function tables such as the Procedure Linkage Table (PLT) or virtual function tables (vtables) in C++ applications gives an attacker enough information to instantiate function-reuse attacks. Thus, Readactor++ chooses to *randomize* entries within both kinds of tables and again uses trampolines to *hide* its contents. Blind probing of table entries is mitigated by inserting booby traps in both PLT and vtables.

2.4   Crash Resistance

Recently introduced attack primitives abused either the ability of programs to restart or their ability to absorb critical access violations [13,14,31]. In both client and server applications, such primitives were used to safely probe the program's address space. Hence, the process does not terminate or automatically restarts if an address is queried that is either unmapped or not equipped with read permissions. Consequently, such primitives can be used to attack any form of *information hiding*: By simply scanning the whole address space, pages containing sensitive information (e.g., shadow stacks, process metadata, or encryption keys) can be unveiled, although no direct references to these sensitive regions exist. Especially probing the complete address space of complex applications, such as web browsers, is achievable within *one single* process, as it may survive erroneous memory accesses [14]. We term this type of crash resistance *intra-process crash resistance*. Scanning for hidden information in network services is possible within several processes, as each new request spawns a new server process [13,31]. Each of these processes may terminate abnormally without terminating the program. To distinguish this case (i.e., multiple processes are used to enable crash resistance), we use the term *inter-process crash resistance.*

3   Caveats of Dynamic Loading

3.1   Attacker Model

For the rest of the paper, we assume that the adversary has found a vulnerability that eventually allows her to read from or write to an attacker-chosen address, the latter with data of her choice (i.e., an arbitrary read/write primitive). We further assume that the attacker operates in a scripting environment (such as JavaScript within a browser) and can interactively respond to events concerning the underlying application. In addition, we assume the attacker to have knowledge about the system configuration, including applied defenses, and the application's source code.

In addition to defensive mechanisms assumed in attacker models of previous works [10,11,30,32], we assume a state-of-the-art exploitation mitigation such as Readactor++ to be in place:

- **Vtable Randomization and Booby Traps.** Vtables are randomized and their entries are hidden behind trampolines and interleaved with booby traps (cf. Sect. 2.3).
- **Writable ⊕ Executable Memory.** The system allows memory pages to be either executable or writable, but not both.
- **Execute-only Memory.** The system is able to mark pages as executable, but neither writable or readable. We expect the target application to mark code sections accordingly (e.g., trampolines).
- **Fine-grained ASLR.** The system provides capabilities to randomize applications at the function level (i.e., we assume a stronger randomization compared to standard coarse-grained ASLR).
- **Brute-forcing Mitigation.** We expect the application to actively respond to a detected attack, for example by preventing automatic restarts in response to hitting a booby trap.

3.2   Attack Overview

The attack makes use of the fact that most of the memory that is used for the dynamic loading mechanism has to be readable. Generally speaking, the attacker is able to re-implement the system's dynamic loading mechanics with the help of available scripting engine capabilities and therefore can obtain the address of critical functions like `system` in `libc` to execute a *function-reuse* attack. Harvesting code pointers is a critical step for most kinds of code-reuse attacks. For one, overwriting a code pointer might eventually enable control over the program counter, whereas proper combination of known pointers is a key ingredient of modern exploit chains. With the recent advance of defense techniques that limit the set of valid targets of an indirect control flow transfer, especially those code pointers become important which point to the *beginning* of a function. Given such pointers, an attacker can set up a *function-reuse* attack which re-uses either whole functions or parts of it, starting from its entry up to a certain instruction [18,25,30]. To be able to re-implement the dynamic loading mechanics and resolve symbols of her choosing, the attacker has to obtain a module base address (ideally the base address of the main module). This can be done with the help of an existing information leak vulnerability or advanced offensive techniques like crash-resistant scanning primitives [14]. Given the module's base address, the attacker is able to parse the binary file format header information and traverse the structures that hold information about the loaded modules and the symbols they export. In case of the *glibc* runtime, the attacker is able to obtain the address of the link_map data structure [17], a linked list. From there, she can traverse the list to obtain the module base of any module loaded into the process (e.g., by comparing against its file name). Then, given the correct module base, she can resolve any exported symbol from the module by parsing the file format in memory with the help of the scripting environment. Since the loader requires these data structures to resolve symbols, they must be present in memory.

Summing up, our attack relies on the fact that symbol metadata, while required by the loader for functionality such as dynamic loading, poses a viable source of function pointer leaks which can be subsequently used when mounting a function-reuse attack.

3.3 Example: Bypassing Readactor++

As an example of how an attacker can abuse dynamic loading in a function-reuse attack against a state-of-the-art exploit-mitigation system, we show how to exploit a Readactor++-protected variant of the Chromium web browser in version 40.0. The software is running on Ubuntu 14.04 with Linux kernel 3.13 patched for EPT support. Note that we re-introduced the same bug (CVE-2014-3176) the original Readactor++ paper protected against [24].

The instantiation of our attack follows the basic steps laid out in Sect. 3.2. However, it has to account for some peculiarities of the exploit-mitigation system in use, Readactor++. The main challenges lie in the randomized layout of virtual function tables and the extensive use of execute-only memory. In summary, we are able to bypass trampolines which hide code pointers by manually resolving addresses of functions of interest. We use this facility to retrieve a function gadget used in a later part of our attack and a critical function used in our payload. Further, we are able to perform vtable *crafting* in order to bypass booby traps (which lie in randomized vtables). This is possible because Readactor++ does not restrict the set of vtables usable at a callsite. As the index into the vtable is randomized at the callsite, execute-probing most likely triggers a booby trap. Effectively, this yields no control over the entry that is called, preventing one from mounting vtable reuse attacks such as COOP [30]. Instead, we *craft* a *fake* vtable. Finally, we employ a new kind of crash resistance to probe the callsite's index and eventually execute our payload. This is implemented by abusing Chromium's process creation model.

Enabling Function-Reuse Attacks. The general idea of our attack is to replace the *xvtable* pointer with a so-called *Entry-point gadget*, as introduced by Göktaş et al. [18]. The gadget (*EP gadget*, for short) designates a sequence of instructions starting at a function entry and spanning all instructions till the first indirect call or jump. To find a suitable gadget, we symbolically execute paths in exported functions that start at function entry and end at an indirect call site. Symbolic execution then lets us filter for paths where the indirect call target—and its parameters—depends on the first parameter of the analyzed function (passed via `rdi`). We found `_obstack_newchunk`, exported by `libc`, which eventually calls `[rdi + 0x38]` with `[rdi + 0x48]` as its first argument. If we can execute the gadget and enforce the following layout on the object in `rdi`, `system` gets called with the correct argument:

```
byte ptr [rdi + 0x50] ← 1
qword ptr [rdi + 0x38] ← &system
qword ptr [rdi + 0x48] ← &system_argument
```

Our analysis is similar to the one used to discover functions for *function chaining* [14]. While our analysis yields several potential gadgets, we did not investigate their feasibility, as one function gadget is enough to successfully mount our attack. Because we target semantical properties only, the approach is invariant to fine-grained diversification as employed by Readactor++ and similar defenses.

Obtaining the Gadget. We obtain read/write primitives by using an out-of-bounds access in `Array.concat()` and predict the allocation address of an object of type `XMLHttpRequest`. As we are equipped with an arbitrary read/write primitive, we can parse metadata of Chrome's allocator, PartitionAlloc, to calculate the bucket the next allocation of said object will be placed in.

The predicted object provides us with a pointer to an *xvtable*. It is important to note that these pointers point into Chromium's module range, so we can use them to deduce its base address. However, we anticipate that in the context of an attacker with crash resistance at her hand, it is hard to prevent leakage of module base addresses, as the attacker is able to scan the memory until a module base address is found. Since the memory is only read during the scan and not executed, active countermeasures like booby traps are ineffective.

Given the module's base address, we first obtain the pointer to the `link_map` structure, which contains information about all shared objects loaded into the process space. We can then walk the list manually to find the base address of the C standard library, `libc`, and resolve the EP gadget by walking the symbol table. Hence, we mimic the loader's functionality from the JavaScript context and manually perform all necessary steps.

Preparing the Object. Figure 1 depicts the modifications we make to the predicted object. Essentially, we utilize *vtable crafting* to perform the attack.

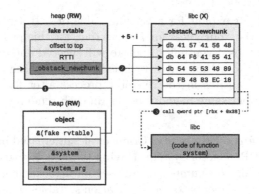

Fig. 1. Schematic overview of our attack: we perform a vtable crafting attack instead of a traditional vtable reuse attack. To this end, we put a fake *rvtable* in memory and modify our object to point to it (edge ❶). Also, we prepare the object according to the semantics of our EP gadget. In the *rvtable*, we replace the *xvtable* pointer to point to our EP gadget instead (_obstack_newchunk, edge ❷). If we hit a callsite to our object with an *applicable* index i, edge ❸ will call system with the given argument.

This is possible since *rvtable* pointers are not enforced to lie in specific memory pages or to belong to a set of whitelisted vtables. Hence, we can craft a *fake rvtable* on the heap and make its *xvtable* pointer point to the beginning of our EP gadget. Concretely, we add an offset $i \cdot (-5)$ to the EP gadget pointer such that the beginning of the gadget lies in some entry within the *xvtable*. Also, we modify the object according to the constraints given in Sect. 3.3. It is crucial to note that by *replacing* the *xvtable* pointer, we bypass booby traps completely. Booby traps in Readactor++ are interspersed among entries in the *xvtable*. Our object interprets the function _obstack_newchunk itself as *xvtable*. Therefore, callsites targeting the aforementioned object cannot trigger booby traps, hence this defense approach does not hinder the attack in any way.

Triggering the Gadget. Having set up the object, triggering the gadget is not as straight-forward due to the randomized vtable layout in Readactor++. Depending on the callsite, the application will call our gadget with an offset of $5 \cdot i$, with $i \geq 0$ unknown (and limited by the number of entries in the *xvtable*). To keep the application alive despite faults due to the unknown vtable offset, we resort to a form of *inter-process crash resistance* by abusing the Zygote process creation model as used in Chromium.

On startup, Chromium forks a designated process, the so-called *Zygote*, to speed-up responsiveness when new tabs are opened [7]. In it, necessary shared objects are already loaded and initialized. If a new tab is opened, the Zygote forks a new process which is responsible for said tab (the *renderer process*). The forked process inherits the Zygote's memory layout and little additional initialization is required. We can use this behavior to our advantage and spawn the function-reuse attack outlined above. To this end, from one main tab, we spawn several tabs, each running our exploit for a varying value of i. If a tab crashes due to an access violation (i.e., our guess for i was wrong for this process), it does not influence any other tabs. Eventually, one tab will succeed and execute system$(\cdot)$ via the EP gadget. Note that our attack is invariant to the fact whether i is randomized for the callsites in the renderer process after forking. We are not dependent on the exact same memory layout in each renderer.

Increasing Bruteforce Efficiency. Crane et al. anticipated bruteforce attacks in the design of the Readactor system. Having to guess i correctly would mean the defender can scale the number of guesses an attacker has to perform linearly by adding more elements to the application's vtables. Considering the soft boundaries on memory usage nowadays, this is a reasonable way to increase the attack complexity a bit. Still, an attacker has multiple options. For one, she can simply choose the smallest vtable she is still able to trigger a virtual callsite for. But what is more, the correct choice of the EP gadget decreases the number of guessing attempts by a factor. In our case, _obstack_newchunk allows execution from offsets 0, +5, and +10 without impacting the semantics of calling the attacker's designated function. This effectively increases the chance of guessing one *applicable* index i by the factor of three.

4   Defense: Symbol Integrity

As discussed in Sect. 2.1, abandoning dynamic loading altogether is not an option in typical environments. Hence, we propose in the following an approach to restrict access to vital symbol information for every piece of code but the loader itself that is also compatible with legacy binaries. This effectively prevents an attacker from discovering any usable call targets using function exports and prevents her from setting up a usable payload.

A related defense is implemented in Microsoft's *Enhanced Mitigation Experience Toolkit* (EMET [23]). Its feature *Export Address Table Filtering Plus* (EAF+) restricts accesses to symbol information coming from blacklisted modules. However, several bypasses exist [2,14,27] which leverage functionality in white-listed modules to access export address tables. Further, since only specific pointers to the symbol table are protected by EMET, it is also possible to scan for symbol tables in memory directly. In practice, EAF+ might also lead to compatibility problems if a legacy module ends up on the blacklist for erroneous reasons. This motivates us to provide a more complete protection that does not rely on blacklists, but builds upon information hiding. In order to prove feasibility, we implemented our approach on top of the Readactor++ system in a tool called *Symtegrity*. Our defense successfully mitigates attacks relying on symbol resolution, such as the one presented in Sect. 3, and can be integrated into existing defenses given that it utilizes an orthogonal defense approach.

4.1   High-Level Overview

The basic idea of Symtegrity is to leverage execute-only memory for hiding information about symbols. More specifically, we replace readable symbol metadata with references to so-called *oracles* that return the symbol address when executed. Since the oracles lie in execute-only memory, an attacker is not able to directly disclose them by reading the corresponding process memory (even in the presence of an arbitrary read/write primitive).

We implemented Symtegrity as a shared object for x86-64 Linux applications using the *glibc* standard library. Our implementation is compatible with legacy software and does not require source code access. Note that the general approach is not necessarily limited to Linux applications, but can also be implemented for different operating systems such as Microsoft Windows.

On startup, our defense processes each shared object needed by the protected application. In this step, the *relative virtual addresses* in symbol metadata (RVAs) are replaced by an index, whereas the RVA itself is stored in an execute-only mapping. Further, this mapping is updated on every shared object load. Entries in the mapping are not stored as data, but code: each entry is an *oracle* that, when executed, yields the data point as return value. The defense also hooks into various functions in the loader which should yield the RVA of the function it has been queried for (the full list is given in our implementation). In each of these functions, the hook re-translates the index back to the original RVA at runtime by querying the corresponding oracle. Thus, at no point during execution, the original symbol RVA is available to the attacker. It is only passed via ephemeral local variables inside those functions in the loader that are responsible for resolving symbols, such as dlsym. If an attacker already gathered the address of this function, she could resolve symbols legitimately. Our defense cannot protect applications that, by themselves, give access to such symbol resolution oracles. In the following, we briefly discuss several implementation details.

Hiding the Mapping. The mapping is allocated at program startup, or, in case of forking applications, at the startup of the child process. This way, we can ensure that we make proper use of ASLR as provided by the OS. Also, we mitigate shortcomings of ASLR implementations in presence of the Zygote model by re-randomizing the child process [20]. Further, the first entry in the mapping does not start directly at the mapping base, but is shifted down by a randomly chosen offset Δ (cf. Fig. 2). Indices are relative to the shifted mapping and do not leak the range of Δ. Even if an attacker was able to deduce the mapping base (i.e., the first page), she would not be able to call the oracle corresponding to an index she retrieved from the symbol table. Finally, in spirit of Readactor++, the mapping is guarded by inserting booby traps in between benign oracles. This prevents an attacker from randomly querying oracles in a page she assumes to be the mapping page and also prevents linear scans via read/write primitives and blind/crash-resistant execution/probing. Effectively, to probe any index, she would previously have to guess Δ in order to obtain the address of the first oracle. All other oracle indices are relative to that one.

However, since she has to resort to execution in order to probe entries, she will eventually hit the booby trap and the attack is successfully detected. Note that this is different from our assumption that an attacker is able to figure out the base address of *modules* of her choice: in this case, she merely reads at particular addresses in a crash-resistant manner. In case of the mapping, however, she has to *execute* code while being able to recover from crashes. Due to the presence of booby traps this is an adversarial scenario, since they actively react to probing attempts. Counteracting this requires a much stronger crash resistance primitive compared to the case of module base discovery.

Updating the Mapping. Upon startup, the defense processes all shared objects which are needed by the application and updates the mapping accordingly. The same happens at runtime once a new module is loaded. Each symbol gets assigned a random, unique index into the mapping (seeded anew for each process). The index indirectly refers to an oracle returning the RVA of the symbol. This is achieved by updating the ElfW(Sym) structure, which stores all metadata related to a symbol. Its st_value field contains the relative address from the module's base address to the symbol itself. Thus, the defense writes the assigned index into the symbol's st_value field and assembles an oracle of the following form in the mapping: mov rax, __real_rva; ret.

Note that during an update, the affected mapping page is unprotected for a small time window. However, we aim to keep that window as small as possible. Concrete empirical measurement results are presented in Sect. 4.2. The results show that the window is far too small to be of practical use for an attacker and we provide a more extensive discussion in Sect. 5.2. To mitigate an attacker deliberately reloading shared objects to increase her chances, one could cache the mapping per object and re-use it. As the mapping remains execute-only, the attacker cannot prolong the update window. However, due to caching, indices would not be re-randomized on the next library load. This does not help the attacker though, as she has no knowledge about the mapping itself.

Symbol Translation. Figure 2 depicts the translation process. While multiple loader functions are hooked, we will describe the process using the example of dlsym; other hooks are implemented in the same way. The hook operates at the epilogue of dlsym. Hence, it obtains both the proper base address the requested symbol lies in as well as the "encoded" index (due to our modifications, dlsym returns a seemingly valid address of the form base + index, from which we can deduce the index). From the index, Symtegrity calculates the offset into the mapping by multiplying it with the size of an oracle. The oracle is then executed and yields the real RVA in rax. The hook now adds the object's base address to rax and returns the resulting value, which is the full address to the symbol.

This sort of translation is applied to all relevant points in the loader and supports all dynamic linking and loading features we encountered in common applications, such as lazy binding, which resolves symbols on demand.

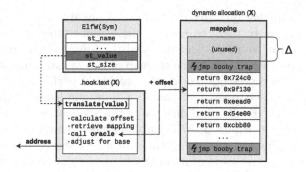

Fig. 2. The `translate` function receives an address encoding the index, with which the defense previously overwrote the `st_value` field. The function proceeds by scaling this index and use it as an offset into the mapping. By simply executing the function at said offset, it receives the original RVA. After adding the corresponding base address to it, the address is returned.

4.2   Evaluation Results

We evaluate the performance of Symtegrity on 64-bit Chromium 40.0 protected with Readactor++. It runs on Ubuntu 14.04 with Linux kernel version 3.13 with the Readactor patch. Due to the hypervisor used in Readactor++, we only use one core of our Core i7 CPU clocked at 1.2 GHz and disabled advanced features such as hyper-threading, an implementation requirement of Readactor++. 8 GiB of physical memory are available on this test machine.

Startup Time. In order to measure the baseline for the startup time, we added a dependency on a custom shared object to Chromium and ensured that this benchmarking library is initialized first. This enables us to measure the exact time throughout all stages of the Zygote process creation model. The library measures the path from the startup of Chromium to the entry point in the renderer process spawned for the initial tab. This includes the time to fork and initialize the Zygote, the Zygote to fork into a new renderer process, and to execute till the entry point of the renderer process. In a second run, we repeat the measurements with our defense applied. Finally, we take the geometric mean over 100 runs.

Overall, Symtegrity induces an overhead of roughly 8% at startup. The unprotected Chromium takes about 6.9 s to finish this measurement, whereas the protected variant takes about 7.5 s on average. Note that this slowdown mostly impacts the startup time of the Zygote, which is done only once when starting the browser. Furthermore, the startup overhead is dependent on the number of dynamically linked shared objects. An application that does not link as many shared objects is subject to a lower overhead on startup. When the Zygote process is already running, the additional delay in opening a new tab with our defense in place is about 0.3 s. This delay is hardly noticeable by a user working with the browser.

Load Time. To further quantify the impact of our defense, we measured the average time Symtegrity takes to update the symbol table of a newly loaded shared object. Hence, we micro-benchmarked the function that processes every object at Chromium startup (i.e., the startup of the Zygote process). Note that the timings are also representative for the workload performed if an object is loaded dynamically via `dlopen`. On startup, Chromium loads 84 shared objects of varying size, which are all linked directly to the application. To set things into perspective, the objects export 51,873 symbols which all have to be processed by Symtegrity. Measuring the processing time for all 84 shared objects loaded on startup yields a geometric mean of roughly 743 µs per shared object. Given that new shared objects are not loaded as often at runtime as during the application's startup phase, we deem the performance overhead reasonable.

Absolute Calls. We counted the number of actual calls dispatched to functions related to symbol resolution. During startup, 7 calls to `dlopen`, 43 calls to `dlsym`, and 217 calls to `_dl_fixup` were recorded. The first two APIs are manifestations of *dynamic loading*, as discussed in Sect. 2.1. We emphasize that these calls do not include shared objects loaded due to *dynamic linking*. The latter API is called when a lazily-bound symbol is requested for the first time.

Mapping Update. Finally, we measured the time in which parts of the mapping are accessible via memory reads. This situation occurs every time the mapping is updated (i.e., a new module is loaded for which oracles are inserted into the mapping). We measured the time from which on write permissions are in place (which imply read access as well) up to the point where permissions are switched back to execute-only. We noticed differences when measuring the window and hence distinguish two phases: one from application startup till the start of the renderer process and another one from that point onwards. For each phase, we averaged the results across multiple runs. For the first phase, covering the application's startup, 468,687 update events have been recorded. The geometric mean of the time window in which the mapping is unprotected is around 1,623 ns, whereas the average value is around 4,149 ns. Consequently, we detected 316 outliers that diverge by more than one standard deviation, where the maximum value lies at 9.948 ms. The second phase covers the time frame from the renderer's entry point to the point where it successfully loaded a page. Naturally, we recorded fewer events. The geometric mean across 7,200 data points is around 2,104 ns, the average value around 2,123 ns. As both timings are close to each other, fewer outliers were found. The maximum value of all 83 outliers lies at 0.0605 ms. While we are unable to give concrete evidence as for the root cause of the higher number of outliers during startup, we suspect them to be due to the high amount of mapping updates and a result of scheduling events. Still, as an attacker does not yet have control over the application during startup, we do not deem this a shortcoming of our approach.

Evidently, the duration in which the mapping is unprotected during an update is far smaller after startup. We argue that this time window is far too small to be of practical use for an attacker. A detailed discussion about the feasibility of this attack and countermeasures is given in Sect. 5.2.

Benchmarks. To evaluate Symtegrity's performance overhead, we ran a SPEC CPU2006 INT benchmark, using SPEC version 1.1. Specifically, we averaged over 10 runs using the *ref* test set and 3 iterations per individual benchmark. The top of Table 1 shows the results (lower numbers are better). It shows the runtime of runs using both the unprotected program (second column) and the one protected by Symtegrity (third column) as well as the relative overhead. The overall overhead is based on the geometric mean of the individual benchmark results. As evident from the table, our prototype implementation incurs almost no observable overhead. This is expected, as the SPEC benchmarks are used to measure performance overhead for computationally intensive tasks. Symtegrity, however, only impacts runtime negatively during startup and upon calls to dynamic loading facilities.

Table 1. Results of the SPEC CPU2006 INT benchmarks (top; lower numbers are better) and JetStream (bottom; higher numbers are better).

SPEC Benchmark	Runtime (s)	+Symtegrity (s)	Rel. Overhead
400.perlbench	259	258	−0.55%
401.bzip2	386	387	+0.22%
403.gcc	246	247	+0.37%
429.mcf	289	288	−0.27%
445.gobmk	390	391	+0.36%
456.hmmer	367	368	+0.38%
458.sjeng	422	422	−0.18%
462.libquantum	316	316	+0.07%
464.h264ref	433	435	+0.42%
471.omnetpp	321	322	+0.39%
473.astar	345	347	+0.40%
483.xalancbmk	203	201	−0.80%
Overall SPEC (geometric mean)	323.62	323.84	+0.0649%
Latency	43.014 ± 3.2720	42.641 ± 0.7330	+0.875%
Throughput	134.82 ± 3.9437	135.36 ± 1.5001	−0.399%
Overall JetStr.	81.934 ± 3.9436	81.812 ± 0.8489	+0.149%

We also conducted a benchmark using the JetStream 1.1 JavaScript benchmark suite [34]. It combines several well-known benchmarks, such as SunSpider, Octane, and those of LLVM, and yields scores for latency, throughput, and an overall score [34]. The bottom of Table 1 shows the results (higher numbers are better). To perform the benchmark, we started the Chromium browser protected by Readactor++ and ran the JetStream benchmark suite to obtain the *Base* column. We repeated the same process using the Readactor++-protected browser with Symtegrity on top to obtain the measurement values in the column titled +*Symtegrity*. JetStream runs each individual test three times and reports a score for each, along with the specific scores shown in Table 1. Evidently, the overall score of our defense lies well within the uncertainty of the base score, indicating that no measurable overhead is introduced when considering the performance of JavaScript in the browser. These results are expected, as Symtegrity mainly affects the browser's startup time.

To quantify the amount of new libraries that need to be hooked by our defense when rendering a web page, we visited the global top 500 pages, as reported by Alexa [1]. We allocated a time span of six seconds for each individual site to load. All in all, only one new shared object, `libfreebl3.so`, would be loaded dynamically, for 9 out of 500 pages. This is also due to the fact that Chromium aims to optimize load times by pre-emptively loading objects on start up, as seen in Sect. 4.2. This supports the fact that at runtime, only few (comparatively costly) updates to the mapping have to be performed by Symtegrity.

5   Discussion

5.1   Scope and Limitations of Our Defense

Symtegrity focuses on restricting access to vital symbol metadata to the respective functions in the loader. It is developed as an orthogonal defense mechanism that is a crucial building block for state-of-the-art defenses that still expose aforementioned data to an attacker. Our approach assumes that the protected application does not expose an oracle to the attacker which is capable of leaking symbol addresses. This covers both intentional oracles, which can be deemed unlikely to occur in common applications, as well as any kind of side-channel. For example, we suggest using *eager binding* in order to prevent exposing an address oracle via resolving functions, such as proposed by Readactor++. Still, detecting such cases in an automatic fashion arguably is hard and thus cannot be covered by Symtegrity. This poses the greatest limitation of our approach.

Furthermore, in a full exploit-mitigation system, one also has to prevent the attacker from disclosing function addresses directly. Since Symtegrity focuses on preventing an adversary from resolving the symbol addresses manually by using the available metadata, attacks using function addresses disclosed previously are out of scope. Hence, Symtegrity is an important piece of the defense puzzle rather than a full-fledged protection system on its own. To this end, we tested an exemplary configuration in which we applied Symtegrity to a Readactor++-protected application. Note that an attacker is unable to use any function pointer in the Procedure Linkage Table (PLT) as it is randomized and interspersed with booby trap entries. Therefore, in the case of Readactor++, she cannot use symbol-resolving functions such as `dlsym` even if the application intentionally exposes them. In the presence of such a defense, more sophisticated attacks that directly scan the remaining readable memory to deduce symbol addresses from its metadata are mitigated.

In the current design, an attacker can potentially correlate the oracle index (found in the st_value field) with the symbol itself, e.g., via the st_name field of the ElfW(Sym) structure. However, it is important to note that possible attack scenarios using this correlation make assumptions that are difficult to satisfy in practice. Assuming that the attacker knows both the symbol mapping's base address as well as the offset Δ into the mapping (at which the first oracle lies), she can query any oracle to retrieve the original RVA. Consequently, in its current state, Symtegrity's security relies on keeping the base address and Δ secret. This is achieved by the underlying system's memory layout randomization capabilities, execute-only memory, as well as booby traps guarding the mapping against execute-probing. Still, the attacker's ability to correlate symbols and oracle indices can be counteracted by extending the current prototype system with two features. First, we can protect the st_name field in the same manner as we already do with the st_value field. A second extension would involve randomization of the layout of the symbol table in memory. This prevents attacks where an attacker assumes the i-th function exported by, e.g., libc, to be system. By applying the same reasoning to the *non-randomized* symbol table in memory, she would still be able to correlate function and oracle index for a specific version of the library, despite the protections in place. However, we assume the current state of protection (randomization of base addresses, execute-only memory, random offset Δ, and booby traps) to be sufficient. Given these assumptions, an attacker is not able to query the oracle corresponding to a symbol of interest in the current approach. As the aforementioned extensions would impact the system overhead negatively, we decided not to include them at this point.

5.2 Data Race on Mapping Update

During dynamic loading, Symtegrity has to change the access permissions of the mapping containing the symbol address oracles. This leaves them unprotected for a small time frame in which an attacker could leak information by direct memory disclosure (see Sect. 4.2). Namely, she would obtain the real symbol RVA returned by an oracle. However, the attacker has to overcome multiple hurdles before being able to do so: First, she must be able to trigger the process in which the mapping gets updated in the first place, i.e., load a new module into the process. This is not a common feature in applications that can be triggered arbitrarily by an attacker. In our tests only one shared object was dynamically loaded after the startup process (see Sect. 4.2). Furthermore, even if the attacker can trigger the dynamic loading of a shared object, she has to be able to do it multiple times in order to win the race. Second, she has to know the base address of the mapping and the random offset Δ upfront. Third, the disclosure has to be fast enough to win the race against the defense re-protecting the affected page with execute-only permissions. We consider these conditions unlikely in practice.

5.3   Applicability of Our Attack

In Sect. 3.3, we presented an exemplary attack on the state-of-the-art exploit mitigation system Readactor++. We argue that our attack is feasible against other defenses and hence we now discuss the applicability of our attack to related approaches which also leverage information hiding for exploit mitigation.

HideM and XnR. Gionta et al. presented *HideM*, a system implementing information hiding in order to mitigate memory disclosure vulnerabilities [15]. This is achieved by leveraging the TLB split mechanism which allows HideM to serve different views into a page, depending on the type of access (data read or instruction fetch). Similarly, Backes et al. presented *XnR* (*Execute-no-Read*) [3], which, to some extent, achieves a similar form of information hiding based on *non-present* pages and a page fault handler. Both approaches aim to mitigate direct disclosure of executable pages by either returning dummy values upon a read or preventing read access altogether. Consequently, our attack is directly applicable to either of the aforementioned systems. At no point during the attack, direct disclosure of code pages is required.

Heisenbyte. Tang et al. presented *Heisenbyte*, along with the concept of *destructive code reads* [33]. The main idea is that upon a read, the operation is served, but the corresponding bytes are replaced by random values. Effectively, this ensures that reads serviced from executable pages do no longer correspond to the bytes that are executed at the very same address. What distinguishes this system from *HideM* and *XnR*, regarding our attack, is the fact that it also assumes load-time fine-grained ASLR. Our attack, however, neither reads executable pages nor does it make assumptions about the memory layout other than the address at which an exported function (such as _obstack_newchunk) lies. Hence, it should be applicable to Heisenbyte as well. Still, we recognize this as an underlying requirement for all fine-grained randomization-based systems: Such approaches have to be aware of any references into the code in order to keep the program intact. A concrete instantiation would be support for dynamic loading and symbol resolution. The aforementioned issue requires such systems to either refrain from randomizing referenced locations such as function start addresses or to deliberately update the references to be synchronous with the new memory layout.

TASR. Bigelow et al. presented *TASR*, a system to re-randomize an application's memory layout at predefined points in time [4]. TASR observes a set of system calls associated with either category and re-randomizes the memory layout every time one of these syscalls is requested. Making a definite statement about the applicability of our attack in presence of TASR is difficult. For one, TASR does not explicitly take JIT engines into account. Consequently, applicability highly depends on where the I/O boundary is placed between the scripting engine and the native context. More specifically, searching the module base would most likely not trigger re-randomization as no syscalls are involved. Still, triggering the object's callsite may very well involve syscalls along the way and re-randomize the memory layout. Also, the validity of obtained symbol RVAs may be affected, depending on the way such references are kept synchronous. In the end, one has to consider trade-offs in order to meet the performance requirements imposed upon the scripting facilities in modern browsers when placing the I/O boundary. Unfortunately, TASR's implementation is not available such that we have to discuss these aspects solely on the claims made in the original paper.

5.4   Limitations of Our Attack

While the attacks presented in Sect. 3.3 primarily serve as a proof-of-concept to demonstrate how an attacker can abuse dynamic loading, we discuss in the following some practical hurdles we came across in the Readactor++ bypass (see also our TR [8]). First, we had to disable Chromium's popup blocker. With the popup blocker in place, our main tab would not have been able to spawn the additional tabs that effectively brute-force the unknown index i. While this is a limitation of our attack against the Readactor++-protected Chromium, it is no inherent limitation of the underlying attack vector. However, spawning several tabs of which one is the succeeding exploit and others abort abnormally is usually prevented, because browsers do not restart on crashes. This was solved with inter-process crash resistance, and could be prevented by locking the system after exceeding a specific number of tab crashes. However, browser vendors trade off usability in favor of security in this case. Note that we only chained together two exported functions: _obstack_newchunk is used as first gadget to execute system at a C-style callsite, to perform our attack. Chaining multiple EP gadgets does not impact bruteforcing, i.e., we do not need to spawn more tabs. This is due to the fact that we can gather exports (code pointers) with *read* instructions (mimicking dlsym) from JavaScript. We only need to bruteforce the randomized index in the fake vtable to *start* the chain (i.e., *execute* a fake virtual function, our first gadget). This is done to circumvent booby traps. The subsequent EP gadgets are called at C-style callsites in the current gadget and are unprotected in *Readactor++*. However, if an attacker wants to chain EP gadgets which call subsequent gadgets at virtual function callsites, bruteforcing attempts would increase drastically, because different virtual function callsites would need to be bruteforced for the appropriate virtual function index. This is likely to reduce exploit success. Hence, we did not pursue such gadget chains further. For our attack, we disabled Chromium's seccomp sandbox. Obviously, it limits our ability to dispatch specific system calls, but does not prevent code execution per se, which was the sole aim of our function-reuse attack.

6   Related Work

We already discussed several papers closely related to our work and review several other related papers in the following. Similar to Readactor, execute-only memory was implemented for mobile devices by LR^2 [5]. By preventing attackers to use load instructions and hiding pointers to code, protected programs become resilient against memory disclosures. While this defense introduces execute-only memory to a different architecture, our approach is complementary as it enables protection of those functions that have to remain at discoverable locations, i.e., exports. Similarly, kR$^\wedge$X introduces execute-only memory to protect against code-reuse in the kernel [28], while our approach aims to protect against adversaries targeting complex userspace programs such as browsers. *Shuffler*, a re-randomization scheme thwarting JIT-ROP, is complementary to our defense, since we target an adversary trying to gather export symbols. It continuously changes code locations, and hence, impedes code-reuse attacks significantly [35]. Due to the time delay between memory disclosures used to build the attacker's gadget chain and its execution, the payload will fail, as the gadgets are elsewhere in the address space. A binary-only code diversifier, dubbed *CodeArmor*, protects code pointers against disclosure and re-randomizes code mappings to hinder code-reuse attacks [6]. Our defense is different as it aims at protecting symbol mappings, without significant run-time overhead. While more narrow in scope, it complements existing (compiler-based) code pointer hiding techniques.

ASLR-Guard [21] also uses information hiding to protect code locations. In contrast to Readactor, it does not require execute-only memory. Their approach assumes fine-grained ASLR and encrypts all code pointers to prevent an attacker from leaking information. The concept of code pointers encryption [22] can alternatively be used for Symtegrity when execute-only memory is not available. Instead of replacing symbol metadata with oracles in execute-only memory, one could encrypt the metadata with a key *hidden* in memory, whose location is only known to the symbol resolving functions. Unfortunately, this approach is vulnerable to adversaries which have a strong memory scanning primitive such as crash resistance at hand.

The attacks proposed by Di Federico et al. [12] are similar in spirit to the one we propose, as they also leverage the *glibc* runtime's symbol resolving capabilities. Instead of manually walking through the symbol resolution process, they use the internal functions responsible for resolving the addresses in the first place and call them on manipulated metadata. However, our attacker model does not cover the case where the corresponding function addresses already leaked to an attacker. Furthermore, their approach assumes that the targeted application is not a position-independent executable (PIE) and lazy binding is used either by the target binary itself or by at least one of the shared objects it depends on. This prerequisite is not required by our approach. Rudd et al. [29] recently propose a novel class of code-reuse attacks. Similar to our work, feasibility of their attack is shown on the example of Readactor and, in particular, indirect code pointers as implemented using, e.g., trampolines. However, instead of brute-forcing the randomized index into a vtable, they *profile* trampoline pointers and are subsequently able to induce malicious behavior using indirect code pointers.

Another defense that targets the loader itself is *Safe Loading* by Payer et al. [26]. They replace the default loader with a hardened one which effectively acts as a user-space sandbox. Modifications include restriction of existing functionality, such as preloading, and the addition of new security-related functionality, such as indirect branch checking. Nevertheless, the symbol resolution process still makes use of a module's symbol table. Consequently, our approach can be used to further refine the safe loader.

7 Conclusion

In this paper, we showed how existing mitigations can still be bypassed by proposing a novel attack vector based on symbol metadata. To demonstrate that such attacks are indeed feasible in practice, we provide a concrete instantiation of our attack against Readactor++ and are the first to demonstrate how the general concept of this defense can be bypassed. Furthermore, we mitigate the attack vector by replacing easily-accessible metadata with oracles located in execute-only memory that yield the corresponding value upon execution. Future defenses need to take symbol metadata into account given that this attack vector turns out to be the Achilles' heel of state-of-the-art defenses.

References

1. Alexa Internet, Inc.: Top 500 sites on the web. http://www.alexa.com/topsites
2. Alsaheel, A., Pande, R.: Using EMET to disable EMET. https://www.fireeye.com/blog/threat-research/2016/02/using_emet_to_disabl.html
3. Backes, M., Holz, T., Kollenda, B., Koppe, P., Nürnberger, S., Pewny, J.: You can run but you can't read: preventing disclosure exploits in executable code. In: ACM CCS (2014)
4. Bigelow, D., Hobson, T., Rudd, R., Streilein, W., Okhravi, H.: Timely rerandomization for mitigating memory disclosures. In: ACM CCS (2015)
5. Braden, K., Davi, L., Liebchen, C., Sadeghi, A.-R., Crane, S., Franz, M., Larsen, P.: Leakage-resilient layout randomization for mobile devices. In: NDSS (2016)
6. Chen, X., Bos, H., Giuffrida, C.: CodeArmor: virtualizing the code space to counter disclosure attacks. In: IEEE EuroS&P (2017)
7. Chromium: Usage of the zygote process creation model in Chromium. https://chromium.googlesource.com/chromium/src/+/master/docs/linux_zygote.md
8. Contag, M., Gawlik, R., Pawlowski, A., Holz, T.: On the weaknesses of function table randomization. Technical report, Ruhr-Universität Bochum (2018)
9. Crane, S., Larsen, P., Brunthaler, S., Franz, M.: Booby trapping software. In: ACM Workshop on New Security Paradigms (NSPW) (2013)
10. Crane, S., Liebchen, C., Homescu, A., Davi, L., Larsen, P., Sadeghi, A.-R., Brunthaler, S., Franz, M.: Readactor: practical code randomization resilient to memory disclosure. In: IEEE S&P (2015)
11. Crane, S., Volckaert, S., Schuster, F., Liebchen, C., Larsen, P., Davi, L., Sadeghi, A.-R., Holz, T., Sutter, B.D., Franz, M.: It's a TRAP: table randomization and protection against function reuse attacks. In: ACM CCS (2015)
12. Di Federico, A., Cama, A., Shoshitaishvili, Y., Kruegel, C., Vigna, G.: How the ELF ruined Christmas. In: USENIX Security (2015)

13. Evans, I., Fingeret, S., González, J., Otgonbaatar, U., Tang, T., Shrobe, H., Sidiroglou-Douskos, S., Rinard, M., Okhravi, H.: Missing the point(er): on the effectiveness of code pointer integrity. In: IEEE S&P (2015)
14. Gawlik, R., Kollenda, B., Koppe, P., Garmany, B., Holz, T.: Enabling client-side crash-resistance to overcome diversification and information hiding. In: NDSS (2016)
15. Gionta, J., Enck, W., Ning, P.: HideM: protecting the contents of userspace memory in the face of disclosure vulnerabilities. In: ACM CODASPY (2015)
16. Giuffrida, C., Kuijsten, A., Tanenbaum, A.S.: Enhanced operating system security through efficient and fine-grained address space randomization. In: USENIX Security (2012)
17. glibc. link.h header file, defining link_map. https://github.com/bminor/glibc/blob/master/include/link.h
18. Göktaş, E., Athanasopoulos, E., Bos, H., Portokalidis, G.: Out of control: overcoming control-flow integrity. In: IEEE S&P (2014)
19. Kuznetsov, V., Szekeres, L., Payer, M., Candea, G., Sekar, R., Song, D.: Code-pointer integrity. In: USENIX OSDI (2014)
20. Lee, B., Lu, L., Wang, T., Kim, T., Lee, W.: From zygote to morula: fortifying weakened ASLR on android. In: IEEE S&P (2014)
21. Lu, K., Song, C., Lee, B., Chung, S.P., Kim, T., Lee, W.: ASLR-guard: stopping address space leakage for code reuse attacks. In: ACM CCS (2015)
22. Mashtizadeh, A.J., Bittau, A., Boneh, D., Mazières, D.: CCFI: cryptographically enforced control flow integrity. In: ACM CCS (2015)
23. Microsoft: The Enhanced Mitigation Experience Toolkit. https://support.microsoft.com/en-us/kb/2458544
24. National Vulnerability Database: Vulnerability Summary for CVE-2014-3176. https://web.nvd.nist.gov/view/vuln/detail?vulnId=CVE-2014-3176
25. Nergal: The advanced return-into-lib(c) exploits: PaX case study. http://phrack.org/issues/58/4.html
26. Payer, M., Hartmann, T., Gross, T.R.: Safe loading - a foundation for secure execution of untrusted programs. In: IEEE S&P (2012)
27. Bania, P.: Bypassing EMET Export Address Table Access Filtering feature. http://piotrbania.com/all/articles/anti_emet_eaf.txt
28. Pomonis, M., Petsios, T., Keromytis, A.D., Polychronakis, M., Kemerlis, V.P.: kR^X: comprehensive Kernel protection against just-in-time code reuse. In: ACM European Conference on Computer Systems (EuroSys) (2017)
29. Rudd, R., Skowyra, R., Bigelow, D., Dedhia, V., Hobson, T., Crane, S., Liebchen, C., Larsen, P., Davi, L., Franz, M., et al.: Address-oblivious code reuse: on the effectiveness of leakage-resilient diversity. In: NDSS (2016)
30. Schuster, F., Tendyck, T., Liebchen, C., Davi, L., Sadeghi, A.-R., Holz, T.: Counterfeit object-oriented programming: on the difficulty of preventing code reuse attacks in C++ applications. In: IEEE S&P (2015)
31. Shacham, H., Page, M., Pfaff, B., Goh, E.-J., Modadugu, N., Boneh, D.: On the effectiveness of address-space randomization. In: ACM CCS (2004)
32. Snow, K.Z., Monrose, F., Davi, L., Dmitrienko, A., Liebchen, C., Sadeghi, A.-R.: Just-in-time code reuse: on the effectiveness of fine-grained address space layout randomization. In: IEEE S&P (2013)

33. Tang, A., Sethumadhavan, S., Stolfo, S.: Heisenbyte: thwarting memory disclosure attacks using destructive code reads. In: ACM CCS (2015)
34. WebKit: JetStream JavaScript benchmark suite. http://browserbench.org/JetStream/
35. Williams-King, D., Gobieski, G., Williams-King, K., Blake, J.P., Yuan, X., Colp, P., Zheng, M., Kemerlis, V.P., Yang, J., Aiello, W.: Shuffler: fast and deployable continuous code re-randomization. In: USENIX OSDI (2016)

Detection and Containment

FraudBuster: Temporal Analysis and Detection of Advanced Financial Frauds

Michele Carminati$^{(\boxtimes)}$, Alessandro Baggio, Federico Maggi,
Umberto Spagnolini, and Stefano Zanero

DEIB, Politecnico di Milano, Milan, Italy
{michele.carminati,federico.maggi,umberto.spagnolini,
stefano.zanero}@polimi.it, alessandro1.baggio@mail.polimi.it

Abstract. Modern financial frauds are frequently automated through specialized malware that hijacks money transfers from the victim's computer. An insidious type of fraud consists in repeatedly stealing small amounts of funds over time. A reliable detection of these fraud schemes requires an accurate modeling of the user's spending pattern over time. In this paper, we propose *FraudBuster*, a framework that exploits the end user's recurrent vs. non-recurrent spending pattern to detect these sophisticated frauds. *FraudBuster* is based on a learning stage that builds, for each user, temporal profiles and quantifies the deviation of each incoming transaction from the learned model. The final output is the aggregated score that quantifies the risk of a user of being defrauded. In this setting, *FraudBuster* detects frauds as transactions that are not simply "anomalous", but that would change the user's spending profile.

We deployed *FraudBuster* in the real-world setting of a national banking group and measured the detection performance, showing that it can outperform existing solutions.

1 Introduction

Financial frauds have been steadily increasing over the past few years, resulting in billions of dollar losses [1]. Malware seems to be evolving through the collaboration between malware creators, growing by 16% since 2016. In 2016 financial malware infected about 2,8 million personal devices, a 40% increase since 2015 [2]. Despite financial institutions rely on fraud-analysis systems, fraudsters keep refining their techniques to remain unaccountable. Automated frauds are typically implemented via specialized malware, sold in underground markets, that can be easily customized to perform and/or hijack money transfers. An insidious type of fraud consists in keeping a "low profile" by stealing small amounts of funds in multiple rounds over time. Due to their stealthiness and recurring nature, we call these attacks as *salami-slicing* frauds, referring to the well-known fraudulent technique [3]. Moreover, Internet banking seems like the perfect venue for this type of attacks, due to the increasing adoption of micropayment systems, with direct debit on the bank account. Detecting these sophisticated schemes requires a robust modeling of the end user's spending patterns to

C. Giuffrida et al. (Eds.): DIMVA 2018, LNCS 10885, pp. 211–233, 2018.
https://doi.org/10.1007/978-3-319-93411-2_10

exclude false positives due to legitimate, small-amount, recurrent transfers (e.g., subscriptions). The detection task is challenging because frauds are dynamic and "blend in" with legitimate transactions. Furthermore, the scarcity of publicly available, real-world datasets makes research in this area a daunting task. Our *state-of-the-art* analysis revealed that existing works presume the existence of periodicities in users' spending patterns, without verifying it on real data.

In this paper, we propose *FraudBuster*, a fraud-analysis system that aims to detect *salami-slicing* frauds by exploiting a precise modeling of recurrent vs. non-recurrent spending patterns. *FraudBuster* is based on a learning stage that automatically estimates the end user's temporal profiles by means of historical (and likely fraud-free) spending patterns and quantifies the deviation of the current user's spending profile from the learned model. In particular, we apply signal processing techniques to extract temporal patterns "hidden" in the time series obtained from the transaction history. We show that temporal patterns exist, and thus a fraud-detection technique augmented by temporal-pattern classification is more effective than conventional detection approaches. First, *Fraud-Buster* classify each user based on its spending pattern. Then if a user is labeled as "periodic" (i.e., his or hers spending patter is characterized by periodicity), *FraudBuster* aligns and averages the observed time series to create a reference pattern model. In other words, we derive the most likely spending activity. Small deviations from strict periodic pattern are accounted by the dynamic time warping (DTW) algorithm [4] that is adapted here to measure the similarity between two temporal sequences up to a small deviation from the reference pattern. For both users with and without periodic spending patterns, *FraudBuster* uses a proper time-windowing analysis of transactions. For each incoming transaction, *FraudBuster* measures the deviation (i.e., anomaly score) of the user's spending activity from the learned model. The final output is the aggregated score that quantifies the risk of a user of being defrauded. By doing this, *FraudBuster* supports the analysts' ex-post analysis (i.e., manual investigation of frauds), making analysts focusing only on highly ranked users and on transactions that deviates most from the user's spending pattern.

We tested *FraudBuster* in the real-world context of a large national bank. Leveraging the domain expert's knowledge, we reproduced *salami-slicing* frauds performed against banking users. *FraudBuster* achieves a detection rate remarkably above *state-of-the-art* approaches, detecting 60% more defrauded users. In addition, we prove the effectiveness of the *time-series* analysis on the detection performance and investigate the robustness of *FraudBuster* against mimicry attacks and real-world *salami-slicing* frauds.

The main contributions are:

- We conduct a case-study analysis on a real-world dataset to show the importance of modeling recurrent vs. non-recurrent spending habits.
- We design *FraudBuster*, an efficient tool to detect *salami-slicing* frauds based on an accurate modeling of the user's temporal profile.
- We provide a comprehensive evaluation of *FraudBuster* and show that it outperforms the state of the art.

2   Background and Motivation

Internet banking services are heavily targeted by cyber criminals. A compromised banking account can be used to directly steal funds from the available balance or can be sold on the underground market. The main tools exploited by fraudsters are the so-called "banking Trojans" or "infostealers," specific types of malware that leverage Man-in-the-Browser (MitB) techniques to intercept and modify web pages, as well as transaction content, at the level of the rendering engine of the browser, in a fully transparent way. Endpoint solutions offer little protection because they are hard to deploy uniformly, due to the variety of devices. Also, modern infostealers are often able to bypass the second factor authentication, if present, by infecting the mobile device and stealing the OTPs. Therefore, effective fraud-detection solutions to identify fraudulent transfers are still a much-needed product. In the context under analysis, frauds can be considered as anomalies in banking transactions. State-of-the-art detection systems rely on statistical and data-mining techniques to detect anomalous transactions and support the analysts during manual investigation. We can broadly distinguish between three main cases of interest. First, a transfer can be anomalous *per se*. For instance, a transfer of two or three orders of magnitude above the maximum amount ever transferred by a given user is clearly anomalous. Secondly, a transaction can be anomalous within a certain *context* (e.g., day, week, time of the year). Third, a *series* of non-anomalous transactions could be anomalous only when observed all together. These are called *collective* anomalies and, according to [5], are the most challenging to detect. Whenever a modern banking Trojan infects the victim's machine, it can execute multiple transactions, either piggybacking while the user is already performing online banking tasks (i.e., transaction hijacking), or simply while the browser is open (e.g., via session stealing). This allows the fraudster to keep a "low-profile" by transferring small amounts of funds in multiple rounds over time, and thus evading even the most advanced detection techniques. Nowadays collective anomalies are growing with the aid of sophisticated malware kits [6]. We use the term *salami-slicing* frauds, referring to the well-known fraudulent attack scheme [3], to indicate collective frauds perpetrated over a given time span (e.g., day, week, month) with the goal of automatically stealing substantial amount of funds from the victims.

2.1   Goals and Challenges

The goal of this work is to propose a practical answer to the aforementioned problem, so as to support the banking analyst dealing with *salami-slicing* frauds. Due to the strict dependency between these frauds and time, the problem can be reduced to an anomaly detection on time series. However, it is difficult to distinguish between users with vs. without periodic spending patterns. In fact, time series obtained from money transfers are characterized by stochastic attribute values and shifts in time, which may conceal the true periodicity. Another challenging aspect is that frauds are dynamic, resembling legitimate transfers (e.g., when performed using the victim 's computers as a proxy), rare, and hidden in each user's transactions. Hence, it is hard to detect frauds with real-world-compliant precision and efficiency.

3   Related Works

Fraud and anomaly detection are a wide research topic for which we refer the reader to [5,7,8]. In this section, we focus on fraud detection from a temporal point of view, showing that the current landscape of fraud-detection solutions is not sufficiently mature to detect stealthy attacks that, similarly to *salami-slicing* frauds, are performed with the goal of evading detection techniques. In particular, we analyze the banking, intrusion detection, and credit card fraud detection contexts that shares many common aspects and, hence, can be compared.

Internet Banking. One of the most recent and effective fraud-detection system for Internet banking is BankSealer [9]. It approaches the problem of detecting frauds from a temporal point of view by tailoring a set of thresholds on time-dependent attributes (e.g., number of transactions, the total amount, and maximum daily number of transactions per time windows). This technique models the spending habits in a simple yet effective way: a transaction is anomalous, in a certain time interval, if exceeds the set of detecting thresholds. However, BankSealer does not consider whether transactions exhibit a periodic and repeating pattern in a reference period (e.g., monthly, weekly, daily). This is reflected in a low detection rate when multiple low-amount frauds (like *salami-slicing* frauds) are observed. The unsupervised approach presented in [1] applies contrast pattern mining considering the dependence between events at different points in time to detect not fraudulent transactions but anomalous activities in the interaction between the bank's customer and the web application.

Intrusion Detection. In [10,11], the authors apply the Discrete Fourier Transform (DFT) on time series to identify anomalous frequencies. In particular, [11] compares the frequency representations by means of Mutual Information [12] to detect anomalies. In the same direction, [13] proposes a novel distance measure to compare two different DFT. However, these works rely on the assumption, not valid in our context, that the normal spectrum, derived from the network time series, is "flat", while the spectrum produced by an attack shows peak for specific frequencies.

Credit Card Fraud Detection. The authors of [14] propose time-based techniques applying a modified version of the k-means clustering algorithm to group transactions in each time window. The centroids of the resulting clusters (e.g., daily, weekly, and monthly cluster) are then used as baselines, and each new transaction's anomaly is quantified as the distance from such centroids. In [15], the authors compare well-known supervised techniques such as support vector machines, random forests and logistic regression applied on a real dataset. To consider time dependent features, they derive attributes by aggregating transactions, employing different time windows length. In [16], the authors aggregate transactions based on time windows of fixed length to extract time-dependent features. Then, they compute the anomaly score of a transaction with a logistic score. In [17], the authors employ the Basic Local Alignment Search Tool(BLAST) [18], a sequence alignment technique that identifies transactions that do not follow the spending pattern of the customers.

3.1 Critics

Existing works face the temporal anomaly detection problem by aggregating data instances in time windows and creating new time-dependent features, or by comparing past time series with the current one by means of the DFT. The main issue is that these methods assume that users exhibit periodic spending habits without demonstrating it. Another issue of the presented works is that they usually consider only few attributes for building user's profile. As demonstrated by our work, a deeper analysis of transaction's feature can be more effective. In addition, the authors in [1] show that classic time-based anomaly-detection methods (e.g., DFT) fail when applied *as is* in the online banking context, which is characterized by mixed scenarios, with users changing their habits over time. Beside this, the presented approaches based on DFT are interesting, but they usually assume an uncorrelated behavior for legitimate user (i.e., flat spectrum) and a "spiked" spectrum for the attacks. As shown in Sect. 4, this assumption does not hold up in our context. A final critic is the high complexity of existing works. They often require a temporal complexity that scales with mn, where n is the length of the historical time series in which we want to search a subsequence with length m. For a real-time analysis, it is impracticable since n is very high. The clustering algorithm proposed in [14] is also infeasible since it considers all the possible permutations in the time windows to solve the shift of transactions.

4 Case Study

4.1 Recurrent Spending Patterns Analysis

Since we found no work that verified the actual presence of periodicities in user's spending patterns we run a case study. We performed a temporal analysis of real banking transactions, looking for recurrent spending patterns. This analysis is

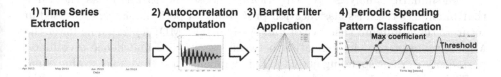

Fig. 1. Time-series analysis and periodic spending pattern classification.

an essential prerequisite for detecting *salami-slicing* frauds effectively. Our goal is to distinguish between *periodic* and *non-periodic* spending patterns. We focus on a "per user" temporal analysis, grouping bank customers and representing their activity with the time series of the daily number of transactions. These time series are characterized by isolated "spikes" (i.e., days in which the user performs transactions), interleaved by long idle periods. Moreover, we notice a minority of low peaks, which can be interpreted as noise, due to the intrinsic randomness of users' activity. As expected, time series present alignment problems between "corresponding" peaks (i.e., events belonging to different time series but "near" from the temporal point of view), due to the shifts in time of user's transactions. These make the analysis a challenging task.

Time Series Analysis and Periodic Spending Pattern Classification.
We consider weekly, bi-weekly, three-weekly, and monthly periodic spending patterns. The selection of "n-weekly" users comes from the need of finding the smallest reasonable recurrent spending pattern (i.e., periodicity), excluding sub-periodicities; i.e., we do not want to consider as monthly users, users which are simply "weekly users" (a month is a multiple of a week and, hence, a weekly user is also monthly users, but not vice-versa). We do not consider longer periods due to the limited timespan of the dataset under analysis. To spot recurrent transactions we rely on the autocorrelation analysis [19,20]. The correlation of a time series with itself at different mutual time-shifts measures their similarity and a high autocorrelation value at given time lag τ implies a temporal pattern with periodicity $T = \tau$. To limit the problem of small shifts in user activity, we smooth the autocorrelation values by applying a convolution with a triangular-shaped Bartlett filter [21] that spreads each transaction spike over its nearby days, implicitly giving a time-tolerance in pattern analysis. With respect to other methods such as DFT or semblance analysis (see [20] for common techniques used in the time series domain), we choose to use Bartlett filter and Autocorrelation since, after an empirical evaluation, they best manage time series characterized by spikes and noise without generating too much ripple in the frequency domain. In order to label a user as "periodic" or "non-periodic", we calculate all the autocorrelation coefficients for $\tau = \{$weekly, bi-weekly, three-weekly, monthly$\}$. Then, we test each user periodic behavior based on the largest autocorrelation coefficient. To distinguish periodic from non-periodic users, we set a threshold: if no autocorrelation coefficient overcomes this value, the user is labeled as non-periodic. The threshold is defined from a percentage of the auto-correlation value in the origin (i.e., for $\tau = 0$), as this sets the reference value for self-similarity analysis. We empirically choose the threshold as the value that minimizes the miss-classification probability of periodic users, expressed in terms of the Minimum Distance of Pair Assignment (MDPA) [22]. The lower the MDPA value is, the closer relation between users exists and hence a common periodicity in their spending activity. This happens for a threshold's value equal to 70%, which produces an abrupt change in the trend of the metric analysis. Figure 1 shows the applied methodology.

Table 1. Periodic spending pattern classification results.

Dataset	Classified periodic spending pattern (%)				
	Weekly	Bi-weekly	Three-weekly	Monthly	No periodicity
April–July	2.7	4.0	5.2	**32.0**	56.1
April–August	2.5	3.2	4.0	**32.8**	57.5

Results. We apply the aforementioned algorithm on the dataset under analysis. For this test, we keep users with at least one transaction per month in order to reduce the artifacts caused by occasional users. As shown in Table 1, most of users (about 56%) do not exhibit any measurable temporal pattern. However, a non-negligible portion of users, about 32% exhibits a monthly periodic spending pattern. If we consider also "n-weekly" users, the total number of periodic spending patterns reaches the 44%. Hence, the percentage of weekly, bi-weekly and three-weekly groups is quite small. From a manual inspection, we noticed that these groups are more subject to noise. This is also proved by the fact that their number largely decrease when considering longer timespan. Since we cannot prove with empirical evidence that these groups are statistically meaningful, we consider only the monthly periodicity. Finally, we test the classification algorithm on synthetic users, with different time span length. This analysis allows us to verify the quality of our classification algorithm, since it provides a ground truth and shows how the classification changes varying parameters and the timespan length. We run several tests, each one on 1,000 synthetic users, varying the time series length and the probability of a user to be *active* on monthly basis. For each of these configuration, we analyze the percentage of monthly users classified. With a longer time span, the percentage of non-periodic users identified as monthly users decreases, while the percentage of monthly users, identified as periodic, increases. This because in short time series the presence of noise and time shifts are much more relevant and leads to a wrong users' classification.

5   Approach Overview

In this section, we describe *FraudBuster*, an analysis system that detects *salami-slicing* frauds by exploiting recurrent vs. non-recurrent spending patterns.

5.1   Training Phase

The training phase takes as input the list of historical transaction and builds, for each user, the profiles that model the spending pattern. As depicted in Fig. 2, given the inputs, *FraudBuster* performs the training in two steps: *recurrent spending pattern analysis* and *temporal profile construction*. This phase is repeated at the end of each time windows (e.g., monthly) to keep into consideration shifts and updates of the user's spending pattern.

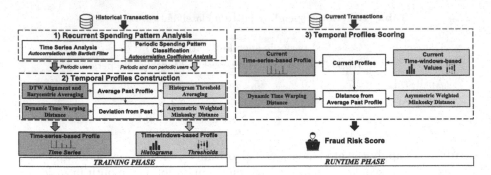

Fig. 2. *FraudBuster* approach: *time-windows-based* profile (light gray) and *time-series-based* profile (dark Gray) that are built for each user.

Recurrent Spending Pattern Analysis. Transactions time series are analyzed to extract user's recurrent spending pattern following the procedure described in Sect. 4. *FraudBuster* first applies the autocorrelation with the Bartlett filter to extract the autocorrelation coefficient. Then, it distinguishes periodic (i.e., monthly spending pattern) from non-periodic (i.e., non-monthly spending pattern) users by means of a threshold: if no autocorrelation coefficient overcomes this value, the user is labeled as non-periodic.

Temporal Profiles Construction. For each user, *FraudBuster* generates two classes of temporal profiles: the *time-series-based* and the *time-windows-based* profile. Each type of profile extracts different statistical features from the transaction's attributes (see Table 2), according to the type of model built.

The *time-series-based* profile is designed for periodic users only and evaluates the deviation of the current user's time series leveraging on their recurrent spending patterns observed in the past. In other words, it compares transactions time series in different time-periods and, therefore, it cannot be applied to non-periodic users since they don't show "similar" patterns that can be compared. Hence, it is built only on attributes that allows an accurate temporal analysis and for which the *time-windows-based* profile is not sufficient to discriminate anomalous transactions from legitimate ones: *Number of Transactions, Amount*, and *Total Amount* attributes.

The *time-windows-based* profile is designed for both users with periodic spending pattern and users with non-periodic spending pattern. It evaluates the deviation of the current user's behavior from the trained one aggregating transactions according to time windows of monthly length in a set of thresholds and histograms. In particular, it considers all features presented in Table 2 and does not compare "patterns" in data but only the aggregated attributes values in the time-windows. For these reasons, it is complementary to the *time-series-based* approach and is applied to both classes of users.

For both profiles, *FraudBuster* computes *the average past profile* and *the deviation* of past profiles from the average one. *FraudBuster* builds the *time-windows-*

based profile by means of the average histograms for categorical attributes and thresholds for numerical ones. The thresholds are built based on the mean and the standard deviation of attribute values. The deviation from the average histogram is computed using the asymmetric weighted Minkowski distance [23]. For the *time-series-based* profile, *FraudBuster* uses the DTW Barycenter Averaging (DBA) [24] method to compute the average time series and the dynamic time warping (DTW) distance [4] for computing the deviation.

5.2   Runtime Phase

At runtime, *FraudBuster* evaluates nearly real-time each new transaction against the trained profiles and ranks users according to the aggregated risk of being defrauded. In particular, it measures the deviation of the current spending behavior with respect to the average profile built during the training phase.

Temporal Profile Scoring. For both profiles, it computes the current temporal profiles and its distance from the trained average one. For the *time-windows-based* profile, *FraudBuster* incrementally builds the current threshold and histogram distribution, while for the *time-series-based* profile, *FraudBuster* incrementally builds the current time series. Then, it computes the distance from the average profile with the asymmetric weighted Minkowski distance for histograms, the percentage gap for thresholds, and the dynamic time warping (DTW) distance for time series. Finally, the anomaly score is defined as the relative difference between the deviation computed during training and the current distance. By doing this, it considers the variance of the user's spending behavior. The final output is represented by the ranked list of users ordered by the aggregated risk score, which keeps into consideration the *time-windows-based* and the *time-series-based* anomaly score of each transaction.

6   System Details

In this section, we describe how *FraudBuster* works, giving a detailed description of the *time-windows-based* and the *time-series-based* profiles.

6.1   Time-Windows-Based Profile

For each numerical attribute, during the training phase, *FraudBuster* builds a threshold on the average plus the standard deviation of attribute value. At runtime, the system computes the anomaly score as the percentage gap between the trained threshold and the current values of incoming transactions.

For each categorical attribute, during the training phase, *FraudBuster* computes the average histogram distribution that counts the occurrences of each attribute value over each time windows and the mean deviation of historical user's spending pattern (i.e., histogram) from the average one. The distance

---

Algorithm 1. Time-windows-based profile training and runtime phases (for user U).

   Input: Historical transactions of user U ;   // Training Phase

1 **for** a *in attributes* A **do**

2   **if** a *in numerical* **then**

3   **for** w *in historical time windows* W **do**

4 | $past\_profile_w(a) = \sum_{t \in w} a(t)$;   // cumulative value of the attribute a

5   **end**

6        $avg\_profile(a) = \sum_{w \in W} past\_profile_w(a)/W$;   // average value

7        $std\_dev(a) = \sqrt{(1/W) \sum_{w \in W} (past\_profile_w(a) - avg\_profile(a))^2}$;

          // deviation

8        $threshold(a) = avg\_profile(a) + std\_dev(a)$

9   **end**

10   **if** a *in categorical* **then**

11   **for** w *in historical time windows* W **do**

12 | $past\_hist_w(a) = hist(a(t)|t \in w)$;   // histogram of the attribute c

13   **end**

14       $avg\_hist(a) = \sum_{w \in W} past\_hist_w(a)/W$;   // average past histogram

15       $avg\_dev(a) = \sum_{w \in W} minkowski\_dist(past\_hist(a)_w - avg\_hist(a))/W$

16   **end**

17 **end**

   Result: $time\_win\_profile(U) = ([threshold(a)], [avg\_dev(a)])$ for a in A

   Input: Current transactions of user U ;   // Runtime Phase

18 **for** a *in attributes* A **do**

19   **if** a *is categorical* **then**

20       $curr\_profile(a) = \sum_{t \in curr\_time\_window} a(t)$;   // current cumulative value

21       $time\_win\_score(a) = (curr\_profile(a) - threshold(a))/threshold(a)$;

22   **end**

23   **if** a *is numerical* **then**

24       $curr\_hist(a) = hist(a(t)|t \in curr\_t\_win)$;   // current histogram

25       $curr\_dist(a) = minkowski\_dist(curr\_hist(a) - avg\_hist(a))$;   // distance

26       $time\_win\_score(a) = (curr\_dist(a) - avg\_dev(a))/avg\_dev(a)$;

27   **end**

28 **end**

   Result: $time\_win\_score(U) = \sum_{a \in A} t\_win\_score(a)$, if $t\_win\_score(a) > 0$

---

is computed with the asymmetric weighted Minkowski distance [23], using a $L - 1$ norm that linearly considers deviations between histograms. For each bin of the histogram we assign a weight based on the normalized frequency of the attribute that gives more importance to previously unseen values. At runtime, *FraudBuster* incrementally builds the current histogram distribution processing incoming transactions and computes the current distance from the average histogram built during the training phase.

The anomaly score is computed for each user, evaluating incoming transactions, and is defined as the relative difference between the current distance and the deviation computed during the training phase. *Time-windows-based* profile training and runtime phases are shown in Algorithm 1.

6.2   Time-Series-Based Profile

During the training phase, for each user, *FraudBuster* builds the average time series using the DTW Barycenter Averaging (DBA) [24] algorithm and the average deviation from the historical time series computing the DTW distance. At runtime, *FraudBuster* incrementally builds a new time series based on incoming transactions and computes the current dynamic time warping (DTW) distance

---

Algorithm 2. Time-series-based profile training and runtime phases for user U.

    Input: Historical transactions of user U ;   `// Training Phase`
1 **for** x *in temporal attributes* X **do**
2   **for** *period* τ *detected in the historical timespan* T **do**
3          $t\_series_\tau(x) = \{x(t)|t \in \tau\}$;   `// past time series`
4   **end**
5        $avg\_time\_series(x) = DBA(t\_series_\tau(x))$;   `// average time series(x)`
6        $avg\_dev(x) = \sum_{\tau \in T} DTW(t\_series_\tau(x), avg\_time\_series(x))/T$; `// average deviation`
7 **end**
    Result: $time\text{-}series\text{-}based\_profile(U) = [avg\_dev(x)$ for x in X]

    Input: Current transactions of user U ;   `// Runtime Phase`
8 **for** x *in temporal attributes* X **do**
9        $current\_time\_series_{\tau'}(x) = \{x(t)|t \in \tau'\}$;   `// current time series`
10       $curr\_dist(x) = DTW(current\_time\_series_{\tau'}(x), avg\_time\_series(x))$;
         `//`   `distance`
11       $time\_series\_score(x) = (curr\_dist(x) - avg\_dev(x))/avg\_dev(x)$
12 **end**
    Result: $time\_series\_score(U) = \sum_{x \in X} time\_series\_score(x)$, if
        $time\_series\_score(x) > 0$

---

from the average time series computed during the training phase. The anomaly score is computed for each user evaluating incoming transactions and is defined as the relative difference between the current distance and the average one. *Time-series-based* profile training and runtime phases are shown in Algorithm 2.

Time Series Comparison and Alignment. In order to compute the distance value among time series, it is necessary to *align* and *compare* them. To perform both comparison and alignment, we adopt the DTW algorithm [4] that computes the optimal alignment (i.e., match) and measures the similarity (i.e., distance) between the two time series. The sequences are "warped" non-linearly in the time dimension to determine a measure of their similarity. More formally, the DTW algorithm finds an optimal alignment between two ordered sequences, $X = [x_1, x_2, ..., x_n]$ of length N and $Y = [y_1, y_2, ..., y_m]$ of length M using a local distance metric $d(X, Y)$ between each pair of events x, y. As local distance we use a $L-1$ norm and for each pair of elements we obtain the cost matrix $C \in \mathbb{R}^{N \times M}$ defined as $C(n, m) = d(x_n, y_m)$. The alignment is a sequence $p = (p_1, p_2, ..., p_L)$ indexing over the pair (n, m) of C under the following constraints: (1) *boundary condition*, $p_1 = (1, 1)$ and $p_L = (N, M)$, requires that the first and last components of the aligned sequence should coincide; (2) *monotonicity condition* $(n_1 \leq n_2 \leq ... \leq n_L$ and $m_1 \leq m_2 \leq ... \leq m_L)$ implies that the ordering must be preserved; (3) *step size condition* describes the relation between the original sequences and the final alignment: $p_{l+1} - p_l \in \{(1, 0), (0, 1), (1, 1)\}$ for $l \in [1 : L-1]$. As a consequence, the cost $c_p(X, Y)$ of an alignment p between X and Y with respect a local distance measure d is $c_p(X, Y) = \sum_{l=1}^{L} c(x_{n_l}, y_{m_l})$. The **optimal distance** $DTW(X, Y)$ between X and Y is obtained by minimizing $c_p(X, Y)$. In addition, we set additional constraints to avoid a wrong time series alignment and comparison. The *first problem* is that time distant elements can be aligned. To solve this, we introduce a global constraint (*Sakoe-Chiba band region* [4]), which considers an alignment admissible if the mutual time-distance

---

Algorithm 3. DTW Barycenter Averaging (DBA).

// $i = \{$ i-th historical time series $\}$, $k = \{$ k-th time series's component $\}$
Input: Time series $t\_series_i = \{x_i(t_{i,j})|t \in \tau, 1 \le i \le N, 1 \le j \le K\}$
1 $avg\_t\_series = \{x(t_{avg,j})|t_{avg,j} \in \tau \ detected\}$;   // average time series definition
2 **for** j *in* K **do**
3      $t_{avg,j} = \sum_i^N barycenter\_time_j(t\_series_i) = \sum_i^N t_{i,j}/N$;   // Barycenter in time
4      $x(t_{avg,j}) = \sum_i^N barycenter\_value_j(t\_series_i) = \sum_i^N x_i(t_{i,j})/N$;   // Barycenter value
5 **end**
Result: $avg\_t\_series = \sum_{i=1}^N barycenter_{value,time}(DTW_{align}(t\_series_i))$

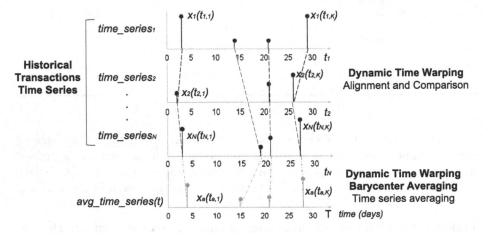

Fig. 3. Average time series computation: dynamic time warping (DTW) alignment method (blue) and DTW Barycenter Averaging (DBA) (green). (Color figure online)

between two values is bounded by a specific time value. The *second problem* is that each entry of the time series can be aligned to more than one entry of the second time series, making *FraudBuster* less resistant to fraudsters that try to simulate user behavior. Hence, we introduce a further constraint in the alignment region not allowing multiple alignment. Finally, the *Boundary condition* can introduce artifacts that are avoided by adding zero elements at the begin and the end of each sequence.

Time Series Averaging. As shown in Algorithm 3 and Fig. 3, the average time series is constructed by aligning the set of time series with the DTW algorithm and computing the barycenter of the attributes values. The algorithm starts aligning two time-series and computing a first "temporary" average time series by considering the barycenter between each of their component (i.e., in time and of the value). Then, it iteratively works in two steps until convergence. In the first step, it applies the DTW algorithm between each individual time series and the "temporary" average time series to find the optimal alignment. In the second step, it updates each element of the "temporary" average time series by computing the "barycenter" in time and of the value of each time series.

6.3 Temporal Profile Scoring

The anomaly scores can be simplified as $time\_windows\_score = \frac{(curr\_val - dev\_thr)}{dev\_thr}$ and $time\_series\_score = \frac{avg\_dist - avg\_dev}{avg\_dev}$, where $curr\_val$ is the feature's value for numerical variable or a distance's value between histogram for categorical variable, avg_dist is the distance between the average time series used as reference and the current one. To mitigate the problem of "divide by zero" that would have led to very high anomaly score even for small shift in user's behavior we add an arbitrary small smoothing parameter. Hence, the final scores are $time\_window\_score = \frac{curr\_val - dev\_thr}{dev\_thr + s}$ and $time\_series\_score = \frac{avg\_dist - avg\_dev}{avg\_dev + s}$.

Final Score Aggregation. Finally, to combine the two temporal profiles outputs in a risk of fraud score, we compute a weighted sum of the *time-series-based* and *time-windows-based* scores. In particular, to make the score less biased from features characterized by high mean and standard deviation we first apply a z-score standardization: $z\_score_{u,f} = \frac{score_{u,f} - mean_f}{std\_dev_f}$, where $mean_f$ and std_dev_f are the mean and standard deviation of scores of the attribute f. We estimate *FraudBuster* parameters by choosing the values that maximizes detection performances. To avoid over-fitting, we conduct this parameter tuning on a subset of the overall dataset (about 3,000 randomly sampled users with at least one transaction per month, to have a more stable dataset).

7 Experimental Evaluation

The goal of this experimental evaluation is to measure the effectiveness of *Fraud-Buster* in detecting *salami-slicing* frauds, (i) comparing the results with the temporal profile of [9], (ii) proving the effectiveness of temporal pattern exploitation in the detection of these frauds, (iii) assessing the robustness of *FraudBuster* against mimicry-attacks, and (iv) evaluating the capability to detect real-world *salami-slicing* frauds. It is important to highlight that for all these experiments we focus on the detection of *salami-slicing* frauds only, since the goal of this work is to provide a mitigation to this insidious menace.

7.1 Dataset Description

The cooperation with an Italian banking group gave us the opportunity to test our system on the real-world *unlabeled* dataset analyzed in [9]. The dataset, summarized in Table 2, contains the fully anonymized record of the transactions performed through the Internet banking services of one of the largest Italian banking groups (i.e., bank transfers, phone recharges and prepaid debit cards) and spans five months, from April to August 2013. As confirmed by our collaborators, it contains no known frauds (i.e., the dataset was preprocessed removing anomalous instances). This dataset allowed us to evaluate the detection power of *FraudBuster* against fraudulent scenarios, to prove the effectiveness of temporal pattern exploitation, and to compare the results with the temporal profile of [9].

Table 2. Number of transactions, number of users, and selected features of the dataset.

Dataset	Transactions	Users	Selected features
Bank transfer	379,242	47,909	# of transaction, total amount, # of new IBAN, IBAN, IBAN_CC, ASN_CC, amount(discretized)
Phone recharge	50,708	15,683	# of transaction, total amount, # of new phone number, phone number, ASN_CC, amount(discretized)
Prepaid debit card	34,583	8,424	# of transaction, total amount, # of new CardID, CardID, ASN_CC, amount(discretized)

We immediately noticed that the transactions are characterized by a "weekly" pattern of five days (working days) with a high value of records, followed by two days (weekend) of lower activity. We also noticed that August has a lower volume of transactions, likely due to the typical Italian summer holiday period.

Dataset Features. Beyond the obvious features (e.g., amount and timestamp), the dataset contains the following attributes: **UserID** that is a unique ID associated to the "author" of the transaction; **IBAN** and **IBAN_CC** of the transaction recipient and its country code (CC); **CardID**, a unique ID associated to each prepaid debit card; **ASN_CC**, the Autonomous System Number (ASN) and its CC from which the user was connected when issuing the transaction. We purposely ignore IP due to its high variance (e.g., dynamic IP address, use of proxy). Personally-Identifiable Information (PII) (e.g., UserID, IBAN) is hashed.

7.2 Evaluation Approach and Metrics

The evaluation of *FraudBuster* is particularly challenging due to the lack of a ground truth. Hence, leveraging on the domain expert's knowledge and on the analysis of some real *salami-slicing* frauds attack schemes, we reproduced synthetically-generated frauds that replicate real attacks performed against online banking users. Following the threat model described in Sect. 2, we assume that the goal of the attacker is to perform frauds while remaining undetected. Therefore, frauds are characterized by low and medium daily amounts, are executed during working hours either from the victim's device that is used as a proxy or from unknown devices (i.e., foreign ASN_CC). For the bank transfer context, we test both the case of national and foreign IBAN_CC. In Table 3 we list all our threat scenarios. We put effort to produce synthetic transactions that resemble the real ones to be as realistic as possible and to avoid the overfitting of our approach to "trivial" fraudulent transactions. For this reason, features' distributions are extracted on the basis of an in-depth dataset analysis to make them "indistinguishable" from genuine transactions. The representativeness of these scenarios was later confirmed by the real-world frauds analyzed in Exp. 4.

We split the dataset following the *holdout* method and using three months for building the profiles and the last month (plus synthetic injected transactions) for the detection performance analysis. Even if *FraudBuster* works near real-time, we decide to evaluate the detection at the end of the month to fairly compare the performance metrics over the same period. As explained in Sect. 6, *FraudBuster* computes, for each incoming transaction, the anomaly score on the basis of the learned model and assigns an aggregated risk score to each user. Finally, it ranks the pair $<user, score>$ in descending order, to support the analysts' ex-post analysis (i.e., manual investigation of fraudulent transactions), by making them investigate only on the top N users of the ranking and on transactions that deviates most from the user's spending pattern. For the first four experiments, after training, we randomly select N users and inject (blindly to *FraudBuster*) the synthetically-generated *salami-slicing* frauds into their transactions belonging to the testing data. Then, we use *FraudBuster* to analyze the testing data and to rank users. To evaluate the detection performance, we consider the top N users in the ranking. The value of N is chosen according to bank workforce, but from our information, the team of analysts is able to analyze around 1–5% of users. Therefore, in these experiments, we consider the top $N = 1\%$ users of the final ranking from those ranked as anomalous. We perform these operations for each threat scenario described in Table 3, which specifies the number, the transaction's beneficiary distribution, and the features' values of frauds injected per user. Moreover, we repeat the test 50 times and average the results to avoid statistical artifacts due to the injection pattern of frauds to random users.

Table 3. Fraud scenarios. The label "Equally" means "frauds are executed toward different accounts with repetitions", "Max one" means "maximum one fraud per account", "All to one" means "all frauds are executed toward one account".

Fraud scenario	#Frauds	IBAN	ASN	Beneficiary distribution	Amount(€)		
					Bank transfer	Prepaid card	Phone recharge
1	10	National	National	Equally	100–500	50–100	5–25
2	10	National	National	Equally	500–1,500	100–250	25–50
3	10	National	National	Equally	1,500–3,000	250–500	50–100
4	10	National	National	**All to One**	500–1,500	100–250	25–50
5	10	National	National	**Max one**	500–1,500	100–250	25–50
6	5	National	National	Equally	500–1,500	100–250	25–50
7	5	**Foreign**	National	Equally	500–1,500	-	-
8	5	National	**Foreign**	Equally	500–1,500	100–250	25–50
9	5	National	National	Equally	2,500–7,500	500–1000	100–200

Under these assumptions and considering as defrauded the top N users in the ranking, a True Positive (TP) is a defrauded user correctly ranked as defrauded, False Positive (FP) is a legitimate user wrongly ranked as defrauded, a False Negative (FN) is a defrauded user wrongly ranked as legitimate, and a True Negative (TN) is a legitimate user correctly ranked as non-anomalous. Then, we compute the well-known evaluation metrics of True Positive Rate (TPR), which compute the percentage of correctly identified defrauded users and False Positive Rate (FPR), which compute the percentage of legitimate users who are wrongly identified as defrauded: $TPR = \frac{TP}{TP+FP}$, $FPR = \frac{FP}{TN+FP}$. We also compute the Average Precision (AP) that summarizes the precision-recall curve as the weighted mean of the precision achieved at every position in the ranking. By doing this, it takes into account the position (i.e., the order) of defrauded users in the ranking: $AP = \frac{\sum_{k=1}^{n} P(k) \cdot F(k)}{R}$, where R is the number of defrauded users, N is the number of user considered in the raking, $P(k)$ is the precision at cut off k, and $F(k) = 1$ if the kth user is fraudulent, 0 otherwise. Since our dataset is highly unbalanced in favor of normal users, we use the Average Accuracy (AA) metrics. The AA is an average of the accuracy obtained for both fraudulent and normal users classes: $AA = \frac{1}{2}\left[\frac{TP}{TP+FN} + \frac{TN}{TN+FP}\right]$. Finally, we graphically represents *FraudBuster* performances with the Receiver Operating Characteristic (ROC) that express the ratio between TPR and FPR.

It is important to highlight that the described evaluation approach and metrics, besides giving an index of the detection performance, allow us to indirectly evaluate *FraudBuster* from the point of view of the cost of challenging frauds and amount of funds protected from defrauding attempts. In fact, while the cost of a FP is the time spent by the analyst in the verification process, the cost of a FN is the stolen amount and the loss of trust in the financial institution. Hence, a high TPR, AA, and AP associated to a low FPR guarantees that *FraudBuster* is correctly ranking frauds while reducing the rate of "false" alarms, which directly impacts the banking analyst activity, and the amount of founds stolen (i.e., TN). Finally, by limiting the analysis to the top $N\%$ positions in the ranking, we are putting a cap on the costs of challenging frauds (e.g., banking analysts).

7.3 Experiment 1: Evaluation Against Fraud Scenarios

In this experiment, we show the effectiveness of *FraudBuster* comparing the results with the temporal profile of BankSealer [9] only, since it detects "stealthy frauds" repeated in times, like *salami-slicing* frauds. For each test, we inject the synthetic frauds described above and summarized in Table 3, equally distributed in the timespan of the testing data. The classification performance is shown in Table 4, while the ROC curve for bank transfers is presented in Fig. 4. We show the detection performance for the bank transfers context only for brevity, but similar results were obtained for the other contexts. Remarkably, Fig. 4a shows that *FraudBuster* outperforms the temporal profile of BankSealer in all fraud scenarios under analysis. In particular, *FraudBuster* reaches a detection rate of 82%, 95%, and 98%, an average precision of 80%, 98%, and 99% and an average

Table 4. Experiment 1 results. Considered metrics: True Positive Rate (TPR), Average Accuracy (AA), and Average Precision (AP). The label *FB* refers to *FraudBuster*, while *BS* refers to temporal profile of *BankSealer*.

| | Bank transfer | | | | | | Prepaid debit card | | | | | | Phone recharges | | | | | |
| | TPR | | AP | | AA | | TPR | | AP | | AA | | TPR | | AP | | AA | |
Scenario	FB	BS	FB	BS	FB	BS	FB	BS	FB	BS	FB	BS	FB	BS	FB	BS	FB	BS
1	69	15	61	12	84	57	90	44	95	33	95	71	97	70	99	78	98	85
2	75	28	70	21	87	63	91	52	95	46	95	75	97	80	99	90	99	90
3	79	40	77	34	89	70	93	60	97	62	96	80	98	89	99	96	99	94
4	82	28	80	21	91	63	91	52	95	46	95	75	98	80	99	90	99	90
5	74	28	69	21	87	63	95	52	98	46	97	75	98	80	99	90	99	90
6	42	16	30	11	70	57	75	31	66	23	87	65	87	61	93	67	93	80
7	79	16	73	11	89	57	-	-	-	-	-	-	-	-	-	-	-	-
8	76	16	79	11	88	57	88	31	90	23	94	65	98	61	99	67	99	80
9	62	16	51	11	81	57	82	55	76	77	91	55	98	87	99	93	99	95
Mixture	70	25	65	19	85	62	85	47	92	41	92	73	96	76	98	85	99	88

accuracy of 91%, 97%, and 99% in the bank transfer, phone recharges, and prepaid cards dataset respectively. These results represent an improvement in all the metrics under analysis that is 30–60% larger with respect to the temporal profile of [9]. Therefore, *FraudBuster* ranks *salami-slicing* frauds in higher position with respect to [9]. ROC analysis shown in Fig. 4c and e, highlights that *FraudBuster* maintains good performance in almost every threat scenario. The best performance is obtained in case of 10 frauds injected per users, considering national beneficiary and low amounts, with a TPR up to 82% for the bank transfers context (95% and 97% for phone recharges and debit card contexts). Moreover, the Average Accuracy (AA) is always particularly high, meaning that *FraudBuster* successfully reduces the number of false positives while maintaining a good TPR. The lowest performance is obtained in scenario 6, since it represents the most difficult to detect due to the low number of frauds and their high resemblance to legitimate transactions. *FraudBuster* shows a TPR of 42% in the bank transfer context (75% and 82% in the prepaid debit cards and phone recharges contexts). However, also in this case *FraudBuster* detects 30% more *salami-slicing* frauds than BankSealer and puts all fraudulent users in the top 3% of the ranking (see Fig. 4e). The results obtained on prepaid debit card and phone recharges are, on average, better with respect to bank transfer domain, since in these contexts frauds toward previously unseen values are easier to spot.

7.4 Experiment 2: Effectiveness of the Time-series-based Profile

The purpose of this experiment is to compare the detection rate of the *time-series-based* profile with respect to the *time-windows-based* profile alone for each

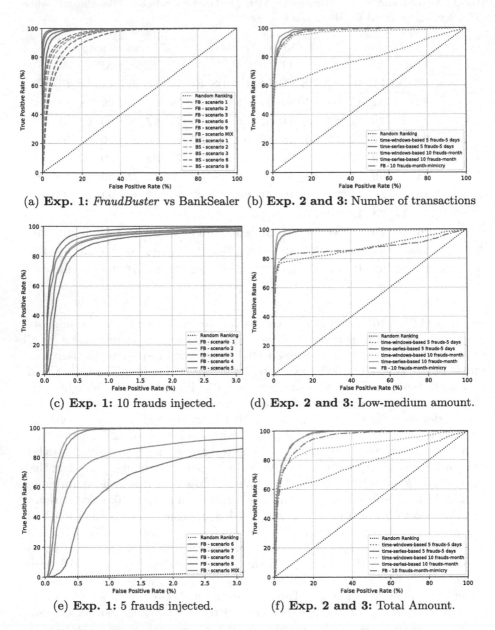

(a) **Exp. 1:** *FraudBuster* vs BankSealer   (b) **Exp. 2 and 3:** Number of transactions

(c) **Exp. 1:** 10 frauds injected.   (d) **Exp. 2 and 3:** Low-medium amount.

(e) **Exp. 1:** 5 frauds injected.   (f) **Exp. 2 and 3:** Total Amount.

Fig. 4. Experiment 1, 2, and 3 Receiver Operating Characteristic (ROC) curves, varying the number N of users considered as defrauded. *FB* stands for *FraudBuster*, *BS* stands for *BankSealer*. Figure 4c and e show an enlargement of the ROC curves.

attribute. Since the *time-series-based* profile is defined only for periodic users, here we design the experiment following the same methodology of the previous one, but keeping only periodic users. We consider two different scenarios: (1) 5 random frauds are injected per infected user over 5 days; (2) 10 random frauds are injected per infected user over the whole month. Figure 4 shows that the *time-series-based* profile and the *time-windows-based* profile have similar performances in the first part of the ROC curves but, after few FP cases, the detection rate of the *time-series-based* profile outperform the one of the *time-windows-based* profile by 20–30%. This is even more evident in the testing scenario with only 5 frauds where both profiles detect "easy-to-spot" frauds, but only the *time-series-based* one, which exploit recurrent temporal patterns, is able to catch "stealthiest" ones. These results highlight the effectiveness of the *time-series-based* profile in the detection of *salami-slicing* frauds.

7.5   Experiment 3: Evaluation Against Mimicry Attack

Though there has been a good amount of research on fraud analysis, the security of these systems against evasion attacks seems not to have received much attention in the banking fraud analysis context. There are many papers proposing new techniques for fraud detection, and authors often try to measure their detection power by testing whether they can detect currently-popular attacks. However, the notion of security against adaptive adversarial attacks, defined as "mimicry attacks" [25], is much harder to measure. In this experiment we investigate the performance of *FraudBuster* under the assumptions that the fraudster knows the detection algorithm and the spending habits of the victim. With this data the attacker can approximate the behavior of the user in order to generate fraudulent transactions to trick the anti-fraud framework and silently commit frauds. Therefore, in this scenario, we inject 10 frauds mimicking user's behavior (i.e., we follow the target user's spending pattern). The results of this experiment are superimposed in Fig. 4 to have a better comparison with *FraudBuster*'s performance. As expected, *FraudBuster* performs worse than the previous experiments since frauds are more similar to legitimate ones and, hence, more difficult to detect. In fact, the mimicry-attack tries to keep a lower risk score, spreading frauds in the ranking. However, it is important to highlight that *FraudBuster* is able to mitigate the mimicry-attack keeping an overall detection rate around 65% and pushing frauds in the top 3% of the ranking. This allows to detect at least the majority of frauds and stop them. The good results obtained are mainly due to the combination of the *time-windows-based* and the *time-series-based* profiles, which require more effort to an attacker that wants to mimicry users' behaviors.

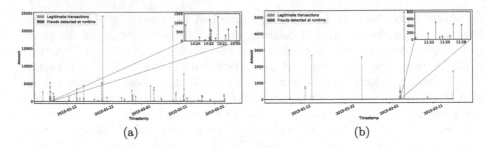

Fig. 5. Experiment 4. Examples of real frauds detected by *FraudBuster*. Legitimate transactions are represented in green, while frauds in red. (Color figure online)

7.6   Experiment 4: Evaluation Against Real-World Frauds

Due to the good results obtained in the previous experiments, we deployed *Fraud-Buster* in the real-world setting of a large national banking group and measured its detection performance. *FraudBuster* analyzed 482,930 bank transfer transactions executed by 58,562 users from October 2014 to February 2015. In particular, similarly to previous experiments, we build the spending profiles on the first two months and analyze the performance on the sequent months, progressively updating the temporal models with legitimate transactions only. In order to have a ground-truth, we ask banking analysts to manually inspect and label frauds in the ranking. *FraudBuster* was able to detect *salami-slicing* frauds, not detected by the other protection system installed, for a total of almost 20 fraudulent transactions. Table 5 contains two different examples of the real frauds detected by *FraudBuster*. The same fraudulent transactions are also graphically presented in Fig. 5, which show (with the red color) the amount of funds stolen in time. The fraudulent transactions in Fig. 5a and Table 5a present amount less than 1,500 € and represents an attacker that exploits different sessions (by hijacking real sessions or deceiving the victims to insert session tokens) to perform his/her frauds. In this case, frauds are executed toward foreign and Italian bank accounts, which, in some cases, are also used twice. These characteristics make these *salami-slicing* frauds as a combination of scenario 4 (single IBAN destination), scenario 7 (foreign IBAN destination), and 9 (medium-high amount) (Table 3). The fraudulent transactions in Fig. 5b and Table 5b present low amounts and are mainly in the same day, except for the last fraud that try to steal a medium-high amount. These characteristics are similar to the ones of injection scenario 5 (small amount, different IBAN destination), summarized in Table 3. Besides *salami-slicing* frauds, *FraudBuster* was able to improve the detection performance of defrauded users by placing in the first 1% of the ranking 8 defrauded users not detected by the already installed detection system.

Table 5. Experiment 4. Examples of real frauds detected by *FraudBuster*. *IP*, *SessionID* (SID), and *IBAN* are hidden for privacy reason.

IP	SID	Timestamp	Amount	IBAN
1..8	1..7	2015-01-07 14:03:06	880.17	GB..8
1..8	5..1	2015-01-07 14:32:17	200	IT..a
1..8	5..1	2015-01-07 14:44:52	55.18	IT..7
1..8	5..1	2015-01-07 14:54:08	159.2	IT..7
1..8	5..1	2015-01-07 14:55:06	1,171.2	IT..5
1..8	5..1	2015-01-07 14:56:15	631.96	IT..d
1..8	5..1	2015-01-07 14:57:16	120	IT..a
1..8	5..1	2015-01-07 14:58:29	561	IT..5
1..8	5..1	2015-01-07 15:07:43	150	FR..c
1..8	5..1	2015-01-07 15:13:11	1,318.82	IT..5
1..8	5..1	2015-01-07 15:29:01	300	IT..d
1..8	5..1	2015-01-07 15:35:17	640	IT..a
1..8	5..1	2015-01-07 15:52:50	780	FR..5
a..5	0..0	2015-01-12 12:01:23	224.74	GB..8
1..1	1..d	2015-01-21 10:07:22	5,187.5	FR..f

(a)

IP	SID	Timestamp	Amount	IBAN
2..7	5..c	2015-02-03 11:20:08	48	IT..a
2..7	5..c	2015-02-03 11:22:23	175	IT..4
2..7	5..c	2015-02-03 11:23:45	495	GB..6
2..7	5..c	2015-02-03 11:24:28	66	IT..2
2..7	5..c	2015-02-03 11:24:59	84	IT..3
2..7	5..c	2015-02-03 11:26:20	93	IT..b
2..7	5..c	2015-02-03 11:26:56	443.52	IT..1
2..7	5..c	2015-02-03 11:28:25	418.88	IT..a
3..a	G..5	2015-02-04 9:52:10	5,300.6	GB..4

(b)

8   Conclusions

In this paper, we provided an in-depth temporal analysis on real data exploiting time series techniques to discern recurrent vs. non-recurrent spending patterns, which is, to the best of our knowledge, the first of such analysis in the literature.

We presented *FraudBuster*, a framework that exploits users' recurrent vs. non-recurrent spending patterns to detect *salami-slicing* frauds. *FraudBuster* automatically extracts end user's spending pattern and evaluates the deviation from its historical one. *FraudBuster* builds two models based on user's periodicity. The first model is the *time-series-based* profile that is designed for users with a periodic spending pattern only. The second model is the *time-windows-based* profile that is designed for all users independently from the periodicity and aggregates user's transactions according to time-windows. For each incoming transaction, *FraudBuster* measures the deviation (i.e., anomaly score) of the user's spending activity from the learned models. The final output is an aggregated score that quantifies the risk of a user of being defrauded. By doing this, *FraudBuster* supports the necessary ex-post analysis (i.e., manual investigation of frauds), making analysts focusing only on highly ranked users and on transactions that deviates most from the user's spending pattern.

We tested *FraudBuster* in the real-world context of a large national bank. Leveraging the domain expert's knowledge, we reproduced *salami-slicing* frauds (in a controlled environment) performed against banking users, and recorded the resulting fraudulent transactions. *FraudBuster* outperformed the state-of-the-art temporal approach considered by detecting up to 60% more defrauded users. In particular, *FraudBuster* was able to reach a detection rate up to 82%, 95%, and 99% respectively in the *bank transfers*, in the *prepaid debit cards*, and in the *phone recharges* context. In addition, we demonstrated the benefits of the time-series analysis and we investigated the performance of *FraudBuster* against mimicry attacks and real-world *salami-slicing* frauds. *FraudBuster* was able to identify real-world *salami-slicing* frauds, for a total of almost 20 fraudulent transactions.

The main limitation of this work is related to the scarcity of data. An analysis of a larger dataset could have revealed more information about user's spending pattern. A future work could be the application of the Matching Pursuit decomposition [26] algorithm that allows to decompose a time series in a linear combination of patterns, hence, detecting different mixture of periodicities. Moreover, to include a more precise prediction of user's activity in windows-based profiles, a numerical prediction based on ARMA process can be implemented. In addition, it was not possible to exploit the semantic data (e.g., name of the recipient, payment description/reason) due to regulatory and privacy reasons. A future extension could be the extraction of privacy-preserving semantic features from the bank side. Finally, the results of the spending pattern analysis of Sect. 4 heavily depend on the modeled country (i.e., what follows a monthly pattern in Italy could follow a weekly pattern in a different nation, or even no pattern at all). Therefore, the findings are not easy to generalize. However, the described methodology is independent from the context and the recurrent spending patterns analysis and classification can applied automatically on any dataset.

Acknowledgments. This project has received funding from the European Union's Horizon 2020 research and innovation programme, under grant agreement No. 700326 (RAMSES project).

References

1. Wei, W., Li, J., Cao, L., Ou, Y., Chen, J.: Effective detection of sophisticated online banking fraud on extremely imbalanced data. World Wide Web **16**(4), 449–475 (2013)
2. Emm, D., Unuchek, R., Kruglov, K.: Kaspersky security bulletin 2016. Technical report, Kaspersky Lab (2017)
3. Bidgoli, H.: Handbook of Information Security, Threats, Vulnerabilities, Prevention, Detection, and Management. Handbook of Information Security. Wiley, Hoboken (2006)
4. Müller, M.: Dynamic time warping. In: Müller, M. (ed.) Information Retrieval for Music and Motion, pp. 69–84. Springer, Heidelberg (2007). https://doi.org/10.1007/978-3-540-74048-3_4
5. Chandola, V., Banerjee, A., Kumar, V.: Anomaly detection: a survey. ACM Comput. Surv. **41**(3), 15:1–15:58 (2009)
6. KasperskyLab: Banking Trojans: mobile's major cyberthreat, September 2015
7. Phua, C., Alahakoon, D., Lee, V.: Minority report in fraud detection: classification of skewed data. SIGKDD Explor. Newsl. **6**(1), 50–59 (2004)
8. Bolton, R.J., Hand, D.J.: Statistical fraud detection: a review. Stat. Sci. **17**, 235–249 (2002)
9. Carminati, M., Caron, R., Maggi, F., Epifani, I., Zanero, S.: BankSealer: a decision support system for online banking fraud analysis and investigation. Comput. Secur. **53**, 175–186 (2015)
10. Chen, L.M., Chen, M.C., Sun, Y.S., Liao, W.: Spectrum analysis for detecting slow-paced persistent activities in network security. In: ICC. IEEE (2013)

11. Aiello, M., Cambiaso, E., Mongelli, M., Papaleo, G.: An on-line intrusion detection approach to identify low-rate DoS attacks. In: 2014 International Carnahan Conference on Security Technology (ICCST) (2014)
12. Cover, T., Thomas, J.: Elements of Information Theory. Wiley, New York (1991)
13. Janacek, G.J., Bagnall, A.J., Powell, M.: A likelihood ratio distance measure for the similarity between the fourier transform of time series. In: Ho, T.B., Cheung, D., Liu, H. (eds.) PAKDD 2005. LNCS (LNAI), vol. 3518, pp. 737–743. Springer, Heidelberg (2005). https://doi.org/10.1007/11430919_85
14. Seyedhossein, L., Hashemi, M.: Mining information from credit card time series for timelier fraud detection. In: 2010 5th International Symposium on Telecommunications (IST), pp. 619–624 (2010)
15. Bhattacharyya, S., Jha, S., Tharakunnel, K., Westland, J.C.: Data mining for credit card fraud: a comparative study. Decis. Support Syst. **50**(3), 602–613 (2011)
16. Krivko, M.: A hybrid model for plastic card fraud detection systems. Expert Syst. Appl. **37**(8), 6070–6076 (2010)
17. Kundu, A., Panigrahi, S., Sural, S., Majumdar, A.K.: BLAST-SSAHA hybridization for credit card fraud detection. IEEE Trans. Dependable Secure Comput. **6**(4), 309–315 (2009)
18. Altschul, S., Gish, W., Miller, W., Myers, E., Lipman, D.: Basic local alignment search tool. J. Mol. Biol. **215**, 403–410 (1990)
19. van der Vaart, A.: TIME SERIES. Technical report, Vrije Universiteit Amsterdam, pp. 67–79 (2010)
20. Oppenheim, A.V., Schafer, R.W., Buck, J.R.: Discrete-Time Signal Processing. Prentice Hall, Upper Saddle River (1999)
21. Bartlett, M.: Periodogram analysis and continuous spectra. Biometrika **37**, 1–16 (1950)
22. Cha, S.H., Srihari, S.N.: On measuring the distance between histograms. Pattern Recogn. **35**(6), 1355–1370 (2002)
23. Tran, N.M., Osipenko, M., Härdle, W.K.: Principal component analysis in an asymmetric norm. arXiv preprint arXiv:1401.3229 (2014)
24. Petitjean, F., Ketterlin, A., Gançarski, P.: A global averaging method for dynamic time warping, with applications to clustering. Pattern Recogn. **44**(3), 678–693 (2011)
25. Wagner, D., Soto, P.: Mimicry attacks on host-based intrusion detection systems. In: CCS02 (2002)
26. Mallat, S., Zhang, Z.: Matching pursuits with time-frequency dictionaries. IEEE Trans. Sig. Process. **41**(12), 3397–3415 (1993)

No Random, No Ransom: A Key to Stop Cryptographic Ransomware

Ziya Alper Genç[✉], Gabriele Lenzini, and Peter Y. A. Ryan

Interdisciplinary Centre for Security Reliability and Trust (SnT),
University of Luxembourg, Luxembourg City, Luxembourg
{ziya.genc,gabriele.lenzini,peter.ryan}@uni.lu

Abstract. To be effective, ransomware has to implement strong encryption, and strong encryption in turn requires a good source of random numbers. Without access to true randomness, ransomware relies on the pseudo random number generators that modern Operating Systems make available to applications. With this insight, we propose a strategy to mitigate ransomware attacks that considers pseudo random number generator functions as critical resources, controls accesses on their APIs and stops unauthorized applications that call them. Our strategy, tested against 524 active real-world ransomware samples, stops 94% of them, including WannaCry, Locky, CryptoLocker and CryptoWall. Remarkably, it also nullifies NotPetya, the latest offspring of the family which so far has eluded all defenses.

Keywords: Ransomware · Cryptographic malware · Randomness
Mitigation

1 Introduction

Ransomware is a malware, a malicious software that blocks access to victim's data. In contrast to traditional malware, whose break-down is permanent, ransomware's damage is reversible: access to files can be restored on the payment of a ransom, usually a few hundreds US dollars in virtual coins.

Despite being relatively new, this cyber-crime is spreading fast and it is believed to become soon a worldwide pandemic. According to [24], a US Government's white paper dated June 2016, on average more than 4,000 ransomware attacks occurred daily in the USA. This is 300% increase from the previous year and such important increment is probably due to the cyber-crime's solid business model: with a small investment there is a considerable pecuniary gain which, thanks to the virtual currency technology, can be collected reliably and in a way that is not traceable by the authorities.

The cost of ransomware attacks on individuals, enterprises, and societies is huge. It has exceeded $5 billion US dollars in 2017, and estimated to raise to $11.5 billion by 2019 [8]. Attacks like the one perpetrated by WannaCry—which infected 300 thousands computers of, among others, hospital, manufacturing,

C. Giuffrida et al. (Eds.): DIMVA 2018, LNCS 10885, pp. 234–255, 2018.
https://doi.org/10.1007/978-3-319-93411-2_11

banks, and telecommunication companies in about 150 countries—suggests that such predictions are not an exaggeration.

Ransomware applications come in different flavours, but *Cryptographic ransomware*, the family studied in this paper, encrypts a victim's files using *strong cryptography* [5]. In this approach, decrypting without the key is infeasible, so the only hope of recovering the files, in the absence of backups, is to pay the ransom.

In the absence of an effective cure for the threat, official recommendations suggest prevention. The US Government, for instance, suggests "to have appropriate backups, so [...] to restore the data from a known clean backup" and in addition "to verify the integrity of those backups and test the restoration process to ensure it is working" [24]. Keeping backups however is a solution that does not scale if the threat becomes world-wide: it is an expensive practice that not all companies implement whereas private users are likely not to follow the practice at all. Not surprisingly, a survey on the practice [11] reports that only 42% of ransomware victims could fully restore their data.

Security experts have looked into the problem. For example the EUROPOL's European Cybercrime Centre and the Dutch Politie together with Kaspersky Lab and McAfee have founded an initiative called "No More Ransom"[1] whose goal is, we quote, "to disrupt cybercriminal businesses with ransomware connections" and "to help victims of ransomware retrieve their encrypted data without having to pay the criminals". But, in case of infection, the initiative warns that "there is little you can do unless you have a backup or a security software in place". Other professionals are offering applications that are capable of some protection, but these anti-ransomware systems leverage from existing antivirus/antimalware strategies rather than re-thinking afresh how to solve the problem. At the time of writing (May 2018), no silver bullet exists to convincingly contain the threat.

Security researchers have also worked to slow down the threat (see Sect. 8), The have approached the problem from a *cryptographic* perspective, proposing strategies that enable decrypting the files. Since decrypting without the key is computationally hard, those works look for smart ways to place in escrow the encryption keys, and use them later to attempt decrypting the files. Let us call approaches of this nature *i.e.,* that attempt to recover the files after damage is done, *"ex post"*, and as *"ex ante"* approaches that attempt to prevent a ransomware from encrypting files in the first place.

Our Contribution. We approach the problem from a cryptographic perspective. Our solution, USHALLNOTPASS, has an *ex ante* nature. It would be the first *cryptographic ex-ante* defense against ransomware that we know about.

Its strategy relies on two fundamental observations. First, the keys-for-money exchange on which ransomware based the success of their business works only if the victim has no other ways to recover the files but paying for the release of the key. To achieve this goal, a ransomware must properly implement *strong cryptography*, which means:

---

[1] https://www.nomoreransom.org/.

- *robust encryption*, that is, well-established encryption algorithms;
- *strong encryption keys*, that is, long and randomly generated strings.

Second, if these are the tools that ransomware necessarily need, one can try to prevent any unauthorized use of them. Nothing can be done to prevent ransomware from using robust encryption: these algorithms are public and ransomware can implement them directly. Thus, we have to focus on denying access to a source of strong encryption keys.

In Sect. 2 we observe that current ransomware gets random numbers from a small set of functions, called Cryptographically Secure Pseudo Random Number Generator (CSPRNG), that modern Operating Systems (OSes) offer to applications. In Sect. 3, we explain the USHALLNOTPASS's essential idea, which is *to guard access to those functions*, let only the authorized applications (*e.g.,* certified or white-listed) use the resources, and stop all the others. In Sect. 4, we discuss how to implement the access control mechanism and its enforcement strategy, while in Sect. 5, we describe all the technical details of our implementation, discussing how we hook the calls to CSPRNG functions and terminate the caller. In Sect. 6, we benchmark our solution for robustness and performance. We ran our solution against 524 *active* ransomware samples obtained from a pool of 2263 real-world malware samples. We stopped 94% of samples in the test set, which includes, among many others, WannaCry, TeslaCrypt, Locky, CryptoLocker, and CryptoWall. Reverse engineering the remaining 6% samples shows that the samples do actually call CSPRNG; so, with a better implementation we should be able to stop them too. Notably, we stop also Bad Rabbit and NotPetya, which came out after we designed our solution. Because of this, USHALLNOTPASS may then have the potentiality to be effective against zero-day threats.

In Sect. 7 we discuss the limitation of our approach. Although having found one common strategy that is capable to block all the hundreds of instances of real ransomware in our possession is in our opinion a considerable finding, we point out that we have not yet proved that we can stop *only* all current ransomware (*i.e.,* no false positive). This investigation requires a different experimental set up than the one taken in this work and is actually our on-going research. We argue that it should not be hard to upper bound the number of false positives to a reasonable quantity. In Sect. 9 we conclude the work: we critically compare what we think are the novel aspects of our solution against the state of the art, given in Sect. 8, and we try to imagine how future ransomware could overcome our solution.

1.1   Requirements

The requirements that inspired and, a posteriori, characterize the security quality USHALLNOTPASS (we use here the terminology as suggested by the RFC 2119 [4]).

(R1) it MUST stop all currently known ransomware;

(R2) it SHOULD be able stop zero-day ransomware;

(R3) it MUST NOT log cryptographic keys and thus:
- it should not introduce the risk of single point of failure that smarter ransomware can try to break;
- it should not endanger the level security of benign applications (*e.g.,* TLS session keys);

(R4) it SHOULD be easily integrated in existing anti-virus software, OSes, and access control tools;

(R5) it MAY be implemented directly in an OS's kernel or in hardware.

2   On Ransomware and Randomness

We answer a fundamental question: why does ransomware need random numbers and from which sources they must necessarily obtain it? The answer will help understand the rationale of USHALLNOTPASS's *modus operandi.*

As any other software virus, a *ransomware*, say R, runs in the victim's computer. On that machine, R finds the files, F, that it will attempt to encrypt. As we saw in Sect. 1, to work properly R needs two tools: a robust encryption algorithm and a means to create strong key, k. With those tools, R has all it needs to encrypt F. The encrypted files will replace F irreversibly and irremediably until the ransom is paid, triggering the release of the decryption key. The diagram in Fig. 1 shows this simple work-flow in picture with some detail that we are going to discuss.

First let us see how R typically acquires the tools it needs. Strong encryption algorithms are publicly available. Current ransomware just makes use of those robust encryption algorithms, either by statically linking third party networking and cryptographic libraries, for example the NaCl or the OpenSSL or by accessing them via the host platform's native Application Programming Interfaces (APIs).

However, to obtain strong keys, R has to access *secure* randomness sources. R has a few alternatives for doing so, but only one is secure. In fact:

(1) R can have a strong k hard-coded, precisely in a section of its binary code, but this solution leaves k exposed. R can probed and have k extracted from it *e.g.,* by Binary Analysis.

(2) R can download a strong k from the Internet. Occasionally ransomware samples employ this technique and download encryption keys from their command and conquer (C&C) servers, but also this option exposes the key. It can be eavesdropped *e.g.,* by Intrusion Prevention System (IPS). Note that although ransomware will likely use secure communication (*i.e.,* an encrypted channel), the problem of establishing the session key remains, looping the argument (*e.g.,* if the key is hard-coded R, there is a way to reverse engineering it, *etc*).

The remaining alternative is to let R generate its own k. But for k to be strong, k must be randomly chosen from a data set with sufficient entropy to make brute-force attacks infeasible and be kept safe. Where, in a computer, R can find that randomness it requires to build strong keys? True randomness is generally unavailable and thus ransomware must resort to those few deterministic processes that return numbers which exhibit *statistical* randomness. These processes are known as *random number generator (RNG)* functions. R can implement them. But, being deterministic algorithm, RNG are always at risk to be error-prone. If they produce predictable outputs the cryptographic operations build on them cannot be considered secure [9] because with a predictable "randomness" all hybrid encryption schemes would be vulnerable to plain-text recovery [3]. History proves that this concern is legitimate. To give a few examples, in the Debian–OpenSSL incident, random number generator was seeded with an insufficient entropy which resulted generation of easily guessable keys for SSH and SSL/TLS protocols [1]. Moreover, DUAL EC random number generator of Juniper Networks found to be vulnerable, allowing an adversary to decrypt the VPN traffic [2]. These incidents shows that extreme care should be taken when dealing with randomness. *Non-cryptographic* random number sources have weaknesses [22], and they should be avoided in cryptography.

The safest way (*i.e.,* the way to avoid that risk of being error-prone in generating pseudo random numbers) is to use well tested and robust functions called Cryptographically Secure Pseudo Random Number Generator *(CSPRNG)*.

In the OSes of the Microsoft (MS) Windows family, CSPRNG functions are available through dedicated APIs (analogous solutions do exist in other OS families, although the name of the functions will change). User mode applications call cryptographic APIs to get secure random values of desired length. Historically, Windows platform has provided the following APIs:

- `CryptGenRandom`: Appeared first in Windows 95 via MS Cryptographic API (MS CAPI), now deprecated.
- `RtlGenRandom`: Beginning with Windows XP, available under the name `SystemFunction036`.
- `BCryptGenRandom`: Starting with Windows Vista, provided by Cryptography API Next Generation (CNG).

Legacy applications call the function `CryptGenRandom` to obtain a random value or, as modern applications do, call `BCryptGenRandom`. When developers do not need a context, they can also directly call `RtlGenRandom` to generate pseudo-random numbers. Moreover, `CryptGenRandom` internally calls into `RtlGenRandom`. While the implementation of `RtlGenRandom` is not open-sourced, a relevant documentation [12] states that various entropy sources are mixed, including: (i) The current process ID; (ii) The current thread ID; (iii) The ticks since boot; (iv) The current time; (v) Various high-precision performance counters; (vi) An MD4 hash of the user's environment block, which includes username, computer name, and search path; (vii) High-precision internal CPU counters, such as RDTSC, RDMSR, RDPMC; (viii) Other low-level system information[2].

---

[2] For the complete list, please see Chap. 8 of [12].

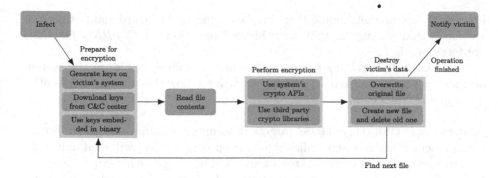

Fig. 1. Generic ransomware functionality.

To be sure the key used is strong, current ransomware takes advantage of the CSPRNG functions that the host OS provides.

Note that, for the same reason, those functions are also used in: (i) Initialization Vectors (IVs): used by both stream and block ciphers (ii) Salts: used in Key Derivation Functions (KDFs) (iii) Paddings: block ciphers (in ECB or CBC modes of operation) and public key encryption algorithms.

3   USHALLNOTPASS' Rationale

From these consideration it should be clear why the idea of this paper of guarding access (*i.e.,* of intercepting incoming calls) to (the APIs of) CSPRNG functions works: any strong ransomware must call those functions sooner or later. All 524 samples we have analyzed call these reliable functions of the OS. Future ransomware might find ways to create keys without calling any CSPRNG function, but that is the topic for future research.

Keys generated by alternative methods may not be so strong and files encrypted with them could be decrypted by *ex-post* defenses like "NoMoreRansom": we plan to test this hypothesis in future work (see Sect. 9).

Thus it should be clear that CSPRNG functions are *security-critical resources*, and hence only authorized processes should have access to them. This means that deciding which processes should be authorized is critical, but is not within the scope of this paper and it will be addressed in future work. Generically speaking, we suggest that authorized applications are those which have been *whitelisted* or *certified*. The process of authorizing an application can be as simple as let the user (or the system administrator) decide about whether s/he trust the application (*e.g.,* as done by [20]), or it can result from an agreement protocol between the operating system kernel's owners (*e.g.,* Microsoft, Apple) and the developers of cryptographic applications, as happens for apps that available in the Apple Store. Whatever the strategy, similarly to what happens in Europe about applications that process personal data, application developers have to gain their authorization/certification. Ransomware, developed for the illegal software market, should therefore be excluded. The third and last consideration is that we suggest that unauthorized requesters of *CSPRNG functions* are terminated.

Thus USHALLNOTPASS prevents ransomware damaging files in the system and no recovery is necessary. In Sect. 6 we will see how this strategy is essential for stopping Not Petya.

Assumptions. USHALLNOTPASS targets ransomware families that follow secure development strategies and utilize strong cryptography. We will deal only with the strongest amongst current ransomware, that is, we ignore insecurely designed and badly implemented ransomware families, for instance those which call `rand` to generate keys or those which encrypt files with home-brew algorithms. For these ransomware we already have solutions able to mitigate their effects.

Currently, USHALLNOTPASS runs as a software component of the host OS and relies on the security of the host. Therefore we assume that the OS on which our system runs is up-to-date. In particular, we require that ransomware does not exploit any zero-day vulnerabilities to escalate privilege. It should be noted that this requirement is inherent to every defense software runs on any OS. Furthermore, an outstanding feature of our strategy is its being obfuscation agnostic, *i.e.,* USHALLNOTPASS targets all ransomware samples from non-obfuscated to highly-obfuscated ones.

4   USHALLNOTPASS' Design

We now describe the inner mechanism of our technique in more detail.

4.1   High Level Description

Essentially, USHALLNOTPASS is an access control mechanism over the CSPRNG of the host system: it intercepts requests to the CSPRNG and queries the ID of the caller. Once the ID is determined, USHALLNOTPASS reaches a decision according to a *system policy*. If the caller process is authorized, it obtains the pseudo-random number. Otherwise, USHALLNOTPASS takes action according to the system policy. In our implementation, the caller is terminated.

Intercepting Requests to CSPRNG. As we argued in Sect. 2, ransomware requires to use CSPRNG of the host system. In the current architecture of modern OSes, there are limited number of resources which provide cryptographically secure pseudo-random numbers. It is feasible to intercept the calls made to CSPRNG functions of the host system and redirect the control to the decision making component of USHALLNOTPASS.

System Policy and Managing Access Control. When a request is made to access the CSPRNG of the system, to reach a decision to grant or deny access USHALLNOTPASS follows a *system policy*, a set of rules, for instance, determined by the system administrator. The system policy can be specified in various ways, depending on the needs and the nature of the host system. Our current design implements it as a *whitelist, i.e.,* list of applications allowed to access CSPRNG which a system administrator determines immediately after USHALLNOTPASS is installed. It can be more complex thought, such as determined by the OS companies in agreement with developers of cryptographic applications and based on accrediations, granted after established security checks.

Further security measures can be necessary. Here we mention two in particular:

- *Digital signatures*: Code signing is a technique to verify the integrity of the executable and the origin of the source. Digitally signed software has therefore higher trust score when evaluated by anti-malware products and OSes. For example, Microsoft uses Authenticode [18] verify the signature of the executables and kernel drivers. Following the same approach, we design USHALLNOT-PASS so that it can be configured to allow applications with digital signatures to access to CSPRNG of the host system.
- *Human interaction*: It may be desired to have a minimal whitelist, and extend it when necessary. So that when an application requests a cryptographically secure pseudo-random number for the first time, it is put on hold and the decision will be made on that time. A similar measure has been described in [20], but it involves the user. Considering this choice unsafe, USHALLNOTPASS instead interacts exclusively with the administrator. USHALLNOTPASS's system policy can be set to force to ask the exclusive permission of the system administrator when an application calls CSPRNG for the first time.

Once the whitelist is created, USHALLNOTPASS will start intercepting the access requests to CSPRNG of the host system. For each request, identity of the owner will be determined and USHALLNOTPASS will decide whether to grant access. If the result is positive, the process is allowed to obtain the pseudo-random number. Otherwise, the request is blocked and the process is terminated.

Needless to say, it is therefore of uttermost important to secure the system policy itself from unauthorized modifications (*e.g.,* stored in a directory accessible only with administrator privileges).

5   Implementation

We implemented a prototype of USHALLNOTPASS which targets Windows 7 OS. On Windows 7, user-mode processes invoke `CryptGenRandom` to get cryptographically secure pseudo-random numbers. Therefore, our implementation intercepts each invocation of `CryptGenRandom` API and determines the identity of caller process. To this end, USHALLNOTPASS consists of two components:

– *Interceptor (INT)* which intercepts calls made to `CryptGenRandom` API, collects and transmits the identity of the caller process to controller, and takes the appropriate action that controller commands.
– *Controller (CTR)* which gets information from the Interceptor and returns grant/deny commands according to the system policy.

5.1   Intercepting Calls to CSPRNG

There are various ways of intercepting calls on Windows platform, including patching System Service Dispatch Table (SSDT), modifying Import Address Table (IAT) and injecting a Dynamic Link Library (DLL) to target process. We followed the DLL injection technique and used Detours library of Microsoft Research for this purpose. The Interceptor of USHALLNOTPASS is hence a DLL module which is loaded into target process on the system. For ease of prototyping, we load the Interceptor into processes using AppInit DLLs technique [17]. Once loaded, it hooks `CryptGenRandom` function, that is, whenever `CryptGenRandom` is called by a process, program flow is routed to the Interceptor.

5.2   Decision of Authorization

The Interceptor calls `GetModuleFileName` to obtain the full path to the module of the caller process, which can point to a DLL or an executable. The file path information is passed to the Controller, whose response is forwarded to the Interceptor. Controller computes the SHA256 digest of the binary file of the module and checks whether it is in the whitelist.

If the result is positive, a GRANT command is returned to Interceptor, or a DENY command otherwise. Once the decision is received from Controller, Interceptor executes it. If the decision was to grant access to secure random API, Interceptor calls `CryptGenRandom` with the intercepted parameters and returns the result and control to the caller process. If the decision of Controller was to deny the request, then Interceptor calls `ExitProcess`, which causes the caller process to end[3].

5.3   Maintaining the Whitelist

Whitelist is implemented as a file which contains the list of SHA256 digests of the binary executables. The integrity of the whitelist is protected by a keyed-hash value, appended to the end of the list. As another security precaution, the whitelist is located in a directory which only administrators has write permission.

The Controller component of USHALLNOTPASS has a graphical user interface (GUI) which provides the basic functionality to the user, such as adding an entry to the whitelist or removing one from it. Controller also logs relevant information about the call events to `CryptGenRandom` API, including time, SHA256 digest of the caller and the action taken.

---

[3] Calling `ExitProcess` can as well cause process to crash, which, eventually ends it.

6 Experimental Results

We tested our USHALLNOTPASS with the aim to verify whether it complied with the requirements we stated in Sect. 1. Compliance with R3 does not need to be tested. It follows from the design: USHALLNOTPASS does not store cryptographic keys (R3). Instead we test compliance with R1 and R2 indirectly by answering the following questions about USHALLNOTPASS:

- **Q1** Does it stop ransomware before they encrypt any files?
- **Q2** Can it protect against zero-day ransomware?

Furthermore we are interested in knowing what is USHALLNOTPASS's performance in time and space resources. A defense system that is not practical to deploy is considered useless.

- **Q3** What is overhead cost in resources of USHALLNOTPASS?

The answer this third question gives evidence for compliance to R4 and R5: if USHALLNOTPASS proves be efficient, it can be easily integrated with existing anti-virus software as an additional run-time control (R4). Its simplicity also suggests that controlling the access to critical functions can be implemented at least at level of OS kernel (R5).

Instead, we have not yet thought about the possibility to implement this mechanism at lower level, such as in hardware.

6.1 Experimental Setup

We conducted a series of experiments to test the robustness of USHALLNOTPASS against cryptographic ransomware. We obtained real world cryptographic ransomware samples from well known sources including VirusTotal[4] and ViruSign[5]. In order to collect executables, we performed a search on these sources with the keywords *ransom, crypt* and *lock* which generally appear in the tags determined by submitters and antivirus vendors. Furthermore, we populated our collection by downloading samples from the links provided by Malc0de[6].

Our initial test set had 2263 malware samples which is labeled by anti-virus engines as ransomware.

Collecting a malware sample is one thing, determining its type is another. A malware sample tagged "ransomware" may not necessarily be an active cryptographic ransomware. Therefore, we needed to check the obtained malware samples one by one and select the active cryptographic ransomware in order to build a valid sample set. For this aim, we utilized Cuckoo Sandbox[7] open source automated malware analysis system. We created a virtual machine (VM)

---

[4] VirusTotal, https://www.virustotal.com.
[5] ViruSign, https://www.virusign.com.
[6] Malc0de, http://malc0de.com.
[7] Cuckoo Sandbox, https://cuckoosandbox.org.

in KVM[8] and performed a clean install of Windows 7 OS. Next, we created a user environment on the VM and performed actions which reflects the existence of a real user, *e.g.*, we installed various popular applications such as third party web browsers (and select plug-ins), office and document software, utilities etc. Moreover, we placed a number of files on the VM that typical ransomware families targets, such as office documents, images and source codes. When possible, we also removed traces of the virtualization, *e.g.*, changed default device names of VM, tuning RDTSC, etc. Finally, we took the snapshot of the VM and finalized the configuration of Cuckoo for managing the VM.

After the test environment was set, we submitted the malware samples to Cuckoo which executed them one-by-one, on the clean snapshot of the VM. Although majority of ransomware samples attack the system immediately after infection, *i.e.*, encrypts the victim's files, we allowed them to run 20 min unless the detection occurs earlier. After each analysis, we inspected if any alteration/deletion of the decoy files observed on the test machine. We call a malware sample as an active ransomware if any of the decoy files has a new SHA256 hash after the analysis is completed. If Cuckoo does not detect any activity or hashes of decoy files are same until the timeout happens, we exclude the sample from our list of active ransomware.

To compare our results to the previous research, and to reason on the techniques used by malware authors, we identified the family of each ransomware sample. For this purpose, we employed AVCLASS [21], an automatic malware labeling tool which performs plurality vote on the labels assigned by AV engines.

We excluded the vast majority of the samples from our test set as they did not show up any malicious activity during the analysis. There are several reasons behind this outcome. Firstly, it is a well known fact that malware authors try to avoid being analyzed and thus malware samples behaves benign if they detect that they are run in a virtual environment. Ransomware authors also follow this strategy. Another reason of inactivity is that malware design may involve a C&C server which may be down for some reason. Finally, ransomware may require certain conditions met before start attacking, *e.g.*, regional settings, wait for a specific date.

To sum up, we built a test set which contains 524 active samples from 31 cryptographic ransomware families to test against USHALLNOTPASS.

6.2   Robustness

In this section, we will analyze the outcome of the experiments to find the answer of **Q1** and **Q2**.

To begin with, USHALLNOTPASS stopped ransomware samples from *all families* in our data set, which includes famous and powerful ransomware families The details are reported in Table 1, where we also report for each family the average number of bytes per calls and the numbers of call, figures that support

---

[8] Kernel-based Virtual Machine, https://www.linux-kvm.org/page/Main_Page.

our argument that employing cryptographically secure pseudo-random numbers is a common property of all the ransomware.

Table 1 shows that USHALLNOTPASS successfully stopped 94% of cryptographic ransomware in our test set, including WannaCry, Locky and TeslaCrypt and remarkably the unmitigated *NotPetya*. The remaining 6% of missed elements looks like be false negative but we have evidence that this is not the case: quite likely we missed them because our implementation of the Interceptor is not perfect. In fact, a dynamic analysis we performed on each representative for all the missed family (*i.e.,* Cryptolocker, Filecryptor, SageCrypt and Yakes) has revealed that the ransomware actually invoke `CryptGenRandom`. Thus, in principle, they should have been stopped. The only conclusion we can draw is therefore that *our* implementation missed to intercept those call for some not obviously apparent technical reason. We looked into that and in Sect. 7 we discuss technical detail about how to improve Interceptor's capacity of intercepting.

That said, we need to comment that USHALLNOTPASS was implemented before the Bad Rabbit and NotPetya ransomware families emerged. Therefore, until proven otherwise, we have at least one evidence that supports R2 that USHALLNOTPASS can be effective on zero-day ransomware.

Case Study: *NotPetya.* We find it remarkable that USHALLNOTPASS was effective against NotPetya, a particular debilitating ransomware that in 2017 was used for a global cyberattack against Ukraine, Germany, Russia, Italy, France and Poland[9]. NotPetya is a ransomware which encrypts victim's disk at boot time (NotPetya has other malware characteristics such as the propagation, exploitation and network behaviors, but those are out of the scope of this paper.) Upon execution, NotPetya generates random numbers to use in the encryption, modifies the Master Boot Record (MBR) of the system disk which allows it to load its own kernel in the next reboot. Next, it restarts the system and shows a fake `chkdsk` screen to the user. Meanwhile, the malicious kernel encrypts the Master File Table (MFT) section of the disk which renders the data on that disk unusable. Since NotPetya loads its own kernel, the solutions proposed by [7,13,14] is bypassed and therefore cannot protect the victim. Moreover, [15] logs the random numbers that NotPetya uses to derive the encryption keys. Nonetheless, the key vault becomes inaccessible as well as other data after the reboot as the MFT is encrypted. On the other hand, USHALLNOTPASS stops NotPetya once it calls `CryptGenRandom` and terminates it before any cryptographic damage occurs.

6.3   Performance

We measured the overhead of USHALLNOTPASS on computing and storage resources to answer **Q3**. Our assessment focuses two points: (i) API level overhead, *i.e.,* the extra time to access secure randomness, (ii) application level

---

[9] https://en.wikipedia.org/wiki/Petya_(malware).

Table 1. Measurements of CSPRNG usage. Next to *Family*, recalling the ransomware's family name, column *Sample* reports the number of elements in the family and the number of samples that USHALLNOTPASS stopped. *CGR Usage* column shows the need of using CSPRNG among ransomware and contains two subcolumns: *Bytes*, the average number of bytes that a sample of ransomware obtains from calling `CryptGenRandom`, and *#Calls*, the number of calls to the function.

Family	Samples (%)	CGR usage	
		Bytes	# Calls
Androm	7/7 (100%)	4125257	178
Bad Rabbit	1/1 (100%)	52	2
Cayu	1/1 (100%)	4216212	20261
Cerber	149/149 (100%)	22393	2786
Crilock	1/1 (100%)	3456637	15
Critroni	1/1 (100%)	4755304	392
Crowti	3/3 (100%)	5231466	14
Crypmod	1/1 (100%)	2167813	20118
Crypshed	1/1 (100%)	5137296	13
Cryptesla	8/8 (100%)	5125627	14
Cryptolocker	8/17 (47%)	2805603	10
Cryptowall	1/1 (100%)	2242370	10
Dynamer	2/2 (100%)	3954293	20118
Enestaller	3/3 (100%)	2127036	82
Enestedel	5/5 (100%)	3871449	61
Filecryptor	3/4 (75%)	64	1
Genkryptik	3/3 (100%)	2506214	11
Kovter	1/1 (100%)	160	3
Locky	55/55 (100%)	5672894	23940
NotPetya	1/1 (100%)	92	2
Ransomlock	1/1 (100%)	2312373	12
Razy	2/2 (100%)	3955	2851
SageCrypt	4/7 (57%)	3417095	9
Scatter	6/6 (100%)	5626959	560
Shade	2/2 (100%)	2900347	12613
Teslacrypt	82/82 (100%)	4351264	14
Torrentlocker	1/1 (100%)	2642555	388
Troldesh	2/2 (100%)	3500127	11
WannaCry	2/2 (100%)	5615288	162
Yakes	23/39 (59%)	2450372	9
Zerber	115/115 (100%)	5542697	70
Total:	495/524 (94%)		

Table 2. Performance impact of USHALLNOTPASS on 100 000 iterative calls to CryptGenRandom

Measurement Mode	Random number length (bits)			
	128	256	1024	2048
USHALLNOTPASS off (seconds)	0.12	0.15	0.20	0.27
USHALLNOTPASS on (seconds)	15.59	15.80	15.84	16.91
Time spent in IPC (seconds)	14.90	15.05	15.05	16.00
IPC discarded (seconds)	0.69	0.75	0.79	0.91
Total overhead (factor)	125.42	105.68	77.69	61.77
IPC discarded overhead (factor)	5.52	5.00	3.89	3.32

overhead, namely, the latency perceived by the users. We conducted the assessments on a Windows 7 OS running on a VM with 2 CPU cores clocked at 2.7 GHz.

Benchmarks in API Level. We measured the time cost of invoking the CryptGenRandom API on the clean machine. For this aim, we wrote a benchmark program that invokes CryptGenRandom to generate 128 bits of random number, repetitively for 100 000[10] times and outputs the total time spent for this action. We observed that it took 0.12 s to complete this task. Then we run the benchmark program on the system that USHALLNOTPASS runs. This time it took 15.59 s to complete the same task. The results states that USHALLNOTPASS introduces an overhead with a factor of 125. According to our analysis, the main reason behind this impact is the significantly slow communication between Interceptor and Controller components of USHALLNOTPASS. We also observed that, if the overhead of communication is discarded, the performance impact happens to be a factor of 5.52. We remark that the observations made on an unoptimized prototype of USHALLNOTPASS. More efficient techniques of IPC and dynamic decision making for access control would result in better performance figures.

Our measurements on API level overhead and detailed results are illustrated in Table 2. It should be also noted that as the length of the pseudo-random number increases, the cost ratio of access control gets lower.

Impact in Application Level. Another important performance criterion is the slowdown in functionality of the software due to USHALLNOTPASS. On our test system, we installed latests versions of select applications which are common in home and office users. Next, we whitelisted and run the applications while USHALLNOTPASS is active. We inspected whether any slowdown occurred during the use of each application and logged the CSPRNG consumption, if any.

---

[10] We have chosen to set the limit of trials to 100 000 as with the current implementation of Inter-Process Communication (IPC), our setup becomes instable beyond this limit.

The test set contains the following applications: 7zip, Acrobat Reader, Chrome, Dropbox, Firefox, Foxit Reader, Google Drive, Internet Explorer, LibreOffice, Microsoft Office, Putty, PyCharm, Skype, Slack, Spotify, Teamviewer, Telegram Desktop, TeXstudio, Visual Studio, VLC, WinRar and WinZip. Among those that called `CryptGenRandom`, we present our observations on the following five:

- **Acrobat Reader.** We created a new digital signature and signed a PDF document. During this period, Acrobat Reader called `CryptGenRandom` 13 times and obtained 64 bytes of random value in total.
- **Chrome.** We observed Chrome's CSPRNG usage by connecting a website over HTTPS. For this purpose, we connected https://www.iacr.org/. Once the TLS connection is established, we stopped monitoring. We recorded 2 calls to `CryptGenRandom` and 32 bytes of usage in total.
- **Dropbox.** After creating a new account, we put 5 files with various sizes, 20 MB in total. During the synchronization of these files, Dropbox invoked `CryptGenRandom` 61 times, obtaining 16 bytes of data in each.
- **Skype.** We monitored Skype when making a video call for 60 s. During this period, Skype performed 13 calls to `CryptGenRandom` and obtained 16 bytes in each call.
- **Teamviewer.** Among the tested applications, Teamviewer was the clear winner in pseudo-random number consumption. In our test, we connected to a remote computer and keep the connection open for 60 s. We observed 128 calls to `CryptGenRandom` which yield 2596 bytes in total.

We did not notice any slowdown or loss in the functionality of any applications nor a program instability.

7   Discussion: Limitations and Improvements

History suggests that malware mitigation is a never ending race: a new defense system is responded with new attacks. We are no exception; cyber-criminals will develop new techniques to bypass USHALLNOTPASS. In this section, we first discuss how they could achieve this goal due to the limitations of our approach. Next, we review the issues may arise during the use of USHALLNOTPASS.

7.1   Alternative Randomness Sources

The results of our experiments suggests that cryptographic ransomware can be efficiently mitigated by preventing access to CSPRNG APIs of the host system. Ransomware authors will try to find alternatives sources for randomness. We anticipate that the first place to look for would be the *files* of victims. Generating encryption keys from files is known as *convergent encryption* [10] and already a common practice in cloud computing. That being said, the feasibility and security of maintaining a ransomware campaign (from point of cybercriminals) based on this approach needs to be studied.

Alternatively, ransomware authors may try to fetch cryptographically secure random numbers (or encryption keys) from C&C servers instead of requesting access to CSPRNG API. As we discussed in Sect. 2 ransomware cannot establish a secure channel with the remote server in this scenario. Such a ransomware may still communicate with a randomness source on the Internet, over an unsecure channel. In this case, however, the random numbers would be exposed to the risk of being obtained by IPSes. This would make it difficult for a ransomware to be successfull in the long term. Having said that, more feasible defense strategies should be developed for home users who will likely not be in the possession of advanced network devices like an IPS.

Lastly, ransomware may statically link a random number generator and use a seed gathered from user space. However, this approach would require higher implementation effort and be error-prone. Again, feasibility and security of this risky approach should be studied.

We leave these challenges as open problems for future works.

7.2 Implementation Related Issues

DLL Injection Method. AppInit DLLs mechanism loads the DLL modules specified by the `AppInit_DLLs` value in the Windows Registry. For ease of development, we utilized AppInit DLLs technique to load Interceptor component of USHALLNOTPASS into target processes. However, AppInit DLLs are loaded by using the `LoadLibrary` function during the `DLL_PROCESS_ATTACH` phase of `User32.dll`. Therefore, executables that do not link with `User32.dll` do not load the AppInit DLLs [17]. Concordantly, USHALLNOTPASS cannot intercept and control any calls made from these executables. During the experiments, we encountered 29 ransomware samples that do not link to `User32.dll`. However, dynamic analysis of these samples shows that they all indeed call `CryptGenRandom` function. This finding suggests that more powerful hooking techniques would yield protection against these sample. We highlight that this limitation only concerns our current prototype, *i.e.,* it is not inherent to the approach, and leaves room for improving the implementation of USHALLNOTPASS as a future work.

Whitelisting Built-in Applications. Modern OSes are installed with components including administrative tools and system utilities. Depending on the nature of the tasks, certain built-in applications may utilize the CSPRNG APIs. To keep the OS stable and secure, and maintain its functionality, these applications should be whitelisted before USHALLNOTPASS launched. To determine which built-in Windows applications call CSPRNG APIs, we performed a clean install of Windows 7 32-bit on a VM, monitored the calls to CSPRNG APIs and identified the caller processes. During this experiment, we executed typical maintenance operations on the clean system, such as defragging hard disks, managing backups, installing drivers and updating the OS.

We detected invocation of CSPRNG API by Explorer (`explorer.exe`) and Control Panel (`control.exe`) which are two of the most frequently used Windows applications. Moreover, Windows Update (`wuauclt.exe`) and Windows

Update Setup (`WuSetupV.exe`) are the only signed applications that consumed secure randomness. Therefore, if USHALLNOTPASS is configured to allow the signed applications to access CSPRNG APIs, these two applications do not need to be whitelisted. Furthermore, Local Security Authority Process (`lsass.exe`) was the only application which calls `BCryptGenRandom`, while others called `CryptGenRandom`. The complete list of applications[11] that called CSPRNG APIs during the experiment is given in Table 3.

Table 3. Windows applications that calls CSPRNG APIs. Most of the applications listed below are located at `%WINDIR%\System32`.

Executable name	File description	Digitally signed
explorer.exe	Windows Explorer	✗
lsass.exe	Local Security Authority Process	✗
SearchIndexer.exe	Microsoft Windows Search Indexer	✗
svchost.exe	Host Process for Windows Services	✗
dllhost.exe	COM Surrogate	✗
wmiprvse.exe	WMI Provider Host	✗
SearchFilterHost.exe	Microsoft Windows Search Filter Host	✗
SearchProtocolHost.exe	Microsoft Windows Search Protocol Host	✗
control.exe	Windows Control Panel	✗
TrustedInstaller.exe	Windows Modules Installer	✗
VSSVC.exe	Microsoft Volume Shadow Copy Service	✗
WMIADAP.EXE	WMI Reverse Performance Adapter Maintenance Utility	✗
wuauclt.exe	Windows Update	✓
WuSetupV.exe	Windows Update Setup	✓
mmc.exe	Microsoft Management Console	✗
MpCmdRun.exe	Microsoft Malware Protection Command Line Utility	✗
dfrgui.exe	Microsoft Disk Defragmenter	✗

Handling Sofware Updates. OS software or installed applications may be updated for various reasons, including patching security vulnerabilities, fixing bugs and adding new functionalities. The update process may also involve replacing the existing executables with newer ones and thus altering their hash values. Therefore, if an OS component or an application which has access rights to CSPRNG API is updated, Whitelist of USHALLNOTPASS must also be updated accordingly to prevent false positives. More precisely, the old hash value should be removed from the Whitelist and the new hash value should be added.

[11] The list of applications may vary on different versions of Windows OS.

Abuse of Digital Signatures. While Code Signing aims to help verifying the software origin, cyber criminals frequently used stolen certificates to sign malware in order to penetrate this defense [6,23]. Furthermore, there is an incidence *i.e.,* a ransomware sample with a valid digital signature [25], which proves that ransomware authors also have this capability. Such a clandestine ransomware sample may evade access control feature promised by our system. Namely, if USHALLNOTPASS is configured to allow digitally signed applications to access CSPRNG of the host system, and the ransomware binary has a valid signature (*e.g.,* the stolen certificate is not revoked yet or Certificate Revocation List (CRL) is not up to date), then the victim's files would be encrypted. Note that utilization of digital signatures is optional and meant to improve practicality and applicability of our system. System administrators should decide enabling this feature according to their systems' needs and capabilities. When ultimate security is desired, this option should be left as disabled so that even digitally signed ransomware would not cause harm on data.

User Interaction. As we discussed above, software applications on host system may be updated or replaced with another one. To prevent interruption in the work flow, USHALLNOTPASS may be configured to ask user permission in case previously unseen process requests access to CSPRNG of the host system. This brings the risk of infection, as the user is involved in the decision making, and may not concentrate well each time. We remark that user interaction is an optional feature of USHALLNOTPASS and is an example of security/usability trade off. If disabled, it would not pose any risk against security.

7.3   Improvements

Our prototype currently hooks into only `CryptGenRandom` API, as our initial findings suggested us that it is widely used by ransomware. To evade detection, ransomware may restrict itself to utilize other CSPRNG APIs such as `RtlGenRandom` and `BCryptGenRandom`. However, adding new hooks is only an implementation effort, that we plan to undertake in a future work.

8   Anti-ransomware: A Critical Review

In Sect.1 we distinguished anti-ransomware defenses according to their *ex-ante* or *ex-post* nature. We also separated *non-cryptographic* from non *cryptographic* approach. In addition, there are two main defense strategies which seem driving the most famous works: *behavioural analysis* and *key escrow*.

Behavioral Analysis. Solutions in this sub-category monitor an application's activity in real-time, searching for indicators (*e.g.,* a process' interactions with its environment, file system activity, network connections and modifications on OS components) that may justify counter-actions such as blocking the application's execution. Approaches differ because of what is observed, how the observation process is designed and executed. Thus, UNVEIL [13] by Kharraz *et al.* generates

Table 4. Comparison of ransomware defense systems

Feature	UNVEIL	CryptoDrop	ShieldFS	PayBreak	Redemption	UShallNotPass
Mode of operation	Proactive	Proactive	Proactive	Key-escrow	Proactive	Access control
Obfuscation resilience	✓	✓	✓	✗	✓	✓
Disk I/O agnostic	✗	✗	✗	✓	✗	✓
Stops NotPetya	✗	✗	✗	✗	✗	✓

an artificial user environment and monitors the potential ransomware there for desktop locks, file access patterns and I/O data entropy. The software decides whether certain activities hide an ransomware by comparing the monitored features with those of benign applications of reference and by applying a similarity threshold of obtained from a precision-recall analysis. Differently, CRYPTODROP by Scaife *et al.* [20] operates in the real environment and observes file type changes and measures file modifications. Malicious changes to file are detected by similarity-preserving hash functions and measuring Shannon Entropy. Continella *et al.* developed SHIELDFS [7] that monitors low-level file system activities and collects the following features: *folder listing, file read/write/rename, file type* and *write entropy*. A ransomware is recognized by comparing these characteristic activity patterns with that of benign applications. SHIELDFS also monitors cryptographic primitives through searching the memory space of a suspicious process for a precomputed key schedule to increase detection speed. Lastly, Kharraz and Kirda developed REDEMPTION [14] which monitors the same indicators as above, but redirects write calls to sparse files. By this way, malicious changes reverted more efficiently than previous defenses.

Works in this category are not cryptographic according to our definition and can have either *ex ante* or *ex post* nature. Which one depends on whether their monitoring happens in a safe virtual environment (so having the possibility to stop the real damage from happening) on in the real system (competing with the ransomware while it has started encrypting).

Key Escrow. Systems adopting this strategy also run in real-time and in the real system so they have an *ex-post* nature. They create the conditions to easy the decryption of the infected files mainly by holding in escrow the encryption keys that the system generates on request. These are many, but in case some requests come from ransomware the keys to decrypt files should be among them. This proactive "protection" is applied only after a ransomware has finished its work.

To the best of our knowledge, the approach of using *key-backup* to combat ransomware is first proposed by Palisse *et al.* in [19] and *independently* by Lee *et al.* in [16]. Later, Kolodenker *et al.* presented the first proof-of-concept of this technique with the PAYBREAK [15] system. It intercepts calls made to APIs of cryptographic libraries, extracting the parameters in those calls and storing them in a secure key vault. To detect statically linked third-party cryptographic libraries in order to extract encryption keys, the system use fuzzy function signatures. In the case of infection, the system tries to decrypt the encrypted files using the stored keys and parameters. Since this defense strategy does not involve any file system trace analysis to construct and evaluate the behavior of a process, PAYBREAK achieves superior performance than the real-time protection systems in the previous category.

Limitations of Current Defenses. To begin with, none of the previous defenses stops NotPetya ransomware. NotPetya performs a disk encryption after the system is booted into its own malicious kernel, thereby bypassing on-line protections.

Besides, solutions that rely on a virtual environment, like UNVEIL, miss ransomware that recognize the presence of artificial system. Such smart ransomware become malicious only when put in real systems while remaining innocuous and bypassing controls otherwise. Anti-ransomware with an *ex-post* nature, like CRYPTODROP, may recognize and stop the ransomware when it is too late. In their experiments over 5100 files, CRYPTODROP's authors report that ransomware could encrypt up to 29 files. The median of this statistics reported as 10. Like other behavioural analysis based solutions, SHIELDFS comes with an overhead that has been estimated to exceed 40% while being 26% in average. PAYBREAK, also *ex post*, needs to correctly recognize the cryptographic functions employed by the ransomware to log the encryption keys and the parameters. While this is feasible for built-in cryptographic functions on the host system, ransomware that utilizes third-party libraries can bypass detection through *obfuscation*. In addition, there are some issues with the logging of crypto APIs. PAYBREAK logs every key, including private keys of TLS and SSH connections. Both protocols offers *forward secrecy* which is build upon employing ephemeral keys. All schemes which counts on application level security (Layer 7 of OSI Model) may become vulnerable in this case. PAYBREAK is designed in such a way that all keys are stored in one place. This may bring the risk of single point of failure as well as a new target for cyber-criminals. Table 4 compares USHALLNOTPASS against the related works herein commented.

9 Conclusion and Future Work

Cryptographic ransomware applications encrypt files and offer to decrypt them after the payment of a ransom. They are getting better and stronger but need randomness to implement strong encryption. So, a strategy to block them is to control access to randomness sources. We propose USHALLNOTPASS, a system that implements this strategy and terminates unauthorized requests to (CSPRNG)'s APIs provided by the host Operating System. On testing, USHALLNOTPASS stopped 495 active real-world samples of cryptographic ransomware (out of 524, so missing only 6%) from 31 different families. USHALLNOTPASS has minimal overhead on system performance which makes it practical to be used in real-world applications.

There is of course room to extend our approach: to improve the intercept capabilities (for example to confirm our conjecture as to why our implementation missed 6%); improve the performance of our decision making method;

studying and preventing other ways that ransomware could generate encryption keys, circumventing calls to CSPRNG, evading our controls; build a practical and automatic white-listing strategy with low false positive rates (an issue that we have only partially assessed in this paper, since it requires a different experimental set up, and we leave this work for the future).

The approach described here has been shown to be highly effective against the current generation of ransomware, but doubtless, (having read this paper), the authors of ransomware will devise new strategies to evade our approach. The race between ransomware and anti-ransomware will continue.

Acknowledgments. We sincerely thank Clémentine Maurice for reviewing our paper. We also appreciate the anonymous reviewers for their constructive feedbacks and comments. This work is supported by a pEp Security SA/SnT partnership project "Protocols for Privacy Security Analysis".

References

1. Debian Security Advisory: DSA-1571-1 OpenSSL - predictable random number generator, May 2008. http://www.debian.org/security/2008/dsa-1571. Accessed 17 July 2017
2. Juniper Networks: Out of cycle security bulletin, December 2015. https://kb.juniper.net/InfoCenter/index?page=content&id=JSA10713. Accessed 17 July 2017
3. Bellare, M., Brakerski, Z., Naor, M., Ristenpart, T., Segev, G., Shacham, H., Yilek, S.: Hedged public-key encryption: how to protect against bad randomness. In: Matsui, M. (ed.) ASIACRYPT 2009. LNCS, vol. 5912, pp. 232–249. Springer, Heidelberg (2009). https://doi.org/10.1007/978-3-642-10366-7_14
4. Bradner, S.: Key words for use in RFCs to Indicate Requirement Levels. BCP 14, RFC Editor, March 1997. http://www.rfc-editor.org/rfc/rfc2119.txt, http://www.rfc-editor.org/rfc/rfc2119.txt
5. Bromium: Understanding Crypto-Ransomware (2015). https://www.bromium.com/sites/default/files/rpt-bromium-crypto-ransomware-us-en.pdf
6. Chen, T.M., Abu-Nimeh, S.: Lessons from stuxnet. Computer **44**(4), 91–93 (2011)
7. Continella, A., Guagnelli, A., Zingaro, G., De Pasquale, G., Barenghi, A., Zanero, S., Maggi, F.: ShieldFS: a self-healing, ransomware-aware filesystem. In: Proceedings of the 32Nd Annual Conference on Computer Security Applications, pp. 336–347. ACSAC 2016. ACM, New York (2016)
8. Cybersecurity Ventures: Ransomware Damage Report (2017). https://cybersecurityventures.com/ransomware-damage-report-2017-part-2/
9. Dodis, Y., Ong, S.J., Prabhakaran, M., Sahai, A.: On the (im)possibility of cryptography with imperfect randomness. In: 45th Annual IEEE Symposium on Foundations of Computer Science, pp. 196–205, October 2004
10. Douceur, J.R., Adya, A., Bolosky, W.J., Simon, D., Theimer, M.: Reclaiming space from duplicate files in a serverless distributed file system. In: Proceedings of the 22nd International Conference on Distributed Computing Systems (ICDCS 2002), pp. 617. ICDCS 2002. IEEE Computer Society, Washington, DC, USA (2002)
11. Gammons, B.: 4 Surprising Backup Failure Statistics that Justify Additional Protection, January 2017. https://blog.barkly.com/backup-failure-statistics. Accessed 17 July 2017

12. Howard, M., Le Blanc, D.: Writing Secure Code. Developer Best Practices, 2nd edn. Microsoft Press, Cambridge (2004)
13. Kharaz, A., Arshad, S., Mulliner, C., Robertson, W., Kirda, E.: Unveil: a large-scale, automated approach to detecting ransomware. In: 25th USENIX Security Symposium (USENIX Security 2016), pp. 757–772. USENIX Association, Austin, TX (2016)
14. Kharraz, A., Kirda, E.: Redemption: real-time protection against ransomware at end-hosts. In: Dacier, M., Bailey, M., Polychronakis, M., Antonakakis, M. (eds.) Research in Attacks, Intrusions, and Defenses, pp. 98–119. Springer, Cham (2017). https://doi.org/10.1007/978-3-319-66332-6_5
15. Kolodenker, E., Koch, W., Stringhini, G., Egele, M.: Paybreak: defense against cryptographic ransomware. In: Proceedings of the 2017 ACM on Asia Conference on Computer and Communications Security, pp. 599–611. ASIA CCS 2017. ACM, New York (2017)
16. Lee, K., Oh, I., Yim, K.: Ransomware-prevention technique using key backup. In: Jung, J.J., Kim, P. (eds.) Big Data Technologies and Applications, vol. 194, pp. 105–114. Springer International Publishing, Cham (2017). https://doi.org/10.1007/978-3-319-58967-1_12
17. Microsoft: Working with the AppInit_DLLs registry value, November 2006. https://support.microsoft.com/en-us/help/197571/working-with-theappinit-dlls-registry-value
18. Microsoft Corporation: Windows Authenticode Portable Executable Signature Format. Technical report, March 2008. http://download.microsoft.com/download/9/c/5/9c5b2167-8017-4bae-9fde-d599bac8184a/Authenticode_PE.docx
19. Palisse, A., Le Bouder, H., Lanet, J.-L., Le Guernic, C., Legay, A.: Ransomware and the legacy Crypto API. In: Cuppens, F., Cuppens, N., Lanet, J.-L., Legay, A. (eds.) CRiSIS 2016. LNCS, vol. 10158, pp. 11–28. Springer, Cham (2017). https://doi.org/10.1007/978-3-319-54876-0_2
20. Scaife, N., Carter, H., Traynor, P., Butler, K.R.B.: Cryptolock (and drop it): stopping ransomware attacks on user data. In: 2016 IEEE 36th International Conference on Distributed Computing Systems (ICDCS), pp. 303–312, June 2016
21. Sebastián, M., Rivera, R., Kotzias, P., Caballero, J.: AVCLASS: a tool for massive malware labeling. In: Monrose, F., Dacier, M., Blanc, G., Garcia-Alfaro, J. (eds.) RAID 2016. LNCS, vol. 9854, pp. 230–253. Springer, Cham (2016). https://doi.org/10.1007/978-3-319-45719-2_11
22. Soeder, D., Abad, C., Acevedo, G.: Black-box assessment of pseudorandom algorithms. Black Hat USA (2013). https://media.blackhat.com/us-13/US-13-Soeder-Black-Box-Assessment-of-Pseudorandom-Algorithms-WP.pdf
23. Szor, P.: Duqu-Threat Research and Analysis, November 2011. https://securingtomorrow.mcafee.com/wp-content/uploads/2011/10/Duqu.pdf
24. US Department of Justice: How to Protect your Networks from Ransomware (2016). https://www.justice.gov/criminal-ccips/file/872771/download
25. VirusTotal: Scan report, June 2017. https://virustotal.com/en/file/81fdbf04f3d0d9a85e0fbb092e257a2dda14c5d783f1c8bf3bc41038e0a78688/analysis/

Hidden in Plain Sight: Filesystem View Separation for Data Integrity and Deception

Teryl Taylor[1]([✉]), Frederico Araujo[1]([✉]), Anne Kohlbrenner[2],
and Marc Ph. Stoecklin[1]

[1] IBM Research, Yorktown Heights, NY 10598, USA
{terylt,frederico.araujo}@ibm.com, mpstoeck@us.ibm.com
[2] Carnegie Mellon University, Pittsburgh, PA 15213, USA
akohlbre@andrew.cmu.edu

Abstract. Cybercrime has become a big money business with sensitive data being a hot commodity on the dark web. In this paper, we introduce and evaluate a filesystem (DcyFS) capable of curtailing data theft and ensuring file integrity protection by providing subject-specific views of the filesystem. The deceptive filesystem transparently creates multiple levels of stacking to protect the base filesystem and monitor file accesses, hide and redact sensitive files with baits, and inject decoys onto fake system views purveyed to untrusted subjects, all while maintaining a pristine state to legitimate processes. A novel security domain model groups applications into filesystem views and eliminates the need for filesystem merging. Our prototype implementation leverages a kernel hot-patch to seamlessly integrate the new filesystem module into live and existing environments. We demonstrate the utility of our approach through extensive performance benchmarks and use cases on real malware samples, including ransomware, rootkits, binary modifiers, backdoors, and library injectors. Our results show that DcyFS adds no significant performance overhead to the filesystem, preserves the filesystem data, and offers a potent new tool to characterize the impact of malicious activities and expedite forensic investigations.

Keywords: Intrusion detection and prevention · Cyber deception
Filesystems

1 Introduction

In today's modern digital age, data theft and compromise remain one of the most severe threats to individuals, governments, and enterprises. Capitalizing on data as the new digital currency, cyber criminals steal personal records [17,26] and hold data ransom [13], costing businesses millions of dollars to regain access to their data [11]. While several specialized filesystem mitigations have been proposed in response to the recent outbreak of ransomware

---

T. Taylor and F. Araujo—Both authors contributed equally to this work.

© Springer International Publishing AG, part of Springer Nature 2018
C. Giuffrida et al. (Eds.): DIMVA 2018, LNCS 10885, pp. 256–278, 2018.
https://doi.org/10.1007/978-3-319-93411-2_12

attacks [16,39,41,44], these protections typically focus on preventing the execution of ransomware, maintaining system backups, or reverse engineering custom cryptography schemes [19,21,34]. Unfortunately, such reactive approaches are inadequate and have not seen widespread adoption, as 71% of the organizations attacked by ransomware still have their files successfully encrypted [13], with less than half being able to recover from backups [15].

Other protective measures, such as decoy files [8,49] and canaries [1,46], have been proposed to detect potential attacks via deceptive breadcrumbs that record unwarranted filesystem accesses. However, in order to be effective, the decoys must not interfere with legitimate uses of the filesystem, which requires that users must either be aware of the decoys or that the decoys must be readily identifiable by users, rendering these defenses easily circumventable and difficult to maintain in shared environments. Moreover, such deceptive files do not prevent cyber criminals from stealing sensitive data. Given the alarming rate and scope of recent attacks [11,39,48], new solutions are needed to identify and dissuade attackers from stealing or destroying targeted data assets.

To overcome these disadvantages, our work introduces a new filesystem, DcyFS, which protects files at their place of rest. DcyFS (1) stops data theft, modification, and destruction by untrusted subjects (e.g., users, processes), (2) resists attack reconnaissance through denial and deception, and (3) embeds a new threat sensor capable of detecting and characterizing many classes of malicious behavior that can be captured at the filesystem level. DcyFS takes a fundamentally different approach to the data theft and integrity problem by monitoring file accesses transparently, hiding sensitive data, creating decoy files, and modifying existing files to provide a fake system view to untrusted subjects. It actively captures filesystem events and correlates them with other system features (e.g., user groups, application name) to create targeted filesystem *views* that hide high-value assets and expose enticing breadcrumbs to detect deliberate tampering with data. Such *context-awareness* minimizes false alarms by curtailing inadvertent, legitimate access to breadcrumbs—by exposing more "truthful" views of the filesystem to trustworthy processes.

DcyFS is a stackable filesystem with a base filesystem and an overlay layer. The overlay is used to strategically inject decoy objects on the filesystem and prevent untrusted modifications to reach the base filesystem, unless explicitly merged. By combining its layered architecture with view separation, DcyFS maintains data integrity and confidentiality. The filesystem can also stop malware from making system-level changes, such as persisting across reboots or creating hidden users, regardless of privilege. Furthermore, DcyFS records all changes made by a given process separately in its overlay layer. Malicious actions attempting to tamper with the filesystem are therefore imprinted in the overlay, which can be leveraged as a powerful tool for extracting forensic summaries that can expedite post-mortem investigations, reveal attributing features of malware, and characterize the impact of attackers' actions.

We demonstrate the utility of our approach by conducting extensive performance benchmarks and analyzing its effectiveness against 18 real-world malware samples spanning five malware categories. Our contributions can be summarized as follows:

- The design of a new *stacking* filesystem to augment standard filesystems with denial and deception capabilities, such as hiding resources from untrusted processes, redacting or replacing assets to protect sensitive data, and injecting breadcrumbs to disinform and misdirect attackers.
- A model that groups applications into ranked filesystem views (called security domains) in order to protect data integrity and confidentiality and avoid merging overlays with the base filesystem. The model specifies an algorithm based on order theory for choosing the proper domain into which an application is run. A root domain provides a single view of the filesystem enabling transparent filesystem operations.
- An evaluation that shows that the approach can detect and resist real attacks from five malware categories. Furthermore, preliminary benchmarks demonstrate that DcyFS can defend against data theft and filesystem tampering without incurring significant overhead.
- The identification and automatic extraction of key forensic indicators of compromise from malware attacks, and their application to use cases, highlighting the filesystem's facility in exposing malware behavior.
- Unlike prior work, our approach enforces file integrity protection without requiring file access mediation. It also supports the implementation of access control policies, and enables the automation of decoy injection in commodity filesystems.

The remainder of the paper is organized as follows. Section 2 presents an overview of DcyFS. Section 3 describes forensic features that are used in conjunction with DcyFS to conduct post-mortem malware analysis, and Sect. 4 outlines our implementation. Section 5 describes use cases on real malware, while performance benchmarks are detailed in Sect. 6. Discussion is presented in Sect. 7. We finish with related work and conclusions in Sects. 8 and 9, respectively.

2 System Overview

We envision a filesystem capable of maintaining file integrity and confidentiality against untrusted subjects, while luring attackers into accessing decoys and leaving forensic trails on the filesystem. To achieve these goals, DcyFS creates customized views of the underlying filesystem on a per-subject basis. Our key insight is that legitimate subjects only require access to directories, files, and file types relevant to their work, and do not need to know about other files on the system.

2.1 Challenges and Design Decisions

There are several significant security and performance challenges that must be overcome to realize DcyFS in practice. For example, a naïve implementation interposes every filesystem event and consults a list of access policies to determine whether to grant subjects visibility of specific directories and files. In a performance-sensitive environment this would be disastrous, imposing unrealistc filesystem overheads. Moreover, the integrity of the system would depend on the correctness and completeness of its access policies.

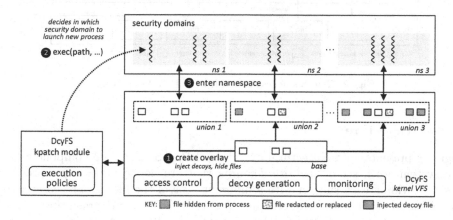

Fig. 1. Architectural overview of DcyFS

Specifically, practical adoption requires that DcyFS (1) prevent all write accesses to the underlying filesystem, (2) curtail read access to sensitive data, and (3) introduce almost no overhead for legitimate subjects, while performing well enough for untrusted subjects to avoid offering overt, reliable timing channels that advertise the deception to attackers. Solutions must be sufficiently transparent that administrators require only a superficial, high-level understanding to specify trust-based configuration policies and inject decoys.

Together, these requirements motivate three main design decisions. First, to protect the integrity of the filesystem data, and impede the destruction and modification of legitimate files, our approach benefits from the synergy between mainstream Linux kernel APIs and the Virtual File System's stackable filesystem architecture to suppress any direct modifications to the base filesystem.

Second, our approach leverages mount namespaces and filesystem layer superposition to inhibit sensitive data exposure to untrusted subjects. This works by enforcing separation of filesystem views, disallowing malicious subjects from accessing legitimate data. The filesystem automatically synthesizes genuine-looking, isolated filesystem layers based on a trust-based policy engine.

Third, the required time performance precludes filesystem access mediation (e.g., runtime access control [24]); instead, we employ a lighter-weight alternative based on the Linux overlay filesystem implementation [9] that enforces data integrity by design. To scale to many concurrent processes, we use OS-level virtualization to deploy launched processes to filesystem views in the kernel, and leverage Linux live patching capabilities [28] to patch the kernel and enable the new filesystem capabilities in running environments.

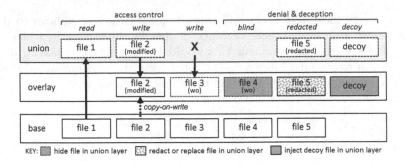

Fig. 2. DcyFS's access control, denial, and deception

2.2 Architecture

Figure 1 presents an architectural overview of DcyFS. The core components of the system are a set of *security domains* that are deployed on a per-process basis, providing each subject with a different *view* of the filesystem—computed as the *union* of the *base* filesystem and the *overlay*. To alter the resulting union, each overlay has the ability to (1) hide base files, (2) modify their content by overlaying a different file with the same name, and (3) inject new files that are not present in the host system. File writes are stored in the overlay, protecting base files from being overwritten. This forms the basis of a stackable filesystem that can be mounted atop different base filesystem types (e.g., block, network) to offer data integrity protection and detection of data-stealing attacks.

Stackable Filesystem. Central to DcyFS's architecture is a stackable filesystem (FS), which combines multiple separate filesystems that are overlaid into a single coherent system. To separate filesystem views, DcyFS transparently combines two filesystems, which we term an overlay and a base filesystem. The base FS is the main host FS and is read-only, while the overlay FS, which is read-write, controls what is visible to a running process. When a file with the same name appears in both FSes, the one in the overlay is visible to the process. When a directory appears in both FSes, the contents are merged in the process view. A file or directory is hidden from view by injecting a character device on the overlay. Figure 2 illustrates this concept, showing the base and overlay mounts, and the resulting union of the two mounts. To hide a base file or directory, DcyFS simply marks it as deleted in the overlay. Decoy files are similarly placed in carefully-chosen locations inside the overlay mount, and existing files can be replaced or redacted for attacker deception.

Per-subject Filesystem Isolation. While the stackable filesystem provides the ability to inject, hide, and overlay files, it alone cannot separate the views of trusted and untrusted subjects To implement this separation, DcyFS leverages *mount namespaces* to transparently isolate filesystem views. A namespace is an operating system construct that wraps a global system resource in an abstraction that makes processes inside the namespace appear to have their own isolated

---

Algorithm 1: Creating the per-subject overlay filesystem.

```
 1 unshare(NEW_NS);
 2 config = getDcfsConfiguration();
 3 mountDir = "/var/namespaces/ns1/rootfs";
 4 makeDir(mountDir);
 5 overlayMount = "/var/namespaces/ns1/overlay";
 6 makeDir(overlay);
 7 populateOverlay(overlayMount, config);
 8 mount(mountDir, base="/", overlay=overlayMount);
 9 innerMountDir = "/var/namespaces/ns1/oldroot";
10 makeDir(innerMountDir);
11 pivot_root(mountDir, innerMountDir);
12 unmount(innerMountDir);
13 removeDir(innerMountDir);
```
---

instance of a global resource [23]. A mount namespace provides an isolated mount point list for any process inside the namespace—a process inside the namespace has a different view of the filesystem than the base system [22].

Algorithm 1 outlines the subject-specific mount namespace creation. The **unshare** system call (line 1) creates and enters a new separate mount namespace from the global mount namespace. Next, a stackable filesystem (specific to an application or user) is created by generating an overlay, and populating it with decoy files, and hidden files (lines 5–7). The overlay and base filesystem are then mounted to a system directory (line 8), and we swap out the existing root filesystem with the newly created stackable filesystem using the **pivot_root** system call (lines 9–11) inside the mount namespace. Finally, we remove the old root filesytem (lines 12–13). Once created, the namespace is persisted using a filesystem mount so that new processes can be placed into the namespace. In this way, a newly launched process is unaware that it runs on a customized view of the host filesystem.

Linux processes are launched using the kernel's **exec** system call. We modify the system call using a kernel patch to create and move new processes into the proper mount namespace according to the mechanism outlined next.

Security Domains. Mount namespaces can be built on the fly for individual processes, or designed for reuse by separate groups of applications. We refer to such reusable namespaces as *security domains*. DcyFS's security domains enforce coherent views of the filesystem, while curtailing issues related to file merging.

Each security domain $\gamma \in (\Gamma, \leq)$ is assigned a rank denoting its level of trust relative to the other domains. Security domains therefore comprise a partially-ordered lattice ordered by trust scores ($\leq$), with the *untrusted* domain (γ_{unt}) at the bottom (denoting untrusted execution), and the *root* domain (γ_{root}) at the top (denoting trusted execution). Meet operation $\sqcap$ denotes greatest lower bound, which is used to determine the proper domain of execution of new programs. DcyFS's filesystem view isolation is policy-driven, defined via associations between mount namespaces, filesystem objects, and users with security domains.

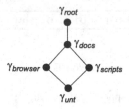

Fig. 3. Security domains lattice example

DcyFS uses this model to determine in which security domain to execute new processes. This decision point extends the semantics of the kernel's $exec(filename, \overline{args})$ function to compute the target execution domain as $\gamma_{filename} \sqcap \gamma_{\overline{args}} \sqcap \gamma_{user} \sqcap \gamma_{ns}$, the meet between the security domains of $filename$, $\overline{args}$ (computed across all arguments denoting file paths), γ_{user} (the set of security domains associated with a user), and γ_{ns} (the parent process security domain, denoted by the current mount namespace). Including γ_{ns} in the security domain determination of a newly launched process caps its execution to its parent process' security domain, thus preventing lower-ranked domains from accidentally or maliciously spawning child processes in higher-ranked domains. In our implementation, this property is seamlessly encoded in the security domains' mount namespace hierarchy.

To illustrate, Fig. 3 describes a simple security domain setup for a client desktop. It includes domains to separate Internet-facing applications ($\gamma_{browser}$), word processing tools (γ_{docs}), and programming environments for scripted languages ($\gamma_{scripts}$). In this context, a web browsers running in $\gamma_{browser}$ may download a PDF document from the Internet, which gets stored in the browser domain. To visualize its contents, a trusted user (γ_{root}) opens the file in a PDF viewer (γ_{docs}). As a result, DcyFS executes the viewer in the browser domain—the greatest lower bound of the domains involved in the security domain determination—so that the potentially malicious PDF file has no access to the user's documents (kept separated in γ_{docs}). Similarly, if a process running in $\gamma_{scripts}$ spawns a second process not authorized to execute in the scripts domain, DcyFS moves the sub-process task to the untrusted domain (γ_{unt}). This is to prevent attacks where a trusted process (e.g., Bash) is exploited to install and launch untrusted malware. The rule also prevents malware from gaining entry to another security domain by running trusted applications.

Profiles. Each security domain has its own profile, which contains the list of files and directories that are viewable within the domain. These include files that are deleted, replaced, or injected in the domain view. The profile also has a list of the directories that are bind mounted to the base filesystem. Such directories are not subject to an overlay and can be directly written. Directories such as the system logs, or a browser's download might be bind mounted to facilitate easy file sharing across domains. In addition to domain profiles, DcyFS also supports application and user profiles that govern domain access. Each profile contains

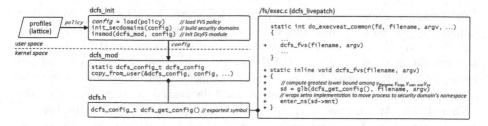

Fig. 4. DcyFS kernel module and live patch, showing main workflow in simplified syntax.

the subject or subjects of the profile, which include user names, binary names, and binary hashes. The profile also contains a list of the domains for which the subject has access, along with a default security domain when an application is run without an open file. Any subject not listed in a profile is designated to the untrusted domain.

Root Domain. While the security domain architecture provides many advantages, we still need a complete view of the filesystem to facilitate copying between domains and to transparently load applications. This is done through the *root* domain, which is a special mount namespace that fuses together a writable base filesystem mount with all the read-only overlay filesystem mounts from the other domains into a single, unified view. This enhances usability by overcoming merging issues that arise from DcyFS's ability to separate filesystem views. Object collisions—when multiple overlays share the same fully-qualified object path names—are handled by stacking overlays according to the trust order relative to each domain. The root domain is reserved for a few special programs such as a file browser, terminal, and file-copying tools. Since the filesystem is a combination of the base filesystem and the overlays of the other domains, the file browser can transparently open files and launch applications in their native security domains to protect the integrity of the root domain. Furthermore, specialized copying tools allow files to be copied or moved between domains as desired.

Security Domains Initialization. Security domains are built hierarchically, taking the same structure as the lattice that describes them. This hierarchical organization is created by nesting mount namespaces via recursive invocations of the **unshare** system call, starting with the root domain, followed by the domains in the next level of the lattice, and so forth. Individual security domains are constructed as described in Algorithm 1. Since the untrusted domain is the leaf namespace of the structure, it must be created in each of the (leaf−1)-level domains and bind mounted to the same overlay. Mount namespaces have the desired property that running processes can only be moved into namespaces down the nested hierarchy. This ensures that a process cannot break the policy enforced by the lattice.

Bootstrapping. Figure 4 shows a simplified view of the kernel modifications that implement the security domains hierarchy and enforcement procedure. Upon initialization, a bootstrap component (`dcfs_init`) ingests pre-defined subject and filesystem view separation (FVS) profiles—denoting the partially ordered lattice of security domains—into a `config` object, which is used to create the security domains and load the kernel module tasked with maintaining the FVS policies. At runtime, `dcfs_livepatch` uses kpatch to modify the kernel's `do_execveat_common` function to call `dcfs_fvs`, which implements the decision procedure to move newly created processes to their appropriate security domains.

Filesystem Denial and Deception. DcyFS provides data integrity by strictly enforcing that all writes are made to the overlay layer. Writes to base files are first *copied up* to the overlay layer before being written using copy-on-write. This has the desirable effect of preserving the base filesystem—changes made by untrusted processes do not affect the base, protecting legitimate users from seeing malicious changes as well as effectively keeping a pristine copy of the filesystem immediately before the malicious process started. DcyFS can hide particular files and directories from the process, thus curtailing sensitive data leaks. Additionally, the filesystem is capable of generating encrypted files and implanting decoys in the overlay to shadow sensitive files in the base filesystem. DcyFS transparently monitors and logs access to such files. Moreover, only the untrusted process is affected by the hidden and decoy files, leaving legitimate users free of confusion.

It is worth noting that trusted processes also benefit from security domains. DcyFS can launch a trusted process atop an overlay to hide unnecessary files and directories, or inject decoys to catch potential insiders. Furthermore, certain directories can be bind mounted from the base filesystem to give trusted processes the ability to directly view and modify them. For example, we might run a database server, providing it with a fake overlay view of the entire filesystem, but giving it direct write access to the directories in which it writes data. As a result, if the database application is compromised, damage is limited to the data directory only.

Filesystem Opacity. DcyFS leverages the overlay infrastructure to conceal its existence from attackers and curtail access to explicit information about its kernel modules, configuration objects, and overlay mounts. This is achieved by bootstrapping the filesystem with configuration rules that hide and redact specific filesystem objects. For example, `/proc/mounts` (`/proc/self/mount*`) and `/etc/mtab` are redacted to conceal overlay mount point information and bind mounts into the overlays, and DcyFS's kernel live patch and kernel module are hidden from filesystem views. Similarly, the filesystem hides its configuration, usermode helper components (e.g., decoy generation, configuration parsing, forensics data extraction), and working directory where overlays and logs are persisted in the base filesystem.

2.3   Threat Model

Attackers in our model interact with the filesystem to perform reconnaissance, steal data, and sabotage their victim's files. Our system does not defend against exploits of kernel vulnerabilities; such protection is outside our scope. We also assume that malicious subjects might attempt to erase story-telling traces of compromise from the filesystem. Misleading the attacker into interacting with an isolated DcyFS overlay is therefore useful for detecting and characterizing the attack, divulging attacker strategies and goals not discernible from a monolitic filesystem. Attacker actions are processed with root- or user-level privileges. The defender's ability to thwart these and future attacks stems from his ability to deflect attackers to isolated, deceptive views of the filesystem, and perform forensic investigations and information gathering.

2.4   Security Goals

Integrity. We define integrity as the infeasibility of alteration of file contents or deletion of files in the underlying filesystem by a subject. More concretely, after DcyFS is initialized, attackers freely interact with their filesystem views, reading, modifying, and deleting filesystem objects. DcyFS enforces file integrity by design—any writes to base files are first *copied up* to the overlay layer before modifications take place. This enables the filesystem to resist data corruption and destruction attacks, and forms the basis for creating efficient recovery strategies.

Confidentiality and Deception. For our purposes, we define confidentiality as the infeasibility of an attacker to learn any information about files stored in the base filesystem, other than files explictly allowed into the subject's view (e.g., via bind mount operations). To prevent data theft and sensitive information leakage, DcyFS implements special operators that *declassify* the filesystem views purveyed to untrusted subjects: *blind* conceals the existence of a file to the upper layer, and *redact* replaces sensitive (classified) file contents or an entire file all together in the subject's view. Similarly, to deceive and disinform attackers, DcyFS introduces a facility to seamleslly inject decoy files and baits into untrusted filessytem views. This affords the filesystem the capability of denying visibility of legitimate files while luring untrusted subjects into revealing their intent and strategies.

3   Filesystem-Aided Forensics

DcyFS offers a valuable tool for post-mortem filesystem forensics. The overlay records all created, modified, and deleted files during the execution of an untrusted process. Such a record provides essential information in piecing together the evidence of an attack. In this section, we investigate some of the key indicators of compromise (IOCs) that DcyFS helps uncover when performing forensic investigations. These indicators are sourced from the ATT&CK for

Enterprise threat model [38], and verified through experiments with 18 Linux malware samples (cf. Sect. 5).

Using these IOCs, we built an analyzer for DcyFS's overlays to identify malicious patterns on the filesystem. Table 1 describes each indicator of compromise along with the list of features the Forensic Analyzer uses to identify malicious activity (e.g., a modified file on the system), and a set of example malware that incorporates such techniques. We describe the entries in more detail next.

Persistence. One of the key goals for any malware is to maintain its presence across system reboots. The exact mechanism for persistence is dependent on whether the malware has root privileges. If it does not, the malware will modify its user's bash profile (e.g., modifying `.bash_profile`, `.profile`, or `.bashrc` files) adding a reference to the malicious application. As a result, when a shell is activated by the user, the malware is launched in the background. Malware running with escalated privileges often modify system-wide configurations in order to persist. This is achieved by dropping initialization scripts into the system run-level directories (e.g., `/etc/rc[0-6].d`), or by modifying the `/etc/rc.local` to add a malicious script. In fact, some malware even installs a modified `/sbin/init` file to launch itself on system startup.

Account Manipulation. Malware, such as backdoors and remote access terminals, create accounts in order to authenticate to systems, escalate privileges, and evade defenses. This requires modifications to the `/etc/passwd` and `/etc/shadow` files, which store username and password information.

Scheduled Tasks. Additionally, malware can ensure persistence and evade detection by creating reoccurring tasks that run at strange hours. On Linux, these tasks are configured through a crontab, and malware will install crontab scripts (e.g., in `/etc/cron.d`), or by editing the `/etc/crontab` system file.

Library Injection. Some malware, like Umbreon and Jynx2, are not executables, but rather libraries designed to be preloaded by system processes. The libraries replace `libc` API calls in order to change the functionality of a running application. In this way, an Apache web server can be turned into a backdoor, or a Bash shell can be hijacked into mining bitcoins in the background. To inject themselves into system applications, malware can add a preload entry into `/etc/ld.so.preload`. This enforces that the malware library will be loaded before all others.

Binary Drop. Cybercrime is becoming a commodity business, where large criminal syndicates rent access to large botnets to other attackers. These bots are designed to download various pieces of malware, such as bitcoin miners or key loggers, to be monetized by the syndicate. With root access, bots will try to download malware in all `bin` directories in hopes the defender will miss one when detected. As a result, newly installed binary downloads on a filesystem are a key indicator of compromise, and our Forensic Analyzer searches for downloaded ELF files.

Table 1. Indicators of compromise (IOC) for forensic analysis of Linux malware.

IOC	Forensic Features	Malware	Malware MD5/Reference
Unprivileged Persistence	.bash_profile .profile .bashrc	Umbreon FakeFile	f9ba2429eae5471acde820102c5b8159 ec301904171b1ebde3a57c952ae58a3a
Privileged Persistence	/etc/rc.local /etc/init.d /etc/rc[0-6].d	XOR.DDOS Trojan.Linux.Rootkit.SU Linux/DDoS-Flood.B	4fdf96368eff70f6dd99bbaa4e30e78c b760b16916edb59b9008cb4900498ad9 03afa3dbd7f1cefdb897ebb05db61e6f
Account Manipulation	/etc/shadow /etc/passwd	Umbreon	f9ba2429eae5471acde820102c5b8159
Scheduled Task	/etc/crontab /etc/cron.d/ /etc/cron.daily /etc/cron.weekly...	Trojan.Linux.Rootkit.SU Umbreon	b760b16916edb59b9008cb4900498ad9 f9ba2429eae5471acde820102c5b8159
Library Injection	/etc/ld.so.preload	Jynx2 Umbreon	c45c761a3482f2a9514aa851dd8fc7b8 f9ba2429eae5471acde820102c5b8159
Binary Drop	ELF file download	TrojanDownloader XOR.DDOS Linux/DDoS-Flood.B	78fae3e208de3bbadabe09f4996f0b44 4fdf96368eff70f6dd99bbaa4e30e78c 03afa3dbd7f1cefdb897ebb05db61e6f
Binary Modifications & Deletions	ELF rewriting	Troj/FKit-A Liora Linux.Zariche py elf prepender	9dba0f36d1d8d8c684579c5e80700337 [40] [6] [36]
Hidden Evidence	.bash_history hidden files delete crontabs	Jynx2 Umbreon	c45c761a3482f2a9514aa851dd8fc7b8 f9ba2429eae5471acde820102c5b8159
File Defacement	encrypted files	Erebus KillDisk	27d857e12b9be5d43f935b8cc86eaabf b9748ec5a7a0e3bc3ca139083ca875b0
Information Measurement	binary differences information gain write entropy	Erebus KillDisk	27d857e12b9be5d43f935b8cc86eaabf b9748ec5a7a0e3bc3ca139083ca875b0

Binary Modifications and Deletions. Aside from downloading new binaries, malware can also alter existing system binaries to make them secretly engage in nefarious activities. For example, when a user runs /bin/ls, the application could exfiltrate all files in the directory without the user's knowledge.

Hidden Evidence. Typically, skilled attackers will try to cover their tracks in order to evade detection. One way to do so is by hiding malware through hidden files, such as any file starting with a period, or modifying programs such as /bin/ls so that malware files are ignored when the contents of a directory are displayed to a user. Another technique for hiding ones presence is to remove entries from the bash history (e.g., .bash_history), or deleting crontab entries that conduct antivirus scans. Finally, killing or deleting anti-virus software is another mechanism for ensuring that malicious activities are not uncovered.

File Defacement. Recent ransomware attacks capitalize on encryption as the main technique to hold their victims' data for ransom. Such attacks often consist in replacing existing files with their encrypted counterparts generated by the ransomware. Our forensic analysis looks for indication of encryption in the overlay filesystem (such as file mimetype) to find evidence of file defacement.

Information Measurement. Attacks can also be characterized by measuring their information footprint in the filesystem. Our forensics analyzer generates three indicators that estimate the impact of filesystem changes introduced by programs:

- *Binary differences:* average percentage of modified bytes across copied up files.
- *Information gain:* average information gain across copied up files, measured as the difference between the entropies of base and overlay files.
- *Write entropy:* average write entropy across overlay files.

4   Implementation

Our prototype was written entirely in C and tested on Linux Ubuntu 16.04 with kernel `4.10.0-27-generic`. To achieve transparency and minimize performance overhead, DcyFS requires a small modification to the kernel along with the installation of a kernel module, which implements monitoring, mount isolation, decoy creation and injection capabilities. The kernel modification is deployed as a kernel hot-patch (patching the kernel while it is running) using kpatch, which modifies the kernel's `exec` family of functions to drop newly created processes into a new mount namespace protected by the union filesystem. We used Linux's OverlayFS [9] union filesystem to implement DcyFS's stackable filesystem, and the Fuse filesystem to implement the root domain.

5   Use Cases

We performed an in-depth investigation of how DcyFS protects filesystems against malware attacks. We analyzed 18 real malware samples designed for Linux, including library injectors, ransomware, ELF prependers, backdoors, and rootkits. The analysis was performed on a Ubuntu 16.04 virtual machine. Each untrusted malware sample executed in its own isolated view of the filesystem.

Library Injectors. Library injectors are malware designed to replace common API calls in system processes with altered functions that perform some nefarious task. We study two library injectors: Jynx2 rootkit [10], and Umbreon rootkit [25]. Jynx2 installs a library at the root of the filesystem which is added to the `/etc/ld.so.preload` file to preload itself into target applications when launched. The library replaces `libc` functions such as `access`, `open` to ignore the directory with the jynx2 library. The library also replaces networking functions, such as `accept`, to turn legitimate servers running on the host into a backdoor. Umbreon behaves similarly, creating a user hidden in `/etc/passwd` through function replacement.

Running these two malware samples atop DcyFS nullifies their ability to hijack system processes and persist privileged users. This is because files like /etc/passwd and /etc/ld.so.preload are only changed in the malware's view of the filesystem, and are not propagated to the base filesystem. A forensic examination of the overlay reveals the injected libraries and directories that Umbreon and Jynx2 try to hide. The mount also shows that the /etc/ld.so. preload and /etc/password files were edited, revealing the newly created user.

Binary Modifiers and Downloaders. While some malware replace API calls to hijack system processes, others simply replace legitimate programs with a modified version. We analyzed binary modifiers, including three ELF prependers, a trojan (Troj/FKit-A [35]), and a binary downloader (TrojanDownloader [42]).

The ELF prependers modify system binaries to inject malicious code. To achieve this, they write themselves to each binary and append an encrypted form of the original binary to the end of the new binary. When a system application is executed, the prepender unpacks the original binary, and transparently runs it. Troj/FKit-A is a backdoor that overwrites system processes, such as ps, to hide its presence from other users. The malware also installs a modified version of /sbin/init to persist execution across system reboots. When these malware samples execute on DcyFS, they have their own view of the filesystem with all modified and downloaded binaries written to the overlay. As a result, these binaries are visible in legitimate views of the filesystem, and are not unwittingly executed by a user. Forensically, the overlay records a copy of all dropped binaries, which could then be analyzed inside a sandbox to understand their behaviors.

Rootkits. We evaluated five privileged and unprivileged rootkits. Privileged rootkits, like Linux/DDOS-Flood.B, and XOR.DDOS [5] require root access to install or modify system files in the /etc/ directory to run across reboots, such as rc.local or crontab. Conversely, an unprivileged rootkit modifies a user's bash profile to ensure it continues running after a reboot. For example, FakeFile [18] is a backdoor that installs itself as gnome-common inside a user's home directory under the hidden directory .gconf/app/gnome-common/ and with an entry to .profile. DcyFS does not stop such malware from deploying DDOS attacks or opening backdoors. However, it can prevent them from persisting across system reboots. Furthermore, the filesystem overlay provides a record of modified files, critical for forensic investigations.

Backdoors and RATs. We also investigated five backdoors designed to view and exfiltrate information from a victim's machine. Basic backdoors such as Turla [3], and Tsunami [33] try to create a connection to external IP addresses to conduct DDOS attacks and accept various commands from a C&C server. Meanwhile, Mokes.A [27] is a spyware that scans a filesystem and repeatedly takes screenshots of the victim's machine to upload them to a remote server. DcyFS does not prevent these programs from executing. However, the filesystem can hide sensitive files, inject decoy documents, and mask real documents with fake versions.

Table 2. Forensic IoCs of malware samples analyzed.

	Bin Drop	Bin Modification	Unpriv Persistence	Priv Persistence	Acc Manipulation	Scheduled Tasks	Library Injection	Hidden Evidence	File Defacement	Bin Differences	Information Gain	Write Entropy
Lib Injectors												
Umbreon	×	×	×		×		×	×	×	20.4	0.025	0.49
Jynx2	×						×			0.87	0.0	0.61
ELF Prependers												
Liora	×	×								24.2	0.05	0.71
Zariche	×	×								24.2	0.05	0.71
Py elf prep	×	×								24.2	0.05	0.71
Trojans												
Troj/FKit-A	×	×	×							1.25	0.001	0.47
TrojanDown	×									–	–	–
Rootkits												
DDOS-Flood.B	×		×							0.22	0.001	0.75
XOR.DDOS	×		×		×		×			0.17	0.0	0.63
Rootkit.SU	×		×							0.44	0.004	0.57
FakeFile	×	×	×					×	×	0.43	(0.17)	0.47
Ransomware												
Erebus	×							×	×	0.0	0.0	0.85
Killdisk	×	×		×	×	×		×	×	1.83	0.31	0.94

Ransomware and Beyond. We evaluated two high profile ransomware samples: Erebus [41] and KillDisk [44]. Erebus uses AES encryption with unique keys to encrypt approximately 433 different file types on a victim machine while ransom notes are left throughout the filesystem notifying victims of their fee. KillDisk encrypts all data files, binaries, and boot loader files. This causes the system to crash, displaying ransom instructions. Unfortunately, encryption keys are not saved and data is permanently lost regardless of payment. With DcyFS, ransomware cannot corrupt important system files even with root privileges, because system changes are only made in its overlay.

Summary. Table 2 shows the results of the Forensic Analyzer on the malware samples. RATs were emitted from the table because their forensic indicators are driven by the actions of a remote attacker. All malware were first downloaded onto the filesystem, resulting in a Binary Drop IOC. Umbreon is the malware generating the most IOCs, modifying files, creating accounts, and injecting itself into system files, all of which are detected by our analyzer. The ELF prependers all perform similar tasks, leading to identical results, while the Forensic Analyzer is able to identify all attempts at persistence by the rootkits.

The Erebus ransomware deletes the original data files on the hard disk, and encrypts them with a different name which is why its entropy gain value is zero, yet the Analyzer is able to identify encrypted files, and records a high value for the entropy of writes. In contrast, KillDisk encrypts all system and user files in-place, including binaries and configurations. As a result, nearly all base files are copied to the overlay. Since the Forensic Analyzer only outputs whether a file has been modified, the encryption of files like /etc/password and /etc/rc.local incorrectly triggers certain rules (marked in red). It is worth observing the high values for information gain and entropy of writes in the case of KillDisk, which is consistent with typical ransomware behavior.

6 Performance Benchmarks

To assess the performance of DcyFS, we performed a set of filesystem benchmarks on both DcyFS and the base filesystem. Overall, our findings show that DcyFS compares to the standard filesystem for smaller files, while performance on large files is largely dependent on whether file operations are executed on the base filesystem or overlay.

Experimental Setup. All experiments in this section were executed on a Ubuntu 16.04 virtual machine with a single-core 2.67 GHz Intel Xeon X5550 processor, 1 GB of memory, 1 GB of swap, and 19 GB of hard drive space. All file benchmarks were done using the *Flexible Filesystem Benchmark* (FFSB) [14] (unless otherwise noted), and experiments were repeated 15 times to minimize performance anomalies. In all experiments, we used the standard ext4 Linux filesystem (installed by default on Ubuntu) for both the base and overlay filesystem mounts.

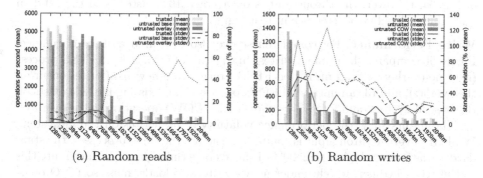

(a) Random reads   (b) Random writes

Fig. 5. Comparing R/W performance of trusted and untrusted processes when varying file size. (a) Comparing random reads from trusted process, untrusted process reading from base, and untrusted process reading from overlay. (b) Comparing random writes from trusted process, untrusted process writing new file, and untrusted process writing existing file (COW).

Read Performance. To compare DcyFS's read performance to ext4, we adopted the methodology described by Tarasov et al. [37]. More specifically, we used FFSB to generate files between 128 MB and 2 GB in intervals of 128 MB.

We then used FFSB with a single thread, and continuously performed random reads on each file using 1 MB I/O blocks over one-minute time intervals. All experiments were done with FFSB acting as (1) a trusted process (i.e., base filesystem, no overlay), (2) an untrusted process (i.e., with overlay) with files read from the base filesystem, and (3) an untrusted process with files read from the overlay. The experiment was repeated with sequential reads.

Figure 5a shows random reads throughput and standard deviations for the three scenarios when varying file sizes. Our results demonstrate that all three processes follow the same general trajectory. Smaller files (less than 896 MB) can fit entirely in memory, leading to read times on the order of 5000 ops/sec. A sudden performance drop off ensues for files larger than (896 MB) because such files are larger than memory—they incur a heavy disk workload.

The results for the trusted and untrusted FFSB (reads from base) are near identical, suggesting that DcyFS does not have a significant impact on random read performance in these scenarios. Indeed, with DcyFS, after a file is open, all operations are directed to the underlying base or overlay layers, allowing for native performance. In contrast, the untrusted FFSB (read from overlay) is outperformed by the other scenarios for smaller files, but its average throughput becomes slightly superior as file size increases. This result is a little misleading as standard deviations are anywhere from 40% to 70% of the mean, suggesting that there is a high fluctuation in throughput between runs. This indicates that performance-critical applications that consume large files may be penalized if files are stored on the overlay.

The results for the sequential read throughput show a similar pattern to that of Fig. 5a. However, the throughput is on average 19% faster than the random case, due to locality of reference in reading.

Write Performance. For completeness, we also measured write performance. Figure 5b compares the random writes throughput of (1) a trusted FFSB process (e.g., no overlay), (2) an untrusted FFSB process to a new file (writes occur on the overlay), and (3) an untrusted FFSB process to an existing file (file exists on the base filesystem, and forces a copy-on-write (COW) operation to the overlay).

The results show the performance volatility of file writes on the filesystem. While the average throughput is comparable across the three processes, the standard deviations are higher than 20% of the average throughput. We attribute this to the I/O scheduler, which, under heavy write workloads, must sort I/O operations to minimize disk movement. Unfortunately, under these circumstances individual writes may get pushed to the back of the I/O queue, thereby hurting write performance. One trend to note is that as files get larger, the throughput of the untrusted FFSB using COW decreases, since the process has to wait for an existing file to be copied from the base to the overlay before it can commence writing. This cost is amortized over the period spanning the file writes, but should be taken into consideration for performance-critical applications.

As with sequential reads, the results for sequential writes resemble those of random writes, but are faster due to locality of reference.

7 Discussion and Future Work

Trust Modeling. We envision the security domains being configured using standard policies inside an operating system in order to mitigate manual user configuration. Default policies could also be attached to software installed from app stores, or repositories such as Linux's *apt*. In the future, we plan to investigate automating this process using different notions of trust (e.g., policy-, reputation-, and game-theoretic based) to enhance DcyFS (cf. Artz and Gil [2] for a thorough survey on the subject). In particular, we plan to extend DcyFS to take into account (1) the identity of the user executing the program, (2) mode of authentication (e.g., remote, local), and (3) past user interactions with the filesystem to determine user trustworthiness. We also plan to investigate how process origin, entry point, popularity, and reputation affects trust, with the goal of automating the creation of a trust model that requires minimal manual intervention.

To protect the filesystem from processes that are exploited, we plan to investigate behavioral modeling to automatically infer process execution profiles, thereby limiting the impact of such attacks through the synthesis of filesystem views that only show data that is necessary for the process to properly function.

Security Domains. We envision an operating system being shipped with default security domains and application lists similar to how SELinux policies are shipped with Linux. These policies can be customized by the user to meet special requirements or security needs. For example, companies often discourage employees from installing unauthorized applications on their work computers. Using security domains, these companies can setup default policies to separate filesystem views for company approved applications, and those installed by the employee.

Decoy Generation. Our current prototype requires decoy files to be generated manually. In the future, DcyFS could automatically create different types of decoy files, such as data that appears to be encrypted, or files containing fake keys or passwords. The system should also learn the content of overlays based on past process behaviors to streamline decoy file generation. Generation of realistic decoy files is still a challenging research problem, and we hope to advance research towards this goal in the future.

Filesystem Bypass. An attacker could bypass DcyFS by executing reads and writes directly to the harddisk device, without using the virtual file system. One way to defend against data theft on the disk is to encrypt it. In order to circumvent attempts to directly corrupting data on disk, a hardware solution is needed to either prevent direct access, or to directly implement the overlay in hardware.

Storage Overhead. A drawback of union filesystems is that they maintain multiple copies of a file on writes. An attacker could append a small amount of data to all files on the filesystem, thereby doubling the number of files on the system. Over time, this can clog the filesystem to exhaust free disk space. Since disk space is reasonably cheap, we do not anticipate this threat as a large impediment for the adoption of DcyFS. We plan to study and monitor how overlays grow, and how they can be maintained and merged into the base filesystem to optimize storage space.

Portability. Our initial prototype was developed for Linux to leverage its virtual filesystem capabilities and mature mount namespace implementation. Recently, Windows Server 2016 was released with native namespace support and an overlay filesystem driver mirroring its open-source counterpart. We are currently investigating ways to port DcyFS to Windows.

Cloud Deployment. Cloud computing environments are an ideal use case to evaluate our approach because they often run very specific and automated workloads. DcyFS can be used to transparently augment container clouds with monitoring capabilities to detect unauthorized user activity, and collect malware binaries, protect system configurations, and conceal visibility of crown jewels to untrusted subjects. We are currently working with research and industry partners to pilot our prototype on a production container cloud environment.

Kernel Upstreaming. Recently, we began investigating ways to upstream DcyFS into Linux distributions by implementing filesystem view separation policies and security domains as a Linux Security Module (LSM). LSM provides security protections to the kernel by implementing a set of function hooks that perform security checks in key system calls. The `exec` function contains binary parameter hooks that could be used to drop a newly created process into a security domain, based on a lattice. We are currently testing our design, and hope to upstream the feature in the future.

8   Related Work

Ransomware Protection. In recent years, most malware work using filesystems has focused on detecting and defending against ransomware. Paybreak [21] allows ransomware to encrypt files on a system, but stores the crypto keys by hooking the Windows Crypto API, so that it can reverse the encryption. While working well against ransomware, it cannot defend against malware that deletes or corrupts data, nor malware that uses its own crypto libraries. UNVEIL [19] runs ransomware in a realistic sandbox environment, and monitors disk access patterns to make a decision about whether a piece of software is indeed ransomware. This approach does not provide host-level detection, nor protection. CryptoDrop [34] can detect ransomware on host machines using I/O based features, but does not provide filesystem protections.

More closely related to our work is ShieldFS [12]. ShieldFS is a copy-on-write filesystem, which enforces that all processes must write to an overlay as protection, until a detector determines that a process is not ransomware based on file I/O stats. Once an application is deemed "benign", based on a model of ransomware behavior, its file writes are merged into the base filesystem. Redemption [20] is similar to ShieldFS except that it uses more features to detect ransomware behavior, including the entropy of data blocks, number of file writes, number of directory traversals, and number of file conversions. While these approaches also provide integrity guarantees against ransomware, they are unable to deal with other types of malware, nor do they deal with data confidentially and deception, which is handled seamlessly by DcyFS. Furthermore, if these filesystems misclassify malware, they will unwittingly allow the malware to destroy the base filesystem. DcyFS does not need a detector and protects the base filesystem by grouping applications into separate security domains.

Filesystem Isolation. Qubes OS [29] is an operating system that isolates applications through virtualization using the Xen hypervisor. Security domains can be setup to run groups of applications in separate virtual machines. These applications are projected onto an administrative domain using XWindows. While providing maximum isolation, Qubes OS sacrifices usability and is not supported natively by commodity operating systems. Similarly, Sandboxie [31] is an application sandboxing platform for Windows which mediates application access to resources, and does not broadly support all applications. By contrast, DcyFS is a native implementation supported by many distributions, provides a transparent filesystem layer which allows users to view files in one location, is lightweight (requiring no mediation), enables deceptive capabilities, is easy to setup, and provides dynamic movement of applications between domains.

Access Control. Complimentary to our work are access control lists (ACLs) [4, 32]. ACLs describe a set of permissions that limit subject (e.g., user, group, or process) access to objects in the system. By contrast, DcyFS limits access by providing completely different views of the filesystem (i.e. filesystem view separation) on a per subject basis, allowing us to hide, replace, or inject objects into the system in order to maintain data confidentiality. An overlay is used to maintain file integrity. ACLs are also susceptible to privilege escalation attacks, whereas root users in a DcyFS environment will only see the filesystem view originally presented to them. Note, however, that ACLs are maintained on top of our filesystem views, adding an extra layer of protection.

Filesystem-Level Deception. Research has also focused on the generation of realistic looking decoy documents [7,8,30,43,45–47,49] to lure would-be attackers into revealing themselves. Yuill et al. [49] presented a system for generating decoy documents (called honey files) and describe four file types that tempt attackers. Bowen et al. [7,8] proposed an automated system for generating and distributing decoy documents to entice and confuse insiders. These documents also contained a beacon so that they could be located when exfiltrated. Whitham [45,46] introduced the notion of canary files which are decoys with beacons, and studied how to deploy documents that are inconspicuous in a real environment. A set of requirements for fake file content generation are described in Whitham [47]. Meanwhile, Ben-Salem and Stolfo [30] and Voris et al. [43] studied the effectiveness of decoy documents in identifying masquerading attacks. While these approaches can notify a defender that they are being attacked, they cannot hide or alter data. Furthermore, decoy documents are seen by all users on a host meaning that users must either be familiar with the decoy documents or they could trigger false positives. By contrast, DcyFS can customize the view of the filesystem on a per process/user basis in order to hide sensitive documents from untrusted subjects, and hide decoy documents from trusted subjects. That said, the above approaches are complimentary to DcyFS.

9   Conclusion

In this paper, we present a new filesystem called DcyFS, which enables the construction of realistic, but completely false, views of the filesystem to untrusted subjects (e.g., processes and users). DcyFS maintains data integrity and data confidentiality by employing a stackable filesystem, injecting decoy files, and hiding sensitive data. Filesystem views are created transparently on a per-process basis, meaning that file modifications by malicious processes are not seen by the global filesystem. In order to eliminate the need to merge files from the overlay to the base filesystem, we describe a security domain model for grouping applications into filesystem views, and a root domain that provides a transparent view of the entire filesystem.

We show the utility of our approach with a thorough performance evaluation. Our results show that DcyFS performs comparably to the host filesystem. Analysis with 18 real-world malware samples indicates that our technique can protect the filesystem from data corruption, and prevent malware from gaining a foothold into the system. Furthermore, DcyFS provides a mechanism for extracting forensic indicators of compromise. We are currently porting DcyFS to Windows, and our future work includes investigating automated approaches to determining trust.

References

1. Thinkst Canary: Canarytokens (2017). https://goo.gl/UcwrPB. Accessed 22 Aug 2017
2. Artz, D., Gil, Y.: A survey of trust in computer science and the semantic web. Web Semant. **5**, 58–71 (2007)
3. Baumgartner, K.: The 'penguin' turla (2014). https://goo.gl/6wAiSo. Accessed 24 Sept 2017
4. Bell, D., LaPadula, L.: Secure computer systems: mathematical foundations. Technical report. MITRE Corporation (1973)
5. Blaze, B.: Notes on Linux/Xor.DDoS (2015). https://goo.gl/RkzNkT. Accessed 24 Sept 2017
6. Bonicontro, G.T.: Linux.Zariche: a Vala Virus (2014). https://goo.gl/6mTCJP. Accessed 24 Sept 2017
7. Bowen, B., Salem, M.B., Hershkop, S., Keromytis, A., Stolfo, S.: Designing host and network sensors to mitigate the insider threat. IEEE Secur. Priv. **7**, 22–29 (2009)
8. Bowen, B.M., Hershkop, S., Keromytis, A.D., Stolfo, S.J.: Baiting inside attackers using decoy documents. In: Chen, Y., Dimitriou, T.D., Zhou, J. (eds.) SecureComm 2009. LNICST, vol. 19, pp. 51–70. Springer, Heidelberg (2009). https://doi.org/10.1007/978-3-642-05284-2_4

9. Brown, N.: Overlay filesystem (2017). https://goo.gl/Fsge3b. Accessed 24 Sept 2017
10. Carbone, R.: Malware memory analysis of the Jynx2 Linux rootkit. Technical report, Defence Research and Development Canada (2014)
11. Chang, Z., Sison, G., Jocson, J.: Erebus resurfaces as Linux ransomware (2017). https://goo.gl/5pJ3yQ. Accessed 12 Jul 2017
12. Continella, A., Guagnelli, A., Zingaro, G., Pasquale, G.D., Barenghi, A., Zanero, S., Maggi, F.: ShieldFS: a self-healing, ransomware-aware filesystem. In: Proceedings of the Annual Computer Security Applications Conference (2016)
13. Crowe, J.: 2017 ransomware trends and forecasts (2017). https://goo.gl/S6BRjx. Accessed 10 Aug 2017
14. FFSB: Flexible filesystem benchmark (2017). https://goo.gl/Qp56Au. Accessed 20 Sept 2017
15. Gammons, B.: 4 surprising backup failure statistics that justify additional protection (2017). https://goo.gl/H3xrPT. Accessed 10 Aug 2017
16. Goodin, D.: Web host agrees to pay $1m after it's hit by Linux-targeting ransomware (2017). https://goo.gl/TwYyzN. Accessed 22 Aug 2017
17. Granville, K.: 9 recent cyberattacks against big businesses (2015). https://goo.gl/LPSWh5. Accessed 22 Aug 2017
18. Information Security Newspaper: FakeFile Trojan opens backdoors on Linux computers, except openSUSE (2016). https://goo.gl/rYfESR. Accessed 24 Sept 2017
19. Kharaz, A., Arshad, S., Mulliner, C., Robertson, W., Kirda, E.: UNVEIL: a large-scale, automated approach to detecting ransomware. In: Proceedings of the USENIX Security Symposium (2016)
20. Kharraz, A., Kirda, E.: Redemption: real-time protection against ransomware at end-hosts. In: Dacier, M., Bailey, M., Polychronakis, M., Antonakakis, M. (eds.) RAID 2017. LNSC, vol. 10453, pp. 98–119. Springer, Cham (2017). https://doi.org/10.1007/978-3-319-66332-6_5
21. Kolodenker, E., Koch, W., Stringhini, G., Egele, M.: PayBreak: defense against cryptographic ransomware. In: Proceedings of the ACM Symposium on Information, Computer and Communications Security (2017)
22. Linux Programmer's Manual: mount_namespaces - overview of Linux mount namespaces (2017). https://goo.gl/ghK9QQ. Accessed 20 Sept 2017
23. Linux Programmer's Manual: namespaces: overview of Linux namespaces (2017). https://goo.gl/djnDWn. Accessed 20 Sept 2017
24. McCune, J.M., Jaeger, T., Berger, S., Caceres, R., Sailer, R.: Shamon: a system for distributed mandatory access control. In: Proceedings of the Annual Computer Security Applications Conference (2006)
25. Mercês, F.: Pokémon-themed Umbreon Linux rootkit hits x86, ARM systems (2016). https://goo.gl/te9PBF. Accessed 24 Sept 2017
26. Moore, H.N.: Why didn't equifax protect your data? Because corporations have all the power (2017). https://goo.gl/PWQvVa. Accessed 21 Sept 2017
27. Paganini, P.: Linux.Ekoms.1 the Linux Trojan that takes screenshots (2016). https://goo.gl/NuRC8G. Accessed 24 Sept 2017
28. Poimboeuf, J.: kpatch - dynamic kernel patching (2017). https://goo.gl/p1VzMu. Accessed 24 Sept 2017
29. Rutkowska, J., Wojtczuk, R.: Qubes OS architecture v0.3 (2010)
30. Ben Salem, M., Stolfo, S.J.: Decoy document deployment for effective masquerade attack detection. In: Holz, T., Bos, H. (eds.) DIMVA 2011. LNCS, vol. 6739, pp. 35–54. Springer, Heidelberg (2011). https://doi.org/10.1007/978-3-642-22424-9_3

31. Sandboxie Holdings: Sandboxie (2018). https://goo.gl/8EBR7J. Accessed 27 Apr 2018
32. Sandhu, R.S., Samarati, P.: Access control: principle and practice. IEEE Commun. Mag. **32**(9), 40–48 (1994)
33. Sandro, A.: Backdoor.Linux.Tsunami.gen or Tsunami is a Linux backdoor that allows remote access to infected machines (2016). https://goo.gl/vzcTNw. Accessed 24 Sept 2017
34. Scaife, N., Carter, H., Traynor, P., Butler, K.R.: Cryptolock (and drop it): stopping ransomware attacks on user data. In: Proceedings of the IEEE Conference on Distributed Computing Systems (2016)
35. Sophos: Troj/Fkit-A (2017). https://goo.gl/5Va1Ld. Accessed 24 Sept 2017
36. t0n1: ELF prepender in python (2015). https://goo.gl/LDepMX. Accessed 24 Sept 2017
37. Tarasov, V., Bhanage, S., Zadok, E., Seltzer, M.: Benchmarking file system benchmarking: it *is* rocket science. In: Proceedings of the USENIX Conference on Hot Topics in Operating Systems (2011)
38. The MITRE Corporation: The ATT&CK matrix for enterprise (2017). https://goo.gl/EHrkZ5. Accessed 24 Sept 2017
39. The New Yort Times: Cyberattack hits ukraine then spreads internationally (2017). https://goo.gl/Av7Hxb. Accessed 24 Sept 2017
40. TMZ: Linux.Liora ELF prepender (2015). https://goo.gl/snRnev. Accessed 24 Sept 2017
41. Trend Micro Solutions: Erebus Linux ransomware: impact to servers and countermeasures (2017). https://goo.gl/o2k84s. Accessed 24 Sept 2017
42. VirusTotal: TrojanDownloader detection results (2017). https://goo.gl/pBNR4M. Accessed 24 Sept 2017
43. Voris, J., Jermyn, J., Boggs, N., Stolfo, S.: Fox in the trap: thwarting masqueraders via automated decoy document deployment. In: Proceedings of the European Workshop on System Security (2015)
44. Welivesecurity: KillDisk now targeting Linux: demands $250K ransom, but can't decrypt (2017). https://goo.gl/paiyvm. Accessed 24 Sept 2017
45. Whitham, B.: Automating the generation of fake documents to detect network intruders. Int. J. Cyber-Secur. Digit. Forensics **2**(1), 103–118 (2013)
46. Whitham, B.: Canary files: generating fake files to detect critical data loss from complex computer networks. In: Proceedings of the International Conference on Cyber Security, Cyber Peacefare and Digital Forensic (2013)
47. Whitham, B.: Design requirements for generating deceptive content to protect document repositories. In: Proceedings of the Australian Information Warfare Conference (2014)
48. Wired: The biggest cybersecurity disasters of 2017 so far (2017). https://goo.gl/GoLpLR. Accessed 24 Sept 2017
49. Yuill, J., Zappe, M., Denning, D., Feer, F.: Honeyfiles: deceptive files for intrusion detection. In: Proceedings of the Annual IEEE SMC Information Assurance Workshop (2004)

Web and Browser Security

Knockin' on Trackers' Door: Large-Scale Automatic Analysis of Web Tracking

Iskander Sanchez-Rola[(✉)] and Igor Santos

DeustoTech, University of Deusto, Bilbao, Spain
{iskander.sanchez,isantos}@deusto.es

Abstract. In this paper, we present the first generic large-scale analysis of different known and unknown web tracking scripts on the Internet to understand its current ecosystem and their behavior. To this end, we implemented TRACKINGINSPECTOR the first automatic method capable of detecting generically different types of web tracking scripts. This method automatically retrieves the existing scripts from a website and, through code similarity and machine learning, detects modifications of known tracking scripts and discovers unknown tracking script candidates.

TRACKINGINSPECTOR analyzed the Alexa top 1M websites, computing the web tracking prevalence and its ecosystem, as well as the influence of hosting, website category, and website reputation. More than 90% websites performed some sort of tracking and more than 50% scripts were used for web tracking. Over 2,000,000 versions of known tracking scripts were found. We discovered several script renaming techniques used to avoid blacklists, performing a comprehensive analysis of them. 5,500,000 completely unknown likely tracking scripts were found, including more than 700 new different potential device fingerprinting unique scripts. Our system also automatically detected the fingerprinting behavior of a previously reported targeted *fingerprinting-driven malware* campaign in two different websites not previously documented.

Keywords: Device fingerprinting · Privacy · Web tracking

1 Introduction

Web tracking is a common practice on the Internet to gather user browsing data for different tasks such as advertisement, personalization, analytics, and identity checking. Despite the fact that web tracking poses a threat to users' privacy and anonymity, it is not considered harmful by itself. Indeed, web advertising companies defend web tracking as a fundamental component of web economy [48]. However, recent reports [44,51] found two different targeted malware campaigns that used a fingerprinting phase to increase the success rate and hide them.

Recent work studied both stateful [32,41,43] and stateless [2,3] tracking, raising a general concern about its prevalence in the web. These studies provided a better understanding of a particular subset of web tracking techniques but they

© Springer International Publishing AG, part of Springer Nature 2018
C. Giuffrida et al. (Eds.): DIMVA 2018, LNCS 10885, pp. 281–302, 2018.
https://doi.org/10.1007/978-3-319-93411-2_13

were not devoted to fully understand and to generically discover web tracking scripts. Another recent work [17], combines some of the previous approaches and ideas to analyze and study both stateful and stateless web tracking. However, due to the nature of these proposed approaches, only concrete web tracking techniques are analyzed and, thereby, a generic web tracking analysis cannot be performed with these methods.

Given this background, we present the first large-scale analysis of generic web tracking scripts. Due to the limitations of current solutions, we build our own tracking analysis tool called TRACKINGINSPECTOR. In contrast to existing solutions, based either on blacklists or static rules, this tool is based on code similarity and machine learning. TRACKINGINSPECTOR automatically detects known tracking script variations and also identifies likely unknown tracking script candidates. We use TRACKINGINSPECTOR to analyze the Alexa top 1M sites [46] to answer the following research questions: (i) how widespread is web tracking on the Internet?, (ii) what is the current ecosystem in web tracking provision and deployment on the Internet?, (iii) can current blacklisting solutions limit or block most web tracking on the Internet?, and (iv) can TRACKINGINSPECTOR discover new web tracking scripts? To what extent?

The major contributions and findings of this paper are three. First, we performed the first large-scale study of generic web tracking. More than 90% of the websites performed tracking and more than 50% of the scripts exhibited a tracking behavior. Second, we present TRACKINGINSPECTOR, the first tool to automatically detect generic tracking scripts through code similarity and machine learning. The results show its ability to automatically detect known tracking scripts and their modifications, and to discover potentially unknown tracking. Our method was able to detect more than 2M known tracking script versions whereas current blacklisting solutions were only able to detect 64.65% of them in the best scenario. This indicates that many variations of tracking scripts are bypassing current solutions. Therefore, we studied these hiding techniques, finding several *script renaming techniques*. Finally, more than 5.5M not previously reported scripts exhibited a tracking behavior. These scripts include over 700 new unique potential device fingerprinting scripts: more than 400 performing canvas fingerprinting, more than 200 performing font probing, and more than 50 exhibiting both. TRACKINGINSPECTOR also automatically detected a previously reported targeted *fingerprinting-driven malware* campaign exhibiting fingerprinting behavior, present in two websites not reported as infected.

2   Tracking Analysis and Detection

2.1   General Description

It is important to remark that the definition of web tracking has been a controversial debate due to the different existing tracking types. In this work, we are going to use Ghostery's[1] definition, which is also used by many other security

---

[1] https://www.ghostery.com/submit-a-tracker/.

and privacy companies: *"Trackers (also commonly referred to as tags) are snippets of code that send and receive information about you to companies to track and analyze your behavior, deliver ads, connect social media, provide comment sections, and more".*

Current Solutions. We evaluated the following solutions for tracking detection: blacklisting (e.g., *EasyPrivacy* [4] and *Ghostery* [9]), the EFF's tool *Privacy Badger* [24] based on simple heuristics, *FPDetective* [3], and *OpenWPM* [18].

Blacklisting tools rely on blacklisted script names, URLs, and domains. Although these methods detect the known tracking scripts and domains, they fail to detect simple variations such as renaming the script or modifying the domain where the scripts are hosted. Besides, they may incorrectly block scripts devoid to tracking but named with the same script name as one within the blacklist.

Heuristics used in the *Privacy Badger* plugin block third-party cookies. This approach raises false positives and only focuses on cookies. Tracking adopts many different forms not covered by this tool.

FPDetective and *OpenWPM* are tracking analysis frameworks based on blacklisting and/or rules to detect tracking. These frameworks solve the main limitations of blacklisting. However, as these techniques are based on predefined rules, the tracking script can be modified with methods that bypass the defined criteria (see Sect. 5 for some examples).

TRACKINGINSPECTOR Solution. Our solution is composed of three components:

- A *Crawler* (Sect. 2.2) to retrieve web scripts and content.
- A *Script Database* (Sect. 2.3) with known tracking scripts.
- A *Text-based Analyzer* (Sect. 2.4) to analyze the scripts using the *Script Database*. It detects both known (or versions) and potentially unknown tracking.

TRACKINGINSPECTOR starts by downloading scripts through the *Crawler*. The *Crawler* waits until every script is downloaded; including third-party, first-party, or HTML-embedded scripts. Then, *Text-based Analyzer* analyzes them using its two components:

1. *Known Tracking Analysis* measures the similarity of each script with the ones stored in the *Script Database*. The script can be a version of a known tracking script or not. This analyzer is intended to be an end-user solution.
2. When no match is found, the *Unknown Tracking Analysis* inspects the script using a machine-learning algorithm trained with the *Script Database* to detect likely unknown tracking scripts. This component is devoted to find new tracking scripts to be added to the *Script Database*.

Dynamic approaches monitor the web behavior during browsing and compare it with specific rule sets for concrete types of tracking [3]. Instead, TRACKINGINSPECTOR uses the *Crawler* to dynamically retrieve the scripts of the site and then, the scripts are analyzed by the *Text-based Analyzer*.

Script Representation. We tested two different approaches: Abstract Syntax Trees (ASTs) and Bag of Words (BOW). While ASTs represented the specific syntax of the functions within the code, the BOW approach captures the token frequencies to model the script. In our preliminary tests, the BOW text-categorization approach behaved better to detect generic tracking behaviors. AST approaches represent the code syntax strictly taking into account also the script structure, while BOW just represent the usage of tokens. Hence, ASTs are worse when dealing with script modifications or new scripts than the standard BOW model. BOW models the scripts using a Vector Space Model (VSM), which represents them as vectors in a multidimensional space whose dimensions represent the possible tokens within the scripts. Scripts are represented as a vector of frequencies of tokens. Since our goal is not to capture the behavior but to detect any type of tracking, other approaches may overfit and fail to detect modifications or new web tracking scripts.

BOW has been used for a broad range of web security problems such as detection of drive-by-download attacks [42], to measure the impact of different models in malware detection [8], or vulnerability detection [56].

2.2   Crawler

Overview. The *Crawler* component automatically retrieves every JavaScript file statically or dynamically loaded in a website. The *Crawler* is based on *PhantomJS* [27], a well-known headless browser. To avoid the detection of the automated browsing when using headless browsers, we adapted existing advanced hiding methods [47] to disguise the browser as a common one. With this adaptation, our *Crawler* is capable of performing transparent and exhaustive browsing. The *Crawler* also deals with obfuscation, and cleans the generated caches and cookies after each website inspection.

Methodology. The *Crawler* starts visiting the frontpage of the site under inspection. It saves all the downloaded scripts, taking into consideration if different scripts have the same name or if they are downloaded multiple times. To retrieve them, instead of waiting a fixed time and gathering them, like previous work on fingerprinting detection [2,3], we analyzed the different script generation behaviors in 250,000 random websites within the Alexa top 1M websites to define a methodology for web analysis and set the adequate times to retrieve every script.

The resulting methodology starts with the *Crawler* waiting until all frames in the website are loaded with a fixed maximum time of 60 s. If all frames are loaded before the 60 s are elapsed, the *Crawler* waits 15 s more (but never more than the maximum time). We added this second waiting time because in several cases additional scripts were downloaded after every frame had already been loaded because other scripts may have called them. If scripts are downloaded during this extra time window, the *Crawler* will wait until the remaining of the 60 s are elapsed. These time frames were selected taking into account the possible redirections within the website or its frames.

Then, the *Crawler* retrieves the resulting HTML code, with all the generated modifications, and gathers the HTML-embedded scripts. Then, the *Crawler* starts a deobfuscation phase and finally, cleans duplicate scripts, files that are not actually JavaScript, or empty files.

De-obfuscation. We implemented a deobfuscator using *JSBeautifier* [33], a well-known deobfuscator as a starting point. Using the techniques implemented in this tool, our deobfuscator tries to unravel the original code, checking in each iteration whether or not the script has been deobfuscated with the specified metrics. Therefore, we can retrieve the original code conserving variable names and structure. Even if many approaches to obfuscate code exist, the analysis of Curtsinger et al. [12] found that the simple `eval` unfolding is the most commonly used, which is included in our deobfucator along with others.

In this way, we can deal with multiple layers and multiple known techniques of obfuscation. In fact, during our work, we found some obfuscators that use others iteratively to perform multiple layer obfuscation. When it is deobfuscated, our method performs an additional step to deal with one obfuscator with a particular behavior. This particular one, when the free version is used, places the original code in an escaped string within the code while the rest of the code is used to call functions in the string and also performs a callback function to notify the authors that this script has been executed. Our method retrieves the code stored in the string and unescapes it, discarding its additional code.

Limitations. This approach may also have its shortcomings. In particular, a dedicated tracker can use more advanced obfuscation to bypass current *JSBeautifier*-based deobfuscation pass.

2.3   Script Database

It stores both known tracking and non-tracking scripts. For the non-tracking scripts, we downloaded scripts from open-source projects and from randomly accessed websites (that did not belong to the Alexa top 1M sites), manually verified afterwards.

Data Sources. To generate the tracking scripts dataset, we retrieved scripts on the following sources:

- **Blacklists:** We used *EasyPrivacy, Kaspersky Tracking List (ABBL)* [30], *ABINE* [1], the tracking version of *AdGuard* [5], the tracking list *FanBoy* [19], and the *Tracking Detection System (TDS)* by van Eijk [16]. These lists were selected because they include scripts and not just domains. We omitted blacklisted domains because our goal is to detect tracking scripts rather than domains. However, this information was used in the large-scale analysis (along with other 6 tracking domain blacklists that will be detailed in Sect. 3) to compare the results and findings of TRACKINGINSPECTOR. Some of these lists included a whitelist composed of tracking scripts that are not considered harmful. Since our goal is to detect tracking behavior, we also included this type of scripts.

- **Open-Source Tracking Projects:** We retrieved several open-source tracking projects: *BeaverBird* [45], *FingerPrintJS* [54], and *Evercookie* [29].
- **Academic Papers:** We also included in our tracking *Script Database* the scripts found in [2,3].

We processed the list of potential scripts and stored the scripts whose complete URL was available. When the scripts were not available, we tried to download them through `archive.org`, removing all the service-related text and code afterwards. When script names were only available, we searched it using several code searchers (e.g., *meanpath* [38], *NerdyData* [13], *FileWatcher* [21]), or common search engines (e.g., *Google* and *Bing*). Then, we manually checked each script to determine whether they performed tracking or not.

Configuration. Since some of the scripts were obfuscated, we deobfuscated them as described in Sect. 2.2. Then, we removed duplicates or different versions of scripts. To this end, we modeled the code using the representation detailed in Sect. 2.1 and computed the cosine similarity of each script within the *Script Database*.

To set a threshold for the detection of versions of original scripts, we conducted an empirical validation over the scripts and selected 85% because it was the lowest one (more coverage), raising no false positives. Then, we added the original scripts to the *Script Database* and also a small number of script versions that presented new functionalities to the original. After this process, 957 original tracking scripts were stored in our *Script Database*. We randomly selected 957 non-tracking scripts from the aforementioned sources.

2.4   Text-Based Analyzer

Overview. The *Text-based Analyzer* is responsible for the detection of tracking scripts. This component is divided in two different sub-components: a (i) *Known Tracking Analysis*, responsible for the detection of versions, or modifications of known scripts stored in the *Script Database* and a (ii) *Unknown Tracking Analysis*, whose goal is to automatically identify tracking script candidates.

Text-Based Web Tracking Detection. Although the goals of known and unknown approaches are different, they both represent scripts using the BOW approach. As in the *Script Database*, the scripts are modeled through a VSM, composed of the terms within the scripts. *Text-based Analyzer* represents each script as a sequence of each term frequencies, using the well-known *Term Frequency* [34] – *Inverse Document Frequency* (TF–IDF) [49] weighting schema.

Known Tracking Analysis detects versions or modifications of currently known tracking stored in the *Script Database*. This component computes the cosine similarity of the script under inspection with known tracking. The cosine of the angle formed by the vector representation of the two scripts is the similarity—if they are totally equal the angle will be zero and their similarity 1, while when the angles are orthogonal and hence they do not share any token, their similarity score will be 0. When the empirically computed threshold of 85% similarity is surpassed, the script is flagged as a known tracking script version.

Unknown Tracking Analysis is based on supervised machine learning. The features used for the machine algorithm are the tokens in the BOW model. Machine learning develops algorithms to learn automatically behaviors from data. Since, in our particular case, data is labeled (i.e., tracking and non-tracking), supervised machine learning algorithms were selected for this task. These algorithms have been extensively used in web security tasks such as detection of malicious websites [7] or malicious JavaScript code [11]. We use the *Script Database* to perform a 10-fold stratified cross-validation experimental evaluation with several well-known machine-learning methods (e.g., Naive Bayes, Bayesian Networks, C4.5, SVMs, and Random Forest) to decide which classifier to use. The best classifier was *Random Forest* [28] configured with 950 *Random Trees*. This ensemble method for classification creates several decisions trees at training and chooses the classification based on the mode or mean of their partial classifications. In the training phase, the bagging technique is used to create the weak random tree learners. To build the aggregate, a similar but more general method is used to select the different high-level splits, also known as feature bagging.

Evaluation. We evaluated the performance of these two components of the *Text-based Analyzer* in terms of tracking script detection, prior to their usage in our large-scale analysis:

- **Known Tracking Analyzer:** Using 85% similarity threshold, did not report any false positives in our tests, being able to detect any version of known tracking at least 85% similar to samples in the *Script Database*. Therefore, we believe that this component should be used in an end-user environment as a replacement of blacklisting techniques. We will compare it with blacklisting solutions in Sect. 3.
- **Unknown Tracking Analyzer:** We consider scripts not detected by the *Known Tracking Analyzer* as *previously unknown*. During the cross-validation evaluation, this component achieved an area under the ROC curve of 0.982, a true positive rate of 94.4%, and a F-measure (the harmonic mean of precision and recall) of 0.935. This method is the first one in the literature able to detect previously unseen tracking and devoted to the discovery of new tracking rather than using it in an end-user environment. This discovery of potentially tracking acts as a filter for a manual inspection to include actual tracking in the *Script Database*. To further evaluate the *Unknown Tracking Analysis* component, an additional evaluation of the method will be performed through a manual inspection of tracking scripts in the wild in Sect. 3.4.

To sum up, both components comply with our initial requirements to be used in the large-scale measurement and analysis.

3   Large-Scale Analysis

3.1   Preliminaries

The goal of this analysis is to answer the next research questions: (i) *how widespread is web tracking on the Internet?*, (ii) *what is the current ecosystem in web tracking provision and deployment on the Internet?*, (iii) *can current blacklisting solutions limit or block most web tracking on the Internet?* and (iv) *Can* TRACKINGINSPECTOR *discover new web tracking scripts and to what extent?*

The *Crawler* retrieved the scripts within the Alexa top 1M and the *Text-based Analyzer* inspected them. When downloading scripts from a removed site, we searched it through archive.org. Since archive.org adds code and also files to the website, we made a cleaning process. 3.67% of the websites were not accessed because its access was restricted (401 and 403), not accessible, or were impossible to find in archive.org.

Some of the scripts flagged as likely unknown tracking scripts by the *Unknown Tracking Analyzer* may be only unknown by TRACKINGINSPECTOR but known by existing domain blacklisting tools. To discriminate between these two cases, we used the blacklisting tracking detection tools *EasyPrivacy, Kaspersky Tracking List (ABBL), ABINE*, the tracking version of *AdGuard*, the tracking list of *FanBoy*, the *Tracking Detection System (TDS), Ghostery, Privacy Badger, Disconnect* [14], *Truste* [53], *Privacy Choice* [50], and *Web of Trust* [52] (the domains classified there as the category 301 - online tracking).

We gathered data about the hosted website and the top-level domains where the scripts were downloaded. We also analyzed the domains, because the hosted scripts in domains influence the trust of the sites [40]. To correctly retrieve the top-level domain names, we used the effective_tld_names.dat by Mozilla [25]. Next, we extracted the country, the ISP, the associated ASs, and the web category of the domains. To determine the category, we used three services: *Cloudacl* [10], *Blocksi* [6], and *Fortiguard* [23]. Their category names are similar, and, after a normalization process, 78 category names were fixed. We also analyzed the reputation of the websites in the *webutation* service [55], that uses users' feedback, comments, and also different analyses such as *Google Safe Browsing, Norton Antivirus* or phistank.com.

For the sake of clarity, we define the terminology that we will be using:

- **Known Tracking Scripts:** We call known tracking scripts to those in the range between 85% and 100% similarity to the ones in the database.
- **Unknown Tracking Scripts:** Scripts that are less than 85% similar to the ones in the script database. These scripts can be either new scripts from scratch or versions of known ones modified enough to be considered *new*. Examples of unknown tracking scripts may include new implementations,

Table 1. Tracking and non tracking behavior prevalence in scripts.

Type	# Scripts	% Scripts
Tracking	11,984,469	57.15%
Non tracking	8,985,457	42.85%
Total	*20,969,926*	*100.00%*

Table 2. Tracking and non tracking behavior prevalence in websites. % W. S. stands for the percentage of websites, considering only websites with scripts. % W. represents the percentage considering every website.

Type	% W. S.	% W.	# Websites
Tracking	97.58%	92.89%	894,779
Non tracking	2.42%	2.31%	22,220
No scripts	N/A	4.80%	46,277
Number of websites with scripts			*916,999*
Total number of websites			*963,276*

added functionalities, or simply scripts never reported and thus never blacklisted. We will also refer to them as *tracking script candidates* or *likely tracking scripts* as the unknown text-analyzer has a small error percentage. We also distinguish between two sub-categories.

- *Unknown Blacklisted Tracking Scripts:* Unknown scripts whose hosting domain is blacklisted but the script is not.
- *Completely Unknown Tracking Scripts:* Unknown scripts whose hosting domains have not been blacklisted.

We also classify them as: (i) *Original*, if in the script database; (ii) *Unique*, different compared by hash; and (iii) *Version/Sample* each download of a script.

3.2 Tracking Ecosystem

General Overview. 20,969,926 script samples (tracking and non-tracking) were downloaded from the Alexa top 1M websites. Impressively, nearly 60% of them were flagged as tracking (see Table 1). In other words, more than half the script functionality in the web is potentially devoted to track users. There were 46,277 websites with no scripts at all. Hence, we measure the tracking prevalence percentage both in every website and in websites with scripts (see Table 2), finding that nearly every website performed tracking.

Only a 20% of the tracking samples were known, whereas the unknown samples were the stunning majority. However, using the previously omitted domain blacklists, 41.11% of these scripts were in blacklisted domains (see Table 3), being unknown blacklisted scripts. The number of samples where neither the script nor the domain were blacklisted, was an impressive 46.90%. Tracking scripts were downloaded from 891,873 different domains.

Table 3. Detected tracking script distribution. *Domains* refer to top-level domains where the scripts are downloaded. *Unknown (blacklisted)* refers to likely tracking script candidates unknown in the Script Database but whose domain is blacklisted.

Type	# Scripts	# Domains
Known	2,439,835	540,369
Unknown (blacklisted)	3,923,615	7,455
Unknown	5,621,019	841,425
Total tracking	*11,984,469*	*891,873*

Website Demographics. For a better understanding, we analyzed different aspects and tracking prevalence. To find the relevance of tracking in each analyzed feature (website, category/*webutation*, and country/network entity origin in domains), we ran several preliminary tests computing the differences of tracking ratios per website to find which ratio could discriminate between the features. The results showed that computing the number of websites with only tracking scripts per each studied feature eased the discrimination, while the number of websites with some tracking and the number of scripts per featured showed the overall behavior.

We computed the following ratios: (i) % of tracking scripts per script in the category, (ii) % of websites performing any type of tracking per website in the category, and (iii) % percentage of websites with only tracking scripts per website in each category. The website categories with the highest tracking percentage were *personal websites, hacking, spyware and adware, social networks*, or *peer to peer*. The top categories with only tracking were *malicious, questionable, unknown*, and *websites with adult content*. Despite it cannot be used to discriminate the maliciousness or greyness, *malicious* or *grey* sites tend to only include tracking.

The relation between websites with some or only tracking scripts with *webutation* hinted that the presence of only tracking affects the reputation of a website. 15.41% of the websites in the *Red* category and 15.31% in the *Yellow* category only used tracking, while only 6.45% and 5.95% of the *Grey* and *Green* categories did. Since users are not usually aware of web tracking, we believe that these results indicate that sites perceived as *bad* by users have a higher ratio of tracking than non-tracking, similar to what happened with categories.

Domain Demographics. We also measured domains hosting tracking, non-tracking, and both tracking and non-tracking scripts (see Table 4). We analyzed domains to understand the provision of web tracking. In fact, previous work found the correlation between the scripts in domains and their nature [40].

We discovered that, similarly to what happened to websites using tracking scripts, domains usually host both web tracking and non-tracking scripts. However, the percentage of them hosting solely tracking scripts is not negligible (10.54%). Regarding the relation of countries with their domains, several small

Table 4. Domain distribution with regards to tracking. *Only Tracking* represents the top-level domains that only contain tracking scripts, whereas *Only non tracking* represents top-level domains with only non-tracking scripts. *Tracking & non tracking* represent the top-level domains that contain both tracking and non-tracking scripts.

Type	# Domains
Only tracking	98,359
Only non tracking	41,640
Tracking & non tracking	793,515
Total	*933,514*

countries surprisingly hosted only tracking. Likewise, we found cases of either AS owners, ASNs, or ISPs whose domains were only used to host tracking. Nevertheless, given the small number of domains, we consider them irrelevant.

As we did with sites, we studied the correlation between the *webutation* of the domain and its hosting of tracking scripts. We found that, as happened with websites, the presence of only tracking in domains affected the reputation: *Yellow* and *Red* represented 22.87% and 23.71% of the domains hosting only tracking scripts while *Grey* and *Green* categories only contained 11.23% and 9.44%.

3.3 Analysis of Known Tracking

To compare the detection capabilities of TRACKINGINSPECTOR with current tracking blockers, we measured the number of known script samples that blacklisting solutions would have blocked. From all the methods, we chose script name and domain blacklisting as the baseline because they provided a broader detection compared to the other alternatives. Another possible solution not used in tracking detection but used in other domains was also compared: code hashing.

Results show that script and domain blacklisting captured 43.80% and 33.84% of the known tracking script versions, respectively. Combined blacklisting solutions blocked the 64.65% of the known tracking scripts while code hashing only would had captured 2.04% of the samples. These results show that current anti-tracking solutions are clearly not enough, not only to fight against completely unknown tracking scripts, but also against modified known tracking scripts.

Moreover, we measured the prevalence of versions of the tracking scripts in the *Script Database*. *Google* related scripts were the most popular: 60.90% of the samples correspond to their scripts, including 29.27% of samples with analytics capabilities. Among other scripts we can find: 20.92% regarding advertisement (*33Across*, *Pzyche*, and *QuantCast*), 3.49% from analytics (*Yandex Metrica* and *comScore*), and 2.00% social analytics samples (*FlCounter* and *Pinterest*). These ones were used by the 84.02% of the websites with scripts.

540,369 top-level domains hosted the known tracking samples (the most popular one was `google-analytics.com`). Their scripts were present in 63.14% of

Table 5. Unknown tracking downloaded from blacklisted domains prevalence in websites.

# websites	646,428
– % in websites with tracking	72.24%
– % in websites (considering sites with scripts)	70.49%

Table 6. 10 most popular blacklisted domains hosting unknown tracking scripts.

Domain	# Websites
facebook.com	177,443
akamaihd.net	176,616
googlesyndication.com	166,469
google.com	156,214
twitter.com	120,843
gstatic.com	114,153
facebook.net	86,299
googleusercontent.com	86,023
googleadservices.com	83,676
ytimg.com	72,571

the websites with scripts. The rest of the domains belonged to Google or to well-known advertisement services. The hosting of known tracking scripts follows a long-tail distribution with a small number of domains (or companies) representing the majority of script downloads.

3.4   Analysis of Unknown Tracking

Unknown Tracking Analysis In-the-Wild Evaluation. TRACKING INSPECTOR flagged more than 9.5M scripts as unknown tracking and more than 5M were not previously known by any blacklist. Albeit we already performed a 10-fold cross validation, we also performed an in-the-wild manual validation.

To this end, we extracted a statistically significant random sample from all the scripts flagged as unknown tracking. The sample was composed of 273 scripts, representing a 90% confidence level and a ±5% confidence interval. According to statistical sampling [22], confidence level measures the probability of the extracted sample to represent the entire dataset given a fixed confidence interval.

With a considerable manual effort, a tracking expert performed an exhaustive analysis of each sample both statically and dynamically, corroborating that 257 out of 273 scripts were actual web tracking (94.1%). These results are nearly the same as the ones obtained in the 10-fold cross validation described in Sect. 2 (94.4%).

Table 7. Distribution of unknown tracking candidates in domain types.

Domain	# Samples	# Uniques
HTML	4,145,542	2,744,244
1st Party	679,319	283,337
3rd Party	796,158	241,578
Total	*5,621,019*	*3,245,238*

Table 8. Popular clusters per domain type.

Domain	Cluster	% Scripts
HTML	Downloader	24.53%
	Statistics	13.47%
	Social sharing	3.33%
1st Party	Statistics	26.70%
	Stateless tracking	15.98%
	Advertisement	11.16%
3rd Party	Statistics	20.86%
	Stateless tracking	15.27%
	Advertisement	14.08%

Unknown Tracking in Blacklisted Domains. Unknown tracking downloaded from blacklisted domains appeared in 70.49% of the websites with scripts (see Table 5). Only 7,455 blacklisted domains (see Table 6 for the 10 most prevalent ones) hosted 3,923,615 of this type. This number is much smaller than in the case of known or completely unknown tracking scripts. In particular, script samples from `facebook.com` were present in 18.42% of the websites with scripts.

New Unknown Potential Tracking

Scripts and Domains. Unknown tracking candidates represented 58.89% of the likely unknown tracking samples flagged by the *Unknown Tracking Analysis*. Their presence varied with regards to whether the domain was blacklisted or not. The prevalence of completely unknown tracking was higher than blacklisted ones: 90.69% of the websites with scripts used unknown tracking (see Table 9).

Due to the high number of discovered scripts, we performed an analysis to understand their nature. To this end, we measured the number of unique scripts and the domain type (third-party, first-party, and HTML-embedded) and performed a clustering analysis to find the most common behaviors.

We removed identical versions through code hashing and measured the number of unique scripts in each domain type (see Table 7). Usually tracking is used with third-party domains, but we found that is not the case for completely

Table 9. Completely unknown tracking prevalence in websites.

# websites	831,677
– % in websites with tracking	92.95%
– % in websites (considering sites with scripts)	90.69%

Table 10. 10 most popular top-level domains hosting previously unknown tracking script candidates.

Domain	# Websites
disquscdn.com	15,185
vk.me	9,228
baidustatic.com	4,848
kxcdn.com	4,189
adformdsp.net	2,958
jivosite.com	2,829
yandex.net	2,739
st-hatena.com	2,399
gtimg.cn	2,384
bitrix.info	2,374

unknown tracking. Most of them (73.75%) were embedded in the HTML, bypassing current blacklisting solutions. 57.73% of the completely unknown were unique by hash. Only a small number of them repeated versions across different domain types (1st and 3rd party, usually), indicating that is not a common practice.

We computed the prevalence of domains hosting unknown tracking. The 10 most popular domains (for the list see Table 10) were different e.g., CDNs, search engines, social networks, or advertisement companies.

Clustering. To understand the 3,245,238 unique tracking candidate scripts, we performed a cluster analysis. To overcome the high overhead of performing a cluster analysis directly on the large number of scripts, we conducted a clustering analysis in two steps. In the first step we clustered the 957 known trackers in our *Script Database* to find the different categories. We chose the *Affinity Propagation* clustering [26] due to its ability to automatically compute the cluster membership of an unknown sample and because it does not need to specify the number of clusters. In the second step, we computed the closest cluster for each of the different unknown tracking script candidates through the previously calculated clusters. The most popular category contained *downloader* scripts which were the 16.53% of the tracking candidates. The second most popular cluster included 12.85% of the scripts and was formed of *statistics* tracking scripts. We also measured the clusters with regards to their hosting (see Table 8).

Table 11. Potential unknown device fingerprinting prevalence.

Type	# Scripts	# Websites	# Domains
Font	25,502	24,873	704
Canvas	2,810	2,776	290
Shared	320	320	45
Total	*28,632*	*27,818*	*1,037*

4   Case Studies

Script Renaming Techniques. Blacklisting techniques only blocked 43.80% of the known scripts versions TRACKINGINSPECTOR detected due to *script renaming*. Over 35% of the samples of each original scripts changed their name. While samples of 200 of the original scripts did not present any change, versions from other 95 original scripts always changed their name. We analyzed three scripts: piwik.js, evercookie.js, and dota.js. 58.33% of evercookie.js samples, 91.13% piwik.js versions, and 99.66% of dota.js changed their name.

Among the script renaming techniques, we defined the following categories: (i) *related script renaming*, (ii) *random/neutral script renaming*, (iii) *functionality script renaming*, and (iv) *misleading script renaming*. *Related script renaming* changes the name to one directly or indirectly related to another service or website using the original script. For example, some versions changed their name to chrysler.js and dodge.js. *Random/neutral script renaming* replaces the name randomly, such as penguin2.js and welcome.js. *Functionality script renaming* modifies the name describing their goal, e.g., fingerprint.js, and tracking.js. Finally, *misleading script renaming* scripts change their names to well-known ones e.g., jquery.alt.min.js and j.min.js.

Canvas and Font Fingerprinting. Canvas fingerprinting [39] and font probing [15] are two device fingerprinting techniques. Due to their relevance, we studied them to determine how many unknown scripts of this type our tool found.

We implemented two experiments for each type. These were designed to filter the potential tracking script samples that match rules for font probing and for canvas fingerprinting. We built two set of rules based on the scripts found by [2,3]. 710 unknown unique device fingerprinting scripts were found: 408 show canvas fingerprinting behavior, 247 font probing behavior, and 55 both.

We also used the new device fingerprinting scripts as the *Script Database* and performed a *Known Tracking Analysis* to measure their prevalence in the Alexa top 1M as well as the domains used for hosting them (see Table 11). 28,632 samples were detected and 27,818 websites used these unknown scripts.

We also analyzed the top potential device fingerprinting unknown script. The most prevalent unknown font probing script was buttons.js. It was hosted by *sharethis.com*, a well-known social widget for sharing content in social networks.

Table 12. Comparison with related work since 2012.

Approach	Type	Stateful	Stateless	Variations	Unknown	Size
Blacklisting solutions	Generic	✓	✓	✗	✗	–
Roesner et al. [43]	Specific	✓	✓	✗	✗	2,098
Cookieless monster [41]	Specific	✓	✓	✗	✗	10,000
FPDetective [3]	Specific	✗	✓	✗	✓	1,000,000
The web never forgets [2]	Specific	✗	✓	✗	✓	1,000,000
TrackingExcavator [32]	Specific	✓	✓	✗	✓	10,000[a]
Englehard and Narayanan [17]	Specific	✓	✓	✗	✓	100,000/1,000,000[b]
TRACKINGINSPECTOR	Generic	✓	✓	✓	✓	1,000,000

[a]They analyzed 500 websites per year in the period 1996–2016.
[b]100,000 stateful and 1,000,000 for stateless fingerprinting.

The most used canvas fingerprinting unknown script was `Admeta.js`, downloaded by 981 websites from *atemda.com*, an ad provider. Regarding scripts containing both techniques, `image.js` was the most common unknown script, downloaded by 131 websites from the domain `magnuum.com`, a content delivery network.

Fingerprinting-Driven Malware. Some reports [44,51] linked targeted malware campaigns with fingerprinting. According to our results, sites with only tracking tend to be questionable and malicious. Hence, we inspected domains hosting only tracking and discovered suspicious scripts. For example, a script performed a fingerprinting step that included identification of the browser, *Java*, *Flash Player*, *SilverLight*, and the presence of a Chinese antivirus and then performed suspicious calls. It is important to remark, that the malicious script discovery was performed manually, based on the fingerprinting behavior and our findings, but we did not build any specific detection technique.

101.99.68.18 and 202.172.54 hosted the script. 101.99.68.18 was allocated in the ISP *Piradious-NET* and 202.172.54 in *M1 Connect Pte. Ltd.*, known for hosting malware. The script was `jquery.min.js`, as in the library *jQuery* and was not obfuscated. Two Chinese sites in the Alexa top 1M (`521if-e.cc` and `examres.com`) contained the iframe used to gather the malicious script.

By searching the iframe name, we found that this script was part of the *Chinad* botnet, as reported by *MalwareBytes* [35,36]. We did not perform a manual malware analysis, since it has already been performed by them. This is a exploit kit that compromised Chinese sites to fingerprint users looking for vulnerable components: e.g., in *Java* (CVE-2011-3544 and CVE-2012-4681), *Internet Explorer* (CVE-2014-6332), and *Flash* (CVE-2015-0311) and downloads versions of the *Chinad* botnet to perform DDoS attacks. To the best of our knowledge, the websites where we found the exploit kit were not previously reported.

5   Related Work

Previous Work

Due to the concern that web tracking raised to users' privacy, a hectic research has been done to analyze these techniques.

One of the first tracking analyses that included HTML cookies was the one performed in [31]. Following this work, Mayer and Mitchell [37] studied different techniques for tracking including their policies and developed a tool to measure web privacy. Roesner et al. [43] presented a taxonomy for third-party tracking using cookies, measuring their presence. Nikiforakis et al. [41] studied three known fingerprinting companies and discovered that 40 websites within the Alexa top 10K sites used techniques such font probing. Acar et al. [3] discovered 404 sites in the top 1M using JavaScript-based fingerprinting and 145 sites within the Alexa top 10K sites using Flash-based fingerprinting. Also, Acar et al. [2] found a 5% prevalence of canvas fingerprint in the Alexa top 1M sites. They also found respawning by Flash cookies on 10 of the 200 most popular sites and 33 respawning more than 175 HTTP cookies. In the topic of web vulnerabilities, a previous analysis of the JavaScript included [40] determined the correlation between the trust of the included scripts as well as the domains hosting the scripts. However, our work differs from this large-scale study since we focus specifically in web tracking rather than vulnerabilities. Lerner et al. [32] presented *TrackingExcavator* and performed a retrospective analysis of tracking evolution since 1996, showing that it increased over time. Englehardt and Narayanan [17] analyzed the Alexa top 100K websites with regards to stateful tracking and the top 1M regarding stateless fingerprinting using blacklists and static rules, finding new device fingerprinting techniques. Our work differs in many ways (see Table 12 for a detailed comparison). We use the following parameters for the comparison:

- **Specific/Generic:** Specific approaches focus on concrete web tracking types using ad-hoc heuristics. A generic approach detects web tracking using a single approach for every type of tracking. Although some previous works deal with both stateful and stateless web tracking, we consider generic approaches the ones that do not rely on specific solutions or heuristics for each type.
- **Stateful/Stateless tracking:** We divide previous approaches into the ones devoted to detect classic stateful approaches, the ones that detect stateless ones, or the ones that detect both types.
- **Detection of Variants:** TRACKINGINSPECTOR detects variants of the known scripts. Other works, normally the ones based on heuristics, may also detect variants but they could not classify them as so.
- **Detection of Unknown:** TRACKINGINSPECTOR also detects potentially unknown tracking. Some heuristics-based methods are also able, but just when the script follows the defined heuristics.
- **Size:** To compare the soundness of our study, we measure the size in websites.

Summarizing, we believe that the major breakthroughs of our work are the following. First, TRACKINGINSPECTOR, a truly generic web tracking detector

```
1  //https://browserleaks.com/canvas
2  var ctx = canvas.getContext('2d');
3  var txt = "exampleText. <canvas> 1.0";
4  ctx.textBaseline = "top";
5  ctx.font = "14px 'Arial'";
6  ctx.textBaseline = "alphabetic";
7  ctx.fillStyle = "#f60";
8  ctx.fillRect(125,1,62,20);
9  ctx.fillStyle = "#069";
10 ctx.fillText(txt, 2, 15);
11 ctx.fillStyle = "rgba(102, 204, 0, 0.7)";
12 ctx.fillText(txt, 4, 17);
13
14 //Extracting image (detectable)
15 md5(ctx.getImageData(0, 0, canvas.width, canvas.height).
       data.toString())
16 md5(canvas.toDataURL())
17
18 //Extracting image (undetectable)
19 imageData = ""
20 for (i = 0; i < canvas.width/10; i++) {
21   for (j = 0; j < canvas.height/10; j++) {
22     imageData += ctx.getImageData(i*10, j*10, 10, 10).
         data.toString()
23   }
24 }
25 md5(imageData)
```

Fig. 1. Snippet of OpenWPM detectable and undetectable canvas fingerprinting image extraction techniques.

that does not depend on blacklists or specific rules but on the previously known tracking scripts. Second, we discovered more than 3 million new unique tracking script candidates, a number higher than any reported previous work. We also found 710 new potential device fingerprinting scripts: 408 canvas fingerprinting, 247 font probing, and also 55 that exhibited both fingerprinting behaviors, a number also higher than previous work. Our tool also automatically detected the fingerprinting phase of a targeted malware campaign for the first time to date.

Empirical Comparison

We also implemented a comparative experiment that consist of 2 specific case studies, showing how our tool can detect instances of tracking scripts that are currently not flagged by other tools.

Canvas Fingerprinting. Englehard and Narayanan [17] analyzed Alexa top 1M websites, using OpenWPM [18], looking for tracking scripts (canvas fingerprinting included). For this specific technique, they proposed a set of 4 rules as a filtering criteria. Even if theses rules could definitely help in the detection process, there is an extremely simple evasion that any script could perform in order to completely avoid detection. The exact rule that allows it, is the following: *"The script extracts an image with* `toDataURL` *or with a single call to* `getImageData` *that specifies an area with a minimum size of 16px x 16px."* If the script performs multiple calls to `getImageData` without exceeding the size determined in the rule, the analysis will erroneously flag the script as non-tracking (see Fig. 1). In order to check if our approach would detect this case, we prepared two different scenarios.

1. We modified a script known for performing canvas fingerprinting (`dota.js`) to obtain the data following the aforementioned evasion technique. Then, we performed a *Known Tracking Analysis* to see if this change would be enough to evade the detection of the script as a variation of the original script. TRACKINGINSPECTOR was able to identify the script with a similarity of 99% and flags it as a modification of a known tracking script present in the *Script Database*.
2. In this case, instead of using a known script as a baseline, we created a new tracking script from scratch, but based on the same idea. As in the previous scenario, we implemented the data retrieval process following the evasion technique described. We performed an *Unknown Tracking Analysis* in this script to verify the effectiveness of the tool in this exact case. TRACKINGINSPECTOR was able to correctly classify the script as an unknown tracking script.

In conclusion, in both of the presented scenarios, our tool was able to detect the tracking script using its different components, in one case to detect the variation and in the other to detect the fingerprinting technique; while the previous approaches failed.

Font Fingerprinting. This type of fingerprinting technique has been extensively analyzed using both OpenWPM [17] and FPdetective [3]. One of the criteria used in these works to classify the script as a candidate of performing this kind of tracking, is the number of different fonts loaded (50 and 30, respectively). However, the work of Fifield and Egelman [20] allows to generate a specific type of font fingerprinting that measures the bounding boxes of some specific Unicode code points. For this case, the technique just needs five generic families (e.g., sans-serif, serif, monospace, cursive, and fantasy). As the number of different fonts used is much lower than the ones specified in their respective rules, neither of the previously mentioned analysis were able to detect them. In contrast to the previous case, this is not a small modification of the technique to avoid detection, but another font fingerprinting approach.

Therefore, we have created a fingerprinting script following this font fingerprinting technique from scratch. Then, we performed an *Unknown Tracking Analysis* to verify if our tool was able to detect this script as a tracking script. TRACKINGINSPECTOR correctly classified this script in the tracking group. As our approach is not based in strict human-generated rules, but in a learning progress with known scripts performing various types of tracking techniques, it can detect different fingerprinting attempts without explicit rules.

6 Conclusions

TRACKINGINSPECTOR measured the web tracking prevalence in websites and domains. The results show that web tracking is very extended and that current solutions cannot detect every known or unknown tracking. We also examined the hiding techniques used to avoid blacklists, finding different script renaming techniques. TRACKINGINSPECTOR detected both known or variations of tracking and likely unknown web tracking. We also found new potential stateless device fingerprinting and their prevalence, showing that even well-known companies provide them. Among the discovered unknown web tracking, we found a previously reported malware campaign targeting Chinese websites, showing that malicious activities may exhibit fingerprinting behavior. We believe that *fingerprinting-driven malware* may become a relevant issue in the future.

Acknowledgments. We would like to thank the reviewers for their insightful comments and our shepherd Nick Nikiforakis for his assistance to improve the quality of this paper. This work is partially supported by the Basque Government under a pre-doctoral grant given to Iskander Sanchez-Rola.

References

1. Abine: Tracking list, October 2017. https://www.abine.com/index.html
2. Acar, G., Eubank, C., Englehardt, S., Juarez, M., Narayanan, A., Diaz, C.: The web never forgets: persistent tracking mechanisms in the wild. In: Proceedings of the ACM SIGSAC Conference on Computer and Communications Security (CCS) (2014)
3. Acar, G., Juarez, M., Nikiforakis, N., Diaz, C., Gürses, S., Piessens, F., Preneel, B.: FPDetective: dusting the web for fingerprinters. In: Proceedings of the ACM SIGSAC Conference on Computer and Communications Security (CCS) (2013)
4. AdblockPlus: EasyPrivacy, October 2017. https://easylist.adblockplus.org/
5. AdGuard: Tracking list, October 2017. https://adguard.com/
6. Blocksi: Web content filtering, October 2017. http://www.blocksi.net/
7. Canali, D., Cova, M., Vigna, G., Kruegel, C.: Prophiler: a fast filter for the large-scale detection of malicious web pages. In: Proceedings of the 20th International Conference on World Wide Web (2011)
8. Canali, D., Lanzi, A., Balzarotti, D., Kruegel, C., Christodorescu, M., Kirda, E.: A quantitative study of accuracy in system call-based malware detection. In: Proceedings of the International Symposium on Software Testing and Analysis (2012)
9. Cliqz: Ghostery, October 2017. https://www.ghostery.com/
10. Cloudacl: Web security service, October 2017. http://www.cloudacl.com/
11. Cova, M., Kruegel, C., Vigna, G.: Detection and analysis of drive-by-download attacks and malicious Javascript code. In: Proceedings of the 19th International Conference on World Wide Web (2010)

12. Curtsinger, C., Livshits, B., Zorn, B.G., Seifert, C.: ZOZZLE: fast and precise in-browser JavaScript malware detection. In: Proceedings of the USENIX Security Symposium (SEC) (2011)
13. NerdyData: Search engine for source code, October 2017. https://nerdydata.com/
14. Disconnect: Tracking list, October 2017. https://disconnect.me/
15. Eckersley, P.: How unique is your web browser? In: Atallah, M.J., Hopper, N.J. (eds.) PETS 2010. LNCS, vol. 6205, pp. 1–18. Springer, Heidelberg (2010). https://doi.org/10.1007/978-3-642-14527-8_1
16. van Eijk, R.: Tracking detection system (TDS), October 2017. https://github.com/rvaneijk/ruleset-for-AdBlock
17. Englehardt, S., Narayanan, A.: Online tracking: a 1-million-site measurement and analysis. In: Proceedings of the ACM SIGSAC Conference on Computer and Communications Security (CCS) (2016)
18. Englehardt, S., Narayanan, A.: OpenWPM, October 2017. https://github.com/citp/OpenWPM
19. Fanboy: Tracking list, October 2017. https://www.fanboy.co.nz/
20. Fifield, D., Egelman, S.: Fingerprinting web users through font metrics. In: Böhme, R., Okamoto, T. (eds.) FC 2015. LNCS, vol. 8975, pp. 107–124. Springer, Heidelberg (2015). https://doi.org/10.1007/978-3-662-47854-7_7
21. FileWatcher: The file search engine, October 2017. http://www.filewatcher.com/
22. Fisher, R.A.: Statistical Methods and Scientific Inference. Hafner Publishing Co., New York (1956)
23. Fortinet: FortiGuard web filtering, October 2017. http://www.fortiguard.com/
24. Electronic Frontier Foundation: Privacy Badger, October 2017. https://www.eff.org/es/privacybadger
25. Mozilla Foundation: Public suffix list, October 2017. https://publicsuffix.org/list/
26. Frey, B.J., Dueck, D.: Clustering by passing messages between data points. Science 315(5814), 972–976 (2007)
27. Hidayat, A.: PhantomJS, October 2017. http://phantomjs.org/
28. Ho, T.K.: Random decision forests. In: Proceedings of the International Conference on Document Analysis and Recognition (ICDAR) (1995)
29. Kamkar, S.: Evercookie, October 2017. https://github.com/samyk/evercookie
30. Kaspersky: Tracking list (ABBL), October 2017. http://forum.kaspersky.com/
31. Krishnamurthy, B., Wills, C.: Privacy diffusion on the web: a longitudinal perspective. In: Proceedings of the International Conference on World Wide Web (WWW) (2009)
32. Lerner, A., Simpson, A.K., Kohno, T., Roesner, F.: Internet jones and the raiders of the lost trackers: an archaeological study of web tracking from 1996 to 2016. In: Proceedings of the USENIX Security Symposium (SEC) (2016)
33. Lielmanis, E.: JS Beautifier, October 2017. http://jsbeautifier.org/
34. Luhn, H.P.: A statistical approach to mechanized encoding and searching of literary information. IBM J. Res. Dev. 1(4), 309–317 (1957)
35. MalwareBytes: Unusual exploit kit targets Chinese users (part 1). https://blog.malwarebytes.org/exploits-2/2015/05/unusual-exploit-kit-targets-chinese-users-part-1/. Accessed Oct 2017
36. MalwareBytes: Unusual exploit kit targets Chinese users (part 2). https://blog.malwarebytes.org/intelligence/2015/06/unusual-exploit-kit-targets-chinese-users-part-2/. Accessed Oct 2017
37. Mayer, J.R., Mitchell, J.C.: Third-party web tracking: policy and technology. In: Proceedings of the International Symposium on Security and Privacy, Oakland (2012)

38. MeanPath: The source code search engine, October 2017. https://meanpath.com/
39. Mowery, K., Shacham, H.: Pixel perfect: fingerprinting canvas in HTML5. In: Proceedings of the Web 2.0 Workshop on Security and Privacy (W2SP) (2012)
40. Nikiforakis, N., Invernizzi, L., Kapravelos, A., Van Acker, S., Joosen, W., Kruegel, C., Piessens, F., Vigna, G.: You are what you include: large-scale evaluation of remote Javascript inclusions. In: Proceedings of the ACM SIGSAC Conference on Computer and Communications Security (CCS)
41. Nikiforakis, N., Kapravelos, A., Joosen, W., Kruegel, C., Piessens, F., Vigna, G.: Cookieless monster: exploring the ecosystem of web-based device fingerprinting. In: Proceedings of IEEE Symposium on Security and Privacy, Oakland (2013)
42. Rieck, K., Krueger, T., Dewald, A.: Cujo: efficient detection and prevention of drive-by-download attacks. In: Proceedings of the Annual Computer Security Applications Conference (CSS) (2010)
43. Roesner, F., Kohno, T., Wetherall, D.: Detecting and defending against third-party tracking on the web. In: Proceedings of the USENIX conference on Networked Systems Design and Implementation (NDSI) (2012)
44. Security Response, Symantec: The Waterbug attack group (2015). http://www.symantec.com/content/en/us/enterprise/media/security_response/whitepapers/waterbug-attack-group.pdf
45. Selzer, A.: Beaverbird, October 2017. https://github.com/AlexanderSelzer/BeaverBird
46. Amazon Web Services: Alexa top sites, October 2017. https://aws.amazon.com/es/alexa-top-sites/
47. Shekyan, S., Vinegar, B., Zhang, B.: PhantomJS hide and seek, October 2017. https://github.com/ikarienator/phantomjs_hide_and_seek
48. Singer, N.: Do not track? Advertisers say "don't tread on us" (2012). http://www.nytimes.com/2012/10/14/technology/do-not-track-movement-is-drawing-advertisers-fire.html
49. Sparck Jones, K.: A statistical interpretation of term specificity and its application in retrieval. J. Doc. **28**(1), 11–21 (1972)
50. AVG Technologies: Privacyfix tracking list, October 2017. http://privacyfix.com
51. Threat Intelligence, FireEye: Pinpointing Targets: Exploiting Web Analytics to Ensnare Victims (2015). https://www2.fireeye.com/rs/848-DID-242/images/rpt-witchcoven.pdf
52. Web of Trust: Crowdsourced web safety, October 2017. https://www.mywot.com/
53. TrustArc: TRUSTe tracking list, October 2017. https://www.truste.com/
54. Vasilyev, V.: FingerprintJS, October 2017. https://github.com/Valve/fingerprintjs
55. Webutation: Open website reputation, October 2017. http://www.webutation.net/
56. Yamaguchi, F., Lindner, F., Rieck, K.: Vulnerability extrapolation: assisted discovery of vulnerabilities using machine learning. In: Proceedings of the USENIX Conference on Offensive Technologies (WOOT) (2011)

JaSt: Fully Syntactic Detection of Malicious (Obfuscated) JavaScript

Aurore Fass[1](✉), Robert P. Krawczyk[2], Michael Backes[3], and Ben Stock[3]

[1] CISPA, Saarland University, Saarland Informatics Campus, Saarbrücken, Germany
`aurore.fass@cispa.saarland`
[2] German Federal Office for Information Security (BSI), Bonn, Germany
`robert.krawczyk@bsi.bund.de`
[3] CISPA Helmholtz Center i.G., Saarland Informatics Campus,
Saarbrücken, Germany
`{backes,stock}@cispa.saarland`

Abstract. JavaScript is a browser scripting language initially created to enhance the interactivity of web sites and to improve their user-friendliness. However, as it offloads the work to the user's browser, it can be used to engage in malicious activities such as Crypto Mining, Drive-by Download attacks, or redirections to web sites hosting malicious software. Given the prevalence of such nefarious scripts, the anti-virus industry has increased the focus on their detection. The attackers, in turn, make increasing use of obfuscation techniques, so as to hinder analysis and the creation of corresponding signatures. Yet these malicious samples share syntactic similarities at an abstract level, which enables to bypass obfuscation and detect even unknown malware variants.

In this paper, we present JaSt, a low-overhead solution that combines the extraction of features from the abstract syntax tree with a random forest classifier to detect malicious JavaScript instances. It is based on a frequency analysis of specific patterns, which are either predictive of benign or of malicious samples. Even though the analysis is entirely static, it yields a high detection accuracy of almost 99.5% and has a low false-negative rate of 0.54%.

1 Introduction

Information Technology is constantly under threat with the amount of newly found malware increasing permanently: over 250,000 new malicious programs are registered every day [11]. Moreover, our Internet-driven world enables malware to rapidly infect victims everywhere, anytime (e.g., Mirai [26], NotPetya [27]). Currently, the most vicious attacks are the so-called crypto trojans (e.g., WannaCry [28]), which often use JavaScript as a payload in the first stage of the infection of the victim's computer. This plethora of new attacks renders manual analysis impractical: defenders remedy this situation by automating the analysis of potentially malicious code. As a consequence, new alternatives based on machine learning algorithms are being explored to obtain a better understanding

© Springer International Publishing AG, part of Springer Nature 2018
C. Giuffrida et al. (Eds.): DIMVA 2018, LNCS 10885, pp. 303–325, 2018.
https://doi.org/10.1007/978-3-319-93411-2_14

of complex data collected from various systems, thereby automatically detecting and analyzing new malicious variants [16,19,30,31].

Many malware families use methods of script obfuscation to evade detection by classical anti-virus signatures and to impose additional hurdles to manual analysis. As a result, analysis tools and techniques constantly need improvement to be able to recognize these obfuscated patterns and to mitigate the threats. A possible approach to detect malicious obfuscated JavaScript relies on lexical or syntactic analyses, which enable an elimination of the artificial noise, e.g., introduced by identifier renaming, created by the attacker while using these evasion methods. While at a textual level, an accurate detection of malicious documents can be foiled by the use of obfuscation, programmatic and structural constructs can still be identified. Therefore, using the way in which lexical (e.g., keywords, identifiers, operators) or syntactic (e.g., statements, expressions, declarations) units are arranged in a given JavaScript file provides valuable insight to capture the salient properties of the code and hence to identify specific and recurrent malicious patterns. Approaches that use lexical [18,21,29] or syntactic units derived from the Abstract Syntax Tree (AST) [7,9,17] to analyze new variants of malicious code have already been proposed. We choose a syntactic approach over the lexical one, as the AST contains more information than the lexical units, allowing us to leverage grammar information for an improved analysis.

In this paper, we present an advanced method based on an AST-level analysis to automatically classify JavaScript samples containing obfuscated code. This implementation responds to the following challenges: resilience to common obfuscation transformations, practical applicability, and robustness against previously presented pollution attacks. We address these challenges by proposing a methodology to learn and recognize specific patterns either typical of benign or of malicious JavaScript documents. The key elements of JAST are the following:

- *Fully Static AST-Based Analysis:* Our system benefits from the AST to extract syntactic features from JavaScript files. Being entirely static, it is also able to analyze samples whose behavior is time- or environment-dependent [25].
- *Extraction of N-Grams Feature:* Using the syntactic features, patterns of length n, namely n-grams, are built and their frequency is analyzed. We find that these differ significantly between benign and malicious samples, allowing us to distinguish them. This approach is resistant to common obfuscation transformations since the intermediate representation used is close to the semantics of the code.
- *Accurate Detection of Malicious JavaScript:* Based on our n-gram approach, applying off-the-shelf supervised machine learning tools can be used to reliably differentiate benign from malicious JavaScript files.
- *Comprehensive Evaluation:* We evaluated our system in terms of detection accuracy, false-positive and false-negative rates, temporal stability, and performance on an extensive dataset composed of 105,305 current and unique JavaScript samples found in the wild: 85,059 malicious and 20,246 benign. It makes accurate predictions (with a detection accuracy of almost 99.50% on

our sample set) and has a low false-negative rate of 0.54% which is more than ten times less than other state-of-the-art systems.

The remaining paper is organized as follows. The implementation of JAST is described and justified in Sect. 2. The detection results as well as the throughput are analyzed in Sect. 3 and further discussed in Sect. 4. Finally, Sect. 5 presents some related work while Sect. 6 concludes the paper.

2 Methodology

The architecture of our JavaScript detection system consists of a feature-extraction part and learning components, as shown in Fig. 1. First, a static analysis of JavaScript documents is performed, extracting in particular syntactic units. Then, substrings of length n, namely n-grams, are produced and their frequency is used as input to the learning components. These components are used to train a classifier or update an existing model with the aim of distinguishing benign from malicious JavaScript samples. In the following section, we discuss the details of each stage in turn.

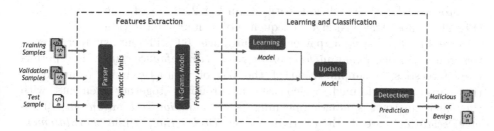

Fig. 1. Schematic depiction of JAST

2.1 Syntactic Analysis of JavaScript Documents

The choice of a syntactic analysis to detect malicious JavaScript instances is motivated by its resilience to common obfuscation transformations. At a textual level, an accurate discrimination between malicious and benign documents can be foiled by this evasion method, but programmatic and structural constructs are still identifiable. Moreover, this parsing process provides a certain level of code abstraction, ignoring, for example, the variable names to consider them as *Identifier*, skipping blank spaces or comments. Therefore, using the way syntactic units (e.g., statements, expressions, declarations) are arranged in a given JavaScript file provides valuable insight to capture the salient properties of the code and hence to identify specific and recurrent malicious (or benign) patterns. The syntactic analysis is performed by the state-of-the-art open source JavaScript parser Esprima [10], which takes a valid JavaScript sample as input, produces an ordered tree describing the syntactic structure of the program (also

```
var Euur1V = this [ "l9D" ] ("ev#333399al")
```

(a) Malicious JavaScript example from [30]

Program

VariableDeclaration

VariableDeclarator

Identifier   CallExpression

MemberExpression   Literal

ThisExpression   Literal

Description	Symbolic name	Value
Identifier	Identifier	15
ThisExpression	Expression	0
Literal	Literal	3
MemberExpression	Expression	0
Literal	Literal	3
CallExpression	Expression	0
VariableDeclarator	Declarator	12
VariableDeclaration	Declaration	4
Program	Program	8

(b) AST produced from (a)   (c) Syntactic units extracted from (b)

Fig. 2. Extraction of AST-based units from a JavaScript sample

known as Abstract Syntax Tree (AST)) and traverses it depth-first post-order, before extracting the corresponding syntactic units. Figure 2 illustrates the parsing process, where the malicious entity from Fig. 2a is transformed into an AST (Fig. 2b), whose traversal gives a sequence of syntactic units (Fig. 2c).

Overall the Esprima parser can produce 69 different syntactic entities ranging from *FunctionDeclaration* to *ImportDefaultSpecifier*. For performance reasons, a simplification of the list of syntactic units returned by the parser is performed. It consists in grouping together elements with the same abstract syntactic meaning (e.g., *FunctionDeclaration* and *VariableDeclaration* are both referred to as *Declaration*, while *ForStatement* and *WhileStatement* are both referred to as *Statement*), also considering one-element families if they could not be grouped with other entities (e.g., *Identifier*, *Program*). It enables a reduction of the number of different units from 69 to 19, while still preserving their syntactic meaning, as each element is analyzed within its context, using n-grams feature.

2.2 N-Grams Model

To identify specific patterns in JavaScript documents, a fixed-length window of n symbols is moved over each syntactic unit previously extracted, so as to get every sub-sequence of length n, namely n-grams, at each position. As shown in the literature, this is a generic and effective means for modeling reports [20–22,29,32–34].

The use of n-grams feature enables a representation of how these syntactic units were originally arranged in the analyzed JavaScript file. Therefore, reports sharing several n-grams with the same frequency present similarities with one another, while reports with different n-grams have a more dissimilar content. As a consequence, analyzing the frequency of these short patterns provides valuable

Table 1. Comparison between the number of all possible n-grams versus the number of n-grams extracted

N-grams	#All possible n-grams	#N-grams considered
N = 1	19	17
N = 2	361	114
N = 3	6,859	570
N = 4	130,321	2,457
N = 5	2,476,099	8,025

insights to determine if the sample is either benign or malicious. To be able to compare the frequency of all n-grams appearing in several JavaScript inputs, a vector space is constructed such that each n-gram is associated with one dimension, while its corresponding frequency is stored at this position in the vector R. For this mapping process, not all possible n-grams are considered, so as to limit the size of the vector space (initially of 19^n according to the length n of n-grams chosen), which has a direct impact on the performance. Besides, not all n-gram combinations make sense, e.g., as the root of the AST, the *Program* unit can only be present once. Therefore, a set S containing n-grams preselected based on their number of occurrences in our dataset is created. For this selection, the suitability criteria defined by Wressnegger et al. [34] were considered: the *perturbation*, as the expected ratio of n-grams in a benign sample that are not part of the training data, and the *density*, as the ratio of the number of unique n-grams in the dataset to the number of all possible n-grams. In particular, we aimed at significantly reducing the *density* of our dataset, while keeping an extremely low *perturbation* so as to limit the number of false-positives induced by unknown n-grams in benign data. This was achieved by only considering the n-grams appearing in our dataset (knowing that currently unknown n-grams can extend the list of n-grams currently considered), which enables a feature reduction of more than 90% for 3-, 4-, and 5-grams, as shown in Table 1.

Formally, the previous vector R is defined using the set S of n-grams considered and the set $S' = (x_i)_{i \in [\![1, |S'|]\!]}$ of JavaScript samples to be analyzed such as:

$$R^T = \{r_1^T, \ldots, r_{|S'|}^T\}$$

$$\text{knowing that } \forall i \in [\![1, |S'|]\!], r_i = \phi(x_i)$$

$$\text{and } \phi : x_i \longrightarrow (\phi_n(x_i))_{n \in S}$$

with $\phi_n(x_i)$ the frequency of the n-gram n in the report x_i.

As a consequence, the ϕ function maps a JavaScript file x_i to the vector space $\mathbb{R}^{|S|}$ such that all dimensions associated with the n-grams contained in the set S are set to their frequency. To avoid an implicit bias on the length of the reports, the frequencies are normalized, such that: $\forall i \in [\![1, |S'|]\!], ||r_i|| = ||\phi(x_i)|| = 1$.

The frequency vector R (defined as $R^{\mathrm{T}} = (r_i)_{i \in [\![1, |S'|]\!]}^{\mathrm{T}}$) is then used as input to the learning components.

2.3   Learning and Classification

The learning-based detection completes the design of our system. Before predicting if a given JavaScript sample is either benign or malicious, the classifier has to be trained on a representative, up-to-date, and balanced set of both benign and malicious JavaScript files. Therefore, a model is initially built using the vectorial representation $R^{\mathrm{T}} = (r_i)_{i \in [\![1, |S'|]\!]}^{\mathrm{T}}$, presented in Sect. 2.2, of the files S' to be classified. This vector is furthermore used to update an old model with newer JavaScript samples, without having to train the classifier from scratch again.

We empirically evaluated different off-the-shelf classifiers (Bernoulli naive Bayes, multinomial naive Bayes, support vector machine (SVM), and random forest) and determined that random forest yielded the best results. Contrary to the two naive Bayes algorithms, random forest does assume independence between the attributes, leading to a higher detection accuracy. It is a meta estimator which combines the predictions of several decision trees on various sub-samples of the dataset: for each tree predictor, an input is entered at the top and as it traverses down the tree, the data is bucketed into smaller and smaller sets. Therefore the whole forest provides predictions more accurate than those of a single tree [31] and controls overfitting, as it classifies an unknown instance according to the decision of the majority of the tree predictors [4].

JAST is implemented in Python and its Scikit-learn implementation of random forest is used to classify unknown data [23]. This Python module integrates a collection of state-of-the-art tools and machine learning algorithms for data mining and data analysis, and provides highly extensible implementations controlled by several parameters (e.g., number of trees in a forest, number of features considered). To optimize the predictions of our learning-based detection, the tuple of hyperparameters yielding an optimal model (that minimizes a predefined loss function on an independent dataset) has been determined. Our independent dataset, which was provided by the German Federal Office for Information Security (BSI) and labeled according to the protocol described in Sect. 3.1, contains 17,500 unique benign samples, and as many malicious ones. This way, it has a balanced distribution and avoids any overfitting. First, random search has been performed with 5-fold cross-validation on this dataset, sampling a fixed number of parameter settings from the specified distributions [3]. This method enabled us to narrow down the range of possibilities for each hyperparameter and in a second step, to concentrate the search on a lower number of tuples. Indeed, grid search has been used on the previous results, exhaustively testing all the resulting combinations with cross-validation, to tune the optimal set of hyperparameters.

The tuple of hyperparameters yielding an optimal model on our independent dataset is presented hereafter. As far as features are concerned, 4-grams have been selected because the length four provided the best trade-off between false-positives and false-negatives. As for the forest, it contains 500 trees having each time a maximum depth of 50 nodes. When looking for the best node's split, $\lceil\sqrt{2,457}\rceil = 50$ features are considered and the Gini criterion is used to measure the quality of a split, based on the Gini impurity [8]. These hyperparameters have been selected because their combination leads to the best trade-off between performance and accuracy.

3 Comprehensive Evaluation

In this section, we outline the results of our extensive evaluation. The success of our learning-based approach comes from the previous well-considered tuple of hyperparameters, and a high-quality dataset. This was confirmed by the high detection accuracy obtained on several unknown datasets. Based on the accuracy of our system's predictions, a study of the temporal evolution of JavaScript files over one year was performed. JAST was also compared to state-of-the-art approaches where its extremely low false-negative rate is without precedent. We also evaluated JAST in terms of run-time performance.

3.1 Experimental Datasets

The experimental evaluation of our approach rests on an extensive dataset mainly provided by the German Federal Office for Information Security (BSI). This dataset, which comprises 105,305 unique (based on their SHA1 hash) JavaScript samples, is in particular composed of 20,246 benign and 85,059 malicious JavaScript files (Table 2) between 100 bytes and 1 megabyte, with a total size of more than 3.6 gigabytes. Our malicious samples mainly correspond to JavaScript extracted from emails, one of the most common and effective way to spread JScript-Loader, knowing that a double-click on the attachment is by default sufficient to execute it on Windows hosts, leading to e.g., drive-by download or ransomware attacks. JavaScript as infection vector is particularly relevant and powerful here since it is especially prone to obfuscation and therefore enables the attackers to build a unique copy of the malicious attachment for each recipient, foiling classical anti-virus signatures. These samples have been labeled as malicious based on a score obtained after having been tested by twenty different anti-virus systems, the malware scanner of the BSI, and a runtime-based analysis. As for the benign files, they were extracted among others from Microsoft products (e.g., Microsoft Exchange 2016 and Microsoft Team Foundation Server 2017), the majority of which are obfuscated, which enabled us to ensure that JAST does not confound obfuscation and maliciousness, but leverages grammar information for an accurate distinction between benign and malicious inputs. For our dataset to be more up-to-date and representative of the JavaScript distribution found in the wild, we also included some open source games written in JavaScript, web frameworks and the source code of Atom [1], tested either using the previous protocol or directly downloaded from the developers' web page. These extra samples extend our dataset with some new, sometimes unusual or specific (e.g., games) coding styles, which shows again that our system does not

Table 2. JavaScript dataset description

JS type	Creation	#JS	Label	Obfuscated
Emails	2017–2018	85,059	Malicious	y
Microsoft	2015–2018	17,668	Benign	y
Games	N/A	2,007	Benign	n
Web frameworks	N/A	434	Benign	N/A
Atom	2011–2018	137	Benign	n

Table 3. Detection accuracy of JAST

JS type	#Misclassified	#Correctly classified	Detection accuracy
Emails	443	81,116	99.46%
Microsoft	71	14,097	99.50%
Games	10	1,997	99.52%
Web frameworks	4	430	99.03%
Atom	1	136	98.98%
Average benign	86	16,660	99.48%

confound unseen nor unusual syntactic structures with maliciousness. Reasons for not including any web JavaScript extracted from HTML documents in this dataset are discussed in Sect. 4.2.

3.2 Detection Performance

In our first experiment, we studied the detection performance of JAST in terms of true-positive and true-negative rates (correct classification of the samples, either as benign or as malicious), false-positive and false-negative rates (misclassification of the samples, malicious instead of benign, or the opposite), and overall detection accuracy. The experimental protocol is the following: 3,500 unique JavaScript files were each time randomly extracted from the email dataset (malicious) and Microsoft dataset (benign), and were used to build a balanced model. The remaining samples were considered unknown and were used to measure the detection performance. We repeated this procedure five times and the averaged results are shown in Table 3. JAST was able to correctly classify 99.48% of our benign dataset, while still detecting 99.46% of the malicious email samples. As both these benign and malicious files were, for the most part, obfuscated, this demonstrates the resilience of our system to this specific form of evasion. More importantly, it shows that JAST does not confound obfuscation with maliciousness, and plain text with benign inputs, but could use differences between benign and malicious obfuscation at a syntactic level to distinguish benign obfuscated from malicious obfuscated files. Indeed, while the former is used to protect code privacy and intellectual property, the latter aims at hiding its malicious purpose without specific regard to the performance. Furthermore, our system offers a very high true-negative rate for the web frameworks, the source code of JavaScript games and of Atom, even though these sample families were not present in the training set. The possible transfer of an email-based model to web samples is further discussed in Sect. 4.2.

Both the false-positive (0.52%) and the false-negative (0.54%) rates are very low for JAST indicating that, based on a frequency analysis of their 4-grams, our classifier is able to make an accurate distinction between benign and malicious samples almost 99.5% of the time. We achieved this optimal trade-off between the false-positives and the false-negatives by using Youden's J statistic, where J is defined as [24,38]:

$$J = \text{sensitivity} + \text{specificity} - 1 = TPR - FPR$$

This index corresponds to the area beneath the curve subtended by a single operating point. Its maximum value is used as a criterion for selecting the optimal cut-off point between false-positives and false-negatives. In our case, Youden's index was determined with 5-fold cross validation on the independent dataset presented in Sect. 2.3. The value we got is 0.29, which means that a sample will be considered malicious if the probability of it being malicious is above 0.29, according to our random forest classifier. Figure 3 presents the evolution of the detection performance when the value of Youden's index varies between 0.19 and 0.95. The best trade-off between false-positive and false-negative rates

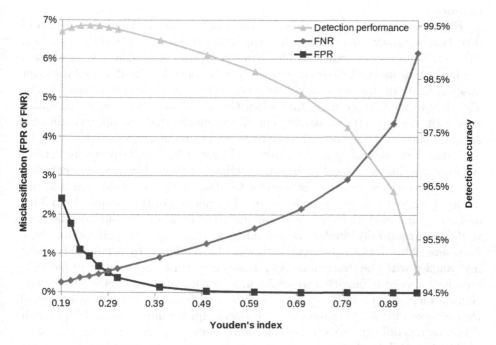

Fig. 3. Detection performance, depending on Youden's index

is obtained for 0.29, while the maximum detection accuracy is obtained for a threshold of 0.25. The value 0.23 is equally interesting, as it represents a reduction of the sharp false-positive rate decline while retaining a low false-negative rate and an extremely high detection accuracy of 99.49%. As for trading an extremely low false-positive rate for a higher false-negative rate, it downgrades the overall detection accuracy extremely rapidly. For the rest of the paper, if no other indication is given, we consider an index of 0.25.

3.3   JavaScript Temporal Evolution

In our second experiment, we focused on the temporal evolution of malicious email-JavaScript received from January 2017 to January 2018. For each month, two steps were performed:

- The labels of the JavaScript samples collected on the current month were considered unknown. The model built in the previous months (the first model being created in January 2017) was used to classify these JavaScript instances;
- The true labels (obtained from other sources such as AV) of the JavaScript samples collected on the current month were used to build a new model, including all the samples of the previous months.

As a consequence, the samples from January 2018 were classified with a model initially built in January 2017 and extended each month, until December 2017 inclusive, with new and up-to-date malicious as well as benign JavaScript instances.

Figure 4 shows the performance of the random forest classifier in terms of detection accuracy –defined by the proportion of samples correctly classified, either as benign or as malicious– for three different thresholds. The prediction decline in June and to a lesser extent in July only depends on malicious JavaScript misclassifications, the mean false-positive rate over the whole period being 0.21%. The decrease gets more important when the threshold increases, which makes sense as it represents the probability cut-off to consider that a sample is malicious. As a comparison, we replaced the complete relearning of a model each month, by an update function adding 100 new trees to the forest built in the previous months. As both experiments presented the same decline in June and July, we concentrated our analysis on these two months to understand where the major changes at a sample level originated from. Indeed, a manual inspection of the samples from June and July, combined with the use of JSINSPECT [14] –a project built on the AST to detect structurally similar code– confirmed that the misclassifications came from several big JavaScript waves, each wave (also referred to as family) containing samples with the exact same AST-based structure. As a matter of fact, the attackers abused obfuscation to send a unique copy of the malicious JavaScript email attachment to each recipient. In this specific case, they only randomized the function and variable names for each JavaScript file they produced: since their SHA1 hash is different, we did not consider them as duplicate, but they are identical at the AST level (variable/function names are represented by an *Identifier*

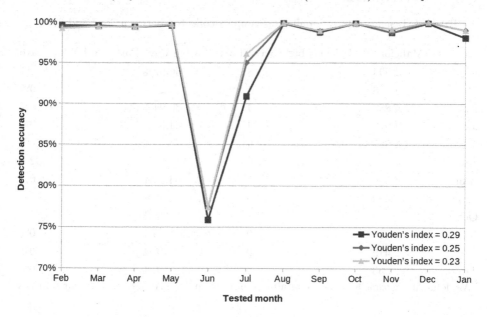

Fig. 4. Temporal evolution of the detection accuracy, depending on Youden's index

node). In June, we can notice in particular the appearance of four such misclassified waves with respectively 213, 355, 578, and 1,049 files in them. If one sample of one of the previous families is misclassified, so is the entire wave, which yielded in our case a high number of false-negatives. A similar phenomenon was observed in July, where two waves respectively containing 107 and 354 samples were received and misclassified. These six specific waves were admittedly composed of malicious samples only, but the classifier labeled each one of them as benign with a probability over 78%. We could have observed the inverse phenomenon, where one sample of a malicious wave would have been recognized as malicious, and therefore the entire wave too (as a wave only contains samples with the exact same AST-based structure), which would have yielded a high number of true-positives (depending on the wave's size). Table 4 indicates that it is globally not the case since the biggest malicious families were rather found in June and July. Besides, we only had big wave (over 300 samples) misclassifications in June and July, the other waves were being correctly flagged as malicious with a probability over 50% (in general even over 75%).

As a second experiment, Fig. 5 presents the evolution of the detection accuracy when the month used to build the initial model varies, the rest of the experiment staying the same. As previously, and for the reasons mentioned before, a decline was observed in June and July. In particular, the differences in terms of detection accuracy in June between a model first built in April and the other ones, or between the different models in July, highlight the presence of these big JavaScript waves (through correct detections or on the contrary misclassifications).

Table 4. Insights into the malicious samples collected between 2017 and 2018

Months	#Malicious	#Malicious big waves[a]	Part of a big wave	Part of a FN big wave
Feb	4,894	8	66.92%	0%
Mar	4,838	4	28%	0%
Apr	4,883	4	30.04%	0%
May	4,922	4	44.64%	0%
Jun	4,987	6	73.73%	39.74%
Jul	4,831	6	53.88%	7.32%
Aug	6,536	6	64.35%	0%
Sep	592	0	0%	0%
Oct	3,610	1	8.8%	0%
Nov	120	0	0%	0%
Dec	419	0	0%	0%
Jan	53	0	0%	0%

[a]We define a *big wave* as a wave containing more than 300 syntactically similar samples

This way, June and July both misclassified several big waves of syntactically similar JavaScript samples, with in particular a wave containing more than 1,000 samples, therefore accounting for more than a fifth of the samples collected in June. Even though it yielded a high number of false-negatives, this is avoidable with a model more representative of the distribution found in the wild. As a matter of fact, another sampling of the *exact same* JavaScript files gave in Sect. 3.2 a false-negative rate of 0.54% (threshold: 0.29, with an equally low false-positive rate of 0.52%). It was not obtained by chance, especially since the training set was significantly smaller, but through models containing more entropy in their randomly-selected samples, in comparison to a few syntactically similar JavaScript waves.

3.4 Comparison with Other Approaches

Table 5 presents a quantitative comparison with closely related work. CUJO and PJSCAN both used lexical units combined with an n-gram analysis to detect malicious JavaScript respectively embedded in web pages and in PDF documents. As for ZOZZLE, it used features extracted from the AST to identify malicious JavaScript samples. We discuss their approach further in Sect. 5. Table 5 shows that JAST is heavily optimized to detect malicious JavaScript instances with its low false-negative rate of 0.54% (threshold 0.29), which is between 10 and 28 times lower than the other tools proposed thus far. Compared to CUJO and ZOZZLE, who also used the results of a dynamic analysis to detect malicious JavaScript samples more accurately, our approach outperforms these concepts. Like the majority of anti-virus systems, they rather traded a low false-positive rate for a higher false-negative rate. Indeed, as indicated by Curtsinger et al.,

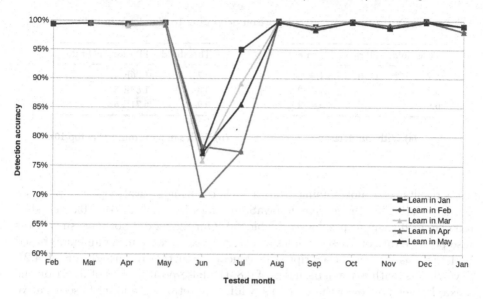

Fig. 5. Temporal evolution of the detection accuracy, depending on the training month

Table 5. Accuracy comparison with closely related work

Project	FP rate	FN rate	Static	Dynamic
JaSt	5.2E-3	5.4E-3	✓	-
Cujo [29]	2.0E-5	5.6E-2	✓	✓
PJScan [21]	1.6E-1	1.5E-1	✓	-
Zozzle [7]	3.1E-6	9.2E-2	✓	✓

given the number of URLs on the web, a false-positive rate of 5% is considered acceptable for static analysis tools, but rates even 100 times lower are not acceptable for in-browser detection. Besides, the low false-positive rate of Zozzle has to be taken with a grain of salt, since this tool rather aims at detecting benign samples. For this reason, it was tested on more benign than malicious files (1.2 million versus a few thousand) which lowered the false-positive rate at the expense of the false-negatives. JaSt on the other hand is designed to detect *malicious* JavaScript files, while still retaining a low false-positive rate of 0.52%.

As mentioned in Sect. 3.2, Youden's index can furthermore be used to shift false-positive and false-negative rates, according to the system's use case and dataset. Therefore, to perform further comparisons with Cujo and Zozzle, we increased the value of Youden's index, so as to lower our false-positive rate. With a threshold of 0.7, our system already had a lower false-positive rate than Cujo's, while retaining a lower false-negative rate (Table 6a). To ensure that

Table 6. Accuracy comparison according to Youden's index

Threshold	FP rate	FN rate
0.7	1.19E-5	2.16E-2
0.8	0	2.91E-2
0.9	0	4.34E-2

Threshold	FP rate	FN rate
0.7	1.26E-4	-
0.8	1.68E-5	-
0.9	6.71E-6	-

(a) With our dataset   (b) With samples from Alexa top 10k

these results were not coming from a lack of benign JavaScript samples, we extracted 119,233 unique benign JavaScript files from Alexa top 10k web sites and classified them as previously (Table 6b). Our model did not have such a low false-positive rate on these samples as before since we were using an email-based model to classify web-JavaScript (this concept is further discussed in Sect. 4.2). Nevertheless, with a Youden's index of 0.8, the false-positive rate of JAST on the Alexa dataset was lower than CUJO's, while still retaining a lower false-negative rate. As for ZOZZLE, a threshold of 0.8 on our dataset provided both a better false-positive and a better false-negative rate. As previously, we also performed this comparison on the samples extracted from Alexa top 10k. With a threshold of 0.9, we had a false-positive rate of 6.71E-4% (standing for 0.8 false-positive, averaged over 5 runs) –admittedly a little superior to ZOZZLE's– but still a lower false-negative rate (Table 6).

Several parameters are responsible for the higher detection accuracy of JAST compared to CUJO and ZOZZLE. First, we did not trade a very low false-positive rate for a higher false-negative rate, which enables our system to accurately detect benign samples with an accuracy of 99.48% and 99.46% for malicious ones. As indicated in Fig. 3, an extremely low false-positive rate significantly degrades the classifier's accuracy. Besides, maximizing the detection accuracy also corresponds to the better trade-off between false-positives and false-negatives. Furthermore, the choice of our random forest classifier has an impact on the detection performance, since it performed better than Bernoulli naive Bayes and SVM –respectively chosen for ZOZZLE and for CUJO– on our dataset. Last but not least, our syntactic analysis also has an impact on the detection accuracy e.g., CUJO is based on a lexical analysis, which does not perform as well as an AST-based one, because lexical units lack context information.

3.5   Run-Time Performance

The run-time performance of our system was tested on a commodity PC with a quad-core Intel(R) Core(TM) i3-2120 CPU at 3.30 GHz and 8 GB of RAM. The experiments have each time been performed 5 times, on 5 different sets randomly selected. The processing time for all stages of our method on 500 unique JavaScript samples (half of which are benign, the other half being malicious), representing 14.9 megabytes, is shown in Table 7. The most time-consuming

Table 7. Processing time for 500 JavaScript samples for different stages of our system

	Parser	N-grams analysis	Learner	Updater	Classifier	Total
Total	96.55s	14.43s	1.79s	0.41s	0.26s	113.43s
Percentage	85.12%	12.72%	1.57%	0.36%	0.23%	100%

Table 8. Throughput characteristics of JaSt

	#Samples	Time	Size	Files per second	Throughput
Emails	85,059	20,247.08 s	2.5 GB	4.20	0.12 MB/s
Microsoft	17,668	6,049.21 s	1.1 GB	2.33	0.18 MB/s
Games	2,007	370.52 s	50.9 MB	5.45	0.14 MB/s
Web frameworks	434	94.39 s	13.8 MB	4.65	0.15 MB/s
Atom	137	30.70 s	5.4 MB	5.70	0.18 MB/s
All files	105,305	26,791.90s	3.67 GB	3.93	0.14 MB/s

operation corresponds to the parsing of the JavaScript files with the open source tool Esprima, written in JavaScript, which accounts for more than 85% of the overall detection time. In comparison, the production of all 4-grams and the creation of a vector of 2,457 dimensions, containing the frequency of each of the previous 4-grams, is quite fast (12.72% of the time). As for the performance of the random forest classifier, it mainly depends on the throughput of Python Scikit-learn algorithms and represents in average less than 1% of the processing time. It includes building a forest of 500 trees (*c.f.* Sect. 2.3) using the previous samples, updating the previous model by adding 100 new trees to the forest –which is more than 4 times faster than creating the original model– and testing the model on unknown samples, the most important part of the detection system and also clearly the fastest. In total, JaSt extracted the syntactic units of 500 JavaScript samples, constructed 2,457 different 4-grams and computed each frequency for all input files (representing 1,228,500 frequencies), built a model based on the previous frequency vector and updated it, before using it to classify 500 unknown JavaScript documents in less than 2 min. Compared to PJScan –implemented in C with its own C library to classify JavaScript entities–, which can analyze a PDF document in 0.0032 seconds, our approach is slower. In compensation, the accuracy of our predictions is significantly better (Sect. 3.4), which primes as the throughput could always be improved by parallelization for a deployment in the wild.

To have a closer look into the performance of our system, we used the models built in Sect. 3.2 to classify our different datasets. Table 8 presents the throughput of JaSt depending on the type of JavaScript file to be detected. The runtime performance is closely related to the number of samples to be analyzed: bigger datasets will have a lower per-file-throughput as smaller ones, since the 4-grams frequencies of all files have to be kept in the buffer before being used for classification purpose. On average, JAST analyzes 0.14 MB/s, which is comparable to the 0.2 MB/s of ZOZZLE for the same amount of features as ours, while still retaining a higher detection accuracy (99.46% compared to 99.20% for ZOZZLE).

4   Discussion

In this section, we first examine the limitations of our learning-based approach, focusing on evasion techniques that might be used by an attacker. We then discuss to what extent an email-based model is able to detect web samples, such as exploit kits provided by Kafeine DNC[1] or JavaScript extracted from Alexa[2].

4.1   Limitations and Further Evasion Techniques

All learning-based malware detection tools will fail to detect some attacks, such as malicious instances not containing any of the features present in the training set. As a matter of fact, machine learning does not always take into account the concept of uncertainty involved in the prediction task [2], and relies in particular on statistical assumptions about the distribution of the training data to construct models, which are then used for future analyses. As a consequence, adversaries could also exploit these limitations to disrupt the analysis process, not to mention engaging malicious activities that could fail to be detected [13]. Our approach is resilient to attacks benefitting from the adaptive aspect of machine learning to design training data that will cause the learning system to produce models misclassifying future inputs, as the system never uses unknown input data as a training set. Attackers could rather try to manipulate a malicious sample to find a variant, preserving its maliciousness, but which would be classified as benign [15,36]. Evasion is made somewhat more difficult because of the absence of a classification score. In particular, our system does preserve a lower false-negative rate than ZOZZLE when confronted to the Jshield samples [6] (80.14% versus 36.7%), admittedly tailored to avoid ZOZZLE's detection. These malicious files have been polluted by an injection of benign features, as it decreases their maliciousness by statistically reducing the impact of their malicious features. To foil JAST, an attacker could rather inject benign functions into a malicious file, which would not change its functionality but would statistically reduce our system's maliciousness rating. Even though it is highly effective (from our 200 malicious samples modified by a transplantation of 100 random benign functions, none of them were detected), we did not have any such false-negatives in our dataset. This would furthermore be easy to detect and avoid, e.g., with dead code elimination or even statically with Esprima, comparing *FunctionDeclaration*'s *Identifiers* with *CallExpression*'s *Identifiers* since these functions are never called. Another attack on JAST might consist of inserting a malicious sample into a –preferably significantly bigger– benign one. Even if it accounted for

---

[1] Malware don't need Coffee, https://malware.dontneedcoffee.com.
[2] Alexa top sites, http://www.alexa.com/topsites.

around a fourth of our false-negatives, it barely represents 0.1% of our malicious dataset, the adversaries rather relying on obfuscation to hide their malicious purpose. A defense against further adversarial attacks could be to combine the predictions of several classifiers (if the throughput is not a constraint). Another possibility consists in adding some parameters to our evaluation system, like the number of (different) nodes in the AST or the amount of different n-grams used, since it has a direct impact on the frequency analysis whom an attacker might try to foil.

4.2 Extension of an Email-Based Model to Detect Web Samples

Section 3.2 presents the detection performance of JAST after having been trained and tested with malicious emails (and Microsoft samples for the benign part). As this model has yielded good predictions on web frameworks, the source code of Atom and also on the peculiar coding style of JavaScript games, even though these families were not represented in the model, it is worth looking at an extension of an email-based model to detect other types of JavaScript. In this experiment, we used the five email-based models, constructed previously, to classify inline JavaScript extracted from malicious HTML email-attachments, exploit kits from 2010 to 2017, and Alexa top 10k web pages. For Alexa, we also extracted third-party scripts and considered that all scripts were benign. While this is arguable in theory, JavaScript extracted from the first layer of the ten thousand web sites with the highest ranking provided us in practice enough confidence for this experiment. Although it has been showed that these web sites could host malicious advertisements, our JavaScript extraction process, which relies on statically parsing the web page with Python and extracting *script* and *src* tags, protected us from these elements generated dynamically. Figure 6 presents the detection accuracy (in terms of either true-positive or true-negative rates) on the previous samples. An HTML page or an exploit kit were considered benign if all the JavaScript snippets they contained were classified as benign. If one malicious JavaScript sample was detected, the whole page was labeled as malicious.

JAST was able to detect 82.31% of the 13,595 malicious web JavaScript, which shows a certain similarity at the 4-grams level between email-JavaScript and web-JavaScript. Further insights into the false-negatives indicated that 14.37% of the previous samples had been *correctly* classified as benign. As a matter of fact, a manual inspection of 80 exploit kits showed that in 21.25% of the cases, the malicious part was *not* embedded in JavaScript samples. Instead, the attack vector was either contained in an SWF bundle or the exploit kit merely included a resource trying to exploit an existing flaw without any scripting code at all. Another issue is related to the quality of JavaScript samples: while analyzing 110 malicious email attachments and exploit kits, we discovered that some files were broken and could therefore not be parsed. In 3.64% of the cases, the *malicious* part could not be parsed, therefore not analyzed. We note that this means that in an attack, this code would not have been executed. As a consequence, when considering only HTML documents and exploit kits which could be entirely parsed and whose malicious behavior was included into a JavaScript snippet, we got a true-positive rate after treatment of 85,18%, which represents an improvement of 3.36%. While malicious email and web samples present some similarities, they also have syntactic differences, which prevented JAST to provide as much confidence in the detection of malicious web-JavaScript as for email-inputs. As a matter of fact, the former tends to contain less malicious patterns and rather have comments at regular intervals, benign snippets next to the malicious part, and a different form of obfuscation than malicious email-JavaScript. While the latter aims at providing a unique copy for each recipient and therefore abuses *variable and function name randomization, data obfuscation* and *encoding obfuscation* [35], malicious web-JavaScript rather tend to identify software vulnerabilities in client machines and exploit them to upload and execute malicious code on the client side. For this purpose, the attackers preferably use *variable and function name randomization* and neatly package their code, which can slightly degrade JAST efficiency.

As for the detection of benign JavaScript extracted from Alexa top 10k, JAST detected 46.11% of them. Instead of grouping all JavaScript snippets of a web page together and labeling the web site as benign if all samples were recognized as benign, we performed a second experiment. We collected every JavaScript snippet of Alexa top 10k (between 100 bytes and 1 megabyte, so as to have JavaScript code with enough features to be representative of the benign or of the malicious class, without downgrading the performance with too big a size) and considered them one after the other. In total, we extracted 119,125 JavaScript samples and got a true-negative rate of 92.79% (averaged over 5 runs) –which is much more acceptable than previously, based on an exclusive non-web-model– therefore a false-positive rate of 7.21%. If we consider that an Alexa top 10k web page contains n JavaScript snippets, we could expect a false-positive rate of $100 - 7.21^n\%$. In average it contains 16 snippets, therefore the probability of getting a false-positive is 69.82%, even higher than the 46.11% we found, since an average value does not give any information regarding the data distribution. However, we envision that JAST would not operate on an unfiltered set of all Web pages, but rather use greyware which already showed some indication of maliciousness (e.g., by instantiating an ActiveX object). This approach was also used by KIZZLE [30].

We chose not to include any web-JavaScript extracted from HTML documents for the training and evaluation part of this paper, but rather discuss the extension of an email-based model to detect web samples for three reasons. First, we did not have any ground truth regarding the position of the malicious entity in the malicious HTML file, which would have required a systematic analysis of our 13,595 snippets to detect and use only the *malicious* JavaScript samples to train our classifier with. For this reason, we decided to exclude them from the evaluation part and instead chose to flag any HTML documents containing at least one malicious JavaScript snippet as malicious. For symmetry purpose, we applied the same treatment to benign HTML files, which thereby reduced the number of benign scripts in our dataset. Last but not least, splitting email

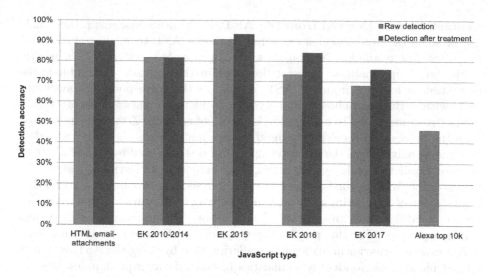

Fig. 6. Detection accuracy of web JavaScript based on an email-model

and web evaluation was a way to show that the syntax-based features can be core in classifying JavaScript: no matter the obfuscation used for hiding their functionality, malicious JavaScript do not necessarily hide their true function.

5   Related Work

In the literature, several systems used essential differences in lexical, syntactic, or other structural properties of JavaScript files to analyze them.

Lexical Analysis. Several approaches benefitted from lexical units and an SVM classifier to distinguish benign from malicious instances. In particular, Rieck et al. developed CUJO [29], a system combining static and dynamic analyses for the automatic detection and prevention of drive-by download attacks. Embedded in a web proxy, it transparently inspects web pages, extracting generic features based on an n-gram analysis of JavaScript lexical units, and implementing a learning-based detection. With PJSCAN, Laskov and Šrndić [21] also combined the extraction of lexical units with an n-gram analysis to detect malicious PDF documents. Contrary to CUJO, the learning phase was performed only on malicious samples, the idea being to build a model of normality and label the files not respecting this model as benign. Beyond pure JavaScript detection, Kar et al. [18] showed with SQLiGoT that a lexical analysis could also be performed to detect SQL injections. This system normalizes SQL queries into sequences of tokens and generates a weighed graph representing the interactions between the previous tokens, before training a classifier to identify malicious nodes.

Syntactic Units Derived from the AST. Some other systems rather made use of some essential features extracted from the AST to analyze JavaScript instances. For example, Curtsinger et al. implemented ZOZZLE [7], a mostly static JavaScript malware detector deployed in the browser. It combines the extraction of features from the AST, as well as the corresponding JavaScript text, with a Bayesian classification system to identify syntax elements highly predictive of malware. To address the issue of obfuscation, ZOZZLE is integrated with the browser's JavaScript engine to collect and process the code created at runtime. A naive Bayes classification algorithm was also used by Hao et al. [9] to analyze JavaScript code by benefitting from extended API symbol features by means of the AST. Beyond a pure malware analysis, Kapravelos et al. [17] rather chose to detect JavaScript samples, which were an evolution of known malicious files, or modified malicious instances, now tailored to be recognized as benign (evasion process). For this purpose, they developed Revolver to automatically detect evasive behavior in malicious JavaScript files, by using the AST as well as a dynamic analysis to identify similarities between JavaScript samples. Besides detecting malicious instances directly, the JavaScript AST can effectively be used to identify a programmer (for plagiarism purpose, or to indirectly detect potentially malicious files, based on the writing skills of a known malware author). For this application, Wisse and Veenman [33] extracted structural features from the AST, used n-grams to describe the coding style of an author and their frequency analysis to recognize the programmer. As for dissimulation techniques, Kaplan et al. [16] quantified with NoFus the fact that obfuscation does not imply maliciousness: this static and automatic classifier can indeed distinguish obfuscated and non-obfuscated JavaScript files, using a Bayesian classifier over the AST. More generally, Yamaguchi et al. [37] used ASTs to identify zero-day vulnerabilities. Indeed, they guided the search for new exploits by extrapolating known vulnerabilities using structural patterns extracted from the ASTs, which enabled them to find similar flaws in other projects.

Other Detection or Clustering Tools. Lexical and syntactic analyses aside, additional tools, benefitting from other features, can be found in the wild. Essential differences in structural properties between benign and malicious files can also be a way for detecting malicious PDF documents, for example, as explained by Šrndic and Laskov [31]. KIZZLE from Stock et al. [30] also aimed at clustering malware samples with a special focus on exploit kits. This malware signature compiler benefits from the fact that the attackers reuse code while delivering it in various kits. Then Kolbitsch et al. implemented ROZZLE [19], a JavaScript virtual machine exploring multiple execution paths in parallel to detect environment specific malware. In practice, it imitates multiple browser and environment configurations while dynamically crawling to detect malware. EVILSEED [12] is an approach designed by Invernizzi et al. to efficiently search the web for pages that are likely to be malicious. Its starts from an initial seed of known malicious web pages to identify other malicious ones by similarity or relation to the seed. Finally, Canali et al. [5] had also been working on a faster collection of malicious web pages with Prophiler. This filter quickly discards benign pages based on HTML-derived lexical features, the JavaScript AST, and an URL analysis.

6 Conclusion

Many malicious JavaScript samples today are obfuscated to hinder the analysis and creation of signatures. To countermand this, in this paper we proposed JaSt, a fully static AST-based analysis to automatically detect malicious JavaScript instances. The key elements of this approach are: (a) an extraction of the syntactic units contained in the files to be classified; (b) a frequency analysis of the n-grams built upon the previous features; (c) the construction of a random forest using the previous frequencies as input to either build a model or classify unknown samples and (d) the evaluation of JaSt on an extensive, up-to-date and balanced JavaScript dataset. In practice, our approach yields extremely accurate predictions (almost 99.50% of correct classification results) and has an outstanding false-negative rate of 0.54%, especially since the system is *entirely* static. Despite this high detection performance, JaSt is also quite fast with a mean throughput of 0.14 megabyte per second, while considering more than 2,400 different features, either predictive of malicious or of benign samples. Besides, this selection of abstract patterns enables our system to be resistant to common obfuscation transformations without having to execute some code. As a consequence, it cannot be foiled by malware variants whose behavior are time- or environment dependent.

To be long-time effective, JaSt has to adapt to new JavaScript instances. This adaptation process is achieved by extending the set of n-grams feature used with new, up-to-date JavaScript samples. As a matter of fact, an analysis of JavaScript instances over a few months showed that building a model each month to detect malicious variants in the current month is only effective if the training set contains enough files representative of the distribution found in the wild, and is not simply a compilation of different JavaScript waves received in the past few months. Last but not least we showed in this paper that the same benign and malicious patterns are partially found in different JavaScript families. As a consequence, a model constructed with malicious emails and benign frameworks can even be used to classify exploit kits, JavaScript games, or other web-JavaScript inputs, highlighting the similarity between different classes of malicious JavaScript.

Acknowledgments. This work would not have been possible without the help of the German Federal Office for Information Security and Kafeine DNC which provided us with materials for our experiments. We would also like to thank the anonymous reviewers of this paper for their well-appreciated feedback. This work was partially supported by the German Federal Ministry of Education and Research (BMBF) through funding for the Center for IT-Security, Privacy and Accountability (CISPA) (FKZ: 16KIS0345).

References

1. Atom: Atom the hackable text editor for the 21st Century. https://atom.io. Accessed 21 Feb 2018
2. Backes, M., Nauman, M.: LUNA: quantifying and leveraging uncertainty in android malware analysis through Bayesian machine learning. In: Euro S&P (2017)
3. Bergstra, J., Bengio, Y.: Random search for hyper-parameter optimization. J. Mach. Learn. Res. **13**, 281–305 (2012)
4. Breiman, L.: Random forests. Mach. Learn. **45**, 5–32 (2001)
5. Canali, D., Cova, M., Vigna, G., Kruegel, C.: Prophiler: a fast filter for the large-scale detection of malicious web pages. In: International Conference on World Wide Web (2011)
6. Cao, Y., Pan, X., Chen, Y., Zhuge, J.: JShield: towards real-time and vulnerability-based detection of polluted drive-by download attacks. In: Annual Computer Security Applications Conference (ACSAC) (2014)
7. Curtsinger, C., Livshits, B., Zorn, B., Seifert, C.: ZOZZLE: fast and precise in-browser javascript malware detection. In: USENIX (2011)
8. Gastwirth, J.L.: The estimation of the Lorenz curve and Gini index. Rev. Econ. Stat. **54**, 306–316 (1972)
9. Hao, Y., Liang, H., Zhang, D., Zhao, Q., Cui, B.: JavaScript malicious codes analysis based on naive Bayes classification. In: International Conference on P2P, Parallel, Grid, Cloud and Internet Computing (2014)
10. Hidayat, A.: ECMAScript Parsing Infrastructure for Multipurpose Analysis. http://esprima.org. Accessed 05 Apr 2017
11. AV-TEST - The Independent IT-Security Institute: New malware. https://www.av-test.org/en/statistics/malware. Accessed 01 Feb 2018
12. Invernizzi, L., Benvenuti, S., Cova, M., Comparetti, P.M., Kruegel, C., Vigna, G.: EVILSEED: a guided approach to finding malicious web pages. In: S&P (2012)
13. Joseph, A.D., Laskov, P., Roli, F., Tygar, J.D., Nelson, B.: Machine learning methods for computer security. In: Dagstuhl Manifestos (2013)
14. Jules, D.S.: JS inspect Detect copy-pasted and structurally similar code. https://github.com/danielstjules/jsinspect. Accessed 19 Feb 2018
15. Kantchelian, A., Tygar, J.D., Joseph, A.D.: Evasion and hardening of tree ensemble classifiers. In: International Conference on Machine Learning (2016)
16. Kaplan, S., Livshits, B., Zorn, B., Siefert, C., Curtsinger, C.: "NoFus: Automatically Detecting" + String.fromCharCode(32) + "ObFuSCateD ". toLowerCase() + "JavaScript Code". Microsoft Research Technical Report (2011)
17. Kapravelos, A., Shoshitaishvili, Y., Cova, M., Krügel, C., Vigna, G..: Revolver: an automated approach to the detection of evasive web-based malware. In: USENIX (2013)
18. Kar, D., Panigrahi, S., Sundararajan, S.: SQLiGot: detecting SQL injections attacks using graph of tokens and SVM. Comput. Secur. **60**, 206–225 (2016)
19. Kolbitsch, C., Livshits, B., Zorn, B., Seifert, C.: Rozzle: de-cloaking internet malware. In: S&P (2012)
20. Kolter, J.Z., Maloof, M.A.: Learning to detect and classify malicious executables in the wild. J. Mach. Learn. Res. **7**, 2721–2744 (2006)
21. Laskov, P., Šrndić, N.: Static detection of malicious javascript-bearing pdf documents. In: Annual Computer Security Applications Conference (ACSAC) (2011)
22. Likarish, P., Jung, E., Jo, I.: Obfuscated malicious javascript detection using classification techniques. In: International Conference on Malicious and Unwanted Software (MALWARE) (2009)

23. Pedregosa, F., Varoquaux, G., Gramfort, A., Michel, V., Thirion, B., Grisel, O., Blondel, M., Prettenhofer, P., Weiss, R., Dubourg, V., Vanderplas, J., Passos, A., Cournapeau, D., Brucher, M., Perrot, M., Duchesnay, E.: Scikit-learn: machine learning in python. J. Mach. Learn. Res. **12**, 2825–2830 (2011)
24. Powers, D.M.W.: Evaluation: from precision, recall and F-measure to ROC, informedness, markedness and correlation. J. Mach. Learn. Technol. **2**, 37–63 (2011)
25. Rao, V., Hande, K.: A comparative study of static, dynamic and hybrid analysis techniques for android malware detection. Int. J. Eng. Dev. Res. (IJEDR) **5**, 1433–1436 (2017)
26. Symantec Security Response: Mirai: what you need to know about the botnet behind recent major DDoS attacks. https://www.symantec.com/connect/blogs/mirai-what-you-need-know-about-botnet-behind-recent-major-ddos-attacks. Accessed 02 Feb 2018
27. Symantec Security Response: Petya ransomware outbreak: Here is what you need to know. https://www.symantec.com/blogs/threat-intelligence/petya-ransomware-wiper. Accessed 14 Feb 2018
28. Symantec Security Response: What you need to know about the WannaCry Ransomware. https://www.symantec.com/blogs/threat-intelligence/wannacry-ransomware-attack. Accessed 14 Feb 2018
29. Rieck, K., Krueger, T., Dewald, A.: CUJO: efficient detection and prevention of drive-by-download attacks. In: Annual Computer Security Applications Conference (ACSAC) (2010)
30. Stock, B., Livshits, B., Zorn, B.: Kizzle: a signature compiler for detecting exploit kits. In: Dependable Systems and Networks (DSN) (2016)
31. Šrndić, N., Laskov, P.: Detection of malicious pdf files based on hierarchical document structure. In: NDSS (2013)
32. Wang, K., Parekh, J.J., Stolfo, S.J.: Anagram: a content anomaly detector resistant to mimicry attack. In: Zamboni, D., Kruegel, C. (eds.) RAID 2006. LNCS, vol. 4219, pp. 226–248. Springer, Heidelberg (2006). https://doi.org/10.1007/11856214_12
33. Wisse, W., Veenman, C.J.: Scripting DNA: identifying the javascript programmer. Digit. Investig. **15**, 61–71 (2015)
34. Wressnegger, C., Schwenk, G., Arp, D., Rieck, K.: A close look on n-grams in intrusion detection: anomaly detection vs. classification. In: ACM Workshop on Artificial Intelligence and Security (AISec) (2013)
35. Xu, W., Zhang, F., Zhu, S.: The power of obfuscation techniques in malicious javascript code: a measurement study. In: International Conference on Malicious and Unwanted Software (MALWARE) (2012)
36. Xu, W., Qi, Y., Evans, D.: Automatically evading classifiers: a case study on pdf malware classifiers. In: NDSS (2016)
37. Yamaguchi, F., Lottmann, M., Rieck, K.: Generalized vulnerability extrapolation using abstract syntax trees. In: Annual Computer Security Applications Conference (ACSAC) (2012)
38. Youden, W.J.: Index for rating diagnostic tests. Cancer **3**, 32–35 (1950)

Bytecode Corruption Attacks Are Real—And How to Defend Against Them

Taemin Park[✉], Julian Lettner, Yeoul Na, Stijn Volckaert, and Michael Franz

University of California, Irvine, Irvine, USA
{tmpark,julian.lettner,yeouln,stijnv,franz}@uci.edu

Abstract. In the continuous arms race between attackers and defenders, various attack vectors against script engines have been exploited and subsequently secured. This paper explores a new attack vector that has not received much academic scrutiny: bytecode and its lookup tables. Based on our study of the internals of modern bytecode interpreters, we present four distinct strategies to achieve arbitrary code execution in an interpreter. To protect interpreters from our attack we propose two separate defense strategies: bytecode pointer checksums and non-writable enforcement. To demonstrate the feasibility of our approach, we instantiate our attacks and proposed defense strategies for Python and Lua interpreters. Our evaluation shows that the proposed defenses effectively mitigate bytecode injection attacks with low overheads of less than 16% on average.

1 Introduction

Programs written in dynamic languages execute in a virtual machine (VM). This VM typically translates the program's source code into bytecode, which it then executes in an interpreter. Some VMs also include a JIT compiler that can compile the source code or bytecode into machine code that can be executed directly by the CPU. The VM usually guarantees that the execution of the script is type and memory safe by lifting the burden of managing the application memory and run-time types off the programmer.

Unfortunately, most VMs are implemented in type and memory *unsafe* languages (specifically, C/C++) which provide direct control over memory. Consequently, memory and type safety vulnerabilities often slip into the VM itself. Malicious scripts may exploit these vulnerabilities to leak information, inject malicious code, and/or hijack control flow. The JIT-ROP attack presented by Snow et al. [1], for example, showed that a single memory corruption vulnerability in a JavaScript VM allowed a malicious script to achieve arbitrary code execution, bypassing the VM's security mechanisms.

To make matters worse, dynamic code generation is naturally susceptible to various types of exploits. The memory region that contains the bytecode or machine code must be writable while the code is being generated. This weakens one of the most effective defenses against code injection, Data Execution Prevention (DEP), as the code cache does need to be both writable and executable

© Springer International Publishing AG, part of Springer Nature 2018
C. Giuffrida et al. (Eds.): DIMVA 2018, LNCS 10885, pp. 326–348, 2018.
https://doi.org/10.1007/978-3-319-93411-2_15

(though not necessarily at the same time). Song et al. showed that it is possible to exploit the time window where JIT'ed code is writable to inject code stealthily [2]. While generating code, the VM also produces intermediate data such as bytecode and data constants which are used as input for subsequent code generation phases. Tampering with this intermediate data may also give an attacker arbitrary code execution capabilities, without having to directly hijack control-flow or corrupt the code section [3,4]. Furthermore, these problems may be worse in bytecode interpreters than in JIT engines. Contrary to JIT'ed code, bytecode does not require page-level execute permissions as it is executed by an interpreter and not by the CPU. Malicious bytecode can therefore still be injected, even if DEP is enabled.

Several recently proposed defense mechanisms mitigate code injection attacks on VMs [2–4]. Frassetto et al. proposed to move the JIT compiler and its data into a secure enclave to defend against intermediate representation (IR) code corruption attacks [4], while Microsoft added verification checksums to detect corruption of temporary code buffers in the JavaScript engine of its Edge browser [3]. However, these defenses focus solely on protecting JIT-based VMs and overlook bytecode interpreters. This is not entirely surprising because there is the belief that the potential impact of a code injection-attack on a bytecode interpreter is limited. It is assumed that injected bytecode cannot access arbitrary memory addresses or call arbitrary functions, for example. We contradict this belief by showing that bytecode injection *is* a realistic attack vector with potentially high impact. Specifically, we present several attack strategies that may be pursued to achieve arbitrary code execution in a well-protected bytecode interpreter, *even if that interpreter employs a language-level sandbox to disable access to dangerous APIs and to introspection features.* Our attack allows scripts to perform operations or to interact with the host system in a way that normally would not be allowed by the sandboxed interpreter.

We implement our attack in the standard Python and Lua interpreters. Python and Lua are widely used to write add-ons and plugins for large applications. Bugs in these applications may allow remote attackers to execute arbitrary scripts (cf. Sect. 3). Attackers can also disguise malicious scripts or packages as benign software and distribute them through standard package managers and distribution channels where users may unknowingly download them [5]. By using the attack techniques presented in this paper, scripts downloaded through such channels can perform malicious actions even if the user executes them in an interpreter with a language-level sandbox (that normally prohibits such actions).

Finally, we present a simple and effective defense against bytecode injection that can be deployed without hardware support and with limited run-time overhead.

In summary, we contribute the following:

- We study the internals of modern bytecode interpreters, uncover several potential attack vectors, and show why bytecode corruption is challenging.
- We present an attack that enables arbitrary code execution in an interpreter by corrupting the bytecode and data caches. Our attack starts with an infor-

mation disclosure step which infers the layout of the heap. Depending on the layout of the heap, we pursue one of four different attack strategies when constructing the attack payload. We implement our attack in two different languages/interpreters with different architectures: CPython and Lua, stack-based and register-based VMs, respectively.
- We propose a defense that protects the integrity of the bytecode caches and evaluate a reference implementation for both interpreters. Our evaluation shows that the suggested defense successfully prevents all four of our attack strategies.

2   Background

Bytecode interpreters translate input programs into bytecode that encodes instructions for a virtual stack or virtual register machine. Most virtual stack machine instructions operate on data that is stored on a stack. An integer addition instruction, for example, typically pops the top two elements off the stack, adds them together, and pushes their sum onto the stack. By contrast, instructions for a register machine operate on data that is stored in addressable registers. An integer addition instruction for a register machine could load its input operands from registers R1 and R2, add them, and store the result in register R3.

Regardless of the type of virtual machine that is being emulated, the size of the bytecode instruction set is small compared to a typical instruction set for a physical architecture. The latest version of the x86_64 instruction set contains well over a thousand instructions, whereas the latest version of the bytecode instruction set used in CPython contains just over a hundred instructions.

2.1   Bytecode Storage

DEP prevents both static and JIT-compiled machine code from being executed while it is writable and vice versa. DEP is ineffective for bytecode, however, because bytecode can be executed even when it is stored on non-executable pages. To prevent bytecode from being overwritten while it is being executed, the interpreter should mark the bytecode as read-only. This is generally not possible because most interpreters store bytecode on the heap, where it typically resides on the same pages as data that must remain writable at all times.

As a consequence of this design decision, it is possible to overwrite the byte-code even while it is executing. It is also easier to discover the location of the bytecode cache than the location of machine code. While the latter requires an arbitrary memory read vulnerability [1], we show that it is possible to discover the location of the bytecode cache with a vulnerability that can only reveal the contents of the heap.

2.2   Data Encapsulation

Interpreters typically encapsulate all program variables, including those of primitive types, into objects. Every object has a header which identifies the type of the encapsulated value. Figure 1, for example, shows two objects representing an integer and a string value. While the integer object only contains one field that stores the actual integer value, the string object has multiple fields to store different properties of the string.

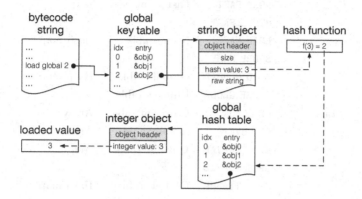

Fig. 1. Loading a global variable through a hash map-like table.

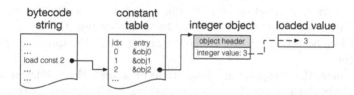

Fig. 2. Loading a value through the constant table.

2.3 Data Access

One of the most notable differences between machine instructions and bytecode instructions is how they access program data. Machine instructions typically encode register numbers, memory addresses, and word-sized constants as instruction operands. Bytecode instructions, by contrast, refer to memory addresses and constants via an indirection layer.

Figure 2 illustrates this difference by showing a bytecode instruction that loads a constant onto the stack. The constant is not embedded in the instruction itself. Instead, the instruction's operand denotes an entry in a constant table. This entry also does not contain the constant itself but instead refers to the address of the object that encapsulates the actual constant. These indirection layers limit the capabilities of an attacker who only can manipulate bytecode. Specifically, an attacker cannot load/store arbitrary constants/variables, call arbitrary functions, or access arbitrary memory locations without the help of built-in tables. To perform a system call, for example, there must be a table

Table 1. Supporting data structures in Python and Lua. Functions have their own constant and locals tables, but share globals tables.

Interpreter	Opcodes	Data structures	Type
Python	LOAD_CONST	Constant table	Array
	LOAD_FAST	Fast locals table	Array
	STORE_FAST		
	LOAD_NAME	Name table	Hash map
	STORE_NAME		
	LOAD_GLOBAL	Globals table	Hash map
	STORE_GLOBAL	Builtins table	
Lua	OP_LOADK	Constant table	Array
	OP_MOVE	Locals table	Array
	OP_GETUPVAL	Upvalue table	Array
	OP_SETUPVAL		
	OP_GETTABUP	Globals table	Hash map
	OP_SETTABUP		

entry that refers to a function object, which in turn contains the address of a system call function. The attacker needs to manually inject this entry and the function object because they are unlikely to exist while the interpreter executes benign scripts.

Table 1 lists the supporting data structures and their related bytecode instructions for Python and Lua. When executing a bytecode instruction supported by an array-typed data structure, the interpreter treats the bytecode's operand as an index into the array. The LOAD_CONST instruction, illustrated in Fig. 2, is one example of such an instruction.

Instructions supported by a hash map-typed data structure, such as LOAD_GLOBAL, shown in Fig. 1, access their target through a triple indirection. First, the interpreter uses the instruction's operand as an index into a key table containing strings. The interpreter loads the string that the instruction points to, hashes it, and uses the hash value as an index into a hash map table (i.e., the global hash table in this case). Then, the interpreter loads the object reference from the hash map table, and loads the data stored in this object.

2.4   Function Calls

Any function that is called from within a script has a function object associated with it. The function object contains a field indicating the type of the function (i.e., bytecode or native), as well as a pointer to the function's executable code (for native functions), or the function's bytecode object (which, in turn, points to the bytecode string).

To call a function from within bytecode, the caller first loads the function arguments onto the interpreter stack. Then, the caller loads the target function object from the name table (which is a hash map-like data structure). Next, the caller uses a function call bytecode instruction to prepare an argument list array, and to invoke the interpreter's call dispatcher function.

This dispatcher function receives pointers to the target function object and the argument list as its arguments. If the target function is a native C function, the dispatcher will call that C function with a context pointer as its first argument and a pointer to the argument list as its second argument. This context pointer is stored in the function object itself, and can therefore be overwritten by an attacker.

Calling Arbitrary C Functions. The set of C functions that can be called by overwriting or injecting function objects on the heap is limited. The reason is that C functions normally expect to find their arguments in certain registers or stack slots, as stipulated in the platform's application binary interface standard.

However, bytecode interpreters pass arguments differently when calling C functions. Specifically, the aforementioned dispatcher function passes pointers to the context and to the argument list structure as the sole arguments to any C function. The context pointer is an implementation-specific pointer that can usually be controlled by the attacker. The argument list pointer, however, cannot be controlled by the attacker. Moreover, unless the C function is aware of the calling conventions used by the interpreter, it will not correctly extract the actual arguments from the argument list.

Consequently, the set of C functions that an attacker can call by corrupting function objects only includes functions that expect less than two arguments and functions that are aware of the calling conventions used in the interpreter.

2.5   Dangerous Interpreter Features

Most bytecode interpreters are designed under the assumption that the end-user will only run benign scripts on benign inputs. These interpreters therefore implement many features that could be abused if either the script or its inputs turn out to be malicious. Recurring examples of such features include the following.

The Eval Function. First introduced in LISP, the `eval` function present in many interpreted languages parses a string argument as source code, translates the source code into bytecode, and then executes the bytecode. Many remote code execution vulnerabilities in scripts are caused by allowing attackers to supply the string argument to `eval` (e.g., CVE-2017-9807, CVE-2016-9949, and scientific literature [6]).

Direct Bytecode Access. Many scripting languages, including Python and Lua, treat functions as mutable objects with a bytecode field that contains the raw bytecode instructions for their associated function. The script can read and overwrite this bytecode field, either directly or through an API. Python scripts, for example, can access bytecode through the __code.__co_code field that exists in every function object, whereas Lua scripts can use the string.dump and load functions to serialize the raw bytecode instructions for a given function object and deserialize raw bytecode instructions into a new function object respectively.

Dynamic Script Loading. Scripting languages often allow loading and execution of additional script code stored in the file system. Python, for example, supports the __import__ function to load modules dynamically, whereas Lua provides the require function for this same purpose. An attacker that controls the arguments to these functions may be able to introduce malicious code into an otherwise benign script.

Native Code Support. Most bytecode interpreters including CPython and Lua support calling native code from the interpreted bytecode through a so-called Foreign Function Interface (FFI). The FFI allows the language to be extended with functionality that is not or cannot be made available within the scripting language itself. From a security perspective, the disadvantage of the FFI is that it can extend the attack surface of the interpreter. Like the interpreter itself, functions called through the FFI are often written in C or C++, which are neither type- nor memory-safe. Vulnerabilities in such functions therefore affect the entire interpreter.

Fully-Featured APIs for Accessing System Resources. Python and Lua both expose APIs for creating, modifying, and deleting system resources such as files, sockets, threads, and virtual memory mappings. The reference interpreters for both languages impose no restrictions on how the script uses these APIs. Typically, the API invocations are only subject to access control checks by the OS itself, and the script therefore runs with the same privileges of its invoker.

2.6   Running Untrusted Scripts

If a bytecode interpreter is used to run untrusted scripts, it is often necessary to restrict or block access to the dangerous features described in Sect. 2.5 or even remove them altogether. Broadly speaking, there are two different approaches to restricting access to dangerous language/interpreter features.

Language-Level Sandboxing. A language-level sandbox restricts access to dangerous features by intercepting, monitoring, and (potentially) manipulating function calls within the interpreter itself. As an example, you can build a language-level sandbox for Java programs based on the Java Security Manager [7]. This Security Manager wraps calls to dangerous functions to perform fine-grained access control checks. Similarly, lua_sandbox wraps internal interpreter functions to disable script access to certain Lua packages and functions [8].

Language-level sandboxing can also be achieved through source code-level transformations. Caja, for example, transforms untrusted HTML, CSS, and JavaScript code to isolate it from the rest of a web page [9]. RestrictedPython similarly rewrites Python bytecode to restrict access to certain APIs [10].

Finally, one can just remove dangerous functionality from the interpreter altogether, which is viable if the sole purpose of the interpreter is to run untrusted scripts. An example of such a stripped-down interpreter is the Python runtime environment in Google App Engine [11], which does not support native code, does not support direct bytecode access, and does not contain certain system APIs (e.g., for writing to the file system).

The advantage of language-level sandboxes is that they can deploy fine-grained access control checks to not just the APIs for accessing system resources, but also to internal functions that can be invoked without interacting with the OS. The disadvantage is that language-level sandboxes lack a hardware-enforced boundary between the sandbox and the potentially malicious script or program. Malicious scripts can therefore escape from such sandboxes if any part of the interpreter contains an exploitable memory vulnerability.

Application-Level Sandboxing. Application-level sandboxes restrict access to system resources by interposing on the system calls made by the interpreter. Since 2005, Linux offers the `seccomp` API for this purpose, while older sandboxes could build on the `ptrace` infrastructure.

The advantage of application-level sandboxes over language-level sandboxes is that they are protected from the interpreter by a hardware-enforced boundary (enforced through the memory paging mechanism). The disadvantages are that they can only restrict access to system APIs, and not to internal interpreter functions. Ideally, an interpreter therefore uses both language-level sandboxing and application-level sandboxing techniques when running untrusted scripts.

3   Threat Model and Assumptions

The goal of our work is to achieve arbitrary code execution through injected bytecode and data. Our threat model therefore excludes attacks that corrupt static code or that introduce illegitimate control flow in the static code (i.e., ROP attacks). Our model is consistent with related work in this area [2,4,12].

Strong Protection for Static Code. We assume that the target system deploys state-of-the-art protection for static code. Specifically, we assume that Address Space Layout Randomization (ASLR) is enabled and applied to the stack, heap, main executable, and all shared libraries. We assume that machine code-injection attacks are impossible because Data Execution Prevention (DEP) is enforced. We assume that code-reuse attacks are mitigated by fine-grained control-flow integrity [13–15].

Memory Vulnerability. We assume that the bytecode interpreter has a memory vulnerability that allows attackers to allocate a buffer on the heap, and to read/write out of the bounds of that buffer. The CVE-2016-5636 vulnerability in CPython is one example that permits this type of buffer overflow. Note that we do *not* assume an arbitrary read-write vulnerability.

Interpreter Protection. We assume that the interpreter deploys a language-level sandbox (cf. Sect. 2.6) that disables all dangerous features listed in Sect. 2.5.

Consequently, we assume that the scripts cannot access or modify bytecode directly. We further assume that there is no application-level sandbox in place. If the interpreter does use an application-level sandbox, then our attack by itself does not suffice to escape from the sandbox. It could, however, serve as a useful building block for a sandbox escape attack.

Attacker. We assume that the attacker can provide the script to be executed by the protected interpreter. The attacker-provided script does not contain any malicious features that will be blocked by the language-level sandbox. We also assume that the attacker knows the version and configuration of the interpreter, and that the attacker can run this same version locally on a machine under his/her control.

3.1   Realism

The assumption that an attacker can provide the script to be executed by the victim is realistic. Many large applications can be customized through Python or Lua scripts, and have App Store-like distribution systems where developers can freely share their scripts with other users of the same application.

Numerous video games [16], including the hugely popular World of Warcraft (WoW), for example, allows users to write Lua scripts to customize the game interface. Developers can upload these add-ons to dedicated fan sites, where they are downloaded by millions of users. Another example is Python's package manager PyPi, where rogue packages have been known to appear [5]. Packages downloaded through PyPi can subsequently be used in any Python-compliant interpreter, including interpreters with a language-level sandbox.

These script distribution systems usually lack the developer verification and malware scanning features that are commonly employed by application stores for mobile platforms. It is therefore relatively easy to disguise a malicious script as a legitimate piece of software, and to distribute it to a lot of users.

An attacker could also inject malicious script code into other (benign) scripts. We studied recent CVEs from 2014 to 2018 and found several examples of vulnerabilities that permit such script injection attacks (e.g., CVE-2017-9807, CVE-2017-7235, CVE-2017-10803, CVE-2016-9949, CVE-2015-6531, CVE-2015-5306, CVE-2015-5242, CVE-2015-3446, CVE-2014-3593, CVE-2014-2331). The CVE-2017-9807 vulnerability in OpenWebif, for example, existed because OpenWebif called Python's `eval` function on the contents of an HTTP GET parameter. An attacker could exploit this vulnerability by submitting a full script as part of this parameter.

4   Attacking Bytecode

Our attack achieves arbitrary code execution in a bytecode interpreter by simultaneously overwriting the bytecode of a single function and the supporting data structures accessed by that function (e.g., the constant table). Overwriting just the bytecode generally does not suffice, because that would force us to reuse only existing constants and variables.

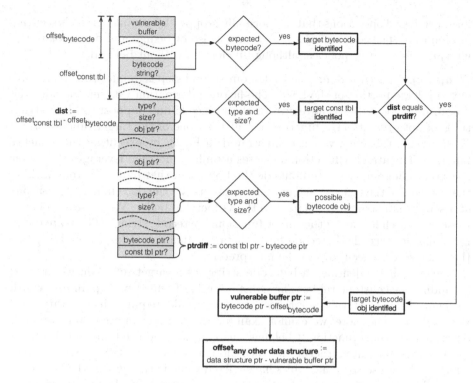

Fig. 3. Overview of our heap layout inference step. By disclosing heap contents and identifying three data structures belonging to the same target function, we can subsequently follow pointers to other data structures by calculating their offset relative to the vulnerable buffer.

4.1 Attack Overview

The attack proceeds in five steps:

Preparation: We load a script that contains an attacker function, at least one target function, and a blueprint buffer for the injected code. Target functions are benign functions whose bytecode and supporting data structures are easily recognizable in memory. Each target function contains a unique sequence of harmless operations that is translated into an easily identifiable bytecode string. We also use a unique and large number of constants and local variables in each target function, which allows us to recognize the function's constant/locals tables.

The blueprint buffer contains the raw bytecode sequence the attacker wishes to inject. In most cases, we cannot inject the blueprint buffer as-is, because its bytecode attempts to load data from data structures we cannot overwrite. We therefore rewrite the blueprint buffer in a later step to ensure that it accesses the correct data.

Note that the attack script itself looks benign to the interpreter. The script does not use introspection features, nor does it call any privileged APIs or perform privileged operations that are normally stopped by the interpreter's security mechanisms. The code we inject, by contrast, is not benign and does violate the interpreter's security policies, although it does so without being detected.

Heap Layout Inference: The goal of our second step is to infer the precise layout of a large portion of the heap. The layout information we infer includes the absolute positions (i.e., addresses) of the bytecode and supporting data structures of both the attacker function and at least one of the target functions.

We begin this step, which is illustrated in Fig. 3, by executing the attacker function. The attacker function allocates a buffer, and then leverages the buffer overflow vulnerability to read outside the bounds of that buffer, thereby leaking the contents of the heap. Based on these contents, we can determine the positions of a set of data structures relative to the vulnerable buffer. We do so as follows. First, we search for one of the target functions' bytecode strings. These are easily recognizable since the bytecode for each target function is known and remains the same across executions of the interpreter.

Once we have identified a bytecode string for a target function, we proceed to finding its constant table. The constant table is filled with pointers, which we cannot follow at this point because that would require an arbitrary read vulnerability. Therefore, we cannot examine the contents of a constant table to determine to which function it belongs. Instead, we read the type and size fields for any potential data structure we encounter. Lua uses a bitfield to encode data structure types, so constant tables have a fixed value in the type field. CPython's type fields are pointers to constant strings, which are always loaded at the same address (relative to the image base). In both cases, potential constant tables are easily recognizable.

Once we have determined that a data structure is a potential constant table, we read its size field. Our attacker script ensures that each target function has a large and unique number of constants in its constant table. We do this by declaring a local variable which stores a list of constant numbers in each target function. The size value of the constant table therefore uniquely defines to which function it belongs.

Having identified the bytecode string and the constant table for a specific target function, we now attempt to find the bytecode object for that function. Again, we can recognize potential bytecode objects based on their type field. Once we identify a potential bytecode object, we can determine if it belongs to the same function as the already identified bytecode string and constant table by verifying that the distance between the bytecode string pointer value and the constant table pointer value in the bytecode object matches the distance between the data structures we identified. If these distances match, we assume that we have found the right bytecode object, and that we now know the absolute addresses of the bytecode object, bytecode string, and constant table we disclosed.

At this point, we can follow any heap pointer to an address that is higher than that of the vulnerable buffer, and we can ultimately disclose the full layout of the heap area that follows the vulnerable buffer. We expect that the attacker will also be able to find at least one code pointer on the heap, thereby identifying the base address of the interpreter's executable code section. This is necessary to locate the C functions we wish to call in our attack. Recent work shows that this is a realistic expectation [17].

Attack Strategy Selection: Based on the heap layout information, we can select an attack strategy and inject the payload. The payload injection is subject to three constraints. First, we cannot write any data at addresses lower than that of the vulnerable buffer, because the vulnerability we are exploiting allows buffer read/write overflows, but not underflows. Second, for the same reason of the first constraint, the payload we inject must be contiguous. Third, we must be careful when overwriting the currently executing bytecode string or any of the data structures that may be accessed by the currently executing code, since doing so might crash the interpreter.

As a result of these three constraints, it is not always possible to overwrite the bytecode string and the constant table of a target function. We have therefore devised multiple attack strategies, each targeting different data structures. We describe these strategies in Sect. 4.2.

Payload Construction: We now craft the attack payload, which consists of a bytecode string, and a data structure containing references to the data the attacker wishes to use in the injected bytecode. We provide more details on the payload construction in Sect. 4.2.

Execution: At this point, we overwrite the bytecode and data structures we identified in the second step with the payload crafted in the fourth step. Finally, we transfer control to the target function we overwrote to trigger our injected code.

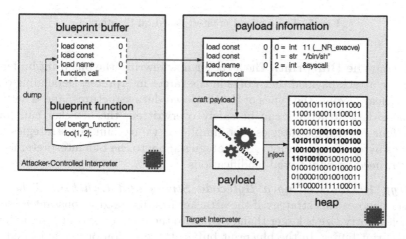

Fig. 4. The attacker creates a blueprint buffer by dumping a blueprint function. The blueprint buffer serves as the starting point for the attack payload construction.

4.2   Crafting the Payload

We craft the payload based on an attacker-provided blueprint buffer. The blueprint buffer contains the raw bytecode string to be injected. The attacker must additionally provide information about the data to be used in the injected bytecode.

Figure 4 shows the process of creating a blueprint buffer, and converting it into an attack payload. The attacker begins by writing a blueprint function in an off-line instance of the interpreter. We assume that this off-line instance of the interpreter is controlled by the attacker, and that it provides access language introspection features (unlike the target interpreter the attacker wishes to attack).

The blueprint function has the desired attack semantics, but does not necessarily operate on the desired data. For example, if the attack should call a C function that is not normally exposed to the scripting language, then the attacker can just write a blueprint function that calls a different (accessible) function instead, dump the blueprint, and adjust the target of the function call while crafting the payload.

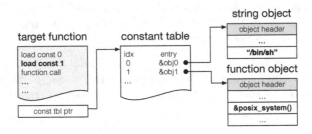

Fig. 5. The payload created based on Strategy 1.

Rewriting the Blueprint. The attacker now rewrites the blueprint buffer into a concrete attack payload that works in the target interpreter. Depending on the inferred heap layout, the types of the disclosed data structures, and whether or not these data structures can be safely overwritten, the attacker can pursue one of four rewriting strategies. For simplicity, we explain our strategies using Python's bytecode convention. All strategies apply to the Lua interpreter as well, however, needing only trivial modifications.

Strategy 1: Overwriting a Bytecode String and Constant Table. The attacker chooses this strategy if the attacker has disclosed a constant table and the table's entry size is larger than or equal to the number of load instructions in the blueprint buffer. In the blueprint buffer, the function object is loaded from the *name table*. The attacker therefore needs to adjust the load instruction to a load from a constant table, i.e., LOAD_CONST $id. The attacker also needs to inject the objects with the prepared data and update the constant table so that each table entry points to the injected object. The resulting payload of Strategy 1 is shown in Fig. 5. LOAD_CONST 0 loads a function argument, "/bin/sh", then LOAD_CONST 1 loads the function object overwritten with the address of *posix_system()* function which is a wrapper function in CPython that unboxes argument objects and calls C system() function with the unboxed arguments. Next, we use a FUNC_CALL instruction to call the injected C function. We could also call the system() function directly because it expects just one argument (cf. Sect. 2.4). In both cases, we are able to launch a system shell, which is normally not allowed in the sandboxed interpreter.

Strategy 2: Overwriting a Bytecode String and Hash Map-Like Table. If the attacker only found a hash map-like table or the target constant table size is too small to cover all the load instructions in the blueprint buffer, the attacker selects this strategy. Manipulating hash map-like structures is challenging, however, due to the multi-level indirections and the use of a hash function (see Sect. 2.3). The underlying idea of this strategy is to simplify the hash map manipulation by making the key table entries point to integer objects instead of string objects. This way, the attacker can access the hash map as if it were an array-like structure.

The implementation details can vary depending on how the interpreter accesses the hash map-like table. In CPython, the interpreter maintains a dedicated key table for all hash map-like structures. The LOAD_GLOBAL instruction fetches a key from the global key table, and then uses this key as an index into the global hash table. In this architecture, the attacker can overwrite the key table so that each key table entry points to an integer object written by the attacker. Lua, on the other hand, requires two bytecode instructions to load data from a hash map, one for loading the key and one for fetching the value. Moreover, Lua does not maintain dedicated key tables for any of its hash maps. Instead, the key can be loaded from any array-like table. The attacker can therefore convert an existing array-like tables into a key table and fill it with references to integer objects.

Similar to Strategy 1, the attacker replaces the bytecode dump of previous load instructions with that of the bytecode sequence for accessing hash map-like structures as described above. The attacker then changes entries in the hash map which point to attacker's objects.

Strategy 3: Overwriting a Bytecode String and Loadable Object. If the attacker is unable to update entries in any tables, he can shape his payload as a single function using this strategy. Instead of using existing tables, the attacker crafts a constant table and adjusts the bytecode and updates the data according as in Strategy 1. The attacker then prepares a bytecode object pointing to the adjusted bytecode buffer and attacker's constant table. To be able to load this bytecode object to the interpreter's stack (or to a register in a register-based machine), the attacker has to overwrite any loadable object with the bytecode object. To do so, the attacker prepares a unique constant object in the preparation step so that its data structure can be easily found in the heap layout inference step. The attacker then overwrites this constant object with the bytecode object, thereby the attacker's bytecode object can be loaded on the stack through the constant table. Based on this loaded bytecode object, the attacker makes a function object which itself becomes the attacker's payload to call the associated function. To do so, the target function's bytecode should be over-written with two bytecode instructions. One is to create a function object using a bytecode object loaded on the interpreter's stack. The other is to call the function in the function object.

Strategy 4: Injecting Bytecode and Overwriting a Bytecode Object. In Strategy 4, the attacker injects bytecode instead of overwriting the existing bytecode buffer. To this end, the attacker injects the bytecode on the heap and overwrites the bytecode pointer in the bytecode object with the address of the injected bytecode as shown in Fig. 6. Before injecting the bytecode, the attacker still needs to adjust the bytecode in the blueprint buffer and update the prepared data according to the available data structures (again, the same step as in Strategies 1 and 2).

5 Defense

We designed and prototyped a defense that thwarts the presented as well as other bytecode injection and overwrite attacks. The main goal of our defense is to protect the integrity of bytecode. The design of our defense is inspired by existing defenses against code cache corruption attacks [3,18]. We propose two defense techniques: making bytecode strings read-only, and verifying bytecode targets during function calls. When combined, this effectively defeats all four of our attack strategies.

First, as shown in Fig. 7, we make all bytecode strings read-only so that the attacker cannot overwrite them. This specifically stops attack strategies 1 through 3, which overwrite the bytecode string of a target function. We implemented this feature by modifying the interpreter's memory manager and parser.

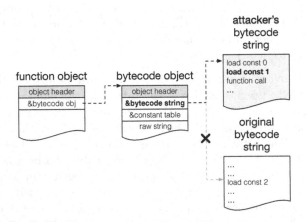

Fig. 6. The payload created based on Strategy 4.

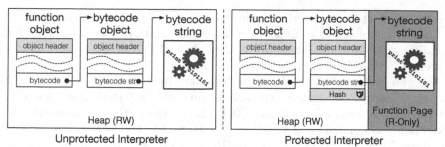

Fig. 7. Overview of our defense. We prevent bytecode strings from being overwritten by placing them in read-only memory. Bytecode injection attacks are prevented by verifying the bytecode pointer hash before executing a function.

Normally, when the interpreter parses a source function and translates it to bytecode, it allocates and stores that bytecode on the heap. We modified the interpreter to allocate a dedicated page for each function's bytecode string, and mark this page as read-only when the source function is fully translated.

This first defense technique prevents valid bytecode strings from being overwritten. However, it does not prevent bytecode injection attacks. Specifically, an attacker can still inject bytecode on the heap, and overwrite the bytecode string pointer in a bytecode object to point it to the injected bytecode instead. We implemented a second defense mechanism that prevents this type of attack. Concretely, we added a bytecode pointer verifier that checks the integrity of a function's bytecode pointer whenever it is called.

We extended the interpreter's parser to generate bytecode pointer checksums whenever it finalizes the translation of a source function into bytecode. We generate these checksums by calculating the hash of the concatenated value: $BytecodePointerValue||BytecodePointerLocation$.

As our hash function, we used the publicly available HighwayHash, which is an optimized version of SipHash. Both SipHash and HighwayHash are keyed hash functions. We generate a random hash key when the interpreter starts and prevent it from leaking by (i) keeping it stored in a dedicated CPU register at all times, (ii) using gcc's `-ffixed-reg` option to prevent reuse or spilling of that register, and (iii) customizing the hash function so it loads the hash key from the dedicated register and so it restores the old values of all registers that we might move the key into. Our bytecode pointer verifier recalculates and verifies the checksum whenever the interpreter invokes a bytecode function. The verifier effectively prevents strategies 3 and 4, which rely on a malicious function call, because the checksum verification will fail before the attacker's bytecode is executed.

6 Evaluation

We implemented our attack and defense for two commonly used bytecode interpreters: CPython 2.7.12 and Lua 5.3.2. We retrofitted a slightly altered version of a known heap buffer overflow vulnerability into CPython (CVE-2016-5636) and added a similar bug to Lua. We constructed an attack that launches a shell by calling `system("/bin/ls")`. We verified that all four of our proposed attack strategies succeed in both interpreters.

We also evaluated the run-time performance impact of our defense by running the Python Performance Benchmark Suite [19] for CPython and the Computer Language Benchmarks Game [20] for Lua. We ran these benchmarks on a GNU/Linux system running Ubuntu 14.04 LTS x64. The system has an eight-core Intel Xeon E5-2660 CPU and 64Gb of RAM. Figures 8 and 9 show our results.

The run-time performance impact of the first part of our defense (making bytecode read-only) is generally negligible. Only `hg_startup`, `python_startup`, and `python_startup_no_site` slow down noticeably. These benchmarks measure the startup time of the interpreter, which is generally short, but do not measure the execution of any bytecode. The other benchmarks do include execution of actual bytecode.

In these other benchmarks, our checksum verification incurs run-time overheads of less than 16% on average. Since our checksum verification checks occur at every function call, the overhead is directly proportional to the number of function calls and returns. `spectralnorm`, and `binary_trees` benchmarks in Lua execute a significant number of recursive functions, which produces numerous function calls and returns, and thus high overhead.

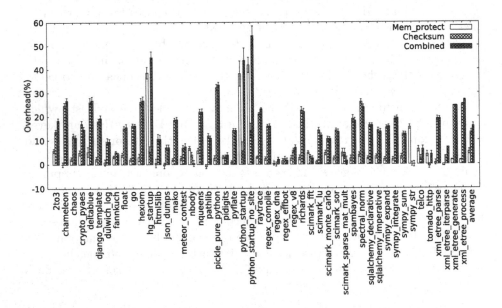

Fig. 8. Run-time overhead in the Python Performance Benchmark Suite.

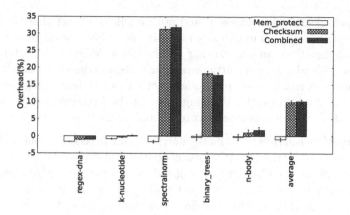

Fig. 9. Run-time overhead in the Computer Language Benchmarks Game for Lua.

7   Security Analysis

While our defense successfully stops all four of our proposed strategies, an attacker could still attempt to bypass it as follows:

Pure Data-Injection Attacks: The current implementation of our defense only protects against bytecode overwrite and injection attacks. While this suffices to thwart all four of our proposed attack strategies, we do believe it might be possible to mount a pure data-injection attack that also achieves arbitrary code execution. In such an attack, the attacker would overwrite or inject new data to alter the behavior of a benign function without overwriting that function's bytecode.

To block these attacks, one can apply the same conceptual techniques we proposed in this paper to protect all of the interpreter's data structures. Immutable data structures such as constant tables can be moved to read-only pages, while mutable structures can be extended with verification checksums.

Partial State Corruption Attacks in Multi-threaded Scripts: The byte-code interpreters we evaluated parse and translate source functions into bytecode lazily (i.e., when the function is first called). Therefore, there is a time window after the interpreter has fully initialized for which source functions may be stored in a partially translated state in writable memory. Recent work by Song et al. [2] and Frassetto et al. [4] showed that it is possible to overwrite this partially generated state in interpreters that support multi-threaded scripting languages. Our defense is, in principle, also vulnerable to such attacks. To prevent such attacks, we could offload the parsing and bytecode translation to an external process, as was done by Song et al. [2].

Checksum Forging: We protect pointers to bytecode strings with a verification checksum to prevent attackers from forging bytecode objects pointing to byte-code strings stored on the heap. If an attacker can create a bytecode object with the correct checksum, our defense would not be able to detect that the bytecode string it points to is stored in writable memory. We prevent such attacks by using a keyed hash function, and by storing the key in a dedicated register which is never leaked. We also prevent attackers from reusing correct bytecode pointers and checksums to redirect one bytecode function to a different, legitimate bytecode function. We achieve this by using not just the bytecode pointer itself, but also the location where it is stored as input to our hash function.

Checksum Alternatives: As an alternative to our bytecode pointer checksum, we could have used a true HMAC (as was done in Subversive-C [18]), or a MAC-AES (as was done in CCFI [21]). We opted not to use an HMAC because our input (i.e., the concatenation of the bytecode pointer and its storage location) is fixed-length. An HMAC therefore does not increase security over our scheme. We did not implement the MAC-AES scheme used in CCFI because it requires many reserved registers, as opposed to just one register in our case.

8   Related Work

Most of the existing work in this area focuses on code-injection attacks and defenses for JIT-based VMs. The security of pure bytecode interpreters has received little attention in the academic community.

8.1   Direct Code Injection

Early JIT-based VMs either left the JIT-compiled code writable at all times, or mapped two copies (backed by the same physical memory pages) of the JIT-compiled code into the VM's virtual address space: one writable and one executable. In both of those cases, an attacker could simply inject code into the JIT code cache by locating it in memory and overwriting it. To prevent such attacks, all major browsers and high-performance JIT engines have now adapted Data Execution Prevention, and they generally only map one copy of the JIT code cache into virtual memory at any given time. The code cache is made writable only while code is being generated, and the JIT engine makes the cache non-writable while executing JIT-compiled code. We enforce the equivalent of Data Execution Prevention for bytecode by moving all bytecode strings to read-only memory. However, Song et al. showed that the timing window during code generation in which JIT'ed code is writable is sufficiently large to still inject code directly into the code cache [2]. The authors proposed to mitigate this attack by relocating the dynamic code generator to a separate process in which the code cache remains writable, while the original JIT process only maps a read-only view of the generated code.

8.2   JIT Spraying

The JIT spraying attack presented by Blazakis injects code indirectly [12]. Blazakis observed that JIT compilers copy constant integers unmodified into the JIT-compiled code region. An attacker can therefore embed instructions into constants used in a script to inject short code snippets into the JIT code cache. The injected code can be executed by jumping into the middle of instructions that encode the injected constants.

This attack was initially mitigated using a defense called constant blinding [22]. Constant blinding masks embedded constants by XORing them with a random constant value before they are used. However, this defense has since been bypassed by Athanasakis et al. [23], who showed that JIT spraying is also possible with smaller constants and that applying constant blinding to smaller constants is prohibitively expensive. Similarly, Maisuradze et al. demonstrated a variant of the JIT spraying attack that uses carefully placed branch statements to inject useful code into the code cache [24]. This attack cannot be mitigated by constant blinding at all.

As an alternative to constant blinding, Homescu et al. proposed to apply code randomization to JIT-compiled code [25]. With code randomization, it is still possible to spray the code cache with machine code that is embedded in constants, but the location of these constants becomes less predictable.

8.3 JIT Code Reuse

Snow et al.'s JIT-ROP attack showed that code randomization for JIT-compiled code can be bypassed by disclosing a pointer to the JIT code cache, and by recursively disassembling the code starting from the instruction pointed to by the disclosed pointer [1]. This technique allows attackers to discover the locations of injected constants, which they can then jump to to execute the embedded code. Execute-No-Read [26,27] and destructive code read defenses [28,29] normally prevent such code-disclosure attacks, but were proven ineffective in the context of JIT VMs [30].

8.4 Intermediate Data Structure Corruption

Theori proposed an attack that corrupts a temporary native code buffer in Microsoft's JavaScript engine (Chakra) [3]. This temporary buffer is used to store machine code before the JIT compiler emits it into a non-writable memory region. Microsoft subsequently added checksum verification logic to the JavaScript engine to verify integrity of the temporary buffer. Similar to this attack, Frassetto et al. corrupt intermediate representation (IR) code which the JIT compiler temporarily produces from bytecode to apply code optimizations and to generate machine code [4]. To defend against this attack, Frassetto et al. proposed a defense called JITGuard, which moves the JIT compiler and its data into an Intel SGX environment that is shielded from the application. JITGuard emits code to a secret region which is only known to the JIT compiler. Since the code is inaccessible to the attacker this also prevents code-reuse attacks targeting JIT'ed code. Our work bears similarity with these approaches in that we corrupt internal data structures of the VM to cause malicious code execution.

Unlike the previous approaches, however, we corrupt *bytecode* which is considered more challenging to manipulate due to its restricted capabilities. Frassetto et al. mentioned in their discussion that corrupting bytecode is challenging and is out of scope [4].

Schuster et al. [31] and subsequent works [18,32] presented whole-function code-reuse attacks that defeat strong CFI and code randomization defenses. These attacks exploit the dynamic dispatch mechanisms present in C++ and Objective-C resp. The general approach is similar to our attack strategies 3 and 4 which rely on a malicious function call. Our defense is also inspired by existing work [3,18,21] that uses hash checksums to verify the integrity of sensitive pointers, runtime metadata, and JIT code caches, respectively.

9   Conclusion

We presented an attack that achieves arbitrary code execution in bytecode interpreters that deploy language-level security mechanisms to prevent unauthorized access to files, sockets, or APIs. Our attack leverages a heap-based buffer overflow vulnerability in the interpreter to leak the contents of its heap, infer the heap layout, and overwrite or inject bytecode and program data. We also presented a defense that thwarts our attack by moving all bytecode to read-only memory pages, and by adding integrity checks to all bytecode pointer dereferences.

We evaluated our attack and defense on CPython 2.7.12 and Lua 5.3.2. Our evaluation shows that our defense incurs an average run-time overhead of less than 16% over a large set of Python and Lua benchmarks.

Acknowledgments. We would like to thank Stephen Crane, Bart Coppens, our shepherd Vasileios Kemerlis, and the anonymous reviewers for their valuable input.

This material is based upon work partially supported by the Defense Advanced Research Projects Agency (DARPA) under contracts FA8750-15-C-0124 and FA8750-15-C-0085, by the National Science Foundation under award numbers CNS-1513837 and CNS-1619211, and by the Office for Naval Research under award number N00014-17-1-2782.

Any opinions, findings, and conclusions or recommendations expressed in this material are those of the authors and do not necessarily reflect the views of the Defense Advanced Research Projects Agency (DARPA), its Contracting Agents, the National Science Foundation, the Office for Naval Research, or any other agency of the U.S. Government.

References

1. Snow, K.Z., Monrose, F., Davi, L., Dmitrienko, A., Liebchen, C., Sadeghi, A.: Just-in-time code reuse: on the effectiveness of fine-grained address space layout randomization. In: IEEE Symposium on Security and Privacy (S&P) (2013)
2. Song, C., Zhang, C., Wang, T., Lee, W., Melski, D.: Exploiting and protecting dynamic code generation. In: Symposium on Network and Distributed System Security (NDSS) (2015)

3. Theori: Chakra JIT CFG bypass (2016). http://theori.io/research/chakra-jit-cfg-bypass

4. Frassetto, T., Gens, D., Liebchen, C., Sadeghi, A.R.: JITGuard: hardening just-in-time compilers with SGX. In: ACM Conference on Computer and Communications Security (CCS) (2017)

5. Willam Forbes: The PyPI Python Package Hack (2017). https://www.bytelion.com/pypi-python-package-hack

6. Rieck, K., Krueger, T., Dewald, A.: Cujo: efficient detection and prevention of drive-by-download attacks. In: Annual Computer Security Applications Conference (ACSAC) (2010)

7. Oracle Corporation: Securitymanager (java platform se 8) (2018). https://docs.oracle.com/javase/8/docs/api/java/lang/SecurityManager.html

8. GitBook: Lua sandbox library (1.2.7) (2017). http://mozilla-services.github.io/lua-sandbox

9. Google Developers: Introduction—Caja (2018). https://developers.google.com/caja/

10. GitHub: zopefoundation/restrictedpython: a restricted execution environment for python to run untrusted code (2018). https://github.com/zopefoundation/RestrictedPython

11. Google Cloud: Google app engine: build scalable web and mobile backends in any language on Google's infrastructure. https://cloud.google.com/appengine/ (2018)

12. Blazakis, D.: Interpreter exploitation: pointer inference and JIT spraying. BlackHat DC (2010)

13. Abadi, M., Budiu, M., Erlingsson, U., Ligatti, J.: Control-flow integrity. In: ACM Conference on Computer and Communications Security (CCS) (2005)

14. Tice, C., Roeder, T., Collingbourne, P., Checkoway, S., Erlingsson, Ú., Lozano, L., Pike, G.: Enforcing forward-edge control-flow integrity in GCC & LLVM. In: USENIX Security Symposium (2014)

15. Niu, B., Tan, G.: Per-input control-flow integrity. In: ACM Conference on Computer and Communications Security (CCS) (2015)

16. Lua: Lua: uses (2018). https://www.lua.org/uses.html

17. van der Veen, V., Andriesse, D., Stamatogiannakis, M., Chen, X., Bos, H., Giuffrida, C.: The dynamics of innocent flesh on the bone: code reuse ten years later. In: ACM Conference on Computer and Communications Security (CCS) (2017)

18. Lettner, J., Kollenda, B., Homescu, A., Larsen, P., Schuster, F., Davi, L., Sadeghi, A.R., Holz, T., Franz, M., Irvine, U.: Subversive-c: abusing and protecting dynamic message dispatch. In: USENIX Annual Technical Conference (2016)

19. Python Performance Benchmark Suite 0.6.1 Documentation: The python performance benchmark suite (2017). http://pyperformance.readthedocs.io

20. Alioth: The computer language benchmarks game (2017). http://benchmarksgame.alioth.debian.org

21. Mashtizadeh, A.J., Bittau, A., Boneh, D., Mazières, D.: CCFI: cryptographically enforced control flow integrity. In: ACM Conference on Computer and Communications Security (CCS) (2015)

22. Rohlf, C., Ivnitskiy, Y.: Attacking clientside JIT compilers. Black Hat USA (2011)

23. Athanasakis, M., Athanasopoulos, E., Polychronakis, M., Portokalidis, G., Ioannidis, S.: The devil is in the constants: bypassing defenses in browser JIT engines. In: NDSS (2015)

24. Maisuradze, G., Backes, M., Rossow, C.: What cannot be read, cannot be leveraged? Revisiting assumptions of JIT-ROP defenses. In: USENIX Security Symposium (2016)

25. Homescu, A., Brunthaler, S., Larsen, P., Franz, M.: Librando: transparent code randomization for just-in-time compilers. In: ACM Conference on Computer and Communications Security (CCS) (2013)
26. Backes, M., Holz, T., Kollenda, B., Koppe, P., Nürnberger, S., Pewny, J.: You can run but you can't read: preventing disclosure exploits in executable code. In: ACM Conference on Computer and Communications Security (CCS) (2014)
27. Crane, S., Liebchen, C., Homescu, A., Davi, L., Larsen, P., Sadeghi, A.R., Brunthaler, S., Franz, M.: Readactor: practical code randomization resilient to memory disclosure. In: IEEE Symposium on Security and Privacy (S&P) (2015)
28. Tang, A., Sethumadhavan, S., Stolfo, S.: Heisenbyte: thwarting memory disclosure attacks using destructive code reads. In: ACM Conference on Computer and Communications Security (CCS) (2015)
29. Werner, J., Baltas, G., Dallara, R., Otterness, N., Snow, K.Z., Monrose, F., Polychronakis, M.: No-execute-after-read: preventing code disclosure in commodity software. In: ACM Symposium on Information, Computer and Communications Security (ASIACCS) (2016)
30. Snow, K.Z., Rogowski, R., Werner, J., Koo, H., Monrose, F., Polychronakis, M.: Return to the zombie gadgets: undermining destructive code reads via code inference attacks. In: IEEE Symposium on Security and Privacy (S&P) (2016)
31. Schuster, F., Tendyck, T., Liebchen, C., Davi, L., Sadeghi, A.R., Holz, T.: Counterfeit object-oriented programming: on the difficulty of preventing code reuse attacks in C++ applications. In: IEEE Symposium on Security and Privacy (S&P) (2015)
32. Crane, S., Volckaert, S., Schuster, F., Liebchen, C., Larsen, P., Davi, L., Sadeghi, A.R., Holz, T., Sutter, B.D., Franz, M.: It's a TRaP: table randomization and protection against function reuse attacks. In: ACM Conference on Computer and Communications Security (CCS) (2015)

Reverse Engineering

ELISA: ELiciting ISA of Raw Binaries for Fine-Grained Code and Data Separation

Pietro De Nicolao(✉), Marcello Pogliani, Mario Polino, Michele Carminati, Davide Quarta, and Stefano Zanero

Dipartimento di Elettronica, Informazione e Bioingegneria,
Politecnico di Milano, Milan, Italy
pietro.denicolao@mail.polimi.it,
{marcello.pogliani,mario.polino,michele.carminati,davide.quarta,
stefano.zanero}@polimi.it

Abstract. Static binary analysis techniques are widely used to reconstruct the behavior and discover vulnerabilities in software when source
code is not available. To avoid errors due to mis-interpreting data as
machine instructions (or vice-versa), disassemblers and static analysis
tools must precisely infer the boundaries between code and data. However, this information is often not readily available. Worse, compilers may
embed small chunks of data inside the code section. Most state of the art
approaches to separate code and data are rooted on recursive traversal
disassembly, with severe limitations when dealing with indirect control
instructions. We propose *ELISA*, a technique to separate code from data
and ease the static analysis of executable files. *ELISA* leverages supervised sequential learning techniques to locate the code section(s) boundaries of header-less binary files, and to predict the instruction boundaries
inside the identified code section. As a preliminary step, if the Instruction Set Architecture (ISA) of the binary is unknown, *ELISA* leverages
a logistic regression model to identify the correct ISA from the file content. We provide a comprehensive evaluation on a dataset of executables
compiled for different ISAs, and we show that our method is capable to
identify code sections with a byte-level accuracy (F1 score) ranging from
98.13% to over 99.9% depending on the ISA. Fine-grained separation
of code from embedded data on x86, x86-64 and ARM executables is
accomplished with an accuracy of over 99.9%.

1 Introduction

Research in binary static analysis—i.e., techniques to statically analyze programs
where the source code is not available—is a thriving field, with many tools and
techniques widely available to help the analyst being actively researched and
developed. They range from disassemblers and decompilers, to complex analysis
frameworks [1,2] that combine static analysis with other techniques, primarily
symbolic execution [3,4], fuzzing [5,6], or both [7]. Binary analysis techniques are

useful in many domains: For example, discovering vulnerabilities [8], understanding and reconstructing the behavior of a program, as well as modifying legacy software when the source code is lost (e.g., to apply security [9] or functionality patches).

A pre-requisite for performing static binary analysis is to precisely reconstruct the program control flow graph and disassemble the machine instructions from the executable file. Unfortunately, perfect disassembly is undecidable [10]: Indeed, modern disassemblers often fall short on real world files. One of the most relevant obstacles to achieve a correct disassembly is to separate machine instructions from data and metadata. Executable files are structured in sections, with some sections primarily containing code (e.g., .text) and some other primarily containing data such as strings, large constants, jump tables (e.g., .data, .rodata). The header of standard file formats (e.g., ELF, PE, Mach-O) identifies the sections' offset and properties. Unfortunately, especially when analyzing the firmware of embedded devices, executables sometimes come in a "binary-blob" format that lack section information. Even if the program comes with metadata identifying the code sections, compiler optimizations make static analysis harder [11]: Often, compilers embed small chunks of data in the instruction stream. Microsoft Visual Studio includes data and padding bytes between instructions when producing x86 and x86-64 code [12], and ARM code often contains jump tables and large constants embedded in the instruction stream [13]. This "inline" data, if wrongly identified as an instruction (or vice-versa), leads to an erroneous analysis.

Motivated by these challenges, we tackle the problem of separating instructions from data in a binary program (code discovery problem). We divide the problem into two separate tasks: First, we identify the boundaries of the executable sections; Second, we perform fine-grained identification of non-code chunks embedded inside executable sections. Separating such problems allows to leverage more precise models, as well as to provide the analyst with the information on the code sections separately from the embedded data information. Our methodology is targeted at reverse engineering (mostly benign) software, rather than at thwarting advanced code obfuscation methodologies such as those found when analyzing some advanced malware. Thus, we are aware that it may be possible to adversarially manipulate the binary program in order to make our methodology output wrong results; we do not explicitly deal with this use case.

Our methodology is based on supervised learning techniques, is completely automated, does not require architecture-specific signatures[1], and is scalable to any number of architectures by appropriately extending the training set. Finally, as our technique trains a different model for each architecture to precisely learn the features of the instruction set, we introduce a preliminary step to automatically identify the target ISA of a raw binary file.

Contributions. In this paper, we present the following contributions:

---

[1] While it is possible to *integrate* our methodology with ISA-dependent heuristics, we show that our methodology achieves good results *without* ISA-specific knowledge.

1. We propose *ELISA*, a technique, based on sequential learning, to separate instructions and data in a binary executable; *ELISA* is able to identify the code sections and, subsequently, to draw out data embedded between instructions;
2. We evaluate our technique on a set of real applications compiled for different processor architectures, precisely collecting the ground truth by leveraging compiler-inserted debug symbols;
3. We complement *ELISA* with a technique for automatic ISA identification, extending a state-of-the-art approach [14] with (optional) multi-byte features, and evaluating it on a large set of executable binaries.

2   Design of *ELISA*

The goal of *ELISA* is to solve the code discovery problem: Given an arbitrary sequence of bytes containing machine instructions and data, without any metadata (e.g., debug symbols), it separates the bytes containing executable instructions from the ones containing data. We start by observing that the majority of executable programs are divided, as a first approximation, into multiple *sections*: one or more containing machine code, and one or more containing data. We follow a two-step approach: First, we *identify the boundaries of code sections*, i.e., sections mostly composed of machine instructions; then, we *identify the chunks of data* embedded into code sections. As we use supervised machine learning models, *ELISA* is signature-less: Its set of supported architectures can be extended by extending the training set, without developing architecture-specific heuristics. The two-step approach gives the analyst both a coarse grained information about the section boundaries, as well as a byte-level, fine grained classification.

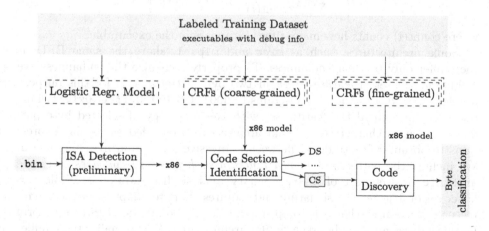

Fig. 1. Overview of *ELISA*.

Figure 1 summarizes our approach. First of all, if the ISA of the binary executable file to be analyzed is unknown, we automatically detect it using a logistic regression classifier. Once the ISA is known, we use a Conditional Random Field (CRF) [15], a supervised machine learning model based on probabilistic sequential learning, to classify each byte of an unknown file as belonging to the code section or not. We train a different CRF model for each of the supported architectures. Then, we perform a post-processing step to eliminate small blocks of code or data by merging them with the surrounding region in order to eliminate the noise in the prediction output. Finally, we use a second set of per-architecture CRFs to classify each byte of the identified code sections as either part of a machine instruction or as data.

2.1   ISA Identification

Whenever the ISA of the analyzed file is unknown, *ELISA* attempts to automatically identify it, including the correct endianness if the architecture supports multiple endianness variants. We adopt a signature-less technique based on supervised machine learning, extending the model by Clemens [14]. We use a logistic regression model to classify a file among one of the supported ISAs.

Feature Extraction. Given an executable binary file, we extract an appropriate feature vector. Since we have no information about the file content or structure, we select features stemming from the frequency distribution of bytes or *selected* multi-byte patterns (using all the byte n-grams would lead to 256^n features).

Starting from the assumption that executables compiled for different CPU architectures have different Byte Frequency Distributions (BFDs), we obtain the BFD of each file, computing the frequencies of the 256 possible byte values. The frequency of a byte having value i is defined as:

$$f_i = \frac{\text{count}(i)}{\sum_{i=0}^{255} \text{count}(i)} \qquad \forall i \in [0, 255]$$

where $\text{count}(i)$ counts how many times i appears in the executable.

Some architectures, such as `mips` and `mipsel`, share the same BFD as they differ only by their endianness. To properly recognize the endianness, we include in our set of features the four two-byte patterns used for this purpose in Clemens [14], i.e., the byte bi-grams `0x0001`, `0x0100`, `0xfffe`, `0xfeff`. Furthermore, we extend the feature set with the frequency of selected byte patterns known to characterize certain architectures, encoded as regular expressions to obtain a fair trade-off between expressive power and matching speed. We include the patterns of *known function prologues and epilogues* from the `archinfo` project part of `angr`, a binary analysis framework [3]. While this latter set of features is a signature and requires effort to adapt to further architectures, we remark that it is completely optional and allows *ELISA* to perform better in discriminating between similar architectures. We normalize the number of multi-byte pattern matches by the file size, computing the multi-byte features as:

$$f_{pattern} = \frac{\#\,\text{matches}(pattern, file)}{\text{len}(file)}$$

Multi-class Logistic Regression. To create a model able to label a sample among K supported architectures (classes), we train a different logistic regression model for each class $k \in \{1, \ldots, K\}$, and use the one-vs-the-rest strategy to obtain a K-class classifier. We use logistic regression models with L1 regularization: given a feature matrix $\mathbf{X}$ and a vector of labels $y^{(k)}$ (where $y_i^{(k)} = 1$ if the sample i belongs to the class k, 0 otherwise), we learn the vector of parameters $w^{(k)}$ for the class k by solving the following minimization problem:

$$\min_{w^{(k)}} \ \left\| w^{(k)} \right\|_1 + C \sum_{i=1}^{n} \log \left(\exp \left(-y_i^{(k)} \left(X_i^T w^{(k)} + w_0^{(k)} \right) \right) + 1 \right)$$

The C parameter is the inverse of the regularization strength: lower values of C assign more importance to the regularization term than to the logistic loss (second term), penalizing complex models. The L1 regularization can generate compact models by setting to zero the coefficients in w corresponding to less relevant features; the model performs feature selection as part of the learning phase, as the learnt model parameters are an estimate of the importance of each feature. For each sample with feature vector X, the set of logistic regression models output a confidence score for each class k, i.e, an estimate of the probability $P(k|X)$ that the sample belongs to the class k; thus, the predicted class is the one with the highest confidence score $k^* = \arg \max_{k \in \{1 \ldots K\}} P(k|X)$.

2.2 Code Section Identification

We formulate the code section identification problem as a classification problem: given a sequence of bytes $(b_1, b_2, \ldots, b_n)$, $b_i \in [0, 255]$, we want to predict a sequence of binary labels $(y_1, y_2, \ldots, y_n)$, $y_i \in \{0, 1\}$, where $y_i = 1$ if the byte x_i is part of a code section, $y_i = 0$ otherwise. To train the classifier, we extract the feature matrix and the label vector for each sample in the labeled dataset; in order to model ISA-specific patterns, we learn a Conditional Random Field (CRF) for each ISA. When classifying an unknown file, we extract the feature matrix, fit the model, and run a post-processing algorithm to remove the noise given by small sequences of code inside the data section (or vice-versa). Doing so, we end up with contiguous, relatively large sequences of code or data.

Feature Extraction. Given a N-byte file, we compute the one-hot encoding of each byte. For example, if $b_i = $ 0x04, we extract $x_i = (0, 0, 0, 0, 1, 0, 0, \ldots, 0)$, a binary vector having length 256. We choose one-hot encoding, a widespread technique to transform numeric features in a set of categorical features, as we are interested in distinguishing one byte value vs. all the others, rather than in the numeric values of the bytes. The files to classify contain both code and data, so we do not attempt to extract instruction-level features using a disassembler. We then consider, for each byte, the one-hot encodings of its m preceding bytes (lookbehind) and n following bytes (lookahead) to account for context-sensitivity, obtaining a $N \times 256 \cdot (n + m + 1)$ feature matrix for each file[2].

---

[2] The parameters m and n belong to the model and can be appropriately tuned; for example, in our evaluation we used grid search.

Conditional Random Fields. CRFs [15] are a class of statistical and sequence modeling methods to segment and label graph-structured data (structured prediction): Instead of separately classifying each item in a sequence, they consider the structure of the problem (i.e., the classification of a sample takes into account also the "neighboring" samples). Thanks to this feature, this model is suitable for separating code from data: Indeed, a byte with a certain value can be interpreted as part of a valid instruction or as data, according to its context.

In a CRF, the dependencies between random variables are modeled as a graph where each node is a random variable; each variable is conditionally dependent on all its graph neighbors, and conditionally independent from all the other variables. In this form, CRFs can be seen as a generalization of a Hidden Markov Model where the distribution of the observation are not modeled, relaxing independence assumptions.

Let $\mathbf{X}$ be a sequence of observations (i.e., the bytes of the binary file), and $\mathbf{Y}$ a set of random variables over the corresponding labels (i.e., code or data). We assume that some variables in $\mathbf{Y}$ are conditionally dependent. A CRF is defined as follows [15]:

Definition 1 (Conditional Random Field). *Let $G = (V, E)$ be a graph such that $\mathbf{Y} = (\mathbf{Y}_v)_{v \in V}$, so that $\mathbf{Y}$ is indexed by the vertices of G. Then $(\mathbf{X}, \mathbf{Y})$ is a* conditional random field *when, conditioned on $\mathbf{X}$, the random variables $\mathbf{Y}_v$ obey the Markov property with respect to the graph: $P(\mathbf{Y}_v \mid \mathbf{X}, \mathbf{Y}_w, w \neq v) = P(\mathbf{Y}_v \mid \mathbf{X}, \mathbf{Y}_w, w \sim v)$, where $w \sim v$ means that w and v are neighbors in G.*

We model the code discovery problem using linear-chain CRFs, a particular case of CRFs where the graph is reduced to an undirected linear sequence: The variable associated with each element $(\mathbf{Y}_v)$ is conditionally dependent only on the observations and on the classification of the previous $(\mathbf{Y}_{v-1})$ and the following $(\mathbf{Y}_{v+1})$ element. Figure 2 depicts the structure of a linear-chain CRF.

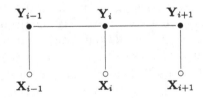

Fig. 2. Graphical structure of a linear-chain CRF [15].

In a general CRF, vertices $i \in V$ and edges $(i, j) \in E$ are associated with a set of feature functions, respectively $f_h(\mathbf{X}, \mathbf{Y}_i)$ and $g_k(\mathbf{X}, \mathbf{Y}_i, \mathbf{Y}_j)$. The feature functions account for features drawn from the observations that can influence the likelihood of the values of the labels. We define a set of feature functions to associate to each vertex $\mathbf{Y}_i$ the feature vector of the associated observation (i.e., one-hot encoded value, lookahead and lookbehind of the byte b_i), and associate the constant 1 to each edge.

Feature functions are used to compute the conditional probabilities. To do so, we associate unary and binary potential functions ϕ respectively to each vertex i and to each edge (i, j) in G. The Markov network model is log-linear, so we can compute the network potentials as the exponential of the weighted sum of the features on the vertices and on the edges:

$$\phi_i(\mathbf{X}, \mathbf{Y}_i) = \exp\left[\sum_h w_h f_h(\mathbf{X}, \mathbf{Y}_i)\right] \qquad \forall\, i \in V$$

$$\phi_{i,j}(\mathbf{X}, \mathbf{Y}_i, \mathbf{Y}_j) = \exp\left[\sum_k w_k g_k(\mathbf{X}, \mathbf{Y}_i, \mathbf{Y}_j)\right] \qquad \forall\, (i, j) \in E$$

where the weights w_i are the parameters learned by the model. Finally, we compute the conditional probability distributions as:

$$P(\mathbf{Y} \mid \mathbf{X}) \propto \prod_{i \in V} \phi_i(\mathbf{X}, \mathbf{Y}_i) \prod_{(i,j) \in E} \phi_{i,j}(\mathbf{X}, \mathbf{Y}_i, \mathbf{Y}_j)$$

Learning CRFs. To learn the parameters of the CRF, we use Structural Support Vector Machines (SSVMs), i.e., soft-margin SVMs with a loss function designed for multi-label classification. The primal problem formulation for soft-margin SSVMs is [16]:

$$\min \quad \frac{1}{2}\|\mathbf{w}\|^2 + C\sum_{\mathbf{x}} \xi_{\mathbf{x}}$$

$$\text{s.t.} \quad \mathbf{w}^\top \Delta \mathbf{f}_{\mathbf{x}}(\mathbf{y}) \geq \Delta \mathbf{t}_{\mathbf{x}}(\mathbf{y}) - \xi_{\mathbf{x}} \qquad \forall\, \mathbf{x}, \mathbf{y}$$

where:

- $\mathbf{w}$ is the vector of weights learned by the model;
- $\mathbf{t}(\mathbf{x})$ is the predicted $\mathbf{y}$ for the input sequence $\mathbf{x}$;
- $\mathbf{f}(\mathbf{x}, \mathbf{y})$ are the *features* or *basis functions*;
- $\Delta \mathbf{f}_{\mathbf{x}}(\mathbf{y}) = \mathbf{f}(\mathbf{x}, \mathbf{t}(\mathbf{x})) - \mathbf{f}(\mathbf{x}, \mathbf{y})$;
- $\Delta \mathbf{t}_{\mathbf{x}}(\mathbf{y}) = \sum_{i=1}^{l} I(\mathbf{y}_i \neq (\mathbf{t}(\mathbf{x}))_i)$ is the number of wrong labels predicted by the model for the input $\mathbf{x}$;
- $\xi_{\mathbf{x}}$ is a slack variable to allow the violation of some constraints when the data is not linearly separable;
- C is the inverse of the regularization strength.

To efficiently solve this optimization problem, we use the Block-Coordinate Frank-Wolfe algorithm [17], an iterative optimization algorithm. Asymptotically, it converges to the solution; we stop it after a fixed maximum number of iterations or when the loss function becomes smaller than a set threshold.

Post-processing. To improve the ability of the sequential classifier to identify code sections, after classifying each byte of a file using our trained CRF, we iteratively remove the smallest contiguous sequence of predictions of code

---

Algorithm 1. Post-processing algorithm

Require: C: list of chunks (start, end, tag), $min\_sections$, $cutoff$
  loop
    $M \leftarrow \max_{c \in C}$ length(c) {size of largest chunk}
    $c_{min} \leftarrow \arg\min_{c \in C}$ length(c) {smallest chunk}
    if $|C| > min\_sections$ **and** length$(c_{min}) < cutoff \cdot M$ **then**
      invert tag of c_{min} and merge with surrounding chunks
      $C \leftarrow$ updated list of chunks
    else
      return C
    end if
  end loop

---

or data (chunk), merging it respectively with the surrounding data or code. We implement this phase as shown in Algorithm 1, which takes two parameters: $min\_sections$, accounting for the minimum number of sections to keep, and $cutoff$, the maximum size of any chunk that can be eliminated (as a fraction of the largest chunk).

2.3   Fine-Grained Code Discovery

Once the code section is identified, we classify its bytes as code or non-code. Similarly to the procedure for identifying code sections, we train a per-ISA Conditional Random Field (CRF) on a labeled dataset, and we use this model to classify previously unseen code sections. We do not apply the post-processing algorithm since we are interested in identifying small chunks of data in the code.

Feature Extraction. We train the model with the same feature matrix used for the code section identification step. We consider the one-hot encoding value of each byte, with m lookbehind bytes and n lookahead bytes.

We observe that, for some architectures, it is possible to improve the performance of the classifier by augmenting the feature set with (optional) architecture-specific heuristics that allow the classifier to solve a simpler problem. For example, in case of fixed-length instruction architecture, such as ARM, we can leverage the fact that every instruction and data block starts an address multiple of 4 bytes. In this case, the problem of code discovery can be stated as follows: classify each 4-byte word of each code section as a machine code word or data. Given this property, we can also extract (ARM-specific) instruction-level features: Using a linear disassembler, we interpret each 4-byte word as an instruction, and we compute the feature matrix considering, for each 4-byte word, both the *opcode* returned by the disassembler (we consider a special value if the word could not be interpreted as a valid ARM opcode), and the *value of the first byte of each word*. We apply one-hot encoding to these features and generate the lookahead and lookbehind as done for the generic feature matrix. In this case, the trained model labels each word, not byte, as code or data.

In the remainder of this paper, we adopt the general feature vector for x86 and x86-64 architectures, and the specialized feature vector for the ARM architecture. Note that we do not consider the case in which Thumb code (which is 2-byte aligned) is also present; that problem is specifically addressed by Chen et al. [13].

3 Experimental Evaluation

We separately evaluate the three stages of *ELISA*: architecture identification, code section identification, and fine-grained code discovery. We implemented *ELISA* in Python, using the machine learning algorithms from the `scikit-learn` library. We implemented the classifiers based on linear-chain Conditional Random Fields using `pystruct` [18], an open-source structured learning library featuring CRF-like models with structural SVM learners (SSVMs). Given the large size of the dataset and the memory space required by one-hot encoding, we use the compressed sparse row representation [19] for the feature matrices.

3.1 Architecture Identification

Evaluation on Code Sections. We obtained the dataset used by Clemens [14], containing 16,642 executable files for 20 architectures; after removing empty and duplicate files, we obtained 15,084 samples. The dataset contains only a few samples for AVR and CUDA (292 and 20 respectively): As this may influence the result, we extend the dataset by compiling the Arduino examples [20] for AVR, and the NVIDIA CUDA 8.0 samples [21], and extract the code sections from the resulting ELF files. To test our tool in a worst-case scenario, we also selected 20 binaries from the challenges proposed in the 2017 DEF CON CTF contest, and compiled them for cLEMENCy [22], a *middle-endian* architecture purposefully designed to break assumptions underlying binary analysis tools: Our model is based on the frequency of 8-bit bytes, while cLEMENCy uses 9-bit bytes.

Table 1 reports the results of our classifier on this dataset. First, to replicate the results by Clemens, we classify the dataset, without the additional samples, considering only the original features, i.e., Byte Frequency Distribution and the 4 bi-grams for endianness detection (Original). Then, we include the additional AVR, CUDA and cLEMENCy samples, and we use the complete feature matrix, including the frequencies of function prologue and epilogue patterns (Complete). In both cases, we use 5-fold cross-validation to evaluate the classifier performance. For comparison, the last column of the table reports the F-measures from Clemens [14]. The detailed precision, recall and Area Under the Curve (AUC) figures are provided for the complete feature matrix only. We obtain a global accuracy of 99.8%. This figure is higher than the accuracy reported by Clemens for both the logistic regression model (97.94%) and the best-performing model, SVMs (98.35%). We observe that this mismatch may be due to differences in the implementations of the logistic regression model: Clemens uses the `SimpleLogistic` implementation in Weka[3], without regularization; instead, we

---

[3] http://weka.sourceforge.net/doc.dev/weka/classifiers/functions/SimpleLogistic.html.

Table 1. Architecture identification performance on code-only samples. To produce the results in the Original column, we removed the samples not used in [14] (clemency and additional avr and cuda programs).

Architecture	#	Precision	Recall	AUC	F1 measure		
					Complete	Original	[14]
alpha	1295	0.9992	0.9992	0.9996	0.9992	0.9985	0.997
x86-64	897	0.9989	0.9978	0.9988	0.9983	0.9983	0.990
arm64	1074	0.9991	0.9991	0.9995	0.9991	0.9986	0.994
armel	903	1.0	1.0	1.0	1.0	1.0	0.998
armhf	904	0.9989	0.9989	0.9994	0.9989	0.9983	0.996
avr	365 (292)	0.9974	0.9974	0.9985	0.9974	0.9808	0.936
clemency	20 (0)	0.9048	0.95	0.9749	0.9268	-	-
cuda	133 (20)	0.9773	0.9699	0.9849	0.9736	0.9	0.516
hppa	472	1.0	1.0	1.0	1.0	1.0	0.993
i386	901	1.0	1.0	1.0	1.0	1.0	0.993
ia64	590	1.0	1.0	1.0	1.0	1.0	0.995
m68k	1089	0.9991	0.9991	0.9995	0.9991	0.9986	0.993
mips	903	0.9978	0.9989	0.9994	0.9983	0.9906	
mipsel	903	0.9956	0.9978	0.9988	0.9967	0.9895	0.886
powerpc	900	0.9978	0.9989	0.9994	0.9983	0.9989	0.989
ppc64	766	0.9987	1.0	1.0	0.9993	0.998	0.996
s390	603	0.9967	0.9983	0.9991	0.9975	0.9983	0.998
s390x	604	1.0	0.9983	0.9992	0.9992	0.9992	0.998
sh4	775	0.9949	0.9987	0.9992	0.9968	0.9968	0.993
sparc	495	0.986	0.996	0.9977	0.991	0.9939	0.988
sparc64	698	0.9971	0.9971	0.9985	0.9971	0.9986	0.993
Total/Average	15290	0.9928	0.9939	0.9969	0.9933	0.9918	0.9566

use a different implementation with L1 regularization. Specifically, we notice a higher difference in the F-measure for MIPS and MIPSEL and for CUDA. We argue that the low accuracy for CUDA in [14] could be due to the very low number of samples available (20). Adding multi-byte prologue and epilogue patterns as features does not improve significantly the performance of the classifier, which already performs well without them: The global F-measure is 99.33% vs. 99.18% of the model without extended features. We also notice that, despite cLEMENCy being an architecture developed with the purpose to break existing tools, *ELISA* still obtain a F-measure of 92%.

Evaluation on Full Executables. We now consider complete "real-world" executables with both code and non-code sections: We use full ELF files, without extracting the code section. Classifying a complete binary is more challenging because the data contained in the non-executable sections may confuse the classifier. We evaluate the classifier on the following datasets:

- Debian. We automatically downloaded 300 random packages from the repositories of the Debian GNU/Linux distribution, compiled for 8 different architectures, and we extracted the ELF executables contained in these packages, obtaining 3,072 samples (note that not all packages were available for all the supported architectures, and some binaries contained multiple ELF files).
- ByteWeight. The authors of ByteWeight [23] made their dataset available online[4]. This dataset contains the GNU coreutils, binutils and findutils compiled for Linux, for the x86 and x86-64 architectures, and using different compilers (GNU GCC and Intel ICC) and optimization levels (O0, O1, O2, O3). The dataset also contains a smaller number of Windows PE executables compiled with Microsoft Visual Studio for the same two architectures and with four levels of optimization; thus, despite being composed of two classes only, it is a rather heterogeneous dataset.

We evaluated the classification performance on both the Debian and the ByteWeight datasets separately, using 5-fold cross-validation. The results are reported in Table 2. Our classifier is accurate even when dealing with binaries containing both code and data sections; we do not notice significant differences in performance among the different architectures (classes).

Table 2. Architecture identification on complete binaries (unpacked and packed Debian GNU/Linux and ByteWeight dataset). For comparison with files with code sections only, the last column reports the F1 measure from the Complete column of Table 1.

Architecture	Debian					ByteWeight		Table 1
	#	Precision	Recall	AUC	F1	#	F1	F1
x86-64	386	0.9922	0.9922	0.9956	0.9922	1097	0.9910	0.9983
arm64	382	1.0	0.9974	0.9987	0.9987			0.9991
armel	385	0.9948	0.9974	0.9983	0.9961			1.0
armhf	385	0.9974	0.9974	0.9985	0.9974			0.9989
i386	386	0.9948	0.9948	0.997	0.9948	1100	0.9908	1.0
mips	384	1.0	1.0	1.0	1.0			0.9983
mipsel	384	0.9974	0.9948	0.9972	0.9961			0.9967
ppc64el	380	0.9974	1.0	0.9998	0.9987			0.9993
Total/Average	3072	0.9968	0.9968	0.9981	0.9968	2197	0.9909	0.9981

Impact of the Sample Size. To study the impact of the file size on the classifier performance, we extract the code section from each sample in the Debian dataset;

[4] http://security.ece.cmu.edu/byteweight/.

then, we extract a random contiguous sub-sequence of s bytes from each file, and we repeat the process for fragment sizes s between 8 bytes and 64 KiB. We evaluate the classifier on each set of fragments via 10-fold cross-validation, considering the macro-averaged F-measure as the performance metric. The results, with a regularization parameter[5] $C = 10000$, are reported in Fig. 3 and show that even for small code fragments (128 bytes), our classifier reaches a F-measure of 90%. For 512-byte fragments, the F-measure is over 95%.

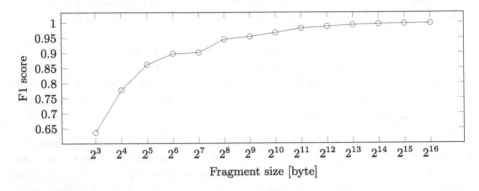

Fig. 3. Impact of the sample size on ISA detection performance

3.2 Code Section Identification

To set the hyper-parameters, we observe that the CRF regularization strength (C) does not influence the prediction if we stop the model after a fixed number of iterations of the Frank-Wolfe algorithm, so we fix $C = 1$. The other parameters are set to: lookahead and lookbehind length $n = m = 1$, 20 iterations, regularization strength $C = 1$, post-processing parameters $cutoff = 0.1$, $min\_sections = 3$. The performance measures are obtained by computing the fraction of correctly classified bytes with respect to the ground truth for each sample, and then by performing an average on the number of samples, giving each sample the same weight, regardless of its size. We also report, for each dataset, the fraction of bytes labeled as code in the ground truth. We extract the ground truth by parsing the header of the original ELF, PE or Mach-O files to retrieve the section boundary information. To obtain the results, summarized in Table 3, we use different datasets, we train a different model for each architecture and for each dataset, and we evaluate the classification performance using 5-fold cross-validation:

- Debian. We select a subset of the Debian binaries used for the evaluation of the ISA identification algorithm. We report the results both before and after the post-processing phase. The F-measure is over 99% for all the architectures with the post-processing enabled. The post-processing algorithm consistently improves the performances of our model by removing noise. If we

---

[5] We determine that $C = 10000$ is the optimal value through grid search optimization.

decrease the number of iterations of the SSVM learner, the contribution of the post-processing algorithm becomes even more important: Thus, our post-processing algorithm allows to reduce the training time of the model without sacrificing the quality of the predictions. Figure 4 shows how the post-processing algorithm compensates for the errors of a model trained with a low number of iterations. We also use this dataset to optimize the lookahead and lookbehind parameters $n = m$ by grid search on a random selection of two thirds of the dataset (the other third being used for validation). As shown in Fig. 5a, we notice that model with the post-processing step enabled always outperforms the model without it, and that the accuracy in the model with post-processing is consistently high: it does not change depending on the choice of the hyperparameter. According to this data, we decided to set a minimal lookahead and lookbehind length of 1 byte for our experiments, and to enable the post-processing phase.

- ByteWeight. We select a subset of the ByteWeight dataset used for the evaluation of the ISA identification algorithm, randomly sampling 40 executables for each architecture from the 2,197 in the dataset.
- Mach-O. We collect 165 system binaries in the Mach-O format from an installation of macOS 10.12 (x86-64).
- AVR. We collect 73 AVR binaries by compiling the Arduino samples [20] for the Arduino UNO[6] hardware.

3.3   Code Discovery

Ground Truth Generation. Obtaining a set of binary executables with bytes pre-labeled as code or data in a fine grained fashion is a non-trivial problem, and previous research use a variety of methodologies to generate the ground truth. Wartell et al. [10] pre-label bytes according to the output of a commercial recursive traversal disassembler, IDA Pro, and evaluate the proposed methodology by manually comparing the results with the disassembler output; Karampatziakis [24] work similarly by using the OllyDbg disassembler for labeling. This method is error-prone: Erroneous ground truth may lead to errors both in the model training, and in the evaluation of the model performance; manual comparison makes the approach non scalable. Andriesse et al. [11] and Bao et al. [23] use a more precise technique: They extract the ground truth from compiler- generated debugging symbols, by compiling a set of applications from source. We use a variant of this latter approach to generate our ground truth.

x86 and x86-64. To show that a sequential learning model, trained on simple byte-level features, can effectively separate code from data, we compiled a x86 and x86-64 dataset with Microsoft Visual Studio, which is known to embed small chunks of data within code. We configured the compiler to generate full debug symbols (by using the `DebugFull` linker option and the `/p:DebugType=full` MSBuild compiler option). As a dataset, we use the C++ projects in the

---

[6] http://www.arduino.org/products/boards/arduino-uno.

Table 3. Code section identification performance.

Architecture	Samples[#]	Code Sec. [%]	Accuracy	Precision	Recall	F1
x86-64	41	40.69	0.9984	0.9969	0.9992	0.998
x86-64 (post-proc.)	41	40.69	0.9995	0.9984	1.0	0.9992
arm64	33	47.83	0.9931	0.9934	0.9922	0.9927
arm64 (post-proc.)	33	47.83	0.9995	0.9989	1.0	0.9995
armel	33	59.22	0.981	0.992	0.9749	0.9832
armel (post-proc.)	33	59.22	0.9983	0.9997	0.9977	0.9987
armhf	46	46.32	0.9847	0.9881	0.9753	0.9813
armhf (post-proc.)	46	46.32	0.9997	0.9995	0.9999	0.9997
i386	40	44.17	0.9946	0.9914	0.9966	0.9939
i386 (post-proc.)	40	44.17	0.9995	0.9985	1.0	0.9992
mips	40	41.51	0.9958	0.9926	0.9955	0.994
mips (post-proc.)	40	41.51	0.9995	0.9983	0.9999	0.9991
mipsel	40	43.64	0.9873	0.9807	0.9943	0.9866
mipsel (post-proc.)	40	43.64	0.9919	0.9901	1.0	0.9941
powerpc	19	57.69	0.9911	0.9858	0.9962	0.9908
powerpc (post-proc.)	19	57.69	0.9992	0.9976	0.9999	0.9988
ppc64el	40	41.66	0.9916	0.9904	0.9924	0.9912
ppc64el (post-proc.)	40	41.66	0.9985	0.9951	1.0	0.9975
x86-64 (ByteWeight)	40	27.13	0.9992	0.9994	0.9987	0.999
x86 (ByteWeight)	40	27.14	0.9998	0.9997	0.9996	0.9996
x86-64 (Mach-O)	165	27.59	1.0	0.9998	1.0	0.9999
avr (Arduino)	73	9.56	0.9999	0.9993	1.0	0.9997

Microsoft Universal Windows Platform (UWP) app samples [25], a Microsoft-provided set of Windows API demonstration applications. We automatically compile the dataset for both x86 and x86-64, parse the debug symbol files (.pdb) with dia2dump [26], and convert the textual representation of each .pdb file into the final ground truth format, i.e., a binary vector that indicates if each byte in the executable file is part of a machine instruction or not, discarding the non-code sections.

We configured the model with $C = 1$, we set the lookahead and lookbehind to $n = m = 1$, and we set 30 as the maximum number of iterations for the Frank-Wolfe algorithm. We evaluate our model on a randomly chosen subset of the dataset (we remark that the samples are large, with a median size of 1.68 MB). We performed holdout testing, reserving 10 executables for training and 40 for testing for each architecture. Table 4 reports the results: Accuracy and F-measure are over 99.9% for both the x86 and the x86-64 architectures. Although the ground truth generation method and dataset differ, this result is in line with the mean accuracy (99.98%) of the approach by Wartell et al. [10].

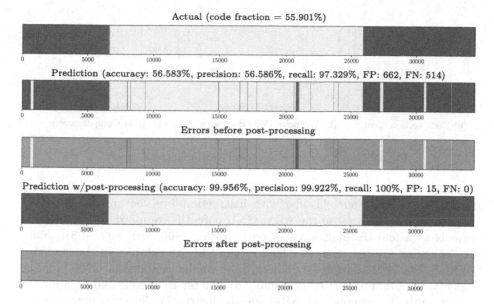

Fig. 4. Results of the code section identification method on a sample (`MIDGsmooth` from the Debian repositories), stopping the Frank-Wolfe algorithm after 10 iterations. While the prediction of the classifier alone is noisy, after the preprocessing phase there are no false negatives, and false positives are significantly reduced.

Table 4. Performance of the fine-grained code discovery method.

Architecture	Samples [#]	Inlined data [%]	Accuracy	Precision	Recall	F1
Windows x86-64	50	27.16	0.9997	0.9997	0.9999	0.9998
Windows x86	50	30.94	0.9996	0.9997	0.9997	0.9997
ARM coreutils -O0	103	5.36	1.0	1.0	1.0	1.0
ARM coreutils -O1	103	7.59	0.9998	0.9998	1.0	0.9999
ARM coreutils -O2	103	7.88	0.9998	0.9998	1.0	0.9999
ARM coreutils -O3	103	7.14	0.9998	0.9998	1.0	0.9999

As a baseline, we evaluated the performance of `objdump` (the linear disassembler included with the GNU binutils) on the Windows x86 and x86-64 datasets, by comparing the output of the disassembler with the ground truth extracted from the debugging symbols. We considered as data all the bytes which `objdump` could not decode as valid instructions, as well as all the decoded `int3` opcodes and those opcodes having "data" or "word" in their names. We found that `objdump` correctly classifies on average 94.17% of the bytes as code or data for the x86 dataset; the accuracy for the x86-64 dataset is higher at 98.59%.

In conclusion, our method is more accurate than a simple linear disassembly approach, which still gives good results on x86 binaries [11].

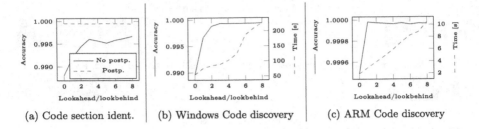

(a) Code section ident.   (b) Windows Code discovery   (c) ARM Code discovery

Fig. 5. Model accuracy vs. lookahead/lookbehind length.

ARM. We evaluate our classifier with instruction-level features for fixed-size instruction architectures on the ARM GNU coreutils compiled with debugging symbols with four different levels of optimization (-O0, -O1, -O2, -O3)[7]. Since the debugging symbols are embedded in the ELF executables in the standard DWARF format [27], we use the linear disassembler included in GNU binutils, `objdump`, to obtain a precise disassembly and to separate code and data for the ground truth. To generate the ARM-specific instruction-level features, first we strip the debugging symbols from the binary using `strip` from GNU binutils; then we disassemble the stripped file with `objdump` and extract our features.

We set the number of iterations of the SSVM learner to 20, and we choose $m = n = 1$ (i.e., 1 instruction, 4 bytes,) for the lookahead and lookbehind. We evaluate the model separately for each level of optimization of the binaries in the dataset, and we compute the performance metrics performing 5-fold cross-validation. Table 4 reports the results: the predictions of our model are almost perfect (accuracy of over 99.9%) for any optimization level. This is expected: Indeed, this problem is easier than code discovery using generic features for x86 and x86-64, as the model can work directly on each 4-byte word, not on single bytes potentially containing a part of an instruction, and the features are generated by a linear disassembler (`objdump`) which can detect the 4-byte words which cannot be decoded into valid ARM instructions.

Lookahead and Lookbehind Tuning. We optimize the lookahead parameter n (and lookbehind, which we choose to set at the same value of the lookahead) executing a grid search for $n \in [0, 8]$. For the x86 and x86-64 dataset (Fig. 5b, 3-fold cross-validation, 10 iterations for the SSVM learner), we notice no significant performance improvement when the lookahead length is higher than 3 bytes. For ARM (Fig. 5c, 10-fold cross-validation on the -O1 binaries, 75%/25% holdout testing), we see that, although the model without lookahead nor lookbehind scores well, a slight improvement can be obtained by setting a lookahead/lookbehind length equal to 1 word.

---

[7] https://github.com/BinaryAnalysisPlatform/arm-binaries.

4   Related Work

Separating code from data in executable files is a well-known problem in static binary analysis. Commercial disassembly tools need to perform, at least implicitly, this task. Andriesse et al. [11] analyze the performance of state-of-the-art x86 and x86-64 disassemblers, evaluating the accuracy of detecting instruction boundaries: For this task, linear sweep disassemblers have an accuracy of 99.92%, with a false positive rate of 0.56% for the most difficult dataset, outperforming recursive traversal ones (accuracy between 99% and 96%, depending on the optimization level of the binaries). Despite this, simple obfuscation techniques such as inserting junk bytes in the instruction stream are enough to make linear disassemblers misclassify 26%-30% of the instructions [28]. Kruegel et al. [29] address the code discovery problem in obfuscated binaries, and proposes a hybrid approach which combines control-flow based and statistical techniques to deal with such obfuscation techniques. More recently, Wartell et al. [10] segment x86 machine code into valid instructions and data based on a Predication by Partial Matching model (PPM), aided by heuristics, that overcomes the performance of a state-of-the-art commercial recursive traversal disassembler, IDA Pro, when evaluated with a small dataset of Windows binaries. The model evaluation is done by manually comparing the output of the model with the disassembly from IDA Pro, because precise ground truth for the binaries in the training set is not available. This limitation does not allow to test the method on a large number of binaries. This approach supports a single architecture (x86), and relies on architecture-specific heuristics: supporting a new ISA requires implementing the new heuristics. Chen et al. [13] address the code discovery problem in the context of static binary translation, specifically targeted ARM binaries; they only consider only the difference between 32-bit ARM instructions and 16-bit Thumb instructions that can be mixed in the same executable. Karampatziakis [24] present the code discovery problem in x86 binaries as a supervised learning problem over a graph, using structural SVMs to classify bytes as code or data.

More in general, machine learning tools have been applied to various problems in static analysis. Rosenblum et al. [30] address the problem of Function Entry Point identification in stripped binaries, using linear-chain Conditional Random Fields [15] for structured classification in sequences, the same model we propose in *ELISA* to tackle the problem of code discovery. Finally, ByteWeight [23] uses statistical techniques to tackle the function identification problem, and Shin et al. [31] use neural networks to recognize functions in a binary.

To analyze header-less files, *ELISA* needs also to identify the ISA. This task is a specialization of the problem of file type classification, well-known in computer forensics. In this context, many statistical techniques have been proposed, usually leveraging differences in the distribution of byte frequency among different file types [32–35]. Forensics techniques usually aim to classify all executable files in the same class, thus are not applicable as-is to our problem. Clemens [14] addresses the ISA identification problem as a machine learning classification problem, by using features extracted from the byte frequency distribution of the files, and comparing different machine learning models on the same dataset. Our

ISA identification step is a variant of this technique. cpu_rec [36] is a plugin for the popular binwalk tool that uses a statistical approach, based on Markov chains with similarity measures by cross-entropy computation, to detect the CPU architecture or a binary file, or of part of a binary file, among a corpus of 72 architectures. A completely different approach leverages static signatures: the Angr static analysis framework [3] includes a tool (Boyscout) to identify the CPU architecture of an executable by matching the file to a set of signatures containing the byte patterns of function prologues and epilogues of the known architectures, and picking the architecture with most matches; as a drawback, the signatures require maintenance and their quality and completeness is critical for the quality of the classification; also, this method may fail on heavily optimized or obfuscated code lacking of function prologues and epilogues.

5   Limitations

We are aware of some limitations to our work. First of all, our classifiers work at the byte level and do not use any instruction-level feature: While this allows *ELISA* to be signature-less, the lack of any notion of "instruction" means that it can mis-classify as code some byte sequences that are not valid ISA instructions. More advanced models could include some knowledge about the ISA and group the bytes corresponding to code into valid instructions. We provided an example of including ISA-specific knowledge with our features for fixed-byte instructions in Sect. 2.1. Also, our code discovery approach for ARM binaries may be extended for the case of ARM/Thumb mixed-ISA binary executables.

Second, our approach is not resilient to malicious attempts aimed at preventing static analysis via obfuscation: For example, large amounts of dead code in the data sections of the file may make *ELISA* recognize the section as code (or vice-versa), and similar approaches may be used to adversarially alter the byte frequency distribution used as a feature to recognize the executable binary architecture. In fact, if we pack the samples of our Debian dataset with the popular UPX [37] packer, discarding any executable not correctly packed, we achieve a very low F1 score (0.282) when we classify the resulting 1,745 files with our architecture classifier trained with a subset of the unpacked Debian dataset. Indeed, the architecture classifier is not robust to classify files with a high quantity of noise, i.e., the high-entropy uniform data of the packed code, with respect to the small unpacking stub that contains the features to be detected.

Finally, although header-less files are common in the analysis of embedded firmware, we decided not to evaluate our approach to real firmware because of the lack of ground truth data and the need of basing the evaluation of a, necessarily inaccurate, manual reverse engineering of each sample.

6   Conclusions

We presented *ELISA*, a supervised learning methodology to automatically separate data from code in stripped, header-less executable files, and to automatically detect the ISA the executable file is compiled for in case it is unknown.

We extended the approach presented by Clemens [14] and obtained better result on the ISA identification problem, while we proposed a novel sequential learning method to perform code section identification and fine-grained code discovery inside the code section. Our experiments show that *ELISA* performs well on a comprehensive, real-world dataset; thus, our work shows that sequential learning is a promising and viable approach to improve the performance of reverse engineering and static analysis tools.

Our work can be extended in various directions. First, *ELISA* aims to separate code from data. Building on this approach, future work can extend our code section identification to the multi-class classification case, in order to distinguish between non-code sections with peculiar patterns (e.g., jump tables, relocations, headers) and, more in general, to computer forensics applications, e.g., the identification of file segments and their classification by file type. Furthermore, our code discovery approach for ARM binaries may be extended for the case of ARM/Thumb mixed-ISA binary executables. Finally, future work may address the challenge of packed executables, raised in Sect. 5, using entropy analysis techniques, e.g., analyzing the entropy of neighbor bytes to detect the presence of compressed data.

Acknowledgements. We would like to thank the anonymous reviewers for their suggestions that led to improving this work. This project has been supported by the Italian Ministry of University and Research under the FIRB project FACE (Formal Avenue for Chasing malwarE), grant agreement nr. RBFR13AJFT; and by the European Union's Horizon 2020 research and innovation programme under the Marie Skłodowska-Curie grant agreement nr. 690972.

References

1. Song, D., et al.: BitBlaze: a new approach to computer security via binary analysis. In: Sekar, R., Pujari, A.K. (eds.) ICISS 2008. LNCS, vol. 5352, pp. 1–25. Springer, Heidelberg (2008). https://doi.org/10.1007/978-3-540-89862-7_1
2. Brumley, D., Jager, I., Avgerinos, T., Schwartz, E.J.: BAP: a binary analysis platform. In: Gopalakrishnan, G., Qadeer, S. (eds.) CAV 2011. LNCS, vol. 6806, pp. 463–469. Springer, Heidelberg (2011). https://doi.org/10.1007/978-3-642-22110-1_37
3. Shoshitaishvili, Y., Wang, R., Salls, C., Stephens, N., Polino, M., Dutcher, A., Grosen, J., Feng, S., Hauser, C., Kruegel, C., Vigna, G.: Sok: (state of) the art of war: offensive techniques in binary analysis. In: Proceedings of 2016 IEEE Symposium on Security and Privacy, SP, pp. 138–157 (2016)
4. Shoshitaishvili, Y., Wang, R., Hauser, C., Kruegel, C., Vigna, G.: Firmalice-automatic detection of authentication bypass vulnerabilities in binary firmware. In: Proceedings of 2015 Network and Distributed System Security Symposium, NDSS (2015)
5. Haller, I., Slowinska, A., Neugschwandtner, M., Bos, H.: Dowsing for overflows: a guided fuzzer to find buffer boundary violations. In: Proceedings of 22nd USENIX Security Symposium, USENIX Security 2013, pp. 49–64 (2013)

6. Corina, J., Machiry, A., Salls, C., Shoshitaishvili, Y., Hao, S., Kruegel, C., Vigna, G.: Difuze: interface aware fuzzing for kernel drivers. In: Proceedings of the 2017 ACM SIGSAC Conference on Computer and Communications Security, CCS 2017, pp. 2123–2138 (2017)

7. Stephens, N., Grosen, J., Salls, C., Dutcher, A., Wang, R., Corbetta, J., Shoshitaishvili, Y., Kruegel, C., Vigna, G.: Driller: augmenting fuzzing through selective symbolic execution. In: Proceedings of 2016 Network and Distributed System Security Symposium, NDSS, vol. 16, pp. 1–16 (2016)

8. Cova, M., Felmetsger, V., Banks, G., Vigna, G.: Static detection of vulnerabilities in x86 executables. In: Proceedings of 22nd Annual Computer Security Applications Conference, ACSAC, pp. 269–278. IEEE (2006)

9. Kolsek, M.: Did microsoft just manually patch their equation editor executable? Why yes, yes they did. (cve-2017-11882) (2017). https://0patch.blogspot.com/2017/11/did-microsoft-just-manually-patch-their.html

10. Wartell, R., Zhou, Y., Hamlen, K.W., Kantarcioglu, M., Thuraisingham, B.: Differentiating code from data in x86 binaries. In: Gunopulos, D., Hofmann, T., Malerba, D., Vazirgiannis, M. (eds.) ECML PKDD 2011. LNCS (LNAI), vol. 6913, pp. 522–536. Springer, Heidelberg (2011). https://doi.org/10.1007/978-3-642-23808-6_34

11. Andriesse, D., Chen, X., van der Veen, V., Slowinska, A., Bos, H.: An in-depth analysis of disassembly on full-scale x86/x64 binaries. In: Proceedings of 25th USENIX Security Symposium, USENIX Security 2016, pp. 583–600 (2016)

12. Andriesse, D., Slowinska, A., Bos, H.: Compiler-agnostic function detection in binaries. In: Proceedings of 2017 IEEE European Symposium on Security and Privacy, Euro S&P, pp. 177–189. IEEE (2017)

13. Chen, J.Y., Shen, B.Y., Ou, Q.H., Yang, W., Hsu, W.C.: Effective code discovery for ARM/Thumb mixed ISA binaries in a static binary translator. In: Proceedings of 2013 International Conference on Compilers, Architectures and Synthesis for Embedded Systems, CASES 2013, pp. 1–10 (2013)

14. Clemens, J.: Automatic classification of object code using machine learning. Digit. Investig. **14**, S156–S162 (2015)

15. Lafferty, J.D., McCallum, A., Pereira, F.C.N.: Conditional random fields: probabilistic models for segmenting and labeling sequence data. In: Proceedings of 18th International Conference on Machine Learning, ICML 2001, pp. 282–289. Morgan Kaufmann Publishers Inc. (2001)

16. Taskar, B., Guestrin, C., Koller, D.: Max-margin Markov networks. In: Advances in Neural Information Processing Systems, pp. 25–32 (2004)

17. Lacoste-Julien, S., Jaggi, M., Schmidt, M., Pletscher, P.: Block-coordinate Frank-Wolfe optimization for structural SVMs. In: Proceedings of 30th International Conference on Machine Learning, ICML 2013, pp. 53–61 (2013)

18. Müller, A.C., Behnke, S.: PyStruct - learning structured prediction in python. J. Mach. Learn. Res. **15**, 2055–2060 (2014)

19. Buluç, A., Fineman, J.T., Frigo, M., Gilbert, J.R., Leiserson, C.E.: Parallel sparse matrix-vector and matrix-transpose-vector multiplication using compressed sparse blocks. In: Proceedings of 21st Annual Symposium on Parallelism in algorithms and architectures, SPAA 2009, pp. 233–244. ACM (2009)

20. Arduino: Built-In Examples. https://www.arduino.cc/en/Tutorial/BuiltIn Examples

21. NVIDIA: CUDA Samples. http://docs.nvidia.com/cuda/cuda-samples/index.html

22. Legitimate Business Syndicate: The cLEMENCy Architecture (2017). https://blog.legitbs.net/2017/07/the-clemency-architecture.html

23. Bao, T., Burket, J., Woo, M., Turner, R., Brumley, D.: ByteWeight: learning to recognize functions in binary code. In: Proceedings of 23rd USENIX Security Symposium, pp. 845–860 (2014)
24. Karampatziakis, N.: Static analysis of binary executables using structural SVMs. In: Lafferty, J.D., Williams, C.K.I., Shawe-Taylor, J., Zemel, R.S., Culotta, A. (eds.) Advances in Neural Information Processing Systems 23, pp. 1063–1071. Curran Associates, Inc. (2010)
25. Microsoft: Universal Windows Platform (UWP) app samples. https://github.com/Microsoft/Windows-universal-samples
26. Microsoft: Dia2dump sample. https://docs.microsoft.com/en-us/visualstudio/debugger/debug-interface-access/dia2dump-sample
27. Eager, M.J.: Introduction to the DWARF debugging format (2012). http://www.dwarfstd.org/doc/Debugging
28. Linn, C., Debray, S.: Obfuscation of executable code to improve resistance to static disassembly. In: Proceedings of 10th ACM Conference on Computer and Communications Security, CCS 2003, pp. 290–299. ACM (2003)
29. Kruegel, C., Robertson, W., Valeur, F., Vigna, G.: Static disassembly of obfuscated binaries. In: Proceedings of 13th USENIX Security Symposium (2004)
30. Rosenblum, N., Zhu, X., Miller, B., Hunt, K.: Learning to analyze binary computer code. In: Proceedings of 23th AAAI Conference on Artificial Intelligence, AAAI 2008, pp. 798–804. AAAI Press (2008)
31. Shin, E.C.R., Song, D., Moazzezi, R.: Recognizing functions in binaries with neural networks. In: Proceedings of 24th USENIX Security Symposium, pp. 611–626 (2015)
32. McDaniel, M., Heydari, M.H.: Content based file type detection algorithms. In: Proceedings of 36th Annual Hawaii International Conference on System Sciences (2003)
33. Li, W.J., Wang, K., Stolfo, S.J., Herzog, B.: Fileprints: identifying file types by n-gram analysis. In: Proceedings of the 6th Annual IEEE SMC Information Assurance Workshop, IAW 2005, pp. 64–71. IEEE (2005)
34. Sportiello, L., Zanero, S.: Context-based file block classification. In: Peterson, G., Shenoi, S. (eds.) DigitalForensics 2012. IAICT, vol. 383, pp. 67–82. Springer, Heidelberg (2012). https://doi.org/10.1007/978-3-642-33962-2_5
35. Penrose, P., Macfarlane, R., Buchanan, W.J.: Approaches to the classification of high entropy file fragments. Digit. Investig. 10(4), 372–384 (2013)
36. Granboulan, L.: cpu_rec: Recognize cpu instructions in an arbitrary binary file (2017). https://github.com/airbus-seclab/cpu_rec
37. Oberhumer, M.F., Molnár, L., Reiser, J.F.: UPX: the Ultimate Packer for eXecutables. https://upx.github.io/

Symbolic Deobfuscation: From Virtualized Code Back to the Original

Jonathan Salwan[1], Sébastien Bardin[2(✉)], and Marie-Laure Potet[3]

[1] Quarkslab, Paris, France
jsalwan@quarkslab.com
[2] CEA, LIST, University of Paris-Saclay, Paris, France
sebastien.bardin@cea.fr
[3] University of Grenoble Alpes, 38000 Grenoble, France
marie-laure.potet@univ-grenoble-alpes.fr

Abstract. Software protection has taken an important place during the last decade in order to protect legit software against reverse engineering or tampering. *Virtualization* is considered as one of the very best defenses against such attacks. We present a generic approach based on symbolic path exploration, taint and recompilation allowing to recover, from a virtualized code, a devirtualized code semantically identical to the original one and close in size. We define criteria and metrics to evaluate the relevance of the deobfuscated results in terms of correctness and precision. Finally we propose an open-source setup allowing to evaluate the proposed approach against several forms of virtualization.

1 Introduction

Context. The field of software protection has increasingly gained in importance with the growing need of protecting sensitive software assets, either for pure security reasons (e.g., protecting security mechanisms) or for commercial reasons (e.g., protecting licence checks in video games or video on demand). Virtual machine (VM) based software protection (a.k.a. *virtualization*) is a modern technique aiming at transforming an original binary code into a custom Instruction Set Architecture (ISA), which is then emulated by a custom interpreter. Virtualization is considered as a very powerful defense against reverse engineering and tampering attacks, taking a central place during the last decade in the software protection arsenal [3–5,23].

Attacking virtualization. In the same time, researchers have published several methods to analyze such protections. They can be partitioned into semi-manual approaches [14,16,20], automated approaches [12,17,22,24,25] and program synthesis [11,28]. Semi-manual approaches consist in manually detecting and understanding VM's opcode handlers, and then, writing a dedicated disassembler. They rely on the knowledge of the reverse engineer and they are time

---

Work partially funded by ANR and PIA under grant ANR-15-IDEX-02.

C. Giuffrida et al. (Eds.): DIMVA 2018, LNCS 10885, pp. 372–392, 2018.
https://doi.org/10.1007/978-3-319-93411-2_17

consuming. Some classes of automated approaches aim at automatically reconstructing the (non-virtualized) control flow of the original program, but they require to detect some virtualization artefacts [12,22] (virtual program counter, dispatcher, etc.) – typically through some dedicated pattern matching. These approaches must be adapted when new forms of virtualization are met. Finally, another class of approaches [7,24] tries to directly reconstruct the behaviors of the initial code (before virtualization), based on trace analysis geared at eliminating the virtualization machinery. Such approaches aim to be agnostic with respect to the different forms of virtualization. Yet, while the ultimate goal of deobfuscation is to recover the original program, these approaches focus rather on intermediate steps, such as identifying the Virtual Machine machinery or simplifying traces.

Goal and challenges. While most works on devirtualization target malware detection and control flow graph recovery, *we focus here on sensitive function protections (such as authentication), either for IP or integrity reasons*, and we consider the problem of fully recovering the original program behavior (expurged from the VM machinery) and compiling back a new (devirtualized) version of the original binary. We suppose we have access to the protected (virtualized) function and we are interested in recovering the original non-obfuscated code, or at least a program very close to it. We consider the following open questions:

- How can we characterize the relevance of the deobfuscated results?
- How much can such approaches be independent of the virtualization machinery and its protections?
- How can virtualization be hardened against such approaches?

Contribution. Our contributions are the following:

- We present a fully automatic and generic approach to devirtualization, based on combining taint, symbolic execution and code simplification. We clearly discuss limitations and guarantees of the proposed approach, and we demonstrate the potential of the method by automatically solving (the non-jitted part of) the Tigress Challenge in a completely automated manner.
- We design a strong experimental setup[1] for the systematic assessment of the qualities of our framework: well-defined questions & metrics, a delimited class of programs (hash-like functions, integrity checks) and adequat measurement besides code similarities (full correctness). We also propose a systematic coverage of classic protections and their combinations.
- Finally, we propose an open-source framework based on the Triton API, resulting in reproducible public results.

---

[1] Solving the Tigress Challenge was presented at the French industrial conference SSTIC'17 [18]. The work presented here adds a revisited description of the method, a strong systematic experimental evaluation as well as new metrics to evaluate the accuracy of the approach.

The main features of our approach are summarized in Fig. 1, in comparison with others works. In particular we propose and discuss some notions of correctness and completeness as well as a set of metrics illustrating the accuracy of our approach. Figure 1 will be explained in more details in Sect. 6.

	manual	Kinder[12]	Coogan[7]	Yadegari[25]	Our approach
identify input	required	required	required	required	required
understand vpc	required	required	no	no	no
understand dispatcher	required	no	no	no	no
understand bytecode	required	no	no	no	no
output	simplified CFG	CFG + invariants	simplified trace	simplified CFG	simplified code
key techno.	–	static analysis (abstract interp.)	value-based slicing	taint, symbolic, instr. simplification	taint, symbolic, formula simplification, code simplification
xp: type of code	–	toy examples	toys+malware	toys+malware	hash functions
xp: #samples	–	1	12	44	920
xp: evaluation metrics	–	known invariants	%simplification	similarity	size, correctness

Fig. 1. Position of our approach

Discussion. While our approach still shows limitations on the class of programs that can be handled (cf. Sect. 5), the present work clearly demonstrates that hash-like functions (typical of proprietary assets protected through obfuscation) can be easily retrieved from their virtualized versions, challenging the common knowledge that virtualization is the best defense against reversing – while it is true for a human attacker, it does not hold anymore for an automated attacker (unless the defender is ready to pay a high running time overhead with deep nested virtualization). Hence, defenders must take great care of protecting the VM machinery itself against semantic attacks.

2   Background: Virtualization and Reverse Engineering

2.1   Virtualization-Based Software Protection

Virtualization-based software protections aim at encoding the original program into a new binary code written in a custom Instruction Set Architecture (ISA) shipped together with a custom Virtual Machine (VM). Such protections are offered by several industrial and academic tools [3–5,23]. Generally, it is composed of 5 principal components, close to CPU design (Fig. 2):

1. **Fetch**: Its role is to fetch, from the VM's internal memory, the *(virtual) opcode* to emulate, based on the value of a *virtual program counter* (vpc).
2. **Decode**: Its role is to decode the fetched opcode and its appropriate operands to determine which ISA instruction will be executed.
3. **Dispatch**: Once the instruction is decoded, the dispatcher determines which *handler* must be executed and sets up its context.
4. **Handlers**: They emulate virtual instructions by sequences of native instructions and update the internal context of VM, typically vpc.
5. **Terminator**: The terminator determines if the emulation is finished or not. If not, the whole process is executed one more time.

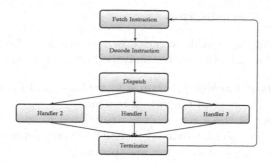

Fig. 2. Standard virtual machine architecture

2.2 Example

Let us consider the C function of Listing 1.1 we want to virtualize it. Disassembly of the VM's bytecode is in comment in Listing 1.1. Once Listing 1.1 is compiled to VM's bytecode, it must be interpreted by the virtual machine itself. The sample of code illustrated by Listing 1.2 could be this kind of VM. The VM is called with an initial vpc pointing to the first opcode of the bytecode (e.g: the virtual address of instruction mov r0, r9). Once the opcode has been fetched and decoded by the VM, the dispatcher points to the appropriate handler to virtually execute the instruction and then, the handler increments vpc to point on the next instruction to execute and so on until the virtualized program terminate. As we can see, the control flow of the original program is lost and replaced by a dispatcher pointing on all VM's handlers (here, only four instructions).

```
int func(int x) {
    int a = x;
    int b = 2;
    int c = a * b;
    return c;
}

/*
** Bytecodes equivalence:
**
** 31 ff 00 09:    mov r0, r9
** 31 01 02 00:    mov r1, 2
** 44 00 00 01:    mul r0, r0, r1
** 60:             ret
*/
```

Listing 1.1. A C function

```
void vm(ulong vpc, struct vmgpr* gpr) {
    while (1) {
        /* Fetch and Decode */
        struct opcode* i = decode(fetch(vpc));
        /* Dispatch */
        switch (i->getType()) {
            /* Handlers */
            case ADD /* 0x21 */:
                gpr->r[i->dst] = i->op1 + i->op2;
                vpc += 4; break;
            case MOV /* 0x31 */:
                gpr->r[i->dst] = i->op1;
                vpc += 4; break;
            case MUL /* 0x44 */:
                gpr->r[i->dst] = i->op1 * i->op2;
                vpc += 4; break;
            case RET /* 0x60 */:
                vpc += 1; return;
}}}
```

Listing 1.2. Example of VM

2.3 Manual De-Virtualization

Manual devirtualization typically comes down to writing a disassembler for the (unknown) virtual architecture under analysis. It consists of the following steps:

1. Identify that the obfuscated program is virtualized, and identify its input;
2. Identify each component of the virtual machine;
3. Understand how all these components are related to each other, especially which handler corresponds to which bytecode, the associated semantics, where operands are located and how they are specified;
4. Understand how vpc is orchestrated.

Once all these points have been addressed, we can easily create a specific disassembler targeted to the virtual architecture. Yet, solving each step is time consuming and may be heavily influenced by the reverse engineer expertise, the design of the virtual machine (e.g: which kind of dispatcher, of operands, etc.) and the level of obfuscation implemented to hide the virtual machine itself.

Discussion. Recovering 100% of the original binary code is impossible in general, that is why devirtualization aims at proposing a binary code as close as possible to the original one. Here, we seek to provide a semantically equivalent code expurged from the components of the virtual machine (*devirtualized code*). In other words, starting from the code in Listing 1.2, we want to derive a code semantically equivalent and close (in size) to the code in Listing 1.1.

3 Our Approach

We rely on the key intuition that *an obfuscated trace T' (from the obfuscated code P') combines original instructions from the original code P (the trace T corresponding to T' in the original code) and instructions of the virtual machine VM such that $T' = T + VM(T)$.* If we are able to distinguish between these two subsequences of instructions T and $VM(T)$, we then are able to reconstruct one path of the original program P from a trace T'. By repeating this operation to cover all paths of the virtualized program, we will be able to reconstruct the original program P – in case the original code has a finite number of executable paths, which is the case in many practical situations involving IP protection.

3.1 Overview

The main steps of our approach, sketched in Fig. 3, are the following ones:

Step 0: Identify input.
Step 1: On a trace, isolate pertinent instructions using a dynamic taint analysis.
Step 2: Build a symbolic representation of these tainted instructions.
Step 3: Perform a path coverage analysis to reach new tainted paths.
Step 4: Reconstruct a program from the resulting traces and compile it to obtain a devirtualized version of the original code.

In our approach, Step-0 (identifying input) must still be done manually, in a traditional way. By input we include all kinds of external interactions depending on the user, such as environment variables, program arguments and system calls (e.g. read, recv, *etc.). Analysts will typically rely on tools such as IDA or debuggers for this step.*

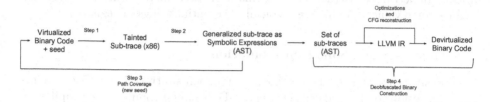

Fig. 3. Schematized Approach

Our approach is based on the tool suite Triton [19] which provides several advanced classes to improve dynamic binary analysis, in particular a concolic execution engine, a SMT symbolic representation and a taint analysis engine.

Dynamic Symbolic Execution (DSE) [9,10,21] (a.k.a. concolic execution) is a technique that interprets program variables as symbolic variables along an execution. During a program execution, the DSE engine builds arithmetic expressions representing data operations and logical expressions characterizing path constraints along the execution path. These constraints can then be solved automatically by a constraint solver [26] (typically, SMT solver) in order to obtain new input data covering new paths of the program. Conversely to pure symbolic execution, DSE can reduce the complexity of these expressions by using concrete values from the program execution ("concretization" [10]).

Dynamic Taint Analysis (DTA) [6,27] aims to detect which data and instructions along an execution depend on user input. We consider direct tainting. Regarding the code in Listing 1.3 where user input is denoted by input, we start by tainting the input at line 1. Then, according to the instruction semantics, the taint is spread into rax at line 1, then rcx at line 3 and rdi at line 4. To resume, using a taint analysis, we know that instructions at line 1, 3, and 4 are in interaction with user input.

```
1. mov rax , input
2. mov rcx , 1
3. add rcx , rax
4. mov rdi , rcx
```

Listing 1.3. x86 ASM sample

Taint can be combined with symbolic execution in order to explore all paths depending on inputs, resulting in input values covering these paths.

3.2   Step 1 - Dynamic Taint Analysis

The first step aims at separating those instructions which are part of the virtual machine internal process from those which are part of the original program behavior. In order to do that, we taint every input of the virtualized function. Running a first execution with a random seed, we get as a result a subtrace of tainted instructions. We call these instructions: *pertinent instructions*. These pertinent instructions represent all interactions with the inputs of the program, as non-tainted instructions have always the same effect on the original program behavior. At this step, the original program behaviors are represented by the subtrace of pertinent instructions. But this subtrace cannot be directly executed, because some values are missing, typically the initial values of registers.

3.3   Step 2 - a Symbolic Representation

The second step abstracts the pertinent instruction subtrace in terms of a symbolic expression for two goals: (1) prepare DSE exploration, (2) recompile the expression to obtain an executable trace. In symbolic expressions, all tainted values are symbolized while all un-tainted values are concretized. In other words, our symbolic expressions do not contain any operation related to the virtual machine processing (the machinery itself does not depend on the user) but only operations related to the original program.

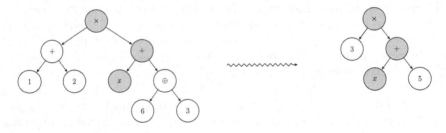

Fig. 4. Concretization of non tainted expressions

In order to better understand what Step 2 does, let us consider the function illustrated in Listing 1.4. Variable x is tainted as well as symbolized and the expression associated to variable var8 is illustrated on the left of Fig. 4 (gray nodes are tainted data). Then, once we concretize all un-tainted nodes, the expression becomes the one illustrated on the right. This mechanism typically allows to remove the VM machinery.

```
int f(int x) {
    int var1 = 1;
    int var2 = 2;
    int var3 = var1 + var2;
    int var4 = 6;
    int var5 = 3;
    int var6 = var4 ^ var5;
    int var7 = x + var6;
    int var8 = var3 * var7;
    return var8;
}
```

Listing 1.4. Sample of C code

3.4   Step 3 - Path Coverage

At this step we are able to devirtualize one path. To reconstruct the whole program behavior, we successively devirtualize reachable tainted paths. To do so, we perform path coverage [10] on tainted branches with DSE. At the end, we get as a result a path tree which represents the different paths of the original program (Fig. 5). Path tree is obtained by introducing if-then-else construction from two traces t_1 and t_2 with a same prefix followed by a condition C in t_1 and $\neg C$ in t_2.

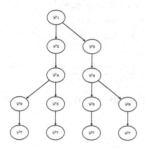

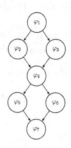

Fig. 5. Path tree   **Fig. 6.** A Reconstructed CFG

3.5   Step 4 - Generate a New Binary Version

At this step we have all information to reconstruct a new binary code: (1) a symbolic representation of each path; (2) a path tree combining all reachable paths. In order to produce a binary code we transform our symbolic path tree into the LLVM IR to obtain a LLVM Abstract Tree (AST in Fig. 3) and compile it. In particular we benefit from all LLVM (code level) optimizations[2] to partially rebuild a simplified Control Flow Graph (Fig. 6). Note that moving on LLVM allows us to compile the devirtualized program to another architecture. For instance, it is possible to devirtualize a x86 function and to devirtualize it to an ARM architecture.

3.6   Guarantees: About Correctness and Completeness

Let P be the obfuscated program and P^* the extracted program. We want to guarantee that P and P^* behave equivalently for each input. We decompose this property into two sub-properties:

- **local correctness:** for a given input i, P and P^* behave equivalently,
- **completeness:** local correctness is established for each input.

---

[2] Such as `simplifycfg` and `instcombine`.

While local correctness can often be guaranteed, depending on properties of each step (see Fig. 7), completeness is lost in general as it requires full path exploration of the virtualized program. Interestingly enough, it can be recovered in the case of programs with a small number of paths, which is the case for many typical hash or crypto functions.

Step	Component	flaw	threats on P^*
1	taint	undertainting overtainting	incorrect too large
2	path predicate	under-approximated over-approximated	incomplete incorrect
3	path exploration	incomplete	incomplete
4	code optimization	incorrect incomplete	incorrect too large

Fig. 7. Impact of each components on the overall approach

3.7 Implementation

We develop a script[3] implementing our method. The Triton library [19] is in charge of everything related to the DSE and the taint engine. We also use Arybo [8] to move from the Triton representation to the LLVM-IR [13] and the LLVM front-end to compile the new binary code. The Triton DSE engine is standard [10,21]: paths are explored in a depth-first search manner, memory accesses are concretized *à la* DART [10] (resulting in incorrect concretization) [15], logical formulas are expressed in the theory of bitvectors and sent to the Z3 SMT solver. Triton is engineered with care and is able to handle execution traces counting several dozen millions of instructions.

Regarding the discussion in Sect. 3.6, we can state that our implementation is correct on programs without any user-dependent memory access, and that it is even complete if those programs have a small number of paths (say, less than 100). While very restrictive, these conditions do hold for many typical hash-like functions, representative of proprietary assets protected through obfuscation.

4 Experiments

In order to evaluate our approach we proceed in two steps. First we carry out a set of systematic controlled experiments in order to precisely evaluate the key properties of our method (Sects. 4.1 to 4.4). Second we address a real life deobfuscation challenge (Tigress Challenge) in order to check whether our approach can address uncontrolled obfuscated programs (Sect. 4.5). Code, benchmarks and

---

[3] https://github.com/JonathanSalwan/Tigress_protection/blob/master/solve-vm.py.

more detailed results are available online[4]. We propose the three following evaluation criteria for our deobfuscation technique:

C_1: **Precision**,
C_2: **Efficiency**,
C_3: **Robustness w.r.t. the protection.**

4.1 Controlled Experiment: Setup

Our test bench is composed of 20 hash algorithms comprising 10 well-known hash functions and 10 homemade ones taken from the Tigress Challenge[5] (see Table 1). The proposed functions are typically composed of a statically-bounded loop and contains one or two execution paths. These programs are typical of the kinds of assets the defender might want to protect in a code.

Table 1. List of virtualized hash functions for our benchmark

Hash	Loops	Binary size (inst)	# Executable paths
Adler-32	✓	78	1
CityHash	✓	175	1
Collberg-0001-0	✓	167	1
Collberg-0001-1	✗	177	2
Collberg-0001-2	✗	223	1
Collberg-0001-3	✓	195	1
Collberg-0001-4	✓	183	1
Collberg-0004-0	✗	210	2
Collberg-0004-1	✗	143	1
Collberg-0004-2	✓	219	2
Collberg-0004-3	✓	171	1
Collberg-0004-4	✓	274	1
Fowler-Noll-Vo Hash (FNV1a)	✗	110	1
Jenkins	✓	79	1
JodyHash	✓	90	1
MD5	✓	314	1
SpiHash	✓	362	1
SpookyHash	✓	426	1
SuperFastHash	✓	144	1
Xxhash	✓	182	1

---

[4] https://github.com/JonathanSalwan/Tigress_protection.
[5] Thanks to Christian Collberg for having provided us the original source codes.

In order to protect these 20 samples, we choose the open-use binary protector Tigress[6], a diversifying virtualizer/obfuscator for the C language that supports many novel defenses against both static and dynamic reverse engineering and devirtualization attacks. Then, we select all virtualization-related binary protections (46) and apply each of them on each of the 20 samples, yielding a total benchmark of 920 protected codes (see Table 2). The goal is then to retrieve an equivalent and devirtualized version of each protected code. All these tests are applied on a Dell XPS 13 laptop with a Intel i7-6560U CPU, 16GB of RAM and 8GB of SWAP on a SSD.

Table 2. Tigress protections

Protecticons	Options
Anti branch analysis	goto2push, goto2call, branchFuns
Max merge length	0, 10, 20, 30
Bogus function	0, 1, 2, 3
Kind of operands	stack, registers
Opaque to VPC	true, false
Bogus loop iterations	0, 1, 2, 3
Super operator ratio	0, 0.2, 0.4, 0.6, 0.8, 1.0
Random opcodes	true, false
Duplicate opcodes	0, 1, 2, 3
Dispatcher	binary, direct, call, interpolation, indirect, switch, ifnest, linear
Encode byte array	true, false
Obfuscate decode byte array	true, false
Nested VMs	1, 2, 3

4.2 Precision (C_1)

The C_1 criterion aims to determine two points **1. correctness:** is the deobfuscated code semantically equivalent to the original code? **2. conciseness:** is the size of the deobfuscated code similar to the size of the original code?

Metrics used: Regarding correctness, after applying our approach we test over 4,000 integer inputs (the 1000 smallest integers, the 1000 largest ones, 2000 random others) whether the two corresponding output (obfuscated and deobfuscated) are identical or not. If yes, we consider the deobfuscated code as semantically equivalent. We also manually check 50 samples taken at random. Regarding conciseness, we consider the number of instructions before and after protections, and then after devirtualization.

---

[6] http://tigress.cs.arizona.edu.

Results: Table 3 gives an average of ratios (in term of number of instructions) between the original code and the obfuscated one, and also between the original code and the deobfuscated one. This table demonstrates that 1. after applying our approach, we are able to reconstruct valid binaries (in term of correctness) for 100% of our samples; 2. after applying protections, the sizes of binaries and traces are considerably increased and after applying our approach we reconstruct binaries sometimes slightly smaller than the original ones. This phenomenon is due to the fact that we concretize everything not related to the user input (Step 2), including initialisation and set up. Manual inspections also reveal that when the original code does not contain any loop, the recovered code exhibits almost the same CFG as the original code.

Table 3. Size and correctness (920 samples)

	Original	Obfuscated	Deobfuscated
Binary Size	min: 78 max: 426 avg: 196	min: 468 max: 5,424 avg: 1,205	min: 48 max: 557 avg: 119
Trace Size	min: 92 max: 9,743 avg: 726	min: 1,349 max: 47,927,795 avg: 229,168	min: 48 max: 557 avg: 143

(a) Sizes

Correctness	Original → Obfuscated	Original → Deobfuscated
		100%
Binary Size	min: x3.3 max: x14.0 avg: x6	min: x0.1 max: x2.8 avg: x0.71
Trace Size	min: x17 max: x1252 avg: x424	min: x0.05 max: x0.9 avg: x0.39

(b) Size ratios

Conclusion: Our approach does allow to recover semantically-equivalent devirtualized codes in all cases, with sizes very close to those of the original codes (even slightly smaller in average, despite loop unrolling), thus drastically decreasing the size of the protected code. Interestingly, our devirtualized codes have also simpler execution traces than the original codes.

4.3 Effectiveness (C_2)

The C_2 criterion aims at determining the effectiveness of our approach in terms of absolute time (required amount of resources) and also in trend (scalability).

Metrics used: We took measure at each step of our analysis and at each 10,000 instructions handled. These metric results can be found in detail in Table 7 (Appendix) and its *Obfuscated* (trace size) and *Time* columns.

Results: Figure 8 is the time-step of our approach on the 920 samples. About 80% of samples take less than 5 sec. to be deobfuscated. The most difficult example takes about 1h10 for approximatively 48 millions of instructions (MD5 with two levels of virtualization).

According to these results, we can see that the time taken by our analysis is linear w.r.t. the number of instructions on the obfuscated traces (*size of the execution tree*). If we focus on the MD5 example[7] and draw a dot at each 10,000

---

[7] MD5 is one of the most involving examples in our benchmark.

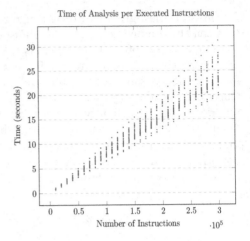

Time of Analysis per Executed Instructions

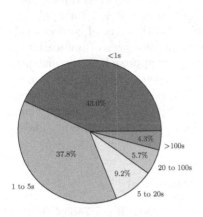

Fig. 8. Time-step (920 samples)

Fig. 9. Time w.r.t. number of instr. (all protections, MD5 algo.)

instructions handled and then for each protections, we get as a result Fig. 9. Each dotted curve of this figure is one of the 46 protections used for our benchmark and each dot is a measure at each 10,000 instructions step. We can clearly see that curves possess a linear aspect.

Conclusion: Our approach has a linear time of analysis according to the number of explored instructions (execution tree), meaning that our approach does not add complexity w.r.t. standard DSE exploration. The more the protection integrates instructions in the binary the more our analysis will take time and RAM consuming but only with a constant evolution. Regarding our samples, we managed to devirtualize lot of them very quickly (only few seconds), and even for the hardest examples we were able to solve them in a short time on common hardware.

4.4   Influence of Protections (C_3)

This criterion aims at identifying whether certain specific protections do impact the analysis more than other protections (correctness, conciseness or performances), and if yes, how much.

Metrics Used: We consider the conciseness metrics, i.e. the number of instructions during the executions of the obfuscated binaries, the deobfuscated binaries and the original ones. We use them on the 46 different protections applied on the same hash algorithm, and then for all hash algorithms.

Results: According to Table 7 in appendix (*Deobfuscated* column), we can clearly answer that the conciseness is the same whatever protection is applied. We get the same result for each one of these protected binary codes. Protections do not influence the number of instructions recovered for all the 20 hash algorithms tested. As an example, Fig. 10 illustrates the influence of different dispatchers analyzed on the MD5 example and we can clearly see that the number of instructions recovered is identical whatever dispatcher is applied. Moreover, previous results in Sect. 4.3 (Fig. 9) have already demonstrated that all considered protections have an effect on efficiency directly proportional to the increase they involve on the trace size.

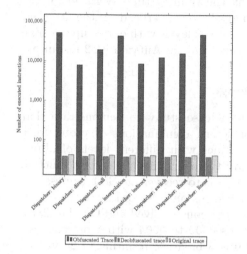

Fig. 10. Influence of dispatchers on our analysis

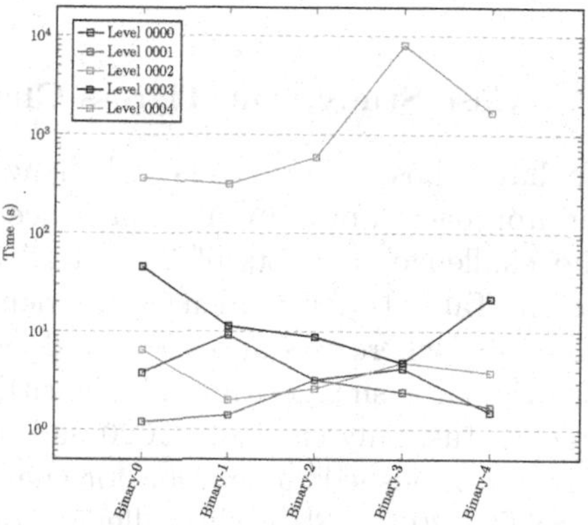

Fig. 11. Time to solve each Tigress challenge

Conclusion: Our approach, in term of precision, is not influenced by the chosen protections and our outputs are identical whatever the protections applied. Yet, as already shown, the protection can influence the analysis time and make the analysis intractable. The previous section shows that such a protection can be effective only if it implies a large runtime overhead - which can be a severe problem on some applications. For example regarding the MD5 example, the execution overhead is 10x with 1 level of VM, 100x with 2 and 6800x with 3.

Discussion on Each Protection In order to really understand why our approach works on such protections, we open a discussion for each category of them.

Complicated VM machinery (opaque vpc, dispatchers, etc.): These protections are mainly introduced to slowdown a static analysis. Yet, using a dynamic taint analysis (Step 1 of Sect. 3.2), we are able to distinguish which instructions are dedicated to the virtual machine and which instructions emulate the original behavior of the program (*pertinent instructions*). The virtual machine's subexpressions are then eliminated through concretization in Step 2 (see Sect. 3.3).

Duplicate Opcodes: This protection makes the VM more complicated to understand by a human, but it does not prevent its exploration (Steps 1 to 3). In our experiments, duplicated opcodes are identified and merged together because of code-level (compiler) optimizations (Step 4) together with the normalization induced by the transformation to symbolic expressions (Step 2).

Nested VM: As already discussed, nesting VMs does not impact the precision but the performance of our method. Hence the defender can indeed prevent the attack, but it comes at a high cost as the running time overhead for the defender is directly proportional to the analysis time overhead for the attacker. As an example, we are able to solve up to 2 nested levels with our setup machine (16GB of RAM), but we solve 3 nested levels using an Amazon EC2 instance.

4.5   Case Study: The Tigress Challenge

We have chosen the Tigress Challenge as a case study to demonstrate that our approach works even in presence of strong combinations of protections. The challenge[8] consists of 35 virtual machines with different levels of obfuscation (Table 4). All challenges are identical: there is a virtualized hash function $f(x) \rightsquigarrow x'$ where x is an integer and the goal is to recover, as close as possible, the original hash algorithm (all algorithms are custom). According to their challenge status, only challenge 0000 had been previously solved and October 28th, 2016 we published[9] a solution for challenges 0000 to 0004 with a presentation at SSTIC 2017 [18] (each challenge contains 5 binaries, resulting in 25 virtual machine codes). We do not analyze jitted binaries (0005 and 0006) as jit is not currently supported by our implementation.

Table 4. Tigress Challenge (each challenge contains 5 virtual machines)

Challenge	Description	Difficulty	Web Status	Our Status
0000	One level of virtualization, random dispatch.	1	Solved	Solved
0001	One level of virtualization, superoperators, split instruction handlers.	2	Open	**Solved**
0002	One level of virtualization, bogus functions, implicit flow.	3	Open	**Solved**
0003	One level of virtualization, instruction handlers obfuscated with arithmetic encoding, virtualized function is split and the split parts merged.	2	Open	**Solved**
0004	Two levels of virtualization, implicit flow.	4	Open	**Solved**
0005	One level of virtualization, one level of jitting, implicit flow.	4	Open	Open[†]
0006	Two levels of jitting, implicit flow.	4	Open	Open[†]

[†]: Jit not supported by our script.

We have been able to automatically solve all the aforementioned open challenges in a correct, precise and efficient way, demonstrating that the good results observed in our controlled experiments extend to the uncontrolled case. Correction has been checked with random testing and manual inspection. Figure 11 illustrates the time and memory consumption for each challenge – again time

---

[8] http://tigress.cs.arizona.edu/challenges.html#current.
[9] http://tigress.cs.arizona.edu/index.htm.

and memory consumption are proportional to the number of instruction executed. The hardest challenge family is 0004 with two levels of virtualization. For instance, challenge 0004-3 contains 140 millions of instructions, reduced to 320 in 2 h with 21GB of memory. More details can be found in [18].

5   Discussion

We first summarize limitations of our approach, together with possible mitigations. Then we discuss how our technique can be defended against (Table. 5)

Table 5. Time (in seconds) to solve Tigress Challenge

	Tigress challenges				
	VM-0	VM-1	VM-2	VM-3	VM-4
0000	3.85s	9.20s	3.27s	4.26s	1.58s
0001	1.26s	1.42s	3.27s	2.49s	1.74s
0002	6.58s	2.02s	2.63s	4.85s	3.82s
0003	45.6s	11.3s	8.84s	4.84s	21.6s
0004	361s	315s	588s	8049s	1680s

5.1   Limits and Mitigations

The main limitation of our method is that it is mostly geared at programs with a small number of paths. In case of a too high number of paths, large parts of the original code may be lost, yielding an incomplete recovery. Yet, we are considering here *executable paths* rather than syntactic paths in the CFG, and we already made the case that hash and other cryptographic functions often have only very few paths – only one path in the case of timing-attack resistant implementations.

Also our current implementation is limited to programs without any user-dependent memory access. This limitation can be partly removed by using a more symbolic handling of memory accesses in DSE [15], yet the tainting process will have to be updated too. Since we absolutely want to avoid undertainting (see Fig. 7 Sect. 3.6), dynamic tainting will have to be complemented with some form of range information. Note that we require only direct tainting, limiting the undertainting effect.

Another class of limitations arises from programs using features beyond the scope of our symbolic reasoning, such as multithreading, intensive floating-point arithmetic reasoning, self-modification, system calls, etc. Extending to these constructs is hard in general as it may require significant advances in symbolic reasoning. Note, however, that there are some recent progress in floating-point arithmetic reasoning, and that (simple) self-modification can be handled quite directly in DSE [1]. Moreover, regarding system calls, adequate modelling of the environment could be useful here – not that much a research question, but a clearly manpower-intensive task. Finally, while completeness is clearly out of scope here, local correctness can still be enforced in many cases by relying on the concretization part of DSE.

Note also that while bounded loops and non-recursive function calls are handled, they are currently recovered as inlined or unrolled code, yielding a potential blowup of the size of the devirtualized code. It would be interesting to have a postprocessing step trying to rebuild these high-level abstractions.

5.2   Potential Defenses

Protecting the VM by attacking our steps. As usual, deobfuscation approaches may be broken by attacking their weaknesses. It is actually a never-ending cat-and-mouse game. Figure 7 (Sect. 3.6) gives a good idea of the kind of attacks our method can suffer from. As the first step of our approach reposes on a taint analysis aiming at isolating pertinent instructions, a simple defense could be to spread the taint into VM's components like `decoder` or `dispatcher`. The more the taint is interlaced with VM components, the less our approach will be precise, as tainted data are symbolized. Especially if we symbolize `vpc` our path exploration step will run into the well-known path explosion problem. We can also imagine a defense based on hash functions over jump conditions (e.g: `if (hash(x) == 0x1234)`) which will break constraint solvers during path exploration. Precise dynamic tainting and more robust crypto-oriented solvers are current hot research topics. Another possibility is to implement anti-dynamic tricks to prevent tracing. This issue is more an engineering problem, but it is not that easy to handle well.

In a general setting, symbolic attacks and defenses are a hot topic of deobfuscation, and several protections against symbolic reasoning have been investigated. Any progress in this domain can be directly re-used, either for or against our method. Yet, these protections are not that easy to implement well, and it is sometimes hard to predict whether they will work fine or not. Especially, the protections have to depend on user input, otherwise they will be discarded by taint analysis. Note also that we do not claim that our method can overcome all of these defenses: we focus only on the virtualization step.

Protecting the bytecode instead of the VM. Another interesting defense is to protect the bytecode of the virtual machine instead of its components. Thus, if the virtual machine is broken, the attacker gets as a result an obfuscated pseudo code. For example, this bytecode could be turned into unreadable Mixed Boolean Arithmetic (MBA) expressions.

6   Related Work

Several heuristic approaches to devirtualization have been proposed (e.g., [22]), yet our work is closer to semantic devirtualization methods [7,12,25]. It has also connexions with recent works on symbolic deobfuscation [1,2,8]. Figure 1 Sect. 1 gives a synthetic comparison of these different approaches.

Manual and heuristic devirtualization. Sharif *et al.* [22] propose a dynamic analysis approach which tries to identify vpc based on memory access patterns, then they reconstruct a CFG from this sequence of vpc. However, their method suffers from limitations. For example, their loop detection strategies are not directly applicable to emulators using a threaded approach. Their approach is also likewise not applicable to dynamic translation-based emulation. Another point is that their approach expects each unique address in memory to hold only one abstract variable, which means that an adversary may utilize the same location for different variables at different times to introduce imprecision in their analysis. Conversely, our method solves this problem since we are working on a trace over a SSA representation, making aliasing trivial to catch up. They also mention nesting virtualization as an open problem, while our method has been shown to handle some level of nesting.

Semantics devirtualization. Coogan *et al.* [7] focus on identifying instructions affecting the observable behavior of the obfuscated code. They propose a dynamic approach based on a form of tainting together with leveraging the knowledge from system calls and ABIs. In the end, they identify a subtrace of the virtualized trace containing only those instructions affecting the program output. Their approach can devirtualize only a single path (the executed one) and cannot be applied on virtualized functions without any system call.

Yadegari *et al.* [25] proposes a generic approach to deobfuscation combining tainting, symbolic execution and simplifications. Their goal is to recover the CFG of obfuscated malware, and they carry out experimental evaluation with several obfuscation tools. Our technique shows similarities with their own approach, yet we consider the problem of recovering back a semantically-correct (unprotected) binary code in typical cases of IP protections (hash functions), and we perform a large set of controlled experiments, regarding all virtualization options provided by the Tigress tool, in order to evaluate the properties of our approach.

Kinder [12] proposes a static analysis based on abstract interpretation built over a vpc-sensitive abstract domain. Its approach performs a range analysis on the whole VM interpreter, providing the reverser with invariants on the arguments of function calls.

Symbolic deobfuscation. Banescu *et al.* [2] recently evaluate the efficiency of standard obfuscation mechanisms against symbolic deobfuscation. They conclude, as we do, that without any proper anti-symbolic trick these defenses are not efficient. They also propose a powerful anti-symbolic defense mechanism, but it requires some form of secret sharing and thus falls outside the strict scope of man-at-the-end scenario we consider here. These two works are complementary in the sense that we focus only on virtualization-based protection, but we cover it in a more intensive way and we take a more ambitious notion of deobfuscation (get back an equivalent and small code) while they consider program coverage. In the same vein, recent promising results have been obtain by symbolic deobfuscation against several classes of protections [1,8,25].

7 Conclusion and Future Work

We propose a new automated dynamic analysis geared at fully recovering the original program behavior of a virtualized code – expurged from the VM machinery, and compiling back a new (devirtualized) version of the original binary. We demonstrate the potential of the method on small hash-like functions (typical of proprietary assets protected by obfuscation) through an extensive experimental evaluation, assessing its precision, efficiency and genericity, and we solve (the non-jitted part of) the Tigress Challenge in a completely automated manner. While our approach still shows limitations on the class of programs that can be handled, this work clearly demonstrates that hash-like functions can be easily5 retrieved from their virtualized versions, challenging the common knowledge that virtualization is the best defense against reversing (Table. 6).

In a near future we will focus on the reconstruction of more complicated program structures such as user-dependent loops or memory accesses.

A Detailed experiments

Table 6. Average of all algorithms per protection

Protection	Traces Size (instructions)			Binary Size (instructions)		
	Original	Obfuscated	Deobfuscated	Original	Obfuscated	Deobfuscated
Anti Branch Analysis: branchFuns	min: 92 max: 9,743 avg: 698	min: 3,047 max: 1,555,703 avg: 121,460	min: 48 max: 599 avg: 122	min: 78 max: 426 avg: 192	min: 935 max: 2,048 avg: 1,641	min: 48 max: 599 avg: 122
Kind of Operands: stack	min: 92 max: 9,743 avg: 698	min: 1,430 max: 381,230 avg: 31,104	min: 48 max: 599 avg: 122	min: 78 max: 426 avg: 192	min: 783 max: 1,139 avg: 979	min: 48 max: 599 avg: 122
Kind of Operands: registers	min: 92 max: 9,743 avg: 698	min: 1,459 max: 425,285 avg: 34,322	min: 48 max: 599 avg: 122	min: 78 max: 426 avg: 192	min: 807 max: 1,182 avg: 1,065	min: 48 max: 599 avg: 122
Opaque to VPC: False	min: 92 max: 9,743 avg: 698	min: 1,430 max: 381,230 avg: 31,104	min: 48 max: 599 avg: 122	min: 78 max: 426 avg: 192	min: 783 max: 1,139 avg: 979	min: 48 max: 599 avg: 122
Opaque to VPC: True	min: 92 max: 9,743 avg: 698	min: 1,600 max: 700,138 avg: 51,405	min: 48 max: 599 avg: 122	min: 78 max: 426 avg: 192	min: 861 max: 1,296 avg: 1,148	min: 48 max: 599 avg: 122
Duplicate Opcodes: 3	min: 92 max: 9,743 avg: 698	min: 1,430 max: 381,230 avg: 31,037	min: 48 max: 599 avg: 122	min: 78 max: 426 avg: 192	min: 783 max: 1,226 avg: 1,063	min: 48 max: 599 avg: 122
Dispatcher: binary	min: 92 max: 9,743 avg: 698	min: 2,449 max: 2,825,359 avg: 195,969	min: 48 max: 599 avg: 122	min: 78 max: 426 avg: 192	min: 814 max: 1,154 avg: 1,010	min: 48 max: 599 avg: 122
Dispatcher: interpolation	min: 92 max: 9,743 avg: 698	min: 2,625 max: 2,592,186 avg: 181,698	min: 48 max: 599 avg: 122	min: 78 max: 426 avg: 192	min: 839 max: 1,183 avg: 1,037	min: 48 max: 599 avg: 122
Dispatcher: linear	min: 92 max: 9,743 avg: 698	min: 2,115 max: 5,804,970 avg: 351,747	min: 48 max: 599 avg: 122	min: 78 max: 426 avg: 192	min: 785 max: 1,125 avg: 982	min: 48 max: 599 avg: 122
Nested VMs: 1	min: 92 max: 9,743 avg: 698	min: 1,430 max: 381,230 avg: 30,104	min: 48 max: 599 avg: 122	min: 78 max: 426 avg: 192	min: 783 max: 1,139 avg: 979	min: 48 max: 599 avg: 122
Nested VMs: 2	min: 92 max: 9,743 avg: 698	min: 37,479 max: 47,927,795 avg: 3,520,624	min: 48 max: 599 avg: 122	min: 78 max: 426 avg: 192	min: 676 max: 1,182 avg: 814	min: 48 max: 599 avg: 122

Table 7. Average of all protections per hash function

Hash	Stat	Traces Size (instructions)			Binary Size (instructions)			Time (s)	RAM (KB)	Correctness
		Original	Obfuscated	Deobfuscated	Original	Obfuscated	Deobfuscated			
Adler-32	min	235	5,385	222	78	665	222	0.4	84,784	
	max	235	2,996,678	222	78	2,001	222	516.0	2,469,276	100%
	avg	235	169,174	222	78	1,092	222	26.6	203,737	
CityHash	min	200	1,455	57	175	571	57	0.1	81,664	
	max	200	37,532	57	175	1,396	57	3.2	93,540	100%
	avg	200	3,555	57	175	938	57	0.3	82,756	
Collberg-0001-0	min	173	4,497	79	167	679	79	0.4	86,008	
	max	173	2,840,513	79	167	3,366	79	494.7	2,339,380	100%
	avg	173	174,703	79	167	1,243	79	26.4	204,447	
Collberg-0001-1	min	326	8,456	167	177	685	96	0.8	102,948	
	max	326	2,066,306	167	177	3,697	96	184.2	883,780	100%
	avg	326	103,599	167	177	1,300	96	9.3	136,964	
Collberg-0001-2	min	227	7,099	84	223	685	84	0.6	93,016	
	max	227	2,132,169	84	223	5,043	84	182.0	899,528	100%
	avg	227	104,401	84	223	1,364	84	9.3	127,183	
Collberg-0001-3	min	262	7,467	68	195	687	68	0.6	90,400	
	max	262	2,071,933	68	195	4,367	68	164.8	898,128	100%
	avg	262	98,637	68	195	1,342	68	8.0	122,732	
Collberg-0001-4	min	228	5,881	100	183	709	100	0.5	86,564	
	max	228	1,510,030	100	183	3,676	100	168.1	896,148	100%
	avg	228	107,831	100	183	1,315	100	12.5	145,051	
Collberg-0004-0	min	372	10,348	190	210	702	99	1.1	116,452	
	max	372	7,804,232	190	210	3,631	99	1431.0	6,306,932	100%
	avg	372	465,758	190	210	1,317	99	74.4	435,567	
Collberg-0004-1	min	147	3,810	67	143	636	67	0.3	85,904	
	max	147	859,278	67	143	2,704	67	71.0	420,912	100%
	avg	147	46,031	67	143	1,165	67	4.1	100,100	
Collberg-0004-2	min	408	11,294	332	219	722	128	1.6	172,760	
	max	408	2,999,784	332	219	4,765	128	275.2	1,243,348	100%
	avg	408	138,738	332	219	1,400	128	13.2	206,449	
Collberg-0004-3	min	203	5,503	78	171	718	78	0.5	86,948	
	max	203	1,439,344	78	171	3,478	78	138.9	755,056	100%
	avg	203	96,331	78	171	1,317	78	11.1	137,375	
Collberg-0004-4	min	307	8,674	146	274	725	146	0.7	103,964	
	max	307	9,279,883	146	274	5,424	146	1,681.6	7,480,952	100%
	avg	307	533,675	146	274	1,452	146	86.6	482,005	
FNV1a	min	143	1,499	57	110	517	57	0.1	80,872	
	max	143	54,846	57	110	1,180	57	4.9	101,828	100%
	avg	143	3,544	57	110	861	57	0.3	82,139	
Jenkins	min	201	5,520	125	79	631	125	0.5	87,572	
	max	201	1,069,111	125	79	1,888	125	83.9	543,272	100%
	avg	201	76,420	125	79	1,076	125	6.2	110,694	
JodyHash	min	92	1,349	48	90	468	48	0.1	79,732	
	max	92	155,637	48	90	1,085	48	25.2	203,072	100%
	avg	92	9,820	48	90	803	48	1.4	86,237	
MD5	min	9,743	173,673	557	314	1,311	557	16.5	266,032	
	max	9,743	47,927,795	557	314	4,828	557	4,226.7	2,688,976	100%
	avg	9,743	2,328,114	557	314	1,857	557	207.5	583,198	
SpiHash	min	364	2,880	160	362	824	160	0.3	89,356	
	max	364	1,694,015	160	362	1,829	160	288.1	1,434,764	100%
	avg	364	100,661	160	362	1,224	160	15.1	159,257	
SpookyHash	min	536	1,784	79	426	788	79	0.1	82,424	
	max	536	140,565	79	426	1,443	79	23.1	193,080	100%
	avg	536	9,571	79	426	1,125	79	1.3	88,364	
SuperFastHash	min	182	1,402	81	144	506	81	0.1	82,572	
	max	182	37,479	81	144	1,331	81	3.1	94,696	100%
	avg	182	3,502	81	144	874	81	0.3	83,540	
Xxhash	min	186	1,672	68	182	691	68	0.6	83,376	
	max	186	103,193	68	182	1,470	68	16.3	164,128	100%
	avg	186	9,310	68	182	1,047	68	1.1	88,478	

References

1. Bardin, S., David, R., Marion, J.-Y.: Backward-bounded DSE: targeting infeasibility questions on obfuscated codes. In: S& P, pp. 633–651. IEEE (2017)
2. Banescu, S., Collberg, C., Ganesh, V., Newsham, Z., Pretschner, A.: Code obfuscation against symbolic execution attacks. In: ACSAC (2016)
3. Codevirtualizer. https://oreans.com/codevirtualizer.php
4. Themida. https://www.oreans.com/themida.php
5. Tigress: C diversifier/obfuscator. http://tigress.cs.arizona.edu/

6. Clause, J., Li, W., Orso, A.: Dytan: a generic dynamic taint analysis framework. In: ISSTA. ACM (2007)
7. Coogan, K., Lu, G., Debray, S.: Deobfuscation of virtualization-obfuscated software: a semantics-based approach. In: CCS. ACM (2011)
8. Eyrolles, N., Guinet, A., Videau, M.: Arybo: Manipulation, canonicalization and identification of mixed Boolean-arithmetic symbolic expressions. In: GreHack (2016)
9. Godefroid, P., de Halleux, J., Nori, A.V., Rajamani, S.K., Schulte, W., Tillmann, N., Levin, M.Y.: Automating software testing using program analysis. IEEE Softw. **25**(5), 30–37 (2008)
10. Godefroid, P., Klarlund, N., Sen, K.: DART: directed automated random testing. In: PLDI. ACM (2005)
11. Jha, S., Gulwani, S., Seshia, S.A., Tiwari, A.: Oracle-guided component-based program synthesis. In: ICSE. ACM/IEEE (2010)
12. Kinder, J.: Towards static analysis of virtualization-obfuscated binaries. In: 19th Working Conference on Reverse Engineering, WCRE (2012)
13. Lattner, C., Adve, V.: LLVM: a compilation framework for lifelong program analysis and transformation (2004)
14. Maximus: Reversing a simple virtual machine. CodeBreakers 1.2 (2006)
15. David, R., Bardin, S., Feist, J., Mounier, L., Potet, M-L., Thanh Dinh Ta, Marion, J-Y.: Specification of concretization and symbolization policies in symbolic execution. In: ISSTA. ACM (2016)
16. Rolles, R.: Defeating HyperUnpackMe2 with an IDA processor module (2007)
17. Rolles, R.: Unpacking virtualization obfuscators. In: WOOT (2009)
18. Salwan, J., Bardin, S., Potet, M.L.: Deobfuscation of VM based software protection. In: SSTIC (2017)
19. Saudel, F., Salwan, J.: Triton: a dynamic symbolic execution framework. In: SSTIC (2015)
20. Scherzo: Inside code virtualizer (2007)
21. Sen, K., Marinov, D., Agha, G.: CUTE: a concolic unit testing engine for C. In: FSE (2005)
22. Sharif, M.I., Lanzi, A., Giffin, J.T., Lee, W.: Automatic reverse engineering of malware emulators. In: S&P. IEEE (2009)
23. VMprotect. (2003–2017). http://vmpsoft.com
24. Yadegari, B., Debray, S.: Symbolic execution of obfuscated code. In: CCS (2015)
25. Yadegari, B., Johannesmeyer, B., Whitely, B., Debray, S.: A generic approach to automatic deobfuscation of executable code. In: S&P. IEEE (2015)
26. Vanegue, J., Heelan, S., Rolles, R.: SMT Solvers in Software Security. In: WOOT (2012)
27. Schwartz, E.J., Avgerinos, T., Brumley, D.: All you ever wanted to know about dynamic taint analysis and forward symbolic execution (but might have been afraid to ask). In: S&P. IEEE (2010)
28. Blazytko, T., Contag, M., Aschermann, C., Holz, T.: Syntia: Synthesizing the semantics of obfuscated code. In: USENIX Security Symposium. Usenix (2017)

Extended Abstract: Toward Systematically Exploring Antivirus Engines

Davide Quarta[✉], Federico Salvioni, Andrea Continella, and Stefano Zanero

Politecnico di Milano, Milan, Italy
{davide.quarta,andrea.continella,stefano.zanero}@polimi.it,
federico.salvioni@mail.polimi.it

Abstract. While different works tested antiviruses (AVs) resilience to obfuscation techniques, no work studied AVs looking at the big picture, that is including their modern components (e.g., emulators, heuristics). As a matter of fact, it is still unclear how AVs work internally. In this paper, we investigate the current state of AVs proposing a methodology to explore AVs capabilities in a black-box fashion. First, we craft samples that trigger specific components in an AV engine, and then we leverage their detection outcome and label as a side channel to infer how such components work. To do this, we developed a framework, CRAVE, to automatically test and explore the capabilities of generic AV engines. Finally, we tested and explored commercial AVs and obtained interesting insights on how they leverage their internal components.

1 Introduction

Antiviruses are still the major solution to protect end users. Despite the importance of malware detectors, there still is a need for testing methodologies that allow to test and evaluate them.

Current AV testing and comparison methodologies, rely on the capability of detection of samples [7,31], and offer interesting insights on the time needed to detected a new sample for a product, but offer no insights in what are the capabilities implemented in an antivirus engine.

Moreover, most previous works focus on testing signature matching, and show how obfuscation techniques are effective against static analysis-based detectors [6,12,26,27,29]. However, modern AVs are complex systems that are not only based on static features and implement heuristics matching and emulation techniques (Fig. 1) [27,31,32]. Other works focus on studying techniques to evade emulators [4,5,11,14,16,17,24,30]. Neither of them focus specifically on AVs, or provide a comprehensive evaluation of AVs emulators. Rather, they look for new techniques to exploit AVs shortcomings. As a consequence, we lack of a recent and comprehensive study on modern AVs and of a complete understanding of how they really work. For instance, today it is usually believed that AVs mainly rely on signature matching while it is still unclear whether and how they

© Springer International Publishing AG, part of Springer Nature 2018
C. Giuffrida et al. (Eds.): DIMVA 2018, LNCS 10885, pp. 393–403, 2018.
https://doi.org/10.1007/978-3-319-93411-2_18

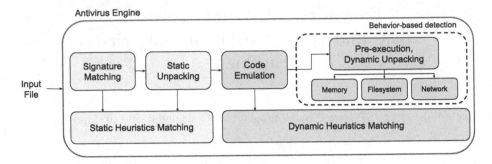

Fig. 1. Overview of a typical AV engine.

leverage emulation engines. This sense of "obscurity" does not help protecting users, because it is hard to understand the features that AVs implement and evaluate their capabilities. Instead, by exploring AV engines and understanding their internals, it is possible, for instance, to identify weaknesses, map the attack surface, or understand how stealthy samples can evade detection.

In this work, we move toward filling this gap by providing a comprehensive methodology to explore and test modern AVs, down to their core components. Our methodology builds upon the techniques devised so far in testing antiviruses [4,6]. Differently from the techniques and frameworks proposed so far, our objective is to allow exploration of the features of antivirus engines both at a coarse and fine grained level. Doing so, we aim at answering the following questions: **(Q1)** Does an AV implement emulation? **(Q2)** Does it implement static unpacking? **(Q3)** Does it implement heuristics matching?

To answer them, the main challenge is that AVs are closed and very complex systems. Hence, performing an in depth analysis is a very complex task and requires deep reverse engineering knowledge. However, this would not scale and cannot be applied to efficiently evaluate many AVs. Instead, we use a generic, black-box methodology that does not make any assumption on the AVs implementation. We consider an AV as black-box system whose inputs are the scanned samples and whose outputs are the outcomes of the scans. First, we craft a set of samples aiming at triggering specific components in the AV engine. Then, observing how the AV reports and labels the input samples, we infer details on how the engine components work internally. Essentially, we leverage the scan outcome as a side channel to gain information about the detection process. In practice, we developed a set of tests in a framework, CRAVE, that, following our methodology, can be used to automatically retrieve the capabilities of a generic AV, requiring manual interventions only to generate peculiar samples such as an undetectable dropper. Specifically, we focused on and implemented three interesting tests: (1) Testing whether an AV adopts an emulation engine. (2) Testing whether an AV performs static unpacking. (3) Testing whether an AV relies on common heuristics.

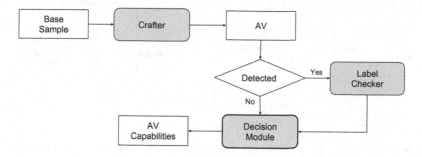

Fig. 2. High-level methodology adopted to explore AVs and extract information about their internals and capabilities.

Armed with CRAVE, we leveraged VirusTotal [1] to perform a large-scale experiment on 50 commercial AVs (including the popular Kaspersky, McAfee, Avast, Symantec). In our experiments, we found that 4 AVs fully implement code emulation. Then, we successfully determined that 20 AVs implement static unpackers. Finally, we verified that our samples mutations trigger the heuristics matching engine and affect the detection outcome.

In summary, we make the following contributions:

- We demonstrated how variations to the samples submitted for analysis to an antivirus engine, combined with the resulting assigned label, constitutes a powerful side channel allowing to infer characteristics of the engines employed for scanning.
- Leveraging this side channel, we developed a framework, CRAVE, to automatically explore AV engines in a black-box fashion.
- Armed with CRAVE, we investigated the current state of AV engines. Specifically, we focused on understanding whether and how AVs leverage different components (heuristics, emulation engines, static unpackers) to process and detect malicious samples.

In the spirit of open science, we make the code developed for CRAVE publicly available [2].

2 CRAVE Testing Methodology and Framework

Our methodology is based on providing AVs with different samples as input and observing how they report such samples. As depicted in Fig. 2, we first craft a new sample by obfuscating and mutating a base sample. Such mutations embed features that under analysis reveal whether specific AV components have been triggered. Then, we provide the AV with our crafted sample and observe the detection outcome. If the AV reports a detection, we also verify whether it

---

[1] https://www.virustotal.com.
[2] https://github.com/necst/crave.

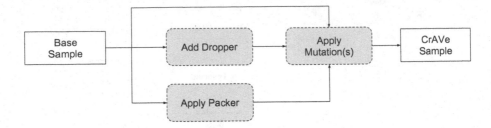

Fig. 3. Crafting phase, different "mutations" are applied on the sample.

labels the sample accordingly—same label of the initial base sample. Intuitively, if the AV correctly detects and labels our crafted sample, it means it managed to properly handle all the mutations and spot the malicious payload.

We implemented CRAVE to support Windows executables. However, our approach is generic and can be applied to any other operating system and executable format. CRAVE is composed by three key components: a *samples crafter*, a *label checker*, and a *decision module*.

2.1 Sample Crafter

CRAVE leverages a set of base samples described in Table 1, on which it applies different mutations to stimulate the AV engine under analysis. Figure 3 shows each step of the crafting process. The base sample goes through a set of different (optional) steps: addition of a dropper, applying a packer, and a set of mutations.

(1) Dropper. We developed a custom dropper with low detection rate to test emulation features. At run-time, our dropper decrypts a malicious sample contained in the resources section using a long (30 bytes) key, stores it on the filesystem and executes it. CRAVE uses the dropper to identify AVs that perform emulation. If an AV is able to correctly identify and label the malicious payload embedded in our dropper, we infer it implemented dynamic analysis features (emulation).

(2) Mutations. We test four popular heuristics usually implemented by AVs [27]. Table 2 describes the samples features that we modify to trigger the heuristics matching. We compare how the detection outcome changes after applying our mutations. We do this for two different purposes: First, applying them

Table 1. Base samples used in our analysis

Sample class	Description
goodware	goodware samples that is not mis-detected
malware	known malware sample (detected)
dropper	simple dropper that decrypts a sample, stores in on the filesystem and finally executes it

to a benign sample to determine whether AV heuristics match such features. Second, on the other hand, applying them to a malicious sample to determine whether such features can be used to evade detection.

(3) Packers. We apply known packers to our base samples in order to understand whether AVs implement static unpackers. Specifically, we pack a malicious sample with a given packer. Then, we edit the packer's stub overwriting its entry point with a RET instruction. Finally, leveraging the detection outcome and label as a side channel, we can infer if the AV employs static unpacking. In fact, if the AV correctly labels the packed malicious sample, it means it successfully unpacked it. However, since we broke the packer's stub, this implies the unpacking has been performed statically.

2.2 Label Checker

The *crafting* phase might change the detection outcome of certain AVs in such a way that the submitted sample is still correctly recognized as malicious, but as a variant of the sample (e.g., W32/Virut.Gen and W32/Virut.X after applying mutations). Note that, CRAVE needs to consider labels matches in its approach. For instance, when testing if an AV performs emulation, we want to verify that the AV correctly labels the dropped payload, and does not simply detect a GenericDropper. Therefore, CRAVE needs to handle little, and irrelevant, differences in the labels of the same sample.

AVClass [28], in its actual state, cannot be used for a direct comparison of two labels, rather it is used to label a sample as a variant of a known family. Thus, we devised a simple method for comparing the labels based on two steps: First a filtering phase in which we remove generic and heuristic labels. Second, a matching phase, based on the aliases for families leveraging AVClass and Metaphone [25]. Metaphone is a phonetic matching algorithm commonly used for indexing and matching text. In our empirical tests, Metaphone performed well on the assigned AV labels. For example, W32/Virut.Gen and W32/Virut.X are both encoded into *FRT*, making the matching process easy and straightforward. When a sample is labeled with a generic signature, this phase discards it to avoid imprecise detections.

Table 2. Features implemented to test heuristics.

Class	Feature	Description
Section Names	random	Randomly generated (alphanumeric)
	randomdot	Random, starts with a dot
	infer	Based on section characteristics and inferred content
Permissions	rwx	Force all sections to have *rwx* permissions
Checksum	correct	Force a correction of the checksum
	broken	Do not correct the checksum

2.3   Decision Module

The decision module compares the detection outcomes and the labels leveraging our Label Checker. In practice, it implements the inferring process described earlier to determine AVs capabilities.

(1) Test Emulation. Comparing the labels assigned to our dropper and malicious payload, the decision module determines whether an AV performs emulation.

(2) Test Heuristics. Looking at new or missed detections of the mutated sample in respect to its original base specimen, the decision module determines whether a certain heuristic can be employed to change the detection outcome.

(3) Test Static Unpacking. Comparing the labels assigned to our packed sample and malicious payload, the decision module determines whether an AV performs static unpacking.

3   Experimental Results

First, we verified whether AVs perform emulations. Then, we verified whether AVs perform static unpacking. Finally, we verified how sample features affect the heuristic engine.

Dataset and Setup. We leveraged VirusTotal to perform a large-scale experiment. Our methodology requires a malware sample that is detected by the tested AV. For this reason we looked for a sample to maximize the number of reported detections in VirusTotal. For our experiments, we used a variant of Virut [3], which at the time of our experiments was detected by 64 out of 67 AVs.

Requirements. Our methodology needs three requirements to be satisfied:
(1) The goodware sample must not be detected as malicious by the AV.
(2) The known malicious sample must be detected by the tested AV.
(3) The dropping logic must not be flagged as malicious by the AV.
These assumptions are easy to meet and we can verify that they hold as a first step of our methodology.

3.1   Testing Emulation

Following our methodology described in Sect. 2, we tested if AVs perform emulation (Table 3). After filtering out all the AVs from VirusTotal that do not satisfy our aforementioned requirements, we reduced the initial list of 64 AVs to 50. Among these 50 AVs, CRAVE identified 4 of them performing full emulation (AV4, AV15, AV16, AV19). Six more AVs were able to detect our crafted dropper, but they reported an inconsistent label. Hence, we could not determine whether they performed emulation.

Dropper Variation (No Execute). We repeated this experiment changing our crafted dropper. Specifically, our new dropper did not execute the dropped

---

[3] SHA256: 06c62c4cb38292fb35f2c2905fce2d96f59d2d461fa21f7b749febfed3ef968d.

file anymore, but it only decrypted it and dumped it on a file. As a consequence, this caused AV4 and AV15 to report it as benign. Interestingly, a new, different AV correctly detected and labeled the new dropper, showing it performed emulation. We could not speculate the reason behind the latter, as this would require deeper investigation.

3.2 Testing Static Unpacking

Following our methodology described in Sect. 2, we tested if AVs perform *static* unpacking. As shown in Table 3, we tested AVs against 5 different, known packers (UPX, MEW, ASPack, kkrunchy, Petite). After filtering out the AVs from Virus-Total that do not satisfy our requirements, we obtained a list of 64 AVs. All in all, we found 17 AVs that statically unpack UPX, 0 MEW, 6 ASPack, 0 kkrunchy, 4 Petite.

Stressing Static Unpacking. We repeated the same experiment as above applying the infer mutation to our crafted, packed samples. The results of this test shows that one AV (AV18) did not unpack ASPack and Petite anymore, suggesting it might rely on sections names to understand the type of packer—for instance, ASPack introduces a section named .aspack.

Goodware. Then, we performed a different experiment by packing our benign helloword and testing whether AVs detect the packers independently if they embed goodware or malware. We found 2 AVs detecting UPX, 16 MEW, 2 ASPack, 26 kkrunchy, 7 Petite.

3.3 Testing Heuristics

We tested if AVs match popular heuristics (Table 3).

Goodware. First, we tested whether applying our mutations (Table 2) to our benign helloworld triggers detection. We found that our infer and checksum do not trigger any new detection. On the other hand, RWX triggers 1 new detection, random 9, and randomdot 10.

Malware. Second, we verified whether applying our mutations (Table 2) to our malicious payload (i.e., virut) causes missed detections. We found that checksum causes 1 missed detection, RWX 1, random 2, randomdot 4, and infer 5.

This experiments show that applying mutations to trigger heuristics matching can affect the AVs detection outcomes, and demonstrate the need for a deeper exploration of such behaviors in future work.

4 Limitations and Future Works

Setup Limitations. While leveraging VirusTotal allows to easily perform large-scale experiments, it also has the limitation of not knowing how each AV is configured. The AVs included in VirusTotal might be parameterized with a different

Table 3. Summary of the results of our experiments on a selection of 20 AVs. For each heuristic, '+' means it triggers new false detections on goodware, '-' means it causes missed detections for a malware.

AV	Emulation	Static Unpacking					Heuristics				
		UPX	MEW	ASPack	kkrunchy	Petite	RWX	random	randomdot	infer	checksum
AV1								+	+		
AV2								-	-		
AV3		✓							-		
AV4	✓	✓									
AV5		✓	✓								
AV6		✓	✓	✓							
AV7							-	-	-	-	-
AV8		✓									
AV9				✓							
AV10		✓									
AV11		✓									
AV12								+			
AV13		✓									
AV14		✓		✓							
AV15	✓										
AV16	✓										
AV17								-		-	-
AV18					✓	✓					
AV19	✓	✓									
AV20		✓									

heuristic/aggressiveness level than the official end-user default configuration [1]. Indeed, we do not aim at providing a quality evaluation of commercial products.

Methodology Limitations. Our methodology cannot fully work if AVs only use generic labels. For instance, in our experiments we found two AVs, that labeled different samples in the same way (e.g., ''Malicious.High Confidence'').

Some AVs might emulate only samples showing specific features (e.g., having a RWX memory area, or a specific sequence of instructions). In this case, we would need to apply or fuzz typical trigger conditions.

Since we cannot control what happens inside AVs engines, when we test if an AV performs emulation, we might face a case in which the emulator fails because of an implementation flaw (e.g., missing emulated API). This would make our methodology infer that the AV does not perform emulation, while it actually does. However, from the detection capabilities perspective this has the same effect: the dropped malware is not detected.

Future Works. Other than addressing the above limitations, we foresee two other research directions. First, studying the differences between local and cloud AVs, and between their free and premiums versions. Second, exploring different side channels that can be used to extract information from AV engines. For instance, writing in memory the extracted information and then reading such information by dumping and inspecting the memory of the AV process.

5 Related Works

Antivirus Testing: Signature Matching. Researchers studied how syntactic obfuscation techniques can defeat signature matching and evaluated AVs capabilities of detecting malware samples that implement such obfuscation techniques [6,9]. However, they did not focus on heuristics and emulation features. The same apply for many other works that focus on techniques to defeat static analysis [12,26].

Evasion of Emulators-based Detection. Several works described techniques to escape from emulators [2,4,5,8,10,13,15–17,30]. However, while they show how emulators can be effectively bypassed, they do not propose any generic methodology or comparison between AVs.

Attacking Antivirus Software. Ormandy revealed several implementation vulnerabilities in commercial antivirus products showing how their complexity often exposes a large attack surface [18–23]. Wressnegger et al. derived AV signatures from malware and proposed a novel class of attacks called "antivirus assisted attacks" that, abusing the byte-pattern based signature matching flow, allow adversaries to remotely instruct AVs to block or delete content on the victim machine [33]. Al-Saleh et al. determined through time channel attacks whether the database of an AV has been updated with certain signatures or not [3].

Emulators Fingerprinting. AVLeak [4] extracts artifacts from AV emulators using a black-box approach. It maps known malware samples to bytes and then leverages custom droppers to leak data by exploiting AVs labeling.

6 Conclusions

In this work, we performed an exploratory study of modern AVs by testing their capabilities. We adopted a black-box methodology that leverages the detection outcome and label as a side-channel to obtain info about the AVs internals. In our experiments on 50 AVs, we found that not all the AVs perform full emulation, that most of AVs implement static unpackers for known packers, and that applying mutations to input samples in order to trigger heuristics matching affects the detection outcome. We believe that testing and exploring AV engines helps reducing that sense of "obscurity" that is often hidden behind AVs. In fact, testing AVs features is a fundamental step in order to evaluate their capabilities, identify weaknesses, or map their attack surface. In conclusion, while we only scratched the surface of AV testing and exploration, our results are promising and show that it is interesting to extend our study in future work. We envision our framework to be extended and used as a reference to test how AVs behave, and how they rely on each internal component.

Acknowledgements. This work has been supported by the Italian Ministry of University and Research FIRB project FACE (Formal Avenue for Chasing malwarE) – grant agreement N. RBFR13AJFT, and by the European Union's Horizon 2020 research and innovation programme under the Marie Skłodowska-Curie – grant agreement N. 690972

References

1. VirusTotal, About Page. https://www.virustotal.com/en/about/
2. Just-In-Time Malware Assembly: Advanced Evasion Techniques. Invincea white paper (2015)
3. Al-Saleh, M.I., Crandall, J.R.: Application-level reconnaissance: timing channel attacks against antivirus software. In: LEET (2011)
4. Blackthorne, J., Bulazel, A., Fasano, A., Biernat, P., Yener, B.: AVLeak: fingerprinting antivirus emulators through black-box testing. In: USENIX Workshop on Offensive Technologies (WOOT). USENIX Association, Austin, TX (2016)
5. Chen, X., Andersen, J., Mao, Z.M., Bailey, M., Nazario, J.: Towards an understanding of anti-virtualization and anti-debugging behavior inmodern malware, June 2008
6. Christodorescu, M., Jha, S.: Testing Malware Detectors. In: SIGSOFT Software Engineering Notes, July 2004
7. AV comparatives: Independent tests of anti-virus software
8. Cova, M.: Uncloaking Advanced Malware: How to Spot and Stop an Evasion (2015)
9. Dalla Preda, M., Maggi, F.: Testing android malware detectors against code obfuscation: a systematization of knowledge and unified methodology. J. Comput. Virol. Hacking Tech. **13**, 209–232 (2017)
10. Economou, K.: Escaping the avast sandbox using a single IOCTL (2016)
11. Ferrie, P.: Attacks on more virtual machine emulators (2007)
12. Ilsun, Y., Kangbin, Y.: Malware obfuscation techniques: A brief survey (2010)
13. Jung, P.: Bypassing sandboxes for fun (2014)
14. Keragala, D.: Detecting malware and sandbox evasion techniques (2016)
15. Marpaung, J.A.P., Sain, M., Lee, H.-J.: Survey on malware evasion techniques: State of the art and challenges, Feb 2012
16. Mourad, H.: Sleeping your way out of the sandbox (2015)
17. Nasi, E.: Bypass antivirus dynamic analysis (2014)
18. Ormandy, T.: Comodo antivirus: emulator stack buffer overflow handling psubusb packed subtract unsigned with saturation
19. Ormandy, T.: Comodo: integer overflow leading to heap overflow in win32 emulation
20. Ormandy, T.: Eset nod32 heap overflow unpacking epoc installation files

21. Ormandy, T.: Symantec/norton antivirus aspack remote heap/pool memory corruption vulnerability cve-2016-2208 (2016)
22. Ormandy, T.: Sophail: a critical analysis of sophos antivirus (2011)
23. Ormandy, T.: Sophail: applied attacks against sophos antivirus (2012)
24. Paleari, R., Martignoni, L., Roglia, G.F., Bruschi, D.: A fistful of red-pills: how to automatically generate procedures to detect CPU emulators. In: Proceedings of the 3rd USENIX Conference on Offensive Technologies WOOT 2009. USENIX Association, Berkeley, CA, USA (2009)
25. Philips, L.: Hanging on the metaphone. Comput. Lang. **7**, 39–44 (1990)
26. Rad, B.B., Masrom, M., Ibrahim, S.: Camouflage in malware : from encryption to metamorphism. IJCSNS **12**, 74 (2012)
27. Rad, B.B., Masrom, M., Ibrahim, S.: Evolution of computer virus concealment and anti-virus techniques: a short survey. CoRR (2011)
28. Sebastián, M., Rivera, R., Kotzias, P., Caballero, J.: AVCLASS: a tool for massive malware labeling. In: Monrose, F., Dacier, M., Blanc, G., Garcia-Alfaro, J. (eds.) RAID 2016. LNCS, vol. 9854, pp. 230–253. Springer, Cham (2016). https://doi.org/10.1007/978-3-319-45719-2_11
29. Sharma, A., Sahay, S.K.: Evolution and detection of polymorphic and metamorphic malwares: a survey. Int. J. Comput. Appl. (2014)
30. Singh, S.: Breaking the sandbox (2014)
31. Sukwong, O., Kim, H., Hoe, J.: Commercial antivirus software effectiveness: an empirical study. Computer, March 2011
32. Szor, P.: The Art of Computer Virus Research and Defense. Pearson Education, London (2005)
33. Wressnegger, C., Freeman, K., Yamaguchi, F., Rieck, K.: Automatically inferring malware signatures for anti-virus assisted attacks. In: Proceedings of the ACM Asia Conference on Computer and Communications Security. ACM (2017)

Author Index

Printed in the United States
By Bookmasters